THE CRYSTAL PALACE
AND THE GREAT
EXHIBITION

The Royal Commission for the Exhibition of 1851

The Royal Commission now functions as an endowed educational trust. It operates a number of competitive schemes for Fellowships and Studentships, and makes other awards to appropriate organisations and individuals. Now in its sesquicentennial year, the Commission is confident that it will continue to support innovation and creativity, in all their forms, well into the future. For further details, contact:

Rear Admiral J. P. W. Middleton, CB
The Secretary
The Royal Commission for the Exhibition of 1851
Sherfield Building, Imperial College
London SW7 2AZ

Tel: 020-7594-8790
Fax: 020-7594-8794
Email: royalcom1851@ic.ac.uk
Website: www.royalcommission1851.org.uk

THE CRYSTAL PALACE
AND THE GREAT
EXHIBITION

ART, SCIENCE AND PRODUCTIVE INDUSTRY

*A History of the Royal Commission
for the Exhibition of 1851*

HERMIONE HOBHOUSE

continuum
LONDON • NEW YORK

Continuum

The Tower Building, 11 York Road, London SE1 7NX
15 East 26th Street, New York, NY 10010

First published 2002
Reprinted 2004

British Library Cataloguing-in-Publication Data
A catalogue record is available from the British Library.

ISBN 0-826-47841-7 (hardback)

Library of Congress Cataloguing-in-Publication Data

Hobhouse, Hermione
  The Crystal Palace and the Great Exhibition: art, science and productive industry, a
history of the Royal Commission for the Exhibition of 1851 / Hermione Hobhouse.
    p. cm.
  Includes bibliographical references and index.
  ISBN 0-485-11575-1
  1. Great Exhibition (1851) : London, England) 2. Great Britain. Royal Commission for
the Exhibition of 1851 – History, I. Title.
  T690.B1 H65 2001
  907.04´421–dc21

                                                                2001035286

Designed by Humphrey Stone

Printed and bound in Great Britain by
Biddles Ltd, King's Lynn
Norfolk

Contents

Colour Plates

Black and White Plates

Figures in the Text

Frontispiece. The Monument to the 1851 Exhibition in the Horticultural Society Gardens, in 1863 (*Illustrated London News*, 27 June 1863)

1. Portrait of John Scott Russell (*Illustrated London News*, 28 June 1851)
2. 'Industrious Boy', cartoon of Prince Albert (*Punch*, 5 June 1850)
3. 'Testing the Gallery Floor' (Berlyn and Fowler)
4. General view of work in progress on the Crystal Palace (Berlyn and Fowler)
5. Fixing cast-iron drain pipes in the Crystal Palace (Berlyn and Fowler)
6. The 'Glazing Wagon', used to transport workmen (*Illustrated London News*, 7 December 1850)
7. Two winning designs for Bronze Medals, to be given to Exhibitors (*Illustrated London News*, July 1851)
8. Plan of Crystal Palace (Berlyn and Fowler)
9. Visitors to the Exhibition on opening day (*Illustrated London News*, June 1851)
10. Portrait of Edgar Bowring, Secretary to the 1851 Commission, 1852–69 (*Illustrated London News*, 28 June 1851)
11. The Commissioners' Estate at purchase (*Third Report*, 1856)
12. 'HRH FM PA at it again', cartoon of Prince Albert (*Punch*, 12 July 1856)
13. Axonometric of South Kensington Museum showing early development (Science Museum)
14. Portrait of Captain Francis Fowke (*Illustrated London News*, June 1862)
15. The Commissioners for the 1862 Exhibition: the Duke of Buckingham, Thomas Baring, Earl Granville, Sir Charles Wentworth Dilke and Thomas Fairbairn (*Illustrated London News*, 1 March 1862)
16. Plan of the 1862 Exhibition Building and the Horticultural Gardens (*The Record of the 1862 International Exhibition*, Elton Collection, Ironbridge Gorge Museum)
17. 'The May-Day Present', cartoon of John Bull presenting the 1862 building to Britannia (Private collection)
18. Portable steam engine by Ransome & Sims (D. K. Clarke, *The Exhibited Machinery of 1862*, Elton Collection, Ironbridge Gorge Museum)
19. Oscillating washing machine by Hussey & Sons, Grantham (D. K. Clarke,

Foreword

BY HRH THE DUKE OF EDINBURGH

A hundred and fifty years ago London witnessed a very remarkable event. It saw the construction of a vast glass 'palace' in Hyde Park for the 'Exhibition of the Works of Industry of all Nations', later to be known as the Great Exhibition. The Crystal Palace was subsequently moved to Sydenham Hill, where it remained a feature of the London skyline until it burnt down in 1936.

The story of the Great Exhibition, and the very active involvement of the Prince Consort, is quite well known. What is not so well known is how it came about and how the Commissioners have responded to their Charter, which requires them 'to increase the means of industrial education and extend the influence of Science and Art upon productive industry', since the Exhibition was dismantled. This book traces the complete story of the organisation of the Exhibition right through to the creation of the South Kensington estate as a centre for national museums and institutions for learning. It also records the continuing involvement of the Commissioners, in spite of many financial difficulties, in the promotion of science and art through scholarships and grants.

This carefully researched book is a tribute to the 'late lamented Prince', who masterminded the Exhibition, and to all the men and women who have served the Commission in one capacity or another for a century and a half.

Acknowledgements

First of all, I must express my gratitude to Her Majesty the Queen for Her gracious permission to use the Royal Archives, which throw a great deal of light on the history of the Great Exhibition of 1851 and the subsequent history of the refounded Royal Commission for the 1851 Exhibition.

I am also very much indebted to Sheila de Bellaigue, Pam Clark and their colleagues at the Windsor Archives, and to Jane Roberts, who has advised me over matters to do with the Print Room, and illustrations from the Royal Archives.

Very important also were, of course, the archives of the Commission itself, and I am very conscious of the debt I owe to successive Secretaries to the 1851 Commission, most recently the current Secretary Patrick Middleton, and Michael Neale, Secretary from 1987 to 1994, who very kindly read the whole manuscript, and provided some very helpful comments. Valerie Phillips, archivist to the Commissioners, guided me through the plethora of documents, and ensured that all relevant material was made available to me. There are a large number of related institutions, which have either been linked with the 1851 Commission, or which are indebted to the Commissioners for financial and other support in the course of their long history, and their librarians and other staff have been very helpful. Foremost among these is the Royal Society of Arts, and their Librarian, Susan Bennett, the Victoria and Albert Museum, where I must mention Anthony Burton, and André Davis, Imperial College and the Science Museum, where Robert Bud and his colleagues were always helpful. There are, of course, an enormous number of other South Kensington institutions to whose archivists and librarians I am beholden for information and help, including the Royal College of Music, and most particularly the Royal Albert Hall.

The Director of the British School at Rome and his staff gave me hospitality when researching in Rome, and assistance in writing up the not inconsiderable part played by the Chairman and staff of the 1851 Commission in the development of the School.

A number of individuals have also assisted with advice and information, as is detailed in the notes. These include Elizabeth Bonython, in connection with her work on Henry Cole, John Kenworthy-Browne for help over Paxton's role, John Greenacombe and other former colleagues from the Survey of London, and fellow members from the Victorian Society. I also must express my thanks to my son Francis Graham, who sorted out the many illustrations and saw the book through the press during my recent illness.

Finally, I must acknowledge my debt to the Chairman and Commissioners of the Royal Commission for the Exhibition of 1851 for entrusting me with the task of writing the history of such an innovative and versatile body. Over the century and a half of its existence it has shown itself to be worthy of its royal founder and his many admirers and followers.

Abbreviations

BM   (Meeting of the) Board of Management of the Commission, preceded by number of meeting, and followed by date, e.g. 123 BM 4.3.1998

BSR   British School in Rome

Com.   Meeting of the Commission, preceded by number of meeting, and followed by date, e.g. 103 Com., 8.12.1973

DNB   *Dictionary of National Biography*

POD   Post Office Directory

PP   Parliamentary Paper

PRO   Public Record Office

RA   Archive material from the Royal Archives, followed by the reference

RC   Archive material from the 1851 Commission Archive, followed by the reference

RSA   Royal Society of Arts

SSC   (Meeting of the) Science Scholarships Committee of the 1851 Commission, e.g. SSC 15.6.1933

WWW   *Who Was Who*

Introduction

The Crystal Palace, in which the Great Exhibition was held, has become a great national icon, and has caught the public imagination twice in British history. First, of course, in 1851, when it was the showplace for a pleased, and somewhat surprised, British public of a unique achievement which gave London international significance. Secondly, under Herbert Morrison and the first Labour government, it was the inspiration for the Festival of Britain, an earnest of the way in which a weary and jaded people would refurbish their war-damaged capital and look again at their country.

Henry Cole, a leading member of the team which brought the Crystal Palace into being, saw it as the greatest promotion of industry since the world began. 'A great people', he wrote, 'invited all civilized nations to a festival, to bring into comparison the works of human skill. It was carried out by its own private means; was self-supporting, and independent of taxes and the employment of slaves, which great works had exacted in ancient days.'[1] A shrewd foreign observer saw it as a more combative occasion: 'Ces sont les tournois de nos temps modernes. Ils sont moins poétiques peut-être que ceux des temps anciens, mais ils ont aussi leur caractère et grandeur.'[2]

The Exhibition itself is only one part of the story of the Royal Commission which, of course, continues in existence today. The formation of the Royal Commission for the Great Exhibition of 1851 is in its own way an epic story. It came into being to meet the needs of a special occasion, being intended like most Royal Commissions to cease upon an appropriate midnight when its work was completed. The prolongation of the life of the Royal Commission and its subsequent history are also the subject of this book, showing how a single initiative was turned into a long-term development programme for British industry and education.

The story of the Great Exhibition, as the Universal Exhibition of the Works of All Nations is known to the British, is the story of amateurs in the best sense of the word, and therefore, perhaps, a particularly British one. The credit for bringing it into being is disputed: it was a matter of dissension at the time, and the claims of various protagonists – Joseph Paxton, Henry Cole, Lyon Playfair, the engineer William Cubitt, or Lord Granville – have been put forward by their biographers ever since.

However, it is probably generally agreed that the leading figure was Prince Albert, not only in his shrewd appreciation of the merits of the scheme for an exhibition when first put to him, but also his enthusiasm for the dedication of the profits to a nationally significant venture.

The original intention in the 1852 Supplemental Charter was the 'furtherance of the general objects for which the Exhibition was designed'. The advice of the Commissioners to the government after the close of the extremely successful Exhibition was that the best way of developing along those lines was 'to increase the means of industrial education, and extend the influence of science and art upon productive industry'. That advice emphasized the importance of international cooperation in the matter, a prime concern for Prince Albert, and one which has remained a concern of the Commissioners, though pursued in different ways over the succeeding years.

The subsequent development of the Commissioners' South Kensington estate was a major achievement, as part of the long-term objective, and its physical appearance and development are a major strand of this book.

The Commissioners have had a long-standing relationship with the policy, or lack of it, developed by successive Government bodies concerned with educational policy, whether artistic, scientific or industrial. Another thread which runs through this book is the relationship and rivalry with scientific education overseas. It was a constant theme in the nineteenth century, particularly where German education was concerned, whether one considers the engagement of Hoffmann by Prince Albert, or, later on, the influence of the Hofschule at Charlottenburg in the setting up of the Imperial College of Science and Technology. With the establishment of the Science Research Scholarships in 1891, the emphasis was on making scientific training available throughout the British Imperial possessions to young scientists, many of whom later played an important part in scientific education and development both in this country and overseas.

I

The Founding of the Royal Commission

The story of the Great Exhibition begins, not in the nineteenth century, but rather earlier with the work of an older institution, and the bringing together of the men who were to promote the Exhibition. The intention was to hold a national exhibition in England of the standing and significance that had been common in France for half a century. This initiative was the work of a group of remarkable men, essentially men of their time, but who could only have flourished in the polymathic and relatively unspecialized mid-nineteenth century.

THE MEN BEHIND THE GREAT EXHIBITION

The group which promoted the Exhibition was brought together by a well-established British organization, known today as the Royal Society of Arts.[1] The Society had been founded in 1754, when a group of 'Noblemen, Gentlemen, Clergymen and Merchants' had met in a coffee-house to found the 'Society for the encouragement of Arts, Manufactures & Commerce'. This had as its objective the giving of prizes for inventions and manufactures which were 'likely to produce great advantages to the nation, by employing many hands, and saving annually large sums of money'. In its early days these were largely concerned with agricultural improvements of various sorts, but there was also a concern for industrial and technical improvements which had an effect on the health of workers. Thus there were prizes for the improvement of land by draining and manuring, for the growing of new winter fodder-crops such as mangel-wurzel and turnips, for improved saw-mills, windmills and carriages, but also for an unsinkable life-boat, and for better ventilation of chemical workshops.[2] The very success of the Society in stimulating arts and industry had led to the foundation of independent artistic and professional organizations; thus the Society, which had held the first exhibition of arts by contemporary artists in 1760, found itself superseded in that role after the foundation of the Royal Academy. Similarly, the formation of the Royal Agricultural Society of England in 1838 provided a new focus for agricultural improvements. By the 1840s, the pace of technological change was too great for even the most enthusiastic voluntary society, and, it has been argued, the Society needed to change direction to survive.[3] Gradually, the holding of lectures to communicate advances in technology, their publication in a journal and the exhibition of successful manufactures became a greater concern than the giving of premiums for inventions.

By 1841–2 this slackening-off of innovative business was being reflected in the Society's income, in its rather ragged organization, and in the difficulty of recruiting active members. The Society was fortunate at this rather low point in its fortunes in finding an energetic new royal President. The Society had enjoyed royal patronage since 1816, when the Duke of Sussex (1773–1843), the sixth son of George III, described by the Society's historian as 'a man of liberal sentiments, genial manners, and intellectual tastes', had become President.[4] He proposed the newly arrived Prince Albert for membership in June 1840. The Prince succeeded as President on the Duke's death in 1843.

Prince Albert of Saxe-Coburg-Gotha (1819–61) who had married his cousin, Queen Victoria, in 1840, did not find his role as consort an easy one. He was largely excluded from formal participation in the work of the sovereign, though he had considerable influence behind the scenes. The Whig aristocracy who largely controlled government were a formidable *cousinage*, who regarded him with amusement, even with humorous contempt. Even *Punch*, with a more bourgeois public, saw him as a convenient and easy butt. However, he found a role and increasing influence through his membership of philanthropic bodies and his interest in educational questions. He took the trouble to cultivate professional men, then just emerging as an influential group, earning the famous Liverpudlian tribute:

> The Prince was at home with such men [Elmes, architect of St George's Hall, and Jesse Hartley, engineer of the Albert Dock] amidst such works. To an architect he could talk as an architect; to an engineer, as an engineer; to a painter, as a painter; to a sculptor, as a sculptor; to a chemist, as a chemist; and so through all the branches of Art and Science.[5]

The Duke of Sussex approved a report which modernized the Society's management, giving power to a council of chairmen of committees and elected members, and appointing a professional secretary. The first of these was a railway engineer, Francis Whishaw (d. 1856), appointed in 1843, and succeeded in 1845 by another engineer, John Scott Russell (1808–82). In 1846, the newly formed Council decided to apply for a Royal Charter, a move duly approved by the President, Prince Albert, and granted in June 1847, though the Society was not entitled to use the prefix 'Royal' till 1908, when Edward VII, as President, granted the right.

The Society had a number of members prominent in public life, such as Colonel W. H. Sykes, MP, FRS, Chairman of the East India Company, J. C. Macdonald, manager of *The Times*, Lord Ebrington, a Liberal Member of Parliament and Secretary of the Poor Law Board, later Lord Fortescue, Sir John Pakington (1799–1880), Conservative Member of Parliament for Droitwich, and a minister under Lord Derby, and Lord Hatherley, Lord Chancellor under Gladstone (1868–72). However, more significant were the members who were also involved with the royal circle, and subsequently with the two major exhibitions of the period in 1851 and 1862, and with the development of South Kensington. These included Charles Wentworth Dilke (1810–69), Richard Redgrave, RA (1804–88), Surveyor of the Queen's Pictures, and his brother Samuel, engineers like Robert Stephenson, Joseph Paxton, and William Fairbairn, and the Scottish chemist, Lyon Playfair (1818–98), who was a founding father of the South Kensington Museum.[6]

THE IDEA OF AN EXHIBITION

The idea of holding an exhibition was not novel. The revolutionary government in France had instituted exhibitions in 1798 to promote French manufactures during the Napoleonic struggle with England. These had proved so beneficial to French industry that they had been continued after the Restoration on a quinquennial basis. An attempt in the closing years of George IV's reign to hold a series of annual exhibitions of 'new and improved productions of our artisans and manufacturers' had proved abortive, though the Royal Dublin Society succeeded in holding triennial exhibitions from 1827 until 1850. However, it was not till 1844 that Francis Whishaw, as Secretary of the Society of Arts, was encouraged by foreign examples to take preliminary steps towards what he planned to call 'a Grand Annual Exhibition of Manufactures'. These exemplars were the French quinquennial national exhibition, and an exhibition held at Leipzig by the newly formed Zollverein of North German States. He started off by promoting two exhibitions of paintings and 'useful inventions', in the winter of 1844–5. This idea was taken up by the Council of the Society in May 1845, which adopted the resolution that

> the experience of foreign countries has proved that great national advantages have been derived from the stimulus given to industrial skill by bringing the manufactures of different establishments into competition with each other, and by presenting Honorary rewards . . . cheapness of production and excellence of material, both in execution and durability, being assumed as the criteria of superiority.

It called for immediate preparations for 'a periodical Exhibition of Works of Industry'. The Secretary reported this to the Society at the annual prize-giving in the presence of Prince Albert, the President, and was duly requested to pursue the matter and report back. This initiative was abortive; as Scott Russell later wrote:

> The public were indifferent – manufacturers lukewarm – some of the most eminent even hostile to the proposition. The Committee neither met with sufficient promise of support in money, sufficient public sympathy, nor sufficient co-operation among manufacturers . . . The attempt was abandoned.[7]

There was one significant consequence of the Exhibition, which was the recruitment of the civil servant Henry Cole (1808–82) as an exhibitor in the Society's own rather modest Art Manufactures Exhibition. Working in collaboration with Herbert Minton, the well-known earthenware manufacturer, whose firm in the Potteries produced everything from drainpipes to bone china, Cole persuaded Minton to send in a beer mug, and he himself 'having consulted Greek earthenware at the British Museum for authority for handles' submitted a design for a tea service. Both the beer mug and the 'Felix Summerly' tea-set won silver medals. This encouraged both Henry Cole and the Society to persist with the idea of an exhibition.

Cole was an assistant keeper at the Record Office, where Prince Albert first came into contact with him.[8] He had made his mark at the Record Commission, as it was then called, by an act of what we would today call 'whistle-blowing'. He had been employed there since 1823 to decipher and transcribe ancient documents for publication, but, in 1835, had had a row with his boss, the Secretary of the Commission. This led to Cole's dismissal, but he fought back by working together with his friends, including the novelist, Thomas Love Peacock (1785–1866), the Utilitarian philosopher John Stuart Mill (1806–73), and the Philosophic Radical Sir William Molesworth (1810–55), Member of Parliament for East Cornwall, and a founder of the Reform Club. The friends orchestrated a campaign which drew attention to the inadequacies of the Record Commission, leading in 1836 to the appointment of a Select Committee of the House of Commons, which was chaired by another friend Charles Buller, also a Cornish Member of Parliament. When the Record Commission was reinstated after the accession of Queen Victoria, the new Master of the Rolls was persuaded to re-engage Cole as assistant keeper of the Records, then stored in 'Carlton Ride', the old riding school of Carlton House. Cole's post as a civil servant did not prevent him from engaging in other activities, and in 1838 he helped Rowland Hill to launch his campaign for the penny post, and, in due course, through his knowledge of printing to assist him in bringing it into being.

In 1843 he published the first Christmas card under his pen name of Felix Summerly. After his success with the Art Manufactures, Henry Cole was encouraged by Scott Russell to join the Society of Arts, becoming a member of various committees, and of Council in 1847. Cole was a significant figure throughout the period: he was very much a man of the age, with a fertile imagination which produced designs for artistic china, projects for national museums and schemes for recycling sewage with equal facility. He also had in equal parts an immense capacity for hard work and getting things done, and for making himself deeply suspect and unpopular. The following year he joined the Council, becoming Chairman in 1850. Thenceforward until his death, in the words of the Society's historian, Sir Henry Trueman Wood, who knew Cole at the end of his life, he exercised 'the strongest personal influence over the Society . . . which, for the first half . . . of this period really amounted to absolute control'. Wood saw him as 'its second founder', considering 'that it was due to his influence and authority that the Society was raised from a state of impotence and insignificance to a condition of prosperity and influence'.[9] In view of the close relation that was to develop between the subsequent Royal Commission, South Kensington and the Society of Arts, Cole's dominance is a matter of considerable significance.

Fig 1. John Scott Russell, Secretary of the Society of Arts, 1845–50,
and then Secretary to the 1851 Commission.

John Scott Russell (1808–82) was a Vice-President of the Scottish
Society of Arts, and was already well-known as the designer of a number
of ships, and an authority on the relationship between waves and floating
bodies. He was a most efficient and energetic secretary, and did a great
deal to reorganize the meetings of the Society during his five-year period
of office. He was an important protagonist within the Society for the
Exhibition, though his part in it has been partly overshadowed by Cole
and Fuller. Once the Commission was appointed he became one of the
secretaries to the Royal Commission. After the Exhibition closed, he
returned to naval engineering, being concerned with both the building of
The Great Eastern, in the Isle of Dogs, and the design of the *Warrior*, the
first of the sea-going armoured frigates.

A third influential, though more ephemeral, figure who joined the
Society in 1847 was Francis Fuller (1807–87), the son of a substantial
tenant of Lord Derby, near Epsom, a surveyor who had been reared as a
farmer, whose obituary records that he saw 'more Derbys than any man
who ever lived'. Initially, he took an interest in the agricultural side of the
Society's work, in such matters as the best way of dealing with buttercups
and dandelions, the best plan for a homestead for a 200-acre farm and
reports on the value to the farmer of rooks and sparrows. However, he
was also a member of the Committee set up to advise the Society on the
feasibility of staging a national exhibition on the French model.[10]

In 1847, the Society of Arts held a successful exhibition in its Great Room, comprising the premium-winning articles, supplemented by exhibits begged from manufacturers visited by Cole and Scott Russell. Upwards of 20,000 people visited the exhibition, and this encouraged the Society to pursue its goal of annual exhibitions, supplemented by periodic national exhibitions. These were to be organized by the Society, but, it was hoped, to be supported by government with a suitable site. Early in the following year, Prince Albert was approached by Cole, but seems to have considered it unlikely that any government assistance would be forthcoming. Undaunted, the Society approached the government direct, first through Henry Labouchere (1798–1869), President of the Board of Trade, who was encouraging, and subsequently through the Chief Commissioner of Works, Lord Seymour (1804–85) (Edward Adolphus, later 12th Duke of Somerset, 1855), in whose gift was a site or building. The Society's exhibitions of 1848 and 1849 were increasingly successful, so that the Society felt confident in announcing a national exhibition for the year 1851.[11]

THE INVOLVEMENT OF PRINCE ALBERT

The exact responsibility for having got the Great Exhibition off the ground is hotly disputed, as is the credit for getting Prince Albert really interested. In the summer of 1849, an exhibition of French industry was held in Paris, and the Society commissioned Matthew Digby Wyatt to produce a report, and he came to play an increasing part in both the promotion and the carrying out of the Exhibition. Matthew Digby Wyatt (1820–77) known to the family as Digby, possibly to avoid confusion with his father, but later made a baronet as Sir Matthew Digby Wyatt, was the son of a non-architectural member of the vast Wyatt clan, and brother to the prolific Thomas Henry (1807–80). His father was Matthew Wyatt (1773–1831), a grandson of Benjamin Wyatt I (1709–72), through a cousinly marriage. Digby was trained in his brother's office, but has been described as 'pre-eminently a committee-man, lecturer, water-colourist, editor and writer'. He spent two years travelling on the Continent, making sketches not only of buildings but also of mosaics, an interest which brought him to the notice of Herbert Minton and Prince Albert. It was this interest in mosaics which brought him into contact with members of the Society of Arts wanting to improve the design of British manufactures.[12]

Wyatt went to Paris with Cole, and Francis Fuller made an independent visit. Returning to Southampton, Fuller met Thomas Cubitt (1788–1855), the London developer and builder, also a member of the Society, who had been visiting Osborne House in the Isle of Wight, on which he had been working for the Royal Family. The two men travelled back together, and, as Fuller later recorded:

> I informed him that we could do a much grander work in London by inviting contributions from every nation; and said, moreover, that if Prince Albert would take the lead in such a work he would become a leading light among nations.[13]

On his return to Osborne two days later, Cubitt reported this to the Prince, who also consulted Scott Russell and Cole. The result was a meeting at Buckingham Palace on 30 June, 1849, at which Cole, Fuller, Scott Russell and Thomas Cubitt were all present.

Because of the importance of this first meeting in the development of the Exhibition project, it is worth trying to apportion some of the credit, first for the recruitment of Prince Albert, and then for the foundation decisions. Cubitt's meeting with Fuller was important, since the great builder was already a member of the Prince's circle, and enjoyed the Royal confidence. Cole records calling at Buckingham Palace, on Friday 29 June, to see Prince Albert 'who agreed that the Exhibition should be a large one embracing Foreign productions; and that a Royal Commission was expedient'.[14] On the other hand, many years later in its obituary, *The Field* paid a tribute to Fuller's 'persuasiveness and tact' and made the point that the other two members of the triumvirate might not have won over the Prince without it.

> The Prince, despite his admiration for Mr. Scott Russell's ability, thought him too talkative, and Sir Henry Cole (as his old friend, Lord Granville, admitted recently in public) had a marvellous capacity for rubbing everyone up the wrong way. Such, however, was Mr. Fuller's elasticity of resource and such his inexhaustible good humour, that, in the end, the firm and steadfast co-operation of the Prince Consort was gained.[15]

The formal minute prepared by Scott Russell at the Prince's request laid down the broad lines on which the group planned to proceed. Most of the difficult questions concerning the Exhibition were in essence 'settled'. The exhibits would be divided into four major divisions, 'Raw Materials of Manufactures – British Colonial, and Foreign, Machinery and Mechanical Inventions, Manufactures, Sculpture and Plastic Art generally'. The site was discussed – the Society had been offered the 'area of Somerset House . . . or a more suitable site on the property of the Crown', and the centre of Leicester Square was also suggested. This was referred to Cubitt by the Prince, but according to Cole, the great developer dismissed it out of hand because of the possible adverse effect on the residents of the square. It seems to have been Albert himself who suggested the vacant ground on the south side of Hyde Park, 'parallel with and between the Kensington drive and the ride commonly called Rotten Row'. Thomas Cubitt suggested the figure of £50,000 for putting up a building, a somewhat low figure, though not as absurdly optimistic as Fuller's £30,000, and it was on this that the Society's estimate of £75,000 was based.[16] Thomas Cubitt was one of the guarantors of the sum lent by the Bank of England in June 1850 (for £5000) but otherwise played little further part. The decision was taken not to limit the Exhibition 'exclusively to British industry. It was considered that . . . particular advantage to British industry might be derived from placing it in fair competition with that of other Nations'. Very large premiums in money, it was thought, would induce manufacturers to develop products, which though not immediately profitable, would be of long-term benefit. The administration necessary was discussed, and though the 'best mode of carrying out the execution of these plans' was thought to be a Royal Commission headed by the Prince, it was agreed that the Society of Arts should be asked to solicit and collect the 'subscriptions on a large scale, for donations'. A draft of the Royal Commission was to be prepared, and a list of Members drawn up, and an additional one compiled of *ex officio* Members drawn from the ranks of government.[17]

PREPARATIONS FOR AN EXHIBITION AT THE SOCIETY OF ARTS

Cole's diary records the constant meetings which followed, supplemented by meals and social meetings with other members of the Society. On Sunday 1 July he took his wife and children to Hyde Park to see the site, and prepared the draft of the Royal Commission. At the request of Stafford Northcote, he went to explain the proposal to Henry Labouchere, President of the Board of Trade. Two weeks later Cole, Scott Russell and Fuller went to Osborne to see the Prince, who had arranged for Labouchere to be present. The Prince showed them his list of Commissioners, which included both Scott Russell and Fuller, with Cole as Secretary. Labouchere offered the support of his ministry, suggesting, however, that the Society of Arts might manage to carry out the work without the necessity of a Royal Commission. This may have reflected the doubts that a number of politicians had about the whole project. However, the idea of proceeding without the proposed Royal Commission was rejected by the three members of the Society, who said that the body running the Exhibition needed to have a sufficiently elevated position so as not to be suspected of being lobbied by competitors. Only a 'tribunal appointed by the Crown, and presided over by His Royal Highness, could have that standing and weight in the country, and give that guarantee for impartiality that would command the utmost exertions of all the most eminent Manufacturers at home, and particularly abroad'.

The plan of operation as submitted by the Society at this meeting therefore envisaged a Royal Commission for 'promoting Arts, Manufactures, and Industry, by means of a great Collection of Works of Art and Industry of all nations, to be formed in London, and exhibited in 1851'. The Royal Commission was to be responsible for determining the nature of the prizes, and the subjects for which they were to be offered, defining the 'nature of the exhibition', and the way it was to be conducted, and finally the awarding of the prizes. The Society of Arts would undertake the raising of funds to finance the prizes and the provision of a building, 'to defray the necessary expenses to cover the risks of the collection and exhibition', and, finally, 'to provide for the permanent establishment of these Quinquennial Exhibitions'. This last objective was to become a very thorny issue.

It was also decided that the prizes should take the form of 'Medals, with Money Prizes so large as to overcome the scruples and prejudices even of the largest and richest manufacturers, and ensure the greatest amount of exertion'. The first prize would be £5000.

Labouchere pointed out that the Cabinet was about to disperse until October or November, and therefore the government could offer little immediate help; however, the Society could usefully employ the time in collecting evidence as to the interest and support likely to be provided by manufacturers.[18]

The Council of the Society met on 26 July, to hear a report of the meeting with the Prince, and to decide what to do next. The outlay required seemed to be about £50,000 for the building and a further £20,000 to provide attractive prizes, sums which the Society could not meet from its own resources. However, there was a feeling that the Society would have more success with manufacturers if it could point to plans for a building.

There was a suggestion that a 'capitalist' might be found who would put up the building and money for expenses as a speculation. It was the adaptable and well-connected Fuller who found these essential figures, through his father-in-law, George Drew, a solicitor from Guildford, with an office in Parliament Street, Westminster.[19] James Munday and his nephew George were described in the contract as 'Contractor for Public Works', but James Munday appears in the Post Office Directory for 1846 more modestly as 'builder' with offices at 26½ Abchurch Lane. Though public opinion about their role later changed, their readiness to take a very considerable risk by investing upwards of £75,000 in an entirely novel and untested enterprise alone made it possible for the Society to proceed.[20] The terms of the contract set out that the contractors were to advance £500 immediately, and to provide £20,000 overall for the prizes to go into a trust fund. They were to erect the building, and to pay all costs of agents, advertising, and printing out of profits. For this they would receive 5 per cent on the receipts, one third of the 'surplus profits' would go to the Society for funding future exhibitions, and the Mundays would receive the balance of four-sixths of the profits. They made it clear that they regarded Prince Albert's involvement as essential to the success of the scheme.

Though the matter was agreed by the end of August, and a draft contract between the Mundays and the Society signed on the twenty-third,[21] a further clause was added stipulating that if the Treasury agreed to provide funding the Mundays would agree to the cancellation of the contract. In return, the Mundays claimed the right to withdraw if a Royal Commission was not issued.

There was one further meeting at Osborne on 1 August, 1849, with the Prince and Colonel Phipps, on the very day on which the Queen was to sail to Ireland on her way north. At this meeting a 'diploma' was drawn up, saying that the holder was to collect opinions and evidence as to an exhibition to be held in London in 1851.[22]

The Society of Arts appointed an Executive Committee to manage the business, consisting of Henry Cole, Francis Fuller, the civil engineer John Farey, and Joseph Woods, architect, geologist and botanist, to work with

George Drew. Meanwhile Cole, Fuller and Digby Wyatt, armed with the diploma, set off for the manufacturing districts to collect opinions and evidence. They travelled to Manchester, the Potteries in Staffordshire, Sheffield, Leeds, Bradford, Rochdale, Huddersfield, Kendal and Glasgow, and then went on to Balmoral to report progress to the Prince.

They reported on the state of the contract, ready for signature, the contractors having already paid the Society's bankers £500, and being ready to invest £20,000 in a trust to provide prize money. The Prince graciously indicated he would be a trustee for the fund. They were able to give a good account of their reception amongst the northern manufacturers, and Cole could add that he had spoken to the Chairman of the East India Company, which was ready to give its backing to the venture. Prince Albert asked for a report, but instructed Cole to check any opinions quoted in the report with the speakers. The Deputation was due to continue to Ireland, where they were instructed to see the Lord Lieutenant.

As soon as the contract was signed on 11 November, 1849, and the prize money of £20,000 paid up, the Executive Committee, with Robert Stephenson as Chairman, and Matthew Digby Wyatt as Secretary, moved into offices provided by the contractors at 1 Palace Yard, Westminster. Essentially their job for the time being was to continue the work of soliciting support and contributions, largely through the promotion of local committees.

The Prince had always taken the view that government should be involved. When he wrote to Labouchere in July about 'a great national and even international Exhibition' which the Society of Arts had in mind, he referred to it as 'of the highest importance and ought not to be approached except in harmony with and under the guidance of the Govt'.[23] A Royal Commission was therefore always part of the scheme, and three days later a draft list of Commissioners was being drawn up, ranging from wealthy aristocrats like the Duke of Buccleuch, politicians such as Gladstone and Peel, the geologist Sir Henry de la Bêche, the agriculturalist Philip Pusey to Scott Russell and Fuller. Cole too, saw the need for the Royal Commission, temporarily delayed by the Parliamentary vacation, but he saw the moment as ripe for approaching manufacturers who were 'thriving and making money and . . . likely to subscribe liberally'. The Prince's secretary, Colonel Phipps, with the difficult task of conveying the Prince's enthusiasm for the project and his readiness to be involved whilst restraining Cole's propensity to take matters into his own hands, and to use the Prince's name too freely, pointed out that it was only the Cabinet that could make it a Government matter.[24] Since it could not be resolved before the return of the Government to London, the Prince's instructions to Cole, Fuller and Scott Russell 'to collect opinions of leading manufacturers and other evidence' were issued in his capacity as President of the Society of Arts.[25]

Meanwhile, Prince Albert had been writing to foreign contacts about the project, to his brother in Coburg, to Quetelet, his statistician friend in Belgium, and to Stockmar about his plan for a World Industrial Exhibition.

> Agents report from the manufacturing districts that the manufacturers hail the project with delight, and will co-operate heartily; and the East India Company promises to contribute a complete collection of all the products of India. The matter will be further advanced in October. To win over the Continent will be no easy matter.[26]

The meeting in Dublin went almost too well, with a hearty welcome from the lord mayor followed by a public meeting at which both Cole and Fuller spoke. Fuller ended by saying that amongst all the men he and Cole had met in the great manufacturing towns 'the best-informed man they came in contact with was the Prince himself'. Phipps was upset by the report, and warned the Prince that this could damage the whole enterprise, making it a further occasion for deprecating the projected public meeting in London. 'A meeting in a private room of some of the leading manufacturers and practical men of science, for the purpose of ample discussion, is, of course, a different thing altogether'. The Prince responded by asking Phipps to remind Cole that 'the strictest privacy was originally observed, and to caution him not to be drawn away by degrees from the original position. Praising me at meetings looks as if I were to be advertised and used as a means of drawing a full house, &c., &c.'[27]

The proposed meeting in London went ahead, at the Mansion House, on 17 October, despite Phipps's concern. Cole made a stirring speech making the points that provincial support had already been expressed, and that though foreign government might support such things by 'compulsory taxation' this was not the English way:

> I believe that no public works are ever executed by any foreign gov-

ernment which can vie for magnificence, completeness and perfection, with those that our countrymen execute for themselves [Hear,
hear] . . . The feeling of the Society of Arts and Prince Albert is, that
it would be far nobler for the English people to do the thing well for
themselves, as far as they can, rather than ask the Government for
assistance.

Seasoned with a few jokes at Scottish expense, the idea of an exhibition,
funded by subscription, but under the management of a Royal
Commission was enthusiastically received. A proposal to form a City
Committee which would include not only the Lord Mayor and the
Aldermen, but also every banker of standing was carried. Public support
for the scheme was such that the proposal for the Royal Commission went
ahead, and on 28 November Labouchere submitted a draft list of
Commissioners and a draft circular letter to them for the Prince's
approval.[28]

THE ROYAL COMMISSION

The proposal at this stage was for the Royal Commission to be responsible for arranging for foreign and colonial products and manufactures to
be included in the Exhibition, choosing a site, managing the Exhibition,
judging the entries and awarding the prizes. The Executive Committee
already appointed would have continued under the control of the Society
of Arts, which would have taken full financial responsibility under its contract with the Mundays. Neither Cole nor Dilke, who would have been
pivotal members of the Executive Committee, was very pleased to see
himself apparently excluded by the Royal Commission, and Grey had to
warn the Prince that both had threatened to withdraw if they were not to
attend the Commissioners' meetings.[29]

A more serious impediment was public reaction to the news of the
Munday contract, particularly amongst the Manchester manufacturers.
In the words of *The Times* it was 'a pity that the element of private speculation should be mixed up with a high national object'. It went on to
criticize the Society of Arts for not putting its faith in public subscription,
and Prince Albert for being 'ill-advised'. There was a feeling that a
national event of that importance should not be funded as a private speculation, together with a degree of suspicion that the whole thing was a
'job' . So great was the concern that a deputation headed by the Mayor of

Manchester, John Potter, planned to lobby the Prime Minister, Lord John Russell. Concern was somewhat allayed by the publication of the terms of the Royal Commission in the *London Gazette*, on 4 January, 1850.[30] The Commissioners included men of all political complexions, of financial standing, and prominence in the arts, architecture, science and agriculture.[31]

Earl Granville, a Whig grandee, and a man much trusted by the Prince was Vice-President and Chairman of the Finance Committee. There were politicians – Lord John Russell, Labouchere and Gladstone representing the government, Lord Stanley, later the 14th Earl of Derby (1799–1869), and Sir Robert Peel the Opposition; the landed aristocracy was represented by the Duke of Buccleuch and the Earl of Ellesmere; the City was represented by Jones Loyd, later Lord Overstone, and Thomas Baring, the arts by Charles Barry, C. L. Eastlake, and Richard Westmacott, science by the 3rd Earl of Rosse (1800–67), President of the Royal Society, Agriculture by Philip Pusey, brother of the better-known High Churchman. There were three *ex officio* Commissioners, the President of the Institution of Civil Engineers, a position first held by William Cubitt (1785–1861), succeeded by J. M. Rendel, and the Chairman of the Geological Society, Charles Lyell, again asked to continue when his term expired, and the Chairman of the East India Company, successively Sir Archibald Galloway, and John Shepherd. William Cubitt was found so valuable that on the expiry of his term *ex officio* that he was appointed in his own right. He must not be confused with the building contractor, Ald. William Cubitt (1791–1863), brother of Thomas Cubitt, to whom he was not related. Robert Stephenson was a later appointment as a Commissioner.[32] There were one or two refusals, including Earl de Grey, and the Duke of Richmond, leader of the agricultural interest alienated by the Repeal of the Corn Laws.

Some care and flexibility were required to adjust to the changed circumstances without losing the skill and dedicated drive of the original triumvirate who had made the running so far. The preamble to the Royal Commission makes it clear how great the contribution of the Society of Arts had been. The Society had already invested the £20,000 provided by the Mundays, in the names *inter alios* of the Marquess of Northampton, and the Earl of Clarendon, and had appointed five City figures including Sir John Lubbock, Samuel Morton Peto, and Baron Lionel de Rothschild, as treasurers for the receipt of donations, three officers of the Society to be treasurers for payment, and an Executive Committee of Robert Stephenson, Henry Cole, Charles Wentworth Dilke the younger, Fuller, and George Drew, nominated by the Mundays, with Matthew Digby Wyatt as Secretary. The Executive Committee members were already installed at 1 Palace Yard, in the offices provided by the Mundays, from which they operated until the offices in the Exhibition building itself were ready. In due course, after the Exhibition Building was closed the officers returned to the offices, partly because they were unlettable. As Bowring later observed, 'it seemed to be the best and the most economical method for us to resume the occupation of our own unoccupied and unlettable House'. Meeting rooms for the Royal Commission itself were found conveniently close, within the as yet unfinished New Palace of Westminster.[33]

THE CONTRACT WITH THE MUNDAYS

At the first meeting of the Commissioners on 11 January, 1850, it was decided to rationalize the relationship between Commission and Society, and also to ask the latter to terminate the arrangements with the Mundays, which had caused so much disquiet. Taking advantage of the clause so fortunately inserted which provided for the cancellation of the contract if the Treasury were prepared to refund the money, notice was given to the Mundays. The Commission in its *First Report* went out of its way to avoiding discrediting either the Society of Arts or the Mundays in the matter of the contract, and in fact, both parties suffered from the cancellation. The Society would have benefited from a third part of the profits, enabling it to fund further exhibitions, and the Mundays, who had taken all the risk when the matter was initiated saw their part removed, with all the kudos and profit going elsewhere. This led them to raise all sorts of difficulties, while the Treasury, not uncharacteristically, made it clear that no money was actually to leave their coffers, until the Commissioners gave an assurance that they would be responsible for the payment. The Mundays felt, not unreasonably, that they had perhaps not done as well as they might have done, and they, too, raised various difficulties, which displeased the Royal Commission and slowed matters further. In fact, the Mundays did not get the money they had advanced repaid until November 1850, some £22,500, with interest. The matter of compensation for 'loss of time, personal service and risk of the contractors' dragged on until the Exhibition had opened. Then by common consent the matter was referred to Robert Stephenson, as arbitrator, who decided on 21 July, 1850, after 'a full inquiry into the circumstances and hearing counsel on the case', that the Mundays should be awarded £5120 and costs of £587 against the Society of Arts.[34] This was repaid by the Royal Commission but the whole matter was felt to have reflected badly on the Mundays, and also apparently on Fuller.[35]

The Royal Commission took over much of the Society of Arts organization, retaining the Executive Committee, though without Fuller and Drew. Drew had been nominated by the Mundays, and both he and Fuller 'declared themselves unable to devote much time to their duties', owing to pressure of other business. They did reappear at the time of opening, provoking a strong reaction from the rest of the Executive Committee.[36] The Commission also made it clear at its first meeting that the status of the Executive Committee was to be altered, the members were to take their orders from the Secretaries to the Commission, and to have little further room for initiative. Correspondence with Government and ministers was to be the province of the Secretaries, and the Executive Committee would be excluded from the deliberations of the Commission.[37] Colonel William Reid, an experienced colonial administrator and a successful Governor of Bermuda[38] was appointed Chairman in the place of Robert Stephenson, who was made a Commissioner. John Scott Russell, Secretary of the Society, and Stafford Northcote, a former private secretary to W. E. Gladstone, were appointed Secretaries to the Royal Commission. Neither in fact spent a great deal of time on the Exhibition, Stafford Northcote because of family problems. He was replaced temporarily, and later permanently, by Edgar Bowring, a civil servant from the Board of Trade. Henry Cole was, of course, already a civil servant, at the Record Office, from which he was given two years absence. He was very unhappy at the loss of contact with the Royal Commission, and also at the loss of status in a project which he had done so much to promote.

The Royal Commission started work immediately, holding weekly meetings, usually chaired by Prince Albert, very much a working President. He was loyally supported by Granville as Vice-President, and Chairman of the Finance Committee. Having sorted out the question of the Mundays' contract, the Commission's first concerns were to raise money by subscription to replace the 'contractors' funds', to obtain a design, and to start the construction of the building on a suitable site, and then to solicit suitable objects from home and abroad to fill it.

The matter of the building was the most urgent, and a Building Committee was appointed at the third meeting on 24 January, 1850 consisting of two noble amateurs, the 5th Duke of Buccleuch (1806–66) and the 1st Earl of Ellesmere (1800–57), both experienced building owners, three architects, Charles Barry (1795–1860), C. R. Cockerell (1788–1863) and T. L. Donaldson (1795–1885), Professor of Architecture at University College, London, and three civil engineers, I. K. Brunel (1806–59), William Cubitt and Robert Stephenson (1803–59). A month later they reported on the choice of site, endorsing the original selection of the area on the south side of Hyde Park, immediately north of the barrack building, and between the newly created Albert Gate and the Prince of Wales Gate.

On 13 March, 1850, the Committee issued an invitation to 'all parties, who are disposed to help them, [asking for] suggestions for the general arrangement of the buildings . . . required for this Exhibition'. They provided a plan of the site for those interested and a set of rules and conditions to guide them, setting out which trees had to be preserved, and suggesting a single story building, top-lit and built of fireproof materials. It was not to occupy more than 900,000 square feet or 65,000 square metres, of which a maximum area of 700,000 square feet could be roofed. 'Contributors' were instructed to confine themselves to a single sheet of drawings of the size of the plan supplied, with buildings drawn to the scale of 1:1000, with a single sheet of explanation. The Committee made its intentions clear:

> Upon the general form of the Building in plan, the distribution of its parts, the mode of access and internal arrangements and contrivances, will depend the convenience and general fitness . . . and it is upon these points that the Committee seek information and suggestions . . .
>
> The Committee think it probable that when the plans are received they may not be limited to the selection of any one plan, but may derive useful ideas from many.[39]

Some 233 designs were returned by the appointed date of 8 April, and a further twenty were received late. The largest number (128) came from London architects, fifty-one from 'residents in provincial towns', six from

Scotland and three from Ireland. Of the thirty-eight from outside the British Isles, twenty-seven were from French architects, of whom twenty received honourable mention, and some 'further higher honorary distinction'. The list contains a number of tantalizing sobriquets – 'Q.', 'Sed quis custodiet Custodes' (185), of which 'A lady with great diffidence submits this plan' (53) is one of the most intriguing, together with a lot of predictable names – J. B. Bunning, the City Architect (194), J. T. Knowles (200), Lockwood and Mawson (77) from Bradford, Thomas Worthington from Manchester (109), together with a number of lesser-known figures, like Benjamin Broadbridge (100), who worked in North Kensington, William Scurry from Pimlico (130), who worked for Thomas Cubitt, and Messrs Soyer and Warrener (165), from the Reform Club, where Alexis Soyer was the chef and had designed the famous kitchens. The designs were exhibited at the Institution of Civil Engineers on 12 June, 1850. Unfortunately few of these designs have survived, though some were published at the time in books and periodicals.[40]

The Building Committee found it possible to select various designs for commendation, including a high proportion of those by French competitors. Two designs were singled out for their 'most daring and ingenious disposition and construction'; these were both iron and glass designs. One was by M. Hector Horeau (1801–72), who had submitted a scheme for an iron and glass building for the Paris markets the previous year, and the other by Richard and Thomas Turner of Hammersmith Works, Dublin (201) one of the great suppliers of conservatories, who had designed and built the Kew Palm Stove.

There was a certain contradiction in these commendations, since, as the *Illustrated London News* pointed out, the Commission's request had been only for 'suggestions' but most of the designs submitted were quite elaborately worked up. The 'plan or drawing sent in was to be a *mere outline sketch* upon a *single sheet*', even one executed on the sheet showing the proposed site, but the Committee had commended the fuller schemes. The *Builder* took an even more disapproving line, quoting a letter from a disappointed competitor. He pointed out how the Committee had praised the 'illustrious Continental neighbours [who] have especially distinguished themselves . . . by compositions of the utmost taste and learning, worthy of enduring execution, examples of what might be done in the *architectural* illustration of the subject'. This readiness to accept designs which ignored all the conditions was seen as 'a palpable act of injustice towards others who, very properly observing the letter of those conditions have been debarred from developing *their* talent' (*Builder*'s italics). Not only had the Committee praised the elaborate and permanent nature of many of the premiated foreign designs, but they had commended a disproportionate number of foreign entries; of the eighteen designs picked out only three came from the British total of 195, with fifteen of the thirty-eight foreign entries being included.[41]

However, as the Building Committee reported, none of the plans actually suited, though it was admitted that they were very useful: 'from some designs the lesson was thus learned of what to avoid, from others much information was gained; since many indispensable requisites had been foreseen, and more or less ingeniously provided for'. The Committee was faced with the problem of a temporary building, which economy demanded should be as reusable as possible, which had to be constructed in a very short time, by then under twelve months. It had not only to be cheap, but also to provide for the display of goods, and the convenient circulation of visitors. A single space would be required to make supervision easy and to give flexibility, a radiating plan would not work, while schemes with rows of parallel counters needed careful handling. A selection of parallel sheds on the site would be monotonous and devoid of variety or grandeur, while 'plans of an architectural character were generally too monumental, too much divided, and far too expensive'.[42]

But the solution seemed obvious, and could not be resisted, and on 9 May, the Building Committee set out to provide its own plan. The chief protagonists appear to have been Brunel, who designed the dome, and Donaldson. Charles Barry, though he afterwards disclaimed responsibility, appears to have had a hand in it, and Paxton wrote to his wife that Barry's 'own Child which you see in the London News is an abomination'.[43] A complete set of plans, working drawings, specifications and quantities was prepared, carried into effect by M. D. Wyatt, who had been seconded from the Executive Committee on 18 April, assisted by Owen Jones and the engineer C. H. Wild 'in preparing the requisite drawings and other particulars . . . and superintending its erection' for which they were to be paid £500 for twelve months' work.[44]

A vast brick palace with a dome 200 feet high was designed, calculated to require between thirteen and nineteen million bricks. It incurred a good deal of public ridicule, often less than charitable. As Cole later pointed out, 'Any *one* of the six [professionals] could have done the work well, acting on his sole responsibility. But the whole nearly wrecked the Exhibition by dispute and delay.' The design has perhaps been attacked too harshly since a decade later a very similar design was provided for the 1862 Exhibition, based on the experience of organizers and exhibitors alike of operating within the Crystal Palace. However, at the time it was a public relations disaster – *Punch* took the opportunity to lampoon Prince Albert by portraying the proposal as based on the infantry hat designed by the Prince .

THE PROBLEMS OF USING HYDE PARK

The completed scheme was put out to tender, but meanwhile on 22 June, 1850, an engraving of the Committee's building was published in the *Illustrated London News*.[45] The very solidity of the scheme alerted the opposition to the use of Hyde Park, at the time not only a lung for Londoners of all classes, but the fashionable parade for metropolitan society. Rotten Row was filled with equestrians and carriages every afternoon, and to be seen 'driving in the Row' was indispensable for social success. The threat to the Park united a powerful coalition of Lord Brougham, the radical former Lord Chancellor, the King of Hanover, better known as the Duke of Cumberland, and the best known, Colonel Charles Sibthorp (1783–1855), Member of Parliament for Lincoln, who had whipped up local anxiety about the prospect of the disruption. Sibthorp was a long-standing opponent of Prince Albert, who had been responsible for moving the reduction of the Prince's parliamentary grant in 1840. He was also an opponent of Catholic emancipation, parliamentary reform, and free trade, which was dear to many of the businessmen behind the proposal for the exhibition.[46] A more practical note was struck by the *Westminster Review*, which pointed out that though the proposed site was 'sufficiently convenient for omnibus passengers coming from the Bank, and within an easy lounging distance of Belgrave-Square and Buckingham Palace', it was a long way from any railway station. 'The expense of transporting heavy machinery from the North of England to Euston-square or Paddington stations will alone be sufficiently serious; but when to this is added the further expense of loading, unloading, conveyance and superintendence through the streets of London' many possible exhibitors would be deterred. It went on to point out the greater convenience of the land lying alongside the northern railway lines near Regent's Park, for both exhibitors of heavy goods and travellers from

Aberdeen alike. This sensible advice was ignored not only in 1851 but by the promoters of several subsequent exhibitions, indicating perhaps that the metropolitan visitor was the real target of the exhibition organizers.[47]

On 27 June, the churchwardens of St George's Hanover Square protested that the use of Hyde Park was 'highly objectionable, and will be attended with very considerable inconvenience', speaking on behalf of residents in Belgravia and Kensington who feared for their silver and their maids' morals. *The Times*, having compared the projected building to the recently extended Buckingham Palace, thundered:

> We are not to have a 'booth', nor a mere timber shed, but a solid, sub-
> stantial edifice of brick, and iron, and stone, calculated to endure the
> wear and tear of the next hundred years . . . Can anyone be weak
> enough to suppose that a building erected on such a scale will ever
> be removed? Under one pretext or another it will always remain a
> fixture.

The public outcry at the prospect of such a monstrosity in Hyde Park distressed the Prince who wrote to Stockmar on 28 June:

> The Exhibition is now attacked furiously by *The Times*, and the
> House of Commons is going to drive us out of the park. There is
> immense excitement on the matter. If we are driven out of the park,
> the work is done for! Never was anything so foolish.[48]

There was also a statutory authority in charge of the park, whose agreement was essential. Hyde Park was managed by the Department of Woods and Forests, under the ministerial control of Lord Seymour. There was obvious anxiety about the use of London's most fashionable open space as a building site, and the initial proposals were very restric-tive. The contractors were only to use one gate, the Prince of Wales Gate, which was to be paved in granite, the Queen's Ride was not to be inter-fered with in any way, either before or during the Exhibition, no drains within the Park were to be interrupted, and no trees were to be cut down without consent. The Royal Commission were to name the date on which they would remove the building, and on failure to do so, the Commi-ssioners of Woods, etc., would be entitled to remove it, and apply the proceeds to the cost. On its removal the Commissioners of Woods would reinstate the ground, and charge the Royal Commission for the costs. So appalled were the Commission by these demands that on 22 June, a top-ranking deputation of Lord Granville as Vice-President, Gladstone, one of Prince Albert's 'men of money', William Cubitt as Chairman of the Building Committee and Robert Stephenson called on the Chief Commissioner of the Treasury, which was acting as broker. More realistic conditions were demanded: some four entrances into the Park were requested, including Albert Gate, and three temporary granite-paved entrances opposite the ground west of the Barracks, one to the west of the Prince of Wales Gate; the use of the Queen's Ride was requested, not least because it was intended to provide access to the north side of the building to the 'walking public'. The Royal Commission formally gave notice that it was intended to close the Exhibition on or before November 1st 1851, and it was agreed that the building should be removed and the ground reinstated within seven months of the closing. It was pointed out that the contract was intended to include a provision for reinstatement, and it was agreed that only if this was not carried out properly should the Department of Woods and Forests employ their own men to rectify matters at the cost of the contractors, though support was provided by the Commission's guarantee, a matter which was to cause considerable trouble after the Exhibition closed. In due course, agreement was given by the Department of Woods and Forests, and a Royal Warrant issued on 26 September to the Royal Commission for the use of the Park. Two royal warrants for the felling of trees were granted, one for nine trees in July 1850, and one for a single tree in January 1851. Because of the complexity of the bodies involved, it was agreed that William Cubitt and Colonel Reid would represent the Royal Commission and Mr Mann, the Superintendent of Kensington Gardens, the Park authorities.[49]

THE INTERVENTION OF JOSEPH PAXTON

Meanwhile, the problem of the building was solved in a way that has grown into legend; there entered 'a man of genius, but no architect or engineer'[50] in the person of Joseph Paxton (1801–65), head gardener to the Duke of Devonshire. Paxton had been working for the Duke of Devonshire since 1826, when the latter had observed him working for the Horticultural Society at Chiswick, and had hired him to work at Chatsworth. From a relatively humble beginning he had, in effect, become the Bachelor Duke's 'Minister of Works', improving the gardens at Chatsworth with splendid water works and two grand new conservatories, one the famous Stove House of 1836–40. He had been concerned in rebuilding the estate village at Edensor, and later he was to extend the Duke's Irish house at Lismore. By 1849, he had become responsible for managing the Duke's financial affairs. From 1831 he had published the *Botanical Magazine*, and had developed a thriving career as an independent consultant, carrying out town-planning and landscape projects, including Birkenhead Park for William Jackson, and Princes Park in Liverpool, a cemetery at Coventry and an abortive scheme for land near the Menai Bridge. He had interests in a number of railway companies, including the Midland Railway and the Chester and Birkenhead and the Chester and Holyhead Railways, in which Jackson had interests. His most innovative building at Chatsworth was under construction in 1850, the Lily House for the enormous water-lily *Victoria regia*, where he had mimicked the ribs of the gigantic leaves in the design of the roof. In his building he used a ridge and furrow system for the roof, and utilized the hollow columns to carry off the water.[51]

Early in June 1850, he seems to have developed the idea of using the design of the Lily House for a building for the Exhibition. Paxton had a large interest in the Midland Railway, and it was on a visit to the House of Commons on 7 June that he first mentioned his idea to John Ellis (1789–1862), Member of Parliament for Leicester and chairman of the railway. Ellis took Paxton to the Royal Commission offices, in the hope of seeing Granville, nephew of the Duke of Devonshire, but in fact he only saw Cole. However, the latter was so impressed that he suggested that when the Committee's own scheme went out to tender very shortly, a proviso should be slipped in to allow tenders for a different scheme also to be submitted. He was able to persuade the Building Committee to adopt this extraordinary proposal.

Paxton returned home, but was only able to devote himself to his scheme after a visit to Stephenson working on the Britannia Bridge in Wales, and another meeting of the Midland Railway on 12 June, at which he did a first sketch on pink blotting paper. Returning to Chatsworth, he drew it up, with the assistance of W. H. Barlow (1812–1912), the Midland Railway engineer, who was later to design the great train shed at St Pancras. He travelled to London on 20 June, in company with Robert Stephenson, who had been involved with the Exhibition project through both the Society of Arts and the Royal Commission, and on his shrewd advice went first to see Lord Brougham, and enlisted the support of this former enemy of the whole Exhibition project. The following day,

Stephenson took him to see Lord Granville, and two days later he saw Prince Albert.

On the same day, Paxton got in touch with Charles Fox (1810–74), a native of Derby, and an experienced railway engineer, who had taken over Bramah's iron manufacturing business. He also contacted R. L. Chance, the Birmingham glass manufacturer, who had supplied the glass for the Great Stove House in 1839. He sent his plans to Fox and Henderson's works in Smethwick for Fox to develop the details. Fortunately he was able to recruit influential allies at the Commission. The Prince had seen evidence of Paxton's competence and ability to handle both buildings and large projects on his visit to Chatsworth in 1843. Stephenson, whom he knew well through his railway interests, 'helped him like a brother', while Henry Cole brought him the exact dimensions of the Building Committee's building to ensure that Paxton's plan would cover the same area. Brunel too had been won over to the idea, and advised Paxton to make sure he met the conditions for the exhibitors' stalls. His original scheme had been devised on a twenty-foot module, while the Commission had stipulated a twenty-four-foot space between the stalls.[52]

Paxton's plan was put to a special Commissioners' meeting on 25 June, proving sufficiently popular to be referred to the Building Committee for consideration. It was difficult for the Committee, already the butt of jokes, and under public attack, to reject their own design, and adopt an outsider's scheme. Worse was to follow: of the nineteen firms approached to tender for the brick design only three had sent tenders by 28 June, though the Committee hoped that with judicious omissions they might get the price down to £100,000.

The following evening Cole, who had been despatched by Lord Granville and Colonel Reid to seek lower tenders, set out on the night mail to Liverpool, Manchester and Birmingham. He drew blank in the first two, but in Birmingham he visited the works of Fox and Henderson at Smethwick, where Henderson said he was prepared to tender for Paxton's design. Cole asked him to consider that of the Building Committee, which the partners duly did, observing, however, that thirteen million bricks would be needed and that the recently completed Euston Station had needed twenty million and taken five months to lay. '3000 cu. yds of water' would need to be dried out of the dome.

Paxton, who was almost as shrewd a publicist as Cole, put forward his scheme through the press, in the *Illustrated London News*, on 6 July,[53] but the matter was already common knowledge two days earlier, when both Houses of Parliament came to debate the question of a site. Anxiety over the possibility of there being a vote against the Exhibition being held in Hyde Park was very great. A concerted attack was mounted in both Houses of Parliament on 4 July, with Lord Campbell, supported by the Chancellor, Lord Brougham, leading an attack in the Lords, and Colonel Sibthorp in the lower House, both basing their arguments on a petition from the speculative developer John Elger, who was the owner of building sites opposite Hyde Park. Much play was made by Lord Brougham of the amount of material to be moved on to the site, and the probable unrest and disorder which might be generated by the Exhibition itself. Sibthorp made the same points, and produced a potentially lethal motion, that the Commons should ask for a report, pending which no further steps should be taken by the Commission. Lord Granville replied in the Lords, and three Commissioners, Gladstone, Lord John Russell and Stephenson in the Commons. The sudden death of Sir Robert Peel, leader of the Opposition but also a Commissioner, had occurred on 2 July, leaving the Prince to fear that the Exhibition would have lost its most effective advocate in the House, but in fact Peel's loss seems to have silenced most of the Exhibition's critics, and Sibthorp's motion against the use of Hyde Park was defeated by 166 to 46.[54]

The Building Committee discussed the matter on 15 July, and agreed to advise the Commissioners to accept Paxton's scheme. At the public dinner in his honour at Derby in August 1851, Paxton described how he also replanned the building to bring the trees into the centre, and devised an arch for the transept to accommodate them, recording how Brunel had brought the measurements of the trees to him at Devonshire House.[55]

MONEY – THE GUARANTEE

The Commission had a site, and the prospect of a building, but money was still a major concern. By getting rid of the Mundays and sidelining the Society of Arts, the Commissioners had taken on themselves the responsibility of financing the Exhibition. They had continued the work of the triumvirate, of Cole, Fuller and Digby Wyatt, by sending out other emissaries to drum up the support of manufacturers, and to collect subscriptions, but there was not enough to fund the building. A report of January 1850 listed the subscriptions collected in the City as £14,408 5s. 0d., of which £5541 12s. 0d. had been paid into the Bank of England, and

£2537 5s. 0d. was on deposit at other banks. By 29 February, of a total of £79,224 13s. 4d., £67,896 12s. 9d. had been paid into the Commission's account.[56]

A series of meetings had been held in London in the winter. On 21 February, one took place in the West End, at Willis's Rooms, to which the ambassadors of the European powers, including France, Prussia and Belgium, and the American Minister, Mr Abbot Lawrence, contributed, with the support of Lord Brougham, and the Bishop of Oxford. The Duchess of Sutherland reported to the Queen that all had gone well, much helped by a stirring address from Lord Morpeth. A month later an even more successful meeting had been held at the Mansion House. The Prince himself made one of his best speeches, painting a picture of universal harmony aided by art and science spread by the growth of technology:

> Nobody . . . will doubt for a moment that we are living at a period of most wonderful transition, which tends rapidly to accomplish that great end, to which, indeed, all history points – *the realisation of the unity of all mankind . . .*
>
> The distances which separated the different nations and parts of the globe are rapidly vanishing before the achievements of modern invention, and we can traverse them with incredible ease; the languages of all nations are known, and their acquirement placed within the reach of everybody; thought is communicated with the rapidity, even by the power of lightning. On the other hand, *the great principle of division of labour*, which may be called the moving power of civilisation, is being extended to all branches of science, industry, and art.[57]

Punch, no more a supporter of Prince Albert than *The Times*, later portrayed him as 'The Industrious Boy' holding out his famous hat for alms, 'Please to remember the Exposition'.[58]

However, once a realistic cost for a building was in prospect it became clear that nothing like enough had been raised. Salvation came from leading businessmen, aware of the potential value of an international exhibition to a nation dedicated to free trade in a protectionist Europe, and as a class, always more supportive of the Prince's ventures than the hereditary politicians. The idea of a guarantee against a loss to supplement the subscriptions had been floated by Lord Granville, and a number

Fig 2. 'Industrious Boy', *Punch*'s cartoon of Prince Albert as
a fundraiser for the 1851 Exhibition.

of Commissioners had guaranteed sums ranging from £500 from Prince
Albert, to £20,000 from the great railway contractor, Samuel Morton
Peto. The latter met Cole on 12 July, 1850, as the question of the building
was being settled, and asked after the fund, saying he was off to Lowestoft
(where he had a house), but would be back in a fortnight. Cole told him
firmly that not enough guarantors had come forward, and that the matter was now urgent. The two men went to the writing room of the
Reform Club, where Peto wrote his now famous letter to the Prince, as
President of the Commission. In this, he stated that in his 'desire to promote the Exhibition' he was 'willing, on behalf of myself and *friends*, to
guarantee the sum of £50,000, or if necessary to advance the same for the
purposes of the Exhibition'. He added a rider to the effect that its success
'would be considerably increased by the adoption of Mr Paxton's plan, if
it is not too costly'.[59] The guarantee was embodied in a legal document,
which was happily never called upon. In a nice touch of sentiment, the
document, which properly was due for destruction after the Exhibition
closed, was saved – a replica being made and destroyed, the original bond
being saved among the Prince's papers.[60]

    The news of Peto's generous offer was given to the Commissioners at
their meeting on 15 July, 1850, and at the adjourned meeting held the following day they agreed to abandon the Building Committee's design, for

which Brassey had tendered £84,141. The Committee itself advocated the adoption of Paxton's scheme, which, as they pointed out, could provide an additional one-fourth of space if equipped with galleries, and with the proposed semi-cylindrical roof would include the trees under the glass. Fox and Henderson tendered £79,800 for Paxton's scheme, with an additional cost of £6000 for the barrel vault, to save some of the threatened trees, which the Commission agreed it would like to accept.

The matter was finally decided at a meeting of the Commission on 26 July, by coincidence the day of another attack by Colonel Sibthorp in Parliament on the use of Hyde Park, happily also abortive. The Commission had before them a somewhat equivocal report from the Building Committee, which reflected dissension between the architects and engineers, and also a justified concern as to whether, in the short time remaining before 1 January, 1851, it would be possible to complete a proposed longitudinal vaulted roof, advocated by Charles Barry. This was in addition to the barrel vault for the transept, needed to save the trees, which were becoming an increasing problem because of the obdurate attitude of Lord Seymour to any unnecessary felling. The Commission met under the chairmanship of Lord Granville, heard from Barry and Cubitt on the concerns of the Building Committee, and from Fox, who said he could complete the building with either the flat or the circular roof by 1 January, 1851. Paxton gave his preference to the flat roof as being 'more easily executed and completed in the time with certainty than the circular longitudinal roof'. The exact responsibility for the idea of the arched transept was hotly disputed at the time, and even since by the biographers of the various protagonists. The idea of a transept appears to have originated with Fox and Henderson, who advocated it for structural reasons. The arched vault is attributed to Barry, who put it forward at the Building Committee as a solution to the problem of the elms. One of his modern biographers has suggested that the idea came from his close friend the engineer, Sir John Wolfe.[61]

The decision was taken that, with the addition of the galleries, it would be possible to shorten the overall length of the building. Agreement was reached without any of the threatened resignations, a definitive plan was signed by Lord Granville, and it was established that Colonel Reid, as Chairman of the Executive Committee, and William Cubitt, as Chairman of the Building Committee would be jointly responsible for the works in Hyde Park.[62]

THE CHARTER

In fact, as the Commission was forced to acknowledge, it was in no position to accept any tender or sign any contract. Fox and Henderson had to
proceed with the construction works solely on the word of Lord
Granville, as Vice-Chairman of the Royal Commission. A problem which
surfaced with the reality of the building was the status of the Commission.[63] Possibly because it was such a novel concept, the First Royal
Commission did not give adequate authority to the Commissioners. They
were instructed to 'make full and diligent inquiry into the best mode by
which the productions of Our Colonies and of Foreign Countries may be
introduced into Our Kingdom', into the most suitable site, and the best
manner of managing such an exhibition, and of selecting and awarding
prizes. Nothing gave the Commissioners the right to spend money on an
expensive building, or even on the prizes, probably because the Society of
Arts and the Mundays had been dispensed with only after the
Commission started work. Very rapidly, on 15 August, a Charter of
Incorporation was issued to the existing Commissioners, giving them the
legal status to carry through the activities relating to the Exhibition, into
which hitherto they had only been qualified to inquire. A stern coda
emphasized the temporary nature of these powers, which were to cease
'when and as soon as all the matters and things entrusted . . . shall be fully
performed . . . then these presents . . . shall be absolutely void'. The opportunity was taken to add Robert Stephenson to the list of Commissioners.
Once the Charter was signed, they were able to negotiate a contract with
Fox and Henderson, finally signed on 31 October, 1850, and to draw on
the Bank of England for funds.[64] Fox later recalled that by the time the
contract was signed, he and his partners had spent £50,000 on the drawings and construction, all without the possibility of legal redress.[65]

DEVELOPMENT OF THE CRYSTAL PALACE

Fortunately Fox and Henderson did not wait for the contract to begin
work, or to set in motion the manufacture of the components for the
building. In essence Paxton had produced a viable project, but a large
number of working drawings were required, as well as some innovative
construction methods. Both at the time and since, it has been pointed out
that amongst the projects submitted to the Commissioners earlier, there
were a number of iron and glass designs on which he could have drawn.

These included those of Horeau and Turner, and even of Charles Harriott Smith, whose widow claimed in her autobiography that Paxton could have stolen the idea from her husband. Equally the plan is very close to that of the Building Committee building. The responsibility for the final detailed design of the building and its success was disputed very publicly, so much so that the *Art Journal* could only observe that the accounts given by Paxton, Fox and Barry 'of their respective shares in the production of the accepted plan, are not strictly reconcilable with each other'.[66] A recent biographer of Paxton has put it less combatively, suggesting that 'it would be more accurate to regard the design and erection of the Exhibition Building as a piece of inspired teamwork by Paxton, Fox, Henderson and Chance', though this perhaps does not give enough credit to the 'home team' of William Cubitt, Wild, Digby Wyatt and Owen Jones.[67] Though the *Art Journal*, like most contemporaries gave the credit for the idea to Paxton, it is very unlikely that it would have come to pass without contractors who were not only prepared to start work at their own risk, without a contract, but were also very experienced in constructing glass and iron buildings, having built nearly 40 acres of glass roofing in the last twelve years.[68] Fox paid an elegant tribute to Barry for 'his invaluable improvement in the architectural beauty of the building'. Paxton himself gave credit to Fox at a lecture given in October 1850 before the building was complete.[69] In a lecture on the building given at the Institute of Civil Engineers, Digby Wyatt summed the process up:

> From the practical experience which they brought to bear upon the subject, designs grew into realities – difficulties were foreseen and remedied – and a high order of mechanized contrivance was displayed, in adaptations of machinery to economise labour and to perfect production.

He also paid tribute to William Cubitt, who, as Chairman of the Building Committee, had been made responsible for approving design and construction on behalf of the Royal Commission. Recalling the 'great services rendered by Mr Cubitt in undertaking so much of the labour of the supervision of the details of the proposed construction, and of the general matters connected with the building', he called him the 'master mind' in the affair.

Other contemporaries took the same view; Weale published a four-part work on the exhibition building by Charles Downes, architect, in which he referred to the 'superintendence of the construction and erection' being 'specially entrusted to William Cubitt'.[70]

The minutes of the Commission make clear that, as the number and variety of the exhibits grew, a great many modifications and improvements were necessary to ensure the building's stability, and to provide all the space needed. It is not recorded on whose initiative all these modifications were made, but it seems clear that Cubitt played a significant part, if only in keeping the Finance Committee in touch with developments. On 14 November, the Finance Committee authorized a further £1000 to provide diagonal bracing and further stability. At the same time the Executive Committee reported a great increase in the expected exhibits, partly due to the addition of Agricultural Implements, and Cubitt, as Chairman of the Building Committee, put forward an ingenious scheme by which additional galleries on alternate aisles would provide an increase of over 2 acres in exhibition space. At the same time he suggested enclosing further space from the refreshment courts, part of which had been left open to protect some of the smaller trees. Much more elaborate staircases to serve the additional galleries and to provide better circulation were required, while to provide greater flexibility in circulation, it became necessary to use planed timber floorboards much more extensively throughout the building. Ventilation too, became more of a concern. The original intention had been to cover the semi-circular heads of the transept with canvas which would have provided through ventilation, but on the decision being taken to fill these with glass, further louvres elsewhere were required.[71]

A great many details were only solved as the building progressed and was put to the test, for example by groups of soldiers tramping over girders in the galleries. Cubitt had as assistants the three men recruited to work up the Building Committee's own drawing. C. H. Wild was responsible for the engineering details, and Owen Jones for decoration. Matthew Digby Wyatt was in charge of general building construction, together with supervision of the fulfilment of the contract, extras and the payment of monthly accounts – what today we might see as project management. In addition, there was a clerk of works, a Mr Earie, and a surveyor, Mr Harwood.

Charles Heard Wild (d. 1857) was a civil engineer, who trained in the factory of John Braithwaite. After working in France on propeller boats, he went to work for Fox, Henderson and Company, in Birmingham. His

Fig 3. A detachment of Royal Engineers testing the strength of the Gallery floors.

skill as a designer and draughtsman was so marked that he was recruited by Robert Stephenson to work on various important railway and other engineering projects including the Britannia Bridge, when he contributed a number of important improvements and new inventions. On Stephenson's recommendation he was appointed to work on the building in Hyde Park, and was in due course to assist in its removal to Sydenham.[72]

Owen Jones (1809–74) was the son of a London furrier with Welsh antiquarian interests, who trained with Vulliamy and at the Royal Academy Schools. He had laid the foundation of his career by travelling in the Levant, Egypt and Spain, a tour which culminated in the publication of a volume on the *Plans, Details and Sections of the Alhambra* (1836–43), which established him both as an expert on decoration, and on innovative colour printing and book production. These interests brought him into contact with Ludwig Gruner, from Dresden, Prince Albert's 'adviser on art', with whom he worked on chromolithographic book production, and Henry Cole, through whom he joined the Society of Arts in 1847.[73] Owen Jones was responsible for the colour scheme, though he himself paid tribute to Barry for his contribution to the design and use of colour. His suggestions were submitted to the Commission in early December 1850. It was agreed that three external coats would be sufficient, and that the 'third coat should be in plain colour' arousing some interesting speculation. The use of flags as external decoration was approved, but the design of these contentious national emblems was checked with foreign missions individually, before drawings were prepared. A subcommittee of Prince Albert, Sir Richard Westmacott and Sir Charles Eastlake were appointed to inspect the samples of interior painting submitted by Owen Jones. They decided on white sash-bars, a white and blue ridge, 'the Paxton gutters to remain as they are, but the red to be of a lighter shade; the columns and rest of the iron-work to remain as proposed by Mr Owen Jones'. This discreet minute may reflect the observation of a contemporary that Jones's 'steady perseverance against a violent and clamorous opposition from the self-appointed arbiters of taste, enabled him to carry out his ideas of the true principles of decorating such a structure'.[74]

However the responsibility for the building is apportioned, the Crystal Palace was one of the wonders of the age, and both contemporaries and later historians have tried to do it justice.

It was essentially a modular building of iron, wood and glass, built of components which were meant to be recyclable, since it was understood from the first that it would be removed after the Exhibition closed. Though such buildings had been constructed before, and indeed at least two had been offered to the Commission among the 245 designs submitted, nothing on such a scale had been contemplated, nor with such a tight deadline. After all its negotiations the Commission obtained possession of the site on 30 July, and the first column was erected on 26 September. Work proceeded throughout the winter; by 1 November, over 1500 workmen were on site daily, rising to 2000 in December and January. For Londoners it was an Eighth Wonder of the World going up in their midst, recorded on a weekly basis by the *Illustrated London News*.

The building stood between the South Carriage Drive and Rotten Row, with the entrance facing towards and in line with Prince's Gate, making the western wing shorter than the eastern. It was constructed on a system of cast-iron columns based on the Commissioners' 24-foot grid. The hollow columns were 19 feet high on the ground tier and 17 feet on the two upper tiers, connected vertically by 3-foot-long pieces. These also provided a horizontal connection with the girders which carried the galleries and provided lateral stability. These girders carrying the gallery were 24-foot cast-iron girders, but wrought iron was used for the larger and more elaborate components in the wider spans. The hollow columns provided drainage, carrying both the rainwater and the condensation

Fig 4. General view of work in progress on the Crystal Palace.

from the glass roof down into a system of specially constructed drainage channels through the park into the existing sewers. This drainage was made possible by the cleverly designed wooden beams, the famous Paxton gutters, in the roof, which not only carried the glass panes, but were channelled to catch the condensation and carry it away before it could drip on to the precious goods or the visitors. Some 200 miles of these sash bars were required to carry the 896,000 square feet of glass in the roof. Both sash-bars and glass were modular, the panes being 16 oz glass, 10 inches by 49 inches. The outside walls were vertically boarded on much of the ground floor, but glazed in the upper stories. Metal louvre panels provided ventilation, placed immediately above the floor at ground level, and at the top of each storey elsewhere. The problem of light and heat, a serious consideration for both exhibitors and visitors, was addressed by the use of cotton cloth in great panels which shielded about half the building area from the direct light of the sun. The temperature was carefully monitored, and in the course of the summer it was decided to remove some ninety sashes 20 feet high by 8 feet wide, to increase ventilation. The Commission's records indicate that despite the numbers in the building, and the summer season, it was usually possible to keep the temperature inside within 2 or 3 degrees of that outside, and even on some summer days below the outside temperature.

Fig 5. Building the Crystal Palace: fixing the hollow cast-iron
columns which carried the water off the acres of roofs.

The timber work was prepared at the Fox and Henderson works in
Chelsea, and at Birch's Phoenix sawmills at Cumberland Market, with
planing machines and gutter-cutting machines creating the wooden components. Hoisting machinery on site was varied, with everything from
three-legged cranes to horse-power, and for exceptional tasks like the
hoisting of the iron ribs into position, massed manpower orchestrated by
Fox himself. Machinery was used wherever possible, for planing and cutting gutters, even for painting the miles of wooden sash-bars, and an
ingenious glazing wagon, devised by Fox, enabled the men to travel safe-
ly across the acres of ridge and furrow roof.[75]

Essentially it was a glass cathedral rather than a Crystal Palace, running east and west on the north side of the South Carriage Drive, 1848
feet in length, stretching from the newly created Albert Gate to west of
the Prince of Wales Gate. The building was 408 feet wide, north to south,
with a further double bay 48 feet wide, and 936 feet long on the north
side. The Nave, running east–west, with a flat roof rather than Barry's
proposed vault, was 64 feet high, flanked with galleried aisles. The 'flat
roof' was in fact roofed on the ridge and furrow principle, for which
Chance filed a patent on Paxton's behalf a week after his design had been

Fig 6. The 'Glazing Wagon', used to transport workmen over the roofs
of the Exhibition building.

accepted.[76] It was intersected in the centre by the Transept, whose semi-
cylindrical roof, devised to save the famous elms, rose to a height of 104
feet. Two courts elsewhere in the building were designed to safeguard
two further clumps. The Nave was 72 feet wide, with smaller avenues
either side some 24 feet wide, rising to 44 feet with galleries, with the outside single-storey aisles only 24 feet high. On either side of the Nave were
galleries at first-floor level, one bay wide, and two storeys high. Next to
them were two-bay aisles to the full height of the two storeys, with a
further first-floor gallery aisle on the outside. Beyond were three further
single-storey bays, on the south side, with an extension on the north. The
floor area, some 19 acres, was four times the size of St Peter's at Rome,
and six times larger than St Paul's. Contemporaries pointed out that the
Nave was nearly twice as wide as that of St Paul's Cathedral, noting that
while the church took thirty-five years to build the present building
would be raised in half the number of weeks. The ground floor provided
some 772,784 square feet, with a further 217,100 square feet in the galleries. There were entrances on the south, east and west, but exits on all
sides at the end of transverse aisles. There was a detached boiler-house
on the western side, to provide power for the machinery in motion. Not

everything could be fitted within the building, and there was a section for the larger specimens of building materials, cement and marble, for specimens of coal, for boats and an obelisk outside at the west end. At the eastern, or foreign end, there was a French fountain, a Swedish cross and a boat. There was a cresting on the roof cornice to provide interest, and further decoration was provided by flagstaffs on the tops of the columns carrying the flags of all the nations represented, an idea attributed to Digby Wyatt.[77]

A particularly Albertian external exhibit was the pair of Model Cottages, designed by Henry Roberts for the Society for Improving the Condition of the Labouring Classes of which Prince Albert was President. The Prince had persuaded the Duke of Wellington to make available vacant ground near the Knightsbridge Barracks, it being impossible to put it elsewhere after the objection to 'bricks and mortar within the Park'.[78] He himself paid the cost of erection, some £458 14s. 7d., and the cottages not only won a Council Medal, but were seen by quarter of a million visitors during 1851, being re-erected in due course as a lodge for Kennington Park.[79]

On 1 February, the *Illustrated London News* could tell its readers that the task was nearly complete, and it had been 'publicly announced that the interior will by next week be ready for the reception of goods, and consequently, the principal work now to be performed lies in the arrangement of the tables, counters, stands, shelves, etc., with the interesting and marvellous objects which will be stored upon them; in the execution of the light and gay decoration adopted by Mr Owen Jones, both inside and outside'.[80] This appears to have been too optimistic, for on 27 February, Cole was drawing Reid's attention to the slow progress of the painters, and through the Commissioner's offer of a further £1000, Fox and Henderson were persuaded to bring in more painters, making the total working in the building over two thousand, until after the opening. This was not the first extra payment that the Commission had to meet. Very considerable additions had been made to the original design in the form of increased space and extended galleries, refreshment rooms, increased offices and staircases, better amenities in gas-lighting and additional ventilation, water for the fountains, and a boiler-house and the arrangements for the Machinery in Motion section. All these had raised the price from the contract sum of £79,800 to £107,780 7s. 6d., agreed by William Cubitt and the officers responsible. However, after the Exhibition closed,

Fox and Henderson discovered that the additional costs incurred by the speed with which they had had to work had necessitated their being less economical in procurement than they had anticipated, and in fact they were likely to incur a heavy loss. Under the circumstances, and in view of the contractors' contribution to the success of the whole enterprise, the Commission paid a further £35,000 to them on 7 November, 1851.[81]

The view from the north-west shows the building in its full glory, between the Serpentine and the Kensington Road, but explains the anxiety of local developers like John Elger, heavily involved in building Prince's Gate, about its effect on the saleability of their fine new developments. On the Serpentine on the north side, there were a number of model boats during the Exhibition.

II

The Great Exhibition of 1851:
Filling the Building

I f we turn from the troubles of getting the right building designed and placed on an appropriate site to the problem of getting it appropriately filled on the opening day, the task was equally heroic. The problem of classification of the exhibits had been addressed at the meeting on 30 June, 1849, when the four great divisions of Raw Materials, Machinery, Manufactures and Sculpture, had been proposed by the Prince and agreed. These made up a logically consistent progression from the 'raw materials which nature supplies to the industry of man', to 'the machinery by which man works upon those materials', then the 'manufactured articles which he produces', and finally 'the art which he employs to impress them with the stamp of beauty'.[1] These had been further divided by Lyon Playfair into thirty manageable classes, but of course there were frequent queries which had to be answered. The problems were considerable: as Lord Normanby had observed with a diplomat's realism, the difficulty was 'how sufficiently to define the description of articles for which the prizes shall be given as neither on the one side to appear to favour the Foreigner nor practically to exclude him from the benefit whilst professing to admit him'.[2] There was also a host of minor decisions, which had to be settled. Thus, were fur coats 'animal products' or 'manufactured articles', and what indeed were wigs? These were adjudicated either by Colonel Reid, by the Local Committees or finally by the Juries. Machinery provided particular problems since many were designs in the course of development, and in the primitive state of patent law at the time, little protection from foreign, or even domestic, plagiarism could be offered to inventors and manufacturers, either British or foreign, and concern about this led to the withdrawal of many articles.[3]

LOCAL COMMITTEES

Early in the tours made by Cole and his friends, the idea of 'Local Committees' in the United Kingdom was adopted. The provincial Local Committees were responsible for drumming up local support and subscriptions at the beginning of the venture, and at the end for encouraging the submission of articles for display, and for selecting those ultimately displayed. After the establishment of the Commission, the work of Cole and his companions in publicizing the Exhibition was continued by agents sent into the provinces, who were paid either £1 a day in the metropolis, or 3 guineas per provincial town. One such agent reported: 'sixteen towns organized; seeds of good sown in five others; one abandoned as hopeless'. He had found three visits necessary to get matters moving in Blackburn: 'I endeavoured not to find the necessity for me to initiate anything, but practically I found I had to do all the work, write the Resolutions, suggest the Members of Committee . . . and get up the whole steam'.[4] Committees were formed in some 297 cities and districts, and the duty of keeping in touch with them was delegated to two Special Commissioners, Dr Lyon Playfair, and Lieutenant Colonel Lloyd, an engineer who had had an adventurous career in South America, appointed through the kindness of Prince Albert.[5] The most useful Local Committee members were elevated to Local Commissioners, of whom a total of nearly 450 are recorded by name.[6] By and large they were manufacturers, engineers or in retail trade, but the name of the occasional banker or architect appears in the list. Some very small towns supported a committee; Melrose with 966 persons was the smallest, but there was a cluster of small towns in Derbyshire, Glossop, Bakewell and Buxton, all with a population of less than 2000. In some cases, the members of the Committees seem to have been recruited through trade associations, as in Edinburgh.[7] The position in London was slightly different since there were over twenty committees, not only for areas like Westminster, which also boasted a 'Ladies' Committee', or Marylebone, but also in traditional manufacturing areas such as Finsbury, Poplar, Tower Hamlets and Lambeth, and as far west as Brentford and Richmond. They were encouraged to drum up support and subscribe, but when the choice of articles came to be made, specialist metropolitan Committees were formed for machinery, textiles and so forth, corresponding to the thirty classes of Playfair's classification. The value of these Committees is attested by the

accounts given in the *First Report of the Royal Commission* of their operation in selected centres – Birmingham, Manchester, Marylebone, and a
specialist Committee from London, dealing with 'Machines for Direct
Use', under the chairmanship of Henry Maudslay.

British Dependencies, as they were termed, were approached through
the Colonial Secretary, except for India, where the East India Company
was involved. The Secretary to the Company wrote a despatch to the
'Supreme Government of India' which was to be forwarded to the local
governments of Bengal, Bombay and Madras, encouraging local manufacturers to put forward their products:

> An occasion will thus be presented for diffusing amongst Europeans,
> a more extensive Knowledge of the Raw Products and Manufactures
> of India. We are at all times desirous of encouraging the develop-
> ment of the resources of that vast Empire, and we attach consider-
> able importance to the formation of a collection of its products for
> public Exhibition, as calculated not only to be of great use to the
> European Manufacturer, but also of essential benefit to our Eastern
> Possessions, which produce many articles little known in this
> Country, yet possessed of valuable properties and procurable in large
> quantities, at a probably cheap rate, if a demand could be created for
> them.

He instructed the 'several Governments' and 'servants' to let this be
known 'throughout India', and to put together a 'Collection of the Raw
Products and Manufactures of India, as may not only be interesting in a
scientific point of view, but may also be subservient to the purposes of
Commerce and Art'. This collection would be coordinated by the
Company to avoid duplication, and to ensure a wide spread of articles and
regions. He suggested amongst others that the following manufactured
articles would be well received:

> Cottons and silks, such as Muslins and Shawls of Dacca and Delhi
> and other districts. Brocades of Benares and Loongies of Scinde, etc.,
> Woollens, such as Blankets of the North Western Provinces and of
> the Himalayas, with the coarse fabrics made of the Wool of the Shawl
> Goat, the Shawls of Cashmere, Dyed articles of Cotton and Silk,
> Mats of Sylphet and other provinces, Paper both of the Plains and
> the Mountains, Pottery from 'Different parts', Tanned Leather and
> prepared skins of different animals, Indian lacquered ware, toys etc.,

work in Metal, using copper, brass and other metals, Embroidered work in gold and silver and other metals, and Jewellery from various parts of India.[8]

If there was an element of mutual suspicion between the metropolis and the British provinces, this was nothing to the problem of dealing with foreign exhibitors, and in the matter of approaching them the Prince's position as husband of the Queen was vital. In fact, it is difficult to see how even the group gathered to promote the Exhibition, influential and full of inventiveness and energy though it undoubtedly was, could have achieved this without the royal connection. The full panoply of Treasury intervention and interdepartmental negotiation had been involved over the use of Hyde Park, where the title 'Royal' was perhaps rather a euphemism, but the Prince's influence was greater where the Foreign Office was concerned. The Royal Family's battles with the Foreign Secretary at this time, particularly when that minister was Lord Palmerston, are legendary, but they stemmed to a large extent from the tradition of royal involvement in dealings with foreign governments, many of which were headed by real rather than nominal 'cousins'.

British ambassadors in all the European capitals were contacted initially through the Foreign Office, which forwarded copies of letters to the Prince, and occasionally more directly through Prince Albert's own office where his secretaries were two well-connected officers, Colonel Charles Grey (1804–70), a son of Earl Grey of the Reform Bill, and Colonel C. B. Phipps (1801–66), brother of the 1st Marquess of Normanby, the statesman and politician, who was British ambassador in Paris.

The attitude of the French was particularly important, since France had the most experience of running exhibitions, albeit only national ones. Normanby had been alerted in the autumn of 1849, when he was able to report that Louis-Napoleon, then President of France, supported the idea. The French were the first to offer congratulations on the project, when M. Sallandrouze de la Mornaix wrote:

Cette noble initiative a été accueillie avec enthousiasme, non seulement en Angleterre, mais dans tous les pays industriels, par les hommes qui apprécient la supériorité des conquêtes du travail et du commerce sur les ruineux et souvent injustes triomphes des années.[9]

Once the Royal Commission had been appointed, it approached the Foreign Office asking for chargés d'affaires and consular officers throughout the world to be instructed to approach their host countries, while diplomats and consuls in London were also alerted. Voluntary organizations were also approached, some of whom found their task difficult: 'the collection of definite information in Eastern countries being a very uncertain and tedious process', explained John Capper, the Secretary of the Asiatic Society, from Colombo, to the Royal Commission in June 1850. In other cases, foreign representatives found the British less than well informed about conditions abroad, like the British consul in Stockholm who pointed out that the Baltic was closed from 1 December to the end of April, making it difficult to forward exhibits to arrive between January and March, as had been requested.[10]

The decision was taken early that all communications with foreign countries would be only through their national committees or Commissions, of which some thirty came into existence. These would be responsible for selecting exhibits, and often subsidizing exhibitors in travel and other expenses.[11] It was of course still the Europe of the *ancien régime*: though a united Italy was to appear within ten years, and a united Germany within twenty. In some cases this reduced the task of those advertising the Exhibition, thus an approach in Vienna enabled communications to be sent throughout south-eastern Europe, including Hungary and Dalmatia, part of modern Poland, northern Italy, as well as the Tyrol and modern Austria; a notice in the *Official Vienna Gazette* announced that exhibits would be collected and forwarded from four centres, each with a Branch Committee, Vienna, Feldkirch in the Vorarlberg, Prague and Milan, at the expense of the government. The seriousness with which participation was seen by the Austrian Commission is shown by the stirring reminder to 'all the brave Agriculturists, Tradesmen, Manufacturers, Workmen, Engineers and Artists of the empire':

> The arrangements which have been made by the London Commission . . . justify the hopes that Foreign Productions will be justly appreciated, and most of the States of Europe have already promised to take part . . . Austria cannot remain behind. It is worth while to maintain the struggle, to defend the Manufacturing and Artistical honour and reputation of our Fatherland, to conquer the place our country has a right to hold in the world, to maintain our

1. *The Royal Commissioners for the Exhibition of 1851* by Henry Wyndham Phillips. This does not in fact show all the Commissioners, but those actively involved in the building; Commissioners, employees and contractors. Standing from the left: Charles Wentworth Dilke, John Scott Russell, Henry Cole, the contractor Charles Fox, Joseph Paxton, Lord John Russell and Sir Robert Peel. Seated: Richard Cobden, Charles Barry, Lord Granville, the Chairman of the Building Committee William Cubitt, Prince Albert, Lord Derby.

2. R. & T. Turner's design for an Exhibition Building, one of the many designs offered to the Commissioners.

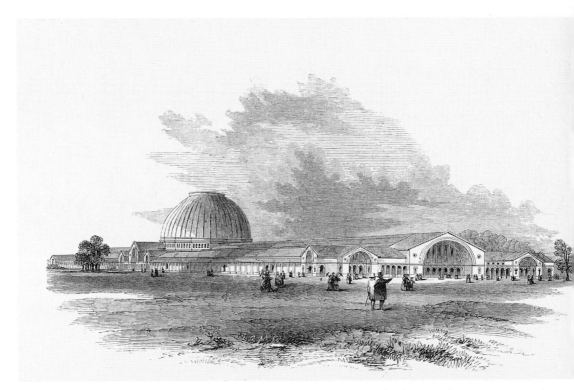

3. The building designed by the Building Committee, who drew on the many suggestions offered to them. It was published by the *Illustrated London News* on 22 June 1850, and caused an immediate outcry, because of its substantial nature and its proposed site in Hyde Park.

TO H. R. H. PRINCE ALBERT,

This simple Design for the proposed Building in Hyde Park is humbly submitted by

THE ARCHITECT.

4. 'To H.R.H. Prince Albert. This simple design . . . is humbly submitted.' *Punch*, never an admirer of Prince Albert, seen as a prime mover of the whole scheme, swiftly published a cartoon drawing on an unsuccessful design by the Prince for an infantry hat.

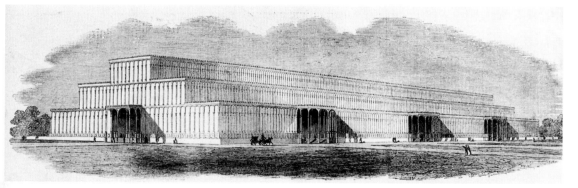

5. Paxton, who had a wide circle of professional and journalistic contacts, took advantage of the controversy to put forward a scheme of his own, in the *Illustrated London News*, on 6 July 1850. He had support from leading figures in engineering and manufacturing.

6. The Exhibition building was essentially prefabricated, components being manufactured both in London and in the Birmingham area, and brought to the site, and assembled. Girders are here being unloaded from Messrs Pickford's wagons with a three-legged crane.

7. A view of the Crystal Palace from the north of the Serpentine.

THE RIBS OF THE TRANSEPT ROOF.

8. The public took a very keen interest in the activity in Hyde Park, and the *Illustrated London News* carried stories every week. An arched transept was provided to avoid having to cut down any of the elm trees on the site. The ribs of the Transept roof were raised under the personal supervision of Charles Fox, the chief contractor.

9. Bird's eye view of the Crystal Palace looking northwards towards Hampstead and the Regent's Canal, drawn by Charles Burton, and published by Ackerman. Though there was a bridge across the Serpentine, the modern north–south route through Hyde Park was only opened for the 1862 Exhibition.

10. This view looking south-east towards Westminster and the City shows the construction of the Crystal Palace very clearly. The success of the buildings beyond, being developed by John Elger and others in Knightsbridge and the Kensington Road, was threatened by the presence of the Crystal Palace and the crowds of visitors.

11. Prince Albert was a keen advocate of model housing for working-class families. He persuaded the military authorities to allow the erection of a sample block of four flats, to demonstrate the advantages of philanthropic housing to visitors to the Exhibition.

12. Marble column outside the east end of the Great Exhibition. A number of large exhibits, including agricultural machinery, and raw materials like stone and coal, were housed outside the Crystal Palace. The heat and light inside were so great on hot days that blinds were hung outside.

13. The Transept looking south, showing one of the elm trees inside the building.

14. Agricultural implements outside the 1851 Exhibition Building, including a
one-horse cart used for transporting heavy materials and a spiked roller
for the cultivation of clay soils.

15. 'London in 1851'. A view from Piccadilly Circus looking west along Piccadilly, depicting London totally swamped by visitors.

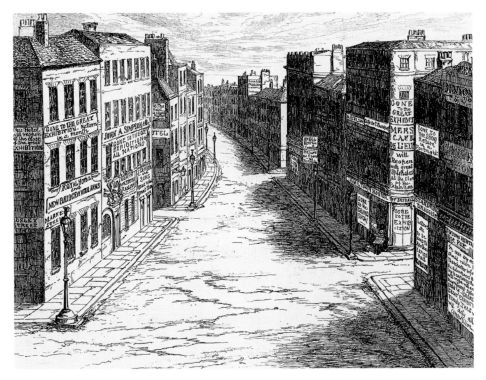

16. 'Manchester in 1851'. The converse fate was forecast for the provinces; it was predicted that tradesmen would be ruined, and the streets emptied of people, as in this view of Manchester.

17. The South Kensington Museum was opened on 22 June 1857. The building was officially known as the Iron Museum, but was almost immediately nicknamed the Brompton Boilers. It contained both art and scientific collections.

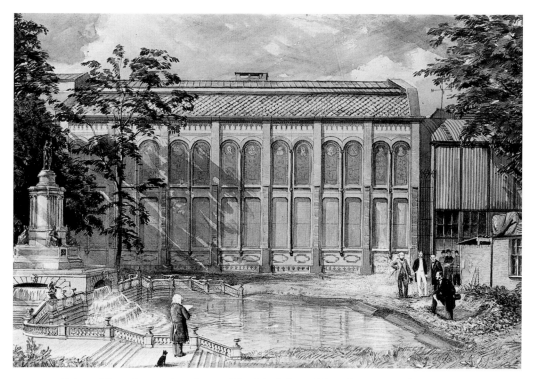

18. Prince Albert inspecting the model of the Memorial to the 1851 Exhibition in 1861. Behind is the Sheepshanks Building of the South Kensington Museum.

19. The Patent Museum, established by Bennet Woodcroft as part of the South Kensington Museum, in 1863, after a watercolour by J. C. Launchberrick. The Iron Museum (Brompton Boilers) can be seen behind.

20. The Iron Museum, nicknamed the Brompton Boilers, under construction. It was designed as a temporary building and a large part was moved in 1867, and subsequently re-erected to create the Bethnal Green Museum.

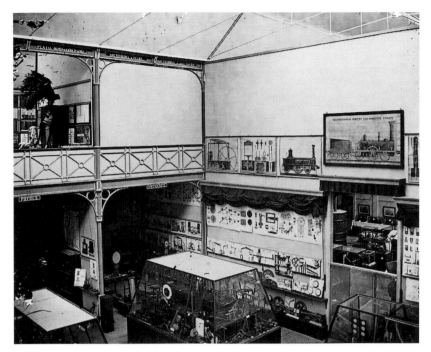

21. The interior of the Patent Museum at South Kensington in the 1860s. This collection contained many important early mechanical and engineering inventions.

22. The first Refreshment Room of the South Kensington Museum in 1857. This was a temporary timber building, designed by Francis Fowke, and paid for by the Commissioners who were anxious to make a success of the new venture. It was demolished in 1867.

23. View looking across the Horticultural Gardens to the arcades on the east, with the Winter Garden on the left. The Memorial to the 1851 Exhibition can be seen in the centre of the gardens.

24. View northwards into the Horticultural Gardens, from the 1862 Exhibition Building, in May 1862.

25. The 1862 Exhibition Building seen across the Horticultural Gardens in January 1862.

26. The Western Dome of the 1862 Exhibition Building, fronting Queen's Gate,
seen from Cromwell Road, 31 March 1862.

27. 'The eighth wonder of the world'. Francis Fowke's proposed Great Hall for the 1862 Building, abandoned because of lack of money.

28. The Nave of the 1862 Building with the Minton Fountain.

29. The 1862 Exhibition Building, 31 March 1862, with exhibits arriving at
the Cromwell Road front.

30. The west end of the 1862 Building with foreign exhibits waiting
to be arranged.

31. The British Picture Gallery in the 1862 Building. The building was intended
as a permanent exhibition gallery for a national museum.

32. Francis Fowke's scheme for refronting the 1862 Building, to make it suitable for a national museum, either to house the National Gallery, or the natural history collections being moved by the British Museum from Bloomsbury.

33. The Winter Garden of the Royal Horticultural Society's Gardens, used by the Albert Hall as an entrance and for receptions.

34. The Albert Hall under construction about 1870, with the Winter Garden, the Horticultural Society Gardens and the Southern Galleries beyond.

35. The Winter Garden from the Royal Horticultural Society's Gardens about 1862.

36. The northern arcades in the Royal Horticultural Society's Gardens about 1862.

37. Natural History Museum, southern frontage in 1881, from a photograph by
Henry Dixon, published 14 November 1881.

38. The Central Hall of the Natural History Museum, as arranged *c.*1900.

39. No. 170, Queen's Gate, built 1888–9 for F. A. White, now the
Rector's Lodging for Imperial College.

40. No. 180, Queen's Gate, built in 1885 for the barrister, H. F. Makins.

41. Cartoon of 'King Cole', by Tissot. Henry Cole's nickname was in use even in royal circles, where he enjoyed a certain amount of protection.

42. Sir Charles Freake, a prominent South Kensington builder and developer, who had a musical wife, and an ambition for a baronetcy which inspired him to build the first National Training School for Music.

43. Lord Elcho, later 10th Earl of Wemyss, 'always a veritable Mother Carey's chicken in everything relating to South Kensington', who managed to get the 1862 Building rejected by Parliament, and expensively destroyed.

44. A. S. Ayrton, Liberal First Commissioner of Works in the early 1870s, with considerable influence in South Kensington, and recruited as an ex officio 1851 Commissioner.

old commercial connexions, to form new ones, and dispel any prejudices against us which may exist.[12]

However, on the other hand, the consul at Warsaw was pessimistic about anything being ready on time, since all communication had to be 'transmitted through the supreme Govt.' in St Petersburg. The position in Germany was complicated, since most states were independent, thus the British Minister in Berlin was not only accredited to the King of Prussia, but also to HRH the Grand Duke of Mecklenburg-Strelitz, and HH the Duke of Anhalt-Köthen, while Lord Cowley, in Frankfort (*sic*), was accredited to the Senate there, to the states of Hesse Cassel, Hesse Darmstadt, Hesse Homburg, and Nassau. In his letter to the various states, however, Cowley suggested that it would be easier to deal with a single organization, the Central Federal Commission, the Zollverein.[13] In the event, the Commissioners in London seem to have kept the different German states separate, although they almost all exhibited under the Zollverein 'masthead', with individual returns for Prussia, Bavaria, Frankfurt am Main, the Grand Duchy of Hesse, Luxembourg, Nassau, Saxony and Württemberg. The only group not included in the Zollverein, described as 'Hamburgh and small states of N. Germany', comprised Hanover, together with the Hanse Towns, Lübeck, Mecklenburg-Strelitz, Mecklenburg-Schwerin, and Oldenburg.[14]

Support from Belgium, where the Queen's uncle Leopold was king, was considerable, as was to be expected, and a Commission was appointed to promote the interests of Belgian commerce and agriculture. The French too had a very elaborate system organized by the Minister of Agriculture and Commerce.[15] The produce of Algeria was displayed under the aegis of the French Ministry of War, which body duly received a Council Medal.

The American minister in London, Abbott Lawrence, took an early interest in the m tter, writing to the Secretary of the American Institute in New York on 22 February, asking that he would pass on the information to other such organizations. He explained that:

> The invitation embraces *all* nations. The plan has met with general approval here, and by the Representatives of the different countries of Europe accredited to this Court . . . I entertain an abiding confidence that *we* possess the material to present at the proposed exhibition such a combination of Science and Art, as will gratify the

highest anticipation of that class of men who have been and will continue to be the creators of wealth, and through their inventions and
labors the civilisers of mankind throughout the world.

If such a response should be given to this invitation as may be
expected, the Exhibition will present . . . a victory gained by a
Congress of Nations, not acquired by arms, or physical strength, but
the triumph of mind over matter.[16]

A further category, though diverse, and not important in terms of
number of exhibits, comprised exotic and sometimes rather distant states
such as Egypt and Turkey, Tunis, China and some of the independent
South American states, including Brazil, Chile and Mexico.

PRIZES AND THE AWARDING OF MEDALS

The original intention in the early discussions had been to attract a wide
and important selection of exhibits by the value of the prizes, an opinion
which had led to the Munday contract, and the prize fund. Unease
amongst the exhibitors about money prizes led to the decision to award
medals rather than money prizes, with an option to give money to an artisan who might have spent a lot of money on an exhibit without any
prospect of reimbursement. Therefore the decision was taken to commission three bronze medals for the various winners and runners–up, but
potential exhibitors then became unhappy at the thought of being blight-
ed by receiving an inferior medal. The Commissioners then decided the
medals should not be ranked, but just given to meritorious exhibits.

The Medals Committee, under Lord Colborne, included a number of
outside experts, including the art historian, Dr Waagen, author of a
guidebook to country houses and their collections, Eugène-Louis Lami
(1800–90), a French artist well known at the former court of Louis-
Philippe, the sculptor, John Gibson (1790–1860), and the archaeologist,
Charles Newton (1816–94), of the British Museum.[17] On 6 July, therefore,
the Committee met to select amongst the designs, which had been submitted anonymously. They chose three: those by Hyppolyte Bonnardel of
Paris (65) and by Leonard C. Wyon (22) and G. G. Adams (105), both of
London.

Inscriptions for the chosen design were a different matter, dealt with
by the Medal Inscription Committee, which met twice as many times.
The members included Gladstone, the historian Thomas Macaulay, the

Fig 7. Two Winning designs for Bronze Medals to be given to Exhibitors.

Revd H. G. Liddell, a well-known Greek scholar, then headmaster of Westminster and domestic chaplain to Prince Albert, Lord Lyttelton, and the Dean of St Paul's.

JURIES

From the framework of Local Committees and national Commissions was developed the system of juries to allocate the prizes. The awarding of prize medals was an even more complex and difficult problem than their design, and the make-up of the juries all-important. Anticipating the various cries of 'foul play' which might arise in a situation where so much national prestige was at stake, an elaborate system of checks and balances was developed. The choice and allocation of jurors were scrupulous, to ensure equal representation of foreign and British jurors on the committees dealing with the different classes, and also a fair and appropriate appointment of foreign jurors. To obviate any charge of favouritism owing to the lack of a national representative on a jury dealing with a sensitive division, there were to be reviews of the medals by committees overseeing groups of classes. Chairmanships were divided equally between foreigners and natives, though vice-chairmen were elected by the individual committees. The resulting Council of Chairmen was charged with the task of laying down the regulations for the conduct of the juries, outlining policy and settling difficult issues.

The problem of the membership of the foreign juries was very shrewdly passed to the local Corps Diplomatique, whose members were asked to agree on the appropriate allocation between the different nationalities of the foreign membership of each of the thirty-four juries and subjuries. Once the proportion was decided, each country was asked to nominate so many members. The foreign commissioners suggested a further safe-guard in that the different juries were grouped into five groups, with the task of confirming any awards made within the group, thus ensuring that there would be a wider spread of nationalities within the group of juries.

The jurors were drawn from a very wide range, usually nationals of the countries they represented, on the whole a distinguished, though some-times heterogeneous group. Much play was made by M. Dupin, the President of the French Commission in London, of the distinction of the French group of Jurors, which included eight Deputies (*Représentants*) who would be needed in Paris in July to settle various 'questions vitales pour la France', and the Duc de Luynes, 'l'un des plus nobles Mécènes de l'art moderne', who had lent one of his own collections to the Exhibition. Most of them held some official position either academic or in the gov-ernment service, and their ranks included the composer Hector Berlioz.[18] The majority of United States jurors came from Massachusetts, Pennsylvania and New York, including Horace Greeley (1811–72), editor of the *New York Herald Tribune*, who chaired the Jury for Class XXII, Iron and General Hardware, which included such diverse objects as Saws, Buttons, Wires, Hinges, Bolts and Pulleys. The southern states, including Texas, Virginia and Alabama, were also represented, by George Peabody (1795–1869), a banker resident in London and a well-known philan-thropist, as a representative of Maryland. The Zollverein, representing most of the German states, produced a large number of experts, official and academic. Other countries settled for representatives already resident in London, like the Russian Imperial Commissioner. Not all of the jurors were nationals of the countries they represented; the Tuscan jurors, for instance, included both Lord Holland (4th Baron, d. 1859), and Antonio Panizzi (1797–1879), Librarian at the British Museum, but born in the tiny Duchy of Modena.[19]

A special Commissioner of Juries, in the person of Lyon Playfair, with five assistants, was appointed to look after the juries, and to attend meet-ings of the Council of Chairmen, and generally to act as secretary to the various bodies.

The deliberations of the juries, which were to result in the awards of the coveted medals, took some weeks, and were only published in August when the accompanying reports were available. An exception was made for the awards for agricultural machinery, published in July at the express request of the agricultural expert, Mr Pusey, since the Royal Agricultural Society of England had generously forgone their own display to enhance that of the Exhibition.[20] Early on the Council of Chairmen came to the conclusion that the allocation of even three medals would necessitate contentious ranking of exhibits, and suggested that one medal only should be awarded by the juries, the smallest should be dropped, and the 'Great Medal' should be given by the Council of Chairmen. This policy was adopted but the Commission decided to put the redundant medal to good use as a reward for jurors, and to commission yet another medal for exhibitors. Despite a helpful suggestion from Prince Demidoff that the medals should be made of 'platina' rather than gold or silver, the Commission stuck to its decision that they should all be struck in bronze. Even in this relatively low-cost material the cost of medals amounted to £3550, with a further £386 for cases, and an award of a further £390 for cash awards. Finally an additional 'service' medal was ordered from Wyon, one of the original designers, making a complete set of five – Council, Prize, Exhibitor, Juror, and Service, awarded to all Commissioners, members of both Executive and Finance Committees, Special Commissioners, Secretaries and Treasurers of the Commission. Medals and Catalogues were distributed to various groups; some fifty individuals, including the sapper officers who had worked at the Exhibition Building, a set to all the participating countries, and some twenty-four Indian rulers of varying degrees.[21]

The impressive *Jury Reports* produced after the Exhibition closed are a tribute both to the hard work and erudition of the jurors, and to the successful way in which this potentially contentious task was carried out. The task of the juries was summarized by Dupin in a farewell epistle from the French Commission. He recalled that some 314 jurors had spent eighty-two days of careful examination and serious discussion in the delicate task of judging the produce of forty nations. It had not been easy, the French jurors had wished to give prizes only for beauty, for grace, for perfection, without being hampered by restrictions, or by being bothered by 'des répulsions, des répugnances, et des appréhensions mercantiles, même en Angleterre'. He ended by extolling the diversity of national characteristics, and concluded:

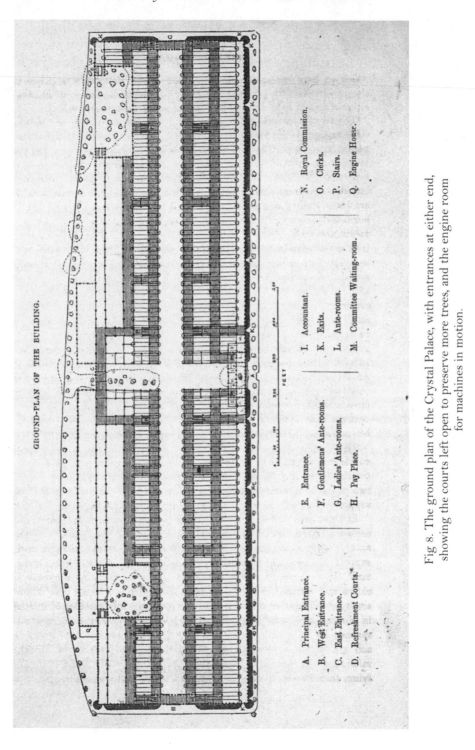

GROUND-PLAN OF THE BUILDING.

A. Principal Entrance.
B. West Entrance.
C. East Entrance.
D. Refreshment Courts.

E. Entrance.
F. Gentlemens' Ante-rooms.
G. Ladies' Ante-rooms.
H. Pay Place.

I. Accountant.
K. Exits.
L. Ante-rooms.
M. Committee Waiting-room.

N. Royal Commission.
O. Clerks.
P. Stairs.
Q. Engine House.

Fig 8. The ground plan of the Crystal Palace, with entrances at either end, showing the courts left open to preserve more trees, and the engine room for machines in motion.

Français, et fiers à ce titre, nous ne sommes pas . . . de ceux qui rêvent pour l'avenir la disparition des types sacrés qui caractérisent les races et les nationalités.[22]

MANAGING THE EXHIBITION: ALLOCATING THE SPACE

Once the exhibitors and exhibits had been identified the problem arose of how to allocate the space. The decision had been taken early on to divide the building into an eastern wing for foreign exhibits, and the western end for the United Kingdom and its Dependencies. There was a central nave running from east to west, with an entrance at either end, and aisles to the north and the south. The Transept had an entrance at the southern end, where the Royal Commissioners and the Executive Committee had offices. There were galleries above the aisles on either side of the nave, which increased the space available, and there were enclosures at the western end where stone and other building materials could be exhibited. Though some ten miles of stands were finally to be available, the business of matching supply and demand had to be addressed early on. Lyon Playfair had been responsible for fine-tuning the classification, Cole for devising the means of dividing up the space. This was, in Playfair's words, the 'best principle which has yet been suggested for allotting space to towns – a question of a remarkably difficult nature'. The amount of space available for each of the four main sections – raw materials, machinery, manufactures and sculpture and fine art – was determined, each exhibitor was asked for his own requirements, and the result was reduced in proportion to the amount available; the sum of the space allocated to manufacturers from each town gave the space available for each town. Playfair insisted that the Commission should retain some space for emergencies. There were also areas which had to be shared like that served by the steam engine, on which Brunel had insisted, in which alone 'Machinery in Motion' could be displayed. This provisional allocation did not prevent the occasional exhibitor who demanded space, and never took the offer up, or the late entrant. Within the sections allotted to each country or town, detailed arrangement was a matter for the national or local committee.[23]

COMPILING THE CATALOGUES

Catalogues were clearly essential, not only for visitors, but as 'an enduring record, in the most perfect shape, of the Exhibition itself'. The matter of the copyright was early considered, and ruled out by doubts as to whether it would be regarded as legally enforceable, and by the practical consideration that 'any Catalogue sold to pay a large profit would be reprinted forthwith, and sold by persons outside the Exhibition and elsewhere', as happened at the British Museum, and had happened at the Exhibition of Cartoons at Westminster Hall in 1843. Wentworth Dilke suggested to the Commission that three levels of catalogue should be available: a very full detailed one, with descriptions provided by the manufacturers, 'omitting obvious self-laudation', complete with woodcuts, running to two or three large octavo volumes, an abridgement of the full edition, selling at four or five shillings, and a 'mere résumé of the collection' costing about one shilling. He advised that the first might be put up to tender, offering the publisher the exclusive right to the manufacturers' descriptions, while the other two he thought the Royal Commission might as well publish and print themselves, since the print-run was as yet very speculative, leading to a low offer from any publisher.[24]

The Commissioners decided to leave the printing to the contractors, and it was awarded jointly to Spicer Brothers, wholesale stationers, and Clowes & Son, printers, for their tender of a lump sum of £2300, and a royalty of 2d. on the small catalogues. In the event, for reasons satisfactorily explained by the printers, not everything was ready on the opening day; only the English edition of the *Small Official Catalogue* for one shilling, and the *Synopsis of the Contents* and the coloured plan, both at 6d., were available, followed on 24 June by the French *Synopsis* and *Small Official Catalogue*, and on 21 July by the German, both at half a crown. The *Illustrated Catalogue* finally appeared in five volumes, only one being ready on 1 May, available separately as they appeared, or as a set at three guineas, at a reduction of two shillings. Cheaper editions appeared later in the Exhibition, including a Popular Guide at 2d. on 2 June, and Hunt's Handbook in parts at 6d. each, at the end of the month. A miscellaneous collection of 'Other Books' were sold in the building. These included priced catalogues of various sections, notably the British, Russian and most of the German sections, of which the Saxony section sold twice as many as any other. There were interleaved versions of the catalogues, and both a Key to the Catalogue and an Index. Tourists could also buy a Cover for their catalogue, and a list of Cab Fares of which nearly eight hundred were bought. Overall 300 sets of the *Illustrated Catalogue* were sold, together with over 7000 copies of the individual volumes, 285,000 copies of the *Small Official Catalogue* in English, 9000 in French and 4000 in German. As had been the experience at the Westminster Hall Exhibition, the smaller cheaper versions did not sell as well, only 84,000 of the *Synopsis* at 6d., and 26,000 of the *Popular Guide* at 2d.[25] In fact, after the Exhibition closed, the printers complained that they had lost money and asked for a supplementary payment.[26] Not all sales took place in the building: there was a City Catalogue Office, which sold over a fifth of the Popular Guides, about a sixth of the 1s. catalogues, and more than half the *Illustrated Catalogues*.

The bland record of volumes printed and sold conceals the enormous effort required to produce the relatively small number of 1s. catalogues promised for May 1st. As Clowes and Son recorded, the information required for the *Illustrated Catalogue* was gathered on colour-coded slips filled in by each of the Exhibitors, corrected by compilers, who also made an educated guess as to the individual class to which the item would be allocated. The resulting information was typeset, and the whole forwarded by 26 April, in proof amounting to 2000 pages, to the Executive, the editor, proofreaders, and the compilers of the small editions in English, French and German. The problem was that until this moment, it was not possible to be certain of the proper class for each article. Each British article had to be placed in one of the thirty classes, into which the United Kingdom was divided, while within the section allocated to each foreign state, the articles had to follow correctly in order within the classes. Nonetheless, at midnight on 30 April, the small edition was ready to go to press, together with a specimen volume of the *Illustrated Catalogue*; five hundred employees were required to sew the 20,000 copies ready for sale the following day. Presentation copies for the Queen and the Prince took highly skilled specialist binders six hours to complete for the opening ceremony.

However, corrections to the text, together with reallocation of objects within the classes and additional exhibits made two further editions necessary before accuracy was achieved. The printers made the point that the work was both complex and very rushed, so that 'the classification which should have been the labour of literary men became the task of the operative printer'. Thus compositors without a word of a foreign language found themselves setting up French and German editions. Possibly not without an eye to the allocation of profits, lists of the different craftsmen were supplied, larger numbers being required for the more complex illustrated works, on which both lithography and engraving were used, some two hundred engravers being employed.[27]

There were, of course, as had been anticipated, a large number of imitative or pirated publications, together with a number of novelties, like Field's *Telescopic View of the Crystal Palace* of which copies have survived in the Museum of London. There were also serious works like *The Art Journal Illustrated Catalogue*, which not only illustrated many works but also included essays by such authorities as Robert Hunt, of the Museum of Practical Geology, on the 'Science of the Exhibition', by Edward Forbes FRS, of King's College, on 'The Vegetable World as Contributing to the Great Exhibition', and a hundred-guinea essay by Ralph Nicholson Wornum of the Government Schools of Design, on 'The Exhibition as a Lesson in Taste'. As well as guides in foreign languages, there was one in Cockney, and Cruikshanks's humorous account of *Mrs Sandboys' Visit to the Great Exhibition*. It also generated a lot of ceramic and other mementoes of various sorts, often featuring the Queen and Prince Albert as well as the Palace itself. These were not produced for the Royal Commission, nor indeed did they benefit the official funds, but they are a powerful tribute to the popular appeal of the Exhibition.

THE ARRIVAL OF THE EXHIBITS

The Commission reported the arrival of the first British goods, on 12 February, with over a thousand articles a week being received from the third week onwards, rising to a crescendo in the seventh to eleventh weeks, with between two and three thousand articles a week. Elaborate arrangements were made with the customs authorities, who agreed to treat the building as a bonded warehouse. Some 11,644 packages arriving through eight ports were forwarded direct to the Crystal Palace, and there opened in front of customs officers. The building was managed by the two hundred sapper officers and men who had been seconded to help with the organization. They were so important in ensuring the success of the project that Henry Cole retained the conviction that the presence of a body of engineers was essential to the success of any enterprise, and this led to the strong military flavour of the early South Kensington.

A Medieval Court had been planned by A. W. N. Pugin, to contain the exhibits of the group of designers and craftsmen who worked for him, Crace, Minton, Hardman and George Myers, the master builder. Thomas

Earley, who carried out the decorative painting, has left an account of the chaos in Hyde Park, which he described as 'the great Babel'. It took over an hour to locate the sixteen cases and four packages already delivered, while the waggon-load of stone which included the medieval effigies and cross had to wait for five hours to get near the building.

On 31 March, Fox and Henderson's men went on strike because they had not received their pay, and order was only restored by the soldiers driving them out of the building. Despite concerns that the building would not be completed on time, and even a threat by the Executive Committee that the sappers would be employed to remove the scaffolding from around the dilatory painters, the building was handed over on time. None of this seems to have deterred the Queen from visiting the Exhibition before it was opened. Even after the opening some 182 articles were taken in. Foreign countries faced a greater challenge and, understandably, more of their goods arrived after the opening. On the other hand, it was not always the most distant countries whose goods arrived latest. Everything from Canada, Nova Scotia and New Brunswick was in place by the opening, most of the 962 Belgian and 303 Dutch exhibits, all of the 247 Spanish and the 50 Egyptian, and all but two of the 216 Turkish items. Doubtless the problem of the Baltic accounted for the few stragglers from Sweden and Norway, and the third of the Russian items which arrived in late May, but it was the three largest foreign exhibitors, America with a total of 1023 exhibits, the Zollverein (comprising Prussia, Bavaria, Saxony, Württemberg and twenty-two other states) with 1874 and France with 3459 articles, whose goods trickled in throughout the summer.[28]

THE VISITORS

Another matter over which the Commissioners were very concerned was the nature of the crowds which would come to the Exhibition building. Though much of the practical concerns fell to the civil servants and officers of the Royal Commission, a certain amount ended up on the royal desk.

The Bishop of London wrote to the Prince to express his concern about the provision of services for 'the unprecedented influx of strangers . . . into this metropolis not only from the British Dominions, but from all parts of the world, and especially from the Continent of Europe'. He proposed opening a subscription to provide prayer-books in foreign languages, together with the holding of services in foreign tongues in schoolrooms. Prince Albert suggested tactfully that foreigners would prefer 'attending divine worship in the manner to which they are accustomed'. Indeed, he suggested, English clergymen might not be able to assist in the matter since while they might adopt a foreign language they could not 'depart from the liturgy', and therefore the problem might not be as great as the Bishop feared. Later the Bishop came to the conclusion that there could be cooperation with 'those foreign churches . . . [which] . . . agree with us in protests against the errors and corruptions of the Church of Rome'.[29]

A more practical concern was expressed on a less spiritual matter by the Prussian envoy, the Chevalier Bunsen, who pointed out that well-connected foreigners would expect to be able to visit the traditional London sights, like St James's and Buckingham Palaces, the Royal Dockyards at Deptford, Portsmouth and Chatham, Woolwich Arsenal, Newgate and Pentonville Prisons and Bridewell and Bethlehem Hospitals. Access was normally gained via the embassies, but time would be short to provide notes of introductions for all these visitors, particularly in view of their likely short stay. He suggested that the embassies should issue certificates to suitable applicants, and the various British authorities should let the ministers and consuls know what hours would suit them for admissions and how many people would be admitted at any one time. A system of cards for entry was duly instituted for most of these sights, with the exception of the London palaces, and the Bank of England, the Royal Mint, and the prisons and hospitals, where admission had necessarily to be restricted.[30]

The reception of foreigners was again a matter in which the Foreign Office was involved, and Palmerston forwarded a number of despatches to Prince Albert. London had long been a safe haven for refugees from the more authoritarian Continental governments, who therefore saw the Exhibition as a dangerous pretext for visits to England. The British envoy William Temple reported that the King of Naples was so alarmed that he was discouraging manufacturers from sending their goods for exhibition, and those applying for passports were being warned that they might not be allowed to return. As Temple explained to Palmerston, it was thought 'that the Exhibition will provide a pretext for all the violent Republicans in Europe and the Neapolitans by mixing in such society would run a great risk of having their minds tainted with revolutionary

. . . doctrines. What danger would be incurred by the goods', he ended, 'does not appear to be quite so evident'. Reaction in St Petersburg had been equally unfavourable; Lord Bloomfield reported that Count Nesselrode was apprehensive about the number of foreigners expected in England, and that they 'will find greater facility in London than else-where for conspiring and plotting against the peace of the Continent'. His remedy, reported the ambassador, had been to deny passports to 'many Persons of Rank and Station', which had caused irritation in the highest circles, while the more astute 'Russian artisans and manufacturers had already left . . . the whole affair, I believe, to be an attempt to throw dis-credit on the object of the Exhibition'.

From Vienna it was reported that the Prince von Schwarzenberg was extremely cynical about the reasons for some tourists heading for London, and was concerned about Mazzini's plans and depots of arms at Chiavara, near Genoa.[31]

A more practical approach was made by various German states who offered assistance in identifying well-known 'dangerous or criminal char-acters who may visit England . . . during the Exhibition'. Eberhardt, 'the best-informed Police Agent in Germany', formerly in Gotha, now in Berlin, was ready 'to point out suspicious characters', while Baron Manteuffel from Berlin was delighted to be asked to supply agents to identify 'dangerous or criminal characters' who might visit England dur-ing the Exhibition.[32]

Normanby reported from Paris on the supposed pan-European nature of the organization:

> I continue to receive numerous communications . . . as to the projects of the Revolutionary party, which has no doubt a much extended European organisation, giving warnings of various Characters as to the use which it is intended to be made of the promiscuous Assemblage of Foreigners to be collected within the next few month in England. Some of these communications only point to the facili-ties thus afforded to the Conspirators for arranging the details of a general movement to be executed afterwards and Elsewhere. Others point to the simultaneous Efforts to be made elsewhere in different populous districts of England to pervert the spirit of that population by Socialist Emissaries, who are to circulate about by the con-veyances established for the purpose of carrying the district popula-

tion to the Exhibition. For the object of corrupting the Manufacturing population, the Agents are Germans, rather than French from their generally speaking the English Language better & with less accent.

He was not much concerned about the effect on British workmen, whom he thought would be otherwise occupied, but concluded by giving the names of German conspirators supplied by the French police, one of whom, the tailor Kessler from Hesse Cassel, had a brother in England, 'établi Aubergiste à Londres. C'est chez ce dernier que viennent loger la plupart des ouvriers Allemands qui arrivent dans cette ville'.[33] The motives of some Continental governments were not always as transparent as they appeared, as Normanby pointed out. Reporting a problem caused by French political refugees being thrown out of Switzerland, though they were offered passports for England or the United States, he mentioned that the French authorities had been ready to give free passage to German revolutionaries. Nonetheless, he was impressed by the widespread interest in getting working-class people to the Exhibition:

> But there is for the first time, this entirely new feature in the intended influx of the Revolutionary party into England, that whatever may be the possible absurdity of their plans, they consider the object sufficiently important to have organised a general subscription in aid of this political pilgrimage . . .
> In all the principal towns similar Subscriptions have been opened, and that the different localities are particularly desired to send 'les hommes d'action'.

Though, he concluded, this might be 'only for organising simultaneous action in their own country' it was significant that this was being done by 'those whose funds are not abundant'.[34]

This concern amongst British diplomats abroad, writing to the relaxed and self-confident Palmerston, explains the almost hysterical note of a letter from the King of Prussia to Prince Albert in April, outlining his concern about the danger to the life of his heir, the Crown Prince William, and the latter's son, if they were both in London,

> in a metropolis the size of a kingdom . . . We should never admit to fleeing *such danger*. But it is true that those godless villains, the *crème* and general mass of whom London, *graces à Vos vieilles lois libérales*, is

full of, would be able to make a fine gesture in their fashion if they caused harm to the Prince of Prussia and his son. I feel with William that he does not have to fear such *dangers*; but *he* and I believe that Your Royal Highness must share with me in feeling that he ought not to be indifferent to a possible danger of this kind.

Though he was prepared to allow the Prussian Royal Family to visit London if precautions had been taken, and would accept the advice of the Queen and Prince Albert on the matter, he could not resist warning them in a postscript that 'countless hordes of desperate proletarians, well-organised and under the leadership of blood-red criminals, are on their way to London now', and enquiring whether it was true, as had been rumoured in Berlin for weeks, that the 'British Government had advised the Queen to leave town for the duration of the Exhibition'.[35]

ARRANGEMENTS FOR THE OPENING

Far from advising the Queen to leave town, the Commission was struggling against pressure to expose her to even greater danger. Whilst dire warnings were arriving from abroad, contrary advice was coming from Lyon Playfair and Cole, now installed in the Executive Office, in 'The Building, Hyde Park'. They advised Grey and Phipps in the Prince's office that the public wanted season-ticket-holders admitted to the opening. Dilke had been unable to persuade *The Times* correspondent otherwise, and Cole reported on the various newspaper reactions. 'The point which seems most distasteful is the proof of distrust which the exclusion of the Public from the inside manifests'. He countered the Prince's argument that there was no ready-made ceremonial for such occasion, by suggesting that the Commissioners should report on their work of creating the Exhibition, emphasizing the importance of the Queen's interest in the matter.[36] Thomas Bazley, a Commissioner and Chairman of the Manchester Chamber of Commerce, wrote directly to Prince Albert, expressing the hope that he would pardon 'the freedom of this communication':

from all parties, I hear the most fervent wish expressed, that if Her Majesty and Your Royal Highness could mingle with the throng of expected Visitors at the Exhibition on the first day of opening, a degree of satisfaction would be produced. . .

Probably no more sublime a scene could be witnessed on earth than a beloved Monarch, like Her most gracious Majesty, in the midst of her subjects, surrounded by all near and dear to her, and by the elite of Europe, surveying the peaceful results of Science Art and Industry, in the productions of her own free and glorious country, and in the contributions of the civilized world, thereby adding dignity to labor (*sic*) and encouraging that elevating principle of industry, the source, under Providence and a wise Government, of a Nation's prosperity'.[37]

Political pressure was added, Lord John Russell writing to the Prince that 'the enemies of the International Exhibition, who are not a few are taking advantage . . . to stir up discontent'. The fashionable society in London might be disregarded, he added, but it would be a pity to alienate the manufacturers and the middle classes. The Prince gave way, and a notice appeared on 28 April, announcing that season ticket-holders would be admitted to the opening.[38]

However, the opening was not to take place without further complication. In an attempt to generate some sort of ceremonial, the idea had been conceived that the Corps Diplomatique should present a formal address congratulating the Queen on the Exhibition. According to custom, such a joint address, usual on a royal birth or marriage, was presented by the doyen of the Diplomatic Corps, in this case, the Belgian Minister Van der Weyer. The approach seems to have been made by Granville on behalf of the Commission, not through the Foreign Office. The programme for the opening was finalized on Tuesday, 22 April, and published on Wednesday, before all the diplomats had been approached and had agreed, and Lord Granville had compounded the problem himself, by having 'left town' before the replies were received. The doyen was the most senior member of the Corps, not necessarily the grandest in rank, or the representative of the greatest foreign power, and Granville's apologetic analysis to Palmerston was that Brunnow, representing Russia, and Koller, representing Austria, had caused the trouble. In a rapid round of visits to his fellow diplomats, Van der Weyer obtained the agreement of most envoys, despite those of Sardinia and Sweden being absent, and that of Spain 'en lit', but was unable to win over the representatives of the two great European autocratic empires. Unusually, Palmerston found himself defending the actions of right-wing governments, suggesting to Russell that the 'Foreign Ministers should be present . . . as *Spectators* and not as *Actors*'.

Prince Albert justified the idea by pointing out the international and unprecedented nature of the exhibition:

it is not a purely English ceremony for an English object, but an international one in which all Nations have taken an active Part: half the Building is in charge of foreign Authorities, half the collection the property of foreign Countries, half the Juries are appointed by Foreign Govts. who have also defrayed the expenses of the foreign Part of the Exhibition. It would have been wrong in my opinion, not to have given the Representatives of these foreign Nations the opportunity of taking an active part also in the opening Ceremony.[39]

THE INAUGURATION OF THE GREAT EXHIBITION

'This day is one of the greatest and most glorious days of our lives, with which to my pride and joy, the name of my beloved Albert is for ever associated'.[40] Thus wrote one of the chief protagonists, but the success of the opening on 1 May has passed into legend. Some 25,000 season-ticket-holders were admitted between nine o'clock and half past eleven, followed by the various official groups, of Royal Commissioners, Executive Committee, Foreign Acting Commissioners, Government Ministers, envoys of foreign powers and royal guests, to await the arrival of the royal party at noon. On arrival Prince Albert joined his fellow Commissioners, in the Queen's words 'a curious assemblage of political and distinguished men', to present an address to the Queen, to which she graciously replied. The address contained a discreet element of self-congratulation that, notwithstanding the magnitude of the undertaking and the great distances from which the exhibits had come, the Exhibition had opened on the day 'originally named for its opening, thus affording a proof of what may . . . be accomplished by goodwill and cordial co-operation among nations'.[41]

The royal procession, duly managed by groups of heralds, was led by Paxton and Fox, C. H. Wild and Owen Jones, and the other active members of the Commission. Despite the irritation of the more active members of the Executive Committee, George Drew and Francis Fuller joined Henry Cole and Wentworth Dilke, preceded by Matthew Digby Wyatt. They were followed by Foreign Commissioners, the Royal

Fig 9. The visitors on the opening day included the famous 'mandarin', in reality
the captain of a Chinese junk moored in the Thames, and national heroes
like the aged Duke of Wellington.

Commissioners, the various representative of foreign powers, without
any part in the ceremonial, members of the government, the Royal
Household, and finally the Queen and the Royal Family. The captain of a
Chinese junk was rounded up by one of the Engineer officers, who had
noticed the absence of any Chinese representative, and included in the
diplomatic group.[42] Also in the procession was the Duke of Wellington
arm in arm with his old comrade Lord Anglesey.

The Queen noted in her Journal:

The sight . .was magical, so vast, so glorious, so touching . . . The
tremendous cheers, the joy expressed in every face, the immensity of
the building, the mixture of palms, flowers, trees, statues, fountains,
the organ (with 200 instruments, and 600 voices, which sounded like
nothing), and my beloved husband the author of this 'Peace Festival,'
. . . . all this was moving indeed, and it was and is a day to live for
ever.[43]

The procession perambulated the Nave and Transept, and the Queen
returned to the platform, the Lord Chamberlain, succeeded by a flourish

of trumpets, announced to the public that the Exhibition was open. The information was relayed to the wider world by a Royal salute fired on the north of the Serpentine, something which concerned the Prime Minister so much that he had advised placing the guns in St James's Park, for fear of shattering glass in the building.[44]

Congratulations to the Royal Family poured in, from other sovereigns, politicians and members of the Royal Household. King Leopold of the Belgians, regretting that he had not been present, congratulated the Queen on 'beloved Albert's work crowned with unexampled success'. The Prime Minister wrote that all had gone very well, 'but the general conduct of the multitudes assembled, the loyalty and the content which so generally appeared were perhaps the most gratifying to a politician'. Lady Lyttelton, for so long Governess to the royal children, understood the Queen's feelings:

> One moment was surely among the brightest of even Your Majesty's bright life – that when you received the address from His Royal Highness – and felt the full success, of so noble, so daring, and so benevolent a plan, his own work – which must cause the name so supremely dear to Your Majesty, to be uttered with admiration and gratitude throughout the nations; and remembered with due honor for ever.

An unknown correspondent, whose letter was forwarded to the royal couple, echoed the sentiment:

> I cannot imagine a more imposing and solemn spectacle – so beautiful in all its varied lights and colouring, so gorgeous a pageant and yet such a subject for deep and solemn thought – we have never witnessed such a scene in the history of the world!
>
> Most justly may the Prince be proud of to day! It seemed more like the realization of the thought of the poet or painter, or some delightful fairy tale . . . I feel so proud that I am an Englishman.[45]

The Clerk to the Privy Council, Charles Greville, went into the park rather than the building, thinking 'it more interesting and curious to see the masses and their behaviour'. Like many later visitors to the Exhibition he was impressed with the well-behaved crowds, 'the countless multitudes, streaming along in every direction; no soldiers, hardly any policemen to be seen, and yet all so orderly and good-humoured'.[46]

Reactions to the polyglot crowd were mixed; Thackeray produced a May Day Ode:

> A peaceful place it was but now,
> And lo! within its shining streets
> A multitude of nations meets:
>   A countless throng,
> I see beneath the crystal bow,
> And Gaul and German, Russ and Turk,
> Each with his native handiwork
>   And busy tongue.
>
> From Mississippi and from Nile –
> From Baltic, Ganges, Bosphorus
> In England's Ark assembled thus
>   Are friend and guest.
> Look down the mighty sunlit aisle,
> And see the sumptuous banquet set,
> The brotherhood of nations met
>   Around the feast![47]

Others were more cynical about the brotherhood of nations; a German commentator, Max Schlesinger, was more aware than the British of the flaws of Prince Albert's insistence on the brotherhood of man, and saw the ironies of the Exhibition:

> All hail to the Colossus of glass! thou most moral production of these latter days . . . which would make believe that all the nations are united by the bonds of brotherhood . . .
>   The flags flutter gaily through the cool of the evening. There the Prussian colours are all but entwined with those of Austria. Here the Papal States touch upon Sardinia. And down there! O sancta Simplicitas! the Russian eagle stretches his wings, and flutters as if impelled by a desire to fraternise with the stars and stripes of North America![48]

Despite an attempt in the previous January on the part of Joseph Paxton to gain support for a policy of free admission, the Commission took the decision to charge for entry to the Exhibition building. Indeed, there was even a hard-line policy about the admission of the press, only defeated by Henry Cole, who appreciated the benefits of friendly and approving journalists.[49] The Exhibition was open on the first day to season-ticket-holders only, of which some 25,000 were present. Numbers are often difficult to estimate, since though season-ticket-holders clearly were present during May, the police did not count the numbers entering the building until 5 June, by which time it had begun to be 'a matter of public interest'. A 'guestimate' seems to have been provided of some 14,500 every day during the 5s. period, and 5000 in the 1s. period at the end of May. For the following two days admission cost £1, and for the next three weeks, 5s. From 26 May, a ticket cost 1s., except on Fridays when it was 2s. 6d., and on Saturdays, when, curiously to modern ideas, it reverted to 5s.[50]

The Queen was a constant visitor, usually with one or two of the children, inspecting one specific section, sometimes with foreign guests. It was not a purely cosmetic exercise: 'Day after day . . . often at much personal inconvenience, has she flattered the various exhibitors by careful examinations of their productions; until it may be presumed that there is scarcely one of her subjects who has more thoroughly inspected all that is worthy of attention'. Such was her interest that she came early on 27 May, to see the admission of the first 1s. visitors.[51] *The Times* commented with pleasure on the occasion in June, when the Queen escorted King Leopold to the Exhibition, in the presence of thousands of shilling visitors:

> By the good management of about a dozen policeman, an avenue was formed down the nave, and the Queen . . . was enabled to pass along living walls of her people as quietly as if she was in her own drawing-room. The effect at this point produced by the thousands of excited spectators was exceeding fine, and all kept their places with an admirable and praiseworthy sense of propriety. Everybody seemed to feel the novelty of the situation, and to desire that justice might be done it. It was, in fact, the first extempore walk of the Sovereign in the presence of her people without other guards than themselves.[52]

The most significant royal tourist was, perhaps, Prince Frederick William of Prussia, permitted to accompany his parents, despite his uncle's apprehensions. Both father and son survived their visit to England, and four years later the young Prince visited Balmoral, and his betrothal to the Princess Royal, Victoria, favourite child of Prince Albert, was approved by the Queen. To Albert's great pleasure they were married in January 1858.

THE EXHIBITS

The building contained over 100,000 exhibits provided by nearly 14,000 exhibitors, of whom nearly half were foreign. The importance attached to it was shown by the trouble taken by foreign nations to ensure a prestigious and fitting display of artefacts and raw materials.

The eastern half of the Crystal Palace was allocated to foreign manufactures, chosen by individual national Committees. The best organized sections were probably the French and that of the Zollverein, both nations accustomed to exhibitions. Some 'countries' appeared in premonitory groupings like 'Italy', a grouping of Rome, Sardinia and Tuscany. 'India' was represented by products assembled by the British East India Company, supplemented by gifts given to the Queen by Indian rulers, though the stuffed elephant on which the Howdah was displayed was found in a museum in a small town in Suffolk. Some of the Russian space was not filled till mid-summer, while Walter Bagehot, who attended the opening, recalled the American section being largely filled with soap.[53]

Overall, however, the Exhibition was a revelation, the first opportunity for many people to see the products of other countries, and often those of distant regions of their own. The products exhibited were extensively described in the *Jury Reports*, and by journalists at the time, and much has been written about it since. We are also fortunate that the Prince commissioned views of the individual exhibits from Joseph Nash, Louis Haghe and David Roberts, and these were published by Dickinson, as chromolithographs, which provide a permanent record of the contents of the Crystal Palace.[54] These were extensively discussed at the time, and have been a subject of study since; this is not the place for a detailed description of the thousands of exhibits.

Preoccupation with taste and design has perhaps blinded some commentators to the value and significance of many of the more industrial objects, including the machinery section. These included printing machines displayed by *The Times* or *Illustrated London News* to Gooch's broad-gauge steam locomotive *The Lord of the Isles*, built for the Great Western Railway, which dominated the Machinery Hall, and McCormick's corn reaper, progenitor of machines in use on arable farms in this country and overseas until after the Second World War. A very large number of useful and practical objects were exhibited, giving rise to discussion about the ability of British industry to compete effectively with foreign competition.[55]

Some exhibits must be mentioned as they have so impressed themselves on visitors or on subsequent commentators. The United States section was substantial, dominated by an eagle. In the centre was a full-sized model of Rider's improved Suspension Truss Bridge, surmounted by a trophy of vulcanized rubber from the Goodyear Rubber Company. Some of its exhibitors were almost caught out by the climate – a specimen of 'red oxide weighing sixteen thousand four hundred pounds from New Jersey' started its journey too late in the year for the frozen waterways, and had to be brought with great difficulty over the mountains to New York, being hauled up by teams of horses, and down by oxen. A large number of manufactured goods were displayed including chairs of various sorts, carriages, usually less showy and more practical than some of the European exhibits, but including a curiosity, a double-ended grand piano for four players. The best known of its exhibits was probably Hiram Powers' 'Greek Slave' in Parian ware, widely copied, but now somewhat of an embarrassment as it is seen as deeply politically incorrect.

Equally well known was the star exhibit of the North German Zollverein section, the zinc casting by Geiss of the famous statue by Professor Kiss of the Amazon being attacked by a lioness, which survived two World Wars, to stand to this day in Berlin – in its own way a gift to cartoonists! Other major exhibits are more familiar to people in this country, as they were given to either the Queen or to British collections. A major Austrian feature was the oak book case carved by M. M. Leistler & Son, and given by the Emperor of Austria to Queen Victoria, and now at the Victoria and Albert Museum.[56]

Though there was a separate fine art section, a critical view was taken of exhibits entered under other headings, one critic observing that ornament was 'now as material an interest in the commercial community as the raw materials'. He went on to comment that there was little new in design in the Exhibition, which he thought was dominated by the influence of France, and therefore by her two favourite styles, the Renaissance and the Louis Quinze, with variations:

The few Greek, or so-called Etruscan specimens, and the Gothic examples, in the singularly styled Medieval court, are almost the only exceptions as regards European design. The best understood style is that which we have been obliged to designate the mixed Cinquecento or renaissance; the apparently most able designers of Italy, France, Austria, Belgium and England, have selected this style for an exhibition of their skill.

He was a somewhat jaded critic, finding too little Greek design, and preferring the 'exquisite designs of Flaxman . . . more beautiful than ever, surrounded as they are by such endless specimens of the gorgeous taste of the present day'.

Wornum was one of those concerned by the relatively poor showing of many British manufactures. He also makes the point that many of the exhibits relied upon expensive materials, concluding that it was:

> infinitely more meritorious in the manufacturer to produce a simple beautiful work . . . within the reach of the world of taste in general, than the accomplishment by an extraordinary effort of an extraordinary work . . . which is beyond the pale of all but regal or princely means . . .
>
>   The Exhibition will do nothing for the age if it only induces a vast outlay of time and treasure for the enjoyment of the extreme few who command immense means.[57]

Not everyone was content with things inside the Palace, the leading Evangelical and reformer Lord Ashley, who had already complained about the version of the Old Hundredth used at the opening, was displeased with the position accorded to the display by the British and Foreign Bible Society. This included copies in 148 languages, of which 121 were printed in languages not before used, and others in 'languages of the South Seas, South and West Africa, and parts of N. and S. America, which *never previously existed in a written form*'.[58] He had already interfered with the display in the Medieval Court, complaining of the position given to a crucifix designed by Pugin.

TOURISM

The Great Exhibition ushered in a new era for London, one of the first occasions on which tourism on a modern scale had to be dealt with. Leaving revolutionaries out of it, there was a lot to concern those responsible for the well-being and entertainment of the expected crowds. There were very few incidents reported of trouble over the presence in London of large number of foreigners, some in unfamiliar garb. In April Palmerston had commented on the report that large parties of French guardsmen in uniform would be coming to London by excursion train, suggesting that it might be better if they left their swords and side-arms 'on the French side of the Channel'.[59]

The large number of guidebooks to London published in 1851 bears witness to a new market. These ranged from ephemeral guidebooks, to more solid productions like Weale's *London Exhibited in 1851*, panned by the *Builder* for its unpatriotic attacks on British *mores* and modern buildings in London[60] and Max Schlesinger's *Saunterings in London*, originally published in Germany, but issued in an English edition in 1853. How much mutual respect and liking was generated between tourists and their hosts, as had been hoped, is a matter difficult to resolve, but clearly the crowds accommodated in 1851 set a benchmark for London police and innkeepers alike.

The Exhibition was visited by over six million visitors, the weekly total rising from the relatively quiet second week in May at 128,000, to over 200,000 in the last week of the month, containing the first shilling days; then to between 288,000 and 300,000 in June and July, dropping off in August and early September, but rising again as the public realized it was about to close. The last two weeks, at the beginning of October, saw the greatest weekly totals, 324,000 and over half a million respectively. Nearly 110,000 visited the building in one day, on 7 October, the last Tuesday, a shilling day, when a second hackney carriage was required to convey the takings to the Bank of England. That was also the occasion on which the greatest number in the building was recorded at any one time, 93,224.[61] *The Times* correspondent recorded on several occasions the pleasure and surprise of onlookers and the authorities at the good temper of the large but well-conducted crowds in the building.

Other tourist attractions were not neglected: London sights which had been open the previous year found their visitor numbers more than doubled, the British Museum from 720,000 to over two million, the Crown Jewels from 32,000 to 209,000, and even Sir John Soane's Museum from 3200 to 7357. Other attractions appear to have opened specially, including St Stephen's Walbrook and the Temple Church. Lord Ellesmere opened the collection at Bridgewater House and the Duke of Northum-

berland opened both Northumberland House at Charing Cross and Sion
House, issuing nearly quarter of a million tickets, and recording that 'no
damage was done to the furniture, or to the numerous articles of *vertu*
and china on the various tables . . . and at Sion not a flower was taken or
a shrub injured'.[62]

The railways came into their own, both for conveying tourists from the
English provinces and foreigners from the Channel ports. The Exhibition
stimulated the railway companies into both competition and a degree of
cooperation. They offered such specially low fares, usually with three
weeks in London, that the Commission came to the conclusion that third-
class passengers often travelled second- if not first-class. Foreign tourists
were much assisted by the cooperation of the railway companies, notably
the South-Eastern Railway and the Chemin de Fer du Nord which started one 'tidal service a day' which cut the travelling time to Paris to eleven
hours, an enterprise which was so successful that on 1 August it was doubled. Other French lines followed suit, reducing travelling time from
Marseilles to 46 hours, at a cost of £6. The Commission tried to estimate
the number of foreigners attracted to the capital, but found themselves in
some difficulties as hitherto no reliable statistics had been kept on the
arrival and departure of foreigners. However, the Committee on the
Working Classes (which seems to have been responsible for compiling
statistics) examined the figures available from those ports with regular
sailings to the Continent, noting that amongst foreigners, Americans, not
requiring passports and looking so like the British, were sometimes overlooked, but that 'a foreigner is so habituated . . . to submit to the strict
regulations that prevail on the Continent that . . . he answers mechani-
cally to the simple inquiries put to him'.[63] Supplementing the figures with
inquiries at the American Legation, the conclusion was that in comparison with an annual number of visitors of 19,340 in 1848 rising to 23,801
in 1850, the summer months of April to September, 1850, brought 15,514
foreign visitors, but the same months in 1851 brought 58,427. They
found this a disappointingly low number, but explained it by the expense
of travel inland on the Continent, the fact that though the French,
Belgians and Dutch were accustomed to come to England, regulations on
travel were stricter elsewhere. They also came to the conclusion that the
official statistics were not totally reliable, pointing out that while the
excess of passengers (in comparison with 1850) listed as arriving by
steam packet in 1851 was some 42,000, the excess of those arriving at the

principal London stations for the Continent was over 80,000. Overall, inquiry at the steam-packet and railway companies conveying passengers to London provided the information that while during the months of April to September, 1850, 2,791,758 people were conveyed to London, the comparable figure for 1851 was 4,237,240.

The Committee endeavoured to put the numbers of Continental visitors into proportion by analysing them by country of origin, and comparing them with the population. On this basis, the largest number of visitors came from France, 27,236 (7.69 per 10,000 population), with 10,440 (6.60) from Germany, which subsumed some residents from other German-speaking countries, like Austria and Prussia, and 5048 from the United States (2.18). The highest proportion came from Holland (9.43) and Belgium (8.75). Despite the difficulties 854 visitors came from Russia and Poland, and 1489 from Italy, including Lombardy.[64]

The Great Exhibition brought to the capital not only foreigners, but many provincial and country people, often more strange to the Londoners than were foreigners from other capital cities. Numbers were swelled by schoolchildren, over 35,000 of whom came in organized groups. Their visits and the names of their schools were meticulously recorded; in the days before universal education, they came largely from national and parochial church schools, and often by the hundred from city parishes and the larger London parishes, though by far the largest single group, of one thousand, came from the Wesleyan and Baptist School, Trowbridge, Somerset. They travelled on the same day, 18 September, as groups from the Tabernacle (122) and the Parish schools (95), also in Trowbridge, two schools from Frome, and the Charity school from 'Bradford Somerset' (possibly Bradford-on-Avon, Wiltshire) (53), together with the charity schools from Wortley (Whatley?) and Nancy (Nunney?), Somerset, which indicates a special train of some sort.[65] This demonstrates the importance of the railways, for the Great Western Railway only reached Frome in 1851.

A number of workhouse children were taken to the Exhibition, mostly from London. Groups of working-class employees were paid for by charitable institutions and considerate employers, like G. P. Baker, a major London builder, singled out by the *Builder* for the way in which he gave 'Exhibition leave' to his workmen for visits, though time was later made up. An interesting account is carried by *The Times* of a visit of a group from Godstone, Surrey, on an excursion. They had each paid 1s. 6d. and the rest of the cost was defrayed by local gentry. The '800 agricultural labourers and country folk', shepherded by their clergy, had travelled to the railway station by wagon, then to London Bridge, and thence to Westminster by steamer. There they saw Westminster Hall, and then

> proceeded on foot and in marching order to the Crystal Palace . . . and at 4 o'clock they took their departure, returning as they had come. The men wore their smartest frocksmocks, the women their best Sunday dresses, and more perfect specimens of rustic attire, rustic faces, and rustic manners could hardly be produced from any part of England . . . The town portion of the assemblage gathered round them as they mustered . . . with looks full of interest, not unmingled with a species of half-pitying interest; and many were the questions put to them as to what they thought of the Exhibition . . . whether they understood what they had seen? . . . After some little marshalling, they left the Exhibition in close order, moving three abreast – an affecting array of young and old, male and female.[66]

The Commission also looked at the length of time spent in London, coming to the conclusion that the visits of the 'middling classes' certainly lasted a week, and with the exception of 'day excursionists' those of the working classes about three days.

Despite the advice of local contacts in the manufacturing districts that the 'artisans were jealous of interference, and would at all hazards prefer to choose their own time and mode of visiting the Metropolis', some special arrangements were made by the Royal Commission and well-meaning London clergy for lodgings. The matter was finally taken into the capable hands of Alexander Redgrave of the Home Office. A Mechanics' Home with one thousand beds was set up, but the Working Classes Committee had to report that never more than a quarter of the beds were occupied. The losses of Mr Harrisson, the owner, were said to be over £4000, and the Finance Committee finally recommended the award of £1000.[67]

Cartoonists made the most of the appalling traffic congestion but it is again difficult to discover just how bad it was. The Metropolitan Police had been consulted before the Exhibition opened as to the likely problems of traffic congestion, and an electric telegraph was installed between the Exhibition Building, the Police Office in Hyde Park and the Home Office in Whitehall, with a branch to Buckingham Palace for the use of Prince

Albert. The Commissioner of Metropolitan Police, Richard Mayne, provided information on two comparable annual occasions, the Horticultural Society Annual Show in Chiswick, and that at the Royal Botanical Gardens in Regent's Park. He reported that the former attracted some 13,000 people, and the carriages waiting occupied some 12 acres. At the latter, which attracted a crowd of 14,500, and which was so near town that a 'great number of the Gentry walked to and fro' and many came in cabs, the waiting carriages, parked at right angles to the road, stretched for 1.5 miles, the equivalent of Apsley House to Kensington Gate.

Where Hyde Park was concerned, there was anxiety about maintaining access for regular riders and those who took carriage exercise in the park, and also for pedestrians. The police were worried about the effect on Hyde Park Corner, where the traffic from Constitution Hill to Hyde Park cut across one of the main London arteries from Piccadilly westwards to Kensington and the Bath Road.[68] The omnibus companies naturally benefited, and the Commission calculated that some 200 additional vehicles were put on the road, while a further 273 altered their routes 'to "Prince's Gate" near the Exhibition'. An extra 350 cabs were calculated to be on the road in 1851, while traffic on the river was thought to have increased by 38 per cent.[69]

The attitude of the French Special Commissioners was always equivocal. The dominance of France is shown by the preponderance of exhibits: 1700 exhibitors showed goods estimated at £294,683 11s. 1d. as opposed to their nearest rivals, Austria with 731 exhibitors and £71,444 worth of goods, then the Zollverein, with some 2000 exhibitors with goods worth £60,645, Russia with 263 exhibitors showing very valuable goods at nearly £59,000, and the United States with 500 exhibitors with £23,000 worth of goods. French firms carried off 54 Council Medals, as opposed to the British score of 78 for exhibits filling half the building.[70] From the first, they had been very involved with the Exhibition, offering advice, sending prestigious and well-qualified Jurors, and MM. Dupin and Sallandrouze had been very ready to offer advice and help to a country which they clearly regarded as a tyro in the matter of exhibitions. After all had not the French been holding national exhibitions for over half a century?

Once the Exhibition was well launched an official invitation to Paris was issued to the Commissioners, Louis Napoleon, still President of France, and not yet Emperor, inviting them in August to a splendid series of entertainments – 'to dine and hear a concert at the Hotel de Ville on Saturday, see the great waters play at Versailles on Sunday, be present at a Fête given by the President on Monday at St Cloud, and dance at a great Ball on Tuesday at the Hotel de Ville'. Though Prince Albert was asked he was unwilling to go without the Queen, and indeed had other engagements in Britain, so the Commissioners, the Lord Mayor of London and the Aldermen and such of the Exhibition staff as could be spared went without him. Happily both Cole and Granville have left accounts of the occasion, which despite its splendours was not without its problems. In a manner with which later generations of mass visitors have become only too familiar, two thirds of the baggage departed in a separate train at Boulogne, leaving the English without their luggage. As Granville recounted to Phipps, Bowring was left to walk the streets in uniform, while Lord Albemarle was reduced to going to evening fêtes in a shooting jacket. The dinner in the Hôtel de Ville was magnificent and Lord Granville replied for the guests, using hints provided by the Prince, whose name was 'received with enthusiasm, the rest of what I said was milk and watery, but being mixed up with a certain amount of butter, was as good-naturedly received as if I had been Demosthenes, speaking to them in the purest Parisian Accent'. Other problems were caused by cultural differences: the Lord Mayor of London was treated with exaggerated respect, 'as a sort of divinity', much more indeed than was accorded Lord Granville himself, a matter which, as he was a member of the Cabinet, upset the other Commissioners more than the equable Granville.

His hosts took him to see the Conservatoire des Arts et Métiers, a museum of technology established under the first Napoleon, an important model for the sort of industrial and scientific museum which was already being discussed in Britain.[71]

CLOSING THE EXHIBITION

There was an inevitable dip in attendance in the Crystal Palace after the London season ended, during which many season-ticket-holders had made almost daily visits, as indeed had members of the Royal Family, and even the aged Duke of Wellington. As the closing date drew near, attendance recovered, but despite the crescendo of interest in September and October, the Exhibition still had to keep to the promised closing date.

Few who were present on the 11th, when the Great Exhibition was closed to the public will forget it. Fifty thousand persons inside took off their hats and sang 'God save the Queen', and those who were outside did so too, and then they gave three mighty cheers . . . and then the bells rang horridly, and the thing was over.[72]

On the Monday and Tuesday, the building was open to exhibitors, jurors and their friends. The formal closure took place on Wednesday 15 October, with a carefully devised ceremony when Viscount Canning, who had acted as President of the Council of Chairmen of Juries, the final authority over the presentation of medals, presented a report to Prince Albert. He explained why the Jurors had decided not to graduate the awards, but to give only the Prize Medal generally, while occasionally awarding the larger Council Medal for some exhibit, remarkable for 'important novelty of invention or application, either in material, or processes of manufacture, or originality combined with great beauty of design'. He referred briefly to the problems this caused with exhibitors used to the French and German National Exhibitions, where prizes were clearly ranked. The thirty-four Juries, each constituted of an equal number of British and foreigners, had considered over an estimated million articles submitted by some 17,000 exhibitors, awarding 2918 Prize Medals, and only 170 of the coveted Council Medals. Each exhibitor took away an Exhibitor's Medal, while each Juror also received a special Juror's Medal. In an equally tactful reply, the Prince thanked Viscount Canning and his team of Jurors, emphasizing the value of the *Jury Reports*, prepared on the 'state of science, art and manufactures in the several branches of the Exhibition'. Thanking Jurors, Exhibitors, members of the various committees, and both foreign and local Commissioners, and members of the Society of Arts, he ended with the pious hope that the same 'singular harmony' which had prevailed so remarkably within the Exhibition might prevail internationally without it.[73]

The medals had proved so satisfactory in solving the problem of rewards to Exhibitors that the same principle was applied to those who had organized the Exhibition. Thus to the Council and Exhibitor's Medals were added the Juror's and Service Medals, using rejected but premiated medal designs. Complete sets of medals and sets of the photographs taken of the exhibits were presented to Commissioners, members of the Executive and Finance Committees, the Special Commissioners, and Secretaries and Treasurers of the Commission.[74] Other awards to the

Commissioners and the Executive Committee were sometimes more contentious.

Colonel Reid and Richard Mayne, as government servants, were made Knights Commander of the Bath, Paxton, William Cubitt and Dilke were offered knighthoods, and Granville suggested that the contractor Fox should also receive a knighthood. The Queen thought that Northcote, Cole and Playfair should become Companions of the Bath, but demurred about knighting Fox, as he was '"*Fox and Henderson*", who have both great merit in the execution of the building, but are only the contractors'. Happily Fox got his knighthood, but Granville had to report to the Prince some days later that Dilke 'was huffy at not being made a Baronet', and had refused his decoration.[75] As Granville also reported to the Prince, the Finance Committee had made generous cash awards to the chief protagonists, £1000 to Paxton, £3000 each to Reid, Cole, Dilke and Playfair, though Granville added that 'Dilke will not hear of money and Reid & Playfair will probably refuse'. Along with a plethora of smaller sums, Owen Jones and Colonel Lloyd both got £1000, and £600 was allocated for scientific instrument cases for the sappers, who were already paid as serving soldiers.[76] The Prince also wrote personally to thank the leading members of the Executive Committee, offering Minton vases to both Granville and William Cubitt as a token of his thanks, while lesser lights got a letter from Colonel Grey conveying the Prince's thanks, and the news that they were to receive a gold medal.[77] Not everyone was content; the Mundays wrote a reproachful letter about the termination of their contract, Scott Russell wrote to complain that alone amongst the secretaries and the executive he had been offered nothing, while the promotion of Lyon Playfair to Colonel Reid's vacated post in the Royal Household irritated the aristocratic Phipps, another member of the Household.[78]

However, those who, like Henry Cole, and indeed Prince Albert himself, had 'originated the design of the Great Exhibition, become its exponent to the public and fought its battles' could enjoy the credit, and reflect on the lessons of its success.[79]

The 'Amazon' has put on her bonnet and shawl, the crystal fountain and the organ have given over playing . . . and the police have left off counting. There is no longer a difficulty in getting a place in an omnibus: the guests are fled, the garlands dead, and Knightsbridge is a deserted village.[80]

Thus wrote the *Builder*, going on to discuss the next problems to face the Commission, the disposal of the handsome surplus generated by the millions of visitors, and the future of the building. There were many suggestions for enjoying the former; the latter was causing a lot of problems.

THE FUTURE OF THE BUILDING

The Office of Woods and Forests were anxious to see the Crystal Palace removed, as promised, and the Royal Commission, too, was committed to its departure, but there were others who saw it differently. It had first to be emptied, and though over 95 per cent of the British Exhibitors had removed their goods within a month of the official closing, the foreign goods were not cleared until 15 January, 1852. Even before the building had taken shape, in the summer of 1850 observers had queried the sense of spending over £150,000 on a building which would disappear in 1852. The *Jardin d'Hiver* in the Champs Elysées was held up as the model of a municipal conservatory for London, though it was accepted that the building could be moved to a site like Battersea Fields.[81]

Once the Crystal Palace had been erected in Hyde Park, the pressure to retain it built up. On 29 July, 1851, the future of the building had been raised by James Heywood (1810–97), Member of Parliament for North Lancashire, who had been briefed, if not primed, by Paxton, and Fox and Henderson, on the good condition of the building, and the possibility of retention. He wished to move a humble address to enable the building to be retained till 1 May, 1852, pointing out to the House that:

> The particular style of architecture called crystal architecture was new to historians, and the magnificent specimen in Hyde Park would, no doubt, be spoken of . . . as one of the great features of the age . . . to be ranked with railways, the penny postage, and other inventions.[82]

He succeeded despite a predictable attack on the Exhibition and its consequences from Colonel Sibthorp, who detailed widespread desecration of the Sabbath, destitution amongst the poor who had come to London to see it and bankruptcy amid provincial tradesmen robbed of their customers. Some influential Members of Parliament took the opportunity to apologize for their lack of belief in the project during the previous year. It was, however, noted that the petitions for the building's retention came from Scotland, Falmouth and Exeter, and not from the capital, and certainly not from the Scottish Member of Parliament who lived opposite it in one of Mr Elger's Houses – Mr MacGregor from Glasgow.[83]

The House of Commons voted to defer its removal, and Lord Seymour, the Chief Commissioner of Woods and Forests, Dr Lindley of the Royal Horticultural Society and the newly knighted Sir William Cubitt were appointed to consider the matter. It was still technically the property of the contractors, though they were financially embarrassed and by early in 1852 had assigned the building to the London and County Bank.[84] The three were asked to consider the cost of purchase, where it should be re-erected and how it should be used. Meanwhile, though nearly empty, it was still a landmark, and Fox and Henderson, finding they had 'incessant applications . . . for permission to view the interior of the Crystal Palace' were proposing to admit the Public at sixpence a time, a proposal which startled Lord Seymour. In February 1852, Paxton put forward proposals for reusing the building as a Winter Garden at an annual cost of £12,000 for maintenance of the structure, and a further £6–10,000 for the provision of 'fresh objects of attraction such as Statuary, Fountains, reliques, Plants, Birds, &c'.[85]

Fox and Henderson continued to try to make some money out of the building, making applications to use it for charity concerts, or public openings, but the Conservative Lord John Manners, who had taken over from the Whig Lord Seymour as Chief Commissioner of Woods and Forests, took a rather harder line.[86] The Commissioners found themselves in the embarrassing position of being threatened with legal action by the government. By April 1852, Fox and Henderson were being charged with having

> used the building for Public Promenades and Concerts; . . . induced a concourse of persons to assemble in the Building, in the park, and in the neighbouring thoroughfares; and that such assemblages have been injurious to the Park, detrimental to property in the immediate neighbourhood, and otherwise prejudicial to the Peace and quiet of the Vicinity.[87]

A last attempt to save the Building *in situ* was mounted by Joseph Paxton and his allies in April 1852. He prepared plans and designs for its enlargement 'for the purpose of converting it to a Winter Garden, and adapting it to other scientific purposes', of which a model was prepared and placed in the Crystal Palace to be seen by all the crowds so contentiously, even improperly, admitted to the building. It involved the addition of four glass towers to house coke boilers for heating, and also two enormous semi-circular additions at either end to provide additional entrances, and open courtyards for the display of sculpture.

On 27 April, a meeting held by a group styled by the *Illustrated London News* as 'the friends of the movement for the preservation of the Crystal Palace' held a meeting at Exeter Hall, presided over by Lord Shaftesbury, supported by the North Lancashire Member of Parliament, James Heywood, Paxton himself, and a number of other notables, mostly from the north-west, the power base of Paxton, and his patron, the Duke of Devonshire. It also included the Duke of Argyll, Lord Harrowby and the Radical Member of Parliament, Joseph Hume. Predictably, they passed a resolution to present a further memorial to the Queen, and to send a deputation to Lord Derby, the Prime Minister, asking for the preservation of the building. They presented the names of grandees prepared to act as trustees, drawn from a surprisingly wide base, including the peers already named, the Duke of Devonshire, the Earls of Carlisle and Burlington, Palmerston, Baron Lionel de Rothschild and the great railway contractor Samuel Morton Peto.[88]

It was followed by an attempt in the House of Commons to have a Select Committee appointed, proposed by the indefatigable Heywood, opposed by Sibthorp and by Lord John Manners, Chief Commissioner of Works, and supported by his predecessor, Lord Seymour and Labouchere, from the previous administration. The motion was defeated by 221 to 103, sealing the fate of the Crystal Palace.[89]

However, Derby could report to the Prince in April 1852 that one of the Exhibition's original champions, Francis Fuller, and a private company were anxious to purchase the building and re-erect it as a winter garden in Battersea Park or some other spot close to the metropolis.[90]

The Crystal Palace was opened to the public on 1 May, 1852, and the public flooded in, though its appearance provided a sad contrast with the earlier occasion. Some ten days later, Grey reported to the Prince that the building had been purchased for £70,000, and the whole of the money paid that very day. The Chairman of the Brighton Railway Company was chairman of the new company, and it was to be moved to Sydenham, and 're-erected entire with such additions as may appear desirable'. Owen Jones and Digby Wyatt were to be retained to supervise the works, and the railway company would guarantee the project, capitalized at £500,000 at 6 per cent, provided the building was re-erected on their land.[91] The contractors were given until 1 November, 1852, to remove the building from Hyde Park, but then came the thorny question of the removal of drains and foundations, and the reinstatement of the ground. Very elaborate drainage, and substantial new sewers, in the innovative oval shape, had been required to drain the 18 acres of glass, and originally the Park authorities had agreed to take some of them over.[92] The matter, made more difficult by the change of administration, dragged on unhappily. Fox and Henderson complained that letters were not answered, Mr Mann from Kensington Gardens criticized the state of the ground, while the Commission attempted to claim that it was a matter only for Fox and Henderson and the Office of Works, which had taken over from Woods and Forests. The Commissioners were finally forced to insist on a bond for £10,000 to guarantee removal being produced by the contractors to satisfy the government. The matter finally went to arbitration at the end of 1853, with Paxton acting for the Commissioners, who paid over £1015 for reinstatement of the ground to the Office of Works.

A sad footnote is provided by a typical Treasury request, coming from the pen of Alfred Austin, the poet, to Edgar Bowring, by then Secretary to the 1851 Commissioners, that the Commission should accept the balance of £7 16s. 4d. to enable his department to clear its books by 31 March, 1859. Bowring finally agreed to accept to pay it over 'to the Assignees of Messrs. Fox & Henderson'.[93]

The Crystal Palace was removed to Sydenham, to open considerably extended and enhanced by a purpose-built park in 1854. It flourished as a 'People's Palace' for over eighty years, the home to exhibitions, concerts, Cruft's Dog Show, and Temperance Demonstrations, until engulfed by fire on 30 November, 1936. Even that disaster was a stylish ending for a nineteenth-century icon: the fire attracted a dinner-jacketed member of the Royal Family, it tempted a photographer to hire an aeroplane, and it was reported that the flames could be seen from Brighton.

III

The Grand Design: The South Kensington Purchase
1852–1857

The Great Exhibition of 1851 confounded the prophets of disaster. It was well received despite the apprehensions of its adherents and the dire warnings of its opponents; it set a standard by which subsequent occasions would be measured; it gave satisfaction to exhibitors and visitors alike; it made a profit, and established the reputations of those associated with it. *The Times* recorded over six million visits in all, nearly 110,000 in one day, with the greatest attendance at any one time being 93,224. The crowds had attended with a decorum which later police forces might envy, and it was remarked that it was not only 'without disorder, but almost without crime'.

None of the predicted disasters occurred. As Prince Albert observed to the Prince of Prussia, mathematicians had calculated the Crystal Palace would blow down in a strong gale, engineers that the galleries would crash to the ground, and others that the presence of so many foreigners in London would lead first to famine and then to plague, and finally to a collapse of morals.

On the contrary, as the *Illustrated London News* pointed out, 'we may justly boast of the good sense and good temper of the British people, who . . . have shown themselves a multitude without becoming a mob'.[1] The foreigners had been accommodated without difficulty, though as the same newspaper observed 'the progenitors . . . might have been terrified at the vast army of observation, of various races and habits, which they have been the means of concentrating around the wealthiest and least defended capital in the world'.[2]

It had raised questions, often uncomfortable, about the quality of the exhibits from the United Kingdom as measured against foreign manufactures. Thus France with a total of 1710 exhibits had carried off some

1043 awards including over 600 Prize Medals and 54 prestigious Council Medals as against the United Kingdom's 2155 awards for 6861 exhibits, with 773 medals and 78 Council Medals.[3] The comparison was made not only in relation to acknowledged leaders of fashion and taste like France, Austria and northern Italy, but also in comparison with products from elsewhere.

In the words of *The Times*:

> The display in Hyde-park . . . shows that in the assiduous and suc-
> cessful cultivation of the fine arts ⌈our own country⌉ is considerably
> in the rear of other nations, and that here she has wide scope for the
> improvement and elevation of her industrial character. It is not only
> in sculpture and bronzes, and such like, that England is beaten . . .
> But the neglect of art among a people tells with most damaging
> effect upon nearly every form of their manufactures . . . The truth is,
> that while other countries have been studying chiefly to render their
> industrial products artistic, we have been struggling to render ours
> cheap and serviceable . . . But it is not the great European commu-
> nities that alone teach us a lesson in this respect − for we cannot
> approach the carpets and rugs of Turkey, Tunis, India, and other
> countries far behind us as they are in general civilisation.[4]

The *Illustrated London News* realized that in a sense the genie was out of the bottle:

> The Great Exhibition cannot fail to exercise a very considerable
> influence upon the art and industry, as well as upon the commerce
> and international relationships of the world.

It quoted Prince Albert's Mansion House speech, acknowledging that communication between nations would accelerate from now on. Broadly it saw the Exhibition as a stimulus to free trade, suggesting that a greater knowledge of both British and neighbours' resources would encourage confidence and respect, and emphasize the value of 'reciprocal dealing'. While British manufacturers hoped to see foreign countries open their markets to British goods in the long term, British shopkeepers were more immediately concerned about the Exhibition as a showplace for foreign goods and designs.

A number of lectures given at the Society of Arts and elsewhere explored these uncomfortable facts, and Playfair, even with the reticence imposed by his role as a Commissioner, pointed out that England was being eclipsed by foreign workmen even in her traditional industries:

> All Europeans nations, except England, have recognised the fact, *that industry must in future be supported not by a competition of local advantages, but by a competition of intellect* . . . The result of the Exhibition was one that England may well be startled at. Wherever – and that implies almost every manufacture – science or art was involved as an element of progress, we saw . . . that the nation which cultivated them was in the ascendant.[5]

Generally, however, the Great Exhibition was approved, even by earlier critics like the Member of Parliament Sir Robert Inglis, who apologized for his earlier cynicism, praising the 'prescient sagacity of the illustrious Prince who . . . had successfully carried it out notwithstanding the luke-warm support of many, and the ill-concealed aversion of others'. The Royal Commissioners felt they could at last relax. In the words of Lord Granville, at a Mansion House dinner in June 1851:

> The Royal Commissioners . . . like people who have been a good deal knocked about, and who . . . had accomplished some good in their time, when they approached old age, and had a large balance at their banker's, they felt that they ought to enjoy their old age with dignity, and they were therefore partaking of the hospitality of their countrymen in banquets and public breakfasts.[6]

Most satisfactory to its projectors was the profit. It had always been intended to produce a surplus, though this had seemed very doubtful at one moment; there was, however, a considerable difference of opinion as to how this could best be spent. The Royal Society of Arts had always intended that the end-product should be a building for future exhibitions, though the undertaking to remove the Crystal Palace dented this aspiration. In addition, as a correspondent to the *Westminster Review* pointed out, the problems of getting triumphs of British engineering, such as Brunel's forty-ton railway engine and tender, down Park Lane behind a team of horses were considerable, and it would be better to have a rail-linked site.

There were other problems over the 'surplus' since it included some £67,000 of subscriptions raised by groups of provincial manufacturers and even mechanics. These were retained although the substantial guar-

antees put up by capitalists like Samuel Morton Peto and Thomas Cubitt
were never called upon. This was a matter which was to be a continual
source of irritation to the great manufacturing cities, who saw the retention of the surplus as a piece of metropolitan opportunism, and was to be
very shrewdly used by Joseph Chamberlain against the Commissioners
twenty-five years later. There were even more outspoken requests for its
return from smaller cities and various provincial bodies, who felt that the
money they had subscribed could well be used locally. The Warrington
Committee wanted theirs for the Building Fund of the Warrington
Museum, while James Macadam from Belfast put it more starkly, saying
that the subscriptions should have been returned as soon as the 'receipts
. . . became sufficient to defray the expenses'.

The Clonmel Mechanics' Institute sent a request on parchment, for
£500, from the surplus of what they termed the 'Museum of the
Mechanical Industry of the Globe', urging the need to 'advance that scientific information among the Irish people without which they cannot
ever take their proper place in the intellectual struggle now going forward among mankind.[7]

However, these matters were ignored in the euphoria which followed
the closing of the building in October 1851. There were, of course, the
proposals for retaining the building, fought hard not only by Paxton's
allies but by Cole also. These, however, had concentrated on the provision
of a winter garden, or an indoor space for equestrian and pedestrian exercise. Among the other schemes suggested to the triumvirate set up to
consider the retention of the building, Lord Seymour, Dr Lindley and Sir
William Cubitt, was one which proposed the housing of objects from the
increasingly crowded British Museum galleries. It was dismissed by the
Head of Antiquities, Edward Hawkins, largely on the grounds that:

> You must not separate the different antiquities: the coins, the medals,
> the bronzes, the vases, the sculptures, all must go together; and the
> library too; for the best collection of antiquities would be almost
> useless, unless you have access to a very extensive library.

However, though not enthusiastic about the Crystal Palace, he thought
that 'an iron and glass building, somewhat like the railway stations, only
rather more finished in its character' would be satisfactory, and, in a way
that presaged South Kensington even more, suggested a collection of
casts in such a building.[8]

THE GRAND DESIGN

Even before the Exhibition closed, the Prince was busy devising a scheme to put the surplus, calculated at between £150,000 and £200,000, to good use. In a long memorandum written at Osborne in August 1851, he made some far-reaching and innovative suggestions for its use, strictly in accordance with the Commissioners' commitment to spending on 'the establishment of future Exhibitions or objects strictly in connection with the present Exhibition'. Because of the importance of these proposals as the blueprint for South Kensington, without which the original Royal Commission would have withered away once the Exhibition was over, they deserve careful examination. They were not all achieved, but it is perhaps more remarkable that so much of his scheme was carried out, particularly if one bears in mind that he was a thirty-year-old foreign prince in a country where he was not universally revered, and was regularly mocked by *Punch* and looked down on by many members of the ruling class.

He felt the original commitment prevented the Commission supporting the proposed retention of the Crystal Palace as a 'Place of Recreation', though he saw no reason why others should not pursue it. He then put forward, very emphatically as his personal view, a detailed scheme, based on the purchase of 25 to 30 acres of ground in Kensington Gore, including 'Soyer's Symposium', a restaurant carried on in Gore House during the Exhibition, which he had been 'assured . . . are to be purchased at this moment for about £50,000'. On this he proposed the establishment of four institutions, corresponding to the four great divisions of the Exhibits, which he himself had originally suggested, Raw Materials, Machinery, Manufactures and Plastic Art, devoted to the 'furtherance of the industrial pursuits of all nations'.

His scheme, which effectually set up South Kensington as we know it today, is worth examining for the light it sheds on contemporary thought on education, as well as its influence on the future development of the Commission's estate. He went on to list the four methods of acquiring such knowledge:

> 1). *personal study* from books, 2). *Oral* communication of Knowledge by those who possess it . . . 3). acquisition of knowledge by *occular* [*sic*] observation, comparison, & demonstration. 4). exchange of ideas by *personal discussion.*

To provide these each institution would have:

1) Library and rooms for study. 2) Lecture Rooms, 3) an Acre of Glass covering for the purposes of Exhibition, & 4) Rooms for Conversationi [*sic*], Discussions and commercial Meetings. The surplus Space might be laid out as gardens for public enjoyment, and so as to admit of the future erection of public Monuments there . . . The Centre might be applicable for a public Conservatory – if wished for.

The Institution for the *Raw Material* would be most usefully subdivided into Metallurgy, Metallurgical chemistry & Animal & Vegetable Physiology (Agricultural Chemistry, Microscopy).

That of *Machinery* would embrace the branch of Polytechnic Science with its subdivisions.

That of *Manufactures* would comprise a School of design & Chemistry as applied to Manufactures.

The Fourth (The Plastic Art) Architecture, Antiquities, Sculpture. Now I find that for all these separate pursuits we have a variety of Public Societies in England, struggling for existence, unconnected with each other, unprovided with any suitable locations,

the Geological Society, Botanical Society, Linnaean Society, Zoological Society, Microscopical Society, Agricultural Society, &c &c

Polytechnic Society, Society of Civil Engineers &c &c

The Society for the Arts, Manufactures & Commerce (from which the Exhibition has sprung & which, after having produced its flower will have exhausted its vital power, & cannot return to what it was before).

The Society of Architects, of Antiquaries, Archaeological &c

Could not these Societies or most of them, containing as they do all that this Country possesses of Talent & Experience in these branches, be united . . .

He saw these institutions as international and suggested that the Exhibitors might be the 'first Life Members of the Institutions'.

By a scheme like this we should insure, that the great Exhibition of 1851 should not become a transitory event . . . but that its Objects would be perpetuated, that the different industrial pursuits of mankind, arts & Sciences, should not again relapse into a state of comparative isolation from each other, in which this progress is necessarily retarded, & that the different Nations would remain in that immediate relation of mutual assistance by which these pursuits are incalculably advanced.

He went on to refer to the proposal to remove the National Gallery, whose valuable exhibits were being damaged by the polluted atmosphere of Central London, and suggested that a larger purchase might be made, and part of it sold to the government for the National Gallery, which might 'assist the study of Art in connexion with Manufacture'. He concluded:

> I am perfectly aware that this is but a very crude scheme requiring mature consideration & practical tests in its details, but I thought it my duty towards the Commission to lay it before them at as early a moment as possible, in order that the remaining weeks of the Exhibition might be employed in investigating it, or that we might be led by that investigation to the discovery of a more feasible plan.[9]

The Executive Committee – Reid, Dilke, Playfair and Cole, with Northcote and Sir William Cubitt – were summoned to Osborne three days later to discuss the Prince's scheme. Though the idea was generally approved, greater realism prevailed, and the number of institutions was cut to one. The group saw more clearly than the Prince the absurdity of trying to get the learned societies to adopt any common course of action, let alone to involve them in the management of such an educational scheme. 'Everybody laughed', recorded Cole in his diary, 'at the idea of making the Antiquarian and Archaeological Societies "commercial", moving them and governing them by the Statistical Society.'[10]

The Prince doubtless hoped to solve other current problems and controversies through the actions of the Royal Commission and the complexity of his proposal. This may have been because he had discovered the efficacy of harnessing existing institutions to the schemes he had espoused – the Great Exhibition of the Industry of All Nations had been just such a success.

The first of these questions was the problem of a site for the National Gallery, which both needed room for expansion, and whose situation had been condemned by experts anxious about the safety of the pictures. Within the last five years concern had been so great that no less than two government commissions and one committee had been appointed to consider the matter. Though by the simple expedient of expelling the Royal Academy which occupied about half the Trafalgar Square building additional space could be found, informed opinion questioned whether removal from 'the smoke and dust of London' might not be better for the well-being of the pictures. None of the three bodies provided a decisive answer, but other sites were canvassed, including two in Hyde Park, but on the north side. The last commission, whose members included Lord Seymour, Eastlake and Westmacott, together with the connoisseur, Lord Colborne (1770–1854), and the Member of Parliament, William Ewart (1798–1869), both politicians keenly interested in the arts, perhaps mindful of the furore over the exhibition building, favoured the purchase of 15 to 20 acres in Kensington.[11]

The learned Societies presented a similar problem: they were housed in Somerset House, which the Treasury wished to repossess to house the Inland Revenue. The bodies affected were the Royal Society, the Society of Antiquaries and the Astronomical and Geological Societies, all of which had a high opinion of themselves though they were not always as highly thought of. Thus, though the Prince had suggested that the societies should move to South Kensington, and welcomed Lord John Russell's information that the Royal Society had manifested 'a desire to move westward', he went on to say that the Society 'as at present constituted has forfeited the sympathy of the generality of the public by its lethargic state and exclusive principles'. It may have been as much comments like this, as the pronounced dislike of Lord Rosse, the astronomer and President of the Royal Society, for South Kensington, that prevented any such move. Lord John Russell saw the danger of a perceived threat from the new 'Industrial University' to the established institutions like the societies or Oxford and Cambridge. 'It is very desirable to keep the objects separate, and the old gentlemen of our scientific societies will be very apt to grumble if they are put out of their way for their evening meetings, and their great elections. They would be much pleased on the other hand with . . . free access to the teachers, collections and libraries of the new institutions.'[12]

Another government body looking for a new home was the Government Schools of Design, founded in 1837 after an earlier bout of concern about the state of industrial and art education in the country. It originally came under the Board of Trade, though transferred in 1856 to the Committee on Education of the Privy Council, a status which reflected its anomalous position under government. It too had been housed at Somerset House, but had been moved by the Treasury to Marlborough House, a temporarily unwanted royal residence, but destined in the not so distant future for the use of the Prince of Wales. On 31 October, 1851, Lord Granville offered Henry Cole the secretaryship of the Government Schools of Design. This post involved the management of a far-flung empire: in London two metropolitan schools, one for males at Somerset House, and one for females in Gower Street, together with a 'museum', essentially a collection of exemplars, and a further twenty establishments from Glasgow and Belfast to the English provinces.

Both Cole and Lionel Playfair provided comments after the meeting at Osborne, on 13 August, 1851. The former's contribution was in the form of a series of questions, chiefly probing the delicate question of who was to deal with the Societies, and how they were to be provided with accommodation, thus identifying the main obstacle to the complete achievement of the Prince's scheme. He also raised the question of whether the Commission could be responsible for developing the scheme, and the Prince's reply made it clear that a new organization would be necessary. Cole's blunt 'Is it not the general desire of this present Commission that it should expire, when it has performed its functions?' elicited 'Yes!' from the Prince – an exchange making the prolongation of the existing Commission six months later, largely with the existing Commissioners, somewhat unexpected, though Cole's proposal later in the paper of 'a new Charter, and the application to Parl^t.' may have pointed the way forward.[13]

Playfair provided a number of 'additions and amendments', pointing out the need to make the case realistically for 'affording instruction to those engaged in the prosecution of Arts and Manufactures'. Improvements in transport and the handling of raw materials had decreased the advantages of having them on the spot, and 'amazingly increased the value of skill and intelligence as the other great element of production'. He described the French system, and the renown of the École Centrale des Arts et Manufactures supported by industry, which annually trained three hundred pupils, who were eagerly sought after, not only in France, but in Belgium and even in Britain. He concluded by pointing out the 'growing necessity that the Nation should afford its Manufacturers the means of acquiring that knowledge without which they cannot long keep foremost in the industrial struggle of Nations'. Diplomatically, he suggested that the range of knowledge of the proposed new institution should be confined to that of 'a technical and practical character . . . supplementary to and not a substitute for the other educational establishments of this country'. The societies for the promotion of abstract and applied science were 'in their very nature and objects cosmopolitan', and would fit well with the proposed international character of the new institution.

Later on, in a note to Phipps, ensconced at Balmoral, Playfair pinpointed the problem of the Societies, whose reluctance to accept 'centralization' could threaten a large part of the scheme, and offered to approach the Royal Society, together with the Geological, Linnaean and others, suggesting they should make an approach to the Prince, explaining their need for joint or at least associated accommodation.[14] Another impediment was the conflict between the establishment proposed to boost British industrial education and the Prince's insistence that, as the Exhibition had been international, so ought the institution to be paid for by the profit. Phipps pointed out that such an establishment in England would be a great national asset. Later on, Playfair was to be confronted with an even greater problem – 'the danger of alarming the Religious world by any avowed *Educational* scheme, which might stir up a storm'.[15]

The final meeting of the Commission before the summer recess was held on 19 August, largely to deal with routine business, the satisfactory balance at the Bank of England, and the arrangements for the closure of the Exhibition on 11 October. The Prince's memorandum was not officially discussed but it was agreed that the opinion of the Law Officers of the Crown was to be sought as to the 'power of the Commissioners under their Charter . . . to dispose of any surplus that may remain in their hands' after paying all outgoings.[16]

CHANGES AT THE COMMISSION

The closing of the Exhibition also meant that the 'Prince's team' – the active members of the Commission and its Executive Committee, was being broken up. Dilke was to remain active, but his refusal of £3000 emphasized his amateur status, as did his refusal of the proffered knighthood. Colonel Reid was knighted for his very considerable contribution to the success of the Exhibition, and returned to his profession as colonial governor – to Malta, where he served for seven years. Cole, who had been seconded from the Record Office to work on the Exhibition, was appointed General Superintendent of the Schools of Design under the Board of Trade. The sapper officer Captain Henry C. Owen, who had supervised the Foreign Department during the arrival and disposal of the exhibits, and then been in charge of the 'general superintendence of the building' throughout the Exhibition, was warmly congratulated and thanked by the foreign delegations. At the close, it was suggested that he should deal with administrative matters like the issuing of *Jury Reports.* He remained with the Commission, as Financial Officer, until he returned to his duties as a sapper officer during the Crimean War. A family connection with South Kensington was perpetuated, however, since his brother Philip Cunliffe-Owen (1828–94) joined the office, and succeeded Henry Cole at the Department of Art, when the latter retired in 1873. Sir William Cubitt, who had truly earned his knighthood for his work on the building, was a Commissioner *ex officio* as President of the Institute of Civil Engineers, but was promptly reinstated in his own right on the expiry of his term of office.[17] The two Secretaries to the Commission moved on. John Scott Russell, who had resigned from the secretaryship of the Society of Arts when he was appointed to the Royal Commission, went to work with Brunel on the ill-fated *Great Eastern.* Northcote had not been present a great deal during the preparation for the Exhibition. Though he later attended the opening, he had surrendered his salary in November 1850 because of 'the desultory nature of his attendance, arising from the circumstances of his private affairs', due to his father's death. His place as Secretary had been effectively taken over by Edgar Bowring, who had been at the Board of Trade as private secretary to Granville, when the latter had been Vice-President in 1848. Bowring seems to have worked for the Commission throughout the Exhibition, but afterwards had had to return to his post at the Board of Trade, where he combined the duties of Secretary to the Commission with that of Registrar to the Board of Trade. Edgar Alfred Bowring (1826–1916) was the son of Sir John Bowring, a north country Member of Parliament who became British envoy to China. He had West Country connections, and was to enter Parliament as Member for Exeter after nearly twenty years at the Royal Commission. He was appointed Acting Secretary of the Royal Commission, and worked closely with Prince Albert on the early development of the Commissioners' estate. Though he was Registrar of the Board of Trade until 1864, he was an effective and hard-working Secretary to the Commission until he resigned in 1869 after he had been

Fig 10. Edgar Bowring, seconded from the Board of Trade to
become Secretary to the 1851 Commission, 1852–69.

elected to Parliament.[18] He became the first of a number of long-serving
and dedicated secretaries who served the Commissioners until after the
Second World War.

The Commission received its Supplemental Charter in December 1851,
and returned to the offices in Whitehall, originally provided by the
despised Mundays, thereafter holding meetings of the Commission at
the Palace of Westminster. A high-powered committee, on which served
the Prince, Granville, Labouchere, Cubitt and Gladstone, was appointed
to consider the future administrative back-up needed, and came to the
conclusion that the Executive Committee could be disbanded, and that a
single part-time secretary would be adequate for the time being, together
with a financial officer, a post taken by Captain Owen. Official sanction
was given by the President of the Board of Trade to Bowring to continue
to work as secretary to conclude remaining business, providing it did not
interfere with his official duties.[19]

The new pattern of administration left Edgar Bowring, working closely with Prince Albert, very much in charge of Commission business. The
Building Committee was dissolved, though Sir William Cubitt remained
one of the Prince's advisers. The Commission itself met less often, usually with Prince Albert in the chair, Lord Granville replacing him when
necessary. The Prince remained a powerful and involved President with a

very clear conception of the task before the revived Commission, working through his private secretaries Colonel Sir Charles Phipps (1801–66), and General the Honourable Charles Grey (1804–70), who worked closely with Bowring. After the Prince's death Grey became the most important advocate for Prince Albert's visionary scheme with the Queen, wrote a life of the young Prince, and became a Commissioner himself in the last year of his life. The Prince involved himself personally in the major projects, but routine business was carried out by the Finance Committee under Granville. This consisted of the purchase and exchanges needed to consolidate the estate, the management of relations with neighbouring landowners over roads, and the manipulation of the complex arrangements for paying the mortgages, and keeping the Commission solvent.

By the time the Exhibition closed, public expectations were high. The *Illustrated London News* carried a story of a surplus of some £300,000.[20] The Commission met two days after the Exhibition had closed, when it was reported that they had £163,308 8s. 9d. at the Bank of England, in addition to money invested in the Funds. They dealt largely with the awards to members of the Committees, and to executive officers, but received the reports of the Law Officers, and appointed a Surplus Committee, chaired by the Prince himself, consisting of Granville, Eastlake, Lyell, Baring, Cobden and William Cubitt.

The Commission put forward a scheme for the surplus on 6 November, 1851, in the form of a report to the Queen, signed by Prince Albert. £505,000 had been derived from various sources: subscriptions £67,400, entrance fees £424,400 and casual receipts £13,200, of which some £150,000 would remain after all expenses had been paid. Though it was admitted that subscribers had been told that the Royal Commissioners intended to apply any surplus 'to purposes strictly in connexion with the ends of the Exhibition, or for the establishment of similar Exhibitions for the future', the Commissioners reported that they had come to the conclusion that the success of the Exhibition had demonstrated that such undertakings could be made self-supporting. Better use of the surplus could therefore be made in 'furtherance of the general objects for which the Exhibition was designed, and in such manner that the advantages . . . may be shared, as far as may be possible, by other countries'. 'The general objects' they considered to have been 'the furtherance of every branch of human industry, by the comparison of the processes employed, and of the results obtained by all the nations of the earth – and the promotion of kindly international feelings, by the practical illustration of the advantages which may be derived . . . from what has been done by others' but the Commissioners had come to the conclusion that the most appropriate objective would be 'measures . . . which may increase the means of industrial education, and extend the influence of science and art upon productive industry'. If this were thought to be a worthy objective, time and thought would be needed to mature such a plan, but meanwhile the Commission needed further powers by Royal Charter to enable it to pursue such a scheme.[21]

Because of doubts about the discretion of some of the Commissioners, the scheme for the purchase of the land at Kensington Gore was not discussed in detail in a full meeting, and Granville wrote to all of them individually for their approval of the purchase of a piece of land somewhat vaguely described as 'a large extent of land . . . partially covered with small inferior houses, but the chief portion is under market cultivation'.[22] Agreement was obtained from the majority of Commissioners, enabling the Prince, with Granville as Chairman of the Finance Committee, and with the support of the small Surplus Committee, to pursue his objective.

When the *First Report* was published, at the end of April 1852, the Commission could hint at its project. The business of the purchase in Kensington Gore appears to have been pursued largely by Prince Albert himself, acting with Bowring, and through his own office and the 'kitchen cabinet' of familiars like Thomas Cubitt and Henry Cole, neither of whom had any official position at the Royal Commission. As Lord Seymour made clear, this was an entirely different matter from any overtures he was making on behalf of the government. A further complication was that Lord John Russell's ailing government finally fell in February 1852, being succeeded briefly by Lord Derby's Conservative administration. The 1851 Commissioner Lord Seymour was replaced as Chief Commissioner of Works by Lord John Manners, who took an even harder line over the removal of the Exhibition building, and Sir Charles Wood, as Chancellor of the Exchequer, by Benjamin Disraeli.

Happily, the choice of Commissioners had, however, been sufficiently bipartisan to ensure that the Prince's scheme met no great opposition. Lord Derby had been one of the original members of the Commission, and Disraeli, as Chancellor of the Exchequer, was rather more supportive of the Prince than had been his Whig predecessor.[23]

After the labours of 1851, the Commission itself met only six times in 1852, and most of the work of dealing with the Kensington Gore purchase fell on Bowring and Prince Albert's private office. Through Dilke[24] the Prince was put in touch with John Kelk, a Mayfair builder and contractor, a partner of John Elger, who had also suffered from the propinquity of the Exhibition over his Prince's Gate development. In order to conceal the identity of the would-be purchaser, Kelk was to be employed, since as a local developer he was known to be interested in building land in the area, and his overtures would not arouse suspicion and raise the price. Kelk, who was already assisting the government over the proposed purchase for the National Gallery, went to Windsor on 22 January, 1852, to brief the Prince about the area.

THE SOUTH KENSINGTON PURCHASE

The site in which government and Commission were both taking an interest lay on the south side of Kensington Road, west of Prince's Gate, partly in an outlying part of St Margaret's, Westminster, and otherwise in the parish of Kensington. Kensington Road had a number of substantial houses on the south side fronting the park; though there were a small number of modest houses behind, and the area behind it had considerable potential, it was relatively undeveloped.[25] The large estate, already identified by the government as a possible site for the National Gallery, fronting on to the road, was the Gore House Estate, about 21 acres in extent, belonging to a Mr Aldridge, who was thought to want about £57,000. To the east, behind Elger's prejudiced houses, were some 11 acres belonging to Charles Freake, also a developer, who was to become very much a South Kensington figure. He had paid £24,000, and it was thought that he might pass on the land at cost, plus expenses.

The largest estate in the area belonged jointly, through somewhat complex lines of inheritance, to two descendants of Sir John Fleming, who had died in 1763, leaving 95 acres in the area. By 1851, the land had descended jointly to the Earl of Harrington and to the wife of a Swiss nobleman, the Baron de Graffenried Villars. The property was divided in 1850–1, the formal order being dated 24 September, 1851, which made it immediately available for development. Because of the scrupulously equitable way the property had been divided, the plots were distributed in a random way between the two heirs. Within a year Lord Harrington had entered into an agreement to lease the whole of his 46 acres to William

Jackson, a Westminster builder with a wharf in Pimlico, and clearly in a big way of business since he was prepared to pay a rent of £100 an acre for the land after ten years.[26]

It was thought by the Commission that the Baron would not be averse to selling, but there were complications since the property belonged to his wife, and it had been carefully tied up in a family trust, stipulating investment only in land or government securities, on which the returns were much lower. One of the Baron's objectives was to obtain an Act of Parliament to alter the terms for investment of his wife's money. He found the arrangements for dealing with English property confusing, and was astounded to be told at a later date that the Royal Commission, which numbered among its members the Prime Minister, the Chancellor of the Exchequer, the Chief Commissioner of Works, not to mention the sovereign's spouse, would be unable to assist him in obtaining the coveted act to break his wife's family trust. The Baron's agent was the surveyor George Pownall, with whom Kelk had been in touch. In the midst of this property was a small outlying piece of the Smith's Charity Estate, used for beating carpets, known as the Carpet Ground.

The Prince would have preferred to employ as agent the great London developer, Thomas Cubitt, his favourite builder, who had just completed Osborne House, and was still working on Buckingham Palace, but was initially persuaded to use the services of John Kelk (1816–86).[27] The meeting with Kelk was followed by one with Lord Seymour, Labouchere and the Chancellor of the Exchequer, Sir Charles Wood, on a site for the National Gallery. Wood was reluctant to commit the government as Lord Seymour had recently produced a new scheme for placing the National Gallery near the end of Rotten Row, but Labouchere backed the idea of the Commission going ahead alone. After 'a long discussion' the Prince and the ministers agreed that a meeting of the Surplus Committee should be called for the following Monday, to sanction the purchase of the Aldridge, Freake and Villars estates. Meanwhile the Prince saw Thomas Cubitt, who said the price was too high, and, in Grey's words, 'rather threw cold water on the scheme by pointing out that there cd. be no return whatever . . . for 4 years . . . However, he was to take the Plan of the ground home with him – get hold of Mr Kelk whom (having been brought up in Mr Cubitt's Office) he was well acquainted with . . . and report the Result to H. R. H.'. The Surplus Committee met and endorsed the Prince's proposed course of action, but the matter was entrusted to

Kelk, who was to report through Sir William Cubitt.

Kelk was successful in the purchase of the Gore House Estate, for which the contract was signed in May, in Kelk's name to ensure secrecy, the Commission paying £60,000 or £2790 per acre.[28]

Dealings with the Baron were less successful, since Sir William Cubitt and Kelk overreached themselves in negotiations with the Baron's agents, with whom they made a building agreement to cover the land with houses, committing their principals to spending £3/4 million on construction, rather than negotiating an outright sale. After some examination of the legal position by the government lawyers, Bowring, Thomas Cubitt and Kelk were sent to see Pownall, and the Baron's trustee, Sewell, to explain that the building agreement was invalid, a difficult interview managed with 'consummate tact and management' by Cubitt, 'who was looked on throughout as *amicus curiae*'.[29] 'Mr Cubitt is going to bid for Baron Villars' ground', Prince Albert wrote to Lord Derby on 14 June, 1852, 'may God speed him, that he may not have to pay too much.'[30]

The market for land in South Kensington was becoming keen, increased not only by the Commissioners' own activities, which gave the impression that more parties were involved than was even the case, but also through the interest of Jackson, who had just obtained a building agreement from Lord Harrington, and saw opportunities in the Baron's property. Cubitt advised the Commission's managers to make it clear that if the prices asked became absurd, they would sell up, and go elsewhere, causing the market to fall. It was fortunate that Derby's government was ready to support the Commission, and agreed to add £110,000 of public money to the Commission's £140,000. Disraeli, as Chancellor of the Exchequer, wrote to the Prince to express his approval of the project as a whole: 'when realised the creation of Your Royal Highness will form an epoch in the aesthetic and scientific education of the people of England'.[31]

Cubitt had been given a maximum of £200,000 by the Commissioners, but his view was that this was too much to pay for the Baron's land, and he and Bowring carried on negotiations throughout July and into August. 'I think Mr Cubitt fully sees how to work it. In fact, his *extreme* judgement strikes me more and more, and makes me more and more regret that we had not his help previously.'[32] Finally, a deal was agreed; the Commission would pay £150,000, together with the Baron's legal fees and those of his agents, together with a contribution towards the Act enabling him to invest more widely. The Commission was to pay a deposit of 10 per cent,

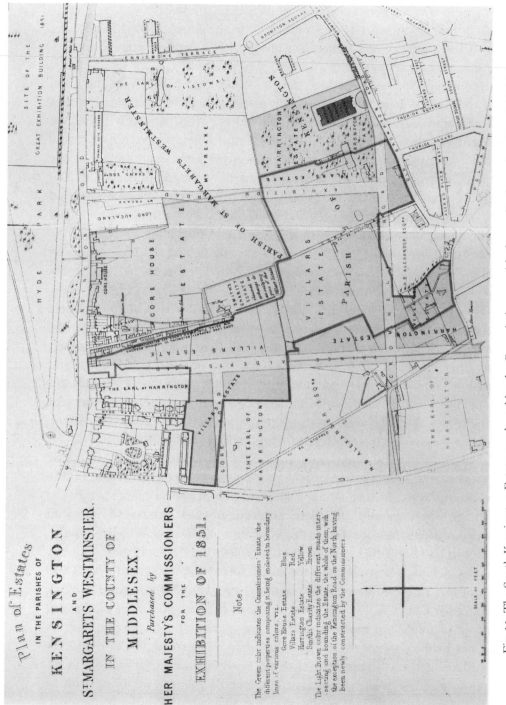

Fig 11. The South Kensington Estate purchased by the Commissioners with the profits from the 1851 Exhibition. The Boundaries were later reorganised by judicious exchanges of land.

and interest of 3.5 per cent from 29 September. Cubitt thought the interest too high, holding out for 3 per cent from March 1852. Finally, the Baron lost patience, and telegraphed from Paris, so Bowring, alone in a London *hors de saison*, realizing that Jackson was in Paris, took the decision to clinch the deal.[33]

Though Kelk could later boast that he had made the best bargain over the Kensington purchases[34] the rest of the negotiations were effectively entrusted to Bowring working with Thomas Cubitt, a successful partnership crowned not only by the acquisition of land for the Commission, but by Bowring's marriage in the following year to Thomas Cubitt's daughter Sophia.

Cubitt wrote to Grey on Christmas Eve, 1852, to apologize for the delay, 'I am afraid that His Royal Highness will think this has been a dilatory business but I have followed it up as much as the very awkward parties I have had to deal with would permit'.[35] Despite the awkwardness of the parties, the Commission acquired a coherent and manageable block of land in Kensington Gore, effectively by the end of 1852, though not all the deals were completed within the year. Seventeen acres were purchased from Lord Harrington, on the south-east side of the property, including Brompton House, and a satisfactory arrangement was made with Smith's Charity over the potentially disruptive Carpet Ground, by the exchange of an outlying piece of the Baron's property to the south. An approach was made to Lord Kensington for his property in Gore Lane, essential if the Commission was to lay out the property in a dignified way. The negotiations for completing the purchase were not concluded until 1857, comprising a mixture of cash and exchange of property and building sites. This was largely to clear the ground of existing buildings, in which several people had interests through leases or ground rents, for the development of what came to be known as the 'main square' of the estate.

The final cost was £153,793 for the Baron's property, and £54,716 for that of the Earl of Harrington, with a payment of £8000 to William Jackson for the loss of over a third of his building land.[36] The Carpet Ground was a straight swap, while £15,000 was paid to Lord Kensington for the freehold interest in his heavily mortgaged property in and around Gore Lane. The leasehold interest in the smaller properties there was compulsorily purchased through an Act of Parliament obtained in July 1854, at a cost of a little over £25,000. The freehold interest in Mr

Aldridge's property on the east of Gore Lane was exchanged for land in Queen's Gate Terrace worth about £500 a year.[37]

Prince Albert was in correspondence with a number of politicians about the educational projects he was promoting. There were a number of disparate museums and teaching institutions which he wanted to gather together, including the Museum of Practical Geology in Jermyn Street, 'arising out of a collection of building stones to be tested by scientific men, before the rebuilding of the Houses of Parliament'. For this reason it was under the control of the Board of Public Works. Through the energy and dedication of Henry de la Bêche, it now had displays of mining equipment, provided lectures for working men, and carried out chemical analyses, and the Prince urged that it should now become part of the Board of Trade, as the Department of Applied Science, in parallel with that of Applied Art. 'I am fully convinced that we cannot afford any longer', he told Lord Derby, 'to be the only country which gives no facilities to its industrial population for the study of Art & Science and that the Government cannot divest itself of its responsibility towards the Nation in this respect.'[38] The Whig politicians were no easier to deal with; Gladstone thought that the School of Applied Art would be better with the Board of Trade where the President was 'necessarily selected with reference to acquaintance with the merits of Trade and Industry, whilst the President of the Council [responsible for education] is not necessarily so, but . . . with a View to Cabinet arrangements, and must be a Nobleman of high rank'.[39] Granville on the other hand thought all education should be under one head, instancing a number of Lords President, who would take education more seriously as it was the only concern of the department.[40] The Prince persuaded Aberdeen to transfer the Museum of Practical Geology to the Board of Trade.[41] He also attempted to get Bennet Woodcroft's collection of patent models, and other objects to do with patent rights, collected under the aegis of the Master of the Rolls at South Kensington, a more difficult task since both would-be curator and the legal department were difficult to deal with, though Woodcroft's collection did finally come to the South Kensington Museum.[42]

Prince Albert had been considerably angered by the premature exposure of his scheme in the summer of 1852 by Sir David Brewster, a Scottish academic, under the title of 'Prince Albert's Industrial University'.[43] In fact, Brewster, who sent a copy of his article to the Prince, said little that was new, but the Prince was clearly concerned that publicity would lead to the sabotage of his plan. Brewster recites at length the charges that the English education system did little compared to Continental counterparts for artisans and skilled craftsmen, thus establishing the need for the Prince's initiative. He gave a long description of the position in France, and the number of people trained by such colleges as the *École Centrale des Arts et Manufactures*, not only for French industry but also for foreign countries including both America and Russia. These criticisms were not new, and he cited not only Playfair, but also Babbage, Davy and Herschell in support of his thesis. He concluded:

> We are all now agreed . . . that the time has arrived when science must be united with skill in the advancement of the Industrial Arts, and that this union can be only effected by a grand effort, individual and national, to establish upon a permanent basis a metropolitan university of arts and manufactures.[44]

Grey and Playfair were more relaxed about the matter, the latter being more concerned about getting together the rudiments of his proposed Department of Practical Science, in competition with Cole's Department of Art, which he complained was 'drawing to the Department of Art, what ought to belong to that of Science'.[45]

THE RELATIONSHIP BETWEEN GOVERNMENT AND THE ROYAL COMMISSION

A Treasury Minute, drafted by Gladstone, set out the relations between the Commission and the government, now in partnership as landowners. Money would be needed to complete the various deals, and parts of the £150,000 would be advanced as needed. The land would be divided equally but for flexibility would all be vested in the Royal Commissioners. 'One moiety . . . shall, by agreement between this Board and the Royal Commissioners, be set apart for such Institutions connected with Science and Art as are . . . supported . . . by funds voted by Parliament.' No such buildings would however be erected without prior consultation with the Commissioners. To provide additional contact, Gladstone further suggested that a number of ministers should sit as Commissioners *ex officio*. This would include the Prime Minister, the Chancellor of the Exchequer, the Lord President of the Council, then responsible for education, the President of the Board of Trade and the First Commissioner of Works. Many of these important figures were at the time already members of the

Royal Commission as individuals, through the Prince's shrewd original nominations, but this would provide a permanent link between government and what might have become an uncomfortably independent body. These provisions were readily accepted and the great Officers of State as listed were elected on 23 February, 1853.[46]

THE COMMISSIONERS' ESTATE

The estate finally purchased by the Commissioners lay a little to the west, and south of the site of the 1851 Exhibition Building itself. Before the exchanges and consolidation which followed the plan for laying out the area, and the Act of Parliament which brought it into being, it was a very irregular shape, stretching down to Old Brompton Road in the east, south to the line of modern Harrington Gardens in the west, with a long tongue of land running westward to modern Gloucester Road.

On the east of the estate was Brompton Park House, the former site of one of the most famous of eighteenth-century nursery gardens, that of London and Wise. It lay east of the later Exhibition Road stretching northward to Charles Freake's land.

There were a number of lanes across the area, all of which were stopped up by Act of Parliament, obtained in 1854. A road called Cromwell Road led to the Cromwell Gardens tea house on the later site of Queen's Gate, while Brompton Park Lane ran northwards a little west of Exhibition Road to cross the parish boundary and to join up with Gore Lane, on the site of modern Jay's Mews, providing access to Kensington Gore. There was a thriving community in Gore Lane, with two public houses, the 'Hand and Flower' and the 'Hind's Head', a Station House, and a Sunday school at the southern end. John Aldridge had eleven houses on the east of the lane, with one or two large houses with extensive gardens, fronting on to Kensington Gore. Then there was Gore House with its extensive gardens, and three more large houses. On the eastern edge, there was Eden Lodge, next to Freake's land. This belonged to Lord Auckland, coveted by the Commissioners but never purchased because Lord Auckland, Bishop of Sodor and Man, did not wish to upset his sister, who was a life tenant, and was unwilling to sell. Later negotiations revealed that he was not anxious to allow his sister to break the entail.

Further west, and largely off the Commissioners' estate, another lane led north-west from the Methwold Almshouses, which lay, in modern terms, on the south-east corner of the junction of Harrington Gardens and Queen's Gate, just north of the later site of St Augustine's Queen's Gate. The lane ran across land remaining in the possession of Lord Harrington, and land belonging to H. B. Alexander, to the modern corner of Gore Road and Gloucester Road. All these rural routes were to disappear under the almost Hausmannic layout devised by Thomas Cubitt for the Commission.

THE NATIONAL GALLERY

The Commission had acquired its estate in partnership with the government, and a major objective was to incorporate a new site for the National Gallery into the scheme. There had been concern about the state of the national collections for some time: both the National Gallery, sharing its premises in Trafalgar Square with the Royal Academy, and the British Museum, housing its mixture of antiquities and natural history in Bloomsbury, had outgrown their accommodation. Though the government contemplated the purchase of Burlington House in Piccadilly, there were other candidates for it, like the learned societies being dislodged from Somerset House, and the Patent Office collection, housed rather uncomfortably within legal accommodation in Chancery Lane. The National Gallery had been the subject of government committees in both 1848 and 1849. A second Treasury Commission sat in 1851, and had pointed to a Kensington Gardens site. Had there not been so much objection to the siting of the Great Exhibition in Hyde Park, this might have been a solution, but though the motives of the opposition to the invasion of Hyde Park in 1850 were not always public-spirited and were often deeply personal, once public opinion had been mobilized it could not easily be reshaped. A further Select Committee on the National Gallery sat in 1853 to hear evidence from a wide-ranging series of experts including the architects James Fergusson, James Pennethorne and Von Klenze, the architect of the new museums in Berlin and St Petersburg, as well the new 'quartier' devoted to museums and colleges in Munich, which so aroused the suspicions of the British public. As well as hearing witnesses in person they sent questionnaires all over Europe to Belgium, Berlin, Munich, Naples, Florence, Rome and St Petersburg. They had a very wide-ranging brief, being concerned over the management of the gallery, the possibility of replacing the present Keeper with a salaried Director, the relationship with the Trustees, the régime for cleaning and curatorship of the pictures, the possible amalgamation of the fine art collections of the British Museum with those of the National Gallery, as well as the situation of the Gallery, including the local atmosphere, and the type of soil on which it was built. The Select Committee was chaired by Colonel William Mure (1799–1860), 'a scholarly Scottish laird'[47] resident in Kensington, and Member of Parliament for Renfrewshire from 1846 until 1855. It included a number of connoisseurs and amateurs of the arts, including Leicester Vernon, nephew of the collector whose pictures had been given to the nation and were to adorn the South Kensington Museum, Monkton Milnes, and Francis Charteris (1818–1914), later Lord Elcho, and from 1883 Earl of Wemyss. Sir William Cubitt spoke for the Commissioners, while Bowring too was deputed to give evidence on the capabilities of the site, supplemented by Thomas Cubitt, who was cross-examined on the suitability of the site for a gallery, and also on the likelihood of working-class visitors making the effort to get to lectures, colleges and museums if sited at Kensington Gore.

Though, as Sir William Cubitt explained, the 'ruling star' had been the intention to find 'sufficient ground in a good situation for . . . a centre for industrial art and industrial science' including 'schools of scientific industry' he was able to convince the Select Committee that there would be ample room for the National Gallery also.[48] The Select Committee voted for a number of changes including the appointment of a salaried Director, and recommended a move from Trafalgar Square, which they felt was not suitable for a new gallery. A change to Kensington was thought to be a good idea, but it was acknowledged that the Gardens or Hyde Park were unlikely to be available, and therefore the Commission's estate 'presents many of the advantages recommended by the witnesses'. However, the Report was far from unanimous, and at the end there was a dissentient minority, consisting largely of Scottish and Irish Members of Parliament, including Mure, and Elcho, who voted against the majority, which included the ministers Labouchere and Lord Seymour.

In the summer of 1853, when most of the land had been acquired, the roads laid out, and when the National Gallery scheme seemed achievable, the Prince produced a more fully worked-out plan for the 'main square' in South Kensington. In this he proposed that the site should be approached from Hyde Park through a handsome architectural screen and gateway, flanked by two large L-shaped buildings 650 feet from north to south, intended for Colleges of Art and Science, leading towards a centrally placed National Gallery (some 190,000 square feet, as compared to the existing building of 28,000). Towards the Brompton Road, there would be two further buildings on either side, for Museums of Art and Science, with 'Architectural Gardens' containing fountains, and surrounded with statues. The southern entrance would be a 'triumphal Arch set back in a Crescent 320 feet wide and 120 feet deep, and ending in two Lodges'. The whole might be surrounded with private houses, and residences for staff for the institutions, and a further site might be earmarked for the Academy of Music, together with a hall for music. He expressed his preference for 'an Italian or Palladian style of Architecture, as admitting variety of outline and invention, with symmetrical architectural lines'.[49]

He appealed for artists to look at these proposals, and to suggest elevations for the buildings. The plans were sent to a number of people, Commissioners, politicians and even Sir Edwin Landseer. Not all of these responded very fully, but there were some pertinent comments, which reveal the state of public opinion towards the scheme, and explain the depth of dislike which 'South Kensington' could inspire.

In his detailed response Sir Charles Barry recited a lot of the objections to South Kensington already circulating, which explain the prejudice against the whole project. It was too far west for general convenience, for artisans and for the evening meetings of the Learned Societies. The site was too small to carry out the 'principle of concentration, as regards both Art & Science', and include the 'National Library and the entire collection of Art and Antiquities at the British Museum' which ought to be included. He pointed out that it would render 'several old-established and popular National Institutions, which have been erected at considerable cost, more or less useless, such as the British Museum, the present National Gallery & Royal Academy, the Museum of Economic Geology & the Society of Arts, etc.' He thought the Kensington site compared unfavourably with the Crystal Palace, 'which occupies one of the most commanding and beautiful situations in the Country . . . placed in the midst of 280 acres of Ornamental Grounds'. He thought it was too low, and suggested that soon as many 'blacks' (sooty particles) would be falling there and polluting the air as in central London. He put forward another scheme by which the national art treasures should go to an enlarged British Museum, though the Natural History Collections would be taken to Kensington, as the nucleus of a 'National College of Science'. He considered that easy access was important for art, but that 'With respect to Science, the Country is *already pre-eminent*' and therefore he

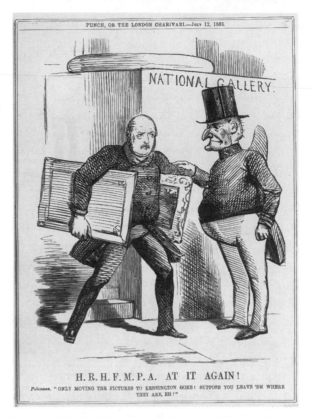

Fig 12. 'HRH FM PA at it again'. Prince Albert defeated in
his attempt to move the National Gallery to South Kensington,
by Mr Punch, expressing public opinion.

thought that those who are interested in Science would be prepared to 'go out of their way'. An extensive list of buildings would be needed, all of which could be fitted into the central block. These included

> Museums for exhibition of Zoological, Botanical and mineralogical specimens, and for patented Inventions, a Menagerie for living specimens in the department of Natural History, a Library of Science, and Theatre with Laboratories for Public lectures in every branch of Science, combined with a Botanical Garden, and accommodation for living specimens of the Animated [*sic*] Kingdom.[50]

Gladstone was concerned with practical points to do with the site and relations with adjacent owners, but pointed out the contradictory nature of some of Barry's statements.

Perhaps understandably, this extremely grand scheme was not realized, and expediency rather than grandeur was to dictate the layout of the central square. It is possible that had the Prince survived, the development might have been more coherently developed, and that opportunism might not have played such an important part.

The encouraging report of the Select Committee was followed in 1856 by a request from the government for a site for the National Gallery, to which the Commission replied with the offer of a site within the main square. Unfortunately this offer was frustrated by Lord Elcho who put forward a motion in Parliament that the matter should again be referred to a Royal Commission. The Royal Commission on the National Gallery, chaired by the elderly liberal, Lord Broughton, decided for the *status quo*, leaving the Gallery in Trafalgar Square, and the British Museum's collections *in situ*. Two years later, the Prince accepted defeat, and the Commission applied formally to Lord Derby's ministry to dissolve the partnership with the government.

This put an end to an important and cherished element in Prince Albert's grand design, but now the Commission were free to go ahead to develop the estate without the handicap of government involvement and political manoeuvring. The National Gallery was never to come to South Kensington, but there were a number of institutions which would replace it. The failure to attract the National Gallery was seen by *Punch* and other opponents as a defeat. A modern historian has suggested that public opinion was influenced by dislike of the buildings going up in South Kensington, and an unfounded suspicion that Prince Albert was personally involved in speculation in the area.[51] The government grant-in-aid was repaid to the amount of £120,000, with the additional grant to the government of the 12 acres of the Brompton House Estate, in which the Department of Science and Art was being installed. The money for the repayment was found by a sophisticated stock mortgage from the Commissioners of Greenwich Hospital, by which the 1851 Commission borrowed £120,000 in cash, on which they paid 4 per cent, agreeing to repay in due course with enough government stock to replace the Greenwich Commissioners' holding of £125,162 19s. 6d., then at 95 7/8 *ex(cluding) dividend.*[52]

IV

The Creation of a 'Quartier Latin'
1857–1869

The failure to establish the National Gallery as the flagship of the Commissioners' estate created a gap in the whole magnificent concept, which took time to repair. South Kensington was always to suffer from a form of schizophrenia in its development, due to the uneasy coexistence of the grandeur of the Prince's original concept with the Commissioners' ability to put it into practice. The reasons for this were several. It can be attributed to the difficulty of carrying out Prince Albert's scheme, based upon a more intellectual approach and the more absolutist Continental tradition, in the context of the empirical and opportunist approach characteristic of the English. As Professor Port points out in his wider study of government building in Victorian London, British anti-absolutist tradition was prejudiced against government planning, and the combination of British attitudes to private property and the Treasury's parsimony made government building on a worthy, let alone a grand scale, almost impossible. There were mischief makers like Colonel Sibthorp, and to some extent Lord Elcho, who appear to have been activated more by the heady charms of opposition for its own sake than by a constructive agenda. South Kensington was never short of powerful personalities, and Henry Cole in his championship of the South Kensington Museum was followed by other museum directors and academics anxious to make the best of things for their own particular constituency. Finally, development on a grand scale requires a 'roi soleil' to push it through against vested interests and private profit, and though Albertopolis had a prince, his powers were limited and his reign short.

Thus measures were forced on the remaining Commissioners, which Prince Albert could have circumvented through his shrewd leadership and the royal influence. However, the Commission succeeded surprising-

I. The opening of the Exhibition of 1851 by Queen Victoria. Because of the pressure of public opinion, season ticket holders were admitted, as well as members of the government and the diplomatic corps.

Opposite above II. The royal party visiting the eastern end of the Nave given over to foreign exhibits. Prominent amongst these is the copy of the famous statue of *The Amazon* being attacked by a lioness, by Professor Kiss.

Opposite below III. The United States Court, which featured a number of raw and manufactured material exhibits, including one from Goodyear of vulcanised rubber. An important exhibit was Hiram Power's statue, *The Greek Slave*.

Above IV. The Transept occupied the centre of the building, and contained a number of statues and Osler's glass fountain. The arch was added to Paxton's original flat-roofed design to accommodate the elm trees.

V. The India Court, with exhibits largely provided by the East India Company. The Howdah was a royal Indian gift to the Queen, but the stuffed elephant on which it was displayed came from a museum in Suffolk.

VI. The Medieval Court, with fashionable ecclesiastical exhibits provided by A.W. N. Pugin and his suppliers.

VII. The Agriculture section featured a number of mechanical exhibits, an area in which British farmers were being challenged by the United States.

VIII. 'Polkas of All Nations', one of the many song sheets featuring popular ditties. As well as the official catalogues and publications, the 1851 Exhibition inspired a lot of popular publications and mementoes.

IX. The opening of the 1862 Exhibition on 1 May by the Duke of Cambridge. The recent sudden death of the Prince Consort on 14 December 1861 precluded any involvement by the Queen or her family. The fashionable decorator J. G. Crace was employed on the 1862 Building, and he used vivid and strong colours.

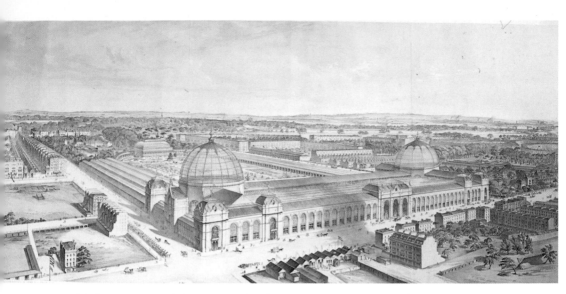

X. 'Bird's Eye View of the Building for the 1862 Exhibition', looking northward from Cromwell Road, showing the striking glass domes at either end, and the annexes which stretched up either side of the Royal Horticultural Gardens. Beyond can be seen the rather heterogeneous development on the northern part of the Commissioners' estate.

XI. Opening of the Royal Albert Hall on 29 March 1871, the largest public gathering which the Queen had attended since Prince Albert's death. A large hall for music and gatherings for the promotion of science and art was an important element in the Prince's vision for South Kensington.

XII. Portrait of Queen Victoria after Franz Winterhalter, 1855.

XIII. Portrait of Prince Albert after Franz Winterhalter, 1855.

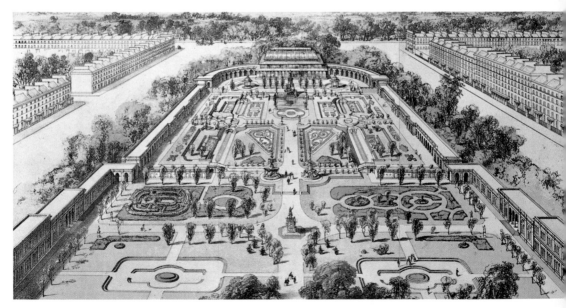

XIV. The Horticultural Gardens in South Kensington as designed by W. A. Nesfield, probably the largest formal gardens ever laid out in England. The Gardens were dominated at the northern end by the Memorial to the 1851 Exhibition, flanked by two bandstands, and the Winter Garden which later became the southern entrance for the Royal Albert Hall. The arcades which surrounded the gardens were used for both temporary and permanent exhibitions.

ly well, often in the face of stiff opposition, in achieving so much of the Prince's scheme after his death.

By 1857, the part of the Prince's scheme which involved the National Gallery had collapsed but there were other parts of the project on which progress had been rapid. The first was the improvement of the facilities for industrial education of which the existing Government Schools of Design were seen as an important part. Though Henry Cole no longer had an official position on the Commission staff, he was Secretary of the Department of Science and Art, part of the Board of Trade. Once the Government Schools of Design had moved to Brompton Park House, he was in a strong position to lobby the Prince, and therefore to affect the Commission's projects. He had an influence on a large number of South Kensington projects, since he was not only Secretary to the Department, but also Vice-President of the Society of Arts, and of the Horticultural Society. In the words of *Vanity Fair*, he felt that he had a 'peculiar mission of reviving the artistic sense among his countrymen . . . His great aim and object has been to provide artistic instruction, and to that end he has founded art schools . . . . He it is who has been the soul and intellect of all those undertakings which have made South Kensington famous'. This was a generous tribute at the end of Henry Cole's time at the Department which accompanied the cartoon of him as 'King Cole'.[1] The article also referred to 'the peculiarity of Mr. Cole's career' as being 'that he has always succeeded in compassing his objects in the face of most fierce and unsparing opposition'. What the article did not need to say was that much of that opposition was generated by his own methods, and it seems likely in retrospect that the Prince's scheme might have had an easier run, had not the 'South Kensington clique' headed by Cole aroused so much suspicion and dislike.

However, as Bowring had told the Select Committee on the National Gallery, there were proposals to make South Kensington 'the great central educational point in science and in art'.[2] The Commission had also made a start on its other major objective, the creation of an educational Trade Museum, in which would be displayed many of the articles purchased from the Great Exhibition. There had been progress in setting up other collections, destined for the new museum, on which reports had been commissioned from experts. The Society of Arts were making a Collection of Animal Produce and Manufacture. At the beginning of 1854, a committee set up under Lord Granville, to consider a Museum of Patented Inventions, had reported. Building on Professor Bennet Woodcroft's advice to Prince Albert in December 1852, they suggested it should include a library and list of specifications, as well as models and machines.[3] They advised that, pending the establishment of a separate museum, the Patent Commissioners should be urged to make such a collection, storing it in their own premises, and, if necessary, in accommodation to be provided by the 1851 Commission.

In a memorandum on the 'Proposed Museum of Manufactures', presented to the Commission in 1854, Captain Owen queried the need for an entirely new Museum of Manufactures. He listed the institutions 'for the promotion of Science and Art' proposed to be collected at Kensington Gore. These included the National Gallery, part of the British Museum, the Museum of Economic Geology in Jermyn Street, the botanic collections at Kew Gardens, the new collections of ornamental manufactures at Marlborough House, and 'as far as it may suit the convenience of the Members' the Learned Societies of London with their collections. He went on to analyse the possible effect of this concentration, which in its mere recital explains a lot of the apprehension aroused in established institutions by the ambitions of 'South Kensington'.

As Owen pointed out, all these existing bodies were in a sense 'Museums of Manufactures', as would be the proposed Trade Museum, intended to 'enable Manufacturers to compare the respective excellences of production', which would involve anything from a seam of coal or an improved harrow or loom to a 'new process in ornamentation'. He pointed out the danger of duplication, and the difficulty of drawing the boundaries:

> It would be difficult to determine whether pottery is more important in a historical, mineral, artistical, or commercial point of view . . . The fact of its being still nothing but pottery leads to the solution of the difficulty, viz., that all pottery should remain together . . . it is purchased, presented, or deposited for the benefit of potters, of porcelain painters, and above all, of those whom it is wished to make wise and discriminating purchasers of pottery . . . one vase may be . . . added from its archaeological interest, another from its graceful form, a third from the peculiarity of some flux used in colouring it, a fourth for its excessive cheapness, and a fifth to illustrate some application of machinery.

He thought that the arrangement should be designed to suit the public visiting the museum, rather than the 'particular view of industry taken by those to recommend the acquisition of such articles'. He suggested to the Commissioners, therefore, that they should consider 'the formation of *one* Museum only at Kensington', of which the existing collections should form the nucleus, comprising 'all that the most competent people consider it advantageous to preserve for the education of the public'. It should, however, be 'based upon a classified census of the population'. 'Thus there would be a Pottery Department for potters, and a Calico Printing Section of a great Cotton Class for calico printers'. He ended by arguing powerfully for a well-arranged museum which would engage the intellectual interest of visitors, rather than one which was a mere collection of objects. He saw as a major objective the education of the public, whose liking for that 'which merely bears the *show* of beauty and excellence, [leads] to a taste which has made us a byword among nations, and deceptive artifices which are a disgrace to our manufactures'.[4] The Commissioners decided to print his report as an appendix, and it is an important foundation document for the South Kensington Museum.

By the middle of 1855, the Commission were applying to the Treasury for help with accommodating all the various government institutions, including the Department of Science and Art, about to be thrown out of Marlborough House. The suggestion was the erection of a modular iron building, obviously inspired by the success of Paxton's building in Hyde Park, to provide the main museum. It was designed by Charles Young of 10 Great George Street, at a cost of £15,000, including £3000 for fitting it out. The Department would also occupy four houses on the Brompton Park estate. The Commission would retain the ground, and would manage the refreshment rooms, and would make a small contribution. The Treasury agreed to pay for the corrugated iron building, nicknamed the 'Brompton Boilers' which served as the first purpose-built building of the South Kensington Museum. The Museum came formally into existence in 1856, when the whole Department of Science and Art passed from the Board of Trade to the Committee on Education of the Privy Council. The South Kensington Museum was formally opened by the Queen in this building on 20 June, 1857.

In April 1856, the Commission issued its *Third Report* recapitulating its achievements in the purchase and laying out of the estate, achievements due in very large part to the personal efforts of the Prince, who

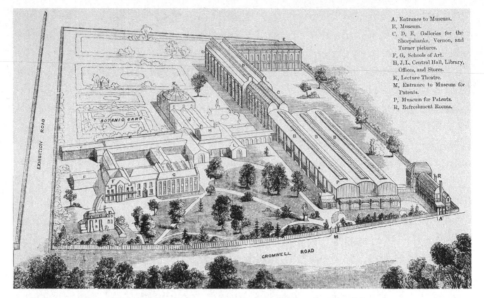

A, Entrance to Museum.
B, Museum.
C, D, E, Galleries for the
    Sheepshanks, Vernon, and
    Turner pictures.
F, G, Schools of Art.
H, J, L, Central Hall, Library,
    Offices, and Stores.
K, Lecture Theatre.
M, Entrance to Museum for
    Patents.
P, Museum for Patents.
R, Refreshment Rooms.

Fig 13. Early development of the South Kensington Museum in
the grounds of Brompton House.

worked closely with Edgar Bowring. They emphasized their partnership
with the Board of Trade in achieving the Commission's major objective,
the 'promotion of Art and Science in their relations to Productive
Industry'. For this reason they welcomed the creation of the Department
of Practical Art under the Board of Trade which effectively combined
many bodies with the same practical objectives, including the Provincial
Schools of Design, the geological institutions established in Jermyn
Street, and two Irish institutions, the Royal Dublin Society and the
Museum of Irish Industry. The two Secretaries of the Department were
happily Henry Cole, already at the Government Schools of Design, and
Lyon Playfair, who had also played an important part in the success of the
1851 Exhibition. They took a very wide view of their responsibilities, and
reported on such matters as the possible establishment of a National
Portrait Gallery, to be promoted through a temporary loan exhibition of
national historical portraits to be held in South Kensington.

On the dissolution of the Commission's partnership with government
after the collapse of the National Gallery scheme, the ownership of the
main South Kensington Museum site passed to the government.
However, the collections soon overflowed on to the west side of
Exhibition Road. The Commission continued to subsidize the Museum's

activities, and the relationship remained close since Henry Cole and other staff of the Museum were much involved on the remaining parts of the Commissioners' estate. The learned societies had been found a new home in 1854 by the government, at Burlington House,[5] and once the partnership with government was formally dissolved in May 1858, the Commission had to seek new tenants.

THE HORTICULTURAL SOCIETY GARDENS

The Commission found a new occupier for the land in another organization in which Prince Albert was involved, the Horticultural Society. This body was founded in 1801, and had pursued a number of projects with varying success since. It had a house at 21 Regent Street, and had run a series of garden exhibitions with considerable success in Kensington and Ealing. In 1822 the Society had obtained a lease of 33 acres of garden ground from the Duke of Devonshire at Chiswick, and it was from this ground that Paxton was so famously recruited by the Bachelor Duke. However, by the 1850s the Society's finances were in very poor order, and they had had to sell their library and the house in Regent Street to pay off their debts. On the death of their President, the 6th Duke of Devonshire, in January 1858, the Society asked Prince Albert to succeed him.

The new Prince-President threw himself into the position, and came up with a proposal for a partnership which must have seemed made in heaven. In the words of the Secretary of the Society, Andrew Murray, the Commission

> had an interest which directly harmonised with, and as it were dovetailed into that of the Horticultural Society. The latter required for their shows and promenades a Garden not wholly in the town, and yet not beyond the limits of London; the former . . . were actually at the same moment contemplating the appropriation of the central part of their land . . . as a Garden, to be surrounded by Italian arcades.[6]

A note among the Prince's papers sets out the likely income and expenditure, even working out the different ticket prices for different days of the week, and also lists the 'Advantages offered'. These included the 20 acres of garden, and 1 acre of glass, not a greenhouse, 3000 feet of colonnade, two refreshment rooms, four dining and meeting rooms, twenty-

Fig 14. Captain Francis Fowke, architect
of the 1862 Exhibition Building.

four shops, a band playing twice a week and the flower shows of the Society.[7] The plan for laying out the garden was prepared by a 'South Kensington' triumvirate of Henry Cole, Richard Redgrave and Captain Fowke, appointed by Prince Albert in May 1858, well in advance of the formal agreement with the Horticultural Society. Redgrave was the Inspector for Art at the South Kensington Museum, and Francis Fowke (1823–65) of the Royal Engineers had been recruited by Cole as an Inspector for Science. Fowke had been asked by Henry Cunliffe-Owen to join the British deputation to the Paris Exhibition of 1855, and when the latter had left to join his regiment in the Crimea, Fowke had taken his place. He had had experience working on the Raglan Barracks at Devonport, and was given the title of Architect and Engineer at the Museum, and he was to play a considerable part in the Museum's expansion, and elsewhere in South Kensington, designing a number of important buildings, not all of which have survived.

The proposal was to lay out the centre of the 'main square', some 20 acres, in a formal garden, and surround it with a 'corridor' which would enclose the garden, providing a *cordon sanitaire*. As Cole explained to the Prince:

> By leaving space for future buildings *outside* the corridor, such buildings may be executed by degrees, without disturbing the laying out of the grounds *within* the corridor.

The arcades forming the corridor, which may be built more or less permanently according to the funds at disposal, furnish a most convenient boundary for the proposed garden; a promenade sheltered at all seasons; and lastly, a convenient means of access under cover, which will unite any buildings to be erected outside of them into a harmonious whole, however different may be their character and style.[8]

The Society applied formally for terms in January 1859, and the matter was settled at a meeting at Buckingham Palace on 27 June, 1859, when the Council of the Society accepted the offer of a 31-year lease of the 20 acres on very generous terms. The Commission undertook to lay out £50,000 on 'a highly decorated Italian Arcade and certain costly earthworks required as the foundation of a Garden'. The Society was to lay out a similar sum on the formation of the garden, including 'a Conservatory of considerable extent'. Though it was intended that the garden would provide an income, the rent was calculated in a complex manner – the Society was not to pay any rent until their own expenses for running the garden, including the interest on their own borrowing of £50,000, had been secured, and then it would pay the interest on the Commission's £50,000. Any surplus arising after that would be split between the two bodies. Effectively the Society was only due to pay £2400, representing the Commission's own outgoings, if takings from exhibitions and so forth provided enough to pay both lots of interest. There was a provision that the lease would lapse should the rent remain unpaid for five years, while if it was paid the Society would be entitled to ask for an extension of the lease. An Expenses Committee, on which both bodies were represented, was to manage the garden's finances, and to assess the amount to be claimed by the Society for its expenses before any rent would be due.

The Commission raised its £50,000 by a further mortgage from the Commissioners of Greenwich Hospital, and the Society by a variety of fund-raising schemes, in which the Royal Family played an important part. Both the Prince and the Queen contributed to the donations, amounting to over £1800, royal life memberships were taken out, which encouraged the recruitment of some six hundred new members, raising £13,000, and a further £40,000 came from an issue of debentures.

The Commission approved the proposed layout from Cole, the architect Sydney Smirke, Richard Redgrave and Captain Fowke, who worked together with the garden designer W. A. Nesfield, 'aided by the constant advice and suggestions of the Prince'. The laying out of the gardens themselves was carried out in conjunction with Charles Wentworth Dilke, Dr Lindley, the Secretary, and J. G. Veitch, representing the Society. Sydney Smirke prepared the 'Architectural Designs'; the garden designer was Nesfield. Only the North Arcades were originally intended to be permanent, while the others were just intended as screens for the buildings behind. Each range of arcades was to be carried out in a different Italianate style. Again the Prince, as a keen gardener, took a great interest, concerning himself with such details as the plan of a proposed labyrinth, sent by Lord Stanhope, and the effect of a proposed avenue of lime trees on the view from the colonnades, and the proper height and going of the steps in the garden, even including a little sketch of trees and colonnade in the letter to Nesfield.[9]

The result was one of the grandest formal gardens ever created in England, which occupied the centre of the 'main square' of the Commissioners' estate, leaving a strip of land some 150 feet or so wide on either side fronting on to Exhibition Road and Prince Albert's Road, for the building of houses or public buildings. At the northern end was the magnificent conservatory, designed by Fowke, flanked by crescent-shaped arcades, in the 'Albani style', giving on to a water garden, in which stood two bandstands, and the foundations for the Memorial to the 1851 Exhibition. The arcades designed by Sydney Smirke continued down the east and west sides, and were designed in the 'Milanese style'. At the southern end the arcades were designed by Fowke in a 'Lateran style', with decoration, both painted and in terracotta, by Godfrey Sykes, another member of the South Kensington Museum staff. There were entrances to the garden through the arcades from east and west, and through the conservatory at the north. Within the arcades were fountains, lawns, a maze, formal beds, all decorated by statues, vases and other ornamental features. The water garden was supplied by an artesian well, sunk by Easton & Amos, who had worked at Osborne, which provided enough water for an ornamental stretch large enough to skate on. The contractor was John Kelk, a successful Mayfair builder who had gone into public works such as docks and railways, and was a partner in the Thames Iron Works and Ship-Building Company of Blackwall, involved in both the construction of warships like the *Warrior*, and in the manufacture of girders and structural ironwork. First involved in Kensington through building houses facing Hyde Park, he had developed a close relationship with Cole, becoming almost 'jobbing builder' to the South Kensington Museum.

Despite some rivalry between Fowke and Smirke over the architectural commissions, the gardens were ready for a formal opening on 5 June, 1861. The ceremony was performed by the Prince Consort, who claimed it was 'a valuable attempt . . . to reunite the science and art of gardening to the sister arts of architecture and painting', an indirect reference to an ambitious scheme to use some of the arcades for the display of sculpture.[10] Though Queen Victoria was absent, being in mourning for her mother, the Duchess of Kent, who had died in March, the opening was a great success, carefully timed just before society left town at the end of the season, so that the *Athenaeum* could report that 'such a gathering of the higher classes has rarely been seen in London, and the expressions of . . . delight in the gardens were universal'.[11]

THE MEMORIAL TO THE EXHIBITION OF 1851

An important feature of the Garden was the Memorial to the Exhibition of 1851, for the design of which a competition had been held. The original proposal put up by the Lord Mayor, Thomas Challis, in 1853, had been to erect a statue of Prince Albert on the site of the Crystal Palace in Hyde Park. This had been turned down firmly by the Prince on the ground that:

> I can say, with perfect absence of humbug, that I would much rather not be made the prominent feature of such a monument, as it would both disturb my quiet rides in Rotten Row to see my own face staring at me, and if it became an artistic monstrosity . . . it would upset my equanimity to be permanently ridiculed and laughed at in effigy.[12]

Once a less personal subject, in the figure of Britannia, was under consideration, the Prince felt he could take charge. However, when the prize-winning design by Joseph Durham was shown to Lord John Manners, as First Commissioner of Works, he refused to have it in Hyde Park, and it was decided to make it the centre-piece of the Horticultural Gardens.[13] The design reflected the ideals of the Exhibition, and the Prince's concept of its international character, Britannia supported by the four quarters of the world. The column was surrounded by four female figures, an African negress, Asia as represented by an Indian princess, decorated with jewels, muslins and other Indian textiles, America was shown resting her hand upon an axe, 'suggestive of clearing of forests and making way for civilisation, the other hand holds the primitive bow and arrow of the Indian; her head is decorated with stars and rice, in allusion to the United States . . . and her mantle bears a clasp with a lion's head (from a design by the Prince Consort), indicative of the British possessions. Europe . . . is the more matronly figure . . . on the right arm she bears a sheathed sword indicating that Europe was at peace in 1851'.[14] The central figure was changed more than once before the monument was erected; first the Horticultural Society requested that Britannia should be replaced by a statue of the Queen, and after the Prince's death, the Queen directed that the column should be surmounted by a statue of the Prince himself. In due course the Prince's statue, at a cost of £8000, was paid for by public subscription. Nonetheless, the memorial clearly commemorates not the Prince but the Exhibition: one face carries the names of all the Commission members, another the list of countries which exhibited; a third the statistics, dates of opening and closing, number of visitors, exhibitors, size of building, and receipts and expenditure. The fourth became a memorial to the Prince. It was unveiled on 10 June, 1863, by the Prince of Wales.

ANOTHER INTERNATIONAL EXHIBITION

The Horticultural Society's quiet enjoyment of the gardens was to be challenged by a new and important neighbour almost before they were opened. The Society of Arts, in which Henry Cole still played an important part, had never given up its hope of holding periodic international exhibitions. They had been disappointed in the removal of the Crystal Palace, and the dedication of the surplus to ends other than the provision of an exhibition building. It is not easy a century and a half later to appreciate how much the concept of exhibitions had grasped the public imagination, and how valuable their role in spreading information was held to be. An advocate of further exhibitions, writing in 1859, could claim:

> What the telegraph and the post are to the merchant and manufacturer, Exhibitions must be to the general public – they are the telegraphs by which the public may be rapidly acquainted with the new products of the Colonies, and the application of those products to our wants.[15]

Thus, at first, the international exhibition was seen as a great opportunity for the advancement of industry and the promotion of trade by a manufacturing country. Competition to hold them became fierce, partly because of the prestige, and also because the manufacturers of the host country got the best opportunity to display their wares. Interest in international exhibitions remained strong, stimulated by that in Paris in 1855, to which an official British deputation had been sent, and on which Cole had written a long report. In March 1858, therefore, the Council of the Society, encouraged by Henry Cole, who wanted a Fine Art Exhibition and Wentworth Dilke, who wanted an industrial one, decided to set in hand preparations for a decennial successor to the International Exhibition. In a report published in April they set out their objectives, and in July they obtained an undertaking from the Prince Consort that he would ask the Commission to guarantee £50,000.

In November they came to the conclusion that the 1851 Commission, having already successfully promoted one exhibition, would be the ideal body to organize the next, and indeed as the beneficiary of subscriptions donated for the 1851 Exhibition, it could be argued it was the Commission's moral duty to do so. They approached the 1851 Commission accordingly, making it clear that what they had in mind, though again an international event, was not to be a mere repetition of 1851, but an exhibition which would display excellence and the progress made in Britain and elsewhere since. Competition came from the Board of the Crystal Palace, inspired by Joseph Paxton, who put in a bid to host the Exhibition, emphasizing the liberality of the terms offered, the suitability of the building and its natural surroundings, the beauty of its terrace gardens, park and fountains, and the access by rail to the site 'which will render it more conveniently and speedily accessible to the great mass of the people'.[16]

General Grey advised the Prince, despite the latter's fear that it might be a failure, that the Commission should take on the 1861 Exhibition on the grounds that it would be a popular thing for the Commissioners to do: 'the undertaking, independently of the popularity that might attend such a course, would go far towards removing the distrust at present felt of them, by those who are opposed to the removal of the national gallery at [sic] Kensington'. Without the Prince's management it might not succeed, but if he took it on he would have Lord Granville's help as he had had in 1851; in any case, whoever was in charge, Grey pointed out, if the project were a failure, responsibility for it would be laid at the door of the 1851 Commission.[17]

The Society of Arts continued to lobby the Commission, pointing out that it had been intended by the promoters of the 1851 Exhibition that it would be the first of a series on the French model, saying with some justice that the public would expect the Commissioners, having been established by the successful 1851 Exhibition, to give a lead in its decennial successor. 'Any beneficial results that the Exhibition of 1851 might accomplish could only be fully known when the condition of general industry should be again tested, after a proper interval, by a similar exhibition.' They emphasized the benefits of the growth in railways, 50 per cent in Great Britain, and much greater abroad, and railway travellers from 85 million a year to 139 million. However, in April 1859, the Franco-Austrian war broke out, and, by June, conditions on the Continent were such that the Society suggested postponing the International Exhibition 'to a more favourable opportunity'.

In November the Council of the Society of Arts appointed a committee of Sir Thomas Phillips, the Chairman, Henry Cole, and Matthew Uzielli, a wealthy resident of Regent's Park, who, with the Prince Consort, was the largest guarantor of £10,000, to try to raise a guarantee fund of £250,000 and to pursue the matter of an international exhibition in 1862. They approached various substantial figures to become trustees of the guarantee fund, the Marquis of Chandos, later the 3rd Duke of Buckingham (1823–89), Chairman of the London and North Western Railway, Thomas Baring, MP, Charles Wentworth Dilke, heavily involved in both the Horticultural Society and the Society of Arts and Thomas Fairbairn, who had been Chairman of the successful and prestigious 1857 Art Treasures Exhibition in Manchester, which had been supported by Prince Albert. Nonetheless, it was felt that further weight was needed, and the ever helpful Granville was approached.[18] The trustees were to raise the guarantee money, and to approach the Commission for a site on their estate, not only to hold an Exhibition, but to build a permanent building in which to hold a series of exhibitions in later years, in short, to rectify the omission which some members of the Society of Arts felt had occurred after 1851. There was a tacit assumption that another exhibition would raise the same sort of surplus as it had in 1851. In February 1860 the Society reported to the Prince, and in March applied to the Commission for a site, but the Finance Committee was not in favour. This

Fig 15. The Commissioners for the 1862 Exhibition:
the Duke of Buckingham, Thomas Baring, Earl Granville,
Sir Charles Wentworth Dilke and Thomas Fairbairn.

provoked an outspoken letter from Cole to Grey, forecasting trouble not merely for a single 'obstructive Commissioner' but for the whole organization including its President; a meeting of the Guarantors of the Fund would need to be called, and would lead to trouble:

It is upon [HRH] rather than the Commissioners that the odium of such a decision will most unjustly fall . . . A large majority of [the Guarantors] are members of the Society of Arts. Several of them are sore and feel that the Society has been ungenerously treated by the Commissioners. Strong opinions are often expressed not only on the policy but even on the legality of spending the Surplus on the purchase of the ground at Kensington. They will . . . show no mercy to the declaration of the Commissioners that they would 'fund the surplus in support of similar Exhibitions'. Some of them, I believe, are men prepared to go to Chancery as well as to Parliament for further discussion . . . The jealous discussions which have taken place in Parliament about Kensington will be trifling in comparison with what is in prospect. The controversy if raised will never cease because every fresh application of the ground at Kensington will revive it in the public mind. Looking at the success of the present guarantee the Commissioners cannot reply that it is merely 'three tailors of Tooley Street' who are calling for Exhibitions and that they are administering a public Trust as they think best; but in the face of Europe they will be called traitors to the cause which gave them birth – traitors who have seized the money & misappropriated it & who resist fulfilling their promise.[19]

Grey responded with a placatory letter, and a potentially explosive and damaging public row between the Commission and another influential body was defused, as so often by the intervention of the Prince and his office. In June when the Society could demonstrate that over £308,000 had been subscribed to the guarantee fund, a favourable response was forthcoming. The Commission agreed to the use of 16 acres, on that part of their estate south of the Horticultural Gardens, north of the Cromwell Road, rent-free for the purposes of the international exhibition. They also gave an undertaking to vest in the Society in due course, at a moderate rent, the coveted permanent building the Society planned to construct, provided it was no more than an acre in extent, and the Society spent at least £50,000 on it. They even undertook to reserve the rest of the ground for an international exhibition to be held in 1872, provided they were paid £10,000 out of the proceeds of the 1862 Exhibition.[20]

Lord Granville, who had been devastated by the loss of his much-loved wife in March, again suggested that the management of the forthcoming exhibition should be taken on by the Commission, but this was rejected on the grounds that the guarantee fund had referred to five specific trustees, and this would be invalidated if others took over. It is clear that Granville himself realized that it was impossible that Prince Albert 'should take the same share of labour and responsibility as ten years ago, and probably several of the most influential of the Commissioners of 1851 would object on the grounds both of principle & expediency to the Commissioners taking any part in the next Exhibition'.[21] Nonetheless, the row rumbled on throughout the summer, with the long-suppressed irritation of the Society of Arts over the earlier use of the surplus finding very frank expression in letters between the Chairman and the President. Bowring was reluctant to take on the responsibility, complaining to Grey:

> Lastly, I presume that when we are asked to conduct the Exhibition 'in accordance with the conditions of the Guarantee' that means that we are to be hampered by the Guarantee List as it stands, good and bad names alike; that we are not to dispose of any surplus ourselves; that the Guarantors are to do what they like with it; and that we are to give the Society of Arts the lease of the permanent buildings just as much as if they themselves carried out the Exhibition and not we.[22]

He added that no immediate answer would be forthcoming as no Commissioners were in town, and Lord Granville, who had been in Paris, had gone to Spain.

Bowring was very concerned about the complex relation between the Royal Commission for the 1851 Exhibition, the Society of Arts and the Guarantors and the new Trustees, particularly as far as the matter of the buildings intended to remain after the Exhibition closed.[23] Though Chandos, Dilke and Fairbairn were willing to go ahead provided a Royal Charter was forthcoming, Granville and Baring still expressed a preference for the matter to be managed by the 1851 Royal Commission since they had managed the earlier event. They requested that if 'His Royal Highness . . . and other Members [felt] they would not be justified in again undertaking the labour and responsibility', the Commission should provide support for the idea of the Exhibition, and advise on the best methods of managing it. At its meeting on 20 November, 1860, the Commission again refused to take over the project, also determining that they would not agree in advance to entrust the proposed 1872 Exhibition to a nominee of the Society of Arts.

Granville was equivocal about the matter, writing to his close friend Lord Canning, the Governor-General of India:

> I have undertaken . . . the management of a new Exhibition in 1862.
> I was much averse to it, and Charles Greville and all my friends predict it will be a great failure. It is impossible to argue the other way; but I believe it will be an absolute success, not a comparative one . . . Pray stir up your people to send us a good Exhibition . . . There are some fearful contingencies. War – in Europe – another bad season – failure of cotton crop – What is going on in America is wonderfully interesting.[24]

However reluctantly, it was accepted that the success of the forthcoming Exhibition was important to all concerned, and that its trustees needed more standing; in fact, they refused to act without it, and as they were all men of considerable substance, Bowring and the Commission had to give way. It was therefore agreed that the Commission would support an application for a charter, and the new trustees were duly incorporated as the 'Commissioners for the Exhibition of 1862', with a closer connection to the Society of Arts than in 1851, under the Prince as President, on 14 February, 1861.[25]

Granville could write more sanguinely to Canning, that despite

> Paxton writing an insidious letter to the *Times* (after a distinct promise of warm support), hitting us between wind and water, just at the moment we required signatures to the Guarantee Fund. We are, however, succeeding with the latter, and have ordered a building designed by Captain Fowke and Cole; from which we have been obliged, to our great regret, to excise a great Hall, which would have been the eighth wonder of the world.[26]

THE BUILDING FOR THE 1862 EXHIBITION

Despite the doubts about the way in which the Exhibition was to be organized, sufficient support had been forthcoming for the Trustees to hold a meeting with Cole in November to consider a design for the building. Though Cole turned down Granville's offer of a job on the new Commission, he eventually took a paid job as adviser for £1500, forgoing three months' pay at the Department. The Secretaryship went to F. R. Sandford (1824–93) a civil servant from the education office, though Cole claimed that without his help Sandford would not have succeeded. The plans for the building, which 'had been maturing since the early months of 1859' were by Captain Fowke, a fact which caused a 'jealousy in the architectural profession', and some very pointed comments by unsympathetic critics like the *Art Journal*.[27] The intention was that the Exhibition should be as large as its predecessor as far as manufactures and machinery went, and at least part of the building was intended to be permanent. A first estimate was £150,000, though later £200,000 was thought to be more realistic, and Kelk offered to carry out the work for that sum. Early in December, the plans were shown to the Prince, and on 22 December were inspected by the engineers William Baker and William Fairbairn, father of Thomas, who thought that the cost might be £295,000.[28]

Very early on, the trustees realized that they could not afford to spend as much as £50,000 on the proposed permanent building, so the terms were altered to provide that the Society could spend the surplus later on to bring the building up to the required standard, reflecting the common assumption that the Exhibition was bound to make money.

The role of the Royal Commission was that of a landlord, who needed only to approve building on his estate, but the matter was confused by the dual roles of several participants, including Granville, who chaired both the Finance Committee of the 1851 Commission and the 1862 Commission, Baring, and later Chandos and Fairbairn, who were members of both Commissions, and of course the Prince himself. As Granville later wrote:

[The public] distinguish little between the mode of management in 1851, and 1862, and although technically wrong they are substantively right. The great idea was his, the whole legislation for both was his, the idea of adding a Picture Gallery to the present one was his, the building and its distribution was modified, and sanctioned by him. Without His Royal Highness, neither the first nor the second would have taken place.[29]

The design approved by the 1851 Commission on 21 January, 1861, was for a very substantial building with a hall behind the Cromwell Road front, intended to serve for ceremonies and a music auditorium, with three tiers of galleries for exhibition space, some 500–600 feet by 200–300 feet wide, and about 200 feet high. The size and importance of the picture galleries has been attributed to the Prince's desire to have the National Gallery at South Kensington, while the hall was presumably an attempt to accommodate the Prince's expressed desire for a hall for music in the complex, met by the later building of the Albert Hall. The drawings were sent out to tender, and history repeated itself; as in 1851, the tenders were much larger than anticipated, ranging from £600,000 to £700,000, with the lowest tender coming from John Kelk in partnership with Lucas Brothers. Paxton made an offer to the 1862 Commission to provide a building, but Lord Granville suggested that 'the same man cannot play the same game twice'.[30] Rescue came from Kelk who offered to carry out a more modest design for £300,000.

Fowke further modified his design, abandoning the proposed hall, and it was agreed that though some of the building was to be permanent like the new French exhibition building in Paris, much of the building would be carried out in wood, though two glass domes were added. The arrangements with the contractors Kelk and Lucas echoed those of 1851, since the contractors effectively agreed to hire the building to the 1862 Commission for £200,000, though if receipts permitted an additional £100,000 might be payable, and the building could be bought outright for a total of £430,000. Bowring had insisted on behalf of the 1851 Commission that the land should be cleared at the end of the Exhibition. Further modifications were made to Fowke's scheme as the contractors provided many of the working drawings, and the interior decoration was entrusted to the fashionable decorator J. G. Crace. The building, as finally constructed, occupied the whole frontage of the Commissioners' property facing south on to the Cromwell Road from Prince Albert's Road (now Queen's Gate) to Exhibition Road, stretching north to the boundaries of the Horticultural Society's gardens, where the southern arcades were modified to accommodate the refreshment rooms for the Exhibition, at the 1851 Commissioners' expense. A temporary annex for machinery exhibits stretched up Prince Albert's Road almost as far as Gore Lane, with a slightly shorter annex on the eastern side approached by a subway underneath the Horticultural Society's council rooms and entrance.

The 1851 Commissioners, though not responsible for the Exhibition,

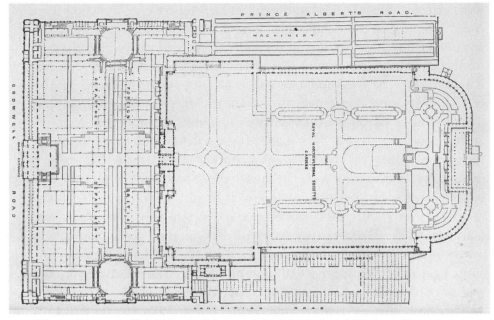

Fig 16. The 1862 Exhibition Building and the Horticultural Gardens. The arcades to the north and the refreshment galleries south of the garden remained after the rest of the 1862 building was removed.

supported it in many ways, not only by providing the site rent-free but also by its undertaking that the Society of Arts might, with certain conditions, retain part of the building for future exhibitions. They also financed at a cost of £47,000 the decorative treatment of the northern side of the building which was to survive as the Refreshment Rooms and the Southern Arcades to the Horticultural Gardens. Indirectly they benefited since they brokered an arrangement by which the Horticultural Gardens were made available to visitors to the Exhibition. Some £8672 was paid to the Society, thus enabling it to make sufficient income to pay its rent, for the first and only time.

The prospect of the Exhibition also concentrated public attention on the roads within the area. The Society of Arts seems to have started the ball rolling by suggesting the need for a road across Hyde Park from north to south, proposing a route from Victoria Gate to the Magazine, over the existing bridge, then in a tunnel under Rotten Row, to a temporary exit at the top of Exhibition Road. Since neither the government, in the person of the First Commissioner of Works, or the local authority, in the shape of the parishes of Kensington or St Margaret's, Westminster, were able or willing to fund it, the Society of Arts offered to build such a road, financing it by debentures. The First Commissioner, the Honourable William Cowper, then proposed a permanent road across the park from Lancaster Gate to the Coalbrookdale Gates, apparently via the Broad Walk. The Metropolitan Police Commissioner, Richard Mayne, the authority most concerned, also wrote to *The Times*, identifying some five or so other bottle-necks liable to give trouble, including the 'narrows' at the southern end of Park Lane, the gardens in the middle of the Brompton Road, 'the tramway or common road connecting railway station near Kensington with Cromwell and Gloucester Roads', the barriers erected in Exhibition and Cromwell Roads to protect the exclusive residents from traffic, and roads as far afield as Sloane Square. Those who had seen the crowds arriving in Hyde Park eleven years before were aware of the likely traffic congestion, despite the building of railway stations nearby in Kensington and Hammersmith, where between 15,000 and 20,000 people were expected to arrive daily.[31]

Though Cubitt had laid out the roads on a grand scale, they had not been engineered to carry heavy and constant traffic, either for building construction, or in the carriage of heavy exhibits, like the cast iron exhibits of 'M. Krupps of Essen in Rhenish Prussia' which weighed over 21 tons. The amount of money spent by both Commissions on the roads, some £13,000, is a tribute both to the amount of road-engineering needed and the long-term improvements generated by the presence of the Exhibition and its six million visitors. A permanent reminder is the road from Exhibition Road across Hyde Park, and the widening of the Brompton Road, but the road improvements elsewhere had to wait for the stately progress of the Metropolitan Board of Works, or even the creation of the London County Council. The real benefit to South Kensington's communications was to come from the building of the Metropolitan Railway. This, in due course, was to enable the South Kensington Museum to compete so effectively with its more 'central' rivals the National Gallery and the as yet undivided British Museum, that on Easter Monday, 1877, they welcomed 27,000 visitors as against their rivals' 20,000 and 19,000 respectively.[32]

THE DEATH OF THE PRINCE CONSORT

Prince Albert opened the Horticultural Gardens in June 1861, with the Exhibition building rising in the background. By the time the Exhibition opened on 1 May, 1862, he was dead. His sudden death on 14 December, 1861, left the country shocked and the Queen inconsolable. 'The most valuable life in the country has been taken', wrote Granville to Lord Canning in India, 'and the public are awakening to the loss of the good and wise man who is gone. The loss to the country is great; to the Queen it is irreparable'.[33]

There were a number of organizations, whose first action was to send official condolences to the sovereign, many concerned with South Kensington, including the two Royal Commissions, the Society of Arts and the Horticultural Society. All of them needed to replace their President, and various solutions and individuals were found, but none of them could replace the active royal presence, which provided such a useful link between diverse and often antagonistic institutions. The Queen attempted to give additional royal support to those bodies in which she believed the Prince had been particularly interested, for instance telling the Horticultural Society that she wished that the gardens 'should be considered as under her peculiar and personal patronage and protection'.[34]

The Prince's place as President of the 1851 Commission was not filled for over two years. Granville continued as the Chairman of the Finance Committee, chairing the Commission on an *ad hoc* basis.

The project most immediately prejudiced by the Prince's death was the 1862 Exhibition. Granville wrote to Phipps that 'his loss throws a gloom over it, which is irreparable from a moral point of view'[35] and it was generally considered that his death, and the consequent lack of Court involvement, was one of the major reasons for the lack of success of the 1862 occasion. There was also the appalling slump in Lancashire due to the dearth of cotton from the war-torn United States, caused by the northern blockade of southern ports. As *The Times* recorded:

> hundreds of lofty many-windowed mills, with closed doors, smokeless chimneys, and deserted streets. . . . But where are they all? They sit in cheerless houses, looking at one another, and the ships.[36]

The Times reminded its readers that in March 1860 some 1,780,000 cwts (89,000 tons) of cotton had been imported, the following year 1,603,000 cwts (80,150 tons), but in 1862 only 296,000 cwts (14,800 tons), dealing a serious blow to Manchester, whence came so much of the impetus for the holding of the Exhibition.

The 1862 Exhibition was very unfortunate in its circumstances by comparison with its predecessor, and doubly damned by having such a success to live up. It would be easier to see it in perspective, if it had been, as intended, the second of a series of decennial exhibitions, but despite the efforts of Henry Cole and the Society of Arts, this increasingly dated aspiration was not realized.

THE 1862 EXHIBITION

The 1862 Exhibition has had a bad press, but it was not dismissed by contemporaries. Though it is clear that the 1851 Commission assiduously avoided taking on the running of the successor exhibition, the personnel responsible for the 1862 event were largely associated with the existing Commission and the rest of the South Kensington institutions. Thus, three of the Trustees and Commissioners for 1862 were members of the 1851 Commission. The other two, Lord Chandos, afterwards Duke of Buckingham, and Thomas Fairbairn, were later elected to the 1851 Commission. The Council of Chairmen of the various specialized committees was chaired by Labouchere, now Lord Taunton, and Playfair fulfilled his old role of Special Commissioner for Juries. Bowring, Spearman and Thring served on the Finance Committee as did Robert Lowe, later Chancellor of the Exchequer, and T. E. Gibson, a veteran member of the 1851 Commission. The Industrial Department included Bowring, Cole and Playfair, as well as the Irish railway contractor William Dargan (1799–1867), the backer, and indeed the main financier behind the 1853 Dublin Exhibition, as well as the Presidents of the main United Kingdom institutions connected with commerce like the Society of Arts, the Royal Agricultural Society of England, the Royal Dublin Society and the Institutes of Civil and Mechanical Engineers. The Mechanical Department, headed by the Duke of Sutherland, included Joseph Cubitt, whose father, Sir William, had been a leading figure in 1851, Captain Galton, and the veteran John Scott Russell. There was a larger Irish involvement generally, the Agriculture Committee, for instance, having two Irish peers, Lords Clancarty and Talbot de Malahide, as well as Lord Portman, whose son was Secretary to the Committee. The Department of Fine Arts, controlled by the various specialized societies like the Royal Academy, was an innovation, but an important element after the success of the Art Treasures Exhibition in Manchester in 1857. The Art Designs for Manufactures, chaired by the 2nd Marquess of Salisbury (1791–1868), father of the Prime Minister, was dominated by South Kensington figures, including Cole, Robinson, Sykes and M. D. Wyatt, together with the painter Maclise and Monkton Milnes. Amongst the other figures involved in the management of the exhibits were Henry Owen, now Commander of the Engineers at Plymouth, and his brother Philip Cunliffe-Owen, who was to succeed Henry Cole at the South Kensington Museum. As in 1851, the Commissioners had requested the help of the Engineers to manage the exhibits and the exhibitors. However, the key figure was missing. *The Times* reminded its readers that:

> The genius of a single man had struck out the great and fruitful idea of calling upon all nations from time to time to estimate their progress in arts and manufactures, to compare their own works with that of their neighbours and rivals . . . but the voice that called us together is mute and the structure which the Prince has intended as the region of his activity has become a mighty mausoleum to his memory.[37]

The Queen was not prepared to open the Exhibition herself, but appointed a number of special Commissioners including the Speaker, the Archbishop of Canterbury, the Lord High Chancellor and the Lord Chamberlain, and the Lords Derby and Palmerston, Leader of the Opposition and Prime Minister respectively. The actual opening was carried out by her first cousin, the Duke of Cambridge (1819–1904), to a trumphant musical accompaniment, very much more carefully planned than it had been eleven years before. Works had been commissioned from Auber, Meyerbeer and Rossini,[38] as representatives of their respective countries, while the host country was represented by Sterndale Bennett, who put an ode by Tennyson to music. Rossini's advanced age made it necessary for him to decline, and though Verdi was approached in July 1861, various changes by the composer in the nature of the music offered combined with delays meant that 'the Music of Italy was without a representative'.

Despite its traditional disapproval of the late Prince's activities, *The Times* was unequivocal in its commendation of the Exhibition, seeing it as belonging to the 'Hyde Park not the Sydenham species', and declaring it

> a great picnic of art and science, a world's gathering . . . There is all the crowding, all the strangely miscellaneous character, all the mixture of the useful and the beautiful, the ingenious, the cheap, and the gay that there was in Hyde Park, but for extent, for convenience, for observation, for beauty of forms and lines, and for drama of colour,

the present building is far, far superior to that in Hyde Park. The former is as a bud is in the rose or the former girl in the woman, . . . it is a simple and beautiful design. The graceful curve of the trusses that support the roof, and the nice choice of colours and tints, make a whole that will stand comparison with the finest edifices in the world.[39]

Though the building was not universally acclaimed – a cartoon shows John Bull presenting it to a somewhat puzzled Britannia and *The Building News* called it 'one of the ugliest public buildings ever raised in this country' – a great deal more thought and experience had been employed on the building than had been available in 1850. There had been two more 'Crystal Palace' type buildings for exhibitions in 1853, in Dublin and in New York, the latter of which had gone up in flames. The example of the Paris and the Manchester Exhibitions pointed to the need for a more solid structure which was better insulated with lower light levels, a mixture of a central permanent structure supported by temporary annexes for large works of art and for working machinery.

The 1862 building was essentially an iron and wooden structure with glazed roofs, set within a substantial edifice some 1200 feet long of load-bearing brick with a series of double-height windows on the north of the Cromwell Road. It was much more substantial than the 1851 building,

Fig 17. 'The May-Day Present', a contemporary cartoon of John Bull, with more than a passing resemblance to Lord Granville, presenting the 1862 building to Britannia.

since the intention was that it should, in due course, provide a permanent home for one or more of the national collections. Critics pointed out that the 16-acre site was very small for the amount of space demanded by the exhibitors, and that the Cromwell Road, of which the southern side was already occupied by houses, was too narrow for such a building. In addition, the time-honoured way in which the road had been made up above the level of the existing ground to allow for the traditional London basement would have prejudiced the appearance of any building. Fowke had had to leave the exhibition building unfinished for the time being, because of the cost, though there was also a presumption that there would be the money to provide decorative elements later. As he explained to one architectural critic, there were intended to be terracotta panels on the 'featureless' wall spaces, and 'the present blank window spaces filled in . . . with a grand series of designs in solid mosaics, rich in colour, emblematic of art and science'.[40]

The main entrance in the middle of the southern façade gave on to a hall 150 feet long and 100 feet wide leading north to the industrial galleries and to an entrance to the Horticultural Gardens, on to which gave the main refreshment rooms. Within the building there was a transverse nave, opening on to a dome at either end, taller than any others except St Peter's, Rome, and St Paul's Cathedral. The internal decoration was by Crace: staircases on either side, painted in 'maroon and subdued reds, with some sage green', gave access to the picture galleries above, in 'a subdued sage-green, relieved along the cornices and strings, ceiling mouldings, etc., by stencilled ornaments in a "vellum colour" [a sort of cream]'. The main building was divided as in 1851, between the British and their Colonies on the eastern side, and the rest of the world on the west. The French had persuaded the organizers that they should be allowed to have a western court to themselves, divided off from the rest of the world, and had also managed to establish a 'French Refreshment Room' on the same side, as a competitor to the host nation's Refreshment Room on the east.

Stretching north from the domed courts behind the arcades either side of the Horticultural Gardens were two *annexés*, much like railway goods sheds, intended to be 'ephemeral', accommodating the Machinery in motion on the western side, and agricultural machinery, animal and vegetable products on the eastern side, regardless of country of origin. These buildings were later to develop a new and important role as the homes of new enterprises, and to generate several new institutions in the life of South Kensington.

The exhibiting countries were the same as in 1851 with some regrouping, Italy now making its appearance to represent the whole country with the exception of Rome, while most of Germany appeared under the Zollverein banner, after France (92,800 square feet) the largest foreign exhibitor in the Industrial Department with some 42,600 square feet, followed by Belgium (31,527), Austria (which had lost her northern Italian possessions (17,600), and Russia (9600), Switzerland (9100), with the war-torn United States reduced to 5800 square feet.

With the addition of fine art, the classes were very similar to those of 1851, and the prizes were again medals rather than cash. Again there were the Juries drawn from different countries, largely those who had been involved in 1851.

The exhibits were in some respects more spectacular than in 1851, particularly those in the section devoted to machinery in motion. This was partly because of the development of large and heavier machines in the decade since 1851, and also because the manufacturers had come to appreciate the value of displaying even large and unwieldy equipment which might be difficult to transport. A reporter from the *Illustrated London News* found it most impressive:

> We do not think there is any point in the whole exhibition the view from which can compare with this in real interest; the array of engines and machines is not only wonderful and beautiful in itself, but every machine exhibited has claims upon our attention as playing some part in our daily wants as luxuries or necessities.

In view of the state of the British cotton industry at that moment, it was ironic one of the most prominent machines was Platt's Mule, which processed cotton from the pod to the spun thread.

It was a wet and disagreeable summer, which doubtless lowered visitor numbers, already affected by Court mourning, and the cotton famine, so bad that the City of London opened a fund to relieve poverty in the mill districts of Lancashire. However, the rain helped to keep down the dust from the roads in South Kensington and the temperature within the building.

In fact, the number of visitors was greater than in 1851, one estimate being 6,211,103, as against 6,039,195, though they did not meet the

Fig 18. Mechanical Exhibits from the
1862 Exhibition. A portable Steam Engine
by Ransome & Sims.

Fig 19. Oscillating Washing
Machine by Hussey & Sons,
Grantham.

expectation of a 25 per cent increase on the 1851 total.[41] These numbers
included 35,570 visitors who came in organized groups from factories,
schools, institutions and various landed estates, paid for by a wide selection of benefactors. Thus two captains of engineers funded groups of
men, with their wives and children from Chatham, Dilke sent 280 children from four Chelsea schools, Chance Brothers sent 1345 workmen
from their Birmingham glassworks, 28 mousetrap makers came from
Selsey, in Sussex, Lady Herbert sent 450 tenants from Wilton, Prince
Louis Bonaparte 40 artisans from Paris, while the 135 girls from the
London Orphan Asylum were paid for by 'A Member of the London Stock
Exchange'. The effect on London generally was difficult to ascertain,
though attendances at the South Kensington Museum were up to 859,000
from 322,000 the previous year, and the number of foreigners visiting
Woolwich Arsenal 3120 from 134.

Despite this sort of organized visiting, the Commissioners were in fact
faced by an anticipated shortfall in the amount of money to be taken, and
by the prospect of having to call on the guarantors, a result which they
felt 'would have been damaging not only to the character of the
Exhibition but also to the prospect of future Exhibitions in this country'.
Therefore, in September they decided to extend the opening from 18
October to 1 November, and to remain open for a further fortnight to
allow the exhibitors to sell their goods. They revised other arrangements
to ensure that no calls were made, including persuading the contractors

to abandon their rights to some of the gate money, and it was agreed that the right to retain a part of the building on behalf of the Society of Arts should be waived. With great generosity Kelk offered to contribute up to £15,000 of his money to protect the guarantors. In addition to other problems, it has to be said that the 1862 Commission had greater calls on their financial resources than that of 1851. Firstly, the 'profits' in 1851 had included some £62,000 of subscriptions, made in advance, and not returned; as in 1851, they had had heavy financial demands for the policing, of over £19,435, and in 1862 the cost of the roads was very heavy. There were three parties interested, the 1851 Commission as landlords, the Department of Science and Art and the 1862 Commission, and the matter was referred for arbitration to the Lord Mayor, William Cubitt, brother to Thomas, who decided that the landlords should pay nothing, the Department make a small contribution, and the majority should be paid by the Exhibition. As a consequence the payment for making up the roads had amounted to £13,358, of which the major part was paid by the 1862 Commission.[42]

As was to be expected, comparison between the two occasions were many, and not always flattering, though the machinery exhibits were larger and heavier: up to 35 tons in weight as against a maximum of nine tons in 1851.[43]

Though the 1862 Exhibition did not produce the expected surplus, and was therefore compared unfavourably with its predecessor, it was not a financial disaster. The *Illustrated London News*, in a lively account of the thriving and flagrantly commercial last fortnight when the exhibitors were allowed to sell their wares, which attracted at least 45,000 visitors, pointed out that though it was 'the fashion to say that it has not been a success' it had had a larger number of visitors, calculated by the *Illustrated London News* as between 50,000 and 100,000 more than in 1851, and it had taken more money.[44] Earlier it had been pointed out that the weather had been more favourable in 1851, being 'abnormally bright and tempting' while 1862 suffered from 'pluvial influence and a chill atmosphere', while a major disincentive to return visits was the access. As yet unassisted by the railways, visitors were forced to use carriages or omnibuses, whereas the Crystal Palace had had Hyde Park for its 'courtyard' and many visitors could just walk across the park. These things were enough, even without the absence of the Court, to diminish the success of the Exhibition.

THE RESULTS OF THE 1862 EXHIBITION

The Receipts were variously computed; by Cole's account they amounted to £469,000, but the 1862 Commissioners' Report gave them as £448,632, with expenditure of £458,848, with a cost for the main buildings of £233,846. The roads, to which the Commissioners had to contribute, cost some £13,358, and the administrative costs were £123,000.[45]

By negotiation with Kelk and Lucas the cost of the building was reduced to a sum which left a deficit of £11,000. This was contributed as a gift by Kelk himself, so the Commission were not out of pocket, and did not have to call upon the guarantors. The Society of Arts which generously undertook the printing of the official *Jury Reports*, edited by Lyon Playfair, which appeared in 1863, had to support a loss of £1033 on the volumes.

Critics like the *Art Journal* were scathing about the lack of a surplus, pillorying 'the liberal use of rose-colour' in the Commission's report, and contrasting the way it described 'the excellence of all the arrangements, the ability, zeal, and assiduity of all the officials, the complete satisfaction of everybody with everybody and everything', the thanks for 'the cooperation of Mr. Henry Cole, and a few other distinguished individuals not actually in office' with more forthright accounts of 'the intense dissatisfaction that prevailed on every side – the heart-burnings, the annoyances, and the blunderings that characterized the official administration throughout'. Despite this it had to admit the Exhibition was in fact a success, though ending with an expression of regret for the absence of the Prince Consort, not only at the opening, but throughout for 'the want of his clear perception and calm judgement and admirable tact most painfully felt in even the minor details of the practical working of the entire Exhibition'.[46]

On the Exhibition's closure there was a similar problem over reinstatement as there had been after the 1851 event, necessitating a sharp letter from Bowring to Sandford, in February 1863, detailing the repairs needed to the Horticultural Gardens, the repairs to the roads, and the actual removal of the buildings.[47] The first was part of the continuing problems of the Horticultural Society, the last had to await the disposal of the site, but the 1851 Commission had already considered the question of getting their magnificent roads adopted. Henry Thring (1818–1907), a leading parliamentary draughtsman, newly elected to the Commission, reported on the varying legal status of the roads: Prince Albert's Road and part of the Cromwell Road had been made under the 1854 Act, which made them public footpaths, but not public carriage roads, while Exhibition Road had been made by Freake and the Commission to serve their own properties, and could therefore be closed by gates by joint agreement by the two owners.[48] An attempt the following year to get the parishes to adopt the roads was only partially successful; though St Margaret's, Westminster, was prepared to adopt the upper part of Exhibition Road, Kensington wanted none of it. In due course, in 1867, the latter parish adopted the rest of the roads but only after they had been thoroughly repaired at a cost of £4000, of which some £706 16s. was paid by the Commission.[49]

THE FUTURE OF THE EXHIBITION BUILDING

On the Exhibition's closure in November 1862, the Society of Arts were unable to make good their ambition to retain a building for future exhibitions, and the contractors were under obligation to remove the buildings, so the 1851 Commissioners again had a site on their hands. In 1860, the Select Committee on the British Museum, concerned with finding a home for the natural history collections, had applied for the terms for a site, and had been offered some 5 acres on Prince Albert's Road, immediately west of the Horticultural Society's Gardens, at £10,000 per acre, except for a small portion at £5000, where the building would have to stand above the arcades of that garden. This price had been below the market price, as Bowring was careful to point out, a generous gesture for an institution which had had to borrow to finance its projects. However, when in March 1862 the Treasury repeated the application, the Commission was prepared to maintain the price, also offering the government an alternative similar piece on the east side of the 'main square' in Exhibition Road, at the same price. Both plots were then in use for the Exhibition of 1862, but in fact the government lost the vote on the matter the following month, so the project was dropped.

The following year negotiations were resumed, in the light of attempts to get the Commission for the 1862 Exhibition to reinstate the ground, and fuelled by a report from the Finance Committee. This pointed out the degree of indebtedness of the Commission, which, in addition to its mortgage from Greenwich Hospital to pay off the government as partners in the original purchase, had taken on a second mortgage of £50,000 for the Horticultural Gardens works, and one for £17,000 to Kelk and Lucas for their work on the refreshment rooms. Though the building leases on the outlying parts of the estate were gradually being capitalized, and the money used to pay off the debt, this was a slow process, and the sale of the ground to the government, solely for 'purposes connected with Science or the Arts', would enable the 1851 Commission to pay off the two last mortgages, and leave some money over for an endowment fund.

Despite its financial position, the Commission remained generous in its terms, offering the site of the Exhibition building, 16.5 acres, worth some £250,000–280,000, for £120,000.[50] The government also had the option of purchasing the Exhibition building, which Kelk and Lucas were prepared to sell for £80,000. New architectural treatments for the permanent parts of the building were supplied, through Kelk and Fowke, by John Johnson who provided a possible recasting in the François Premier style.

The Cabinet decided in May 1863 to proceed with the purchase of both site and building, though not without the royal influence being invoked to ensure the safe passage of the measure. They obtained the support of Disraeli and the leaders of the Opposition, but failed to anticipate the level of backbench opposition. The opposition was led by two mavericks, Lord Elcho, 'always a veritable Mother Carey's chicken in everything relating to South Kensington', and William Gregory (1817–92) an Irish landowner who was Member of Parliament for Galway. Gregory had been instrumental in getting a Select Committee on the British Museum set up in 1859, to enquire into the problems of space for exhibition and storage, conservation and management of the collections, in the course of which he had crossed swords with Gladstone. He was appointed Chairman, and was instrumental in bringing in a report which favoured the retention of the natural history collections in Bloomsbury and expansion of the existing site, in line with a 'grand idea of Mr. Layard to have one Great Hall for Antiquities'. This was against the opposition of both Gladstone, and the formidable librarian Antonio Pannizzi, who was anxious to get rid of the 'scientific men, with whom he had no sympathy'.[51] The Report was not put into effect, but when in 1863 government and Opposition together brought the matter again before the House, Gregory had his revenge. The two proposals for the purchase of the site and the purchase of the buildings were taken separately within the House of

Commons. The purchase of the site went through on 15 June, 1863, but he, Lord Elcho and others decided to concentrate on the proposal to purchase the buildings for £105,000:

> I opposed the vote . . . to purchase the whole of the buildings from the contractors, and to patch up those hideous structures for . . . the natural history collections for Bloomsbury. I gave a full account of the bad condition of these buildings – their unfitness, unsightliness, unsuitability, etc.[52]

Partly because of Gladstone's inept handling of the matter, the opposition was so effective that the vote for the purchase of the building was thrown out by backbenchers from both sides of the House on 2 July. Behaviour in the House was so boisterous that Disraeli was said to have lost control of his party for the first and only time in his life. The opposition was generated partly by a growing dislike of what Gregory described as the 'craving, meddling, flattering, toadying and self-seeking clique that had established itself at South Kensington', and the atmosphere of 'Court job' which was thought to have surrounded the choice of Fowke as architect. It was stirred by a group, identified by Palmerston as 'artists and architects who . . . expect that their body corporate will obtain employment and reap honour and fame from the erection of buildings to be substituted for the present one'. The result was that the government got an excellent site at a knockdown price, and the two Commissions and the contractors were left with the problem of clearing away the 'disused sheds'.[53] The contractors sold the temporary buildings and the salvageable materials to the Great Northern Palace Company, in which both Kelk and Lord Chandos, together with the London and Northern Western Railway Company had an interest, for use in the Alexandra Palace, Muswell Hill. The picture galleries and the main building proved to have been so substantial that Fowke's military training had to be called on to blow them up, 'and nothing could be grander than when . . . the massive buildings, amidst deathlike silence, suddenly uplifted themselves from the ground . . . and finally fell to the ground with thundering crashes'.[54]

HOUSING THE NATURAL HISTORY COLLECTIONS

A competition for a new building was held that same year, won to some public embarrassment by the abused and unpopular 'South Kensington' favourite, Captain Fowke. Cowper, the First Commissioner of Works, behaved very honourably, and upheld the judges' award in the face of the British Museum's preference for the second-prize design by Robert Kerr. The Museum authorities then asked Fowke to provide modifications to his design, but he died in December 1865 before they were completed. Alfred Waterhouse (1830–1905) was asked to complete the designs. The matter of the Natural History Museum dragged on for another decade, while government and Museum toyed with the idea of placing the new building on the Embankment near Charing Cross Station, a project put forward by a select committee chaired by Lord Elcho. Several grandiose designs were produced, but the scheme foundered on the fact that the Embankment land had been compulsorily purchased for 'purposes of public recreation', a criterion not met by either a Natural History Museum or its proposed companion, the New Law Courts. In the event, the latter were placed in the Strand and the former returned to its waiting home in South Kensington.[55]

A further attack on the Commission was mounted by A. S. Ayrton (1816–86) the Radical Member of Parliament for Tower Hamlets, who proposed a motion for abolishing the Commission altogether and using its assets, computed at £320,000, for the benefit of the public. This threat was taken very seriously by the Commissioners who drafted a reply setting out first the lack of competence of the House of Commons to end the Commission, which could only be terminated by the same authority which had brought it into being, the Crown acting in concert with the Lords and the Commons, and then only in the case of proven illegal or improper action. More constructively, they went on to enumerate the Commission's achievements over the last ten years, which included the development of the 'new, popular, and rapidly extending district of . . . "South Kensington"', which had risen in value from £350,000 to between £750,000 and £1,000,000 in value, largely owing to the way in which it had been developed, with magnificent roads, and the Horticultural Gardens as a new 'lung' for London. Twenty-seven acres had been dedicated to 'purposes connected with Science and the Arts' including a Museum which had attracted some four million people since its foundation. In fact, of the original 85 acres, 27 acres had been laid out in the gardens, 11 in the roads, 10 or 11 in beneficial development designed to fund the repayment of the mortgages, and only 15 acres remained unallocated. In conclusion, the Commissioners reminded their critics of the 'respect due to the memory of the late Prince Consort', and that the five great Officers of

State were amongst the *ex officio* members, emphasizing the absurdity of the proposal to transfer responsibility to the First Commissioner of Works, a minister who was already 'a member and a regular attendant at the meetings'. In marked contrast to the earlier debate, the motion was thrown out by a majority of four to one (165 to 42), establishing that the Commission itself still commanded public respect.[56]

The Commission continued to recruit new members, electing Fairbairn and Chandos in 1861, presumably through their connection with the 1862 Exhibition, but remained without a President till 1864. Part of the delay was due to the Queen's choice of Derby rather than Granville. The former refused the office when it was first offered in January, saying that he had played little part compared to Granville, who had managed the Commission's affairs as Chairman of the Finance Committee, and he would not wish to supersede 'one who has devoted much time and attention to the business'. However, Derby was elected to the Finance Committee as a first step, and the problem was sorted out by a royal letter to Granville, explaining that though the Queen was far from forgetful of Lord Granville's 'long and zealous services' to the Prince, 'other considerations' made it desirable that Lord Derby should be President. Derby was elected President in April 1864, being given the task of sorting matters out with the 1862 Commissioners immediately on his appointment.[57] He continued as President till his death, even during his time as Prime Minister in 1866–8, when the Commission met at 10 Downing Street.

COMMEMORATING THE PRINCE CONSORT – THE ALBERT HALL

After the sudden death of the Prince, there were various ideas for commemorating his life and work amongst those close to him. However, appropriately for a man always more popular with the middle classes, it was the Lord Mayor of London, William Cubitt, brother to Thomas, who started the fund-raising for a national monument to the Prince. Despite some irritation that the City had taken the lead, other bodies like the Society of Arts joined in, and in February a four-man committee of William Cubitt, Lord Derby, then leader of the Opposition, Lord Clarendon and Eastlake was appointed. However, the matter was largely managed by Albert's former secretaries, Colonel Grey and Colonel Phipps. Various types of memorial were canvassed, including a simple obelisk, but the final conclusion was that something practical and associated with his ideas for South Kensington should be included, and that therefore not only a statue, placed in the centre line of the Horticultural Gardens, and also in line with the site of the 1851 Exhibition, but also a hall should be raised to his memory. The would occupy part of the important site at the north of the Commissioners' estate, originally intended for the National Gallery. Seven established architects were asked to provide schemes for a hall and for a statue within Hyde Park. In June, Eastlake wrote formally to the Commission, enclosing the report by the seven architects, and asking for a site for a hall, some 150 feet by 60, on a direct line between the centre of the conservatory and the proposed monument in Hyde Park. The Commission responded warmly, expressing their pleasure that the National Memorial was to be associated with the Commission's estate. By early in 1863, some £60,000 had been raised by public subscription, to which Parliament voted to contribute £50,000 in April 1863, but it was clear that this would only fund the monument, so the matter of the hall was allowed to lapse. Though many connected with South Kensington and the Commission were involved with the Albert Memorial, including Derby himself and John Kelk, who was the contractor, only the Hall concerned the Commission directly.[58]

The matter of the Hall then became a personal objective of Henry Cole, who used his trips to the Continent, primarily intended to acquire objects for the South Kensington Museum's collections, to investigate halls for music. The Hall had been intended to furnish the hall for music wanted by the Prince, but was also seen as a meeting place for the various South Kensington institutions, for learned societies, which it was hoped to attract, and also for the international exhibitions which Cole and others hoped to hold. The original scheme seems to have been to connect the hall with a block either of chambers, or of shops and restaurants, and George Gilbert Scott, as the designer of the Memorial opposite, was asked to provide a design for the contiguous north front of the building. In June 1864 Cole, as so often, took the initiative, and drew up a prospectus for the Hall, which he sent to Grey with the intention of enlisting royal support. This was forthcoming, Grey urging Derby to see Cole and hear his views, adding that the Queen 'knows that he is unpopular – but she also knows his devotion to the objects which the Prince had at heart – his immense fertility of resource – and his great administrative abilities – his patience and his perseverance – by which he is in fact developing the South Kensington Museum and Schools, into the greatest Art Institution in Europe'. Without getting much overt support from Lord Derby, Grey continued to urge that the Commission should play an active role, pointing out that the Hall was not merely part of the National Memorial scheme, but would supply a lack which 'had been recognised by the Prince as a great Public want'. Perhaps more fruitful was his correspondence with Bowring, to whom he furnished arguments for the Commission spending its funds on the Hall; he thought that in pursuit of objectives which 'advance science or Art, *they have the full power so to apply it, without looking for any pecuniary return'*. Grey reported to the Queen that Bowring had drawn up a favourable financial statement, which he hoped would influence Derby to 'take the question of the hall up zealously and effectually', ending with a reminder that 'A word from Your Majesty . . . would doubtless do much good'.[59]

Cole had advertised for subscribers for seats, in effect to a freehold, in what he wished to call the South Kensington Hall, enrolling Granville, and Thomas Baring, as well as Coutts the bankers, and Sir Anthony de Rothschild. By the end of 1864, he had enlisted fifty vice-presidents, and was able to approach the Prince of Wales to become President. Though many people thought that Scott, as designer of the National Memorial, would also be asked to design the hall, Cole preferred to work with his trusted ally Henry Scott. The design was based on the amphitheatre at Nîmes which Cole and Fowke had visited together in 1864.[60]

In January 1865, Cole and Richard Redgrave successfully lobbied the Prince of Wales on a visit to Osborne, equipped with the sketch by Scott, and a model by Fowke of the hall itself. Thenceforward the scheme had the official support of the Queen, as well as that of the two royal secretaries.

The spring of 1865 saw a renewed attack by the Prince's former secretary on behalf of the hall, after Derby reported that at a meeting of the Commission it was agreed that the hall was a reasonable objective. Progress had been made by establishing that 'a Central hall, adapted for purposes of Science and Art, on the proposed site' was a legitimate use for the Commission's funds. Further correspondence from Grey and the Queen herself saw the royal influence employed to 'keep [Lord Derby] up to a sense of the responsibility which he has assumed in accepting the Presidency . . . to promote the realisation of the Prince's idea, in a manner worthy of its great Author'.[61]

Success crowned the campaign, and at a meeting of the Commission in

May 1865, chaired by Derby, Bowring's report for the Finance Committee, recommending support for the proposed hall, was presented. It was felt that the hall was part of the original scheme, and would help to promote the Commission's objectives. A hall seating 5000 to 7000 persons would 'provide ample accommodation not only for above objects but also for the exhibition of pictures and other temporary Exhibitions and for great musical performances'. The cost of this was estimated at about £200,000 and the Committee recommended that the Commission should support the project by guaranteeing a quarter of the money needed for the construction and completion of the building, and by providing a free site, worth some £60,000. There were various safeguards, thus the balance of the money would have to be subscribed within eighteen months, and any subscriptions between £150,000 and £200,000 should be used to diminish the Royal Commission's contribution, while funds over £200,000 should be used to establish a maintenance fund. They proposed that a charter of incorporation should be sought, and that £2000 should be advanced for advertising and to raise subscriptions.[62]

By the end of the following month a 'working committee' had been formed, presided over by the Prince of Wales, supported by Derby, Granville, Henry Austin Bruce, MP (1815–95), and later the first Lord Aberdare, George Moffatt, MP, one of the Treasurers, Thring, Bowring, and of course, Cole, with Lieutenant Colonel H. Y. D. Scott of the Royal Engineers as Secretary, seconded to help Cole.[63] This was the first official appearance of a man who was to become an important and influential member of the Commission staff, serving the Albert Hall and the Royal Horticultural Society as Secretary, and succeeding Bowring as Secretary to the Commission itself in 1869.[64] Later that year, efforts were made to recruit more widely, particularly among the 'artistic element' including representatives from the Royal Academy, the Royal Institute of British Architects and the Institution of Civil Engineers, and such 'outsiders' as Elcho, Layard and William Tite.[65]

Fowke, who had produced the plans for the inside of the hall, fell ill in the latter part of the year, and died suddenly in December 1865. Various solutions to fill the gap were canvassed, Herbert Fisher (b. 1827), Private Secretary to the Prince of Wales from 1863 to 1870, saw it simply as a matter of having 'to select some eminent architect . . . to carry out in all its splendid features, the design already sanctioned . . . leaving him free, with the same [financial] limit, to reconsider the external architecture and especially the north front'.[66] Cole had other ideas, even suggesting that the Dresden architect Gottfried Semper, much admired by the late Prince, should be invited to design the exterior. Derby warned the Prince of Wales that to introduce Semper would be seen as 'a slur on the whole body of British architects', while he regarded the only British 'eminent architect' so far involved, G. G. Scott, as having an 'expensive turn, and a love of elaborate work' which would cause 'funds to fall lamentably short'.[67] Grey could report back to Derby in February 1866, after a visit to Cole, that Fowke's draughtsmen had been at work 'completing plans and drawings from the memoranda and drawings which he had left, & models are in course of execution both to show the interior & the plan of the staircases and entrances to the boxes, stalls, &c, & the exterior eleva-tion. It will save . . . a great deal of expense, if the Committee when it meets, shall be satisfied with the plans so submitted to it, & not think it necessary to call in any other architect'.[68] The matter was thus solved in a typical South Kensington manner through Cole's influence, and Fowke's plans were completed by his draughtsmen working with Colonel H. Y. D. Scott. Conveniently for Cole, G. G. Scott withdrew his own design for the elevation on the grounds that it transgressed 'one of the primary laws of architecture that the external elevation should be the *result* of the internal plan, circumstances led to this law being, in the pre-sent case reversed'.[69]

Despite some concern on the part of Derby about the quality of the architecture, and keenness amongst the architectural profession to get involved in this prestigious scheme, Henry Scott was left to complete the Hall, with the help of a 'committee of advice' including Richard Redgrave, the architects William Tite, Fergusson and M. D. Wyatt, and the well-known civil engineers John Fowler and John Hawkshaw, together with other members of the South Kensington team, leading to some confusion as to the responsibility for the design both at the time and in retrospect.[70]

Another concern was the recruitment of suitable patrons and seat-holders; though a prospectus had been drawn up by June 1865, together with a draft list of possible vice-presidents, approaching them was a mat-ter of some delicacy. It was an ambitious list; it ranged from the Archbishops of Canterbury and Dublin, two royal princes, six dukes, some of whom were Commissioners, through a number of other noble-men, many connected with learned societies, Antony Panizzi of the British Museum, the Governor of the Bank of England, and a number of

City figures, and manufacturers, including a partner of Herbert Minton, and Titus Salt, the famous Bradford manufacturer.[71] By December Scott could report to Grey on efforts 'to stir up' the Vice-Patrons and 'other men of wealth and mercantile position', but also on the need to 'bring some weight to bear upon the great world and to bring in a large proportion of the aristocracy & of fashionable people'. Sir Morton Peto had assured Lord Derby, who had originally recruited him, that the project was feasible, and 'only wanted a little energy now to make it a brilliant success, which would reflect credit on all engaged in it'.[72] With great care the prospectus was sent out to coincide with the return of both Houses of Parliament in February 1866, and though it was well received, there was some criticism of the way in which it was put forward. The *Pall Mall Gazette* commented:

> As South Kensington is becoming the nucleus of everything scientific and artistic, and as London is spreading more rapidly in that than in any other direction, probably this is the best site that can be found; and the historical associations of the two International Exhibitions appear to demand the permanent dedication of a palace to Art and Science in the neighbourhood . . . The site of the building is as well chosen as the patronage of the design.

It found reprehensible, however, the way in which the project was being promoted, and the emphasis on the letting of the seats and boxes, as 'a highly remunerative investment', which they felt rendered the 'whole design a little more fit for the Stock Exchange than the patronage of the heir-apparent'.[73] Grey was more sanguine, urging Cole in April to hold a meeting, and put out the prospectus: 'I feel confident that its dissemination with the long list of peers at the head, will in this democratic Country, bring in shoals of fresh applicants'.[74] This confidence weathered the Overend and Gurney crisis of May 1866, which brought down a number of firms, including that of Sir Samuel Morton Peto, a leading supporter of the hall project, and dealt a blow to the recruitment of patrons.

Despite these problems, the prospectus was sufficiently successful for the Commissioners at their meeting on 30 July, 1866, held at 10 Downing Street, currently occupied by the President, to be able to consider both a draft Charter of Incorporation for the Hall, and a generous offer from Messrs Lucas to the Executive Committee for the construction of the building. Though Cole had recruited a large number of prestigious names from the Court, Parliament and industry,[75] only £110,000 had been subscribed; taking into account the £50,000 promised by the Commission, this left a shortfall of £40,000, which Lucas were prepared to fund, taking sittings to the value of £40,000 in lieu, if necessary.

Further emphasis on the importance of music in South Kensington was given by a report from a Committee on Musical Education, ostensibly from the Society of Arts, but containing many names familiar locally, including not only the ubiquitous Cole, but Donnelly, Scott, Redgrave, Sandford and Bowring, urging that help should be given to the Royal Academy of Music. This was an initiative that came to nothing, the Commission declaring a year later that though they could provide a free site on the estate, they would not grant the £10,000 also wanted by the Academy.[76]

In April 1867, a contract was signed with Lucas, who had taken over Kelk's South Kensington projects from his former partner. On 20 May, 1867, the Queen laid the foundation stone of the Hall, and in the same month, the Provisional Committee of the Albert Hall was able to present the Final Charter for approval by the Commission. As well as music and concerts, the proposed uses for the hall were to include congresses and *conversaziones* concerned with science and art, exhibitions of all sorts, industrial, artistic, agricultural and horticultural, and 'any other purposes connected with Science and Art'. The Corporation was entitled to raise donations and subscriptions, but any profits were to be ploughed back into the Hall. The subscribers were to be Members of the Corporation, and a tariff was established for the different boxes: £1000 bought a ten-seat box in the first tier, £500 a second-tier box of five seats, £100 a seat in the amphitheatre. The Prince of Wales was to be the first President, and the Executive Committee consisted of Prince Alfred, Duke of Edinburgh and later Duke of Saxe-Coburg-Gotha from 1893 to 1900, Grey, Bruce, Cole, Bowring and Thring.

The building was opened by the Queen on 29 May, 1871, an occasion which she found 'trying and "émotionnant"', as did Cole. The Hall, whose final external appearance indeed reflected its arena-like interior, was elliptical in shape, filling the space between Kensington Gore on the north and the top of the Horticultural Gardens on the south. The Horticultural Society's magnificent conservatory provided the southern entrance to the building, with portes-cochères on the other three sides.

Within the building were three tiers of boxes, seats in the amphitheatre and above the boxes, with an arcaded gallery at the top, intended for exhibitions. Though gas-lighting was provided the hall was originally lit by a glass dome. The construction of the cast-iron and glass dome was a considerable challenge to Colonel Scott, who applied for help to the two engineers Fowler and Hawkshaw, who provided advice and the services of experienced assistants. The cast-iron ribs were made by the Manchester firm of Fairbairn Engineering, being assembled on the ground in Manchester before transfer to London. Lucas Brothers' own men carried out the construction of the brick structure, externally clad in red-facing bricks and terracotta details, but the mosaic frieze which encircles the Hall was designed by decorative artists from the Department of Science and Art, Reuben Townroe and James Gamble, and made by the ladies of the South Kensington mosaic class for the contractors, Minton, Hollins & Co.

Though the Albert Hall is probably now best known for its connection with the BBC Promenade Concerts, it was not primarily designed as a concert hall, being intended, as the prospectus set out, to have a multiplicity of uses. Queen Victoria, in a letter to Lord Derby in 1865 when the project was at an early stage, explained that she had no objection to its use for music 'of the highest kind – Classical music for instance – which decidedly belongs to Art & the promotion and encouragement of which the beloved Prince was most anxious about'.[77] This attempt at versatility is often blamed for the difficult acoustics, which made themselves apparent early in the Hall's history, and which were only partially solved by the well-known mushrooms installed after the Second World War.

THE WOOING OF THE ROYAL ACADEMY

Though the Commission was successful in establishing the Albert Hall, seen as an important part of the Prince's scheme, an attempt to achieve another element in the original project failed. The question of the National Gallery resurfaced in the summer of 1866, a key element being the divorce from the Royal Academy with which it was sharing the building in Trafalgar Square. As Bowring summed it up to Grey, 'The whole matter is a triangular duel for 3 sites for 2 Institutions, and we must play *our* game very cautiously'. Though Eastlake, himself a member of the 1851 Commission as well as President of the Royal Academy, had been expected to raise the question with his colleagues, on his death in the

autumn of 1865, it was revealed that he had never done so officially.
Encouraged by Grey and Bowring, Derby wrote formally, on 14 May,
1866, to the members of the Academy, to offer them a site. Their
President Sir Francis Grant found himself in a dilemma, since it was not
clear whether the Academy or the National Gallery would remain in
Trafalgar Square, and then what the displaced institution would be
offered in its place. Though he wished to please the sovereign who was
the Patron of the Academy, and was tempted by the size of the site, of
some three acres, offered in South Kensington, Grant was not sure the
Academy could finance a new building there. In addition, it was very
dependent on takings from exhibitions, which the members considered
would fail in South Kensington. Grey persevered, trying to get an undertaking from Cowper, First Commissioner of Works, that he would not
flaunt the offer of Burlington House before the Academicians, trying to
persuade the Commission to subsidize a grandiose new building, even
writing to Grant about 'the difficulty fast growing of crossing Piccadilly,
with safety' for pedestrians visiting the exhibitions.[78] However, whether
it was the jealousy of Cole and the South Kensington 'clique' as identified
by Bowring, or the charms of Burlington House, the members of the
Royal Academy refused to move to Kensington.

The Commission issued its *Fifth Report* in 1867, and though inevitably
it dwelt on the 'irreparable loss' of the Prince Consort, it could point to
solid achievement in the five years since his death. The Memorial to the
1851 Exhibition had been completed, the building of the Central Hall had
been put in train, largely through the financial support of the
Commission, and, though they did not dwell on this, the 1862 Exhibition
had achieved a considerable success in terms of exhibits and exhibitors,
under very unfavourable circumstances, incidentally enabling the
Horticultural Society to capitalize on its grounds, and display its garden
to full advantage. The sale of the 1862 site to the government, albeit on
very generous terms, had enabled the Commission to pay off much of its
outstanding debt, leaving it cash for an endowment. Regular building
agreements on the land outside the 'main square' had created improved
ground rents, whose sales were gradually reducing the main debt to the
Greenwich Commissioners.

An analysis of the financial position in the following year by the
Treasury official Alexander Spearman was on the whole satisfactory, the
Commission had cash reserves of some £30,000, an excess of annual

income over expenditure of £2500, a mortgage reduced from £187,000 to £77,000 and real estate valued at about £437,000. There were liabilities of £50,000 to the Central [Albert] Hall, of which only £2000 had been met, but even so the future looked quite secure. There were two items which underlined a significant worry: there was no allowance made for rent from the Horticultural Society, and the site of the gardens had been included as potential building land at a value of £250,000. However, for the time being the Society under its ageing President, the Duke of Buccleuch, was still endeavouring to make a success of the gardens. An important consideration in giving the Society time to sort out its affairs was doubtless the knowledge of how dear to Prince Albert had been the creation of the gardens, something which would have weighed with those who had worked with him closely, Bowring, Derby as President, and Granville as Chairman of the Finance Committee, and above all Grey, the Prince's former Secretary.

THE ROLE OF EDGAR BOWRING

Bowring was elected to Parliament in the Liberal interest in 1868, and decided to resign his post as Secretary after nearly nineteen years. Until 1864, he had also served in the Board of Trade, which he left with some irritation at the 'shabbiest manner' in which the Treasury had behaved over his pension. As he explained to Grey, his departure from the civil service also meant that 'red tape objections have hitherto prevented my getting a room in Whitehall for our Commission business', and he was reduced to working from home in 69 Westbourne Terrace, but calling every day at the Board of Trade offices for his letters.[79] He hoped to get a room at 10 Downing Street with Lord Derby, but without success. However, though peripatetic in its meeting places, the Commission seems to have met fairly frequently at 32 Abingdon Street between 1866 and 1870, later moving to 5 Upper Kensington Gore, in 1871.

During his time Bowring had seen the Commission transformed from an *ad hoc* body set up to manage an untried and speculative venture to an established private corporation which had significantly changed British national attitudes to industrial education, and had promoted a number of important institutions. His post had been salaried, albeit remaining at the part-time figure of £400 per annum, and though he realized it was not incompatible with a seat in Parliament, he felt he ought to resign. Granville accepted his decision, but welcomed his offer to continue his connection with the Commission, and Bowring was elected a Commissioner in 1869, together with General Charles Grey, Lyon Playfair, and Sir Francis Sandford, former Secretary to the 1862 Commission, now back in Whitehall at the education office. These four appointments signal a change in the make-up of the Commission, from a preponderance of major political figures to civil servants and middle-class movers and shakers, a trend which became more marked as the original grandees died off. In the nineteenth-century way, there were no retirements on the grounds of age, and few resignations, and a limit on either age or length of service was only introduced in the 1980s.

The Prince of Wales was elected a member of the Commission and President in succession to Derby, on 18 February, 1870. Bowring, who expressed apprehension that his parliamentary duties would interfere with the growing demands of the Commission's work[80] was replaced by Lieutenant Colonel Scott, the architect of the Central Hall, and one of Cole's most trusted lieutenants, a significant change for he had not worked with the Prince. Two more deaths further severed the connection with Prince Albert, Lord Derby dying on 23 October, 1869, and General Charles Grey, the man who had perhaps done most to ensure that his master's grand design was carried out, in March 1870. Acting with the discretion natural to a royal servant, he had called the royal influence to his aid to encourage laggard Commissioners, and to keep poor Derby awake at nights worrying over the Central Hall; and by a combination of discreet flattery and gentle bullying he had kept the main lines of the grand design before the Commissioners, despite their individual predilections and outside preoccupations. The connection with the Royal Household was maintained by the election as Commissioners of Major-General Thomas Biddulph (1809–78), former Master of the Royal Household, and now Keeper of the Privy Purse, and Colonel Henry Ponsonby (1825–95), former Equerry to the Prince Consort, and Private Secretary to the Queen.

V

'The Late Lamented Prince': Reassessment after the Death of the Prince Consort 1869–1878

The first meeting after Lord Derby's death was held on 10 February, 1870, at 32 Abingdon Street, which served as the Commission's office. The Commissioners – Bazley, Baring, Gibson, Playfair, Sandford and Vignole, *ex officio* as President of the Institution of Civil Engineers, together with Bowring, appearing as Commissioner for the first time, elected as Chairman A. S. Ayrton (1815–86). Ayrton, who had been Radical Member of Parliament for Tower Hamlets since 1857, and Secretary to the Treasury (1868–9), was now an *ex officio* member, as First Commissioner of Works, since 1869.[1] Though not without ruffling a lot of feathers, he had done a great deal to reorganize the Office of Works in reforming it to reduce the money spent on outside architects, and to ensure the effective use of public money. Despite being the author of an attack on the 1851 Commission some years earlier, he changed his ways, and as Bowring commented, 'in his new position he applied his talents to the service of his quondam foe'.[2]

Lieutenant Colonel Scott had been appointed Secretary the previous July, taking over from Bowring, at the same salary of £400 per annum. Henry Young Darracott Scott (1822–83) was a Devonshire man, educated at Woolwich, who had a successful career in the Royal Engineers at the Royal Military Academy Woolwich, where he assisted in the reorganization of the school, and had trained young engineers in sketching and surveying.

On Fowke's death he had been seconded to work at South Kensington for the Commission, and had inherited the latter's mantle as architect for the Albert Hall. This somewhat curious system was the result of Cole's conviction, gained during the Great Exhibition, that it was essential to have the assistance of Royal Engineer officers and detachments in running the various projects at South Kensington. Like so many South Kensington figures, Scott held a number of interlocking posts, with associated bodies. As an employee of the Commission since 1865, he was simultaneously the architect in charge of the Albert Hall, assistant to Cole as head of the architectural office in the Department of Science and Art, and Honorary Secretary of the Royal Horticultural Society. He was very conscious of his debt to Cole, and was seen as something of a satellite, at least at the beginning of his career.[3]

It was not an easy moment to be taking office at the Commission, since a number of major projects were facing serious problems. Though the South Kensington Museum, the Albertopolis flagship, was still ploughing its aggressive and often irritating way under Henry Cole, the Horticultural Society was unable to fund its rent for the gardens satisfactorily, and there was doubt about the future for the Albert Hall. The government too had proved a poor neighbour; having forced the Commissioners to destroy the 1862 Exhibition Building at considerable expense so that they could build their own museum, 'for seven years the land had remained waste, a sort of potter's field, and a scandal to that part of the metropolis'.[4]

THE NATURAL HISTORY MUSEUM

The Commissioners were forced into very tough action indeed to persuade the government to embark seriously on the construction of what became known as the Natural History Museum. The Bloomsbury natural history collections were never a direct responsibility of the Commission, and therefore their detailed history is not a subject for this book. It was, however, one of the projects where the Commissioners assisted government by providing a site on extremely easy terms, and where, as often happened, the government of the day was damagingly slow to respond. The idea of a separate building for the British Museum's important natural history collections had been put forward by Professor Richard Owen (1804–92), Superintendent of the Department, almost on his arrival there in 1856. He had much of Cole's ability to lobby and interest the great in his projects, but also some of Cole's ability to infuriate and upset his colleagues. The question of additional space for the natural history collections was a sensitive one at the British Museum, where the librarian Antonio Panizzi was the senior official, and the merits of extending Smirke's building or building on a new site were hotly debated. In 1860, the Trustees had accepted the idea of a new building, put forward by Owen the previous year, and had voted to move to South Kensington. The Commissioners had offered them a site on the western side of the main square, where the Western Annexe was later to stand, some 5.5 acres at the favourable price of £10,000 an acre, half its market value. However, the inevitable Select Committee was appointed in 1860, but conflicting statistics about the cost of the move were presented[5] and the presence of William Gregory as Chairman and Elcho ensured that the outcome was unfavourable to South Kensington. Two years later, the bill to remove the collections from Bloomsbury was thrown out by the House of Commons, and the Act authorizing the removal was not passed till 1878. Though the government bought the site of the 1862 building, without the building, in 1863, a change of administration, followed by a grandiose scheme for putting a number of government institutions including the Natural History Museum on the Embankment, delayed matters until 1870. This delay did not assist matters in Bloomsbury, but was even more disastrous in South Kensington, where the whole Commissioners' estate was preju-diced by the view of the empty site. In fact, the state of the area was still a matter for comment in 1907, when Edward VII drew Sir Arthur's Bigge's attention to it.[6]

The original competition had been won by Fowke, on whose death the young Alfred Waterhouse (1830–1905) was appointed to carry out the design. After a number of changes, brought about by financial and admin-istrative decisions, he produced a Romanesque design for a building based on Owen's original plan of accommodation in 1859. The Commissioners were increasingly worried by the government's lack of progress, but gov-ernment economy meant that the building was not started till 1872. Even then, because of inflation in the building trade, the wings on to Exhibition Road and Queen's Gate were cut back. Waterhouse used terracotta exten-sively for the exterior ornament of beasts, birds and plants, using draw-ings and models provided by Robert Owen, the Director of the Museum, for the rarer and extinct species featured both inside and outside the building. This type of decoration had been specified by Owen, and this turned it into a sort of medieval cathedral to the natural sciences. Unfortunately, the difficulty in obtaining the enormous quantity of terra-cotta and other materials meant that the building was delayed and the contractors went bankrupt.

However, the Museum was completed to the Commission's relief in

1881, providing not only an important architectural element in the district, but increasing the scientific content of the estate, something about which the Commissioners were becoming increasingly concerned.[7]

The death of the Prince Consort on 14 December, 1861, had come as a shock to many in England, and nowhere had 'the want' been more keenly felt than in South Kensington. The Prince had not only been able to guarantee royal enthusiasm and government compliance, if not approval, but had also been a very active President of at least three organizations involved in the area. He had gained the respect of a wide range of politicians, not only of like-minded men like Gladstone and Peel, but more volatile figures like Disraeli and Palmerston, who were ready to back him in schemes like the removal of the National Gallery. The tributes of men who had worked with him, like Edgar Bowring, and his files of correspondence at Windsor, make it clear how many schemes originated in his busy mind, or came across his desk. He was seen as a conduit for projects by men like Bennet Woodcroft, and the enthusiasts of the Society of Arts, who promoted the 1851 Exhibition. He was also able to influence if not to control his 'kitchen cabinet'. This ranged from Lord Granville, who had worked loyally to make a success of the Commission for the International Exhibition of 1862, to Henry Cole, who, as Bowring recalled, 'managed, as he himself would be the first to allow, to tread on many toes, leading at times to loud outcries and the discharge of vials of wrath on many innocent heads'.[8] The Prince's influence remained strong in the development of South Kensington as long as those who had worked with him, like Granville, Derby, Grey, Bowring and Cole, remained in positions of influence, but after 1869 they gradually disappeared from the scene, through death or retirement. Henceforth, the Commission would work to a new agenda, no longer with the Prince's Grand Design so constantly before them: even the management of the Commission's business was to change.

The tasks facing General Scott, as Secretary, in 1870, were well rehearsed: as well as the day-to-day running of the Commissioners' estate, the main items were the management of relations with the Horticultural Society, of which he was also Secretary, and the continuing attempt to make it possible for it to meet its financial obligations to the Commissioners, and the preparations for the series of Annual International Exhibitions, on which he had been working with Cole. There was also concern about the finishing of the Albert Hall, where

Scott was executive architect. At this first meeting, in February 1870, the main agenda was the report of the Finance Committee, putting into effect the Commission's decision to embark on the Exhibitions. This had been taken the previous year, at the last meeting chaired by the ageing Lord Derby, at his house in St James's Square.[9]

CHANGES TO THE COMMISSION

At the 89th Commission meeting, held on 18 February, 1870, with Lord Granville in the chair, three new members were added to the Commission – the Prince of Wales, later Edward VII, Prince Christian of Schleswig-Holstein (1831–1917) husband of Princess Helena, who was felt by the Queen to need occupation, and the 15th Earl of Derby (1826–93), who had had a distinguished Conservative political career as Lord Stanley. The Prince of Wales was then elected President, renewing the direct connection between the Commission and the Royal Family. Though General Grey's death, on 31 March, 1870, deprived the Commission of one of its links with the Prince Consort, the connection with the Royal Household was maintained by the election of Colonel Henry Ponsonby (1825–95), Private Secretary to the Queen.

The following meeting was held at Marlborough House, chaired by the Prince, possibly because a deputation of French Commissioners appointed by imperial decree for the 1871 Exhibition was present. As always, the French took foreign exhibitions very seriously; they wished to erect a their own separate gallery, they had appointed a committee of distinguished experts and civil servants for each of the classes of exhibits – the architect Viollet-le-Duc being in charge of 'dessus-industrie'.

1870 saw an unusual number of meetings; another meeting was held in July to elect further Commissioners, the Prince of Teck (1837–1900) husband of Princess Mary of Cambridge, first cousin of the Queen, Earl de Grey, already an *ex officio* member, the architect William Tite and the connoisseur Alexander Beresford-Hope. The Finance Committee was strengthened by the addition of de Grey, Northcote, Sandford and Playfair.

ANNUAL INTERNATIONAL EXHIBITIONS

The nature of international exhibitions was changing, as had been manifested by the Paris Exhibition of 1867, where a much more commercial approach had been developed. To the processes of manufacture had been added fine arts, theatrical performances and various sports intended to demonstrate national characteristics. Nonetheless, though the 1862 Exhibition had put paid to the proposed series of decennial exhibitions on the 1851 model, regular exhibitions were still the objective of many in South Kensington and at the Society of Arts at this time. The idea of annual international exhibitions had been promoted by the Provisional Committee of the Royal Albert Hall, on which Cole was a powerful figure, occupying as he did the position of Vice-President at both the Society of Arts and the Royal Horticultural Society. He had found supporters in Granville, Grey, Thring, Bruce and Bowring, assisted by Henry Scott. Cole had produced a report, which suggested a series of exhibitions, no longer universal but each concentrating on a number of separate classes of exhibit. They were planned to commence in 1871 with an exhibition of Fine and Industrial Art, the former with a wide remit to include painting and sculpture of all kinds, engraving, architecture, designs for manufacture, copies of ancient painting, sculptures and objets d'art, with the rider that 'Scientific Inventions and New Discoveries of all kinds will be admitted'. 'Industrial Art' was rather more restricted, to 'Pottery of all kinds, including that used in building'; 'Educational Works and Appliances', defined as books and maps; 'School Fittings, Furniture and Decoration, Appliances for Physical Training, including Toys and Games, Specimens and Illustrations of Natural History and Physical Science'; and 'Wool and Worsted Fabrics with raw Produce and Machinery for manufactures in the same'.[10]

Cole had never lost sight of the original Society of Arts objective of regular exhibitions, and had gone in for one of his extensive campaigns of lobbying influential figures, including on this occasion the Duke of Buckingham and Chandos, and Earl de Grey, as well as old allies like Lord Granville and General Grey. However, the public appetite for large universal exhibitions had been somewhat satiated, while manufacturers were less ready to support them. The loss of both the 1862 building and the site made it necessary to find another venue on the Commissioners' estate, and Cole and Scott together devised a way of using the as yet uncompleted arcades round the Horticultural Gardens. The project was given impetus by the deliberations of the different national Commissioners meeting at Paris in 1867, which Cole had attended, who set out regulations for the smaller exhibitions which were becoming more popular. In July 1868, together with Grey and Henry Scott, Cole lobbied Lord Derby, getting him to agree that if such smaller exhibitions were to be held the Commission would be the proper authority to conduct them, and promising support to the tune of £50,000.

Four days later, Cole got a formal resolution passed by the Provisional Committee of the Albert Hall, who saw the building as a venue for exhibitions and scientific and academic meetings, as much as for concerts.[11] Scott, too, was a key figure in the project; as a colleague of Cole and architect to the Hall he was an obvious choice for the necessary design work. The Horticultural Society had a lot to gain from regular exhibitions; the profits from the 1862 Exhibition had demonstrated the financial benefits of visitors' use of the gardens. Indeed this alone enabled them to pay the rent due to the Commissioners. By April 1868 Cole could tell Grey that the Society would cooperate over the annual exhibitions and associated flower shows.

The original scheme for housing the exhibits, devised apparently by Scott and his assistant, J. W. Wild, was for a large glass building to the south of the garden, together with glass galleries on top of the arcades. This scheme was estimated to cost some £175,000, which was beyond the means of the Commissioners, and had to be cut back. The latter had been unwilling to commit more funds to a project in which there was not a great deal of faith. However, the Queen had intimated her support, because both hall and gardens had been projects of Prince Albert's. To further attract the royal attention, Grey had reported that he had put up the Prince of Teck, for the Horticultural Society, with the idea that in due course he might follow the Duke of Buccleuch as President, He also suggested that once the exhibitions were established, there would be little difficulty 'in giving Prince Christian [husband of Princess Helena] much interesting occupation in superintending & directing part of the preliminary arrangements'.[12] Under some royal pressure, and with Grey added to the Commission in June 1869, the Commissioners agreed to back the project, but within the limits proposed by Sir Alexander Spearman (1793–1874) in his report on their finances.

THE COMMISSIONERS' FINANCES

It was estimated that an additional £100,000 would be required to finance such a series. Sir Alexander Spearman had investigated the possibility of borrowing such a sum the previous year. He reported that a further debt might cripple the Commission's activities, particularly if they had to find a second mortgagee. The Commissioners were already committed to further expenditure on the Albert Hall, where seats were not selling as fast as Cole had hoped. There might also be the opportunity of purchasing the Eden Lodge Estate which lay between the Commission's land and that of Freake to the east. If the Exhibitions were as profitable as Cole had anticipated in his report, Spearman conceded that there would, of course, be no difficulty, but if the Commissioners were not in a position to pay the interest regularly, the lender might foreclose on the more desirable parts of the estate. He suggested two further sources of funds: the government might be persuaded to buy the refreshment rooms which been constructed for the 1862 Exhibition for some £20,000, or to sell back at the original price the still vacant site of that Exhibition, which he thought the Commissioners could use a great deal more profitably. The Finance Committee, which seems at this time to have taken many of the major decisions as well as being responsible for all the day-to-day activities of the Commission, was not deterred by this gloomy forecast, and arranged to borrow the further £150,000 from the Lords of the Admiralty on the existing security at 4 per cent. They had also approached a number of noblemen and gentlemen to form a General Purposes Committee to bring the exhibitions into being. It was to be chaired by Earl de Grey and Ripon (1827–1909), later the Marquess of Ripon, Lord President of the Council, and therefore responsible for the Department of Science and Art. He was supported by several other peers, the indefatigable Granville, the 5th Marquess of Lansdowne, Lord Devon, and Lord Northbrook (1826–1904), nephew of Thomas Baring (1799–1873), and the statesman W. E. Forster, then Vice-President of the Council and much involved with education, together with a number of South Kensington veterans, Stafford Northcote, Bruce, Sandford, Bowring, Gibson, Cole, Playfair and Henry Thring.

    Financial limitations dictated that Scott's proposals were cut back to completing the arcades in the Royal Horticultural Gardens, building galleries behind the eastern and western ranges and using the arcades as terraces for his first-floor galleries. Lucas Brothers, successors to Kelk, won the contract, and arrangements were entered into with the Horticultural Society for the use of their gardens during the Exhibition. Provision was made for the individual national commissions to build additional galleries on the vacant land next to the arcades on the east and west. Care was taken not to impair the possible development of the frontages on to

Fig 20. The South Kensington Contractors: Mr, later Sir, John Kelk (centre) and the
Lucas Brothers, who were not only the contractors for the 1862 Exhibition Building
but also built elsewhere in the area, including the South Kensington Museum,
the Albert Memorial and the Albert Hall.

Prince Albert and Exhibition Roads, and the point was made that the
presence of buildings between the Horticultural Gardens and any new
private houses would prevent the owners of the latter complaining about
such buildings in the future.[13]

Cole suggested that roads to connect the hall with the northern
entrances of the Horticultural Gardens should be constructed, but as this
created problems of intrusion on existing tenants, the matter was left to
the Finance Committee.

The Finance Committee reported on the arrangements for the Ex-
hibition, including regulations for any national Commission, not only the
French, who wished to erect supplementary galleries outside the arcades.
They had added Prince Christian and Ponsonby to the General Purposes
Committee. They reported that they were arranging for a tunnel to con-
nect the railway station with the site of the 1862 building, something for
which both the promoters of the Albert Hall and the General Purposes
Committee for the 1871 Exhibition had been pressing.[14]

Because of concern over the pirating of inventions, an Act was passed
in July 1870 to ensure some protection for inventors of new products

exhibited at the series of annual exhibitions, or at similar exhibitions to be promoted by the Board of Trade to promote British art or industry.

THE 1871 INTERNATIONAL EXHIBITION

Foreign affairs were to intrude again, as they had in 1860–1, and a special meeting was held at Marlborough House in April 1871 to assist French exhibitors unable to bring goods from a beleaguered Paris 'under the existing impediments'. M. Sommerard, Commissioner-General for France, attended the meeting, armed with a defiant letter from French manufacturers:

> Besides, if our arms have been unsuccessful against numbers, it should be well understood abroad that France is not downcast – that she has not lost the rank which belongs to her in civilized Europe . . . she is prepared to give signs of existence by showing the powers of her productive resources.

A number of British collectors of French works of art, including Matthew Digby Wyatt and John Kelk, were invited to the meeting to be asked to lend items from their collections.

The 1871 Exhibition was opened on the traditional 1 May by the Prince of Wales, and in due course welcomed over a million visitors. It was a success, acclaimed by press and public, and netted the Commissioners a handsome profit. The Commission reported confidently to the Home Secretary on its opening, explaining that drawing on the experience of the last twenty years, they had made a number of changes in the organization. Many of the recent exhibitions had been too large and contained a number of undistinguished objects, while the giving of prizes often depended more on the national make-up of juries than on the merits of the objects exhibited. For these reasons, henceforth the numbers of categories exhibited would be smaller, though every year works of Fine Art, Scientific Invention and Horticulture would be included, and the objects would be exhibited by class or category, rather than on a national basis. With the intention of making things easier for the exhibitors, particularly perhaps those without a well-oiled national organization behind them, considerable investment had been made on fittings, furniture and cases for the exhibition galleries. The Commissioners pointed out that it had always been the Prince Consort's wish that objects should had be exhibited by class rather than by country, but had to admit that in the current year it had been unable to carry this rule out without exception in the Fine Art classes. They proposed to abandon the giving of prizes together with the jury system.

A month later, the General Purposes Committee was able to report that the Exhibition had opened satisfactorily. The finances were apparently promising, and they hoped to be able to pay back some £20,000 of the expenditure on the buildings, £75,000 on the permanent galleries and £15,000 on the temporary. Their optimism was such that they had suggested the use of 4 Upper Kensington Gore, next to Scott's office at number 5, as offices for the staff administering the international exhibitions, while they submitted proposals for an ambitious programme for the annual exhibitions, with different types of exhibit each year.

The categories of exhibit seem somewhat ill-assorted, apparently intended to attract a wide range of manufacturing interests, but may have just been rather miscellaneous – a long way from the heady 'universal' days of 1851. Thus 1872 would feature 'Cotton and all its uses, Jewellery, Musical instruments, Acoustical Apparatus and Experiments', and 'Paper, Stationery and Printing' in all its forms from 'Paper, Card and Millboard' through 'Account Books' to 'Letterpress, Plate, and all other modes of Printing'. The 1873 list included 'Silk and Velvet', 'Steel, Cutlery and Edge Tools', 'Surgical instruments and Appliances', 'Carriages not connected with Rail or Tram Roads', 'Substances used as Food' and 'Cooking and its Science'. By 1876 'Philosophical Instruments, and 'Processes depending upon their use' and the 'Uses of Electricity' were included, and for 1880 was planned the exhibition of 'Chemical Substances and Products, and Experiments, Pharmaceutical Processes' together with 'Articles of Clothing comprising Hats and Caps, Millinery, hosiery and Gloves, and Boots and Shoes'.[15]

THE MANAGEMENT OF THE COMMISSION

The 1871 Exhibition was a success, and inspired a hope that the exhibitions would provide an income for the Commission. Henry Thring, who was to be one of the longest-serving Commissioners (from 1861 until 1907), wrote a report on the Commissioners' estate in 1871, reviewing the first twenty years of the Commission's existence. He was able to point out how shrewd the purchase had been: it had cost £342,000, and though thereafter some £450,000 worth of land had been disposed of, it had nonetheless been valued recently at £500,000. However, he had to point out that the Prince Consort had been wrong in putting his faith in either dealing with government or attracting scientific or artistic national societies to the area. He concluded that 'neither the Scientific Societies nor the Government can be expected to take the initiative [in] the South Kensington Estate', and that 'Science and Art, by themselves, will not yield a profit'. It was therefore up to the Commissioners themselves to develop South Kensington, and, again, they alone would have to find the funds. One of the opportunities for the Commissioners to make money out of Science and Art was through the International Exhibitions, which should be allowed to develop a commercial aspect, though this element of the 'Bazaar' should not be made too obvious. He also pointed out the importance of coordinating the management of the Albert Hall, the gardens and the International Exhibitions so that they were mutually supporting. He also pointed out the opportunity for 'making at South Kensington a square unrivalled in any city for beauty and utility', and how important it was for the development of the estate to retain the open space provided by the gardens. This required development in partnership with government, which the Commissioners could reasonably expect in view of the way that they had subsidized government through the 'valuable Collections presented for public use . . . and the great pecuniary sacrifice made by them in selling the land . . . to the Government'. He felt that the government had betrayed the Commissioners, once by not making an effective and impressive use of the 1862 Exhibition site, sold at such a generous price, and secondly, by refusing to let the Commissioners buy it back and develop it. Therefore, since the Commissioners alone were able and ready to develop the estate for the benefit of the country, they would have to take the only means at their disposal of improving the financial position of the Commission, promotion of the International Exhibitions.[16]

The following year, visitor numbers fell by a half, causing concern about the financial position of the Commission. On 10 July, 1872, Granville, as Chairman of the Finance Committee, reported to the Commission that the Committee had appointed Spearman, Bazley and W. Anderson 'to inquire into and report on Financial State of the Affairs of the Commission'. A fortnight later the first report was presented, saying that on present showing the Annual Exhibition accounts were balancing, pointing out that though the Commissioners' capital debt was just under £210,000, its capital assets could be computed at over £600,000 in houses and lands, over £4500 in stocks, and eight hundred seats in the Albert Hall, valued at £80,000. On the other hand, the income and expenditure account was not satisfactory: the Commissioners spent some £9744 per annum in mortgage and debt charges, management and office expenses, while their income from rents and stocks was not above £5000. It was felt that the notional income from the Horticultural Gardens and the Exhibitions was too speculative to be relied upon.

They also considered a report from the Commission's Surveyor, Henry A. Hunt, CB, advocating a more aggressive attitude to development of the estate, to provide capital to pay off the mortgage debt. The three employees, Cole, Hunt and Scott, were asked to leave and the Commissioners were left to deliberate. Their conclusions were not surprising: they were almost all senior politicians or civil servants in a generation when the solution to any problem was the appointment of at least a Parliamentary Select Committee, if not a Royal Commission, followed by the publication of a 'blue book'. A further committee of Ripon, Sandford, Playfair and Thring was appointed to report on the 'best system of executive management of the affairs of the Commission'.[17]

THE COMMITTEE OF MANAGEMENT

With an expedition and authority surprising to a modern generation, the Cabinet minister and the three senior civil servants reported a fortnight later at an unfashionable August meeting. They pointed out that the affairs of the Commission in three different spheres were handled by three different committees, thus dislocating the interests of the Commission, dividing responsibility and introducing confusion into the accounts: the Exhibitions were managed by the General Purposes Committee, the Horticultural Gardens by the Expenses Committee and the Albert Hall by the Council of the Hall attended by nominees of the Commissioners. They suggested a radical reform of Commission business: the annual appointment of an executive committee of not more than seven Commissioners with powers to borrow money, and to manage the Commission's financial affairs, one of whom should be appointed as a salaried Executive Officer, and paid a percentage of the profits on the management of the estate. The Committee should meet weekly, and to provide continuity the Commission itself should meet not less than once a month. Another Commissioner, not a member of the committee, should be appointed Treasurer, to countersign every cheque. The Committee would be responsible for expenditure, the conduct of the Exhibitions, and the related negotiations with foreign governments, the management of the estate, and for coordinating the Commission's interests in the different spheres, Hall, Exhibition and Gardens.

Their choice for Executive Officer was Cole, with whom they had entered into negotiation. Though 'most willing to advance the interests of the Commission' he was not prepared to accept payment for his services at the moment, though he had told them that when he retired from his government post, he would be ready to 'meet the wishes of the Committee'. Until then they accepted he should continue to work unpaid, but suggested he should be elected a Commissioner, put on the Committee of Management and given the title of Acting Commissioner. Meanwhile, until the appointment of the Executive Officer, the Secretary should attend the meetings of the Committee, and carry out its instructions. They added a rider that the money, £121,000, spent on permanent works for the Exhibitions might be capitalized, making the annual deficit less serious, and that plans for the 1873 Exhibition were so advanced that despite some prospective difficulties it would have to take place. The recommendations were accepted, Cole and Anderson were appointed Commissioners and the Duke of Edinburgh, Sandford, Playfair and Thring were appointed members of the Committee of Management, with the proviso that others might be added by the absent President before the first meeting scheduled for November.[18]

This is quite a startling series of recommendations, which perhaps hints at an element of the Augean stable about the Commission's office practices. Certainly the Commission had developed in a very 'topsy-like' manner, increasing its responsibilities with each development at South Kensington, without necessarily ever analysing its role or the way it was carrying it out. The Commission's own office, in one of the eastern Kensington Gore houses at this moment, appears to have been staffed by Scott as Secretary, who was paid a separate, and larger, salary for his work for the Annual International Exhibitions, L. C. Sayles, Clerk to the Commissioners, and an accountant, James Richards, who seems to have also worked for the Royal Horticultural Society. The committee of enquiry does not seem to have been critical of Bowring, who was appointed Treasurer, or of the other long-serving figure, Lord Granville, who, though the Finance Committee, of which he had been Chairman since 1850, had been discontinued, continued to play an important role.

It is also a tribute to the way that Cole was seen by his contemporaries: Playfair had, of course, worked with him for twenty years, though the two men had different backgrounds, and different objectives. Henry Thring was a leading parliamentary draughtsman, the first parliamentary Counsel to the Treasury ever appointed, and ultimately a member of the House of Lords. Sandford had been Secretary to the Commission for the Exhibition of 1862, and, now at the Department of Education, was able to judge of Cole's work at South Kensington. The Earl of Ripon, son of the Prime Minister Lord Goderich, a Christian Socialist and follower of F. D. Maurice, a path which somewhat unexpectedly led him ultimately into the Roman Catholic Church, had had a distinguished ministerial career under Palmerston and Gladstone.

Cole had been a dominating figure in South Kensington, earning the sobriquet 'King Cole', even used by the Princess of Wales, and for ever enshrined in the Tissot cartoon of 1871. Though he was less close to the Royal Household than he had been in Grey's lifetime, Cole knew a number of Commissioners personally, several of whom had held ministerial office at the Privy Council, and were therefore responsible for the Department of Science and Art. He had stayed with his various chiefs at their country homes, at Studley Royal with Earl de Grey, at Highclere with Earl Carnarvon, at Althorp with Earl Spencer, been welcomed to Walmer Castle by Earl Granville, and even spent a Friday to Monday at Sandringham to celebrate the birthday of the Prince of Wales. These visits provided an opportunity to pursue various projects, and to lobby for different interests, a practice which did not always make him popular with his colleagues.

At its next meeting, the Commission reconsidered the burden they proposed to lay on the members of the Committee of Management, and decided to pay them an attendance fee of three guineas, up to a maximum annual expenditure by the Committee of £1000. The Committee was to report at its first meeting on the Commission's relations with the different committees and societies, and 'to submit a scheme for the future conduct of the business of the Commission'.[19]

The new committee met first on the 13 November, 1872, with a quorum of William Anderson, Francis Sandford, Playfair and Thring. Edinburgh, the nominal Chairman, was not present, but he was to be asked to appoint a deputy in his absence. The first conclusion the members came to was that it was doubtful whether members of the

Commission could accept any payment, a matter pursued through several meetings, and finally settled, in the negative, by an appeal through Fladgate, the Commission's solicitor, to the Attorney-General. Though reluctant to work without payment, the members of the Committee met almost weekly, dealing with every aspect of the Commission's affairs from organization of the 1873 Exhibition to fixing the salary of Sayles at £350 per annum, and paying him a gratuity of £100. They took over the job of the General Purposes Committee, as far as the Exhibitions went, and that of the Finance Committee, and had to deal with a particularly difficult period in the Commission's relations with the Horticultural Gardens. The burden seems to have fallen on Playfair, Sandford, Anderson and Cole, with Scott in attendance. It was agreed that the Earl of Carnarvon (1831–90) would join the Committee as Chairman after Easter 1873. One of his first acts was to change its name to the Board of Management, and he chaired the Board until the following year when his duties as Colonial Secretary made it impossible. He was succeeded by Earl Spencer (1835–1910), who served as Chairman until 1881.

In the summer of 1873, Cole finally retired from the South Kensington Museum, accepting that under the ruling about payment he would have to retire as Commissioner if he were to be paid. He resigned on 17 June, 1873, retaining the title of Acting Commissioner, and was awarded a salary of £1000 per annum, subsequently raised to £1500. He thus became a paid member of the Commission staff again after some twenty years at the Department of Science and Art. He played a very important part in the work of the Commission during this period, something in which he took great satisfaction. He recorded in his diary that on one occasion, when he was dining with Lord Carnarvon at the Travellers' Club, the latter explained his view of the office organization:

> He shwd me his draft of arrangements between Scott & myself. He admitted that the Commn. were only lawmakers. Bd of Management were the Ministers. He Secy of State. Scott Parliamentary Secy, I permanent Secy. . . . He sd he wd not be Chairman of the Bd to have Acts of Management repudiated by Commissioners.

This was not approved by Scott, who took the view that 'all executive action was wrong and that Lord Carnarvon ought not to sign letters'.[20]

THE INTERNATIONAL EXHIBITIONS

The major concern was the organization of the current Exhibition, over-shadowed by the major international exhibition in Vienna to which other countries were sending their best products. The French Commission refused to participate at all in London in 1873, and even objected to a local French voluntary committee[21] so their Annexe was given over to an exhibition of carriages. The Commissioners attempted to recruit new exhibitors in the Japanese and the Danes, and an Exhibition from the Australian Colonies was put together to fill the Belgian Annexe. A wide-ranging Cookery Exhibition was a feature, the organizers developed the attractions, including a demonstration of German military cookery by a small detachment of the imperial army, and other cookery designed for specialist constituencies like workhouse inhabitants and prisoners. The most damaging issue was the turmoil at the Royal Horticultural Society which led to a total refusal to permit any use of the gardens for visitors to the Exhibition, and necessitated expensive and inconvenient alterna-tive arrangements.

The first exhibition in 1871 had been a success, attracting over 1,140,000 visitors and netting the Commissioners a handsome profit, of £17,671 3s. 1d. The following year saw a fall in visitor numbers by a half to 647,000 and a loss of over £5000. Visitor numbers were just below half a million in 1873 and 1874, with even more disastrous financial con-sequences, turning the 1871 profit of nearly £18,000 to a loss of £17,000 in 1874. The Commissioners estimated they had spent £126,383 on the construction of the galleries, including the conservatories, the connection with the Royal Albert Hall in which some of the exhibits were housed, the refreshment rooms, the provision of lighting, heating, the glass cases and other fittings, including hangings, curtains, blinds, druggets and so forth.

There were other extra expenses including £1840 for medals given in 1873 and 1874, £2065 for the opening ceremonial for 1871 and 1872, and £278 12s. 8d. for arrangements for the Shah of Persia's visit in 1873. The Commissioners had continued the earlier policy of buying some of the most interesting exhibits for display in British collections. They calculat-ed they had lost some £22,254 over the series.

However, it was far from being a total disaster, and, as Cole pointed out, some 2,755,901 visitors had seen the four exhibitions, and if one divided the loss by such a number it could be calculated that each person

had been enlightened at a cost of under 2d. each, which compared well
with the cost of visitors to the British Museum at 4s., and to 1s. 3d. for
visitors to South Kensington Museum.[22] Despite the failure of the series,
the Commissioners do not seem to have blamed Henry Cole for the de-
bacle though he had been a leading light in putting the project forward,
from its inception in 1869, when he was still Secretary of the Department
of Science and Art.

THE END OF EXHIBITIONS

At the first meeting in 1874, the Commissioners decided to put an end to
any further exhibitions after the one then preparing, the Prince of Wales
saying that he wished to get rid of exhibitions, and that 'his father, the
wisest of men, wished not to have any more'. Lord Carnarvon resigned
because of his duties as Secretary of State for the Colonies, warning the
assembled Commissioners that the work was only just begun, and that
the difficulties were perhaps greater than before. He considered that 'the
future conduct of the affairs of the Commission would require constant
attention, care and wariness; the property was . . . large, and the interests
involved in its administration large and most important'.[23] Lord Spencer
was elected to the Commission, and immediately took on the chairmanship; other members of the Board of Management were the 5th Marquess
of Lansdowne (1845–1927), Bartle Frere and Sir William Anderson.

THE SPECIAL COMMITTEE OF ENQUIRY

Carnarvon's words so alarmed the Prince of Wales, that he immediately
set up a further special committee of inquiry including Granville, Ripon,
Spencer, Carnarvon and Playfair. Its terms were very wide – it was to
investigate 'the general financial policy and position of the Commission,
and its relations for the future with the Annual International Exhibitions,
the Royal Albert Hall, and the Royal Horticultural Gardens; and also
with regard to any further uses which be made of the buildings and property of the Commission for the advancement of the objects intrusted to it,
and to offer suggestions for the future management of the business and
property of the Commission'.

The Committee met a month later at Lord Granville's house in Bruton
Street, hearing first of all from Henry Cole. They recommended that
Cole's engagement should be terminated at the end of the year, but that
he should be paid £2000 for his work for the exhibitions before 1873.[24]

In the event, despite the difficulties with the Horticultural Society the exhibition that summer was not the least successful. However, Cole refused the money for reasons that are not clear, and spent much of the year working out his scheme for the future of South Kensington.[25] The Committee of Enquiry, realizing the two bodies duplicated their functions, eventually took over the management of the Commissioners' business from the Board of Management in 1876. They provided a series of reports which altered the emphasis of the Commission's work and was to lead in due course to a new role.

Cole's departure from an active role in South Kensington, possibly accelerated by some disagreements with Scott, was not unforeseen, and was more than welcome to many, both from South Kensington itself and in government. Ponsonby wrote to his wife of Lord Ripon's loaded joke at breakfast at Balmoral, that the vacancy on the Spanish throne could be conveniently filled by Cole. Cole did not fight for the exhibitions, but immediately started work on proposals for an industrial university, and to develop his views on the future of South Kensington.

Cole's methods and projects had irritated many at South Kensington, as did his 'retirement' to 33 Thurloe Square just across the road from the Museum, whence he visited it or the gardens nearly every day. However, Cole had virtually created South Kensington, and as Bowring reflected, 'revolutions in the administration of art and science are, I suppose, not to be effected by rose-water, any more than are French revolutions'. However, at this time, a number of threatened changes much alarmed Cole, including Treasury economy over purchasing objects, proposals to put the expenditure on building under the control of the Office of Works, and even the threat to give control of his beloved South Kensington Museum to the Trustees of the British Museum. He identified the author of these economies as Robert Lowe (1811–92) Gladstone's Chancellor of the Exchequer from 1868 to 1873, whom he attacked in a public and official speech in London in 1873 to the embarrassment even of Lord Granville. Cole compounded his problems by suggesting publicly that it might be best if the government were to buy the Commissioners' estate, for national objects, though retaining the Horticultural Gardens as a public garden, a scheme which he later worked into a pamphlet.[26]

It fell to Ponsonby to explain Cole's grievances over what was happening in the area to the Queen, who had always taken a great interest in Cole's welfare, as one of the Prince's 'most useful Agents'. Indeed, on these grounds, some ten years earlier he had been bailed out by a gift from the Queen, when he had debts of over £1200.[27] By 1873, even the Queen could not save him, and Ponsonby did not feel that she would want to listen to Cole's 'indignant denunciations of Mr Lowe', though he advised her that

> no change in the Constitution of South Kensington should be made without giving Your Majesty ample time to consider it . . .
>
> It appears that Mr. Cole has hitherto exercised despotic power at South Kensington. The President of the Council has never been strong enough to oppose him, and he has always had his own way. The Government (some of them) object to this and wish to place the Museum under the Trustees of the British Museum.[28]

The Cabinet itself was divided on the future of the Museum, not all of the government approving of the idea of giving the British Museum control of South Kensington. In the event, it remained under the control of the Education Department, with which it was 'virtually merged'. Overall control passed to the Secretary of the Education Department, Sir Francis Sandford, himself an old South Kensington hand, with the Macleod of Macleod as his deputy. Philip Cunliffe-Owen (1828–94), brother to Captain Henry Owen, succeeded Cole as Director of the Museum, with Major Donnelly as Director of Science, and Richard Redgrave in charge of art.[29]

Another problem which exercised some of the Commissioners was an honour for Cole on retirement. As Ponsonby told his wife, the Prince of Wales

> sees his faults but maintains with some truth that the success of South Kensington is entirely owing to him and is urgent that he should be made a K. C. B. I know that Gladstone is not eager about this and last year convinced the Queen that it was not desirable, chiefly because any honour to Cole would have immediately opened the vials of wrath of all his enemies upon him and Cole K. C. B. would have been more obnoxious to them than Cole C. B.

Gladstone avoided the matter for some time by claiming that there were no vacancies in the second class of the Bath, but Disraeli, though commenting that 'these civil servants are no longer content with the simple honor of knighthood', which had satisfied Sir Isaac Newton and Walter Raleigh, finally found a vacancy for Cole in 1875.[30]

Even after he retired Cole could not leave South Kensington alone, and provoked further irritation by publishing a pamphlet in 1876 on the use of the ground at South Kensington, on the lines he had earlier developed. He had two main preoccupations, the first the iniquity, as he saw it, of the Commissioners selling off land worth £103,500 for plots for private building, citing many authorities from Prince Albert to Bowring and Disraeli to show that 'the main square' within Prince Albert and Exhibition Roads had always been intended for public purposes only. Pertinently he quoted the Prince on 'the evils which have unfortunately so often arisen in practice in this country from *a want of foresight* in this respect, attention having generally been confined to the absolute and pressing requirements of the moment without providing for their inevitable extension'. He reminded the public of Bowring's plea to government in 1852 for further funds, on the grounds that the Commissioners were 'very sensible of the extreme importance of securing, for the national objects to which it is proposed to devote the whole of the estate purchased by them, *the absolute possession of all the land that is included within the main roads*'.

Cole's second concern was with the position of the Horticultural Society, the future of the gardens, and the losses which could be incurred by the debenture-holders, who might be led to 'regret having placed their confidence in the plans of the Prince Consort, and lent their money to realise them'. He went on to propose various schemes for solving the problems of the Commissioners without aborting the Prince Consort's grand design. He estimated the present value of the galleries and the gardens within them at £675,000 – one scheme was to sell the area to the government at half its value, some £337,000–350,000, on condition that they paid off the debentures. The part of the open space not wanted for public buildings would be preserved. The conservatory should be removed southwards to the gardens proper, enabling the Royal Albert Hall to build a more suitable southern entrance. The ante-garden to the south could then become the site for a 'Museum of Industrial Science, allowing modern inventions in Science and Machinery in Motion to be exhibited as at the *Conservatoire des Arts et Métiers* at Paris'. This would be 'a cheap purchase for the public', would enable the Commissioners to pay off their mortgage, the debenture-holders would be reimbursed, and the Horticultural Society be relieved of its embarrassments. He felt that the government, already maintaining nearly twenty parks and gardens in the London area, could easily manage one more. He seems originally to have suggested that the Commissioners might remain in control of part of their estate, but concluded 'I consider that the sale of the whole to the Government at a moderate price the preferable arrangement'.

Ponsonby enquired discreetly what various Commissioners thought about Cole's scheme. It does not seem to have been dismissed out of hand though he found a certain cynicism about Cole's attitude.[31] The Duke of Edinburgh, the Queen's second son, was very outspoken:

> I felt that there must be some dangerous and underhand proceedings going on the part of Sir H. C. and wished Sir T. [Biddulph] and yourself to be forewarned and forearmed so that the Q. might not find herself in the position of unnecessarily or unknowingly lending her hand to upsetting a Royal Commission apptd by herself of which the P. of Wales is President in succession to my father . . . I may add that [in] nearly every case in which any blame could possibly attach itself to the Commission the acts were brought about by Sir H. C. and that now (his not being a Commissioner) his present action is simply meddlesome interference.

Lord Spencer was discreet, saying that he would rather talk than write on the subject, but was perhaps more dismissive of Cole than of his proposals:

> [Cole] is always driving at something and one never knows where and when his explosion will come.
>
> I hardly think that the Government would like the land but if they would I as a Commissioner would not object to being relieved of the duties attaching to the position.
>
> I hope that matters will be allowed to remain quiet at S. Kensington for the present. We must reconsider our position in 3 years or less now, when the India Office lease concludes & until then if we can it is desirable to sit still, but a final smash of the Horticultural [Society] or the Albert Hall might hurry the crisis.
>
> Our position is financially strong, but what duties belong to the Commissioners are not agreeable to perform or easy.[32]

In April 1876, Cole appears to have suggested to Ponsonby that the Commissioners

> should dissolve themselves, the reason for this suggestion in Sir Henry Cole's opinion being, that they have ceased to carry out the wishes and intentions of the Prince Consort . . . moreover the Albert Hall itself is now in very eminent danger of being diverted to purposes entirely at variance to the Memory of the Prince Consort, and Sir Henry thinks that the Commission as such ought not to exist when this is done. Sir H. Cole has a scheme that the Government should purchase the whole of the Ground that remains in the hands of the Commissioners and make it Government or Crown Property.[33]

Little further action seems to have been taken over this scheme which in some ways echoed that put forward by Ayrton some ten years before.

DOMESTIC DEVELOPMENT ON THE ESTATE

Development on the estate had also been intended to follow a strict plan. The 'main square' between Kensington Gore and Cromwell Road, and Exhibition Road and Prince Albert Road, had always been seen as the focus of the Commissioners' interest, with the outlying portions regarded as sources of funds for the central development. Though the possibility of developing the Western and Eastern Annexes, the land on the extreme east and west, had been considered, they were safeguarded for possible sites for institutions. There was, however, increasing concern over the size of the Commissioners' mortgage to the Lords of the Admiralty (who had succeeded the Greenwich Hospital Commissioners), of £208,500, on which they were paying £8744 per annum.

In 1872, Henry A. Hunt, the government surveyor who managed the Commissioners' estate, advised the Commissioners that the estate, even after the generous sales to the government, and the lease to the Albert Hall, was worth over £500,000, and urged them to pay off their debt. Without interfering with the annexes, seen as useful adjuncts to the forthcoming Annual International Exhibitions, he suggested that some land at the north end of Prince Albert Road (now Queen's Gate) should be sold for building. The Commission owned a small strip of land on the west side of Exhibition Road, which lay between Eden (now Lowther) Lodge and the roadway, and this was sold very profitably to Mr Lowther.

The other land facing north on to Kensington Gardens and Hyde Park, either side of the Albert Hall, he suggested should be sold for 'Building Leases at Ground Rents'. Ground rents on the existing leasehold property should be capitalized at a relatively generous thirty-three years' purchase, leaving untouched the rack-rented property, which provided a good return. The Horticultural Gardens should not be disturbed, but he advised the letting or sale of the South Galleries, the former Refreshment Room to the 1862 Exhibition.[34]

In 1878 the Commissioners could report that by such sales they had reduced the debt to £162,039 13s. 2d. in gilts (cash equivalent about £155,000), thus improving their income. They had also taken steps to let building sites at the north-west corner of the estate on the eastern side of Prince Albert's Road (now known increasingly as Queen's Gate), and a large site on the east of the Albert Hall.[35] This site was particularly important in terms of the Commissioners' revised approach to development. A deal had been struck with a commercial developer from Kensington, Thomas Hussey, for the whole site at a rent of £3150 a year; in addition, Hussey was to make the necessary road from Exhibition Road round the back of the Horticultural Society Garden arcades. Hussey's original proposal was for a row of large houses on the important site facing the park and Kensington Road. Lord Spencer had some misgivings about the design, and the Commissioners stipulated that the design should be 'vetted' by Norman Shaw, who had recently completed the adjacent Lowther Lodge, and was working on a series of distinguished and prestigious private houses in Queen's Gate. As so often happens, there were a number of changes of plan and design before the development was complete. Though Hussey also employed Driver and Rew, a commercial firm, it was Shaw who was employed to design the final scheme, submitted to Lord Leighton in February 1880 for approval. This was not one large block in imitation of Queen Anne's Mansions in Westminster, but three blocks of flats, erected between 1879 and 1887, and skilfully designed to provide an impressive façade to the park, and yet give the maximum of accommodation.[36] The later block on the more southerly site, now Albert Court, was to turn out a much more difficult matter.

The private houses on the estate designed by Shaw are well described elsewhere, but they are such an important and interesting group that they deserve mention, both for their own importance and their significance to the estate. The four owners were all friends, belonging to the same *haute bourgeois* circle. The first house (1874–6) was number 196, Queen's Gate, designed for J. P. Heseltine, an acquaintance of William Morris and the Whistler circle, followed in 1884–5 by number 180, a wittily designed and elegantly equipped house for Colonel H. F. Makins, an owner rich enough to make his own road off Queen's Gate to serve the mews. Frederick White, a cement manufacturer who was much involved in both the planning and the external appearance of his house, at number 170, went first to Philip Webb, then to Shaw on the grounds the latter was more open to suggestions from the building owner, resulting in 'the most masterly in restraint of any of Shaw's houses'. White's interest in architecture was also demonstrated in the way in which fireplaces and other fittings from demolished buildings from Millbank and elsewhere in London were incorporated into the building. The last of the four was number 185, of 1890, for William Vivian, a connection of the Makins family.[37]

These houses rank with any that Shaw designed in Chelsea, or with the George and Peto Arts and Crafts houses in Harrington Gardens, and indicate that Queen's Gate was beginning to be seen as fashionable among the intelligentsia. They made curious neighbours for the earlier stucco-fronted houses of Douglas and other 1850 developers, some of which indeed had to be refronted in brick before they would sell.

NEW INSTITUTIONS ON THE ESTATE

Having decided to terminate the series of exhibitions, the Commissioners had to find new uses for the land and buildings. Though they were able to sell some of the glass cases, and other fittings, from the Exhibition, they had to purchase the purpose-built Belgian and French Annexes. However, the two lines of galleries some 600 feet long, behind the arcades, did in fact complement the latter, and provided the surround to the gardens, which had always been thought desirable. The centre of the estate was beginning to show a certain coherence, with the Albert Hall at the north linked through the great Conservatory and the Northern Arcades to the Eastern and Western Galleries and Arcades. The southern end of the 'main square' was occupied by the site of the 1862 Exhibition, the 'potter's field', on which the Natural History Museum was slowly rising. Between it and the more elaborately laid out part of the Horticultural Gardens was the 'ante-garden', bounded on the south by the former refreshment rooms of the 1862 Exhibition, and entered from the east via the offices and rooms of the Horticultural Society. The gardens themselves were very popular with the members of the Society 'living in the South Kensington district', but who were anxious that the public should be excluded.

The growing institutions of South Kensington were hungry for space, and the Commissioners found it easy to find new uses – the Eastern Galleries were leased by the Secretary of State for India to accommodate the Indian Museum, subsequently part of the South Kensington Museum. It remained in the Eastern Galleries, as the Indian Section of the Victoria and Albert Museum, until after the Second World War, when the Galleries themselves were demolished. The Southern Galleries went to the Office of Works at £1500 a year, while the Western Galleries were acquired in due course by the Department of Science and Art, for the display of a collection of scientific instruments.

The failure of the International Exhibitions was a catalyst bringing a number of changes to the Commission and in the broader context to South Kensington. Cole was right, as so often, about the need for effective solution of various South Kensington dilemmas, and probably right in his implied conclusion that the Commissioners might not be setting about solving them in a very effective manner. The two most vulnerable institutions were, of course, the Horticultural Gardens and the Albert Hall.

THE ROYAL HORTICULTURAL GARDENS

Had the Exhibitions succeeded it would have made all the difference to the future of the Horticultural Gardens. Under the terms of their agreement, the Society were due to pay £2400 a year to the Commission, a sum which represented not a ground rent, but merely the interest at 4 per cent on the amount borrowed on mortgage by the Commissioners to lay out their share of the arcades and other buildings. Even so, the Society was not liable until after it had paid its own costs, a matter decided by the Expenses Committee on which both Commission and Society were represented. There was a provision that if the Society failed to pay its rent for five years, the lease would be forfeit, while success would entitle the Society to an extension for thirty-one years. In 1862, an arrangement by which the visitors to the Exhibition had been able to use the gardens had brought in £30,000, enabling them to pay the rent for the first and almost only time. Again in 1871 was the system set up by which entrance to the gardens was included in the ticket for the Exhibition, and a penny in the shilling was paid to the Society. The rent was paid successfully for that season, but by 1872 the rent was again unpaid. The problem was exacerbated by the fact that the Society was also burdened by a debenture debt incurred by their own outlay on the garden of £50,000, on which they had only paid off £300 by 1876. Some Fellows felt that the Commissioners and the Society might have been partners, but 'went hand in hand, much as the giant and the dwarf did in the fable, and that while the giant (the Commissioners) will get all the credit, the dwarf (the Royal Horticultural Society) will get all the blows'.[38]

The matter came to a head at the annual general meeting in February 1873, when the members were presented with a scheme devised by the Commissioners to enable visitors to that year's exhibition to enjoy the amenities of the gardens, combined with a system to ensure that the increased revenue was applied to paying the rent, and to reducing the debenture debt. As the Council itself admitted:

> The number of fellows is now so great, viz. 3572, and the motives which led them to join the Society are so different, and in some respects contradictory, that it has been difficult to conduct its affairs so as to satisfy all parties. Regard for science, love for flowers and flower-shows, social motives, the convenience of using the gardens at South Kensington, and the International Exhibition privileges, have each a share.[39]

A series of adjourned meetings in the spring of 1873 brought to a head the grievances of discontented groups within the Society, notably the London or 'Kensingtonian' group led by two baronets resident in Cromwell Place, Sir Coutts Lindsay, artist and dilettante, and Sir Alfred Slade, and the 'horticulturists', of whom the Revd Reynolds Hole and Shirley Hibberd appear to have been the most vocal. The latter objected to the way in which the Society's Chiswick garden was being reduced in size, and felt that not enough attention was being paid to the scientific pursuit of horticulture, while the others, many of whom seem to have joined the Society for the benefits of its magnificent Kensington garden, had a more parochial agenda. Sir Alfred Slade detailed the concern of local residents, claiming that the Exhibition 'instead of being an advantage to the neighbourhood . . . would drive people away . . . not the Fellows alone, but the owners of property, who would be certain to have it deteriorated'. He went on to accuse the Commissioners of 'opposing the wishes of the trading community, [and] the wishes of all the respectable inhabitants'. Attention was drawn to the way in which Commissioners were also on the Council of the Horticultural Society, a matter made more complicated by the fact that Scott was Secretary to the former, and Honorary Secretary to the latter. The rebel members stopped short of dismissing the ageing Duke of Buccleuch, who had been the Queen's choice as President, but a new series of Council members were elected, and Scott was forced to resign.[40] In fact, the Duke of Buccleuch resigned to be succeeded by Viscount Bury (1832–94), until in 1875 Lord Aberdare took over the presidency, gradually bringing the Society into better relations with the Commission, of which he had been a member since 1866.

This refusal to come to terms with the Commissioners, in the words of Slade, 'signed the death warrant' of the International Exhibitions, but also of the Horticultural Gardens. Visitors to the exhibitions held in 1873 and 1874 were denied the use of the gardens, and made to use a passage across the gardens between the East and West Galleries. Some members were so disturbed by the dissensions within the Society that they resigned, so that membership, and therefore income, fell. A protracted series of negotiations failed to provide a solution which would satisfy all the different groups within the Society, let alone the interests of the Commissioners. The Society attempted to set up a money-making skating rink in 1874, which the Commissioners felt was too popular a recreation, and used their authority as landlord to stop it, though later on, in 1879, lawn tennis was permitted.[41]

The Society put up a series of schemes for the use of the gardens, which the Commissioners felt they could not accept, and the members who had led the 'coup' in 1873 resigned in 1875. Though the Society had failed to pay any rent since 1871, was £5000 in debt, and the buildings needed £2000 spent on them in maintenance, under the terms of the lease if the Society managed to pay its rent in 1875, it could continue for another five years. The Commissioners had been warned that the 'Kensingtonians' were likely to put a payment of rent together, thus obtaining another five years for the Society, and they took decisive action. They offered to postpone the right of re-entry from June 1876 till 1878, provided the Society could raise its annual subscription income from the present inadequate £7000 to the necessary £10,000. Lord Aberdare, a South Wales coalowner who as Henry Austin Bruce had served as Member of Parliament for Merthyr Tydvil, rising to hold the posts of Home Secretary and Lord President of the Council, was elected Chairman. He was also involved with the Albert Hall, and as Ponsonby reported to the Queen at Balmoral, had 'taken the matter in hand . . . He finds that the few members who live at South Kensington, and who . . . have greater enjoyment of the Gardens . . . are in the habit of lending out their tickets and admitting whole families on their tickets. He proposes to stop this'. However, those Fellows who had left in 1873 seemed to have refused to return, while the 'horticulturists' were not keen on South Kensington. By August 1876, the Society had acknowledged defeat, and were asking the Commissioners for terms for surrender of the lease. The gardens were particularly dear to the Queen, who saw them as a key project in her husband's scheme, but Biddulph had to tell the Queen that he saw little hope of them being maintained. Even if the Commissioners were prepared to pay off the debenture-holders, this would not 'resuscitate the Horticultural Gardens. When the thing comes to a crisis, and the Gardens entirely fail, some new scheme may be proposed . . . the Commission of 1851 have a most valuable property, but of which the Gardens are part'. Mindful of the Queen's interest, he added, 'Your Majesty is a Debenture-Holder, having inherited the Prince's debentures, but not to an amount which is of any great importance'.[42] The same year the Commissioners put together a scheme, possibly inspired by Cole, to sell the gardens to the government at a discount with the proviso that a large part would be kept for a public garden, while the rest would provide a site for a proposed Science Museum across the garden. This offer, which would have left one of the most attractive parts of Prince Albert's original scheme largely in place, was linked to a new initiative for Science and Technical Education at South Kensington (see Chapter VI) and was probably the last opportunity to save even part of 'the finest quadrangle in the metropolis'. One can be cynical about the way in which a Treasury-dominated administration would have maintained such an expensive gift, but the idea was immediately frustrated by the refusal of the debenture-holders to agree to the scheme. The lease was terminated at the end of 1878, but the Society refused to vacate because of what its Council saw as its obligation to the debenture-holders. Therefore the Commissioners had to take its tenants to court, and the Society was technically evicted only after legal proceedings in 1882. Even then, by arrangement with the Commissioners and the managers of a new series of exhibitions, they remained in occupation of the offices, and the Conservatory and gardens for meetings and occasional shows, until 1888.[43] Despite a final appeal from the Society to the Queen in 1887 for 'encouragement and support in its endeavours to establish itself at South Kensington on a permanent . . . basis' it had finally to vacate the offices and garden, and to move to Victoria Street. Even after it was clear that the Society would have to move, the Commissioners attempted to save the garden, offering them to the government without any rent providing that it was maintained as a public park, pointing out that it 'would not only be an agreeable resort for visitors to the Museums, but would prove an inestimable boon, in their intervals of rest, to a large number of young persons annually subjected to the severe strain upon mind and body entailed by a lengthened examination'.[44]

Sad though it is to contemplate one of the major losses sustained by the estate, it seems to have been due to a mixture of over-optimism and poor management by the Society, and the lack of a clear policy on the part of the Commissioners. As Bowring commented, for sixteen years the Society had occupied a piece of land valued at between £300,000 and £500,000, virtually rent-free, and had only managed to produce a surplus of £500. The situation was not made any easier by the fatal South Kensington habit of indulging in conflicting interests. From Prince Albert downwards the early figures involved in the Commission and its related bodies seem to have made a practice of getting involved in bodies with opposing objectives, which led on occasion, as at the Horticultural Society, to unmanageable tension.

THE ALBERT HALL

The finances of the Albert Hall had also benefited from the International Exhibitions, since there had been concerts associated with them, and some rooms had been used for housing exhibits. The Hall had experienced financial problems since its beginning. It had not found enough subscribers to take seats, and the building had only been finished through the generosity of the Commissioners, who had taken five hundred seats, and the contractors, who had taken three hundred in lieu of £30,000 owed to them, later sold on to the Commissioners. It suffered a little from the prejudice against South Kensington, which, *The Daily News* reported, had 'become a synonym for jobbery and intrigue', an attitude borne out by some of its nicknames, which included the West End Alhambra, Kensington Circus and most unkind of all, 'the Cole Hole'.

However, the Queen had opened the Hall to great acclaim on 29 March, 1871, some years ahead of the associated Albert Memorial opposite, 'inaugurated' in August 1872, but without its principal statue until 1875. The First Commissioner of Works, Ayrton, despite parliamentary opposition and some popular outcry, had realigned the Kensington Road between the Memorial and the Hall, straightening out a small local curve and moving it slightly to the north to give the Hall more space.

The Provisional Committee at the Hall put forward a final report in March 1872, listing the costs of the Hall's construction, its use for that year's International Exhibition and the schemes which they considered should be followed for the Hall, listed as 'a series of cheap concerts for the people', a society of amateurs of all classes for instrumental music, and a national training school for music. In this connection the formation of the Albert Hall Choral Society had already been begun, and the Committee was planning a series of popular lectures on science and art, as well as further use as an exhibition hall. They also put forward, under the terms of the Charter, a constitution for the Hall which was agreed by the members of the Corporation in the same month. Despite the fact they had arranged to increase the seating in the Hall from 5600 to 7100, to increase the potential revenue available to any impresario taking the building, the financial problems continued. A series of concerts put on by Messrs Novello had to be supported by the seat-holders at a loss of £2 a seat. The matter was addressed by a private Act of Parliament, which entitled the Corporation to raise an annual rate for the maintenance of the building.

With the support of the Commissioners, the Council of the Hall had pointed out in 1875 that the funding of the seats had been altogether too favourable to the seat-holders; no provision had been made for the maintenance of the building, and an endowment fund to maintain the building was urgently required. Though a voluntary subscription of £2 per seat was paid that year by the Commissioners on their eight hundred seats, together with other seat-holders, it was clear that only an Act of Parliament could ensure the necessary annual payments. By the Act, passed in June 1876, a majority of seat-holders could set a compulsory annual rate, not exceeding £2 per seat. To prevent the Commissioners dominating the proceedings, the Act limited their voting powers to one vote per fifty seats in the election of the Council and the matter of the seat rate.

During the series of Annual Exhibitions, parts of the Hall, including the Picture Gallery running round the top of the auditorium, and galleries connected to the Conservatory at the southern end, had been used for display purposes. In addition, the Hall had been open to the public, and these uses had been both popular and lucrative for the Hall since the Commissioners had subsidized them. During the 1871 Exhibition, the Commissioners had paid £30 a day for the daytime use of the Hall, while under the particularly difficult conditions of 1873, when they were making use of the crush-rooms as well as the Picture Gallery, they had paid all the maintenance of the Hall. When the Exhibitions came to an end in 1876, they were lobbied by Warren de la Rue, a seat-holder and member of Council, deploring the under-use of 'the noble structure', and suggesting that the picture gallery and even the crush-rooms, 'if not used for one of the national collections of pictures, would be most valuable for a complete library of Physical Science in contradistinction to the library of Natural History'. This plea was addressed to Lyon Playfair, who represented the Commission on the Council of the Hall, and was taken up by the Commissioners, who agreed to forgo all their revenue from their eight hundred seats, in return for an arrangement with the Hall for the use of their galleries. These were offered to the government in the hope that this would stimulate the development of a Museum of Science comparable to the art collections being put together on the east of the Exhibition Road. Previously the Commissioners had had an arrangement by which their eight hundred seats had been placed at the disposal of the Hall's management, receiving two-sevenths of the net profits of the Hall on each occasion.[45] Had the offer to the government been taken up, the Hall would have lost the 'considerable income' from visitors viewing the building, and therefore in anticipation the Commissioners also offered to pay off the Hall's outstanding debt of £4000. To service the capital, eighty of their seats were surrendered to the Hall in return for the cancellation of the seat rate on them, which was equal to 4 per cent on the loan of £4000.[46]

Ever hopeful of government acceptance of their generous offer, the Commissioners left this complex arrangement in being till 1884, then reluctantly decided to give it up in despair. By 1889, they were beginning to find the seat rate a heavy burden, since the returns on their seats did not justify it. However, as the Hall continued to be used for the exhibitions put on in the gardens during the 1880s, the seat-holders derived considerable benefit from those uses of the Hall.[47]

ACCESS TO THE HALL — THE SUBWAY

Like the rest of Albertopolis, the Hall was far away from the centres of London population, and competing with other better known, well-established concert halls like the Hanover Rooms off Regent Street, or St James's Hall in Piccadilly. One of the problems was the approach for passengers from South Kensington station. This station was a joint project of the Metropolitan and Metropolitan District Railways, and had been authorized by a railway Act passed in 1864 with the Commissioners' support; it was intended to be 'a first-class ornamental station' with a prestigious façade towards Exhibition Road. It was opened in 1868, and an early attempt was made to connect it to the Commissioners' estate by a service of horse omnibuses up and down Exhibition Road for the Exhibition, from May to September 1871. These were supplied by the two railway companies, lost money, and were abandoned. The next attempt at supplying a link to the 'main square' and to the Albert Hall came from a company set up to exploit the invention of T. W. Rammell, patentee of a pneumatic railway system, of which Lord Henry Gordon-Lennox, MP, was a director, which obtained the South Kensington Railway Act, in 1872. There was to be a tunnel from the railway station to the Albert Hall, about half a mile (four furlongs and three chains). Two other railway companies were competing; the Metropolitan Railway Company proposed to provide a tramway under the road and gardens to the Hall, the Metropolitan District Railway merely a foot subway to the entrance of the gardens. The Act of Parliament obtained in 1884 permitted the second, and the subway was constructed in 1885, proving useful for the short run of exhibitions and for the Hall. A tunnel ran from the station as far as the entrance to the Horticultural Gardens, when the visitor to the Hall could take shelter in the Arcades towards the Conservatory and the Hall. The subway opened in May 1885, charging each passenger a 1d. toll, but closed the following year, being only opened for special occasions thereafter. The major alterations in the late 1880s disrupted the connection with the Hall, but the Commissioners planned to safeguard a further length of subway to the Hall, as contemporary plans indicate, for the time when they or other interested parties could carry out the necessary works. Though the tunnel was continued northwards for a short distance, the need for space amongst the South Kensington institutions meant that the safeguarded space was never surrendered to the railways or the Hall, but absorbed into laboratory space under Imperial College. A further attempt was made in 1906 to reopen the project for a connection with the Albert Hall under a new railway act, but it was abortive, and the subway which today ends at the junction of Imperial Institute Road and the Exhibition Road was opened again in 1908, without charge.[48]

THE SUPPLEMENTAL CHARTER FOR THE HALL

Quite apart from the problems of distance and access, another problem was the 'character and objects' of the 'Hall of the Arts and Sciences', expressly for the 'promotion of the Science and Art' which excluded some of the more popular and lucrative forms of entertainment. There was a certain fortunate lack of clarity about exactly what entertainments could take place in the Hall, which even Thring who had drafted the documents could not elucidate.[49] More popular acts crept in later, apparently supported by the Prince of Wales, who, happily for the Hall's finances, took a more relaxed view than his mother. However, Ponsonby had to report in 1886 that without the support from the current exhibition, financial difficulties would arise:

> The concerts given there are too expensive and select and the public do not visit the Hall.
>
> It is now proposed that popular Concerts should be given there with the Bands of the Guards; and other attractive performances while at the same time maintaining high class music. The Prince of Wales thinks this would be most desirable.

Whatever the programme on offer, seat-holders' rights were always an obstacle since they could insist on occupying their own seats even for privately organized balls. The Chairman of the Corporation, H. C. Rothery, wanted to promote 'popular concerts, Balls and Entertainments', an idea supported by the Prince of Wales, while other members upheld the more austere views attributed to the Duke of Edinburgh, who objected to popular entertainment.[50]

Sir John Somers Vine, official agent for the International Health and International Inventions Exhibitions, put forward a programme for popular concerts, which alarmed some of the seat-holders, and was hotly debated the following year. All these objectives indicated the need for a Supplemental Charter. There was a body of opinion which objected to each of the objectives: the seat-holders supported by Cole wished to exert their right to take their seats on all occasions, a party led by the Duke of Edinburgh and Dr Mouat were concerned about the likely nature of some of the entertainments being proposed, while another party, led by Sir John Somers Vine, wished the Hall to lease or purchase the grand Conservatory at the southern end of the Hall, part of the Horticultural Gardens, which served as a South Porch, together with part of the gardens, reputedly to acquire and display items from the Colonial and Indian Exhibition, epitomized as threatening to 'Cremorne' the Hall. The Supplemental Charter finally acquired by the Hall on 25 October, 1887, gave the Council the vital power to exclude seat-holders from not more than ten occasions a year, and to make arrangements to exchange boxes and seats in the Hall, and it extended the definition of the entertainment which could be given in the Hall, including Volunteer Balls, 'operettas, concerts, balls, or any other than theatrical entertainments for the amusement and recreation of the people'. The proposals to add powers to lease and manage the land to the south seem to have vanished from the Charter, apparently because of the opposition of the Kensington Vestry, at the time the statutory local authority in the area.[51]

The popular entertainment finally went a little far, and Ponsonby, who had been consulted before the entertainer was booked, found himself apologizing to the Queen in November 1889, saying that he had seen no objection 'in Sampson performing his feats of strength there . . . He knew nothing about the Comic Songs etc., with which it is stated the performance was accompanied. But he thought that exhibitions of strength were such as could be legitimately performed there'.[52]

THE NATIONAL TRAINING SCHOOL FOR MUSIC

Not all the projects intended to support the Hall came to fruition, but one was to have lasting consequences. There was a long-standing interest at the Society of Arts in musical education, led by Henry Cole, and the Society produced a report on the Royal Academy of Music, whose funding and standards were causing concern, in 1861. The Academy's accommodation in Tenterden Street was in a poor condition, and a move to South Kensington would have also met the desire in Albertopolis for a national musical academy comparable in standing with that in Paris, to parallel the teaching institutions for science and art. It had been part of the Prince's grand design, and in 1865 the Commissioners were lobbied by the Society of Arts, who appointed a committee to examine the need for a national musical training scheme.[53] The initial proposal to bring the Royal Academy of Music to South Kensington fell through because neither the Treasury or the Commissioners were prepared to provide a subsidy. After the completion of the Albert Hall, the decision was taken in 1873 to found a National Training School for Music, independent of the Royal Academy of Music, and based at South Kensington. Henry Cole was the prime mover, and the instrument was the Society of Arts, whose Committee was led by the Duke of Edinburgh, who was genuinely interested in music and a personal friend of Sir Arthur Sullivan (1842–1900). Though the original intention was to follow the debenture route, whereby supporters would lend money on the security of the land and buildings, Cole was fortunate in finding an ally in Charles Freake (1814–84), a major local developer with a musical wife. He had told Cole that he would fund the building himself, if the Commissioners were prepared to give the site. A vacant site to the west of the Hall was found, leased to Freake for £80 a year for ninety-nine years, and the Duke of Edinburgh laid the foundation stone in December 1873. Despite Cole's official departure from the Science and Art Department, the construction followed a familiar pattern: the design was done by a Cole nominee, in this case his son, H. H. Cole (1843–1916), a lieutenant in the Royal Engineers, with decorative *sgraffito* work carried out by F. W. Moody and his students at the National Art Training School. Included on the Committee were Major J. F. Donnelly, now head of the Department of Science, Prince Christian and Lord Clarence Paget, but the building was carried out under the direction of a subcommittee of Henry Cole and the Duke of Edinburgh, who laid the foundation stone in December 1873, and opened it formally on 17 May, 1876. It still stands today, one of the most distinguished little buildings on the Commissioners' estate, though no longer an academic institution.

The founders of the School were ambitious – their stated aim was 'the cultivation of the highest musical talent in the country', and to found a school 'which shall take rank with the state conservatories of Milan, Paris, Vienna, Leipsic, Brussels and Berlin'. There were thirty classrooms planned for three hundred pupils, each to be funded by a scholarship of £40 a year, but though they decided that they could open with 100, the numbers never rose above 93 (in 1880). Arthur Sullivan was the first Principal, assisted by four other Principal Professors, including John

Stainer (1840–1901) as organ professor, and fifteen other teachers.

Though the Commissioners welcomed the new institution on to the estate, they were no more ready to fund it than they had been the Royal Academy of Music; an appeal to supplement the eighty-two scholarships of £40 and £50 which were providing pupils for the school, either through their own funds, or by encouraging government largesse, was met by the reply that the school could be extended by taking paying pupils. Moreover, the Commissioners pointed out that they had hoped to see the Royal Academy of Music attracted to South Kensington, rather than the creation of a rival organization, adding that they looked forward to the amalgamation of the two musical institutions, then being promoted by 'a movement' led by the Prince of Wales and Prince Christian. The problems rapidly became worse for the funds subscribed were all used as scholarships, and nothing went into an endowment.

THE ROYAL COLLEGE OF MUSIC

It did not help that the School, which had for its patron Prince Alfred, the Duke of Edinburgh, destined to succeed his childless uncle Ernst II as Duke of Saxe-Coburg-Gotha, had to compete with a separate but comparable institution promoted by the Prince of Wales. The Commissioners seem to have abandoned any hope of persuading the Royal Academy of Music to move to South Kensington, and on 13 July, 1878, at Marlborough House, the formation of the Royal College of Music was announced. A Charter was procured in 1880 for the formation of 'a central representative body, charged with the duty of providing musical education of the first class, and having a capacity to exercise a powerful influence on the cultivation, practice and regulation of the art of music'. The National Training School had opened in 1876, but could not survive more than five years for lack of funds, and at Easter 1882, the Duke of Edinburgh handed over the school's assets, the building and some £1100 to the Royal College of Music, claiming:

> Though we have not been able to do what we would, we have honestly done what we could, and that our school has rendered excellent service to the cause of musical education in the country, and may fairly claim to have been the true pioneer of the Royal College of Music.[54]

The Duke of Edinburgh became a member of the Council of the new body, together with Prince Christian, since 1881 Chairman of the Board of Management, both Archbishops, the Duke of Westminster, and a number of other figures in public life, including Baron Ferdinand de Rothschild, a personal nominee of the Prince of Wales.[55]

The Prince of Wales was a very active patron, believing that the College should have an adequate endowment fund, and for this he insisted that there should be a campaign all over the country, sending the Duke of Edinburgh to open the campaign in Manchester at the Free Trade Hall. By the time the College opened in Freake's building, on 7 May, 1883, over £110,000 had been subscribed, and though the Commissioners had turned down the National Training School's request, they readily subscribed £500 a year. Sullivan was also added to the Council by the Prince, but the first Director was George Grove, of the *Dictionary of Music* fame.[56]

In 1887, Freake handed over his interest in the building to the Prince of Wales who seems to have taken over his brother's patronage of the musical institution, which in 1882–3 had become the Royal College of Music. The same year, Freake was awarded the coveted baronetcy by Gladstone, rather than the knighthood offered earlier.[57] However, the original building was proving too small, and a search for a larger site was on.

QUEEN ALEXANDRA'S HOUSE

Another benefactor attracted to the area was Sir Francis Cook (1817–1901) a successful City merchant, who was a patron of the architect J. T. Knowles, whom he had employed to build a villa at Cintra, in Portugal. In 1883, he approached the Commissioners through Sir Philip Cunliffe-Owen, Director of the South Kensington Museum, and they were told that he had deposited £30,000 at the London and Westminster Bank for the building of a hostel for female students attending music and art schools in South Kensington. Accommodation for female students had long been a matter of concern, and the Commissioners readily granted him a large piece of back ground in Kensington Gore, behind Freake's building, west of the Albert Hall, subject to the building of a road, from Prince Albert's Road (now Queen's Gate), to the west side of the Hall. The building was designed by C. Purdon Clarke, Keeper of the Indian Collections, and a later Director of the South Kensington Museum, who went to the United States to research students' hostels there. He prepared a design for the building, with which he was assisted by a 'Mr Down' also apparently from the Department. It is a substantial red brick building in a subdued Arts and Crafts style, with some remarkable terracotta and faience panels. The students were provided with 'sets' of rooms, two bed-rooms with a shared sitting room, and there were public rooms, not only a drawing room and dining room, concert hall and practice rooms, but also a gymnasium. Appropriately the honours were done by the Princess of Wales, who laid the foundation stone in June 1884, and together with the Prince declared the building, now known as Queen Alexandra's House, open in March 1887. The cost of the building was some £60,000, a munificent figure seen as a bribe by Gladstone's secretary, but which nonetheless won Cook a baronetcy in 1886.[58]

NEW TENANTS FOR THE ESTATE

The collapse of the International Exhibitions had left the Commissioners with additional buildings, but these did not remain vacant for long, pro-viding accommodation for bodies, many of which after spending time in South Kensington, as it were *in utero*, moved on to became national insti-tutions in their own right. Thus though the Commissioners leased the South Galleries to the Commissioners of Works, other buildings in South Kensington were used for temporary exhibitions, like the West Galleries which accommodated a display of scientific instruments in 1876. Many of these bodies originated in temporary exhibitions, like the National Training School of Cookery, or the National Portrait Gallery, while oth-ers happened to be in need of space, when the Commissioners had some to spare.

The National Portrait Gallery started in the Southern Gallery in 1865, and though in 1876 the Commissioners wanted to move it to the Albert Hall, it stayed on in the Southern Gallery till it went to Bethnal Green in 1885. Another was the Royal School of Art-Needlework, under the Presidency of Princess Christian of Schleswig-Holstein. This had been founded in Sloane Street in 1872, with the object of 'restoring ornamen-tal needlework, for secular purposes, to the high place it once held among decorative arts'. In 1874 it took a lease of the former Belgian Galleries, in Exhibition Road, from the Commissioners, moving in 1903 to a purpose-built building by Fairfax B. Wade.

Similarly the Secretary of State for India had taken the East Galleries, built for the abortive series of International Exhibitions, to display the magnificent and historic collections of the East India Company, now taken over by the government. Supplementary space was provided in the northern end of the former French Court, lent by the Commissioners.

The National Training School of Cookery emerged directly from the Industrial Division of the 1873 Exhibition which included 'Food'. The Committee which was asked to organize this class suggested lectures in connection with it. These were so successful that when the Exhibition closed, the Committee, under their Chairman, Frederick Leveson-Gower (1819–1907), younger brother of Lord Granville, urged on by Cole, founded the school. It too enjoyed the patronage of the Prince of Wales, and had as President the first Duke of Westminster. Its object was the training of teachers 'to give instruction, in public schools, in cookery suitable to the wants of the middle and lower classes', though they also included paying pupils 'in the more elaborate branches of the art'.[59] Women pupils only were taken, from a wide range of backgrounds, from Lady Florence Gower, daughter of the Duke of Sutherland and cousin of Lord Granville, to cooks paid for by their employers. By the end of his life, Leveson-Gower could point to the success of the school, which had trained nearly 100,000 pupils, and had been imitated in America and the Colonies.

VI

'For Science, there is no adequate provision'. The Battle for Scientific Education in South Kensington 1878–1896

The 1878 Report of the Commissioners marks a turning point in their development of South Kensington: they were addressing the problem of scientific education as such for the first time, and also putting forward an initiative of their own, as opposed to backing a scheme from an outside party or pursuing a programme laid down by Prince Albert. The report is a clear and concise summary of the Commission's achievements to date:

> To the foresight and wise counsels of the His Royal Highness the Prince Consort . . . may be chiefly attributed the improvement in the artistic cultivation of the present generation . . . The provision made by the Government for instruction in Art may fairly be considered to be commensurate with the wants of the country. For Science, however, there is no adequate provision, and we believe it to be our duty to promote its study and diffusion, so far as our means will permit us.[1]

The means proposed were the erection of a building for 'Scientific and Technical Instruction, to contain Laboratories for study and research, a Collection of Scientific Instruments and a Library of works on Science' to be transferred to the government for those purposes, together with the use of other existing galleries in South Kensington. It was also proposed that ownership of the larger part of the Horticultural Gardens should pass to the government 'as a place of recreation for the public'. When the Commissioners' funds were in better shape, they proposed to devote the proceeds of the estate rents to science scholarships for bright scholars from provincial schools to study in the metropolis.

In some ways this was a report which acknowledged failures on the part of many bodies involved in South Kensington, but it also signalled a growth of independence in the Commissioners. Though they referred back to the Prince Consort's conceptions, they were no longer repeating his ideas as a mantra, entirely properly, since a quarter of a century had elapsed since the successful 1851 Exhibition. They could point to the establishment of some dozen institutions on the estate, but they also saw a very serious gap in their provision. No longer were they happy to establish museums for a miscellaneous selection of objects; they had identified science and technology as the real need. The long battle to get the British government to address the needs of scientific education had begun in earnest; the sceptical may wonder whether it has yet been won.

SCIENTIFIC INSTITUTIONS IN SOUTH KENSINGTON

Though the leading figure at the Commission during the 1870s was Earl Spencer, Chairman of the Board of Management from 1874 till 1881, when he left the country to become Lord Lieutenant of Ireland, he was ably seconded by Playfair, as 'virtual Deputy Chairman'. The Prince of Wales held an annual meeting of the Commission, and was active over institutions with which he had a personal interest like the Royal Albert Hall and the Royal College of Music, but left the general direction of the Commission to the Board of Management and the Secretary. For Playfair scientific education had long been a priority. He had addressed a letter on the subject to Labouchere, now Lord Taunton and Lord President of the Council, in 1867, on his return from the international exhibition in Paris, where he had been a juror, lamenting the British showing:

> A singular accordance of opinion prevailed that our country had shown little inventiveness and made little progress in the peaceful arts of industry since 1862 . . . out of 90 classes there are scarcely a dozen in which pre-eminence is awarded to us . . . the one cause on which there was most unanimity . . . is that France, Prussia, Austria, Belgium and Switzerland possess good systems of industrial education for the masters and managers of factories and workshops, and that England possesses none.

He had consulted the French expert, Dumas, senator and President of the Municipal Council, who had demonstrated that many prize-winning exhibits had been produced by men trained at the École Centrale des Arts et Manufactures, while another French expert had vouchsafed that Austrian workmen were the best trained, other Continental countries being better at managerial education. Playfair ended by urging an official inquiry into the matter of industrial, and, by implication, scientific education in Britain.[2] Through Lord Granville's intervention, the letter was published in *The Times*, while Playfair's views were supported by other experts consulted by Lord Taunton in his capacity as Chairman of the Schools Inquiry Commission. These included manufacturers, a lecturer from the School of Mines and two professors from the Royal Institution, one of whom ended on the Cassandra-like note:

> In virtue of the better education provided by continental nations, England must one day . . . find herself outstripped by those nations both in the arts of peace and war. As sure as knowledge is power this must be the result.[3]

Chemistry was seen as a discipline on which a large number of industries depended, from agriculture, where new types of manure were being used to increase fertility, to the whole range of manufactures from textiles through soap to iron and steel. However, even the scientific community was not at one on what sort of training in chemistry was required, or even how best to increase the numbers. Though the Scottish universities, where Playfair had been educated, provided training in chemistry, and there were a number of institutions in England, including the Museum of Practical Geology in Jermyn Street, and the Royal College of Chemistry, in Hanover Square, founded in 1845, there was a rift between those who believed in an academic training, and those who felt that chemistry was a necessary practical training for such as pharmacists, industrial chemists and factory managers.

Playfair was not alone in his campaign; the Society of Arts had been concerned for some time about education for arts and industry, while there was pressure in Parliament from both sides, from the Conservative Lord Robert Montagu (1825–1902), Vice-President of the Education Committee (1867–8), and the Liberal Member of Parliament, Sir Bernhard Samuelson (1820–1905), a Midland ironmaster and promoter of technical education. Samuelson chaired a Select Committee in the summer of 1868 to which both Henry Cole, and Donnelly, Official Inspector for Science, who had replaced Playfair at the Department of Science and Art, gave evidence.[4]

Though the Committee was intended to enquire into scientific education in relation to industry, it ended by concentrating on the training of teachers, who would in turn educate artisans. The Committee heard from Edward Frankland (1825–99), trained in Germany, who had taught chemistry at Owens College, Manchester, from 1851 to 1857, from H. E. Roscoe (1833–1915), who had succeeded him, both of whom took the view that 'applied science' was merely 'pure chemistry' applied to industrial ends. Playfair, with his Scottish background and German training, took a more elevated view of 'applied science' which he thought could be seen as an academic subject in its own right.[5] Nonetheless, all three men in their evidence to Samuelson supported the idea of more training for teachers at polytechnic level, rather than the extension of tertiary training at the older universities, unsurprising in view of the fact that compulsory elementary education was only introduced in Britain in 1870. Though the Committee did not accept Playfair's view that the poor showing of British industry was due to poor training, it did accept that educational provision was needed for those working in industry at all levels, and that an elementary education was required to enable workmen to take advantage of the help offered by mechanics' institutes to mature students. They felt that secondary schools needed to include more science in their curriculum, while the most advanced pupils would be catered for by regional colleges with a national college in London, very much on the pattern of the existing Royal College in Dublin. These proposals would require an expansion in the training of teachers, both at polytechnic level for school teachers, and at university level for those leading the discipline.

Samuelson went on later, in an education debate, to propose the amalgamation in South Kensington of three existing government institutions – the Royal School of Mines, housed at the Museum of Practical Geology in Jermyn Street, the Royal College of Chemistry in Hanover Square and the newly built School of Naval Architecture, part of the Department of Science and Art – to form a normal school for training teachers.[6]

The implications of the Samuelson Report were so important that under W. E. Forster, the architect of the Education Act of 1870, a Royal Commission was set up on Scientific Instruction and the Advancement of Science, under the 7th Duke of Devonshire (1808–91), Chancellor of the University of Cambridge. It sat for the next five years, issuing some eight reports, the first of which dealt with the three government institutions in London. It had a difficult path to tread, since these, particularly the South

Kensington bodies under the Department of Science and Art, were resented as government-funded institutions competing unfairly with private colleges. There were also rivalries at the Museum of Geology between the Geological Survey staff and the lecturers like T. H. Huxley teaching ancillary subjects. On the other hand, there was evidence that demand for science teaching had outstripped supply, at least in London. Some scientists like A. W. Williamson (1829–90), dean of science at University College, London, emphasized that the proper route was the study of pure science at a university or a college followed by its application to industry or teaching, and therefore polytechnic-style schools, on the French model, were not needed. The Devonshire Commission endorsed the proposed amalgamation in South Kensington, and further development of the three government institutions to train teachers of science.[7]

Not all of these institutions stood on land belonging to the Commission, but the Devonshire Report was enormously important in its influence on the development of South Kensington. Cole could point to the demand for art teachers stimulated by the work of the Department for Science and Art, but there was less interest in science teachers, though there was an awakening public and political concern over the consequences of this gap between art and science. France had been the main rival in 1851, but now two other industrial giants were on the horizon, Germany and the United States, challenging the comfortable assumptions of 1851 about British pre-eminence in manufacturing, if not in artistic manufactures.

EDUCATION IN SOUTH KENSINGTON

The building in which the Report recommended the centralizing of the science teaching programmes of the three government institutions, originally known as the Normal School of Science, part of the Department of Science and Art, stood in Exhibition Road. It was a recent building (now known as the Henry Cole Building), suggested by Cole in 1865 to an unwary Treasury, and, as was the South Kensington practice, designed by Fowke and his successor Scott, and other members of the Department. It was destined for training in Naval Architecture, a campaign for which had been waged by Scott Russell and others through the Society of Arts. It was intended that pupils should be provided by the Board of Admiralty, to be educated in a polytechnic system, modelled on the École Impériale du Genie Maritime in Paris, alternating with work in a shipyard. Though

ostensibly for training naval architects, it was well supplied with laboratories, designed largely on the advice of Hoffman and his successor
Frankland, being based on research into the laboratories at Bonn,
Heidelberg and Stuttgart. It was so admired that it became a model for
later scientific buildings in the 1880s, along with the Cavendish Laboratory at Cambridge, and the buildings of Owens College, Manchester.[8]
The laboratory provision was one of the attractions for T. H. Huxley, who
occupied the post of naturalist, connected with the palaeontological side
of the Geological Survey, at the Geological Museum in Jermyn Street.
This had been built in 1847–8 to accommodate the Survey, and the related Royal School of Mines, seen as an important national service to enable
Britain to exploit its own natural resources and those of the growing
number of Colonies. Huxley was responsible both for the management of
the museum collections and for teaching natural history, but the building
was proving inadequate because of the increasing importance of ancillary
disciplines like natural history and chemistry, which demanded not only
lecture theatres, but also laboratory space for teaching and for pupils to
replicate experiments. Another problem was the use of the building by
both of the two great rivals in the field of natural history, Huxley and
Robert Owen of the British Museum's natural history collections. Huxley
was a member of the Devonshire Commission, and he had ensured that
witnesses had made clear the shortcomings of the Jermyn Street building,
the inconvenience of the chemistry laboratory based near Oxford Street
and the general confusion caused by the dispersal of government provision for scientific training. The attraction of the laboratory space and
other facilities in the Exhibition Road building were too obvious to reject,
and as so often, another of Cole's far-sighted and somewhat disingenuous
schemes had achieved its objective. Huxley started teaching in the
Exhibition Road on an *ad hoc* basis in 1871, and in 1872 the Council of the
Royal School of Mines agreed formally that the disciplines of natural history, chemistry and physics should move there, leaving Sir Roderick
Murchison, head of the Geological Survey, who had opposed the proposed
removal to South Kensington, with the Survey and the Museum in
Jermyn Street. The naval architects never set foot in the building at all,
being removed to Greenwich in 1873, Huxley took the whole of the top
floor for his biology teaching, and the lower floors were allocated to
physics, geology and chemistry, giving them the opportunity to develop
in their new home.[9]

This move brought another powerful new player into South Kensington: T. H. Huxley was not only an original thinker and a very important scientist, he was also a man who had a wide network of friends and acquaintances, including such diverse figures as the polymath Member of Parliament and banker, Sir John Lubbock (1834–1913), the biochemist Edward Frankland, the botanist Sir Joseph Hooker (1817–1911) from Kew, John Tyndall (1820–93), well known for his investigation into magnetism, the philosopher Herbert Spencer and the architect James Fergusson (1808–86), many of them members of a dining club, know as the 'X Club'.[10] Once established as Dean of the Normal School of Science from 1881 to 1895, Huxley was to play an increasing part in the development of scientific education in South Kensington, though he only became a member of the 1851 Commission in 1891, at the end of his life.

Externally the 'Huxley Building' is recognisable as a product of the 'South Kensington School of Architecture' in brick with terracotta ornament, arcades on the street frontage, and on the top floor. It towered over the other buildings in the Exhibition Road, until matched by Aston Webb's more grandiloquent buildings for the Victoria and Albert Museum. It was known as the Normal School of Science in imitation of the French system on which it was supposedly based until, in the 1890s, the older title of the Royal College of Science was reinstated. Christened the Huxley Building in 1931, when the scientists finally moved out in 1974, it was taken over by the Victoria and Albert Museum and renamed the Henry Cole Building.

The curriculum was dedicated to training science teachers, of which a large number were demanded by W. E. Forster's Education Act of 1870, which set up elementary education for all children up to the age of 12. H. G. Wells who studied in the building, though he never took a degree, has left an account of teaching methods in the new laboratories:

There was a long laboratory with windows giving upon the art schools, equipped with deal tables, sinks and taps and, facing the windows, shelves of preparations surmounted by diagrams and drawings of dissections. On the tables were our microscopes, reagents, dissecting dishes, or dissected animals as the case might be. In our notebooks we fixed our knowledge. On the doors were blackboards where the demonstrator, G. B. Howes, afterwards Professor

Howes, a marvellously swift draughtsman would draw in coloured chalks for our instruction.[11]

Thus, when the Commissioners made their comment about no provision for science, there was in fact a growing scientific element in South Kensington, on both sides of the Exhibition Road, epitomized by two great rivals in the field of natural history, T. H. Huxley at the Royal College of Science, and Robert Owen at the Natural History Museum. Neither man would have elected to move to the Commissioners' estate, but both accepted that it offered space for development not otherwise available in London, a tribute to its royal founder's foresight.

SCIENTIFIC COLLECTIONS

Nonetheless, the Commissioners were correct in identifying the need for a properly organized museum for science. There were a number of collections, but these were in a sense episodic, acquired for all kinds of reasons, but without a guiding philosophy, as perhaps had informed the art collections. There was also some confusion as to what such a museum should contain; was it, for instance, a technological collection on the lines of the long-established Musée des Arts et Métiers in Paris, or was there also a place for collections of food and animal products. In addition, it is important to remember the tradition of basing teaching on collections, a tradition which had started with the teaching of art, but had been adopted for scientific studies, as at the Museum of Practical Geology. This had indeed been the pattern to which the Prince's original scheme had aspired, with museums of art and science, coupled with ancillary teaching institutions; the only problem some two decades later was that the scientific collections were ill-assorted and not as impressive as those on the arts side.

The first deliberate attempt to put together a collection of scientific objects for the South Kensington Museum came about as a result of the Royal Commission on Scientific Instruction. In its 1874 report, the Commission recommended the formation of a 'Collection of Physical and Mechanical Instruments', adding that it should be considered 'whether it may not be expedient that this collection, the Collection of the Patent Museum, and that of the Scientific and Educational Department of the South Kensington Museum should be united and placed under the authority of a Minister of State'.[12] This was taken up by the Council of

Education which formed an Advisory Committee of distinguished scientists, including Huxley, Clerk Maxwell and the distinguished physicist, the 3rd Lord Rayleigh (1842–1919), to consider the matter. They reported on the various scientific collections then at South Kensington. These included several which owed their origins to the 1851 Exhibition, like Animal Products and Food, both of which contained exhibits from the 1851 Exhibition, assembled by Playfair. In 1863 Frank Buckland had been asked to comment on the two collections, and they were then enlarged by a further collection demonstrating the merits and products of fish culture.

The best-thought-out collection was the Educational Collection, seen as an aid to science teachers, assembled on the instructions of the 1851 Commissioners, and supplemented by gifts from manufacturers. A collection of Building Materials was formed from models and specimens shown in 1851, and by gifts from the Paris Exhibition. Henry Cole and the architectural and building department at South Kensington carried out experiments, the results of which were published in the catalogue. In 1864, a collection of machinery, marine engines and naval models, some of the latter lent by the Lords of the Admiralty, was put together, including some seminal objects like the Jacquard loom and the Babbage calculating machine. Though the marine objects were moved to Greenwich in connection with the school of naval engineering in 1873, the rest remained.

Perhaps the most interesting collection, and the one nearest to the French national technological collections, was a private collection put together by Bennet Woodcroft (1803–79). Woodcroft was another great Victorian civil servant built in the same mode as Cole, 'ambitious, combative and often awkward in his dealings with other people'.[13] He was an inventor, engineer, patent consultant and historian of technology, who was appointed to the specification division in the newly created Patent Office in 1852. He was born in Manchester where he went into business with his father, a textile manufacturer, which led to his patenting a number of inventions for textile machinery and printing techniques. He also invented a patent propeller, used on Brunel's steamship *The Great Britain* with great success in 1845. He joined the Society of Arts in 1845, and was a member of the Society's 1851 Exhibition Committee. Though eclipsed by other members of that committee, he played a more active role on the Society's Committee on patent reform, together with Cole, Playfair and Charles Dickens, appearing in 1851 before a Select Committee on the

Patent Law Amendment Bill. The following year, he was appointed an Assistant to the Commissioners for Patents, at the substantial salary of £1000 per annum. In December 1852, he was summoned to Windsor by Prince Albert, who had identified him as an ally in his project of setting up a collection 'where models of new inventions might be deposited and preserved, and where lectures might be given on manufactures and machinery', confirming the Prince's view that British 'manufacturers even the greatest of them were, as a class, entirely ignorant of the principle and nature of their own work'. This ignorance, as Woodcroft pointed out, was largely due to the lack of published information on the existing patents. At the end of the interview he agreed to investigate possible support among the manufacturers for the Commissioners' scheme.

This support was forthcoming, though his report had to be rather carefully tailored to accord with the South Kensington objectives.[14] Woodcroft's own work in setting up the Patent Office Library, and in publishing the long list of patents dating back to 1617, did not prevent him pursuing the project for a patent collection. The suggestion had been welcomed in the Commissioners' *Third Report* in 1856, but there were a number of practical difficulties, not least being the aggressive characters of the two men on the spot, Woodcroft and Cole. The former was anxious that his Patent Museum should be available free, while the South Kensington Museum had accepted the principle of charging. The upshot was that the Patent Office Museum, belonging not to the Department of Science and Art, but the Patent Commissioners, was 'crowded into an unsightly shed, which was always open free. So', as a contemporary observed, 'the authorities had their way, and nobody suffered except the public'.[15]

The so-called Patent Office Museum contained a great deal of material belonging to Woodcroft himself. He was a dedicated collector, a real creator of a museum, of the sort not often allowed their head under Treasury funding. It is to Woodcroft that we owe the preservation of the *Rocket* and the *Puffing Billy*, and a more remarkable rescue – that of the Symington marine steam engine of 1788, the 'parent engine of steam navigation'. The unorthodoxy of his collecting methods, and the lack of distinction between his own property and that of the Patent Office was to cause confusion on his death in 1879, but he is perhaps the real begetter of the technological collections of the Science Museum as we know it today.

Though the Report of the Royal Commission on Scientific Instruction was somewhat dismissive of the existing collections, it made the point that taking the British Museum, Kew, and Jermyn Street into account, only at South Kensington was there any attempt to 'collect together in a museum, objects illustrating the experimental sciences'. The Commission received evidence from a number of instrument makers, emphasizing the difficulty of finding examples of existing patterns for comparison. As Colonel Strange, one of the military witnesses, put it:

> I think that if [students of the physiology of instruments] had such a collection to go to, it would materially aid them in the choice of . . . apparatus . . . and would tend enormously to advance exact experiments. There is no doubt that some years ago there was no nation that could compete at all with England in such matters, but we have taught the rest of the world, and the pupil has become somewhat in advance . . . of his master.

The Commission also quoted from a House of Commons Committee on the Patent Office Library and Museum, which suggested that patent fees, which had been accumulating till they were not far short of £1,000,000, might be dedicated to the upkeep of the Patent Collection. They also added a rider to the effect that the South Kensington collections should be reviewed critically to ensure that all the objects were of 'national interest or utility'.[16]

It was decided to hold a Loan Exhibition of Scientific Instruments in 1876, to help in establishing a better collection for the South Kensington Museum. It was intended to hold it at the Museum, but this was impossible, and the 1851 Commissioners had to offer the organizers the Western Galleries, now empty because of the cessation of the Annual International Exhibitions.

The Exhibition was very successful, and enabled a large number of people to see the progress that had been made not only in Britain but elsewhere in the world. The emphasis on the scientific rather than the industrial nature of the exhibition meant that the catalogue could be divided by category rather than by nation. Despite the success of the Exhibition, the opportunity to acquire objects was not taken as enthusiastically as had been done for previous groups of exhibits, and generally the Museum does not seem to have been as inspired by the success of the Scientific Instruments Exhibition as had been hoped by its promoters.[17]

THE PROPOSAL FOR A SCIENCE MUSEUM

However, it did stimulate the Royal Commission to make its extremely generous offer to erect a building for a Science Museum. This was also to include a library, and provision for scientific education generally, including examination rooms, at a cost of £100,000. Meanwhile the Commissioners offered the Western Galleries as a temporary home for the Scientific Collections, a role they were to perform for the next seventy years. This proposal was supported by a letter from the President and members of the Royal Society to the Lord President of the Council, the Duke of Richmond, urging the establishment of a Museum of Science, and the amalgamation of the Patent Collection with the other South Kensington collections. Though the Commission returned to its offer in 1878, and made it the keynote for the *Sixth Report* of 1878, the government of the day was not minded to accept the offer. After a long delay a formal refusal was received in March 1879, explaining that the 'liberal character of the offer' to build and donate a 'Museum of scientific objects and a national scientific Library of reference', had been recognized, but alarm had been caused by the expansive tone of the memorial from the Royal Society. This had alerted the Lords of the Treasury to the fact 'that the scheme was one of considerable magnitude, and one that would entail a large expenditure, not only for setting it on foot . . . but also continuously in future for maintaining it'. A departmental committee had been considered, but further problems had arisen, and the immediate prospect of 'depression of trade at home and complications abroad' made it necessary to decline the offer.[18] However, the matter was not entirely forgotten, and the generous offer of the 1851 Commissioners in 1878 was to prove a considerable embarrassment to their successors.

THE PROVINCIAL DEPUTATION

Other interested parties had realized that the Exhibition Commissioners were reconsidering their options, and a powerful deputation of mayors, chairmen of free libraries and other municipal representatives, from twenty-seven major provincial cities in England and Wales, led by Joseph Chamberlain, Member of Parliament for Birmingham, attended the Commission at Marlborough House in June 1877, to urge on them the realization of their property and the distribution of the funds for the benefit of municipal art galleries and scientific museums. Though the first steps had been taken by the Free Libraries and Museums Committee of Birmingham, representatives of almost every major manufacturing city in the country were involved. In some senses the deputation reverted to the ancient grievance, first expressed in the aftermath of the 1851 Exhibition, that though the provinces had subscribed heavily to the costs of the Exhibition, the benefits had all been spent in London. The Commission was urged to sell its land in whole or in part to the government, and to give the proceeds, estimated at between £350,000 and £720,000, directly to the municipalities for them to make use of in building local museums and endowing them with exhibits, rather than to offer scholarships to provincials to study in London. There was also a marked distaste for the idea of attracting scholars to London, rather than providing funds for them to study locally. Indeed, though there was a reference in the Memorial to the provision of scholarships for 'advanced students' to study at both provincial centres and in London, this proposal was withdrawn at the meeting.[19] Though the Prince of Wales, as President, received the deputation, it was Lord Granville who replied for the Commissioners. Welcoming the 'wholesome jealousy of anything like over centralization in this country' and admitting that the government of unreformed London was 'perhaps worse than that of any of the boroughs represented', he went on to point out that London had four million inhabitants, that the decision not to return the funds had been taken a long time ago, and in their offer to fund a national Museum of Science in London the Commissioners had taken the advice of a Royal Commission and of the President and Fellows of the Royal Society. He also suggested that it could be a mistake to liquidate the Commissioners' estate in a hurry, adding that there was a sentimental attachment to the place where the 1851 Exhibition had taken place; 'we should dislike to sever the memory of the Exhibition entirely from its local habitation'.[20]

Though the Commissioners did not do as the deputation wished, it had an effect on their future policy, possibly because of the need for greater public accountability, and because of the reluctance of the government to respond to their offer of a site for a Science Museum. There was also concern about the level of borrowing by the Commission and of the need to balance the books.

THE CITY TAKES A HAND: THE CITY AND GUILDS
TECHNICAL INSTITUTION

There was however, another educational establishment of significance which came to South Kensington at this time. The historic City Companies, responsible in medieval times for apprenticeship, had gradually lost their connection with training and education, and indeed much of their *raison d'être*. Some, like the Mercers' Company, supported schools, a few, including the Fishmongers' and the Goldsmiths', retained a connection with the trades they represented, but most of the rest had virtually become dining clubs. Indeed, a Royal Commission reported in 1884 that, of a gross income for the City Companies of between £750,000 and £800,000, some £200,000 was trust income, and of the rest about £100,000 was spent on 'entertainments'. In response to growing criticism, a committee under Lord Selborne, a member of the Mercers' Company, and a former Lord Chancellor, was set up in 1878 to consider the best way to advance technical education. They turned for advice to six experts on technical education, including Donnelly, Inspector of Science at the Department of Science and Art, Douglas Galton, the chemist H. E. Armstrong (1848–1937), Trueman Wood, Secretary of the Society of Arts from 1880–1913, and Huxley. They advocated the establishment of a 'Central Institution or a Technical University for training technical teachers and providing instruction for advanced students in applied art and science'. Huxley pointed to the superior training available 'in every German state (even the smallest)' and in 'Switzerland, with two-thirds the population of London and infinitely less wealthy', concluding that the 'condition of England in these matters is simply scandalous'. His 'complete system of technical education' envisaged the training of artisans, teachers and apprentices to a very high standard in their chosen crafts by awarding exhibitions for further study. The Institution was incorporated in 1879, and started by establishing technical classes at the existing schools in Cowper Street, Finsbury, and at the Lambeth School of Art, as well as by subscribing to other existing craft and technical schools. A building fund was started supported by four of the Great Companies – the Goldsmiths', Fishmongers', Clothworkers' and Cordwainers', to build a Central Institute in Kensington and a technical college in Finsbury.[21] Initially a site nearer the City and closer to the areas from which the students might be expected to come was favoured, either in Finsbury, or even on the Embankment, then being developed. However, the latter was unavailable. The knowledge of the 1851 Commissioners' conversion to the cause of scientific and technical education reached the City, and Lord Selborne approached Earl Spencer.[22]

A member of the Clothworkers' Company visited General Scott on 31 October, 1878, when a fairly frank exchange of views took place, the 'Cit' explaining to Scott that it was thought by 'most of his confrères that everybody who comes within the clutches of the ruling powers in that neighbourhood (South Kensington) received unceremonious treatment'. Scott emphasized the Commissioners' intention to assist Technical Education, pointing out that in the case of 'a corporate body appointed by the City *if they maintained it with their funds*, no fear need be felt of the Commissioners wishing to interfere roughly with them, or deprive them of any glory to which they would be justly entitled'. He explained the Commissioners' scheme for 'a Museum of "Arts et Métiers"', which he did not think the government would accept, and suggested that '*if the City Companies could ensure funds to maintain* the Institution', the Companies and the Commission might go into partnership. The City Companies, threatened by a Royal Commission inquiry into the use of their considerable income, had set up their own Committee, which reported in favour of a Central Institute, amongst other means to support technical education. They were naturally anxious that two competing institutions should not be set up at the same time, and reluctant merely to donate funds to existing bodies like King's College, and University College, London. Meetings continued between Scott and the City emissaries, F. J., later Sir Frederick, Bramwell, Secretary to the Institute, and John Watney of the Mercers' Company. Scott was very conscious of the 'fiasco' of the Horticultural Gardens which had landed the Commissioners in a great deal of trouble and expense, suggesting that the Institute should be able to 'act independently of the caprice of a clique of City magnates'. This informal approach was reported to the Special Enquiry Committee, then effectively managing the business of the Commission, after which the City and Guilds made 'certain "suggestions"'.[23] These embodied an offer to provide £50,000 for a building to be erected in the next five years 'for a central institution for the teaching of advanced branches of Technical Science'. For their part, the Commissioners would be expected to provide a site for 999 years at a peppercorn rent. Early on the City and Guilds had fancied a site in Queen's Gate, but this was not acceptable to the Commissioners, since it might have damaged property values there, and they settled on one in the Exhibition Road, between the School of Cookery and the French Court, about half way between modern Prince Consort Road and Imperial Institute Road, asking the Commissioners also to safeguard a further site of a similar size to the north for the next twenty years for a possible extension. The Commissioners estimated that the value of such a site would be £100,000 on the open market, but agreed that it was a scheme of such great potential value that they should discuss it further. There were certain serious points of difference: since the City Companies only subscribed 'during pleasure', the City and Guilds could not guarantee the £5000 needed annually to support the Institute over and above any fee income.[24] The Commissioners were donating a valuable site on a prominent part of their estate, and wanted to be sure that it would be competently managed, so they suggested the nomination of experts to serve on the Council, either from their own ranks or from recognized learned bodies. The City Companies were not ready to accept nominees of their landlords, but finally agreed 'to offer seats in every grade of the governing body to the Presidents of the Royal Society, Society of Arts, Civil Engineers and the Chemical Society'.[25] Huxley urged Scott to accept this concession, warning him of the damage to the Prince of Wales and the Commissioners that would ensue, if the offer were declined, in the opinion 'of a public which is actually incompetent to judge the rights and wrongs of the case'.

Lord Spencer, writing from Algiers on 24 February, 1880, gave his approval, 'provided that the new Institution has a Constitution which will make it national, and a governing body which will be efficient and suitable to [its] purposes'.[26]

Once agreement on a prominent site in Exhibition Road was reached, the design of the building was also a matter of negotiation. Waterhouse had been appointed architect in preference to Shaw and G. E. Street, presumably because of his experience at Owen's College, Manchester, and the Yorkshire College, Leeds, and he found himself working with Huxley, who was much more closely involved in the Central Institution than he had been in the Normal School, though ironically it was to be used much more for the training of industrial engineers and chemists than the school teachers in whom Huxley was interested. By 1883 President of the Royal Society, Huxley played an important part in persuading the City Companies to guarantee the funds required to keep the new institution in being, reminding them that the mere erection of the building was only the bones, there was still the matter of filling it, 'the making of a soul for this body'. The Royal Commission chaired by Lord Derby was appointed on 29 July, 1880, and the Report with a major 'Dissent Report' signed by Sir Nathaniel de Rothschild, and two other City figures, was published on 28 May, 1884. Huxley's task was doubtless made the easier since Lord Derby's Commission was just about to report their findings on the Livery Companies and their finances.[27]

Waterhouse's design was submitted to Lord Leighton, who had become a Commissioner in 1879, and approved by the Commission. Though plain, the building was worthy of the prominent position, soberly built in red brick and red terracotta, well planned for its primary use as a scientific building, for which it became a model. It was a long narrow building extending northward along Exhibition Road, with laboratory accommodation off a central spine, somewhat curtailed at the back by the need not to deny light to the Eastern Galleries. Because it was originally to include an architectural school, it had a large space for a 'museum' on the first floor. Intended to cost about £50,000, the original building was estimated to cost a further £16,000, but the Institute was persuaded to find the extra funds on the grounds of foreign competition, epitomized by the founding of the Berlin Technical High School at Charlottenburg in 1879. It was opened by the Prince of Wales in June 1884, though internally it took longer to complete. Waterhouse had the advice of not only Bramwell, and Abel, the later Director of the Imperial Institute, but also of the existing professors in South Kensington, W. E. Ayrton, O. Henrici, W. C. Unwin and H. E. Armstrong.[28] Philip Magnus (1842–1923), sometime Superintendent of the Department of Technology at the Central Institution, and later Member of Parliament for London University, was appointed Organizing Director in 1880, but even so the institution suffered from a slow start, having only seventeen students at the outset, barely a tenth of those anticipated. Donnelly was able to reproach Huxley over this, and indeed suggested that the students might be better studying in Finsbury, and the City and Guilds should let the South Kensington establishment take over the Central Institution building. However, though the building was not used for teacher training as Huxley had hoped, or for architecture as Banister Fletcher had proposed, once it was taken over in 1899 as an engineering school of Imperial College, it prospered.[29]

THE FUTURE DEVELOPMENT OF THE ESTATE

A radical proposal had been urged on Lord Granville by Cole after his retirement in 1874, when the failure of the Horticultural Gardens was becoming obvious. At the conclusion of a detailed printed account of the development of different institutions on the estate, he had suggested the sale of the Horticultural Gardens to the government, thus enabling the debenture-holders to be paid off. The conservatory was to be moved, and the Albert Hall given a new southern entrance. Lord Granville's reply perhaps justifies his nickname of 'Pussy'; acknowledging Cole's nine-page account, he commented:

> It seems to me right that you should put on record the work you have done for the Royal Commission of 1851.
>
> You are aware that I appreciate the industry, ability and fulness [*sic*] of resource which that work has shown.[30]

Cole had gone on to refine and develop his proposals, causing the 'vials of wrath' to open in the accustomed manner, but the Commissioners do not appear to have taken note, ignoring Cole's refinements which would have saved the Horticultural Gardens for posterity.

The Commissioners' own proposals were less radical than Cole's scheme, which must, however, have influenced theirs. In 1876, they offered the Horticultural Gardens to the government, subject to the outstanding rights of the Royal Horticultural Society, at half their market value, but the government only wanted the Eastern and Western Exhibition Galleries. The Commissioners proposed to sell the Western Annexe as building land immediately, and also the Eastern Annexe, if the government did not want it for the Indian and Colonial Museum. £100,000 of the money realized by these sales was to be dedicated to the building of the proposed Science Museum, which was to be offered to the government on condition that they would maintain it. If the new museum were placed immediately north of the Natural History Museum in the ante-garden, taken together with the South Kensington Museum, now acknowledged as largely dedicated to art objects, it would complete the trio of museums established at South Kensington. Taking into account the Gardens, the Albert Hall, the suggested Science Museum on the south, and the gardens flanked by the India Museum in the Eastern Arcades, and a Gallery for temporary exhibitions on the west, the

Commissioners could then take pride in having brought to fruition much of the Prince Consort's original scheme.

Though this scheme was laid before the Queen by the Prince of Wales at Balmoral in September 1876, and duly approved, the government refused the offer.[31]

The refusal of the government to accept the ante-garden as a site for the Science Museum, and the uncompleted business associated with the Horticultural Society, left the Commission in limbo as far as their larger schemes were concerned. The Special Committee addressed itself to the matter of the estate, deciding in principle to lay out the Eastern and Western Annexes for building, then to build on the ante-garden on the southern side of modern Imperial Institute Road, and finally to sacrifice the central portion of the garden 'looking on a square of some 7½ acres' for development. The two-storey arcades in which the Annual Exhibitions had been held were let to the government – the Eastern Arcades to the India Office for the Indian Collections, and the Western and Southern to the Office of Works for the housing of various scientific collections and temporary displays, like that of the famous Crace Collection of views of London, later transferred to the British Museum. The Commissioners were, in fact, instrumental in keeping the India Collection together, since the Secretary of State for India warned them in 1879 that he was contemplating splitting up the contents amongst the British Museum and other institutions.[32] Lord Spencer intimated to his fellow Commissioners that the Indian government might be tempted by the offer of a lower rent, and an offer was made, linked to the suggestion that though the specimens of economic botany and natural history might go to Kew and elsewhere, 'the objects illustrating art-manufactures, and industries, as well as antiquities and sculptures, should be kept together . . . to illustrate in an efficient manner the Art and Industry of the Indian Empire'. It was further suggested that the government might work with either the British Museum or the South Kensington Museum 'in retaining a Museum which might be of much value to the Indian Empire and to the manufacturing industries of this country'. The proposal was accepted, the collections passing to the Department of Science and Art the following year, remaining in the Eastern Galleries until the latter were demolished in 1956 for the extension of the Imperial College of Science, when some of the exhibits were destroyed, and others put into store, to be later displayed at the Victoria and Albert Museum.[33]

The Special Enquiry Committee, appointed on an *ad hoc* basis in 1874, had in effect run the Commission for five years since 1876, when the Board of Management, realizing it was duplicating the Committee's activities, had wisely withdrawn. The Committee was in fact the most distinguished single group in political terms to have run the Commission, with the possible exception of the smaller group actively involved in the 1851 Exhibition; they included one political grandee who had held all the major Cabinet posts except that of First Lord of the Treasury (Granville), one who later governed Ireland (Spencer), another who was a Liberal Colonial Secretary (Carnarvon), and a fourth who went on to be governor-general of India (Ripon),[34] together with Playfair, one of the ablest and most politically astute of nineteenth-century scientists. In 1881, the Special Committee submitted its twelfth and final Report, detailing the major problems they had dealt with – the Royal Horticultural Society, the Annual Exhibitions and the Royal Albert Hall. Not all of these had been completely disposed of, and the Commission's finances still occasioned worry. However, new policies had been put in place, and with Lord Ripon already in India, and Spencer off to Ireland, they could hand over to the reconstituted Board of Management in July 1881. The Board was to be chaired by Prince Christian of Schleswig-Holstein (1831–1917), Carnarvon and Playfair would continue to serve, with the addition of A. J. Mundella (1825–97) a Nottingham manufacturer who had become an important figure in educational matters, the 5th Earl of Rosebery (1847–1929), later Liberal Prime Minister, and Sir Bartle Frere (1815–84), who had served in both India and South Africa in various capacities, and had been the leader of the Prince of Wales's successful tour of India in 1875–6. For reasons of health, in 1882 Bowring resigned the post of Treasurer, which he had filled for ten years, being replaced by Lord Aberdare.[35]

Henry Scott, who appears to have been ill for some time, died on 16 April, 1883. In view of the serious state of the Commission's finances, the Board of Management decided to accept Playfair's offer to act as Honorary Secretary, with the assistance of the experienced Clerk to the Commission, the lawyer L. C. Sayles, who had been in post since 1868, who was promoted to Assistant Secretary, remaining in the service of the Commissioners till 1904. Playfair set himself to retrieve the Commission's finances, which he achieved in a remarkably short time, through making a number of much-needed changes, not merely through saving Scott's salary.

CHANGES ON THE ESTATE

The City and Guilds proceeded to erect the Central Institution building, a very up-to-date home for science teaching. The leading figures were elected to the Commission – Lord Selborne (1812–95), happily also President of the Council, and therefore responsible for education, Sir Sydney Waterlow (1822–1906), a former Lord Mayor and Member of Parliament, Treasurer of the City and Guilds, and a well-known philanthropist, and F. J. Bramwell. With the Central Institution was associated a School of Art-Wood-Carving, a body much nearer to the earlier concept of Science and Art as related to Manufactures. The other slightly disparate body on the western side of Exhibition Road, the National Training School of Cookery, survived there till 1889, before moving to a site in Westminster.

Even after the law suit against the Horticultural Society was won in 1882, the Commissioners did not throw the Society out, realizing that though they might intend in due course to build on the gardens, this would take time, and they would need professional maintenance in the interim. Commissioners and Society came to an accommodation by which the arcades would be used for exhibitions while the Society continued to maintain the gardens, and use them for their annual shows, utilizing part of the arcades for the sale of fruit and flowers.[36] Rather curiously by modern perceptions, the Albert Hall also contained both exhibition and office space, paid for by the Commissioners and used partly by their staff and partly for exhibitions.

INTERNATIONAL EXHIBITIONS

The gardens, together with other spaces on the Commissioners' estate, thus provided a venue for an interesting series of exhibitions between 1883 and 1886, significantly on scientific themes, organized, initially, by an independent Executive Committee, headed by the Member of Parliament Edward Birkbeck and the Marquis of Hamilton. It was anxious to hold an International Fisheries Exhibition in 1883.[37] This exhibition was such a such a success, that it was followed by three further annual exhibitions, making use of the same buildings. Health, Food and Clothing in

1884 was organized by a committee under the Chairmanship of the 3rd Duke of Buckingham and Chandos (1823–89), who had been a Commissioner since 1861, and a leading figure in the 1862 Exhibition. International Inventions followed in 1885, managed by a new South Kensington figure, Sir Frederick Bramwell, but though visited by 3,750,000 people, the costs of putting it on were so much higher that it lost nearly £6000.

The final Exhibition in the series was to leave a lasting impression on the Commissioners' estate – that of the Colonies and India, nicknamed the 'Colinderies', under a Royal Commission headed by the Prince of Wales as President. The Treasurer was Sir John Rose (1820–88), a statesman who had made his name in Canadian politics, and the Secretary Sir Philip Cunliffe-Owen, Director of the South Kensington Museum. It was expressly devised with the Queen's Golden Jubilee in mind, an anniversary the more significant because her Silver Jubilee had fallen in 1862, and been totally overshadowed by the mourning for the Prince Consort. The contractors were the Knightsbridge firm of Humphreys, who provided iron buildings for hospitals and churches, and had worked on a number of exhibitions both at South Kensington and elsewhere in England and abroad. The Exhibition featured a number of Indian courts and colonial exhibits of various sorts, but also a street of houses known as 'Old London'. These had been provided for the Health Exhibition as a delicate tribute to the City and some of the Livery Companies, who had taken part. They were 'no fanciful restorations from written records, but are faithful delineations from actual drawings derived from authentic sources', copies of real buildings, 'erected from the drawings and under the superintendence' of George H. Birch, ARIBA, a former Secretary of the London and Middlesex Archaeological Society. The official report claimed that these were no 'pasteboard and painted canvas delusions, but honest structures', copied from drawings of such well-known London icons as the Oxford Arms, and houses occupied by Oliver Cromwell and Dick Whittington. They were a practical feature since they also provided the Colonial Exchange and Writing Room provided by Messrs Cook, offices for the various Colonies exhibiting, such as Fiji, or Western Australia, and for the Fire Brigade or St John's Ambulance. The gardens were magnificently lighted, through the good offices and specialist skills of the Electric Lighting Committee, by the contractors, Messrs Galloway of Manchester. There were over 10,000 lamps in all, in the arcades and the gardens – 1500 in the Conservatory, and 1550 scattered round the upper gardens, including the bandstands and the trees, the Memorial to the 1851 Exhibition also being floodlit. Power was provided by generators, some of which had been displayed at the previous year's Technical Inventions Exhibition, including three large Siemens' dynamos. Additional interest was provided in the evenings by specially arranged jets of water illuminated by different coloured beams. Held during the summer of 1886, the Exhibition was visited by 5,500,000 visitors, including some 1,232,010 working-class visitors on 'artisan's certificates', and resulted in a surplus of £35,000.[38]

The 1851 Commission benefited directly from the rent for the gardens, also receiving a share of the proceeds payable for the three profitable exhibitions, charging rent too for the Western Annexe ground, together with payments for dilapidation and damage. A Royal Commission under the Prince of Wales was in charge, and though the 1851 Commission's role for all the exhibitions was officially that 'of landlords only . . . taking no share in the management', as so often happened in South Kensington, the role of the 1851 Commission became inextricably mixed up with that of other bodies operating in the area.

THE ESTATE AS REORGANIZED BY PLAYFAIR

Despite the earlier stated objective of paying off part of the mortgage and making the Commission's funds available for the support of scholars, the Commissioners had slipped further into debt, having had to borrow further from the Bank of England. When Playfair took over as Honorary Secretary in 1883, the loan to the Bank of England stood at £10,000, the mortgage to the Admiralty at a nominal £162,039 13s. 2d., the face value of the gilts which would be needed to be replaced. This meant that if the price of gilts was low, the real debt would be lower, or if higher correspondingly higher. In the event, when the Commission paid off its debt the price was above par, with a corresponding additional cost to the Commission. There was a further debt to Sir Charles Freake of £5000 for money which he had lent to the Royal Horticultural Society, and guarantees to the Royal Albert Hall, and the Royal College of Music which were capitalized at over £60,000, giving a total capital debt of £243,686 as against 'Cash and Realisable Assets' of £411,901. The position was almost worse in income terms, since there had been a deficit of £1423 in 1882. The Commission had given away so much land at a peppercorn rent that only the house-property, mostly let at ground rents, and the galleries, let to various branches of government, provided any return.[39] The government was often a late-payer, and the Horticultural Society had long ceased to pay any rent, so the earnings from the various exhibitions on the annexe ground and in part of the arcades were useful. For a long time, the philosophy had been that the Commissioners' main duty had been to fill up their estate with useful artistic and scientific bodies, after which they would presumably have handed ownership to the government, as indeed so many commentators from Ayrton to Cole had suggested. Now, largely driven by Playfair, a new policy was being pursued which involved the realization of sufficient assets to pay off the debt, and give the Commission some freedom of action.

The financial situation had become increasingly anomalous, since the original mortgage to the Commissioners for Greenwich Hospital had been secured on the whole estate when it was worth considerably less. Now their successors in title, the Lords of the Admiralty, had a lien on the whole estate, now valued at over £650,000, for a mortgage of about £156,000. This meant that every sale or lease required the agreement of the mortgagees, which was expensive and cumbersome. The rate of interest was 4 per cent, high at current rates, but the Admiralty would not allow the Royal Commission to pay off the principal other than with the proceeds of ground-rents.[40] Naturally the Board were anxious to rid the Commission of this incubus, which they saw as practicable in view of the improving financial position, and, in a very optimistic review of the Commissioners' estate in 1887, the Board suggested it would be able to create a sinking fund for extinguishing the mortgage debt, as well as creating a fund for the technical scholarship scheme. In March 1888, they came to an agreement with the Bank of England for a ten-year mortgage of £140,000, secured only on the existing house-property and the land then being let in Queen's Gate. This replaced the Admiralty mortgage, which had had to be redeemed at £152,919 12s. for the nominal £148,834 9s., owing to the high price of gilts at the time. A further benefit to the Commission was the lower rate of interest charged by the Bank, 3.75 per cent instead of 4 per cent. Thus by the time that Playfair resigned as Honorary Secretary in the spring of 1889, the Commission could take pride that their financial position was much stronger: the debt was only some £134,000, and the annual surplus was £5000, something they attributed entirely to Playfair's skilled management.[41]

There was a further influence on the Commissioners' policy towards the estate. The trouble with the members of the Horticultural Society in 1873 was largely engendered by members living locally, and this alerted the Commission to a significant and growing local public opinion. When once South Kensington had suffered from its suburban and empty character, the increase in residents, both on and off the Commissioners' estate, had led to 'a feeling . . . against the further aggregation of public institutions in a locality already possessing so many'. This had manifested itself in opposition to the site suggested for the Imperial Institute and the Commissioners attributed the removal of the National Portrait Collections, which had sojourned in the Southern Galleries from 1865 to 1885, to the public preference for 'a site within a mile and a half of St James's Street', based they felt on such a prejudice.[42] They also detected a movement towards more local museums, which had already led to the setting up of the Bethnal Green outpost of the South Kensington Museum, and which was to inspire C. R. Ashbee's plea for a museum within walking distance of every home.[43]

The conclusion to which this pointed was the opening of the sacred 'main square' to private development, and no longer reserving it for national institutions. In 1879 the Commission had decided to let the ante-garden for building as soon as possession could be obtained, though only in 1882 were they able to ask Sir Henry Hunt to lay out the area accordingly. He suggested a road 80 feet wide through the ante-garden, somewhat to the south of the modern Imperial Institute Road, leaving sites for houses on either side. However, he warned that the necessary infrastructure of road and sewers was to cost some £7000, and the sites might remain empty for up to ten years. The Board were also aware that sites in the Western Annexe had not been taken up 'in consequence of the want of demand for building sites for large mansions', and therefore no action was taken. The problem of the upper and central gardens was temporarily solved by the new series of exhibitions, and its management by the Royal Horticultural Society. This continued until 1888, when the Society finally vacated their offices and library on 25 March, moving to offices in Victoria.[44]

The Board also decided to consolidate their holdings, and purchased a small plot of land from the government, part of the former 1862 Exhibition site on the Queen's Gate side, which they persuaded them to sell back at the low rate at which the Commission had parted with the

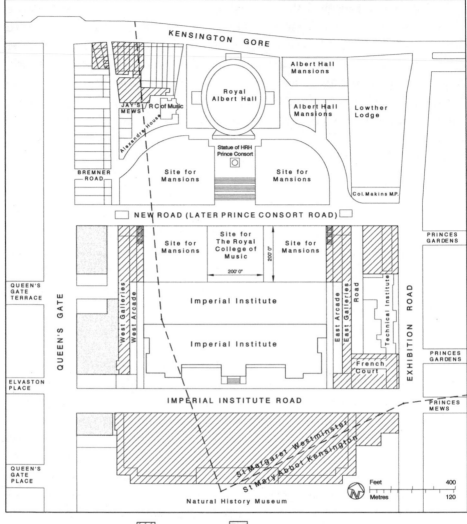

Fig 21. The Commissioners' Estate in 1889, showing the Commissioners' developments to date, and the effect of the intended developments like the Royal College of Music, and the proposed buildings in Prince Consort Road.

whole site back in 1864. In 1885, they acquired a rather larger site in Jay's Mews (the former Gore Lane) for £4715, which belonged to the Duke of Bedford, presumably as mews for Thorney House in Palace Gate, which the 8th Duke had built in 1869.[45] These were intended to improve other property, and make the potential sites more attractive.

Sites for development were therefore identified on either side of the

Albert Hall, and in the Western Annexe on the eastern side of Prince Albert's Road, now known irrevocably as Queen's Gate, after the entrance into Kensington Gardens at the northern end. Though, in principle, the Eastern Annexe on the west side of Exhibition Road was also available for building, in fact the French and Belgian courts were occupied by educational institutions, and the City and Guilds were developing a large site for their Central Technical Institute in the area, so very little was available there.

Playfair was very clear about the importance of focusing on providing funds for the intended scholarships, and the need to ensure that no new venture should take precedence financially. In a memorandum for the Prince of Wales about a site for the Imperial Institute, he catalogued the existing buildings – including a possible Conservatoire des Arts et Métiers, adding that an 'Imperial Institute may be an important supplement but it should neither compete nor dispense with them'. He suggested that the Institute should have a site to the north of the proposed new road, '9 acres being available without touching the proposed Gardens of the Albert Hall'. He urged the necessity of the Institute providing space for a series of exhibitions which would enlist the essential support of manufacturing interests, both at home and in the Colonies. The attraction of these he maintained would be increased by the gardens and the music. Rather ominously, the memorandum was approved by the Prince 'with a reserve as regards that part of it which relates to the Gardens'.[46]

The problem of communications within the main square was a matter of increasing concern for the Commission, as buildings within the main square proliferated. Access to the Royal Albert Hall from Exhibition Road was a difficulty as it was only possible to provide a road 30 feet wide, and the Metropolitan Board of Works insisted on a minimum of 40 feet. The projectors of the newly arrived lodging house for female students, Alexandra House, agreed to provide access for it from Queen's Gate, but it was increasingly obvious that development within the main square was dependent on passage through the gardens for both east–west and north–south communication. The management of the Albert Hall was particularly concerned over convenient, and to some extent protected, access for their seat-holders and patrons. As long as the garden arcades were open much of the walk to the Hall from South Kensington station could be done under cover. Though an underground railway for both pedestrians and rail passengers from South Kensington station northward to the Albert Hall was projected in 1883, opposition from the Office of Works over the Natural History Museum, and difficulties over the grant to the company of a passage under property mortgaged to the Lords of the Admiralty, made the proposal abortive. Another later projected scheme for boring a railway under Hyde Park was defeated by the physicists working at the Central Institution, who claimed their instruments would be rendered useless by the vibration.[47]

The Board of Management pressed ahead with leases for building plots, showing a greater fastidiousness over design and the choice of developer and architect than previously. Sites for single houses in Queen's Gate were let to wealthy building owners and the site to the east of the Albert Hall was let in 1889.

THE IMPERIAL INSTITUTE

The last of the major South Kensington Exhibitions, the extremely successful Colonial and Indian Exhibition, generated further demands for an 'official site'. The new objective was the establishment of a Colonial and Indian Institute, suggested by the Prince of Wales to the Lord Mayor in September 1886. A report on this was prepared by a distinguished committee sitting under the chairmanship of Lord Herschell (1837–99), a former Lord Chancellor, appointed a Commissioner in 1887. This included the Governor of the Bank of England, Lord Rothschild, and Lord Revelstoke, the Lord Mayor, the President of the Royal Academy Sir Frederick Leighton, Carnarvon and Playfair from the Commission, the Liberal Unionist Member of Parliament and lawyer Sir Henry James, later Lord James of Hereford, and two Members of Parliament, who had been colleagues of the Prince of Wales on the Royal Commission on the Housing of the Working Classes, G. J. Goschen and Henry Broadhurst, a working-class Radical Member of Parliament

The Committee early came to the conclusion that the proposed Institute would have to cater for the mother country as much as for the overseas dependencies. The Hall and Conference rooms would be shared but certain galleries would be reserved for permanent displays of colonial and Indian products and manufactures, with other galleries for occasional special exhibitions, while on the United Kingdom side there would also be exhibited manufactured goods, and other objects intended to promote British trade. Colonial and Indian libraries on the one side, and a library for industrial, commercial and economic study with standard works and reports on the other, were advocated. There would be facilities for scientific study and investigation of the products of the Empire and the Colonies, and for examinations in technical subjects. There was a proposal, reminiscent of the early ideas for South Kensington, that the Royal Colonial Institute and the Royal Asiatic Society should be persuaded to join 'in some form'. Another organization which it was thought would be advantageous to attract was the 'recently formed Emigration Department', which could use the resources of the Institute to encourage would-be settlers in the Colonies. The original idea of a body to display and encourage the productions of India and the Colonies seems to have been somewhat diluted by the desire to encourage British manufactures and commerce. Space would be shared fairly between the home country and the Colonies, as would representation on the governing body of the Institute.

With remarkable candour the Committee reported that the costs of a preferred site of about 2 acres in central London, ranging from £250,000 in Whitehall to £400,000 on the Embankment, would be beyond their means. Then turning to South Kensington, 'though sensible of the objections', they accepted that the possibility of obtaining a 'sufficient site virtually free of cost' would outweigh the disadvantages. The proximity of the existing institutions was also an attraction in view of the scientific elements in the Imperial Institute scheme. They expressed the desire that the Institute might help to promote technical education in connection with the provinces in due course; meanwhile they went on to suggest that the Commissioners should use their proposed scholarship scheme to the tune of providing £3000–4000 per annum for working-class students to study in the metropolis, and possibly to extend its influence 'to promote the foundation of scholarships both in connection with the Colonies and provincial centres'.[48]

The intention was that the Institute 'would form a fitting memorial of the coming year' symbolizing the increase in the Queen's dominions, uniting the whole of her people by advancing 'the industrial and commercial resources of every part of the Empire'. As such, it was hoped that it would attract subscriptions from both wealthy individuals connected with the Colonies and India, and from the various colonial governments, an objective only partially achieved.

A charter was granted on 12 May, 1888, giving the new institute wide powers of staging exhibitions to show progress in agriculture, commerce and trade throughout 'Our Empire, and the comparative progress made in other countries', together with the provision of commercial museums, sample-rooms and intelligence offices in London and elsewhere in the Empire, and the promotion of trade generally. In line with South Kensington's objectives was the furtherance of technical and commercial education, and of the industrial arts and sciences, but to this was added 'the furtherance of systematic emigration'. These objectives could be pursued in a wide variety of ways through the provision of accommodation, scholarships, donations or gifts, but before any expenses were incurred the charter stipulated the establishment of an Endowment Fund of at least £140,000, the income of which was to be made available to the Corporation of the Institute. The latter was to be governed by a president, initially the Prince of Wales; the members of the Organizing Committee as named in the charter and any subscribers of £500 or more were to be members of the Corporation. This in turn was to be managed by its governing body. Until the Institute was in being with a building and a fund, its affairs were to be managed by an Organizing Committee, chosen from the original members, of which five was to be a quorum. The original members consisted of Lord Herschell, Playfair and Thring, the Members of Parliament G. J. Goschen and Henry Hartley Fowler, various figures from the City, and representatives of India and the Colonies based in London and the presidents of bodies like the Royal Society and the Royal Academy. The Governor of the Bank of England was a member *ex officio*, as was the President of the London Chamber of Commerce.

By the beginning of 1887, the Board was faced with the anticipated request for a prominent site. It therefore set out proposals for laying out the whole estate, reluctantly providing for the Imperial Institute, concluding that this most recent tenant would take a site worth more than £100,000, making a total of over £450,000 donated to public undertakings.

A comparatively small area will then be left to the Commissioners, and . . . the time has, perhaps, come when they should desist from their policy of providing sites gratuitously for institutions to be managed by other bodies, and should in future rather look to raise a substantial income to be devoted to the advancement of technical education in such manner as they may think best.[49]

However, it had been made clear from the outset that the Prince of

Wales expected a site to be provided for his pet project, to which the Board acceded but with fairly strict provisions. Though accepting that no payment would be made for it, they stipulated that such a site of 7 or 8 acres would only be made available subject to the appropriate mortgage debt, and any necessary roadways should be paid for by the Institute. They offered a prime site on the south side of the gardens, north of the new road earlier proposed by Henry Hunt, to run east–west through the estate, effectively between the gardens and the ante-gardens. This position gave the Institute much of the same prominence in the South Kensington plan as the National Gallery would have occupied in Prince Albert's 1853 scheme. The Board made it clear that this was the extent of their generosity, concluding their 1887 Report by repeating that all surplus income was now to be dedicated to the creation of technical scholarships, and no funds would be appropriated to the new body, thus snubbing a request from the Imperial Institute Committee for scholarships to enable provincial students to make use of the new Institute's facilities.[50]

THE IMPERIAL INSTITUTE BUILDING

The Prince of Wales had embarked on fund-raising both in the City and more widely, though he had not received as much help from Lord Salisbury's administration as he had hoped. The problems for those drawing up the brief for the building were essentially the same as for those drawing up a brief for the functions of the Institute – there was considerable confusion as to what it was for. Initially, it was seen as a sort of museum or showplace for products, both of the Colonies and India, and of the mother country, and departments for emigration and commercial intelligence were amongst the first to be set up. There was also an idea that colonial products could be tested and examined in the building, something that did in fact take place, so laboratory space was also needed. This was an element to which the Commission did, in fact, give some assistance. A Building Committee was formed in January 1887, on which served Lord Herschell, the chemist Frederick Abel (1827–1902), who became the first organizing secretary and director, the ageing Lord Leighton, and Waterhouse, in whom the Commissioners had considerable confidence, though he never became a Commissioner. The brief was ambitious: the building was to serve as a conference centre so the Building Committee expected a library and three reading rooms with 'intelligence offices', a 'fine reception hall', conference rooms, committee rooms,

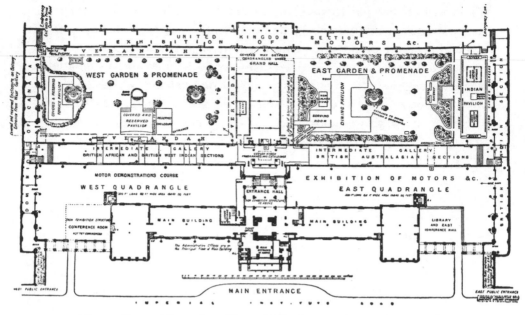

Fig 22. Ground floor plan of Imperial Institute, as in use *circa* 1900 for
an exhibition of motors.

refreshment rooms and offices. Because of the testing of products, scientific facilities, sample rooms and laboratories would also be needed.

A competition was held, sixty-six architects applying to compete, and six were chosen for the limited competition: Rowand Anderson from Edinburgh, A. W. Blomfield, T. E. Collcutt, T. N. Deane & Son from Dublin, Aston Webb and Ingress Bell, and T. G. Jackson. Each competitor was to prepare a scheme within three months, £200 being awarded for the work. The assessors were largely lay: Herschell, Carnarvon, Abel, Leighton, with Waterhouse the only professional. As a commentator pointed out, all the entries were very different in character, possibly because 'the world has not seen an "Imperial Institute" and no one appears yet to know what it is for'.[51]

The winning entry came from T. E. Collcutt (1840–1924), a London architect who had won competitions for provincial town-hall and library buildings, in what has been described as a 'free Tudor style leaning towards Early French renaissance'. His design was liked for its massing and silhouette, and it fitted the magnificent site, the most impressive left on the Commissioners' estate. Its central tower was flanked by two wings, extended to cover the ends of the Eastern and Western Galleries, which had been truncated by Imperial Institute Road, and which were crowned by cupolas designed by Collcutt. The exterior was built in Portland stone and brick, and for the interior Collcutt used exotic marbles, mosaic work and 'red-gauged brickwork used as if it were an entirely decorative material'. The magnificent staircase with its painted panels and the vestibule were well-recorded by contemporary photographers and artists, but there were also individual rooms inspired by various parts of the Empire – a panelled Canadian room, and the British India Conference Room, decorated by J. D. Crace. In the words of a twentieth-century critic, who saw and admired the building:

> The whole building is a *tour de force*, combining as it does extreme delicacy of detail with breadth and grandeur in its general effect. The principal tower is extremely elegant in silhouette, admirably proportioned in itself.[52]

Its tower was so important that it was seen as one of the most striking additions to the London skyline of the 1890s.[53] Collcutt is said to have refused to lower it to provide the necessary economies. Ironically, the tower, the only part of this magnificent imperial showpiece to survive, is reported to have so displeased the royal patron, that Collcutt never received the knighthood which should have crowned the design of so important a building.

A Fellow who wrote a description in 1898 gave a splendid picture of the building whose 'sphere of operations includes eleven millions of square miles of territory, with three hundred and seventy millions of inhabitants. In the galleries of the Institute there is now represented such a view of the peoples, countries, products and resources of this Empire as has never been available before . . . The visitor, passing from court to court . . . is enabled to form a conception of his fellow-subjects, such as he could not obtain . . . in any other place'. This could be supplemented by curators, libraries holding official reports and journals, maps and samples of products, lectures held at frequent intervals, and even 'ex-Colonists available who will personally give him the benefit of their experience', not to mention a school of oriental languages. For those who wished to become Fellows, all 'the advantages of a good club' were provided, 'including reading-room, writing-room, library, billiard and smoking room, newsroom, dining and refreshments rooms . . . evening concerts in the great hall in winter, garden concerts in summer, lectures, entertainments'.[54] However magnificent, and indeed ultimately practical, the far-flung objectives, all these attractive features could not fill the building with enough Fellows to provide the running costs to get the project off the ground.

The initial budget of £250,000 for the building was reduced to £150,-000, partly because of the Commissioners' insistence on an endowment fund, and partly because of the costs of the road and the foundations. The contract price from Mowlems was finally accepted at £161,597, to accommodate the tower. Collcutt's elevation for the southern façade was built as designed, but other changes took place: the great Imperial Hall which was to have occupied the northern wing was never built, a conference room and library combined in the east wing being substituted, but two sets of galleries connecting the building to the existing Eastern and Western Galleries were added to the north of the main block. The most northerly gallery was financed by the government and intended to house the British Collection, now at the Tate Gallery, but was soon taken over for the Indian Museum. The half-finished building was informally opened in June 1892, and formally by the Queen in May 1893.

Sir Frederick Abel, an industrial chemist and a War Office expert on explosives, who became the first Director of the Imperial Institute, intended its role to be very practical in its work of retaining 'a competitive place for the Empire against the industrial power of Continental and American rivalry'.[55] He saw one way of achieving this by testing imperial products and thus improving them, and managed to persuade the Commission to provide an annual contribution of £1000 towards its laboratories.

The project was faced by a series of difficulties, starting from a disappointing response to the appeal, intended to raise £500,000, which only reached £426,000 followed by the considerable overspend on the contract. The Commissioners' contribution was not enough to meet the shortfall, caused partly by lack of interest from Indian and colonial administrations, and by a falling off in membership by Fellows of the Institute locally. Though some subscriptions were received from maharajas, the failure of the Indian and individual colonial governments to support the Imperial Institute determined its ultimate fate, and so disgusted its Royal President that according to his biographer, the 'Prince of Wales lost all interest'.[56]

The financial position was made worse by draconian demands for rates from the two new Metropolitan Boroughs of Westminster and Kensington, which absorbed much of the income. In the last months of his life Playfair advised the Commission not to increase the subvention, despite a powerful plea from Abel.[57]

By 1900, the Institute, far from having absorbed the Commission which some had postulated, was in such financial difficulties that it had to find another occupier for part of the building. Through the good offices of the Scottish lawyer and Liberal Member of Parliament, R. B. Haldane (1856–1928), the University of London, then moving out of Burlington Gardens, took over half the building. The lease was effectively surrendered to the Office of Works, which became the Commissioners' tenant. Moreover, in 1902 the Institute itself was taken over by the government, whose functions with regard to the Colonies it was thought to duplicate, and became part of the Board of Trade, being transferred to the Colonial Office five years later.

Another national museum nearly found its way to the Commissioners' estate in the 1890s, in the shape of the proposed National Collection of British Art, a representative collection modelled on the same lines as the Musée du Luxembourg in Paris. It was initiated by a memorandum from the Earl of Carlisle, an artist himself, and an artistic and architectural patron of considerable standing, to Goschen, as Chancellor of the Exchequer. He suggested that a representative collection of British artists might be formed from collections already belonging to the nation in the National Gallery and the South Kensington Museum such as the Sheepshanks and Chantrey Bequests. He pointed out that the Eastern and Western Galleries were the best-lit fireproof galleries in London, and only needed a Cross Gallery to connect them. Arrangements were made in December 1890 to build the gallery with a contribution from the Commissioners and some readjustment of the boundaries of the Imperial Institute, the galleries and the Royal College of Music. The Commission granted a new lease to the government to include the new cross galleries 25 feet wide on two floors, to which the Commission had made a substantial contribution, not entirely covered by the increased rent. However, a powerful scientific lobby caused the government to change its mind about the site for the British Art Collection, but the Board were philosophical about the enforced change of plan, taking the view that the Commissioners would be as happy for the new gallery to be used for scientific exhibitions.[58]

Under the Commissioners' plan as set out in 1888, a sizeable plot would be left south of the new road, to leave an important site for sale to the government, adjoining the Natural History Museum and its other land. North of the Institute site, enough of the gardens would remain to provide an attractive open setting for the Memorial to the 1851 Exhibition and for the fountains, south of the Albert Hall, whose Council was anxious to acquire the area as a venue for exhibitions and functions. Substantial sites for private development, needed to improve the financial position of the Commission, could be allocated east and west of the truncated gardens, north and south of the route of the modern Prince Consort Road. There was still space on the Western Annexe, the east side of Queen's Gate, intended for private houses, but the Eastern Annexe, the western side of Exhibition Road, was increasingly occupied by institutions, often in former exhibition buildings.

The National Training School of Cookery, in the former French Court, sometimes seen as South Kensington's contribution to the training of women in practical art and science, had become so successful that it needed more space. The Commission, however, found itself unable to offer it more than a small piece of the land purchased from the Duke of Bedford near modern Jay's Mews, so the school moved to a site in the Buckingham Palace Road found for it by its President the Duke of Westminster. The Royal School of Art-Needlework, occupying part of the former Belgian Court, was also doing well and looking for more permanent buildings.

THE GROWTH OF THE ROYAL COLLEGE OF MUSIC

The Royal College of Music, which had taken over the premises of the National Training School for Music west of the Albert Hall, was complaining of lack of space. Part of this was due to the building of Alexandra House directly to the west, which the College felt prejudiced its chances of expansion. Moreover, it had found yet another sponsor anxious to earn royal favour and obtain a baronetcy, a Mr Samson Fox of Leeds, and was therefore able to ask for a larger site.

A number of new sites were considered. In early 1887, Sir George Grove approached Playfair[59] and was offered a site in Exhibition Road south of the Central Institution, a possibility, but one which involved inconveniencing or even moving both the National School of Cookery and the Royal School of Art-Needlework. A year later, the College Council set out its requirements in a memorial, complaining of the lack of space in the existing building, which had no rooms suitable for anything but the teaching of lessons, none for 'waiting, eating, examinations, or meetings of the governing body, or the Reference Library', while some of the existing rooms had been deprived of light and air by the newly completed students' home, Alexandra House. The College had to resort to using accommodation in the Albert Hall and even in the aforementioned Alexandra House. There was no room for expansion, and the building was already too high, so they requested the grant of a site for the erection of a new and commodious building, with provision for extension as the College grew and came to 'embrace more and more of the musical education of the Country', reminding the Commissioners that their President, the Prince of Wales, also the President of the College, had promised a site in 1882, as soon as the funds were forthcoming.[60] In a covering letter, Grove said the Exhibition Road site was not large enough, referring to 'Mr. Fox's magnificent gift . . . £30,000 was not his ultimatum . . . without being over-sanguine we hope to have *ultimately* a fine group of buildings . . . forming a College worthy of the name'. He went on to express his approval of the alternative which he had discussed with Playfair, 'the ground . . . about the Conservatory south of the Albert Hall . . . obviously the very place', the semicircular northern end of the Gardens, immediately north of the new road (Prince Consort Road) about to be made.[61] Sir George Grove called in the architect, J. J. Stevenson, discussing the use of the Festspielhaus at Bayreuth or the conservatoire at Brussels as a model. This use of the proposed site was not entirely congenial to the Council of the Albert Hall, chaired by the Duke of Edinburgh, who had aspirations to manage the rump of the gardens themselves, and possibly the architect of the new college had plans of his own too. By May 1888, Grove was writing to Prince Christian, who was also involved with the Royal College of Music, in his capacity as Chairman of the Board of Management, to ask for land south of the Imperial Institute Road, which he and the architect had visited together in search of 'a more remote spot out of earshot of dwelling houses'. He concluded by pointing out that 'it brings the two institutions in which the Prince of Wales is most directly concerned near to one another'.[62] Colonel Ellis, then a member of both the Prince of Wales's household and the Board of Management, sent out a three-line whip for the next Board meeting in July 1888 – he himself would come up from Sandringham, Ponsonby from Windsor, and the Prince hoped that Thring, Mundella and Childers

would attend. The Prince, Ellis told Playfair, did not 'hold to the conservatory site – and is inclined to the view that unless Mr Fox comes with a
sufficiently assured large sum in his hand – it wd. be wiser to offer Sir G.
Grove & Co. the other site'. Ponsonby's view was 'for leaving the conservatory site *open* – and letting the crescent of houses (wh. are to produce
income) be extended – leaving a clear view . . . of the P. Consort's Statue
from the s. entrance of the Albert Hall . . . and relegating Chateau Fox to
the other site'.[63] Some days later an agreement was come to between the
Board and the Executive Committee of the College, supported by Fox, for
a site in Exhibition Road, north of the Central Institute, 224 feet in
frontage and 125 feet deep, though Playfair explained that the site would
not be available till vacated by the Schools of Cookery and Art-
Needlework.[64]

A building committee was set up, on which Fox served, and research
was done into academies as far afield as Leipzig, Vienna, Rome and Cin-
cinnati, Ohio, and a competition was under contemplation. Samson Fox
made his offer of £30,000 towards a new building, and the Commissioners
toyed again with the idea of siting the College immediately south of the
Albert Hall facing south to the proposed new road. However, Grove and
Fox decided the site was not large enough, and the Commissioners
offered them a large site on the south side of the new road, occupied by
the fountains and the Memorial to the 1851 Exhibition, the centre piece
of the gardens. This was accepted, and by February 1889 the College was
in treaty with the Board of Management over the details of the design.

The new plan for the development of the estate was essentially that of
1886, with the significant addition of the Royal College of Music which
was to occupy the remaining part of the Horticultural Gardens, now to
be totally destroyed, a major loss to the planning of the South Kensington
estate, and one which no subsequent management has succeeded in recti-
fying. The Horticultural Society vacated their offices on 25 March, 1888,
leaving the gardens on which they had spent £80,000 'with no benefit'.
It is not clear why the Board of Management decided to give up the idea
of preserving any part of the former Horticultural Gardens, but possibly
they were influenced by the failure of the Albert Hall's bid to administer
them, as well as by the weight of royal patronage. The Prince's attitude
to the garden had perhaps been indicated by his response to Playfair's
memorandum setting out his scheme for a site for the Imperial Institute,
which would have preserved the gardens in a reduced form.[65]

Fig 23. Perspective of Royal School of Music, by A.W. (later Sir Arthur) Blomfield.

Once the Royal College of Music had secured its site, it rejected Stevenson, and turned to A.W. (later Sir Arthur) Blomfield for its new building, subject to the approval of Waterhouse on behalf of the Commissioners. Blomfield claimed to have been selected by the Prince of Wales, and was clearly a safe pair of hands, but provided a dull design. Thus, not only did the College deal the deathblow to the finest formal garden in the capital, it added little of architectural moment to the area. It was a difficult site, on the lower side of a high road, which necessitated two basements to adjust the levels. The plain red-brick façade had to be raised an extra storey because of the anticipated blocks of flats either side. Behind the north-facing front, there was a temporary hall, replaced shortly afterwards with a two-storey building containing an examination room in the basement and a multi-purpose hall above. To his fury Blomfield was not offered the later commission, owing, it was hinted, to difficulties over his fees for the earlier building. Fox also was disappointed, never getting his title, dying plain Mr Fox in 1903.

The gardens were dismantled, the buildings and plants being sold in April 1889; ironically the features which had been provided at such a cost as almost to bankrupt the Royal Horticultural Society, and to weigh the Commissioners down with a heavy burden of debt for many years, fetched less than £2000 under the hammer. The statue plinth, and some of the balustrading and paving, were retained for reuse elsewhere on the estate, but everything else seems to have gone. The two bandstands were sold for £300, to the London County Council Parks Department, which re-erected them in Southwark Park and at Peckham Rye.[66] The conservatory, though offered as a single lot, was sold in bits, the materials fetching £75 5s. There were even some early electric lights, with lenses and coloured glass, and glazed lights from the fountains. Some of the statues, though they are not identified in the catalogue, must have come from some of the contemporary exhibitions. A marble group of the *Eagle and Child* together with a plaster bust on a wooden pedestal fetched £1. 4s., plaster figures 4ft 9ins high 13s., while specimen conifers in pots went for a relatively higher sum. *Araucaria cunninghamii* 3 feet high fetched 15s. each. One of the best-known of the statues, *Youth at a Stream* by Foley, found its way to the Albert Hall. The main ornamental feature of the garden, the Memorial to the 1851 Exhibition with the statue of Prince Albert on top, together with its flanking stonework, was ultimately resited on the terraces immediately south of the Albert Hall, but owing to problems with the development of the whole area, it was to be some time before it was re-erected.[67]

This was the final destruction of one of the grandest public gardens ever laid out in London, probably in the British Isles, which the Prince Consort had envisaged as the centre piece of the estate. Worse, in the plan for its removal, no provision was made for north–south communication through the 'main square' of any sort so the original axis on which both the Albert Hall and the Albert Memorial were laid out was nullified.

Any visitor to South Kensington is painfully aware of the absence of a tangible centrepiece to the estate. The lack of physical communication within the Commissioners' estate seems to be increasingly reflected from this time on, by its occupation by individual institutions with little formal relationship, often literally jockeying for position and desirable sites.

In 1889, the Board found a developer to take the four blocks in Prince Consort Road for private development, a Mr Sarl, who had committed himself to the two northern sites (now occupied by Albert Court on the east, and by the Beit Building on the west). However, the prospect of more domestic buildings in the area provoked an immediate reaction amongst interested parties. Within two months, five memorials had been addressed to the Prince of Wales, suspiciously similar in form, and as the Board reported, thought to be 'the result . . . of a wide canvass of Chambers of Commerce, Corporation, Guilds, and Educational Institutions throughout the country'. Nothing, the Board reported to the Commission, had been heard from the governing bodies of the South Kensington institutions whose interests the memorialists purported to defend. The Board had despatched a reply to each of the memorialists, explaining that many institutions had already been established on the estate, and that as the benefits were meant to be national rather than metropolitan, this could be achieved in the form of scholarships from the Commission's increased income.[68]

Despite the memorials, the letting of the sites to Sarl on the northern side of the new road, east and west of the Albert Hall, went ahead. He employed an architect called Frederick Hemings (*c.*1855–94) who submitted two schemes for him. Sarl sold the scheme on to a surveyor called George Newman, who sold it on to his firm George Newman and Company, backed by Jabez Balfour's Liberator Building Society. Hemings' schemes were approved by Waterhouse on behalf of the Commissioners, and work started shortly. However, in the autumn of 1892, the Liberator Building Society collapsed, bringing down a number of enterprises, and leaving Newman bankrupt with a half-completed building some four-storeys high on the northeastern site. In the course of the subsequent bankruptcy proceedings, it was alleged that in addition to the £16,000 Newman had paid to Sarl for the scheme, he had disbursed a further £10,000 to the Commissioners' staff and agents. This led the Lord Chancellor Lord Halsbury (1823–1921) to declare that 'considering the mode in which the contract had been obtained for the Commissioners . . . in the public interest it is positively necessary that some investigation should be held'.

At a further hearing on 14 March, 1895, Mr Justice Vaughan Williams, who had heard the original bankruptcy case, pressed by the famous advocate Marshall Hall appearing for the Commissioners, made it clear that there was no evidence that the 'paid officials, secretary and under-secretary and solicitors' had received any money. However, some curious facts emerged: it was clear that it was a purely speculative deal and the sale on to Newman had netted Sarl, together with his solicitor Byron Johnson and a third party, £4000 in cash and £12,000 in bills, which they had shared out on Fladgate's premises, where they had gone to obtain an agreement for Newman. It was also said that a firm of surveyors, Buckland & Garrard, valued the land at 1s. 2d. a foot, while the Commission had valued it at 10d. The statement by another surveyor that he could not claim to influence the Commissioners' Surveyor, Henry Hunt junior, and that he was no more than a 'club acquaintance', but that he had pocketed a commission for introducing Newman, does not improve the image of those dealing in land on the Commission's estate. It also became clear that the sale to George Newman went against Commission policy, which was to avoid agreements with limited companies.[69] These proceedings not only touched the Commission with scandal, but also made it impossible for them to proceed with the potentially lucrative development for some time. Finally, they annulled the arrangement with the disgraced Newman and repossessed the sites. Though advised by Hunt to complete the building themselves, they had little stomach for it, and a firm called the Albert Court Syndicate, of which Hussey was a director, made them an offer, obtaining 'a very good bargain' according to one observer.[70] Another director was the architect R. J. Worley, who was responsible for designing the completed building. The lease of the building was granted in 1897, and the following year the Commissioners sold the freehold, probably compounding the 'bargain'.

THE TERRACES BELOW THE ALBERT HALL

The Commissioners had agreed to provide for new terraces below the Albert Hall and to replace the demolished conservatory with a new southern entrance to the Albert Hall, the cost of which would be split between the Commission and the Hall.

The use of the rest of what came to be known as the 'Central Space' or the '150 feet space', between the two development plots, was problematic for some time, since it had been assumed that it would be taken by the Newman consortium and developed as a part of their 'take'. However, it was left on the Commissioners' hands, and in late December 1897, Henry Roscoe, who had agreed to inspect it on behalf of the Management Committee, found that the South Porch and the new roadway round the back of the Hall were still incomplete.[71]

The account of the development of the area has survived in the Commission's archives, and it shows that little had changed in the way in which the Commission's business was managed, or in the 'hands-on' approach of the Commissioners themselves. Henry A. Hunt, who had succeeded his father as Surveyor, considered that providing a new site for the Prince Consort's statue and a garden would cost at least £10,000. There was a fifteen-foot drop from the Hall to Prince Consort Road, and though the space could be filled in with earth, he advised that the best and most immediate solution was to build vaults to carry the statue, the steps and the paving. Though made ground would be some £2000 cheaper, nothing could be laid on it for three or four years. In addition, he had hopes of finding a tenant for the vaults. By mid-summer 1898, Higgs and Hill, the contractors, had fifty workmen on site and over 100,000 bricks had been laid since work commenced on 20 May. Sir Henry Fowler, who had taken over the running of the Board of Management from Playfair, was concerned over progress, a concern which turned to dissatisfaction the following year, when the Queen visited the area, and the work was still incomplete. Hunt defended the contractors, pointing out that cement could not be laid in wet weather or frost, and that there had been a late frost on 26 May; however, he added, there were now twenty Italians at work, starting work at four in the morning, and all would be finished in a week. In the event, Hunt saved the Commissioners £77 17s. 5d. on the contract sum of £11,999.[72]

An approach was made by Sir Frederick Bramwell a short time later, on behalf of the Kensington and Knightsbridge Electric Lighting Company, for the use of the vaults for 'electric batteries and transformer machines', with assurances that no generating machinery or steam engines would be employed.[73] Though the vaults were advertised more widely for use as wine cellars, for the use of 'Refreshment or Ball Contractors', or, a most up-to-date suggestion, 'Motor Agents', the only firm interested was the electricity company, which needed an early reply as they had contracted to light the Natural History Museum. Concern was expressed about the noise and vibration likely to be caused, and the Board of Management turned to its scientific experts, Professor W. E. Ayrton and Sir Henry Roscoe, to deal with this problem. After considerable bandying of expert opinions on the acoustic properties of double-glazing, sufficient assurances were obtained from the company for a lease to be granted of the vaults in 1900.[74]

However, some five years later, further problems surfaced, with a complaint from the Kensington and Knightsbridge Electric Lighting Company that the vaults were leaking. F. J. Stevenson, who had succeeded Henry A. Hunt as Surveyor to the Commission, attributed the problems to settlement of the brick vaults, assisted by the vibration of the transformers, and the way in which the iron staunchions were being used to move the company's equipment. Further examination with the assistance of a civil engineer led Stevenson to conclude that the 'movement in the Terrace and the Vault below . . . must have been known to the late Surveyor as far back as 1900'[75] and that the damage was due, not to the effect of the Albert Hall sliding down the hill as feared by the resident engineer of the electric company, but 'primarily to faulty design and bad construction of the Contractors who carried out the work', with the vibrating machinery a contributory cause, but one difficult to prove.[76] In consequence, the brick vaults on to Prince Consort Road were causing the pavements to bulge. Holloway Brothers were called in to carry out repairs to the tune of over £1000.

By July 1906, the new team of Sir Arthur Bigge and Shaw were reporting to the Board on the damage. Stevenson was authorized to build new vaults on the south side of the Albert Hall to remove dampness at a cost of a further £1600 to £2000. Stevenson then came to the conclusion that the Council of the Albert Hall had not carried out its obligation to excavate the areas immediately south of the Hall thus leaving a great mass of earth sliding downhill on to the vaults further south. The responsibility for the deferring or postponement of this work was hotly disputed by Verity working for the Hall, but the whole episode does not reflect well on Henry A. Hunt. The carrying out of this work began in mid-summer 1907, but the payment for it became irrevocably confused with the larger question of the Commissioners' financial relationship with the Hall, which was sorted out in 1908. The terraces continued to give trouble through movement and dampness, and to cause problems between the Commissioners and their tenants. In the early 1920s they were vacated by the electricity company, and Shaw, who was anxious to relieve the Commissioners of the liability, was able to negotiate a sale in 1926 to the London Country Freehold and Leasehold Properties, the owner of Albert Court.[77]

THE MEMORIAL TO THE 1851 EXHIBITION

Above the vaults, a series of terraces were created below the Albert Hall, which provided a new site for the Memorial to the Exhibition of 1851. The Memorial, on its original plinth and surrounded by some of the original balustrading and stairs from the gardens, was re-erected in 1908, soon after its repair by the well-known metal-working experts Barkentin & Krall of Regent Street.[78] According to Shaw this repair was due to a caustic royal comment on the statue's condition by the Prince of Wales (later George V), when riding round the estate with Stamfordham.[79]

45. The Prince Consort Gallery in the South Kensington Museum *c.*1876.

46. The Horticultural Gardens in use for the International Fisheries Exhibition in 1883, when they were covered by extensive temporary exhibition buildings.

47. The opening of the International Health Exhibition in May 1884. It featured a street known as 'Old London', whose buildings provided useful accommodation for officials and visitors to the Exhibition, and offices for St John's Ambulance and the Fire Brigade. There was a genuine attempt to represent historic structures correctly, and this seems to have been an early manifestation of concern over the demolition of historic buildings.

48. Sketch for the interior of Holy Trinity, Prince Consort Road by G. F. Bodley.
The church was a belated initiative by the Church Commissioners to provide
an ecclesiastical centre for the 1851 Estate.

49. The National Training School for Music, later the Royal College of Music.
It was designed by Lieutenant Henry Cole. When the Royal College moved to a
larger building, it became the home of the Royal College of Organists.

Mansions Lowther Gardens Queen's Gate.

J.J.Stevenson
A.J.Adams } ARCHITECTS.

First Floor Plan

Ground Floor Plan

50. Mansions, Lowther Gardens, a development by a private developer adjacent to the Commissioners' Estate, but later purchased and used as offices by the Commission.

51. Laying the Foundation Stone of the Royal College of Music, 8 July 1890. The group round the base of the Memorial to the 1851 Exhibition, included Sir George Grove, hatless, seated in the middle of the back row, Sir C. Stanford, in a white top hat, immediately below him, and Sir Hubert Parry, in a rakish black top hat, again to the left and below. Sir Frank Bridge is in the front row, third from the right.

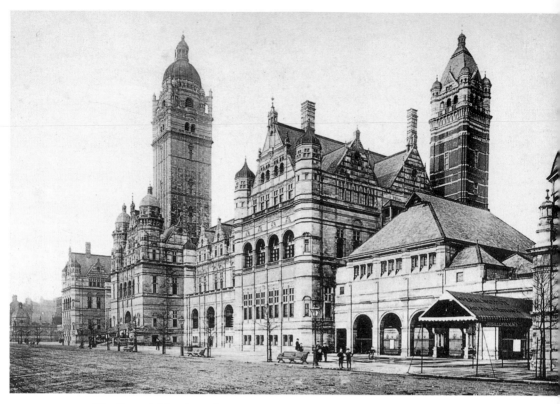

52. The Imperial Institute from Imperial Institute Road about 1890. On the right is the entrance to the Eastern Galleries.

53. The Imperial Institute, view through the main entrance looking north to the vestibule.

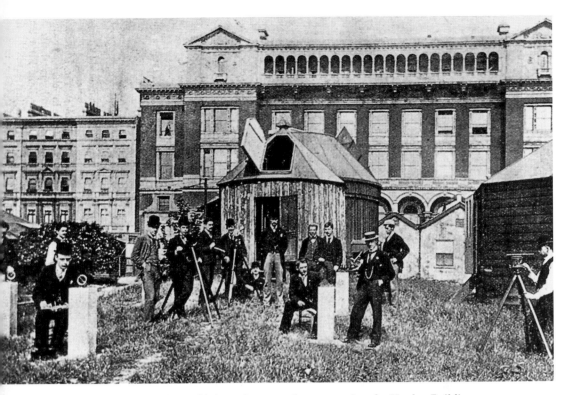

54. The Royal College of Science in 1891, then occupying the Huxley Building,
now the Henry Cole Building of the Victoria and Albert Museum. In front
can be seen the Solar Physics Laboratory.

IMPERIAL INSTITUTE

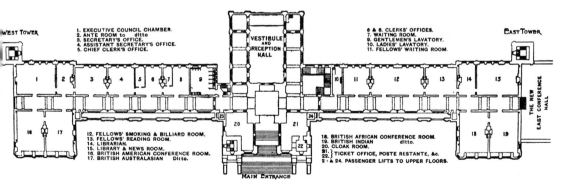

PLAN OF THE PRINCIPAL FLOOR

55. Plan of the Principal Floor of the Imperial Institute, which provided
conference, library and club accommodation.

56. Perspective of the new Royal College of Science, on the south side of Imperial Institute Road, as designed by Aston Webb in 1900.

57. Central Institution of the City and Guilds in Exhibition Road, designed by
Alfred Waterhouse, 1881–4, later part of Imperial College.

58. Royal School of Art Needlework, on the corner of Imperial Institute Road and
Exhibition Road, about 1900. The building was later taken over by Imperial College.

59. Sir Lyon Playfair, KCB, FRS, later Lord Playfair, who became Honorary Secretary to the Commission from 1883 to 1889. He reformed the Commission's finances and pioneered the 1851 Scholarship scheme.

60. Major General H. D. Y. Scott, Secretary 1869–83, who played a number of roles in South Kensington, being also Secretary to the Royal Horticultural Society, architect to the Albert Hall and to the South Kensington Museum.

61. Major General Sir Arthur Ellis, GCVO, who combined the Secretaryship of the Commission during 1889–1907 with duties in the Royal Household.

62. Sir Arthur Bigge (1849–1931), later Lord Stamfordham, Secretary 1907–10. He was an important member of the Royal Household, serving as private secretary to George V, as Prince of Wales, and as King, from 1903 to 1931.

63. Reginald Brett, 2nd Viscount Esher (1852–1930), Chairman of the Board of Management, 1910–30, responsible for interesting the Commissioners in the British School at Rome, and for a number of other educational initiatives.

64. Sir Richard Glazebrook, a Commissioner from 1911, and Director of the National Physical Laboratory, 1900–19.

65. Sir Norman Lockyer, Professor of Astronomical Physics at the Royal College of Science, and Secretary to the Duke of Devonshire's Royal Commission on Scientific Instruction, a keen supporter of the Science Museum.

66. Sir Evelyn Shaw, KCVO, Secretary to the 1851 Commissioners, 1910–47.

67. A group of physicists at Cambridge in 1932, a number of whom were 1851 Scholars, including Professor Lord Rutherford (front row, centre), J. Chadwick (front, third from left), Sir Harrie Massey (second row, third from left) and Sir John Cockcroft (front row, extreme left).

68. The southern part of the Exhibition Road about 1900.

69. Perspective of the main elevation of the Science Museum, designed by J. H. Allison.
On the right can be seen the Post Office, so disapproved of by the Commissioners,
but which has survived as part of the Science Museum.

70. The Imperial War Museum started its existence in the Western Galleries, here seen in 1926, with military vehicles outside.

71. The Science Museum collections were originally housed in the arcades of the Royal Horticultural Gardens, before the new Science Museum was built. Part of the Agricultural Collection in Gallery 39, in October 1928.

72. The Exhibition Pavilion by Edwin Lutyens, Rome Exhibition, 1911.

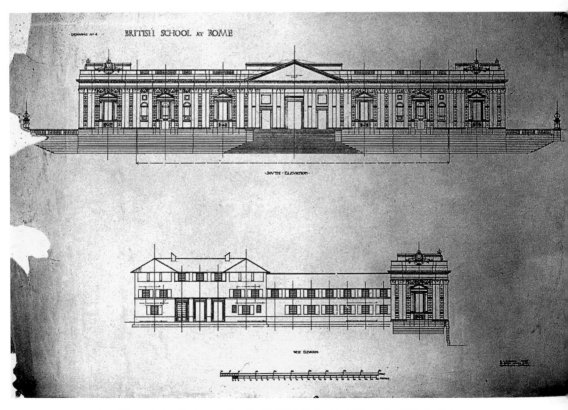

73. The original scheme for the British School at Rome by Edwin Lutyens.

74. The main façade of the British School at Rome as built, by Edwin Lutyens.

75. British Scholars, funded by the 1851 Commission and other bodies, in the courtyard of the British School at Rome in 1928.

76. An aerial view of the Commissioners' Estate in South Kensington in 1939, with the Albert Memorial in Hyde Park beyond, the Albert Hall at the north end, flanked by the Beit Quadrangle to the left, Albert Court to the right, and below the Imperial Institute. On the south side of Imperial Institute Road is the Royal College of Science, with to the east the main blocks of the Science and Geological Museums fronting Exhibition Road. Outside the Commissioners' Estate are the Natural

77. The Commissioners' Estate in 1988, showing the effect of post-war redevelopment.

78. The new Geological Museum in 1935, built to replace the Museum of Practical Geology in Jermyn Street, and now part of the Natural History Museum.

79. Royal College of Art, New Building by Hugh Casson and H. T. Cadbury-Brown fronting Kensington Gore.

80. The Queen's Tower, the tower of the former Imperial Institute, from Imperial
College Road, *c.2000*.

81. The main frontage of the Victoria and Albert Museum looking on to Cromwell Road, designed by Aston Webb.

The Memorial has, however, always been vulnerable both to pollution and to interference from local students, and, in the Second World War, to the attention of American GIs. In 1920, the Commission turned for help to the Office of Works, which had a large number of statues in its care. Evelyn Shaw, then running the Commission, was appalled by the extravagant advice of the Office of Works, which ran:

> I feel I ought to point out that an occasional overhaul once in 8 years cannot be regarded as the proper way to treat an open-air statue . . . it should be cleaned at least three times a year . . . This works out at more than the occasional repairs which you have indulged in so far, but a statue looks presentable all the time and its life is prolonged.

The statue was thoroughly cleaned and repaired in 1928, but Shaw settled for an annual clean, fearing his Commissioners 'would faint at the idea of having it done every four months',[80] a system which remained in place until the outbreak of war in 1939. After the Second World War, very thorough restoration was required, not least because of the paint daubed on the Memorial 'by troops or other revellers'. Shaw deplored the way in which the pre-war Office of Works' annual cleanup, costing some £17, had risen to the 1948 estimate of £117 from the private firm, Messrs Reparations Ltd.[81]

By 1959, Prince Albert, on his Memorial plinth, was included by *The Times* in an article listing London statues 'in need of cleaning', in sad contrast to the Albert Memorial which had recently been thoroughly restored, though it would appear the matter had already been put in hand by the Surveyor, 'Roy' Holroyd Chambers.[82]

MAJOR–GENERAL ARTHUR ELLIS AS SECRETARY

In 1889, Playfair resigned as Honorary Secretary, pleading the need to reduce pressure of business, since he was nearly seventy. The Commission appointed Major-General Ellis as a paid Secretary, with a salary. Arthur Edward Augustus Ellis (1837–1907) was a member of the Prince of Wales's household and had been a Commissioner since 1877. He came from an old West Indian family, whose grandfather had married the only child of the Earl-Bishop of Bristol. He himself had fought in both the Crimean war, and in India in 1859–62, returning to England to marry Labouchere's daughter in 1864. In due course, he became an important member of the Prince of Wales's household, accompanying him on many visits abroad. He was a talented draughtsman, commemorating many royal occasions, from a visit to Disraeli in Downing Street to the Prince of Wales riding on an elephant during his Indian tour in 1875–6. In 1901, he became Comptroller of Edward VII's household, playing a significant part in the reorganization of the Royal Household, which had become antiquated and very out-of-date under the old queen, and reforming the Lord Chamberlain's Department, responsible for ceremonial matters and royal receptions.[83] As Secretary to the 1851 Commission, Ellis received the modest salary of £300 a year, less than that of L. C. Sayles, on the grounds that the work was only 'moderate', in fact being part-time.[84]

Playfair remained on the Board of Management, as Deputy Chairman, together with the Chairman Prince Christian, Thring, Childers, Mundella and a new member of the Commission, Henry H. Fowler (1830–1911) Liberal Member of Parliament, and former mayor for Wolverhampton, who had held various government posts in Gladstone's administration. Playfair's time as Honorary Secretary had been directed almost entirely to improving the Commission's finances, and he was able to leave the secretaryship with a statement confirming his success, together with a new plan for the estate, calculated to continue the rise in the income available for scholarships, to which £5000 a year was initially to be devoted.[85] Ironically, despite its new drive towards financial self-sufficiency and increased income, the Commission had to borrow in 1892 because it was undertaking a large number of projects related to the development of the estate. In fact, the income and expenditure had increased so much and become so complex that the decision was taken by the Board to terminate the arrangement by which Mr Farrell of the Bank of England had audited the accounts for the Commission, and to employ a firm of chartered accountants, Messrs Deloitte, Dever and Company, at a fee of £20.[86]

THE SETTING UP OF THE SCIENCE SCHOLARSHIPS

Unmoved by the memorials against the development of private homes, the Commission issued its *Seventh Report* in July 1889, proclaiming its intentions both for the estate and the science scholarships. Under the new pattern of meetings, which was to see the Board under Prince Christian and Playfair taking the decisions and reporting to increasingly infrequent and formal meetings of the Commission, a new policy was developed. The Board set up a new Science Scholarship Committee under Playfair, on which A. J. Mundella represented the Commission, with a number of scientific experts – Professor William Garnett, T. H. Huxley (1825–95), J. Norman Lockyer (1836–1920), appointed Professor of Astronomical Physics at the Royal College of Science in 1890, Sir Henry Roscoe (1833–1915), Professor of Chemistry at Owens College, Manchester (1857–85), and Sir William Thomson, later Lord Kelvin (1824–1907), telegraph engineer and inventor and President of the Royal Society (1890–4). The invited members were offered an honorarium of £25 to defray the expenses of attending the meetings.

The Science Scholarships Committee reported to the Board on the proposed scheme in 1890. They had been advised that a number of scholarships now existed, and since it was important not to discourage private benefactors, the Commission should therefore give scholarships of 'a higher order', and 'their functions should begin where the ordinary educational curriculum ends', on the existing French model. They therefore recommended scholarships of £150 a year, tenable for two years in the first instance, occasionally extended for a third, 'limited to those branches of science (such as physics, mechanics, and chemistry) the extension of which is especially important for our national industries'. These would be tenable at any university at home or abroad, but the holder must agree to dedicate himself whole-heartedly to the object of the scholarship, and not to seek any paid position during the period. In due course, suitable colonial and provincial colleges would be given the power of nominating senior students to scholarships. The whole scheme would be managed by a 'committee of advice'.

This report was approved by the Board, in the absence of any meeting of the Commission, and the Committee proceeded to select the participating universities. They were bound by the Commission's instructions that provincial universities alone should benefit in acknowledgement of the provinces' unrewarded contribution to the success of the 1851 Exhibition. The three national universities of Oxford, Cambridge and Dublin were excluded because of their large endowments, but colonial institutions were included. The initial seventeen scholarships were to be awarded annually to universities and colleges throughout the British Isles, and in Canada, Australia and New Zealand, who would themselves nominate the Scholars. Some bodies were awarded an annual scholarship, others had to share: thus the three Welsh colleges, of Bangor, Aberystwyth and Cardiff, shared one scholarship every year, McGill

College, Montreal, and the University of Toronto had to share, as did Aberdeen and St Andrews, while the sharing of two scholarships out between the four Irish colleges of Belfast, Cork, Galway and the Dublin College of Science must have presented problems.[87]

The Science Scholarships Committee did not let the grass grow under its feet, and the first sixteen scholarships were awarded in 1891.[88] The list and the scheme were given retrospective approval by the Commissioners, and they agreed that when funds permitted the scheme should be increased from seventeen to twenty-five Scholars.

The colleges in which the first group of winners chose to study are interesting: of the fifteen men and one woman, ten chose to spend at least the first year at their own college, though they were all advised to move for the second year. Of the others, one, from Dublin, opted for Glasgow, while the other five decided to go to German universities; Berlin, Leipzig, Würzburg, Munich, Heidelberg. Of those to choose a different college for the second year, one elected to go to South Kensington, the rest to Germany. The following year, the Scholarships Committee were able to report considerable success: only one Scholar had resigned, five were still at their sponsoring university, the rest had gone to German institutions. The subjects chosen were various; a number were related to magnetism, some were working in the field of organic chemistry, one was working on the chemistry of dyeing and fermentation, another on the thermodynamics of the steam engine. Once launched, the scheme proceeded smoothly, though occasionally a full number of scholarships could not be awarded for lack of suitable candidates. Another problem was the shortage of money, caused to some degree by the Newman *imbroglio*, and in 1892 the funds, some £5000, had to be borrowed.

By 1894, Playfair was able to report that the Science Scholarships Committee had adopted a system of auditing the work of the Scholars by submitting their reports to outside experts for their opinion, most of which had been satisfactory. Other universities and colleges were added to the list, Queen's University, Kingston, Canada, and Dalhousie University, Nova Scotia, and at Playfair's suggestion, University College, London, all in 1893, but Calcutta University, though proposed in 1894, was never included. Its merits, together with those of the other Indian colleges of Bombay, Madras, Allahabad and Lahore, were discussed in the Science Scholarships Committee in 1896, but the members came to the conclusion that Calcutta and the affiliated colleges were examining rather than teaching bodies, and that scholarships could only be awarded to 'institutions which actually teach science'.[89] The South African College, later the University of Cape Town, sent a Scholar from 1904 onwards, but otherwise the Commission seems to have kept to their original list of colleges. In due course, the selection of colleges for study broadened, the first Dalhousie student electing to go to Cornell University, New York State, while the Central Technical College, South Kensington, also received Scholars in 1894.

As the Science Scholarships scheme settled down, inevitably modifications followed; the experts' reports were outspoken, and not always as favourable as they might have been. One, John J. Sudborough, from Mason College, Birmingham, was thus assessed by Professor Armstrong: 'While . . . Mr. Sudborough has considerable ability and experience as a practical worker, I fail to find any evidence that he is possessed of originality.' Nonetheless, Sudborough went to Heidelberg, and returned to teach, first at Nottingham, then as Dean of Science at Aberystwyth, and finally as Professor of Organic Chemistry at the Indian Institute of Science, Bangalore.[90] The Scholars were chosen carefully, and only the best were allowed the precious third year.

THE DEPARTURE OF PLAYFAIR

In June 1896, Playfair, now aged 78, and a member of the House of Lords, resigned both as Deputy Chairman of the Board of Management, in effect the chairman when the actual Chairman was a member of the Royal Family, and as Chairman of the Science Scholarships Committee, though remaining a member of both bodies. Characteristically, he left a comprehensive memorandum on the lines he thought that the Commission should follow to manage its finances and its estate, and the larger role for which it had been set up. Possibly because of his scientific bias, his legacy was in a sense one-sided: though he had reformed the Commission's finances, and set up the successful scholarship scheme which was to point the way forward for the future work of the Board, it has to be said that his stewardship of the estate was not so far-sighted. Whatever the pressures from other members of the Board, and even the President, his time as Secretary saw the final destruction of the fine horticultural centrepiece planned for the estate by Prince Albert, and the abandonment of any coherent town-planning for the area, a lapse of judgement whose results can be felt to this day.

Playfair suggested that the Board needed strengthening with some new members, and nominated his successors – Henry Fowler as Vice-Chairman of the Board, and Henry Roscoe as Chairman of the Science Scholarships Committee. He could not resist commenting on the changes in the membership of the Commission: a number of important figures had died since the last meeting – Huxley, Lord Aberdare, involved with both the Horticultural Society and the Albert Hall, and Treasurer since Bowring's resignation, Lord Leighton, and Henry Ponsonby, who had fulfilled the difficult task of liaison between the Commission and the Royal Household, and the Liberal statesman, Hugh Childers, who had served on the Board of Management.

Playfair was much concerned over the finances of the Commission, which he still saw as precarious. He felt that under Bowring and Scott, the Commission had spent too much on capital improvements to the estate, the erection of new buildings for which there was no return, a policy which got the Commission into debt. The debt was now extinguished, and the Board had been in a position to invest nearly £10,000 in stocks and shares in 1896.[91] Though he felt that there existed a 'satisfactory clear revenue to aid the objects for which we act as trustees', he advocated the setting up of a reserve fund of £20,000, before any further generosity to South Kensington institutions or an increase in scholarships. Those scholarships had 'removed the discontent . . . manifested by deputations, memorials, and questions in Parliament', and felt in the provinces because they failed to share in the profits of the Great Exhibition. This was not the only benefit, and the Commissioners, who were already aware of the distinction of Ernest Rutherford[92] could take pride in what they were doing for scientific education:

> New and important discoveries have been made by our Scholars . . . Suppose, for instance, by this system one great discoverer like Faraday or Stephenson were to appear among the young Scholars, thus encouraged by £150 annual grants, a gift would have been presented to this country which would have been cheap had the nation contributed a million sterling to his production.
>
> This promotion of research is the reason why Germany is running us so hard in commercial competition, and our Scholarship Scheme is doing an important work in this country . . . by encouraging young scientists with capabilities of original discovery.[93]

VII

Changes at South Kensington:
The Victoria and Albert Museum
and Imperial College
1896–1910

Playfair's resignation as Chairman of the Board of Management in 1896 ushered in a number of changes in the Commission itself; at the same period external forces were to change the Commissioners' estate and South Kensington for ever. As the nineteenth century and the Queen's reign ended, new players and new attitudes were to sweep away a lot of the characteristics of Albertopolis, including some of its small-town qualities, the nepotism, its interwoven employment and interests – what we might call its 'cronyism'.

Because of the Commissioners' success in attracting and developing institutions on the estate, their own control of the area was diminished. In some matters, their prestige was no longer so great, as shown by the refusal of the City and Guilds to accept any 1851 Commissioners as members of their Council. Much of the estate was occupied by independent bodies like the Natural History Museum, controlled by the Trustees of the British Museum, while the increasing influence of the Board of Education, headed by the formidable civil servant, Robert Morant (1863–1920), meant that the independence of other South Kensington bodies, like the South Kensington Museum, was being curbed. The Commission had became a wealthy landowner, using its profits for scientific grants, an important role, but no longer a strategic one as in the 1850s and 1860s. Its financial contributions were often solicited, and always welcome, as in the case of the Imperial Institute, but its ability to attract new bodies was somewhat inhibited by the lack of space available and its reputation for high-handed treatment of newcomers. Increasingly it was the government, now taking education more seriously, though checked as always by Treasury parsimony, which was to shape the area in future.

THE COMMISSIONERS

With Playfair's retirement, the last of the original group which brought the Commission into being disappeared from South Kensington, though Playfair remained active over some matters like financial support for the Imperial Institute till the year of his death. Over the previous five years a number of veterans had died, including Earl Granville, Earl Carnarvon, and Lord Sandford. The composition of the Commission itself was indeed changing, and the politicians and men of business who had dominated the Commission in the 1870s and 1880s were being succeeded by scientists and other experts drawn from the various institutions in South Kensington, or recruited through the Science Scholarships Committee. Thus in 1891, new Commissioners elected included Sir William Thomson (1824–1907), later Lord Kelvin, Sir Henry Roscoe (1833–1915), the astronomer Professor Norman Lockyer (1836–1920), and T. H. Huxley (1825–95), as well as the royal nominees, the 9th Duke of Argyll (1845–1914), husband of Princess Louise, and former Governor-General of Canada, the Duke of Fife (1849–1912), husband of Edward VII's daughter, Princess Louise, and Baron Ferdinand de Rothschild (1839–98). There was still a regular addition of politicians and those involved in government; in the course of the 1890s the Commission recruited the Members of Parliament Sir Henry Campbell-Bannerman, H. H. Asquith, Leonard Courtney, Charles Spencer, half-brother of the 5th Earl Spencer so important at the Commission in the 1880s, and the civil servants, Lord Welby, Permanent Secretary to the Treasury from 1885 to 1894, Sir Fleetwood Edwards and Sir Edward Hamilton. The artist John Millais (1829–96) was an unusual Commissioner drawn from the arts world. An increasing number of Commissioners were to come from local South Kensington institutions, like Lord James of Hereford from the Imperial Institute, Dr Garnett from the Royal School of Art-Needlework, Sir Sydney Waterlow representing the City and Guilds Central Institute, or F. G. Ogilvie of the Education Department. Nonetheless, Ellis, writing to Lord Esher in 1902, could say that the 'Commissioners are many and comprise every pattern of "big wig" in England', going on to say that 'the duties are therefore *very few* and far between but the members are dying off and the King wisely wants fresh blood'.[1]

ADMINISTRATION

There were also the *ex officio* Commissioners, the Presidents of the Institute of Civil Engineers and of the Geological Society, appointed in 1850 by the first charter, some of whom continued to attend and to be welcomed to meetings of the Commission. Several government ministers were still *ex officio* Commissioners because of Gladstone's intervention in 1853 – the Lord President of the Council, the Prime Minister, the Chancellor of the Exchequer, the President of the Board of Trade, First Commissioner of Works, and until 1899, the Vice-President of the Council on Education. They do not seem to have attended many Commission meetings, but in George V's time as President their 'accessions' were reported to the assembled Commissioners. Quite frequently an interested *ex officio* member would be asked to join the Commission, as Winston Churchill was in 1912, after serving *ex officio* as President of the Board of Trade in 1908. Some of the *ex officio* members continued to sign the Reports until after the Second World War, as in 1951 when Clement Attlee and Hugh Gaitskell, as ministers, appended their names to the *Tenth Report.*[2]

The administration of the Commission developed a more regular pattern from this time forward. As with Playfair as Honorary Secretary, under Ellis the Board of Management became increasingly important, making most of the decisions, which were reported to annual meetings of the Commission and usually nodded through.[3] In the 1890s the office was based at 18 Victoria Street, on the north side just east of New Tothill Street, where it was housed with the Army Medical Service. In 1901, the office moved to number 16, moving to number 54 in May 1905.[4] Board meetings were peripatetic: for meetings of the Commission, or for meetings of the Board if any of the royal members were present, Marlborough House, the official residence of the President, the Prince of Wales, was used, otherwise they met at the Commission office. At this time the most important figure in the office was the Assistant Secretary, L. C. Sayles, a man with a barrister's training. He had been with the Commission since at least 1868, when he had occupied one of the Kensington Gore houses.[5] His importance is demonstrated by the fact that when Ellis was first appointed his salary was £300 per annum as against Sayles's £400, though in due course Ellis's salary rose to £500, Sayles's only to £450.[6] He retired in 1904, on the grounds of ill-health, and was replaced as

Assistant Secretary by Evelyn Shaw (1881–1974), appointed at a salary of £150 per annum, a man who was to have more influence on the Commission than any other employee except Edgar Bowring. Sayles ran the office, dealing with a large number of routine matters, which fell outside the province of either of the Commission's professional advisers, the solicitor or the surveyor. Both of these men attended almost all the Board meetings from 1898 and carried out a number of regular duties for the administration of the estate, for which they received fees. At this time, as initiated by Playfair, there was a regular programme of sales of ground rents, sometimes of the freeholds, of Commission house property, and of the investment of the proceeds either on deposit or in suitable stocks and shares. This policy involved both surveyor and solicitor, as did the changes in the estate layout caused by the building over of the garden, and the creation of Prince Consort Road.

The Commission's first solicitor had been William Mark Fladgate (1805–88), who had been appointed in the Commission's early days through his friendship with Charles Wentworth Dilke, largely to deal with routine conveyancing. In the early days of the Commission, difficult legal questions seem to have been submitted to Commissioners with expert skills, like Henry Thring, later Lord Thring, Commissioner from 1861 to 1907, who was Counsel to the Treasury, and a leading lawyer, though later the Commissioners adopted the more usual modern practice of submitting controversial legal matters to counsel through their solicitor. William Francis Fladgate (1866–1937), later Sir Francis, succeeded his father in the family firm.[7]

Similarly, the first Surveyor to the Commission was the Surveyor to the Office of Works, Henry Arthur Hunt (1810–1889), later Sir Henry Hunt. He retired in 1887, and was succeeded by his son Henry A. Hunt who was to occasion some concern over his handling of the Newman affair. When the younger Hunt died in 1904, his partner Steward 'having regard to his health and other engagements' turned down the job, and the Commissioners appointed Frederick J. Stevenson as their surveyor, who served the Commission from 1905 to 1921.[8]

THE BUSINESS OF THE COMMISSION

It could be argued indeed that at this time there was little business which required the advice of 'big-wigs', except for the odd strategic decision on which there would be a lot of lobbying and occasional intervention at the highest level. The successful Science Scholarship scheme was forging ahead under the management of the Science Scholarships Committee, with the annual expenditure rising gradually from £5000 odd in 1892 to over £6000 in 1908.[9] The Board of Management was mostly concerned with a regular programme of sales of ground rents, and their investment in gilts, colonial and provincial stocks, and the occasional railway preference shares. The changes to the estate plan through the building over of the Royal Horticultural Society Gardens and the creation of the Prince Consort's Road meant considerable expenditure, through such payments as those for the building of a new southern entrance to the Royal Albert Hall, or the adoption of roads by Westminster City Council. There were also small subsidies to tenants or prospective tenants.

HOLY TRINITY CHURCH

Rather late in the day by the standards of responsible Victorian ground landlords, the Commissioners established a church for the area, stimulated by the building up of Queen's Gate, and the decision to use the four plots in Prince Consort Road, for housing rather than institutional use. The initiative came from outside, from Lord Ashcombe (1828–1917), Thomas Cubitt's eldest son, who had eschewed the building trade, becoming a Surrey country gentleman, a Member of Parliament and a Church Estates Commissioner. He approached the Commissioners in 1898 to ask whether there was a site on the estate to which the name and assets of the redundant Holy Trinity Chapel on the north side of Knightsbridge might be moved. This was followed by an application from the incumbents of the two Knightsbridge parishes, All Saints and Holy Trinity, saying that the site of the latter was to be sold to finance a new church on the Commissioners' estate. The Board offered them a 9000 square foot plot in Prince Consort Road, but only for sale at £5000, or to rent at the appropriate interest. Even a complaint from the Bishop of London about the high price did not move the Board, though they did concede that the parish would not be liable for the maintenance of either the 'central space', the terraces or the West Quadrant Road. The design of the church was to be subject like other buildings to the artistic approval of Alfred Waterhouse. Bodley's request for a further ten foot strip on the site increased the price to the Ecclesiastical Commissioners by £1000, possibly reflecting the Board's priorities, but his design was approved in June 1901, and the church, one of his most elegant in a flowing fourteenth-century style, was consecrated two years later.[10] It was completed after Bodley's death in 1907 by his assistant Cecil Hare. Because of the very cramped site, it is very much a town church built into the hill, with a blank 'south' wall, and the 'west' wall as a piece of street architecture. Inside however it was completed by Arts and Crafts fittings: altar, pulpit and choir stalls from Rattee and Kent, together with a new organ case to take the old organ, somewhat enlarged, from the demolished Holy Trinity Chapel, and glass to Bodley's design from Burlison & Grylls.

The Board proved more helpful to the Royal College of Art-Needlework, which embarked on a prestigious but expensive new building in Exhibition Road, but this may have merely reflected the significance of the adjective 'Royal', which came from the patronage of the Princess Christian. The school had been one of the tenants found for the redundant annexes of the 1871–4 Exhibitions, and had moved to the Belgian Annexe in 1875. In 1892, it secured an important site on the north side of Imperial Institute Road at the ground rent of £200, and a design was produced by the Arts and Crafts architect Fairfax B. Wade, who happened to be the brother of the Lady Superintendent. Though the design was approved, and originally intended to cost £12,500, in 1898 the school approached the Commissioners for a loan of £16,000, half the estimated cost of the building, to be secured by interest at 3 per cent. This was to be funded by letting part of it to the City and Guilds. Work did not start till 1899, when the Prince of Wales laid the foundation stone. There were further problems over the building and its funding, which were only solved by providing well-equipped engineering laboratories for the Central Institute of the City and Guilds, the rent for which went straight to the Commission to service the debt. The Commission's money was further safeguarded by the letting of another part of the building to the School of Art-Woodcarving.[11] The route of the tunnel to provide access under cover to the Albert Hall was safeguarded by the Commission, but this project was ultimately defeated by the objection of the occupants of the engineering laboratories to any vibration or interference from railways of any sort.[12]

Another building over which questions were raised was the Post Office in Exhibition Road, which was reconstructed in 1905 to replace a temporary District Office. It was placed on a site leased exclusively for buildings connected with science. Schomberg McDonnell (1861–1915), the

well-connected successor to Esher in the Office of Works, enquired discreetly as to whether Commissioners would object to such a use on this
site, and possibly assuaged by the inclusion of a Meteorological Office,
the Commissioners decided to leave the matter to the Office of Works.

Though there were no large new sites left in the 'main square', there
were a few vacated sites, which had to be reassigned, often because their
previous owners had outgrown them or moved away. One of these was
H. H. Cole's building for the National Training School for Music on the
west of the Albert Hall, vacated by the Royal College of Music. There was
some competition over this, since, though it was requested by Donnelly
for the School of Art-Woodcarving in 1898, the Royal College wanted to
retain it, and had not moved out. Donnelly's application was refused, and
the building went to the Royal College of Organists, whose request was
supported by Hubert Parry from the Royal College of Music. Five years
later, the organists were granted a ninety-nine-year lease at a peppercorn
rent.[13]

On the domestic side of the estate, the Board of Management had all
the usual concerns of ground landlords: the conversion of over-large private houses into apartment blocks, service flats and private hotels, all
requiring modifications or additions to leases. South Kensington seems to
have been early into motoring, and by 1903, tenants were anxious to convert mews stables into 'houses for motor-cars'.[14]

THE ROYAL ALBERT HALL

There was one major concern which the Commissioners needed to bring
to a satisfactory conclusion, and this was their relationship with the
Corporation of the Albert Hall. This had been very close since the building of the Hall; the Commission had had offices in the building for some
of the smaller exhibitions, and at one stage had intended to use the
gallery for some of the scientific exhibits. They still held eight hundred
seats, under rather complex arrangements; they did not exercise the full
number of votes, they paid the seat rate but the seats were marketed by
the Hall Corporation which took a large percentage of the profits, five-
sevenths as against the Commissioners' two-sevenths, plus a payment for
keeping the Hall open. The Commission had lent money to the Corporation in 1878 to enable it to pay off its initial debt, and lent more to assist
the Corporation of the Hall to build a new Southern entrance to replace
the Conservatory. The cost of this was estimated at £5000 in 1891, which

the Commission had undertaken to provide, £3000 being a further loan to the Hall at 4 per cent. The seat rate was far higher than the profits, as was shown annually in the accounts, £1440 as against £250 in receipts in 1891. Seven years later it was worse: the same seat rate and receipts of only £144 5s. 7d. The Board, pointing out that the Commission had spent some £170,000 on the Hall for which they received no benefit, asked for leave to sort the matter out.[15]

The approach, made by Fowler and Ellis, was not well-received by those managing the Hall, who claimed that any change in the arrangement would expose them to grave financial embarrassment; though notice was given for March 1902, it was deferred for a further year, but the parties could not even agree on the name of an arbitrator. Fowler took the view that the Hall should not have a divided management, writing to Edward VII on his views against 'dual control of the Commissioners and the Council and the necessity that one or the other should have entire ownership'. The matter dragged on until 1908, when the Council of the Hall under their President the Earl of Pembroke obtained extremely generous terms from the Commissioners. The latter surrendered all eight hundred seats, thus relieving themselves of the seat rate, and in order to compensate the Corporation for the net loss of between £500 and £1000 a year agreed to extinguish two earlier loans totalling £8540. They also agreed to fund the Corporation's share of the new southern entrance with a loan of some £2500, at 4 per cent. The Commission retained its interest in the Hall, continuing to nominate a member of the Council, still seeing the Hall, to which they estimated they had contributed £180,000 over the years, as a flagship for the neighbourhood.[16]

THE CHANGE OF PRESIDENT

The accession of the Prince of Wales as King-Emperor in January 1901 inevitably brought changes, though he did not immediately relinquish control. He had recruited a number of royal relatives to the Commission, and his intended successor, the Duke of York (later George V) joined in 1896. His brother-in-law, Prince Christian, was the nominal Chairman of the Board for twenty-three years, but the real work was done by the Deputy Chairman, first Lyon Playfair, and then Sir Henry Fowler, who succeeded the Prince as titular Chairman in 1904. Henry Hartley Fowler, 1st Lord Wolverhampton (1830–1911), was a Liberal Member of Parliament, former mayor of Wolverhampton, President of the National

Telephone Company, President of the Local Government Board in 1892, and Lord President of the Council, 1908–1910. He has gone down in history as the first Methodist to sit in the Cabinet.

Though possibly a little prone to push favourite projects like the Imperial Institute or the Royal College of Music ahead of the interests of the estate generally, Edward VII, as Prince of Wales, had served the Commission well as President, and his last service as President was to provide some first-rate members and yet another well-connected and astute secretary. On 10 February, 1903, the Commissioners met to elect the Prince of Wales as President, and to welcome two important new recruits. Reginald Brett, 2nd Viscount Esher (1852–1930), and Sir Arthur Bigge (1849–1931), later Lord Stamfordham. Bigge, son of a Northumbrian vicar, and a professional soldier, was a former Private Secretary to Queen Victoria, and Private Secretary to the new Prince of Wales, in due course taking on the role of Secretary to the 1851 Commission. Both of these appointments were very much by royal command, Ellis's letter to Esher ends, 'I shd. like to be able to report to the King that you will accept H. M.'s suggestion He says your joining will be *most valuable* – which is only true'.[17]

Esher is indeed one of the most interesting and influential of any of the 1851 Commissioners, both as a personality and in the part he played in the Commission. Educated at Eton and Trinity College, Cambridge, Reginald Baliol Brett started his career as private secretary to Lord Hartington, later 8th Duke of Devonshire, then sat as Member of Parliament for a Cornish constituency from 1880 to 1885. He then withdrew from public life, becoming part of the royal circle round Queen Victoria. In due course, he edited the Queen's letters, and later was appointed Keeper of the Royal Archives. From 1895 till 1902 he was Secretary of the Office of Works which gave him responsibility for matters as diverse as the design for the rebuilding of Waterloo Place, the Diamond Jubilee celebrations and Queen Victoria's funeral. On the last occasion he was instrumental in ensuring that all went smoothly at the interment at Frogmore, after the unhappy shambles on Windsor Hill, when the horses had jibbed. He went on to be a member of the Imperial Defence Committee and Deputy-Constable of Windsor Castle.[18]

THE DEPARTMENT OF SCIENCE AND ART

However well-connected the Commissioners were, there were an increasing number of events outside their control, even on their own estate. One of these was the removal of the Department of Science and Art from South Kensington to Whitehall, and the final split between the art and the science sides of the South Kensington Museum.

Since Cole's retirement in 1873, his joint holding of the posts of Secretary of the Department of Science and Art and Director of the Museum had been divided. The bureaucrats of the Department were in control, while without a man of Cole's irresistible energy in charge, it was difficult for the museum staff to obtain authority to expand the space available to house the acquisitions. A letter to *The Times*, from the French Inspector-General of Fine Arts, Charles Iriarte, was widely read and noted:

> Today, for all us foreigners South Kensington is a Mecca. England there possesses the entire art of Europe and the East, their spiritual manifestations under all forms, and Europe has been swept into the stream in imitation of England.

However, he continued,

> The splendour of the start (excessive as it seems to me) contrasts with the inertia of the last fifteen years; the inconceivable treasures are becoming so much heaped up as to be a veritable obstacle to study.[19]

The art collections and its associated training school for practical art were, however, admired in other countries, and, as Barbara Morris has pointed out, as far afield as Philadelphia, Vienna and Bohemia, institutions were founded in imitation of the Department of Art.

The science collections were equally inspiring; the young German engineer Oskar von Miller (1855–1934) from Bavaria visited South Kensington about 1880, and found it so impressive that he went back and founded its great rival the Deutsches Museum in Munich. The matter was approached with more expedition in Germany, the foundation stone was laid by Wilhelm II in 1906, and though, like that of the Science Museum building, its completion was delayed by the Great War, Hindenburg opened the Munich building in 1925, two years before

George V opened the first purpose-built Science Museum in Exhibition Road.[20]

In 1890 the decision had been taken to hold a public architectural competition for extensions to the South Kensington Museum building to provide more space. This had been adjudicated by Waterhouse, who had himself declined to compete, and was won by Aston Webb against stiff competition in 1891 from architects such as Collcutt, T. G. Jackson and William Young, seen as a Scottish representative. However, because of hesitation on the part of the Treasury over money, and a falling out with the Office of Works over other matters, the actual building was not started until after 1897.

Meanwhile, concern over other aspects of the management of the museum collections in South Kensington grew, both within the museum world and in Parliament.[21] The muddle and confusion in the collections provoked a campaign, headed in Parliament by David Lindsay, Lord Balcarres (1871–1940), who was to gain a great reputation for his life's devotion to the interests of national museums and art galleries. He sat as a Conservative Member of Parliament from 1895 till 1913 for his family's seat of Wigan where the Lindsays were influential coal owners. After a successful Oxford career, he had spent time doing social work in the East End, where he had met figures from more modest backgrounds like the London Member of Parliament John Burns, who had become a great personal friend. He came from a wealthy family well known for its art collections, but was influenced by wider concerns over the South Kensington collections.

Changes at the Department of Science and Art were demanded because its main concern was not with the museum collections, but with its responsibilities for the running of secondary schools concerned with scientific and artistic training. 'Nepotism, sinecures, the purchase of forgeries, absence of cataloguing, employment of untrained staff', combined with its costs and its administrative methods, were among the charges against the management at South Kensington.[22] It was attacked by the Radical Member of Parliament, John Burns, in the House of Commons in July 1896, as 'a nest of nepotism and a jungle of jobbery'.[23] Together with the Balcarres campaign, this had provoked the setting up of the Select Committee.

The Department was a complex one; Sir John Donnelly was the Secretary of the Department of Science and Art, and there were

Directors for Science and Art, as well as Directors for the two South Kensington Museums. The two Museums had had separate directors since 1893. In 1898, these were Major-General Festing for the Science Museum, and Mr Purdon, later Sir Purdon, Clarke for the Art Museum. It also controlled the major provincial museums, notably the Dublin Museum of Science and Art, the Edinburgh Museum of Science and Art, the South Kensington satellite Bethnal Green Museum, and the Geological Museum in Jermyn Street attached to the Geological Survey. There were also teaching institutions, the Royal Colleges of Art and Science, both based in South Kensington, whose role was to train teachers for the provincial schools. The Department of Science and Art ran the public examinations in the various subjects, whose success or otherwise reflected the work of the Department, holding examinations throughout the British Isles, and elsewhere in the British dominions, including Tasmania, Guernsey, New Zealand, Natal and South Australia. It also supported schools with grants at various levels. There was an increasingly vigorous campaign to break up this educational colossus; in 1897 the Scottish Schools were transferred to the Scottish Education Department, and elsewhere the newly established County Councils, particularly the London County Council, were becoming important educational authorities. The Department's Report reflects its efforts to establish a satisfactory working relationship with the other bodies.[24]

In 1897 the Committee for the Museums of the Science and Art Department took the decision that a Select Committee should be set up to inquire into the museums. The Select Committee included both Balcarres and Burns, and Sir Mancherjee Bhownaggree (1851–1933), a leading Indian lawyer, one of the first Indians to sit in the House of Commons. The Chairman was Sir John Gorst, one of the ministers responsible, but feelings ran so high that he resigned as Chairman, and was succeeded by Sir Francis Powell (1827–1911), a barrister and a Conservative Member of Parliament from the West Riding.

The Select Committee was only charged with inquiring into the museums but was clearly concerned by the confusion and the jockeying for position that occurred throughout South Kensington, as well as on the Commissioners' estate. There had been some division of the massive Department earlier on; in 1885 the Department had decided to call the science collections housed in the Southern and Western Galleries the 'Science Museum' though it remained under the overall control of the director of the South Kensington Museum Sir Philip Cunliffe-Owen till he retired in 1893.

The result of the Select Committee's deliberations was to redesign much of South Kensington's existing institutions, to curb the freelance behaviour of the flagship, the South Kensington Museum, and to bring its activities under the control of government, and of the Board of Education in particular. Its first Report in April 1898 was brief and urgent, recommending that the whole of the eastern side of Exhibition Road, with the exception of the Royal College of Science building (then the Huxley building, now the Henry Cole Building) 'be exclusively devoted to the Art Museum and the Art Library, with provision for . . . the business connected with Loans of Art Objects, and the Art Schools'. The other side should be similarly allocated to the needs of Science. This decision may have been precipitated by concern over the increasing competition for sites in South Kensington. This had led in 1891 to such agitation from prominent scientists led by Lord Rayleigh against the incipient Gallery of British Art, now the Tate Gallery, that it had been discouraged from settling in the South Kensington area at all.[25]

The Select Committee's *Second Report*, which appeared the following year, was very much concerned over the danger of fire, advising that the Fire Brigade rather than the traditional corps of sappers should be in charge of fire protection, and indeed that the long-standing relationship with the Royal Engineers, dating from Cole's day, should be dissolved. They urged more specialization and training for the staff, to encourage expert knowledge among the museum personnel, in order to avoid the need for expensive outside advice. They were critical of some of the practices which had grown up, including the recruitment and training of staff, where they felt too many new recruits were related to the existing staff, calculating that one fifth of the staff were related to others. They were also concerned by the widespread dispersal and confusion of the collections, and the lack of space generally. There were also criticisms of the arrangements for expenditure and the keeping of records.[26]

The Committee also considered that hardy perennial among proposals, the transfer of the South Kensington Museum and the Bethnal Green Museum to the control of the British Museum. They rejected this on the grounds that the South Kensington collections were intended for teaching purposes unlike those at the British Museum, and were extensively used for circulation amongst other museums and provincial schools at various educational levels.

Donnelly refuted many of the criticisms in a series of 'Observations upon the *Second Report*, which were loyally backed up by the Ministers, the President of the Committee for Education, the Duke of Devonshire and the Vice-President Sir John Gorst, who pointed out they alone were responsible to Parliament for the administration of the Department. Nonetheless, the Report presaged a large number of changes in South Kensington, both physical and administrative – as Balcarres noted in his diary on 28 July, 1898:

> Carried the report of the select committee on the museums of the Science and Art department. It has given me hard work during two whole sessions: my next objective must be to carry into effect some of the reforms we have suggested.[27]

The planned rebuilding of the South Kensington Museum buildings got under way only after a radical Treasury proposal to incorporate galleries for the science collections was defeated by the Office of Works in 1898. Further changes were made by Aston Webb, and these were approved sufficiently rapidly for Queen Victoria to lay the foundation stone in May 1899, when the new name of the museum was given royal approval. There was some confusion at the start since those responsible for the Science Museum assumed that both museums would share the new title, and that museum bore the title 'Victoria and Albert Museum, Science Museum' until the new building was opened and the two museums were finally separated.[28]

Aston Webb had a complicated brief for the Victoria and Albert Museum, Though some of the existing buildings were to be replaced, there were other permanent galleries on the site, many of them originally squeezed in around the existing Brompton House. The site was an awkward trapezoid, with the buildings provided since 1860 lining up either with Exhibition Road or with the site of the Oratory to the east. The junction between Exhibition Road and the part of Cromwell Road on the south, known as Cromwell Gardens, was at an awkward angle. As Webb himself put it in a guide to the Museum:

> The planning . . . has been laid out on as simple lines as a building of this scale will allow, and the necessity of conveniently linking it up to and adapting it to the various levels of the old building were

considerations which greatly increased the difficulty of the problem.[29]

Under these difficult circumstances, Webb's buildings read surprisingly coherently, as he used the option of a simple classical plan, as across the road at the Natural History Museum, or at the British Museum, for the main front. There is an element of confusion when this meets the older galleries and Courts. Happily his choice of materials, red brick and Portland stone, consorted respectfully with Fowke's red brick and beige terracotta. In one case, a stretch of the original façade to the central garden quadrangle, left unfinished by Cole's team, was completed in keeping with the original, a very early example of historicist respect for the South Kensington style.

The new building, though kept simple internally out of consideration for the exhibits it was to house, was highly decorated externally with statuary, and some ceramic and marble was used on staircases indoors. It has been described meticulously by John Physick in his exhaustive study, *The Victoria and Albert Museum, The History of its Building*, and indeed its extension is not strictly part of the history of the Commissioners' estate; on the other hand, the effect of its rebuilding and the divorce from the science side was to change Henry Cole's South Kensington for ever. Webb's building provided the museum with a splendid and worthy public façade to the south and west, and doubled the space available for exhibits. It had also the effect of encouraging a radical reorganization of its contents, their classification and conservation. Part of the new building was ready for at least partial occupation by the end of 1906, and was formally opened by Edward VII in June 1909, though the external sculpture was not fully in place for a further two years.

Though the art collections were magnificently housed in the new Victoria and Albert Museum, and rearranged according to a new system, nothing was done for the science collections, to which the Commissioners had drawn attention twenty years before. This was an omission which outraged many scientists. However, there was an increasing interest in expanding science teaching in South Kensington, in which the Commissioners' estate was to be much involved, and where the Commissioners were to act as honest brokers.

THE CREATION OF IMPERIAL COLLEGE

In January 1903, an important new project was put to the Commission by
Edward VII, still President, as the Prince of Wales (the future George V)
was not appointed till the following month. This was the scheme for a
national technical college, nicknamed the 'Charlottenburg Project' after
the much-admired Charlottenburg Technische Hofschule in Berlin, and
reflected the increasing concern over technical and scientific competition
with Germany.

The project had been set out in August 1902 by an influential triumvirate – the Duke of Devonshire, Lord Rosebery and A. J. Balfour – in a
memorandum to the King, forwarded by him to the Board of
Management.

> The scheme is one for the provision and organization in the
> Metropolis of the Empire of a School for the application of Science
> to Industry at least as effective and comprehensive, in regard to the
> highest class of experts, as any of the Schools in Berlin, or in the
> great cities of other Countries . . .
>
> The United Kingdom is at present specially deficient in the provi-
> sion of advanced instruction and of original investigation in the
> whole range of the application of science to industry, and to the
> higher branches of commercial education. In other countries special
> attention has long been paid to the highest Technical training of
> those who will become, if not the captains of industry, the skilled
> lieutenants and confidential assistants in every branch of commerce
> or manufacture.

The point was driven home by describing the position 'of the great
College of Applied Science at Charlottenburg, alongside the University of
Berlin'

> erected at a cost of £500,000, and costing £55,000 a year. From its
> portals there issue every year some 1200 young men of 22 or 23
> years of age, equipped with the most perfect training that science
> can give, as experts in Chemical Technology, Electrical
> Engineering, Metallurgy, Shipbuilding, &c. . . . . the great industrial
> combinations of the German Empire . . . owe their remarkable suc-
> cess in no small degree to the quite exceptional wealth of scientific
> knowledge and training . . . at their disposal.[30]

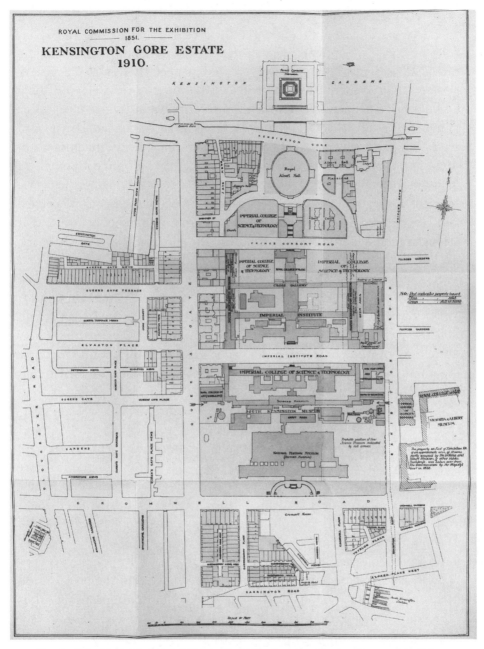

Fig 24. The Commissioners' Estate in 1910, showing the development in Prince Consort Road. The Victoria and Albert Museum is shown as such, while the scientific galleries are still labelled South Kensington Museum. The Royal College of Art is housed behind the Victoria and Albert Museum with a modelling department in Queen's Gate.

The advocates of the scheme pointed out that in Germany, and to a lesser degree in France, Belgium and Switzerland, 'widely lavish expenditure by the government had left England far behind', while in the United States private donations met a similar need. It was also a matter for shame that students from Canada, Australia, South Africa or India could not find adequate training within the Empire.

Though this project was seen as meeting a national need, it was also seen as helping to provide training for the seven million inhabitants of 'the larger London'. The newly founded London County Council, of which Rosebery had been an early Chairman, and which had an energetic Technical Education Board under Sidney Webb, was much concerned about the matter. The Committee came to the familiar conclusion that 'various branches of industry have, during the past twenty or thirty years, been lost to this country by the competition of foreign countries . . . that London, in particular, has distinctly suffered; that these losses are to be attributed in no small degree to the superior scientific education provided in foreign countries'.[31] Now that London University had been set up under the 1898 Act, it was felt that the way was clear for creating a new body which could provide technical education to a high standard. The memorandum included a plan of the South Kensington estate identifying three sites still available in the Prince Consort Road, and a further two in Exhibition Road, all already allocated to other interests. It was suggested that the Commissioners might be prepared to give the site, without which no further progress could be made, provided that £300,000 could be raised to build and equip the College. The Commissioners' estate already housed the Royal College of Science, the Royal School of Mines and the Central Technical Institute of the City and Guilds which made it the ideal site, and it was thought that £200,000 might be raised to build and equip the college, and that the London County Council would contribute £20,000 a year towards upkeep.[32]

The Board of Management was somewhat sceptical of the project, and perhaps unwilling to surrender the last three potentially profitable sites on the estate even for a national need so glowingly portrayed. These were valued by the surveyor at £140,500, so they would be making a very substantial contribution to the new scheme.[33] The King set up a committee with Sir Francis Mowatt representing the government, Lord James, Fowler and Ellis representing the Commission, and R. B. Haldane and Rosebery representing London University. By July 1903, Mowatt could report that a number of contributions had been promised – £100,000 from Wernher, Beit & Co., £50,000 from the Trustees of the Bessemer Memorial Fund, and £40,000 from other sources.[34] The following year the Prince of Wales made it clear at the annual meeting of the Commission that the Board of Management was expected to back the scheme, though their report only undertook not to develop the requested plots for the time being, until a government Departmental Committee, chaired by Sir Francis Mowatt, had reported. Matters were not helped by Mowatt's serious illness at the end of 1904, though his place was filled by R. B. Haldane (1856–1928) a prominent lawyer and Liberal Member of Parliament who was an advocate of civic universities. A subsequent change of government further delayed matters.

The Board was somewhat wary of government schemes for institutions on their estate in view of the past history of such projects – the long delay in building the Natural History Museum on the 1862 site, once the government had secured it, the refusal to take up the offer of a site for the Science Museum once the Treasury had made an estimate of the running costs, and the underutilized site on the south side of Imperial Institute Road. Fortunately perhaps for the formation of the 'Central College for the application of Science to Industry, in connection with the University of London' the Commissioners refused to make any commitment until adequate funding for buildings and annual income was in prospect.

The Departmental Committee reported in January 1906, making many familiar points about the lack of proper scientific education and training, attributing this to the lack of facilities for instruction, and the 'absence of such co-ordination among existing institutions of technological education' as would facilitate concentration of courses, and the inability on the part of employers to recognize the value of such courses. It concluded that

> the opportunities for research in our technological institutions are inadequate to the needs of the Empire, owing not to any want of ability on the part of the professors, but to the fact that much of their time is frequently absorbed in the giving of comparatively elementary instruction in Pure and Applied Science.

Predictably the Report selected South Kensington as the best situation for the new institution, largely because several sites had already been provided for scientific and technical education on the estate, and these institutions – the Royal College of Science, the Royal School of Mines and the Central Institute of the City and Guilds – were destined to become part of the new college. It included a graceful tribute to the work of the Commissioners for the Great Exhibition of 1851,

> who, by the manner in which they have executed their trust through-
> out the half century of their existence, have been intimately associ-
> ated with, and in a large measure responsible for, the educational
> developments of South Kensington, and who are now crowning
> their services to higher scientific education by their willingness to
> place an extensive site on their estate at the disposal of a scheme
> designed to carry out the objects contemplated in our Recom-
> mendations.[35]

The subtle change in the job description of the new college is interesting, since the Departmental Committee was also instructed to consider 'the promotion of higher scientific studies' as well as the technical training emphasized by the 1902 memorandum, though its preliminary Report in February 1905 referred to an Imperial College of Technology and Applied Science.[36] The Final Report in 1906 reported that adequate funding was available, and the Board of Education decided to go ahead.

A further complication, causing some embarrassment for the Board of Management, was that an application was received from Arthur Rücker on behalf of the University of London for a site for a medical school to give preliminary training to young medical students for which there was seen to be a need.[37] The Senate had approved the 'Institute of Medical Sciences' project, and he described the proposed curriculum which included chemistry, physics and biology (preliminary), and intermediate subjects of anatomy, physiology and possibly pharmacology. He was able to reassure the Board that 'Anatomy necessarily includes dissections but it may be stated that no-one not using the building would be aware that any part of it was assigned to what purpose and certainly not any of the residents in the neighbourhood'. Anatomy departments, he added, were usually placed at the top of the building, top-lit not side-lit, and no post mortems were to be carried out.

The Goldsmiths' Company had promised £10,000 for the college, conditional 'upon a site being granted at South Kensington', and, Rücker added, the Prince of Wales 'who is much interested in this movement, is anxious no risk should be run of the above named sum being lost'.[38] The following year Bigge reported to the Board that the Prince of Wales was interested in the project, and did not want all the available sites given away to the proposed National Technical College.

Meanwhile the 'Charlottenburg scheme' had run into demarcation problems: the existing institutions were run by the Board of Education or the City Companies and were not part of London University, which seems to have had a somewhat 'red-brick' municipal image in its early days. As Morant explained to Ellis there were 'difficulties . . . in the way of securing a completely harmonious cooperation between the different institutions interested in the scheme . . . [and] if once the Institution were started on a basis of autonomy and separation, it would inevitably develop separatist tendencies, and render less and less possible any subsequent incorporation'. However, any reorganization of the newly formed university would cause delay, and he added for good measure, that there was a view that 'the idea of merging what was meant to be the greatest Imperial Institution of Technology in a local University was in itself to be deprecated'.[39]

The promoters of the New Technical College had earmarked the three plots in Prince Consort Road, that on the north-west, and the two on the south, plus, it would appear, any other vacant or unoccupied sites which could be acquired, and the Board had long agreed that no development should take place until the Departmental Committee had reported. The 'delicate nature of the difficulties involved in any reorganization of the University' delayed progress until Reginald Mckenna (1863–1943) was appointed President of the Board of Education in November 1906, when they appeared to have been solved. The Board of Education applied to the Commission for the three sites, but some questions were raised by Ellis and Fowler as to whether it was in accordance with the 1851 charter. Fowler insisted that only a meeting of the Commissioners with the President could sanction the grant, so on 28 February, the Prince of Wales called what was in effect an extraordinary meeting of the Commission to deal only with the question of the two proposed new bodies. The Commission obediently resolved to 'appropriate Plots A, C, and D, for the purposes of the New Technological Institution', but a plot of ¾ acre, formerly occupied by the Royal School of Art Needlework, fronting on Exhibition Road, was reserved for the Institute of Medical Sciences.[40]

This appears to have cleared the way for the granting of a charter to the new Imperial College of Science and Technology. This led ultimately to the unification of the existing scientific teaching institutions on the Commissioners' estate, though the City and Guilds Central Institute was not formally incorporated till 1910. Some of the problems were solved by elaborate patterns of representation from all the different bodies concerned. The official Commission representatives were Esher and Bigge, who had succeeded Ellis as Secretary on the latter's death on 11 June, 1907. Other Commissioners represented other bodies, in the Albertopolis tradition of cross-representation, Mowatt the government, and Rücker and Roscoe the University of London.

The separate Science Library, which had since 1883 served as the library of the Royal College of Science, was taken over by Imperial College on its foundation, in 1907.[41]

IMPERIAL COLLEGE BUILDINGS

The buildings which were to form the new institution were varied in both origin and date. Soon after the Commissioners had sold the government the area on the south side of Imperial Institute Road, the Royal College of Science had persuaded the Board of Education that the accommodation in the Huxley Building was inadequate, and that part of the new site should be utilized for teaching physics and chemistry. A number of schemes and projects were discussed in 1890, but finally Aston Webb was commissioned to design buildings to stand south of the Imperial Institute. While the larger negotiations were going on to found the new college, a fine new range of buildings was rising to house science teaching. One of the most architecturally impressive buildings dedicated to science in the area, it was however equally admired by the professors who used it because of the excellent planning and layout which had resulted from Webb's research into the needs of its occupants. Webb had consulted Arthur Rücker on the physics side, and his colleagues on the chemistry side, and the results were well received. The building, in his preferred red brick and Portland stone, stretched the length of the Imperial Institute, and though the *place* shown in an early scheme was never created, the two buildings 'nodded', with the two east and west entrances facing each other. The three-storey central block with its blank attic storey was used to house the Science Library. The careful planning and fine proportions were supplemented by elegant detailing; the lighting fittings were supplied by the Bromsgrove Guild.[42] The roadway was lined with plane

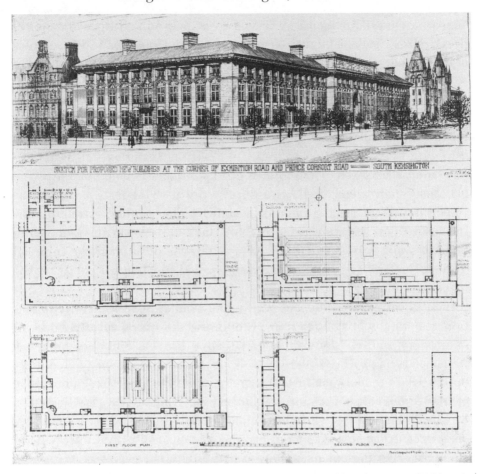

Fig 25. Perspective of the new Royal School of Mines Building by Aston Webb, drawn by T. Raffles Davidson.

trees, and the road took its place as one of the grandest streets in South Kensington, and worthy of the epithet 'Imperial'.

The satisfaction of the Royal College of Science with their new buildings may have led the newly created Imperial College to turn in July 1908 to Aston Webb for the most urgently needed accommodation. This was more space for the Royal School of Mines, needed for training engineers, for whom he built on the prominent corner site in Prince Consort Road, opposite the ill-fated Newman development. The Board considered the drawings for the new building on March 1909, not without some irritation, since Webb's plan involved cropping the northern end of the Eastern Galleries, breaching the party wall with the Royal College of

Music, and building over a narrow strip of land intended for a roadway north of the City and Guilds. Negotiations with the Office of Works were characteristically difficult, since, though they did not mind surrendering 40 per cent of the galleries, used for the 'art collections' of the South Kensington Museum, they wished to be relieved of 40 per cent of the rent. The Commissioners felt that the rent had been set at a generous level, and was very low anyway, so the Office of Works' reaction was seen as niggardly. Needless to say, Imperial College did not expect to have to pay, and as usual the Commission paid for most of the changes. The Commissioners were very trusting in the form of the lease they gave to Imperial College, since they omitted some of the traditional safeguards – thus there was no provision to protect the foundations of neighbouring buildings, since the Board 'having regard to the position of the Imperial College . . . felt assured that the point would not be overlooked by the Governing Body'.[43]

The Royal School of Mines was again a building worthy of its situation, this time wholly in Portland stone, and decorated with two groups of statuary by P. R. Montford, incorporating busts of Sir Julius Wernher (1850–1912) and Alfred Beit (1853–1906). It was an expensive building, both because of its substantial and ostentatious construction and because of its equipment. Much of the latter was funded by the Bessemer Memorial Committee, who contributed £100,000 for the eponymous laboratory, The façade was extended to the east end of Prince Consort Road to incorporate the extension to the City and Guilds College. This was funded by the Goldsmiths' Company as they had undertaken when the project was first mooted. It cost a great deal more than the £10,000 first discussed, their contribution finally rising from £37,000 to £50,000.

At the other end of Prince Consort Road, the building was designed in a Tudor domestic style by Webb, reflecting its original role as the Students' Union, but it was in effect put to a number of uses – the northern range (1910–11) was built as a hostel, the east range (1912–14) for botany and plant physiology, and the west side, for biochemistry, was completed only in the 1920s.[44] It took the name Beit Quadrangle after the mining magnate, who gave a substantial sum, reflecting the importance attached by the 'Rand lords' to proper training in mining and metallurgy.

THE SCIENCE SCHOLARSHIPS

The Commissioners were supporting a number of educational bodies at this time. They had loyally supported the Imperial Institute laboratory, which they had regarded as a centre for research, contributing some £18,000 in all, until the entire institution had been taken over by the government. They withdrew their support for it in 1906, feeling it was not their place to support government bodies.[45] They had provided a grant of £1000 in 1905 to a short-lived ginger group under the patronage of the Duke of Devonshire, the National Association for the Promotion of Secondary and Technical Education. They promoted musical education on a modest but regular scale through the long-standing annual grant of £500 to the Royal College of Music.

However, the Commission's major work for education at this time was through the Science Scholarships, which supported over three hundred Scholars from some thirty institutions, in various research projects between 1891 and 1910. The Scholars came from colleges all over the English provinces and from nine institutions in important cities in the Empire, largely those selected in 1891. Many of these had graduated during the twenty years of the scholarship scheme from colleges to independent universities. Another sign of the increased importance attached to scientific education in England was the greater number of institutions within Great Britain to which the Scholars could elect to go, including the Cavendish Laboratory at Cambridge.

The institutions in which the Scholars spent part or all of their time did not vary greatly over the first twenty years. Including the home colleges in which some students elected to spend their first year, about 45 per cent of the institutions were in the British Isles, and about 35 per cent in Germany. In the earlier decade more time, about 5 per cent, was spent in various colleges in the British Empire, again because a number of award-winners in the early years spent their first year in the home college. The same proportion elected to go to American universities. In the second decade colonial students seem to have been more enterprising and fewer stayed at home, but again 5 per cent chose United States institutions. The remaining colleges and research institutes selected were in other European countries, notably in Austria, France and Switzerland, but including the University of Stockholm, and the Zoological Laboratory in Naples.

One or two of the Scholars made their mark very early, like Ernest Rutherford from New Zealand, 1895–8, who was elected a Fellow of the Royal Society in 1903, and won the Nobel Prize for chemistry five years later. Many of the Scholars went into teaching, some in secondary schools, but more usually in technical colleges and universities, often in far-flung parts of the Empire and the Colonies, from New Zealand and India to South Africa. Several went into the Meteorological Survey of India, one went to the Poona Agricultural College. Robert Holt from Liverpool, having studied mechanical engineering, became Vice-Principal of the Engineering College, at Gizeh, in Egypt. Some of the Scholars stayed in their host countries, like Edward Glauert who stayed in Charlottenburg to do private research, and John Lloyd who resigned his scholarship at Würzburg on being offered a job with an aniline dye company at Ludwigshafen-am-Rhein. The same was true of some students at American universities; some Canadian students who elected to go to Cornell, or Columbia, seem to have remained at American universities. John Simpson from Manchester, trained in Norway and at Göttingen, joined Scott's ill-fated British Antarctic Expedition in 1910. A number went into industry, some with well-known companies of national importance like Brunner Mond, while Norman Picton from Wales trained at Leipzig, and went to work for a furriers in Bermondsey.

A few women were given scholarships, but are often recorded as having married or given up research for other reasons, though several went into secondary teaching in girls' secondary schools. Unusually, Alice Embleton from South Wales, having worked at the Balfour Laboratory in Cambridge, went on to work on cancer research at the Royal College of Science in South Kensington.

The original scholarship project was supplemented by an imaginative bursary scheme, introduced in 1900. This was devised to deal with the problems of scientists with potential as researchers, who were too poor to support themselves through to a level of scholarship, which would enable them to demonstrate their ability. These Research Bursaries were for one year and funded almost to the same level as the scholarships. Taken all in all the Commissioners could congratulate themselves on the work of the Scholarships Committee and the success generally of their innovative scheme.[46]

THE SCIENCE MUSEUM

The same concern for scientific education, which been so successful in grouping the existing institutions in South Kensington into Imperial College, was to bring about the creation of the long-gestated separate Science Museum.

An important figure in this campaign was the astronomer, Sir Norman Lockyer, both a Commissioner and a member of the Science Scholarships Committee, who had been the Secretary of the Duke of Devonshire's Commission in 1874. He had been battling for the establishment of a Science Museum for over thirty years, and returned to the matter with a memorandum reviewing the activities of the Commissioners and other parties in South Kensington in regard to the various proposals for a museum. He pointed out that by 1874 provision had been made for museums of art and natural history, while science was still neglected, and that the land offered by the Commissioners had been accepted by government, and yet no Science Museum had been provided:

> We have now arrived at the year 1907, and . . . in spite of the Commissioners' repeated efforts, we have no Science Museum, and the Commissioners have no more land to offer.
>
> Is, therefore, the realisation of the Prince Consort's idea impossible? . . . on the contrary, the present time is an appropriate one for a renewed effort on the part of the Commission.

Pointing out that the Commission had endowed the new Imperial College with old and new plots of land to the tune of £400,000, he pointed out that the existence of this new body made the need for a museum yet more imperative. He appended a plan and photographs to show the way in which a new building would look at the southern end of Exhibition Road where a frontage of 360 feet would be available. A problem had arisen in that the Office of Works under Schomberg McDonnell had plans to put a post office on the site, in defiance of the earlier expressed intention to reserve it for scientific use. As an alternative he suggested that 'were the dangerous spirit museum removed to a safer site, such as the Natural History Museum Gardens, some distance west', then a site would be available on the site of the old Southern Galleries. There was an urgent need for the resolution of the question, 'because if any buildings are erected on the spaces referred to, any such Science Museum as the

Commissioners have had in contemplation during the last thirty years, for which they have freely given their land and offered money, will be impossible of realisation, to say nothing of future extension'.

He suggested that the best way forward might be for the Commissioners to take up the cudgels again, reinforcing their concern with 'the renewal of the offer, already twice made, to provide a money contribution to the building'. 'Speaking as a Commissioner', he concluded, 'I can conceive no more worthy expenditure, as it will give full effect to the great purposes the Commissioners have had in view . . . in carrying out the late Prince Consort's wise advice as to the best use of their property in the nation's interest. *Finis coronat opus*.'[47]

The matter was taken up by the elderly Henry Fowler, created Lord Wolverhampton in 1908, still an active member of the Liberal Cabinet as Lord President of the Council. On 4 February, 1908, Lockyer was invited to attend the Board of Management, to discuss reviewing the activities of the Commissioners in regard to the various proposals for a museum. The Board took the view that having no longer a site of their own to offer, they would have to discover what were the views of government before taking any action. However, a fortnight later, Fowler as Chairman asked Bigge to 'see the officials of the Board of Education about the Science Museum. I think you must intimate to them that we cannot *initiate* any proposal'. He went on to say that if the government were 'prepared to make a substantial offer I should advise our Board to meet them liberally'. Any payments should be by instalments over the period of construction.

Sir Henry Roscoe too took the matter up, with Reginald Mckenna, then at the Board of Education, who, he reported to Fowler, 'looked with favour on the matter'.[48]

The matter was given further impetus by a memorial presented to the Board of Education in July 1909, signed by over two hundred concerned public figures and men of science, urging the government to provide adequate accommodation for the nation's science collections. It was a wide-ranging group including Lord Rosebery, Lord Avebury, the Lord Chief Justice, the Master of the Rolls, a preponderance of professors holding important posts in scientific institutions, manufacturers like Ludwig Mond and Sir John Brunner, a large number of engineers including the Honourable C. A. Parsons, and the presidents of the various engineering institutes. A number of 1851 Commissioners supported it as individuals, including Mowatt, Leonard Courtney, now Lord Courtney of Penwith, Lord Rayleigh, Sir Arthur Rücker, and Sir Archibald Geikie. The memorialists 'being deeply interested in the practice and progress of British Science, desire to bring before you the importance of the proper housing of the Science Collections at South Kensington'. They went on to point out that the handsome 'permanent buildings now erected provide accommodation for Art Collections only: to complete the scheme a suitable building for the Science Collections is a necessity'. There were now 'models and copies of historical and modern philosophical apparatus of the greatest value to all interested in the progress of British Science, and a large number of machines, instruments and models of great interest as illustrating the origin and development of our most pregnant British inventions'.

Permanent accommodation would not only make it possible to display all the exhibits in the museum, but would encourage those with suitable items to fill the lacunae to donate them more readily. They pointed out that though the site sold to the government by the 1851 Commission in 1890 had been largely used for other scientific purposes, there was still a long strip between the new Royal College of Science building and the Natural History Museum site with a frontage to Exhibition Road, which would be both convenient and suitable.[49]

The government had a more pressing problem in the budget struggle with the House of Lords, and the snap election of 1909, so the matter of the Science Museum was not immediately settled.

The following year Fowler, now Lord Wolverhampton, was gathering information on the Commission's financial position, in response to a request from the government for a contribution of £150,000 towards building the Science Museum. There was also a very serious suggestion that the Commission, having effectively disposed of its estate, might be wound up. Bigge told Esher in March 1910 that he felt that the suggested contribution was in order, 'but *the* question is as to the disposal of the rest of our funds. HRH absolutely declines having a Select Committee & says that the whole question of "winding up" & the various grants must be considered 1) by the Board of Management & 2) by the whole Body of Commissioners'. Esher had his doubts about the level of financial support for the museum, but Bigge reminded him that the 'proposed establishment of a Science Museum meets with entire approval of the highest Scientific Authorities'.[50]

The Commission had investments worth about £200,000, and an income from rent of about £14,000, but the removal of three-quarters of its investments to support the new museum would leave it with little income. Outgoings included £5000 for the Science Scholarships, which could well be increased, and £500 to the Royal College of Music, while Imperial College was hoping for 'a substantial grant'.

However, the Prince of Wales's views seem to have hardened. Bigge, in an undated letter, written in April or early May, 1910, set them out:

> His Royal Highness is opposed to the winding up of the Commission, as he considers that the funds which the Commissioners have at their disposal can be made use of on behalf of undertakings connected with Art and Science which could never be helped from public monies . . . future schemes may be proposed . . . which might seem to give greater effect to what His Royal Highness believes to have been the ideals of his grandfather, and under these circumstances he feels that the Commissioners should hold their hands.

More specifically, the Prince was against 'spending money in bricks and mortar', since he felt that 'this Museum ought to be built quite as much as the Victoria and Albert Museum or the Natural History Museum', both of which were paid for by the public purse. However, as the Commission had offered £100,000 in 1876, he was not against that sum being offered. He was also against giving money to Imperial College, but was keen on the Science Scholarships, and suggested that they could well be increased, devoting 'a considerable amount of our income in extending the Scholarships and Bursaries to enable students of promise to continue their studies at Imperial College'.[51]

The Board of Management met in April 1910, and decided to repeat their 1876 offer of £100,000 towards the museum provided that the government would provide a site and the rest of the money to erect the buildings. The Commission seems to have reached a turning point, because at the same meeting the Board considered the proper application of their surplus funds 'to further the objects of their charter and to give continued effect to the general policy of the Commission'.

Bigge, in one of his last letters as Secretary, wrote to Walter Runciman, now President of the Board of Education about the offer, adding:

May I in return for your own private ear say how extraordinarily liberal I feel the Commissioners are, especially when the ground upon
which you will build your Museum was practically given to you at
half its value. . . . the public will realise that our policy was a sound
one – not to spend all our money in bricks and mortar, but to hold
on to it and make use of it in a way which will be the envy of any
Government who unfortunately can never lay their hands upon
funds in the manner which now suggests itself to the
Commissioners, namely in Scholarships and Bursaries, and so enable
latent talent to be fostered and used to the profit of the State.[52]

Aware that they had not reported for twenty years, though an
'Epitome' had been printed in 1908, the members of the Board decided to
draft a report for the Commissioners, 'containing a restatement of the
policy which they have hitherto consistently pursued, and such expansion
of their policy which appears to be demanded by recent developments in
Science and Art'. It should specially refer to certain important projects
like the establishment of a Science Museum, the extension of scholarships
and bursaries, and the establishment of professorships at the Imperial
College of Science and kindred institutions.

However, before the Report finally appeared the following March, all
the leading figures in the Commission had disappeared from the scene.
Edward VII died in May 1910, depriving the Commission at a stroke both
of President and Secretary. Even earlier in the year it had become obvious that a new Chairman of the Board of Management was needed, since
Wolverhampton was now nearly eighty, and the Prince of Wales (soon to
be George V) wanted Esher as Chairman.

Esher had not been enthusiastic about the prospect; it was a minor
appointment for a man who had been one of Edward VII's most trusted
advisers, and an important figure in the Committee of Imperial Defence.
He set out his doubts frankly to Bigge in June, saying that though he was
very much flattered and honoured by the 'King's kind proposal' that he
should become Chairman, he was very pessimistic as to whether the work
of the Commission could continue.

After carefully considering the matter I am more than doubtful
whether [without the Prince of Wales and with] a weakened secretariat, it will be possible for the Commissioners to hold their own
against those members of the Government, and those high Officials

in the Civil Service, who think the day has come for the Commission to be superseded by some very different authority.[53]

Despite his pessimism, Esher was won over, whether it was by the knowledge that the King 'was so much pleased with the view that you took to the future policy', or with Bigge's offer to continue as Secretary 'for a time' to help him.[54]

Wolverhampton resigned from the Cabinet at the end of June 1910, and in a letter acknowledging this, Bigge effectively gave him his *congé*:

> With regard to the *1851 Commission*, important alterations must be made in its officers. The King is about to nominate Prince Arthur of Connaught as President, and a successor must be found to me as Secretary . . . His Majesty could not think of your undertaking any work of the Commission, let alone the fatigue of a journey to London.[55]

There remained the problem of the secretariat. 'Young Shaw' was holding the fort, writing a formal report with the help of Fladgate for the Commissioners to present on their future policy. He suggested a 'Secretary of the same standing as of yore', and suggested that F. G. Ogilvie, although a civil servant at the Board of Education, might take the Commission job on as well, on a small salary. However, in due course, Shaw himself was offered, and accepted, the position, at Esher's first Board meeting on 18 July, 1910.[56] Bigge returned to his position as a Commissioner, and Shaw was instructed to find himself an Assistant Secretary at £150 per annum. This meant a change in the post of Secretary which now became a full-time professional job. All the previous holders had combined it with other jobs, taking policy decisions, but relying on a more modest figure like Sayles to do the day-to-day work.

In Esher, the reprieved Commission had acquired one of the most remarkable figures of the epoch at its head, a man seen by *The Times* in a millennium article as one of the most outstanding politicians of the century – the *éminence grise* who had helped the Royal Family to adapt to the new century. He was to do the same for a more modest institution, enabling it to survive radical changes in government attitudes to education and training, and to continue to provide assistance for projects outside the concerns and remit of government.

VIII

New Initiatives in Education
1910–1921

L ord Esher took on the Chairmanship of the Board of Management at a difficult moment. However, more perhaps than any other man in charge of the Commission was he capable of dealing with complex and difficult situations. To Thomas Jones, a senior civil servant who knew him during the First World War, and a Commissioner from 1921 to 1950, he was the 'perceptive Reginald Brett' who 'refused high offices in the State, and preferred multifarious secretarial and advisory background activities; he knew everybody; he anticipated and smoothed out difficulties for his royal and administrative superiors and dispensed shrewd and sound advice'.[1] However, the problems facing the Commissioners could well have daunted a less able man. Not only was he faced by the interregnum forced on the Commission by the succession of the President to the throne, but he felt that the organization was threatened by menacing external forces:

> I am very doubtful whether the work of the Commissioners can be satisfactorily carried on at all. It was one thing having the Prince of Wales to preside over the Commission, but it is a totally different thing having Prince Arthur of Connaught . . . With the Prince of Wales at the head of the Commission in his great position, and with his determined character, it would have been easy to make a fight, and a successful one, against that body of opinion which holds that the Commission, dating from so long ago, should be wound up and its responsibilities transferred to a Government Department under the control of Parliament.[2]

NEW CHAIRMAN, NEW PRESIDENT

However, he accepted Prince Arthur of Connaught as President, though he took steps to have him replaced by the Prince of Wales in due course. Fortunately George V retained a great interest in the work of the

Commission, vetting prospective Commissioners even after he had handed over as President, and he took a very strong line against any attempts to wind it up.

Esher held his first Board of Management meeting on 18 July, 1910, attended by a number of veterans, Lord James of Hereford, the civil servant Sir Francis Mowatt, the Chairman of the Science Scholarships Committee Sir Henry Roscoe, F. G. Ogilvie of the Board of Education and, despite his retirement as Secretary, Sir Arthur Bigge. The officers were also present as usual, the newly appointed Secretary Evelyn Shaw, the solicitor William Francis Fladgate (1853–1937), the surveyor F. J. Stevenson, together with Aston Webb, who was involved with the plans for the new buildings for Imperial College in Prince Consort Road.

Most of the problems which had vexed Lord Wolverhampton's last meeting remained on the table, only the matter of the contribution to the Science Museum having been settled, by the intervention of Bigge, at the King's request, to give the Commission's formal agreement to the donation of £100,000, half the Commissioners' liquid resources, to the government for the purpose. The Science Museum question was to continue to trouble not only the Commissioners but also South Kensington for years to come, since the scientific community could not agree on its siting, and the Treasury was, as always, backward in producing the promised money. As the Commissioners pointed out, they had sold an ideal site for such a museum at the southern end of Exhibition Road to the government in 1890, at less than half of its market value. In July 1909, a deputation of eminent scientists had lobbied the government, complaining about the lack of provision for a Science Museum, in contrast to the elegant new buildings arising on the east of Exhibition Road, dedicated to the national collection of decorative arts. However, the moment the site on the west of Exhibition Road was suggested, a protest, encouraged, if not initiated, by the British Museum scientists at the Natural History Museum had complained of the congestion likely to be caused by their own additional accommodation, the Royal College of Science buildings and the prospective Science Museum buildings all being squeezed into the area south of Imperial Institute Road. Nonetheless, despite all these protests and delays, the Commission agreed to stand by its offer of £100,000, made almost *in absentia*.[3]

The Science Museum was an important matter for the Board of Management, but other even more significant decisions about policy were taken at its meetings in 1910, and confirmed by a meeting of the full Commission on 13 March, 1911. The publication of the *Eighth Report* to the government at that same meeting also provided an opportunity to remind government of the Commissioners' achievements over the past two decades, and to restate the Commission's objectives. The Commissioners could point to the successful establishment of the 'Great College of Applied Science' on their estate, and the amalgamation in Imperial College of a number of discrete institutions already in South Kensington. This was the thirteenth in the list of institutions established on the property since the Commission had acquired it, many of national significance, and all of educational utility. The Commissioners could also point to a most satisfactory restoration of their finances, from the mortgage-ridden days of 1889 to the ownership of a portfolio worth over £200,000. This had enabled them to redirect their efforts from bricks and mortar to supporting individual scholars in science and arts. They could take particular pride in the Science Scholarships, which had helped to train 336 scholars from all over Britain, the Empire and the Colonies. They could also set out the 'fresh departure' of the 'bursaries for young scholars, not to be chosen for their aptitude in research work, but selected as men likely to prove useful and capable captains of industry', an initiative which the new King, when President, had supported together with the Naval Scholarships scheme.[4]

At his second meeting as Chairman in November 1910, Esher stated the Commissioners' position, which 'deprecated any diminution of the corpus of the Commissioners' estates or any permanent alienation of their income'. A 'more definite policy in the administration of the funds' was required, and also a more tentative approach over the giving of scholarships and bursaries, so the effects of these were properly assessed after a few years, to ensure that they were producing the desired results. Administrative changes were made: the Commission's substantial investments had been held by trustees, only one of whom was still alive, the elderly Sir Dighton Probyn, a former member of Edward VII's entourage, and it was decided that these were to be held under corporate seal in future.[5]

The range of scholarships proposed was widened: in technological subjects at Imperial College and elsewhere, in Naval Architecture, in Architecture, Sculpture and Decorative Painting, with the addition of some Industrial Bursaries for practical scientific training. Whether it was a sign of the increased emphasis on practical science, or just a desire to husband their resources, the Board turned down requests for help from A. J. Balfour towards the study of genetics at Cambridge, and from Mowatt for a chair of vegetable physiology at Imperial College.

The 138th meeting of the Commission held at St James's Palace elected the new President, Prince Arthur of Connaught (1883–1938), eldest son of the Duke of Connaught, Queen Victoria's third son, who was married to the Duchess of Fife, herself a granddaughter of Edward VII. It also reappointed Bigge as a Commissioner and a member of the Board of Management, adding the aeronautical engineer Richard Glazebrook and the physicist Sir Arthur Rücker to the Board. The Science Scholarships Committee remained under the chairmanship of the Manchester chemist Sir Henry Roscoe, with much the same membership, which included the 3rd Lord Rayleigh, a physicist and pioneer in the study of radioactivity, Lord Courtney of Penwith, Geikie, Lockyer, Rücker, Garnett, Glazebrook, Horace Brown and Professors Collie and Cormack. The Commission also formally endorsed the new policy put forward by the Board in its report. This pronounced against any further use of resources for building at South Kensington, and, without disturbing existing provision for scholarships, decided to seek a wider range of objectives: 'the present funds should be so used as to give a further impetus to scientific and artistic training . . . most helpful to those who may forward the applications of Science and Art in industrial enterprises'. There was also an impetus towards more directed financial help: 'Scholarships and Bursaries, endowed not for all time but for limited periods, and directed especially to encourage not only research work but also the training of "Captains of Industry"'. It was decided that the Commissioners should direct their funds towards schemes which found it difficult to attract help from 'ordinary sources'. The Board recommended that help to the fine arts should be given by the adoption of similar methods as to those the Commissioners had found helpful in the scientific sphere.

The report from the Science Scholarships Committee shows that the chosen destinations of the successful candidates in 1910 remained much the same. Though the two Canadian Scholars elected to go to Harvard, eight went to universities and Technical High Schools in Germany, and of the nine selecting home universities, six chose to go to Cambridge. The 1911 Report, the first to report on the Science Scholarships, gave a list of 336 Scholars with a brief account of their studies, and subsequent careers.

Roscoe could claim that over half of the past Scholars were engaged as professors, assistant professors or lecturers, some ninety-two had gone into manufacturing, seventeen were involved in private research, and of the remainder three were with the British Antarctic Expedition under Captain Scott.[6]

Despite the established success of the Science Scholarships, the 1911 Report clearly proclaimed the new policy of encouraging art as well as science as far as industry was concerned, and of seeking shorter-term initiatives. Though the Commission could report growing investments, and an increasing balance at the bank, as opposed to the earlier dependence on mortgages and bank overdrafts, an accompanying map showed how the estate had shrunk. The only areas still in hand were the plots either side of the vaults below the Albert Hall, and a little piece of 'no-man's land' between the Royal School of Needlework, the City and Guilds Institute, and the Eastern Galleries occupied by the Indian Collections. Much of the rest had been disposed of: the area between Imperial Institute Road and the Cromwell Road sold to the government at a discount, much of Queen's Gate sold off to private owners, together with the little group of houses on the corner of Harrington Road and Queensberry Place, and the north side of Queen's Gate Terrace. Some of these houses were still technically owned by the Commissioners as they were on long leases, particularly the block on the south side of Kensington Gore, and the east side of Queen's Gate. The east side of Queen's Gate was still largely residential, but in Exhibition Road academic buildings of various sorts filled the western side of the block between Prince Consort Road and Imperial Institute Road. Prince Consort Road itself was largely occupied by blocks of Imperial College, and the ill-fated Newman block of flats. Relatively little remained for the Commissioners to realize, so the promised donation to the building of the Science Museum would have to come from its investments, leaving it with its funds halved.

THE STRUGGLE TO CREATE A SCIENCE MUSEUM

The value placed on the Commissioners' offer is attested by its formal and enthusiastic acceptance by Sir Robert Morant, the Permanent Secretary at the Board of Education. The Commissioners' subsequent behaviour over the offer is difficult to understand, unless one looks back at the struggle for a national Science Museum, which had been in play almost as long as the Commission itself.

The Commissioners' role in the long and not altogether impressive history of the establishment of the Science Museum was critical, and on the whole praiseworthy. Despite the efforts of Playfair and others concerned with science in South Kensington, the science, or as they were sometimes known the 'non-art', collections were never as well-supported as their art rivals. They had been banished to the Southern Galleries, owned by the government, and the Western Arcades of the Horticultural Gardens rented from the Commissioners, and even to the Bethnal Green Museum, while the art collections were increasingly concentrated on the Brompton House site. There were a number of reports supporting the national importance of the science collections, and the valuable way in which they afforded 'in the best possible manner information and instruction in the immense variety of machinery in use in the manufactures of this country'. A further boost was given by the Royal Commission on Scientific Instruction and the Advancement of Science, under the 7th Duke of Devonshire, which reported in 1874 on the need for a 'Collection of Physical and Mechanical Instruments', going on to suggest the amalgamation with it of the Patent Museum, and the Scientific and Educational Collections of the South Kensington Museum, all to be under the control of a Minister of State. This had been capped by the 1851 Commissioners' approach to government to sell a site for a science museum in 1876, coupled with the offer of £100,000 towards the building and equipping of such a museum, but the Treasury had turned a deaf ear. An important loan exhibition of scientific apparatus was assembled in 1875 in South Kensington, promoted by an influential committee of experts in science, industry and engineering, including the Astronomer Royal Sir G. B. Airy, the industrialist C. W. Siemens and Lord Rayleigh. This provoked the 1851 Commissioners to repeat their earlier offer in 1878, this time formally refused by the government. Finally, in 1888, the Commissioners offered to convey the land south of the Imperial Institute Road for a third of its value of £200,000 to the government on the understanding that it was used for purposes connected with science and the arts. This was accepted the following year, and it seems to have been tacitly understood that this was a site for the projected science museum.

Repeated efforts were made by the scientific community, supported by Colonel J. F. D. Donnelly as Secretary of the Department of Science and Art from 1884, to get collections of scientific and industrial objects together, and arrange for them to be properly housed and looked after.

Various sites in South Kensington on the Commissioners' estate were suggested, but such collections as there were housed in the Southern and Western Galleries. Sir Frederick Bramwell chaired an inter-departmental committee in 1884, which estimated the needs of the nation's science collections at some 120,000 square feet as opposed to the 69,000 square feet currently occupied. His Committee suggested the site on the south side of Imperial Institute Road stretching from Exhibition Road to Queen's Gate, which could have provided almost twice the area.[7] A dissenting report from A. B. Mitford (later 1st Lord Redesdale), Permanent Secretary to the Office of Works from 1874 to 1886, took a different view, suggesting the practical utility of the collections was small, and that the favourable opinions of the various professors were suspect, since 'prophets who have been invited to bless are seldom so uncivil as to curse'. Despite the support of South Kensington scientists such as Huxley and Donnelly for the recommendations of the main report, George Goschen, the Conservative Chancellor, was able to turn down the recommendation that £220,000 should be spent on a new building to house the collections, on the grounds that the committee was not unanimous.[8]

Nothing official was done in line with the Report, though the collections themselves were 'weeded' to reduce the pressure on space. The Patent Museum collections, largely put together personally by Bennet Woodcroft, came to the Science Museum in 1883; the Educational Collection was sacrificed, as was the Structural Collection, though to later regrets, while the Buckland Fish Collection was also considered out of place in a scientific collection largely made up of mechanical exhibits. Some administrative changes were introduced; expert scientific committees were appointed to advise on the different collections, while in 1885 it was decided that the Science Collections should be known as the Science Museum, though it was only in 1893 that a separate Director was appointed.

The rivalry between the Natural History Museum, then part of the British Museum, and the other South Kensington scientists did not assist in convincing the government that the scientific community was at one in feeling that a Science Museum was indispensable. However, any threats from outsiders were resisted, as when Henry Tate's British Gallery was suggested as a suitable occupant of the vacant space on the south side of the Imperial Institute Road. This was seen as earmarked for scientific interests, including the Royal College of Science as well as the long-heralded Science Museum. The scientific community launched an acrimonious correspondence in both *Nature* and *The Times*, and a delegation led by Sir William Thomson managed to make the point with the Chancellor of the Exchequer and the Lord President of the Council.

As earlier recorded, the 1898 Select Committee recommended the division of the collections along the line of Exhibition Road, but this seems to have provided an opportunity for the Treasury to put the Science Museum 'on hold' until the newly named Victoria and Albert Museum had been paid for and opened. This is the more curious, in view of the concerns of some parts of the government, not only the scientific and educational establishment, over the increasing superiority of German scientific education, and consequently that country's industrial and naval progress.

One part of the scientific collections which developed separately, and rather more successfully, was the Science Library, based on the Educational Collection, begun in 1857 for the use of the Education Inspectors. In 1883, the non-geological holdings of the library of the Museum of Practical Geology in Jermyn Street were transferred to South Kensington, and in 1886 patent specifications were added. This collection served as the library for the students of the Royal College of Science, and was therefore absorbed as a matter of course by the Imperial College of Science, having spacious quarters provided in Webb's fine building in Imperial Institute Road.

THE BELL COMMITTEE REPORT

Once the Victoria and Albert Museum had been opened in 1909 by King Edward VII, a ceremony that made clear the art collections' monopoly of the name, the Board of Education could respond in an active way to the 1907 deputation, and the subsequent agitation. The response of Walter Runciman, then President of the Board of Education, was to appoint yet another Select Committee in March 1910, under the industrialist, ironmaster and coal owner, Sir Hugh Bell (1844–1933) to report on both the Science Collections and the future of the Museum of Practical Geology in Jermyn Street. It comprised a very distinguished group, largely of scientists, though there were also civil servants like Sir Schomberg McDonnell, Secretary of the Office of Works from 1902 to 1912, and men of business, many of them already involved with South Kensington and with the 1851 Commission. Commissioners included Sir Archibald

Geikie, and Richard Glazebrook, Director of the National Physical Laboratory from 1899 to 1919, while F. G. Ogilvie was the Secretary, in the light of his post at the Board of Education, as Secretary for the Science Museum, Geological Museum and Geological Survey. When the Director of the Science Museum, W. I. Last, died in August 1911, Morant added the post to Ogilvie's duties, despite the fact, according to some authorities, that he had a not very high opinion of Ogilvie. The long-term interests of the museum were well served by Ogilvie's insistence on having an assistant, which brought Henry Lyons (Director 1920–33) into the museum's service in 1912.[9]

The Bell Committee reported initially on 22 March, 1911, in a document which has been called 'the greatest and most significant single influence in the history of the Science Museum', which dealt with both general principles for the rehousing of the collections, and with the state of those collections. The latter comments were not a matter for the 1851 Commissioners, though their general tenor bears out the need for the Commissioners' persistence in urging the case of the science collections. The Committee saw the collections 'of exhibited scientific instruments and apparatus, machines and other objects' as affording 'illustrations and expositions of the various branches of Science within its field and of their applications in the Arts and Industries', thus serving both students of science and the general public. The report emphasized the importance of providing for the latter, stipulating that 'objects should be so selected and exhibited as to arouse the interest of these visitors, and to afford them in as simple and attractive a form as possible an opportunity of obtaining at least general ideas on the subjects which the Collections illustrate'. Though many of the individual collections were praised for their historical and educational importance, the report was less admiring of the conditions under which they were housed, saying of the Mechanical Engineering sections that 'all these valuable exhibits are so crowded that they cannot be properly inspected, and actual offers to present objects of no less interest in the progress of invention cannot be accepted until additional space is available'. Some recently developed areas like electrical engineering were therefore inadequately represented: 'in no area is there more urgent need of early action to secure for the Museum examples of instruments and appliances that have marked a new era in invention and industry'. Areas which were very underrepresented included transport engineering in various areas such as docks, roads and tunnels, and even signalling systems, and municipal engineering showing progress in drains and sewerage systems, which had done so much to make cities healthier and more agreeable.[10]

The proposals put forward in the report held wide implications for the future development of South Kensington. It made both a number of proposals for the amalgamation of collections held by different bodies in a number of locations, and suggestions for the better management of those collections. Though it made a number of proposals for public demonstrations of various scientific appliances, and for relating the collections more closely to teaching, it proposed that the practice of lending exhibits to schools should cease. Instead it suggested the building up of a collection of lantern slides for teaching purposes.

Firstly, the report urged the removal of the geological collections to South Kensington so that they could be united with similar holdings at the Natural History Museum, and in the Science Museum. For this, agreement with the British Museum authorities was necessary, finally achieved soon after the publication of the first part of the report. They offered a contiguous site on the west side of Exhibition Road, and this defined the site available for the science collections.

At the time, the science collections occupied the Western and Southern Galleries, hidden behind the new buildings of the Royal College of Science which faced the Imperial Institute across the Imperial Institute Road. The projected site for the Science Museum occupied the whole area behind the Royal College of Science, including the existing Southern Galleries. A triumvirate of Henry Tanner, architect to the Office of Works, the President of the Royal Institute of British Architects Leonard Stokes, and his predecessor Ernest George, advised the Committee on the best site and form for the building. The final decision was for a tripartite building, running from Queen's Gate to Exhibition Road, to be built in three *tranches*, starting at Exhibition Road, linked to the proposed new Geology Museum to the south, and backing on to the Natural History Museum. Immediately to the south was the 'spirit building' of the Natural History Museum in which was kept the museum's collection of thousands of specimens stored in spirit. This was detached from the main building because it was seen as a fire risk, and the Office of Works therefore suggested it should be demolished and replaced by a building erected elsewhere on the Natural History Museum site, at a safe distance. A monumental row ensued between the Trustees of the British Museum and the

Office of Works which had to be taken to the Cabinet for solution, reported in a document that began 'For many years the existing Science Museum at South Kensington has been a scandal'. The outcome was that the 'spirit building' was allowed to stay while the Science Museum was to have no windows to the south, a more serious impediment in the days when the preferred lighting for museums was daylight. The eastern block was planned to occupy the space between the roadway, the existing Post Office-cum-meteorological building, and in line with contemporary practice, a large hall was an important feature of the building. This was to be single storey with a light well above which would provide daylight for the surrounding three floors of gallery. Possibly the most significant matter for the Commissioners was that the division of the project into three meant that only some £40,000 was demanded immediately by the government.

Even so, Esher, struggling with the problems presented by the costs of other Commission projects, attempted to avoid this commitment. In 1912, influenced by the success of the Industrial Bursaries Scheme, and alarmed for the Commission's ability to continue if its capital base was eroded, Esher wrote a personal letter to Lloyd George, then Chancellor of the Exchequer, asking him to forgo the debt. Esher did not dispute the 'honourable liability' incurred by his predecessor Lord Wolverhampton, but he made the case '*in misericordiam*' that 1851 money would be better spent on the Industrial Bursaries than on bricks and mortar. He pointed out that the Commission's funds were very much more flexible than those of government.

> I do not believe that any scheme started in connection with the practical education of our people has ever shown greater promise than the plan of these industrial bursaries . . . a very remarkable record of fine work performed by boys of 19 and 20 years old under adverse pecuniary conditions. These young lads are all of them the sons of poor parents unable to afford any assistance to their children . . . I have a great hope that this appeal may not be in vain knowing how much you have at heart the welfare of those classes who are at the same time industrious and poor.

Characteristically, Esher, in a note to Shaw, asked for details of Welsh students, 'as I think a little demonstration of that kind would appeal to the Chancellor'. The equally wily Chancellor could only reply that the government estimates had included the scheme for the museum, and Parliament had already been told of the £100,000 from the Commission.[11]

THE BUILDING HISTORY OF THE SCIENCE MUSEUM

At this time the practice of government offices was changing, and the Office of Works was building up a new Technical Branch, which attracted ambitious young architects, and the Office was therefore increasingly ready to use its departmental staff. Thus, though an attempt was made by the President of the Board of Education to organize a competition for the Science Museum, comparable to that held for the Victoria and Albert Museum, this was resisted by Lord Beauchamp (1872–1938), First Commissioner of Works from 1910 to 1914, who wanted to employ his own staff. The new building for the Science Museum was therefore allocated to Richard Allison (1869–1958), 'one of the brightest of the younger men in the office' and eventually architect to the department. He visited the Royal Scottish Museum in Edinburgh, and science museums in Brussels, Paris and Munich. He chose Coignet concrete as the construction material in imitation of the Deutsches Museum, designed by G. von Seidl, whose foundation stone had been laid by the Kaiser in 1906. The design for the eastern block, faced in heavily rusticated Portland stone, was approved after a number of modifications necessitated by economies demanded in the House of Commons in March 1913. Parts of the Southern Galleries had to be cleared for demolition, and this was done by the same time. The contract for the reinforced concrete frame was won by the Kensington firm of Leslie & Company, but building was delayed by a strike until the following year. It was delayed again by the outbreak of the First World War, but the carcase was sufficiently completed for the government to take it over in 1918, behind a temporary front, for government offices.[12]

INDUSTRIAL BURSARIES

The Board of Management meeting on 3 May, 1911, threw itself into the new projects, a separate subcommittee being set up to deal with all of them – industrial bursaries, the proposed postgraduate scholarship in naval architecture, and the scholarships in architecture, sculpture and decorative painting. The Board had before it a report by the Secretary, who had toured the provincial universities to research the proposed

Industrial Bursary scheme, telling Lord Esher that 'your scheme received a *very warm welcome* wherever I went. *There is nothing like it* and everyone admits that such bursaries will do much to help to get able scientific men into industrial employment'. There was even a suggestion that perhaps the Commissioners had done enough:

> In giving grants both in land and in specie to the Government for the purposes of museums and schools ... more has been done in this direction than should have been done. The housing of museums of national importance is essentially the work of the Government and of Parliament and the Prince Consort's idea was undoubtedly that the funds [should not be used] for purposes for which the House of Commons could very properly be asked to provide in the annual estimates.

Despite pressure from the universities to allow further time for study there before the Bursars embarked on their industrial career, the subcommittee, chaired by Esher himself, was adamant that the purpose of the bursaries was to enable poor graduates to go into industry, where, at that time, young men with no experience, without private means, were too poorly paid to be able to take up apprenticeships or training posts in manufacturing.

The target was some twenty-five bursaries annually. The bursaries were open only to British subjects under 25, who had spent three years studying science, and who were of a sufficiently practical bent to do well in industry, but too poor to finance themselves. The Industrial Bursaries were between £70 for those living at home, and £100 for those living away. The bursary was generally for two years, though exceptionally it might continue for three years; the candidate had to report on his year's work, and a report from the employers was required to validate the work done by the candidate. A satisfactory number of the candidates were able to resign their grants early on being appointed to posts with higher salaries.

Of the seventeen successful candidates in the first year, three went into railway companies, and three into mechanical engineering, two each into electrical and civil engineering, and chemical research for industry, others into 'general colliery work', structural steel work and the weaving and dyeing industry. The reports set out the financial circumstances of the candidates, who came from very varied backgrounds, one being the son of a clerk in Holy Orders with an income of £270 and a dependent child, one of a retired engineer with £300 and two dependent children, and others the sons of a farm labourer or of a butcher 'with income just sufficient to support family'.[13]

THE NAVAL SCHOLARSHIP

The scholarship in naval architecture had been a particular project of George V as President, and fitted in well with the decision to finance no further buildings, but to dedicate the income to scholarships for both arts and scientific students. The single annual postgraduate scholarship was for British graduates under thirty, who had been employed for at least three years as apprentices or similar, and had already studied naval architecture, who wished to investigate problems or some development in shipbuilding, either at home or abroad. It was tenable at the Royal Naval College, Greenwich, or the universities or colleges of Glasgow, Newcastle and Liverpool, and was to be monitored by the Institution of Naval Architects. It was particularly important at the time, not only because of the investment in the naval arms race, but also because of the competition between the shipping lines at home and abroad for control of the Atlantic trade. Three scholarships were awarded in 1911, 1912 and 1913, but the scheme, like so much else, was rendered otiose by the outbreak of the First World War in August 1914, when the Naval Scholar went to work for Swan Hunter. Though the scheme was suspended for the duration of the war, it was revived after 1919.[14]

PROPOSED SCHOLARSHIPS IN ARCHITECTURE, SCULPTURE AND ART

The most innovative of the three new schemes espoused by Esher was that of the scholarships in monumental art, comprising architecture, sculpture, and decorative painting, because it helped to develop a new institution abroad, a truly international development, very much in the Prince Consort's original concept of an area of learning not confined to the British Isles. It also moved the Commissioners away from their increasingly exclusive involvement with science.

By July 1910, Evelyn Shaw was already hard at work collecting information on the sorts of scholarships available as far as sculpture, architecture and decorative arts were concerned.[15] He consulted widely, with Frank Heath at the Board of Education, and Frederick Kenyon, Director of the British Museum, and three others at the top of their professions – the architect Aston Webb (1849–1930), Thomas Brock, RA (1847–1922), sculptor of the Victoria Monument and later President of the Society of British Sculptors, and Edwin Austen Abbey (1852–1911), who had painted the official picture of the coronation of Edward VII, and a series of murals for the Pennsylvania State Capitol. The Board decided to adopt the resulting report, which fleshed out Esher's proposals for the three Art Scholarships, in November 1910, and this was confirmed by the full Commission in March 1911. A subcommittee of Esher, Ogilvie, Rücker and Glazebrook was established to bring these proposals about, and on 7 April, 1911, it met Aston Webb, Brock and Edwin Austen Abbey to discuss the details. It appears to have been Webb who suggested that the Director of the British School at Rome might be asked to supervise the Scholars. This was taken up in a later meeting with the School's London representatives and it was agreed.

At the following meeting on 3 May, 1911, the Board met with a report from Shaw on Esher's scheme before it. Shaw's research had established how modest and restricted were the existing awards by the Royal Institute of British Architects, the Royal Academy and the Society of Sculptors, and how necessary was further provision. The British School at Rome had been approached for help in supervising the students, though it was made clear that if the responsibilities were too heavy the Commissioners would have to make provision for additional staff. A revised constitution for the British School at Rome was proposed, based on the French Academy which gave the Prix de Rome. The scheme was for a two-year term in Rome, at £120 a year to cover studio accommodation, materials and so forth, open to students under thirty years of age from the British Empire. These scholarships were to be awarded under competitions to be devised by the three artistic bodies. The Commissioners would contribute the funds, and also provide for an additional officer of the School to look after the Scholars – 'to advise, report on, and in some measure, control the scholars and supply them with the means of obtaining studio accommodation and working materials'.[16]

At the same meeting, the Board effectively gave the subcommittee, of Esher, Ogilvie, Rücker and Glazebrook, the go-ahead for the proposal. In due course, they held a number of meetings, concerned with ascertaining the existing arrangements for the staff and pupils at the School, and with obtaining larger premises. In fact, however, a proposal was already being discussed which was to provide the British School in Rome with new premises on a prestigious site.

THE BRITISH SCHOOL AT ROME

The British School at Rome was a more modest institution than either the German or the French establishments, both of which were funded by government. Even the recently established American Academy had an extensive site on the Gianicolo, with a prominent building by McKim, Mead & White, thanks to the personal involvement of the architects, and a generous private benefactor. The British School had been founded at the beginning of the century through the efforts of several British archaeologists, impressed by the work being done in Rome by Rodolfo Lanciani of the Commissione archaeologica communale on the remains of Ancient Rome, discovered under the rapidly expanding suburbs then being developed. It was modelled on the successful British School at Athens, founded in 1884, whose members had encouraged the foundation of a similar institution in Rome. The Rome school was started through the initiative of Henry Pelham (1846–1907), Camden Professor of Ancient History at Oxford, with very modest support, from some British institutions, and from the British Ambassador, Lord Currie. The school was intended to promote Roman and Graeco-Roman Archaeology, and also to be a centre for the study of 'the language, literature, antiquities, art and history of Rome and Italy'. The first Director G. M. Rushforth was appointed in March 1900, but it seems to have been his successor as 'Acting' and then Assistant Director, 'Titus' Ashby (1874–1931), a pupil of F. J. Haverfield of Christ Church Oxford, who kept the School going through the difficult early years. Ashby had worked with Lanciani and published extensively in the *Papers of the British School at Rome*, but his 'gruff manner' did not endear him to the members of the School. He had been made Director in 1906, but found it difficult to get on with his colleagues. However, he was rescued to a large extent by the return to Rome of Mrs Strong, widow of the former librarian to the 8th Duke of Devonshire, who had succeeded her husband in the post. Eugenie Strong (1861–1943) was an archaeologist of repute, who had studied in Athens and Munich, and published on Roman sculpture, well connected both socially and academically, who smoothed out a number of personal problems, and worked with Ashby happily as Assistant Director from 1909 onwards.[17] Sir Rennell Rodd (1858–1941), an author and historian as well as a most successful diplomat, thought highly of her, commending her to Esher as 'a very remarkable woman and in her own subjects a really first-rate authority. Besides which she is not in the least a pedant, and is almost a woman of the world, inasmuch . . . that she is adaptable to all societies and excellent company'.[18]

Proposals for extending the academic base of the School were made from time to time, and from 1907 onwards the School provided a centre in Rome, at its quarters in the Palazzo Odescalchi, for scholars from the Royal Institute of British Architects and the Royal College of Art. The Royal Institute of British Architects considered the means of extending the School as a base for art students of all sorts, on the model of the École des Beaux Arts, but it was difficult to get the government to increase its modest grant.

THE ITALIAN EXHIBITION OF 1911: THE BRITISH PAVILION

The opportunity to enlarge the School came with the 1911 Exhibition, staged in Turin and Rome to celebrate the fiftieth anniversary of the unification of Italy in 1861. A Royal Commission was set up to manage both the British contributions to the 1910 Brussels Exhibition, and to the two Italian ones, under the Presidency of the Prince of Wales. Earl Lytton was Chairman, and his brother-in-law, Edwin Lutyens, who had designed the British pavilion for the Paris Exhibition of 1900, was Consulting Architect. The foreign pavilions were placed on an open space in the Valle Giulia, and the British were allotted an excellent position. The Board of Trade, which was in charge, decreed that the design of the pavilion should be based on the west front of St Paul's Cathedral. Lutyens visited Rome with his brother-in-law in October 1909, and, soon after, he was officially asked to design the pavilion. He produced a typical witty Lutyenesque design based on the upper part of St Paul's, as the façade for an iron-framed building built internally out of breeze and pozzuolana, and externally clad in fibrous plaster. Fire resistance was a concern because there had been a fire at the exhibition in Brussels, and the British pavilion had been engulfed, destroying a number of valuable exhibits.

The structure was, of course, a temporary one, an iron frame manufactured by the Knightsbridge firm of Humphreys who had built up a large and prosperous business all over the British dominions in 'iron buildings', from 'tin tabernacles' and cottage hospitals to exhibition building of all sorts. The firm owned a large area in Knightsbridge where stood the exhibition building known as 'Humphreys Hall', and had been involved in the series of South Kensington Exhibitions in the 1880s, Fisheries, Health and Inventions, and even the 'Colinderies'. They had worked abroad at the American Exhibition of 1887, the Italian Exhibition in the following year and at Paris in 1900. The firm had been established in 1834, and built up by Colonel J. Charlton Humphreys from a modest family building business in Southwark to an organization nationally known for its ability to provide temporary buildings for any eventuality. It had become a public company in 1891, and Humphreys himself was known for his gentlemanly interest in the Southwark Yeomanry, but it was still very much a family company.[19]

The British Pavilion in Rome, though temporary, so dominated the Valle Giulia with its impressive portico, and was so admired that the Syndaco of Rome, Ernesto Nathan, approached the British Ambassador Sir Rennell Rodd (1858–1941) with a suggestion that the site of the exhibition pavilion should be donated to the British authorities on the understanding that it was rebuilt to the same design in a permanent form as an exhibition centre. Sir Rennell, who had been promoting the idea of expanding the artistic, as opposed to the archaeological, side of the British School, thought that it might be even more suitable for the British School in Rome, to provide a base for the proposed art and architecture scholarships. He communicated this scheme to Lutyens on 15 April, 1911, suggesting that the latter should get the Royal Institute of British Architects to buy the building, and fit it up. This proposal was apparently welcomed by Aston Webb.[20] Lutyens himself was delighted:

> The excitement of the day has been my seeing Aston Webb who is very excited about Rennell Rodd's proposal about the British School … If it comes off – the Rome affair – it will be a great feather in my cap.[21]

The proposal 'came to Lord Esher's knowledge' in April 1911. Counsel's opinion was taken as to whether the Commissioners were entitled to hold land outside the 'King's Dominions', and fortunately the answer was in the affirmative. The Commissioners discussed the proposal at their meeting on 3 May, and that day Esher telegraphed to Rodd that the Commissioners would like to acquire the Pavilion together with additional ground at the rear. He asked for an option for a month 'to enable them to ascertain cost of and to make provision for adapting and especially for making provision for maintaining a building for British School'.

The Syndaco was accommodating, the only stipulation being that the building should be used for education, or otherwise revert to the City of Rome, and an agreement was signed by Rodd and Nathan in July 1911.[22] The land was finally vested, not in the School, but in three British trustees – Prince Arthur of Connaught, Lord Esher and Sir Rennell Rodd. The Commissioners' proposal that it should be used as the base for a reconstituted institution was adopted but various bodies with an interest in the School had to be consulted. Soon after an agreement was reached by which the 1851 Commission was to provide a London office for the British School, and the Secretary of the Commission was also to be the Honorary General Secretary of the British School, an arrangement which was to last for seventy years. This made Evelyn Shaw the linchpin of the scheme, operating a complex relationship between various academic bodies in England, Esher and Rodd, both powerful figures used to getting their own way, an architect in London and contractors in Rome.

NEW HEADQUARTERS FOR THE BRITISH SCHOOL AT ROME

Converting the pavilion was less straightforward than had been hoped. Lutyens was approached to redesign his work to make it permanent. The contractor, Colonel Charlton Humphreys, who technically owned the building, donated it to the Commissioners, and was duly awarded the contract for the reconstruction. In May 1911 Lutyens went out to Rome, and went over the building with George Freeman, a director representing Humphreys.[23]

Even with two such accomplished diplomats as Rennell Rodd and Lord Esher, it was difficult to reconcile the various interests involved in the School. Rodd, a classicist and a protégé of Granville, who had served with distinction in both Berlin and Cairo, as well as Rome, was always conscious of the needs of the established Faculty of Archaeology, History and Letters, and anxious that they should not be put in the shade by the proposed new Arts Faculties. His advice over Italian practices and local customs was invaluable. Esher was essentially interested in promoting the newer Faculties, but was also to take a real interest in the future progress of past students, as in his introduction of Bradshaw to Lionel Earle. Both men followed the comfortable Edwardian practice of retiring into summer seclusion, in Rodd's case to the Villa Rosebery at Posilippo, in Esher's to his beloved Roman Camp at Callander, leaving Shaw to struggle on by telegram and letter.

The brief for the plans of the School was drawn up by a number of hands, with Ashby and Mrs Strong, with some intervention from Rodd, presenting the practical needs of the students in Rome, and Lutyens the architectural scheme from London, with the assistance of Albert Thomas in his London office and of the Resident Architect in Rome William Squire. Considerable problems were presented by the fact that Lutyens was understandably far more interested in his magnificent New Delhi project, which had materialized almost as soon as the project for the British School had begun. It became clear that his office was not accustomed to take decisions in his absence.

Lord Esher had put before his subcommittee the Commissioners' agreement to the scheme on the understanding that the cost would be between £6000 and £10,000. This seems to have assumed that most of the structure could be strengthened and reused, so that the Pavilion would remain roughly as it was with some alterations to the galleries to make them suitable for students, and the Director's House and the Students' Hostel would be built at the rear. It became clear, however, that unfortunately no more land was available, and that a more radical and more costly treatment of the Pavilion would be necessary, by which the façade would be reconstructed and the interior adapted for working purposes, and a hostel for twenty-five students and quarters for the Director would be built on the existing site, behind the façade. A new design was prepared, but Humphreys estimated that even without the extra foundations, drainage, sanitary fittings, lighting and heating, the cost would be about £32,000, that is some £10,829 for the façade, £8133 for the interior of the School and £12,271 for the hostel. The matter was embarrassing for Lutyens, and a very public *bêtise*, about which Baker could tease him the following year, when the two were about to collaborate over the Viceroy's House at Delhi. Despite Lord Esher's personal efforts, with the assistance of Sir Aston Webb, it was only possible to get the cost down to £25,000. The subcommittee met for the third time on 29 November, 1911, together with Frampton, Webb and Poynter representing the Royal Academy, Blomfield and J. W. Simpson representing the Royal Institute of British Architects, Brock and Stirling Lee for the Sculptors, and the representatives of the existing British School, Professor J. S. Reid, A. H. Smith and Baker-Penoyre, and the portrait painter John S. Sargent. They were mostly concerned with such matters as the Constitution of the revamped School, and a list of the 'great and the good' to be invited to serve on the Council.[24]

It was the Board of Management at their meeting in December 1911 who had to struggle with the financial problems. The members decided to spend £15,000 on 'reconstructing the façade and making such alterations to the interior as would provide for the working accommodation required as well as for the lighting and heating'. They appointed Aston Webb and Blomfield to advise the subcommittee on the plans; Esher, Rücker, Ogilvie and John Singer Sargent were to be the Commissioners' representatives. They also considered the proposals of the different professional bodies for the competitions to be held for the scholarships, and decided to send Shaw to Rome early in the new year.[25]

Lutyens was also in Rome, based at the Embassy, and described his visit and the *dramatis personae*:

> Ashby lunched, then palace-hunting with Evelyn Shaw, and a tea party at the British School. Mrs. Strong, once so keen, is now depressed and thinks the new building will be too far out from Rome – and is making things difficult. Ashby is keen. I have likened Mrs. Strong to a great big retriever and Ashby to a small wire-haired terrier that trots round after her.[26]

Lutyens's revised design after he 'had revisited site and made himself familiar with requirements of institution' came out at £40,000, without heating or lighting. Undeterred, the Special Subcommittee decided to expend the £15,000 available from the Commission on 'reconstructing the main portion of the façade, omitting the construction of the wings, and leaving the galleries as they were'.[27] This work was to be superintended by William Squire, based in Rome, appointed at ten guineas a week. The programme for the School was endorsed by the Board and then the Commissioners, at their consecutive meetings at St James's Palace in June 1912, when Prince Arthur of Connaught made the 'British School at Rome and the proposed Art Scholarships' the key note of his speech. He recalled his visit to the International Exhibition, the generosity of the Syndic and the Municipality of Rome, and congratulated Lord Esher and the Board of Management on 'bringing into existence an Institution which . . . will place us on a level with other nations in the matter of artistic education, and can do for British students under wise and careful guidance what has been done by means of similar institutions in Rome for the art students of other countries'. The School had been incorporated and granted a Royal Charter earlier in that month so it was now a going concern. An Executive Committee had been appointed to run the hostel side of the School's work, while the 'purely artistic and archaeological work of the school is under the supervision of four Faculties of Experts'.

The Special Subcommittee was also responsible for the other new projects, like the Industrial Bursaries and the Naval Scholarship, where the first Scholar, Arthur Cannon, had been appointed in December 1911. A large part of their report was, however, devoted to the Art Scholarships, 'designed especially for the encouragement of Monumental Art'. It defined the role of the Commissioners in the reconstitution of the British School, as 'bringing into it fresh elements representative of the Fine Arts, with a view to establishing an Institution . . . which would in itself be worthy of the support of the Commissioners as contributing materially to the advancement of higher education in this country'. The School, it pointed out, would be 'in no sense a teaching Institution' though guidance and supervision would be at hand, and technical and other interests would be 'afforded their due share of control'. The problem of the adaptation of the Pavilion for the school buildings had been somewhat eased by the gift of £10,000 by an anonymous donor found by Lord Esher, with the promise of more should 'the progress of the scheme be satisfactory'.[28]

In November 1912, the Board approved the regulations for the three scholarships, and these were awarded in 1913, though as yet the accommodation for the three Scholars was not complete. Candidates had to be British subjects under thirty when they took up the award, of £200 a year for three years. The procedure for selecting Scholars was elaborate and time-consuming. For architecture, for instance, a number of institutions were entitled to nominate up to four candidates each; these included the Royal Academy and the Royal College of Art, two London and five provincial schools of architecture; in addition, the chapters of the Royal Institute of British Architects in the Colonies were allowed to propose candidates, and the holders of a number of long-established scholarships given by the RA and the Royal Institute of British Architects were eligible to apply, while anyone not included in these lists had to pass a qualifying examination. These nominees entered a First Competition, for which they had two months to prepare drawings on a subject selected by the Faculty of Architecture of the British School. From these, ten were selected for the Final Competition, which took place 'en loge' in London for a period of two weeks, again with the subject decided by the Faculty.[29]

The building of the British School at Rome, though it took up much of the time of both Chairman and Secretary until the outbreak of the First World War, and a large part of the Commissioners' financial resources, was not the only preoccupation of the Board. In 1912, the Science Scholarships Committee completed its twenty-first year, and they celebrated by offering annual scholarships, instead of alternate ones, to three Antipodean universities, Sydney, Melbourne and New Zealand, and by inviting McGill University, Montreal, to nominate a candidate.

Lord Esher's drive to restore the balance between art and science did not preclude the Commissioners responding to other appeals for assistance, and in 1912 they funded a considerable extension to the buildings and work of the National Physical Laboratory. The Laboratory had been established in 1899, under the aegis of the Royal Society, in buildings at both Kew and at Teddington, to carry out physical and engineering research of national importance for which there were no facilities elsewhere, in such fields as the 'standardizing and verifying of instruments, and the testing of materials'. By 1912, more accommodation was needed – the work had expanded, and the staff had increased from 30 to 150, and, in addition, the old Observatory at Kew was now needed for meteorological research. The Office of Works had agreed to provide more buildings at Teddington, at a cost of some £30,000 with a further £5000 for equipment, to which the Treasury was prepared to make a single contribution of £15,000, leaving the rest to be found from private benefactions. Members of the Commission and the Science Scholarships Committee, including Geikie and Rayleigh, were members of the General Board, while Glazebrook was the Director of the Laboratory. As the Funds Committee pointed out, private individuals including prominent businessmen, such as Sir Julius Wernher and Sir John Brunner, had already contributed to the setting up of the existing buildings, and the Laboratory carried out a good deal of work for government departments under contract. Over £3000 was needed to complete the buildings while some £5000 was still needed to equip the laboratories.

Lord Rayleigh made an urgent appeal to the Board in December 1912, in which he emphasized the Commissioners' role in the application of science to industry and manufacture, pointing out that the Commissioners

> by their scholarships, their industrial bursaries and their general policy have had no small success in enforcing this lesson on the nation. The Laboratory . . . is a unique Institution, national in its character, distinct from all Technical Colleges and Universities. It pursues . . . one of the main objects of the Commission, the greater good of the nation through the applications of science.

He went on to list other connections with the Commission, since five former Scholars were 'prominent members of the staff'. He anticipated one response to the request – that such a national work ought to be undertaken by the government and paid for out of national funds. He pointed out that the Executive Committee was inhibited from using this argument as the Treasury had offered £15,000 on the understanding that the balance would be met from elsewhere. As he concluded, it 'was surely better to try and do a needed work rather than leave it undone because the Government declined to find all the funds'.[30] Faced with such an appeal by a prominent member of the Science Scholarships Committee, and with the Director a member of the Board, the Board agreed to give the necessary £5000 towards completing the buildings.

Members of the Board could feel considerable satisfaction at its achievements: not only were they carrying out their charter obligations through the promotion of both scientific and artistic projects of national significance, but some long-standing problems relating to the estate had been solved. Westminster had finally agreed to take over the Commissioners' roads, at a cost to the Commission of £6000 for repaving, and the Royal Albert Hall had finally paid off the temporary loan made in 1908 in connection with the South Entrance. The Board's finances continued to improve, though they had had to set aside not only the £15,000 for Rome, but the promised £100,000 for the Science Museum. The difficulties that had been surmounted are perhaps most clearly reflected in the Board's tribute in its 1912 report to Shaw 'to whose unwearied zeal and tactful handling of most difficult negotiations', the success to date had been largely due.[31]

BUILDING THE BRITISH SCHOOL AT ROME

The Special Subcommittee had investigated the existing arrangements for the British School very thoroughly, detailing the pay and emoluments of both Ashby and Mrs Strong, their contribution towards the servants and the cost of lighting and heating their accommodation. The proposal was that both should live on the premises with the assistance of a part-time manager, unpaid, who would be responsible for running the establishment in return for accommodation rent-free. It is possible that this stricter organization was one of the things that had upset Mrs Strong, who took the view, according to Lutyens, that 'our School is going to be too big for her and she is terrified of the architectural students. Why she picks out the architectural ones I don't like to think'.[32]

It was hoped that the building would be completed quickly, and the first Scholars for Architecture, Painting and Sculpture came out to Rome in 1913. H. Charlton Bradshaw (1893–1943) was the Architecture Scholar, Colin Gill (1892–1940) the holder of the Decorative Painting Award and Gilbert Ledward (1888–1960) the Sculptor.

The building took much longer and much more in the way of resources than the Board had planned. A realistic assessment by Esher in 1912 acknowledged that, Lutyens's estimate being £45,000, 'there is no immediate prospect of our being able to carry out the Architect's design for the complete scheme'. The alternatives were to raise further donations sufficient to enable the building to be adapted to house twenty-four to forty scholars, or to use the building as working quarters for art students only, an alternative opposed strongly by Rodd, on the grounds that this would be unfair to the old-established archaeological faculty. An endowment for maintenance would be required: it was calculated that the existing endowment of £10,000 at 4 per cent would provide enough to maintain the buildings as working quarters for the art students, who needed extensive studio space, particularly for the sculptors. A further £25,000 would provide £1000 per annum, enough to fund working quarters, hostel and administrative staff. The cost of administration in London would be met for the time being by the 1851 Commissioners, who would allow their offices to be used as headquarters by the Executive Committee and the three Faculties of Art. However, the note continued, prophetically, 'it should be borne in mind that the school will one day be independent of the 1851 Commissioners, when a fund will have to be provided for office and administration expenses in London'.

Lutyens's original scheme for the School had been to extend the building on plan by adding a further bay to the wings of the main south elevation between the central portico and the end pavilions, and extending
east and west wings northward behind the end pavilions to a residential
north wing. The centre would have been part courtyard, and part exhibition rooms, lecture theatre, and studios. The original exhibition galleries
would have been converted to studios, and the east and west wings would
have housed the servants, dining room and library. Separate accommodation was to be provided for Director and Assistant Director at the rear of
the plot. The wings at the back would have been in a different style in a
sort of South of France-cum-Northern Italian classical style, with white
walls, red roofs and green-shuttered windows. The east and west walls
were more formal in treatment with screens of coupled columns on the
ground floor. The double-height library had a domed roof and an elegant
first-floor gallery with a bronze railing. An early scheme for the garden
with box-fringed parterres, clipped limes, groves of ilexes and cypresses
showed that Lutyens was anxious that the new building should match up
to the work he was doing for both corporate and private clients, not only
in Britain, but throughout the British Empire.

The shortfall in both the land on offer behind the building and the
money available made considerable changes in both the planning and the
size of the building necessary, despite Esher's resourcefulness in obtaining a substantial contribution from Edwin Abbey's widow, and from elsewhere.

The final plan was less extensive, and again modified before completion; the finishing of the façades and the interiors considerably more
modest. After a meeting of the Board in February 1913, the scheme was
cut back drastically to the original shorter façade of the pavilion, despite
the fact that the foundations for the extended version had already been
provided. The 'Revised Plan submitted in accordance with Instructions
given at the meeting, Feb. 5 1913' bears a slightly irritated note 'dotted
line denotes line of former scheme now dismantled'. The new curtailed
scheme involved the rebuilding of the exhibition pavilion façade only
behind the left wing on the west side. The new buildings, too, were more
modest, in a more vernacular Italian style. Immediately behind the façade
on this side was the library, less grandly finished than originally
designed, and in the west wing were the flats for Director and Assistant

Director with the accommodation for students on the third floor. The north side was occupied by two ranges of studios with north lights, in truth a great improvement on the original plan of providing studios in the original gallery space. Immediately behind the central portico was an Exhibition Hall, giving on to an open courtyard through a colonnade with paired Ionic columns. The courtyard behind was dominated by an elegant niche, containing a bust of Edwin Abbey, whose widow had given so much financial help. The eastern side of the courtyard had to remain open until funds accumulated after the First World War, when the buildings were extended by H. Charlton Bradshaw, the first Rome Scholar for Architecture.[33]

The many changes caused delay as did the war, but the management of the contract was not exemplary, nor assisted by the fact that Lutyens made four visits to New Delhi, between April 1912 and May 1915, when it was difficult to get replies from the London office. Squire claimed to have written twenty-nine letters to Thomas about 'the Drainage Question', without getting a satisfactory reply. Occasionally Lutyens travelled via Rome to see the School, and generously did not claim all his expenses. However, the costs of the project were high, and Lutyens was not at his best when working to a tight budget. Equally his specification was based on traditional English materials, English oak and Baltic softwood were stipulated, expensive in Italy at all times, but almost impossible in the course of the First World War. Rodd was very indignant that more local materials and craftsmen were not used, urging the use of Italian walnut, locally worked, for the library, while Esher and Shaw were very wary of Lutyens's preference for expensive finishes. Thus when the library was being carried out in a more modest way, with funds provided by the Archaeological Faculty, to Squire's design using local softwood instead of English oak, Shaw told Squire to be cautious since 'it would not be advisable to give Lutyens the chance of making any suggestions which are pretty sure to involve the expenditure of more money than you possess for the purpose'.[34] Lutyens's letters to his wife show his increasing irritation with the matter.

Many of the materials and fittings were intended to be sent from England, and the outbreak of war made this difficult. Ashby, the Director of the School, joined the Ambulance Corps and went to the north where the Italian Third Army was fighting the Austrian troops. Both Humphreys and the resident architect or clerk of works, William Squire, complained of the lack of information from Lutyens's office. Lutyens, for his part, regarded Squire as useless. 'his supervision is nil. His diplomacy is fatal. He is very stupid, very nervous, and has little technical knowledge and no power of organisation whatsoever'.[35]

Part of the problem seems to have been a certain insularity in the approach to equipping the building, and the Commission's files contain details of furniture for the students' bedrooms to be supplied by London emporia, though Mappin & Webb had a branch in Rome which was also to be patronized.[36]

However, by 30 April, 1916, the building was completed and available for occupation, after three and a half years, and as Shaw could report to Lord Esher, within the 'funds available'. It had been 'a close thing' however, and Lutyens had had to forgo 'his nominal fee of £350' for out-of-pocket expenses, and Squire acted in an honorary capacity for the last five months of his three and a half years in Rome. 'Mrs. Strong', Shaw added, 'is strangely silent.' Shaw and Esher, with Rodd, Ashby and Squire in Rome, could take credit for the achievement of a project, which, in 1911, must have seemed ideal and well within the capacity of a quasi-official body acting with the support of the British government, but was a very different matter after the outbreak of war.

THE 1851 COMMISSION IN THE FIRST WORLD WAR

When war broke out in August 1914, Esher, who had been a member of the Committee of Imperial Defence for the last ten years, found himself effectively recalled to the colours. As President of the County of London Territorials, he threw himself into the task of recruiting volunteers, but was soon asked by Kitchener to act as liaison officer between him and the British Commander-in-Chief, Sir John French. Later he was posted to Paris to fill the same sort of role between the British and French High Commands. These duties of national importance left little room for the Commission but, in fact, as soon as it was clear that the war was not 'going to be over by Christmas', the work of the Commission closed down almost entirely. Lord Esher spent much of the war in Paris, and most members of the Board and the Scholarships Committee and their charges were engaged in work of national importance. The supply of Scholars and Bursars dried up as all able-bodied men were called up, and potential Bursars found paid employment under the government.

The Board met twice in the course of the war, with very little business to transact except for completing the building work at the British School at Rome, which benefited from the surplus income from the vacant Rome scholarships, by 1917 amounting to some £3000. The Rome Scholars, including the sculptor Sargeant Jagger who was wounded at Gallipoli, had enlisted; of the forty Industrial Bursars in 1914, nine had enlisted, five resigned, and twenty-four had found chemical and engineering work, mostly 'in the manufacture of War Supplies'.[37]

Shaw presented a brief report to Esher in 1915, recording a most satisfactory financial state of affairs, including 'surplus cash of £19,000', which he thought would enable the Commissioners to meet the promised payment for the Science Museum without spending capital. Several Scholars and Bursars had had their army pay or their salaries made up, as had the Assistant Secretary McClure who had enlisted.

POST-WAR CHANGES

After the Armistice, the Commission took a long time to reorganize; a number of Commissioners had died during the war, and a whole raft of new and younger faces appeared at Commission meetings after 1921. Esher, now approaching seventy, was playing a less active part in both court circles and in government. Increasingly he was spending time in Scotland, at Callander, but the competent Shaw kept him in touch with major problems. Happily for the Commission, Esher had a realistic attitude to the changes in society, in government and the passing of control in the country from the pre-war governing class. He was able to steer the Commission into new roles, and to enable it to continue to use its resources in an effective and innovative way to best effect.

In the short term, the Commissioners had benefited financially from wartime conditions, as they had not been able to spend much of their income, since there were no recipients for scholarships or bursaries. Money from rents had accumulated, but this was balanced by a depreciation of some £18,000 in the value of the Commissioners' portfolio of investments. However, under post-war conditions they had to raise the value of the bursaries and scholarships by 20 to 50 per cent. This was possible in 1919 and 1920 because of the cash accumulated during the war, but would have to be reconsidered in due course. The value of the estate was also affected by inflation, and, even before the war, the Board had been considering getting it revalued for the 'modern Domesday Book' under the 1909–10 Finance Act.[38] The problem of the contribution to the Science Museum had only been postponed by the war: some £19,000 of the first *tranche* of £40,000 had been paid, and now that work was resuming on the carcase of the building, further demands had to be anticipated.

One great improvement could be reported, in that for the first time for many years, the Commissioners had an office on their own property. Since the 1880s the staff had been lodged in Victoria Street, apparently rent-free in government buildings, by 1886 at number 2, on the north side close to New Tothill Street, a building which they appear to have shared with the Board of Trade Bankruptcy Audit Office. When Victoria Street was renumbered, it became number 18, and by 1900 they shared it with the Army Medical Service.[39] In 1905 the Commission office moved further west to number 54, a block with a multiplicity of tenants, including the Inland Revenue, the Marine Department of the Board of Trade and the Mutual Life Insurance Company of New York.

Esher was always concerned about the future of the Rome Scholars, and by 1920 he was looking for a suitable place for the Rome students to exhibit their drawings and works of art.

'I want to have a "Museum" of our own', he wrote to Shaw, 'but you will have to find a nice office. I am not in love with Victoria Street.' He toyed with the notion that Lionel Earle (1866–1948), then Permanent Secretary at the Office of Works, might find the Commission a suitable office, but finally abandoned the idea, in favour of Shaw's suggestion of purchasing a lease. 'Probably you could get the sort of place we require fairly cheap. It is only *small* houses that are expensive these days.'[40] Victoria Street was convenient when the Board and the Commission included a large number of politicians and civil servants closely involved in government, but with more scientists than politicians, and with the growing importance of South Kensington as a scientific centre, a new office was needed further west.

No. 1, Lowther Gardens was on the edge of the estate, on the grounds of Eden Lodge, which the Commissioners had failed to secure at the time of the South Kensington purchase. It was one of a pair of houses which had been built on the bottom of Lord Lowther's garden by Colonel Makins to the design of J. J. Stevenson in 1877. He had built number 1 for himself, and number 2 as a speculation at the same time.

In 1920, number 1 belonged to a Scottish landowner, Graeme A. Lockhart Whitelaw of Strathallan Castle, Machary, Perthshire, who was putting it up for auction in May 1920. Substantial houses requiring a large staff were less attractive to private owners in the reduced post-war circumstances, and Lowther Lodge had already been sold, in 1912, to an institution, the Royal Geographical Society, but space was at a premium on the Commissioners' estate. At the end of March, Shaw informed Finch, the Commissioners' solicitor, that Lord Esher had 'decided in his own mind to purchase No. 1 Lowther Gardens', and was anxious not to lose the freehold. Leslie Vigers, who was to succeed Stevenson as the Commissioners' Surveyor, valued the building at £18,000, but warned that there were restrictive covenants that would operate against office use. Though the Board supported Esher in his decision, there was a problem in the shape of Imperial College, whose Rector Sir Alfred Keogh, a former Surgeon-General, was 'anxious that no private person should get the house', in case they should interfere with the future expansion of the College. However, he did not feel that the College should 'compete against the Commissioners', and the upshot was that it was agreed that the Commissioners should buy the building, and as they needed only the ground floor and basement, Imperial College would take the top floors, largely to prevent them being turned into flats. A reluctant and unenthusiastic partnership was formed between Keogh, who 'frankly admitted he regretted our intervention', and Shaw, responsible to Esher, and encouraged by Stamfordham, who found Keogh's attitude bizarre. 'He wants the house', he told Esher, 'but he does not know what for. He was prepared to outbid anyone, without knowing its value.'[41] Negotiations continued on Gilbertian lines; Shaw, having opened negotiations through Fladgate, had been told that Whitelaw had paid £24,000 and wanted £30,000, for premises valued at between £16,000 and £20,000. He then approached the auctioneers anonymously through John D. Wood, which deceived no one. An additional problem was the ownership of No. 2, whose owner would have the right to enforce the restrictive covenants. This was complicated by the fact that Mrs Radcliffe, the elderly owner, was unable to make any competent decisions. However, Shaw obtained sufficient undertakings from her man of business and her likely heirs to pursue the Commission's objective of No. 1. This came up for auction, with the highest genuine bid being some £15,000, and in due course Shaw secured it for £20,000, earning Esher's commendation for his 'skill and patience'.

Shaw was able to obtain an office use for the Commission by drawing the attention of the London County Council to the fact that 'other large houses were vacant in the vicinity', identifying a trend in South Kensington which was going to affect the Commissioners' estate greatly.[42]

The building was to provide a convenient and prestigious office for the Commission for over sixty years. It was too large for the diminished staff, and though Lord Esher had expressed his preference for the upper floors to be used as a hostel, they were occupied by 'the new Aeronautical Department' of Imperial College under Richard Glazebrook.[43]

Though the Commissioners did not meet again till 1921, this seems to have been due to an anticipated change of President, with the election of the Prince of Wales, later Edward VIII. It was Esher who saw Prince Arthur who was about to go out to South Africa as Governor-General, and persuaded him to 'place himself in the King's hands'. 'He is quite willing to resign', he told Shaw, 'but Lord S. [Bigge had been made Lord Stamfordham in 1911] might approach him again. Only we should try to get the thing *settled*.'[44]

Because of the imminent change of President, there was no meeting of the Commission in 1920, but the Board was able to hold its winter meeting in the new offices, convening a joint meeting with the Scholarships Committee in order to review the scheme, now some thirty years old, in the light of changed post-war circumstances. The priorities were to 'maintain the prestige of the Commissioners' Scholarships' and for this purpose they were to be compared with scholarships given by other bodies. There was, however, no reviewing of the position over the Science Museum, where they refused a request from the Treasury to increase their grant.[45] There were changes in the staff – Leslie Vigers took over as Surveyor from the sick and ageing Stevenson, while McClure left to pursue a full-time legal career at 5 Paper Buildings, being replaced by Stanley Quick as Assistant Secretary. Quick joined an office staffed by Shaw as Secretary at £1000 per annum, himself at £350, a senior clerk and bookkeeper at £225, and a clerk at £130 per annum.

IX

Serving the British Empire
1921–1947

The Commission and the South Kensington estate over which the young Prince of Wales was to preside was a world away not only from the body which had bought the rural estate under his great-grandfather, but indeed from that presided over by his own father ten years before. The war had impoverished victors and vanquished alike, and though England had avoided the revolutions which had destroyed so much of familiar pre-war Europe, a great deal had changed. The rich were no longer so rich: as Esher pointed out to Frederick Ponsonby, visitors to Hatfield were no longer met at the station by a carriage with outriders. More pertinently, as he said to the Cabinet Secretary Hankey: 'There is no chance of the future resembling the past. That is the first point. England, and the Empire, can never again be the England and the Empire that you knew.'[1]

The Commission, too, had to adjust to a new England and a new Empire, and use its resources to serve a changing world. Despite Esher's semi-retirement at Roman Camp, he was still able to provide a surprisingly enlightened leadership in these changes, and to ensure that the Commissioners and those running the various scholarship schemes never lost sight of the main objectives.

The Board members who met for the first time in the new offices at 1 Lowther Gardens had all been associated with the Commission for over ten years. As well as Esher, and Stamfordham, who had retained an active interest despite his important position in the Royal Household, there were the financial adviser Lord Revelstoke, Ogilvie and Glazebrook (1914 list), though Mowatt and Roscoe had died since the last Commission meeting. The policies they followed were well-tried ones, and were to direct the Commission's activities until the outbreak of the Second World War. As the Commissioners performed their allotted tasks, they left themselves less and less room for manoeuvre: most of the estate had been virtually alienated on long leases to suitable institutions, the lines of scholastic patronage had been set out in an even-handed manner and the various interests on the Board were sufficiently well balanced to maintain a settled programme.

The full Commission had not met since March 1914, when it had met at St James's Palace under the presidency of Prince Arthur of Connaught. It met early in 1921 in its own offices under the Prince of Wales. The distinction between the full Commission and the Board was emphasized by separate appointments. The convention of formally electing prominent politicians to the Commission was maintained by the election of Lord Birkenhead (the former F. E. Smith), Lloyd George, then Prime Minister, Earl Curzon and Viscount Haldane. On the academic side were elected men representing a wide range of interests, the historian H. A. L. Fisher, the Rector of Imperial College Sir Alfred Keogh, the Director of the British Museum Sir Frederick Kenyon, who had been involved with the British School, and one of the earliest Science Scholarship-holders, the Nobel Prize-winner Sir Ernest Rutherford. New Commissioners were added to the Board of Management, Lord Buckmaster, Professor J. B. Farmer, already on the Scholarships Committee, and Thomas Jones, former Assistant Secretary to the Cabinet. The veteran civil servant Sir Francis Ogilvie, and Sir Richard Glazebrook, Chairman of the Science Scholarships Committee, had already been recruited to the Board.

The reports of the Board and the Science Scholarships Committee were the main business at this meeting, and set out the future pattern by which the Royal Commission was to transact only formal business, the real work being done by the Board and subcommittees.

The Reports to the Commission set out the agenda for the next two decades, the maintenance of the South Kensington estate, and the continuation of the pattern of scholarships: the Science Scholarships, the Industrial Bursaries, the Naval Architecture Scholarship and the Art Scholarships at the British School at Rome, where the final bill for building had been £20,000, well over the original estimate. However, thanks to the dearth of candidates for scholarships in the war, the Commission had been able to accumulate funds.

In post-war conditions, the Board found it had to rethink its commitments, but there were few avenues open to it. Though it had been able to save money during the war, post-war inflation demanded that Scholars were paid more, while the capital value of many of its investments had declined. However, the needs of potential science scholars were still there, and the Board felt justified in continuing its existing scholarships in Decorative Art, Architecture and Sculpture at Rome, and in Naval Architecture, while it was anticipated that the demand for the Industrial Bursaries would continue.

THE INDUSTRIAL BURSARIES

These had atrophied during the war as all adult males were usefully employed on national service, and a new generation of students ready to take up apprenticeships had not yet emerged since the war. However, in 1920, the Board had been able to appoint some twenty-three Bursars of whom three had resigned on obtaining 'remunerative employment'. Consultant engineers at the time would expect apprentices to earn their training by working for two years or more without pay. The bursary enabled the candidate to take on a training job on a pittance, which would enable him ultimately to aspire to a management post. This useful method of enabling talented but poor graduates to make their way in industry was to prove essential until the outbreak of the Second World War. In the 1930s, the situation became worse, as some employers attempted to reduce the pittance they paid their employees. Thus Metropolitan-Vickers Electrical Company in Manchester, a regular employer of Bursars, lowered pay from £130 to £13 a year.[2] The Board's reaction was draconian – they refused any Industrial Bursaries in connection with Metropolitan-Vickers until the policy changed in 1937, when the firm was again eligible to take Bursars.[3] During the two interwar decades the Board funded about twenty bursaries annually, renewing about half for the second year, and about a third for the third year. The candidates had all to be nominated by their universities, and their varying backgrounds are catalogued by the Commission – the son of a farmer's widow with four dependent children, children of lowly paid or deceased fathers, post-office sorter, Wesleyan minister, vocalist at £230 per annum, occasionally an assistant secretary at £450 p. a., or a managing director, but with dependent children. The majority of them came from the families of skilled workers, clerks and tradesmen, with the occasional unfortunate from a professional home, where the breadwinner was dead or disabled. The family income on average was about £225, with 39 per cent under £156, and 18 per cent over £365, and the families had done all they could to supplement a scholarship through college or university, while there were often younger children to assist.

This was a scheme which did indeed apply science to industry, since it enabled those who had already achieved a scholarship to the university for their scientific training to put it into practical effect by enabling them to bridge the gap between graduating and having enough experience to be worthwhile as an employee. A Record of the Science Scholars had been published since the early days of the scheme, and the Industrial Bursaries were recognized by a similar publication in 1929, cataloguing the achievements of some 303 award-holders. They went into various forms of applied science and technology such as civil and electrical engineering, posts in the coal, oil and other extractive industries, with a minority working for manufacturing chemists, and in textiles and other manufacturing industry.

An indicator of the correctness of the Board's choice was the speed with which the Bursars were able to resign their awards in favour of paid employment. Of the 350 Bursars appointed between 1911 and 1929, 50 were able to resign before taking up the appointment, but the Board monitored the careers of the remainder. In 1929 the Board could point to the important posts filled by ex-Industrial Bursars – those of the Chief Turbine Engineers of C. A. Parsons and Metropolitan-Vickers, the Chief Engineer of Shell, and of the Director of Research for the British Cast Iron Research Association. Some of them had gone into the public service or into research; one was the Professor of Civil Engineering at Imperial College, and another, an organic Chemist at the National Institute for Medical Research who had become a Fellow of the Royal Society.

As so often, the Commission was pointing the way, and industry itself was providing the solution. By 1934, the Board could report that some of the larger manufacturing concerns had 'learnt the wisdom of opening their doors to the best talent available' and were paying a living wage to promising youngsters, a trend which was, in due course, to enable the Industrial Bursaries scheme to be discontinued.[4]

CHANGES TO THE SCIENCE SCHOLARSHIPS SCHEME

By contrast, the Science Scholarships scheme had been suspended in 1915, but reinstated in 1919, though with some problems. In 1920, the Committee, now under the chairmanship of Sir Richard Glazebrook, felt that after thirty years of successful operation, a review of the scheme was due.

The Committee could point to the success of the scheme through the professional careers of the 415 Scholars assisted so far, of whom 63 were employed 'professionally in Imperial, Colonial and foreign government establishments', 74 as working chemists, managers, engineers and designers in industry and manufacturing, and some 206 in teaching posts from professors to school masters and mistresses. The scheme had been commended by a parliamentary committee which was addressing the problems of providing scholarships for higher education, which had concluded that though the 'number of workers thus subsidized has been small in comparison with the needs of the nation . . . we believe it will be universally admitted that the results have far more than justified the expenditure'.[5]

One problem was the increase in the number of teaching institutions in both the provinces and the Colonies whose staff wished to be allowed to nominate students, but this would have meant an increase in the number of Science Scholarships, and the money was not available. Whereas before the war £150 a year enabled the Scholar to devote his entire time to research, post-war conditions meant that £200 now barely paid for maintenance. As the Science Scholarships Committee frankly admitted, the awards were so low that applications had fallen, and in addition, demand for competent scientists had increased so that many would-be researchers were turning down research grants in favour of better-paid working appointments, or resigning them early. The Committee recommended to the Board of Management that the scheme should be thoroughly reconsidered.[6]

Research disclosed that the 'field in which the Commissioners had done the pioneer work was being extensively developed' by the government since the war. The government scheme was operated by the Department of Scientific and Industrial Research, and was intended 'to build up the laboratory system in this country by providing professors with research workers from among [promising] science graduates. The war had shown the many weaknesses in the scientific bases of our industries', according to Frank Heath, Secretary to the Council of the DSIR, and the intention was to build up a better base for research in British institutions. For this reason, 'they did not, under their scheme, encourage a student to go abroad'. Formerly, they had 'aimed at promoting the prosecution of researches which interested them. This side of the [Council's] activities was being gradually restricted and they had decided in future to limit

grants for individual research workers to a selected few whose researches were of special scientific value to the Nation'.[7]

Esher had been keen from the beginning that the Commissioners'
scheme should put the 'Dominions in front of our operations'. The 'Great
Dominions' of Australia, New Zealand and South Africa should each have
one Research Scholar, and Canada two. The 'Mother country' should be
treated differently with five 'Research Scholarships apportioned to scientific subjects, on the lines of our Art Scholarships for Painting, Sculpture
and Architecture'. He suggested that the value of both sorts of scholarship should rise to £250 per annum, with additional travelling expenses.
Shaw was somewhat cynical about the government's commitment to
spending on research, suspecting that this might 'one day be rudely curtailed. I do not believe that the G. will, except as a war emergency measure, justify its expenditure on the scale presently allowed . . . ⌈scientific
training will have to take its chance and⌉ its place in the national scheme
of education, whatever the McCormicks and Ogilvies think'. He pointed
out that though the Department claimed to spend £50,000 on grants, if
the Commission withdrew its £9000, questions would be asked by the
Treasury. It was hoped that the government schemes would perform 'the
same service as the Commissioners' system in enabling students to pursue their studies abroad' though it was felt that the '1851 Scholarship . . .
had always been regarded as the blue ribband ⌈*sic*⌉'. New awards had thus
become available, and the Commissioners wished to continue the tradition of supplementing rather than competing with other institutions.

The matter was finally decided by a conference of the Board and
Committee members, in which Lord Esher played a significant part,
supplemented by a later Conference between Glazebrook and Shaw and
representatives of the Department of Scientific and Industrial Research,
Sir William McCormick, Sir Frank Heath, Ogilvie, and a Mr Lloyd, three
of whom were present or future members of the Commission. At a
subsequent private meeting between McCormick, Chairman of the
University Grants Commission, and Shaw, the latter summarized the
relationship between the wider government scheme and the more modest
Commission scheme, in a simile which serves for many of the
Commission's contemporary initiatives:

> I made it quite clear to him that we were acting as sort of advance
> force for his large army which was gradually spreading itself over

the country we had left behind. I made him realise that unless his forces followed close upon our heels there would be a dangerous sap which we could not get back to defend.

In reply, McCormick assured him that the 1851 Commission would not regret leaving 'the ordinary training field in the hands of the Research Department'.[8]

As usual, the bland account in the formal minutes conceals meticulous groundwork by the Secretary, with constant urging from the Chairman. The Science Scholarships Committee proposed the foundation of a small number of Senior Studentships tenable by the 'exceptionally talented' established scientist to enable him or her to devote their time to research, to meet the needs of the universities in the United Kingdom. Esher put in a plea for the consideration of the claims of the Welsh Colleges, but the Senior Studentships were awarded on merit, without any geographical considerations.

It is difficult to quantify the value of the five annual Senior Student-ships, tenable for up to three years, though some holders seem to have been head-hunted before their results were fully proven. A number of distinguished figures emerged from their ranks, including the anthro-pologist, L. S. B. Leakey (1928), and (Sir) William Penney (1931), while others like (Sir) Alexander Todd later served as members of the Science Scholarships Committee.

Though this award was available only through institutions based in the United Kingdom, talented students from overseas could be, and were, nominated by home universities. The system was also changed for over-seas universities. The continuation of the existing system in the domin-ions and Colonies was felt to be the best answer, but a simple increase in the number of scholarships available to include all the new science-teach-ing institutions which had developed in the last two decades was impos-sibly costly. The solution ultimately adopted was to abandon the system by which individual institutions were approved, and encouraged to nom-inate candidates, and to substitute the allocation of awards to the four Dominions, Canada, three, Australia two, and South Africa and New Zealand, one each.[9] A thorny problem arose in the case of Ireland, which was in the throes of establishing the Irish Free State. The matter was finally resolved in 1923, by the inclusion of the University of Belfast in the Senior Studentship scheme, while a new scholarship was established for the southern Irish universities – the Royal College of Science (Ireland), Dublin, Cork, Galway, the National University of Ireland, and Trinity College, Dublin.

Though the Commissioners reserved the right to reject candidates whom they did not feel sufficiently qualified, the choice was left to the recommending countries. The conditions for candidates were not changed, and they were expected to devote 'their whole time to the prosecution of research in order to fit themselves for practical service to the academic or industrial world'. The Scholars were not allowed to hold any paid post incompatible with their obligation to the duty to the Commissioners. Some assistance was given for travel, and later on the Commissioners found it possible to get help from the great British shipping lines – P & O, Cunard, the Canadian Pacific and Union Castle.[10]

The new scheme came into effect in 1922, and at the same time the Committee decided to publish a new edition of the *Record of Scholars*. The big change in the scholarships was, of course, in the institutions where they were held. Before the First World War, a large number of them had been held in German or in other European universities, whereas the 1919 and later intakes of Scholars almost all went to British institutions, with the occasional American place of study. It was obviously partly due to prejudices generated by the war, but it reflected the better opportunities available at United Kingdom institutions due to the British government's increased perception of the need for scientific education and facilities for research.

The postgraduate scholarship in Naval Architecture, established in 1911 with the personal encouragement of George V, continued to provide scholarships to enable ship designers to devote two years to the study of one particular problem associated with the design of ships or their engines. A review in the 1930s confirmed the merits of the scheme, since all the award-holders had found jobs in government institutions or shipbuilding firms.

THE BRITISH SCHOOL AT ROME

The 1851 Commission had a close connection with the British School at Rome through the shared premises and a shared secretariat in London. It subscribed a regular sum of £4500, as against the £5000 per annum for the Senior Studentships, making it the second largest demand on the Commission's resources. It nominated four representatives on the School

Council, and was involved in the giving of the Scholarships for Decorative Art, Architecture and Sculpture. The fourth Art Scholarship, for Engraving, was funded by Sir Stephen Courtauld.

Esher and Shaw were concerned that the returned Art Scholars should get as much help as possible, and their work should be displayed. Enquiries were made about gallery space on the estate, and attempts were made to find work for them. Lionel Earle was consulted about work for the architect H. Charlton Bradshaw, and he seems to have been found work at Lympne for Philip Sassoon through Esher's influence.

The buildings for the British School in Rome had been completed to a much reduced scale for a variety of reasons, though their erection had cost more than the budget, and very soon it became clear that more space was needed. The Royal Commission was not directly involved in fund-raising, though they gave a further £5000 towards the cost of the buildings and paid off some accumulated debts. They raised their grant for maintenance over and above the scholarships from £500 to £1000 a year.

The building as completed by Lutyens had a west wing, housing the Director and Assistant Director, running from the grandiose south elevation overlooking the Valle Giulia, connecting with the north wing containing studios and students' accommodation. The east side of the courtyard had been left unbuilt because of cost. For the time being, two of the studios had to be used for dining room and common room. Accommodation for students soon became a problem since, even after the art scholars had been provided for by building galleries in the studios, there was not enough room for students of the older established archaeological faculty. A partial solution was provided by a scheme, designed by Bradshaw, to provide a dining-room-cum-common room behind the east end of the façade, digging down into the sloping hill on which the School stands to provide a semi-basement kitchen. This scheme obviated the need to build in the courtyard whose central open space today provides an agreeable centre for the School. Work was completed in 1923, making adequate provision for students and staff.

Staff changes brought a certain amount of turbulence, since late in life Ashby found himself a wife, who unfortunately did not get on well with Mrs Strong. Esher, writing to Shaw about the matter, was as usual out-spoken:

Why did that ass Ashby marry? He ought to have lived clandestine-ly with his Art Director. Then we should have had a *Pax Romana*.[11]

There was however, no 'Pax Romana' and the Council only renewed the posts of the combatants until 1925, when both Ashby and Mrs Strong left. There followed a number of short-lived and somewhat unsatisfactory appointments, the Directors either returning to take up appointments elsewhere or being unsuitable for other reasons. In 1936, a former archaeological student Ralegh Radford (1900–99), who had been Inspector of Ancient Monuments for Wales, was appointed Director. It was during his time, under the leadership of Rodd, that the buildings were completed. Even after his retirement and election to the House of Commons, Rodd always kept in touch with the School, maintaining that it was important not to forget the needs of the Faculty of Archaeology, History and Letters, with its London office separate from the Faculties of Art. It was funded by the Treasury and the subscriptions from various archaeological institutions, with two biennial scholarships. At this time, the School was largely funded by the Commission, and the older Faculty of Archaeology, History and Letters was dependent on the Commission's administrative support to supplement its government grant.

There were two appeals for the School in the late 1930s, headed by Rodd, now Lord Rennell of Rodd, and supported by Lord Macmillan for the 1851 Commission. It was therefore partly for increased funds for archaeology, with a more general one for the completion of the School buildings. This scheme was again to the design of Bradshaw, though in a style respectful of and compatible with that of Lutyens. He designed a three-storey eastern range, which provided both a new common room and writing room on the ground floor, and more accommodation for students above. At the same time, additional library space was provided to accommodate the books and papers of Thomas Ashby, who had died in 1931. Despite increasing political tension which caused the students to withdraw, first to Spain and then to Athens, building went ahead. The contract was carried out very rapidly, to Bradshaw's design, but under the supervision of an Italian architect, the Commendatore E. Rossi. Contracts were placed in July 1937, and the wing was opened in October 1938, in the presence of King Umberto of Italy.[12]

The School was closed in the following year, on the outbreak of war, but the buildings were well looked after, first by the Roman authorities, and then after Italy declared war in July 1940, by the 'Protecting Power', the Swiss, and the School's vigilant guardian, the steward Bruno Bonelli. When the Allies reached Rome, it served as accommodation for staff from the British Embassy, until the students returned. A happier period for the School followed on the appointment of an archaeologist who had worked throughout the Mediterranean region from Malta to North Africa. J. B. Ward-Perkins (1912–81) remained at the helm of the British School for twenty-eight years, until 1974, giving it a period of stability and growth through a period when one of its most constant supporters, the 1851 Commission, was to experience doubt as to the loyalty due to one of its creations.[13]

MEMBERSHIP OF THE COMMISSION

Membership of the Commission was increasingly divided between the traditional recruits from the political world, a relic of the days when active politicians took an interest in the work of the 1851 Commission, and the 'working members' who made up the Board of Management. The important figures in the 1920s were Esher himself, Stamfordham, despite, or perhaps because of, his position as a member of the Royal Household, Sir Francis Ogilvie, Glazebrook as Chairman of the Science Scholarships Committee, supported by J. B. Farmer and Rutherford, Thomas Jones and Lord Buckmaster (1861–1934), a distinguished lawyer, who became Chairman of the Governors of Imperial College in 1923. Lord Revelstoke (1863–1929), a partner in Baring Brothers, and a director of the Bank of England, served from 1912 till his death, in his capacity as the Commission's Financial Adviser. Sir Archibald Geikie (1835–1924), a former Director-General of the Geological Survey, who had been a Commissioner since 1908, retired in 1922, and Sir Francis Ogilvie (1858–1931), appointed at the same time, virtually died in office, after twenty-three years of service to the Commission on the Science Scholarships Committee and the Board as well as being a Commissioner. This was true of many of his contemporaries, for whom retirement was not usual, and indeed it was not till 1988 that a limit was set to the term served by members of the Board of Management.

Esher, well aware of the value of active politicians of all parties, also recruited from the other familiar constituencies – members of the Science Scholarships Committee, heads of institutions on the estate, important benefactors like Sir Alfred Mond, and retired civil servants who would provide sound advice, and good contacts. He showed a surprisingly modern approach in one matter, however, which he raised with Stamfordham in April 1924.

'I should rather like to have a woman on the Commission. Preferably one of these Socialist women. I wonder what the King would suggest. He knows them all and has sized them up.' He went on to suggest either Beatrice Webb (1858–1943), or Margaret Bondfield (1873–1953), later the first woman to sit in the Cabinet, and asked for suggestions. Stamfordham's reply was brisk:

> Doubtless you will regard me as a reactionary: but really I do not see the necessity to put a woman upon our Council, and, in any case, not what you call 'one of these socialist women', certainly not Mrs. Sidney Webb. However, if you still think that we shall be better for female influence, we should do better to take one who is not a specialist, political, educational, or social, but a woman of broader outlook and of more general knowledge and experience.

He went on to suggest Lady Buxton, 'who has knowledge of the Dominions and interests herself in educational and social problems'. Esher's reply was shrewd and to the point:

> I do *not* regard you as a 'reactionary', but I am facing certain facts which it is difficult to ignore.
>
> In educational matters women are now a very important factor. Take this country – There is no doubt that the Duchess of Atholl *is*, whether we like it or not, the first and leading authority in all matters of Education, and Miss Haldane is a good second. The men are simply 'others ran'.
>
> Our Commission exists for the purpose of contributing all we can, to the furtherance of Education in Science and Art; and we have at present no representatives of the larger half of the population on our Commission. I felt and feel that we are a little open to criticism on this account. There is no necessity, of course, to appoint at our forthcoming meeting a woman member.

Stamfordham saw the need to make an appointment: 'I quite see your point and should be all in favour of making the lady appointment *now* – rather than wait for the suggestion to come from outside. But the great thing would be to get the exactly right and suitable person.' He went on to suggest Miss Lilian Faithful, former Principal of Cheltenham Ladies' College (1907–21), and Vice-Principal of King's College Women's Department (1894–1907), 'an outstanding personage – a woman of wide sympathies and also of artistic tastes'.

Esher, suffering from gout at Roman Camp, decided to let the matter rest, proposing the antiquarian Montague James for the vacancy. He pointed out that he was 'Provost of Eton . . . He is a notable Archaeologist, scholar etc., so I don't see who can object'.[14]

There the question rested, and apparently no suitable 'representative of the larger half of the population' presented herself for nearly sixty years, when, by coincidence, a great-niece of Beatrice Webb became the first woman Commissioner and member of the Board of Management.

The appointments to the Commission were shrewd, if occasionally old-fashioned; the choice of politicians as active members of the Commission, as opposed to *ex officio* members, was always thorny, and Shaw and Esher turned down some political nominees, particularly if they felt they were unsuitable; as Shaw put it, what was needed were:

[Persons] useful as representing (1) Science, (2) Art, and (3) their applications in Industry – what we exist to promote.

With the exception of the energetic minds needed to direct the affairs of the Commission and to look after its technical work, the principal qualification for membership . . . is, after all, to act as a Trustee of a Royal Educational Trust.

Firebrands and tub-thumpers would be a very great nuisance in a Body which gets its work done very well by a few wise and efficient administrators.[15]

Esher and Shaw recruited Ramsay MacDonald (1866–1937), Philip Snowden (1864–1937) and the labour leader William Graham (1887–1932), as well as Stanley Baldwin (1867–1947) and Walter Elliott (1882–1956). Sir William Bragg and Sir Frank Heath who had both served on the Science Scholarships Committee were appointed to the Commission in 1924, as well as the distinguished Scottish lawyer Hugh Pattison Macmillan (1873–1952), who was to succeed Esher as Chairman of the Board of Management. Slightly more old-fashioned in flavour was the appointment of a number of peers, including the Marquis of Hartington (1895–1950), later the 10th Duke of Devonshire, the conservationist Earl of Crawford and Balcarres (1871–1940), the Marquis of Londonderry (1878–1949), and a royal appointment, the Earl of Harewood (1882–1947), husband of Princess Mary, Princess Royal (1897–1965), herself a later President of the Royal Commission.

The year 1930 saw a number of important changes, most significantly the death of Lord Esher in March, a man who had done more to shape the Royal Commission than anyone except its royal founder, and perhaps Henry Cole and Edgar Bowring. In Stamfordham's words, he 'had regarded the affairs of the Commission almost as his special child and devoted considerable time and labour to quiet unassuming work in its interests. In this gifted versatile nature the Commission have lost an able Chairman and a valued friend'.[16] Esher had gradually modernized the Commission during a period of unprecedented change, showing real fore-sight in selecting new causes for it to espouse, and refusing to contem-plate its winding-up or a take-over by government. Ably supported by Shaw, he had spotted the important role which the Commission could play in filling the gaps in government provision and in developing pilot schemes for deeper-pursed institutions.

An almost greater break followed in 1931, with the death of Lord Stamfordham, who had been connected with the Commission in various capacities for nearly thirty years as a Commissioner. He had been the last 'Honorary' Secretary, and, even after he had resigned, 'no decision of any consequence on policy or administration was ever taken without his advice and approval'. His influence was equally significant at the Science Scholarship Committee, where Glazebrook could recall that in 'times of difficulty he had proved a most sympathetic adviser, in times of success, he had been the first to congratulate the Committee'.[17] His death broke the very close connection the Royal Commission had always enjoyed from its earliest days with the Royal Household, though the appointment of Sir Clive Wigram (1873–1960) in 1934 did something to restore it.

Esher had been shortly predeceased by Lord Revelstoke, who had maintained the Baring tradition on the Board of Management as the Commission's financial adviser since 1912. He was in turn succeeded by Sir Edward Peacock (1871–1962), also from Barings. The distinguished Scottish painter and engraver, D. Y. Cameron (1865–1945), who had been involved with the British School at Rome, was appointed a Commissioner, together with a number of scientists, Sir Henry Lyons (1864–1944), the founding father of the Science Museum, Sir James Jeans (1877–1946) and Sir Frank E. Smith (1879–1970). The 1934 Commission meeting saw the appointment of the distinguished biochemist and Nobel Prize-winner, Sir Frederick Gowland Hopkins (1861–1947), who had studied as a young student at South Kensington, his fellow scientist Sir James Colqhoun

Irvine (1877–1952), together with Sir Josiah Stamp (1880–1941), a former Inland Revenue clerk who had risen to be Chairman of Nobel
Industries, and a Director of the Bank of England. The former diplomatist, Sir Godfrey Thomas (1889–1968), who had become a member of the
Prince of Wales's household, was recruited in 1930, as were the politician
the 3rd Viscount Halifax (1881–1959) and the diplomatist, Sir Edward
Harding (1880–1954).

The last series of appointments before the outbreak of war reflected
the bodies with whom the Commission had to deal – Lord Greene (1883–
1952), a lawyer with connections with the Pilgrim Trust, Sir Warren
Fisher (1879–1948), Permanent Secretary at the Treasury and head of
the civil service, apparently appointed in the wake of the agreement over
the Science Museum contribution, and Sir Henry Dale (1875–1968), a
distinguished doctor who had run the Wellcome Laboratory, who was a
member of the Museums and Galleries Commission. The 11th Marquess
of Lothian (1882–1940), who had held a number of political and diplomatic appointments, and was Secretary to the Rhodes Trustees, became a
Commissioner in 1937, as did Lord Eustace Percy (1887–1958).

THE ROLE OF THE SECRETARY

The distinction between the Commissioners and the two committees
which did the work – the Board of Management and the Science
Scholarships Committee – grew throughout the period, as the meetings
of the Commission itself became fewer. The work of the committees was
underpinned by the work of the office at 1 Lowther Gardens, which ran
both the scientific awards and those for the British School at Rome. The
Secretary to the Commissioners was throughout the period also Honorary General Secretary of the British School at Rome, and involved in both
the annual awards and the building activities which continued throughout the period. Shaw had been Secretary since 1911, and the Commission
paid tribute to his twenty-seven years service in 1931, reminded by the
deaths of Esher and Stamfordham of how much support their Secretary
had provided to those two formidable Commissioners. His assistant
McClure had left to pursue a full-time legal career, and been succeeded by
Paul Burrows. He had left in 1931, because of ill-health, and had been
replaced by Digby Sturch, who, in due course, was to serve the Commission as Secretary. The office was supplemented by the work of the

Surveyor, Leslie Vigers, who had succeeded Stevenson in the 1920s, and A. F. Moir, the Solicitor from Fladgates, who dealt with the complex and changing world of London property, where increasing regulation was eroding the traditional control of ground-landlords.

THE COMMISSION'S AWARDS

The Commission had changed its scheme for scientific scholarships in 1922 because of the alternative schemes elsewhere, but despite the increasing competition no further changes were made before 1939. In a review of the Senior Studentships scheme in 1937, the Committee emphasized the benefits of working with the Department of Scientific and Industrial Research, which often found assistance for runners-up of ability from the Commissioners' scheme. They were also able to report on the 'increase in the general level of ability' in the students from the Dominions. They had also added a stipulation that unless facilities for some specific research project were only available outside Great Britain, in Europe or the United States, overseas Scholars should spend part of their time in the United Kingdom – 'otherwise the award is of purely scientific value, and in no way contributes to the promotion of friendship and understanding between this country and the Dominions'. Indian students had always been eligible for the Senior Studentships, but in 1937, by dint of finding more money, the Commissioners extended the Overseas Scholarship scheme to India. They could point to another Nobel Prize-winner, J. Chadwick who won the Nobel Prize for Physics in 1935, and the list of recent Scholars included Dr A. R. Todd, a Senior Student in 1931, and (Sir) William Penney, in 1933.[18]

The influential scientific monthly *Nature* published an article by Sir Francis Ogilvie, which set out the history of the Commission's scholarship schemes and the approach adopted over the eighty years since the Exhibition. He claimed that the Commission had led the way in a number of fields:

> Their primary and their large aim was the development of 'system' [as in 'a system of encouragement to local institutions for Practical Science'] . . .
>
> The Royal Commission has been, in its years, prospector, promoter patron – patron in the centuries-old sense of extending wise guidance and limited assistance to persons on projects that appeared

capable of furthering science or the arts, or of stimulating inventions or industries. In the nature of things the ideas of the Commissioners have occasionally been too much in advance of the times to secure effective response. Yet, when prospects improved and the idea still seemed good, it was tabled again with any modifications that seemed desirable.[19]

The article in *Nature* coincided with another reminder of the Commission's genesis. At the suggestion of the Persian expert Sir Arnold Wilson, Chairman of the Executive Committee of a Persian Art Exhibition being held at the Royal Academy, it was decided to issue a general invitation to all those still living who had actually visited the Great Exhibition in Hyde Park in 1851. Some 370 survivors took tea at Burlington House on 6 March, 1931, all of them over eighty years old, and were greeted by Lord Macmillan, Chairman of the Board. Some of the guests brought with them relics of the Crystal Palace. Thanks were duly returned by the 94-year-old Canon Wilson (1836–1931), former headmaster of Clifton College and father of Sir Arnold.

A Scholars' Dinner held in New York in 1929 brought together past award-holders working either in Canada or the United States, and emphasized the far-flung nature of the scheme, and its success in creating a corps of award-holders. Two years later to coincide with the centenary of the British Association in London, the distinguished chemist Sir James Irvine, an award-holder (1899–1901), suggested the holding of a celebratory dinner for 1851 Scholars and award-holders. Some 120 gathered at the Mayfair Hotel on 28 September, presided over by Lord Rutherford, probably the best known of the Commissioners' award-holders, who had won his scholarship some thirty-six years before.[20]

The Commission had published a further volume on the Scholars in 1930. Their scheme continued to attract graduates of great potential, though the Commission did not have the pick of Dominion scientists, or indeed the field to itself, any more. In addition, as Rutherford pointed out, to be a successful researcher under modern conditions required a much longer training and probably the help of collaborators; a researcher could no longer so easily achieve results on his own.[21]

The Commission had changed its focus to some extent as conditions changed. There was a complaint from a New Zealand scientist that the bright young men attracted to scholarships in the United Kingdom did not return home. Surely, he complained to the Commissioners, they did not wish to 'drain the Dominion of its most intelligent men'.[22] This attack caused concern to the members of the Science Scholarships Committee, who replied that a subsidiary objective of the Overseas Scholarships scheme was to inculcate a feeling of *camaderie* among scientists from the different Dominions, by ensuring that their studying was done, if practicable, in the mother country. Nonetheless, the Committee agreed to consider the New Zealander's suggestion that scholarships should be extended to pay for some work to be carried out in the country of origin at the end of the Scholar's tenure of his award.

THE MUSEUMS AND GALLERIES COMMISSION

The connection of so many Commissioners with other grant-giving bodies reflected the changed atmosphere, and the way in which the need for scholarships to enable poor students to further their education was more generally recognized. The government set up a number of new bodies, like the Department of Scientific and Industrial Research and the University Grant Commission, to deal with funding of higher education. They also set up a Royal Commission to report on the state of the national museums in London and Edinburgh, seen as an educational resource. Headed by Lord d'Abernon (1857–1941), a distinguished financier and politician, who had been the first British ambassador to Berlin after the First World War, the members, who included Sir Lionel Earle and Sir Richard Glazebrook, were all well-known figures. Their terms of reference were very wide, betraying considerable disquiet about the condition of the repositories of national treasures, ranging from the physical condition of the buildings, and the way in which they were administered, to the legal conditions which governed their trust, and whether they were doing a good job, particularly in the educational field. It also considered the question of funding, including the cost to the Treasury, and the question of whether museums should charge for admission. Four national museums were then based in South Kensington, and the Report and the evidence on which it was based give an interesting picture of the Commissioners' estate at the time. The Royal Commission's recommendations also affected the development of the estate over the next half century, either through new proposals, or by their insistence that existing proposals should be honoured both by the Treasury and by the institutions themselves.

It is clear from the terms of reference that the condition of many of the exhibits within museums was giving rise to public concern, while the prospective cost of putting things in order alarmed the Treasury. There was a strong hint that a recommendation of consolidation or unification would be welcome in some cases, while in other cases there was a concern that the institutions were out of control, and perhaps pursuing paths of collection which overlapped with similar bodies.

The Museums Commission cast its net very widely, consulting the German museologist, Dr J. M. Friedlander, the French expert Dr S. Reinach and the American collector and connoisseur Bernard Berenson, as well as asking the British ambassadors in all the major European countries and the United States to report on conditions in their host countries. The heads of all the national museums were asked for interview, and, memoranda were submitted by selected outside bodies like the Royal College of Art, the National Art Collections Fund and the 1851 Commissioners, as well as art journalists, and pressure groups like the Sudeley Committee, a forerunner of the later National Heritage pressure group founded in 1971 by John Letts to focus public attention on museums. The questions asked by the members of the Commission, and indeed the answers, revealed that all was not well at South Kensington. However, the Report went out of its way to commend Prince Albert's initiative, pointing out that through his vision and 'the enlightened labours' of the 1851 Commissioners there had been erected in the course of three generations

> not only some of the greatest of the National Museums, the Victoria and Albert Museum, the British Museum (Natural History) and the Science Museum, together with the Art & Science Libraries attached to those Museums, but a number of other institutions . . . all illustrating in their several ways the Prince's idea of an intellectual centre dedicated to the study and application of Science and Art.

It was less complimentary about those responsible for funding national museums and galleries in more recent times, pointing out that the British Museum had received over the last five years on average £40,000 in private gifts, as against a purchase grant of £25,000. The national museums

> have for long been treated as the Cinderella of the Social Services . . . the cost of these institutions has hardly increased during the period of a generation . . . They began by being the first educational insti-

tutions which the Government thought proper to assist. They are now the last. Yet without them the educational fabric of the State would be quite incomplete. To the scholar they afford the indispensable material for study in almost every domain of learning, to the artist inspiration, and to industry the resources of science.[23]

The Commission set up two subcommittees to deal with areas over which the members were particularly concerned, one for Scotland, and one for South Kensington, headed by Sir Richard Glazebrook. Evelyn Shaw's evidence urged that the three scientific institutions – the Science Museum, the British Museum (Natural History) and the Geological Museum whose move to South Kensington had been agreed in principle – should be regarded as integral parts of a National Exhibition of Science. To facilitate this he suggested the use of the proposed new Geological Museum building as a physical link between the two existing institutions.[24] Ironically, though connecting bridges through the new building were provided, a later report from the Standing Commission on Museums and Galleries pointed out that these areas had been the ones selected to be blocked off to house staff and surplus exhibits.[25]

Another point made by Shaw was the anxiety that the 1851 Commissioners felt about the ultimate disposal of the Imperial Institute building, and of the Western Galleries, then occupied by the embryo Imperial War Museum. This last had been brought into existence by command of the War Cabinet on 5 March, 1917, and opened by George V at the Crystal Palace in June 1920. It had moved to South Kensington in 1924, where it been housed in the Western Galleries, let to the Office of Works on a lease due to expire in 1941. The collections were originally intended to display only *matériel* from the First World War, a somewhat limiting concept, and difficult to implement, since as the Curator, Charles Ffoulkes, pointed out, some of the weapons used in the war were regarded as obsolescent even in the last century. He had had great difficulty in housing a growing library, the enormous collection of objects, some 100,000 photographs and over 4000 works of art, many by well-known artists such as Sargent, Orpen and Lavery, and even including some Cubist works. However, he had also taken over a small iron gallery from the Victoria and Albert Museum, and had recently acquired number 178, Queen's Gate as an annexe.

Like all competent curators he was always looking to expand his collections, and had been offered a number of exhibits, including historic firearms from the Enfield firearms factory. The collection attracted some 200,000 visitors a year, and had become an important player on the South Kensington scene.

The Museums Commission, starting from the premise that museums had an equal responsibility for research and education, produced an interim Report on British National Museums in 1928, dealing with the most urgent problems. They recommended the expenditure of £3000 on the completion of the Science Museum lecture theatre, and £250,000 each on the library accommodation at the British Museum, and on the British Museum's Natural History Collections. At the last, they were concerned about the storage of valuable fossils, mammals and birds, needed for research and stored away in places inaccessible to students. The collection of animals and birds, preserved in spirit, was a constant source of trouble to its neighbours as it was considered a fire risk, and affected the development plans of other institutions.

Though it was pointed out that the recommendations had been relatively modest financially, and that indeed one, the removal of the Geological Museum to South Kensington, would not embarrass the Treasury because of the value of the site it was vacating, there were several significant criticisms of the administration of national museums. These were to mean considerable changes in future in the way which they were managed by government, with repercussions in South Kensington as elsewhere.

Attention had been drawn by several commentators to the anomalous way in which the professional director might be overruled by his trustees. Friedlander contrasted the way in which

> in Germany the official, trained in History of Art, the scholar, has fairly independent control . . . is generally appointed for life, pensionable, and cannot be dismissed . . . In England, on the other hand, and still more in the States, the power is partly in the hands of the Trustees, who, as private collectors, connoisseurs and independent personalities of rank and authority, control and correct the 'Direktor' in all his actions, even in taste.[26]

A number of changes followed in many institutions as a consequence of this thoroughly researched and far-reaching report, one of which was the creation of the Standing Commission on Museums and Galleries, which continued to press for changes in South Kensington and elsewhere until it was absorbed into the Departure of Culture, Media and Sport in 2000.

THE DEVELOPMENT OF THE ESTATE

The Report of the Museums Commission had pointed out that most of South Kensington was let on long leases to government or to individual institutions, but the 1851 Commissioners still had a role in its development. The Commissioners were mindful of their role as ground landlords in South Kensington, but they had decreasing control over their estate. They had been concerned over its contribution to their funds, and Lord Buckmaster even suggested that their properties were less valuable than their investments.[27] Vigers, the new surveyor, pointed out that the comparison was unfair, since the funds obtained from the sale of ground rents, and the occasional freehold, had all been invested in government funds, and on the Stock Exchange, thus giving the impression that the investments had risen more than the land. The question of the real value of the estate had been raised earlier, since for many years it had appeared in the books at an 1889 valuation. The Commissioners had even considered an offer made through Vigers for the remaining leasehold estate in the 1920s, but had turned it down.

As a consequence of Buckmaster's raising the issue, in June 1930, Vigers was asked to prepare a brief report and a new valuation. As with all leasehold estates in London, the income could not be increased or the capital value of the estate drawn upon until the long leases expired. Most of 'the main square' had been leased on 999-year leases at low rents to institutions, and the Commissioners had little control, except through restrictive covenants and in matters of management. Much of the estate outside the central block had been sold off, the value of much of the rest somewhat impaired by occasional sales which reduced the Commissioners' holdings of potentially valuable large blocks. Vigers had managed the Kensington Gore properties to the west of the Albert Hall very astutely, so that all their leases were extended to fall in simultaneously in 1944. Elsewhere the problem was that the large properties in Queen's Gate no longer attracted the wealthy and fashionable, and the Commissioners found themselves continually granting licences for new uses – ladies clubs, private residential hotels, conversion into maisonettes, and so forth. Only a few private residents, such as the Makins family in their magnifi-

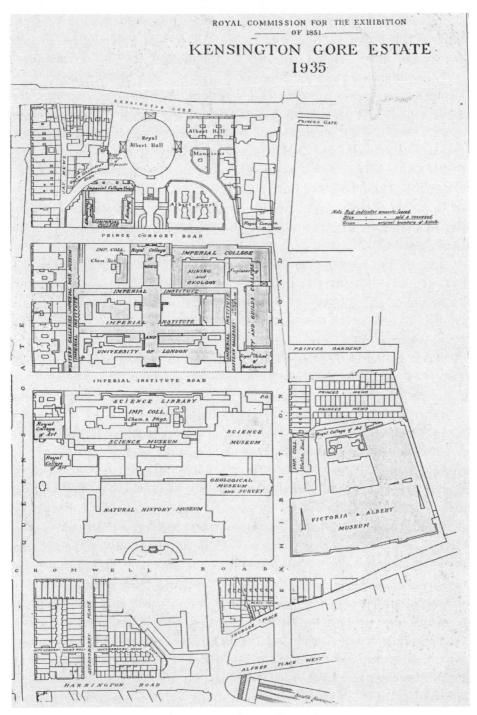

Fig 26. The Commissioners' Estate in 1935.

cent Norman Shaw house at number 180, Queen's Gate, remained to remind the Board of Management of the former splendours of their estate. The mews had not had their complement of horses for some time, and conversion to 'motor houses' and garages had begun before 1914. However, a new problem was the conversion not to garages housing the showy vehicles of the affluent, but to working garages where repairs were carried out. The Surveyor warned that all these conversions to commercial uses could well make the Commissioners liable to make generous payments to their tenants for goodwill, when the leases finally came to an end, unlike the occupiers of private houses, who could usually be expected to pay heavily for dilapidations. He endeavoured to avoid this by trying to ensure that licences to carry on trades incorporated a disclaimer about goodwill.

Nonetheless, the valuation reveals that the Commissioners' estate was still extensive – Albert Hall Mansions, on a ninety-nine-year lease till 1978, 11–25 Kensington Gore, mostly with stabling attached, nearly twenty houses on the east side of Queen's Gate, mostly with garages in Jay's Mews, as there was no space for mews behind them because of the Western Galleries. There were a number of domestic properties in Queen's Gate Terrace and in the mews behind, whose leases were due to fall in in the 1950s. All these represented a modest income, but a potentially large capital gain in some twenty-five years' time.

At this time, the future development of the 'main square' exercised the Commissioners, since they felt that they had assisted government very greatly in the past to establish the museums in the area, and were anxious that the task should be properly completed. Some years earlier, Ogilvie had raised the question of the proper development of the land north of the Imperial Institute Road, pointing out that the Office of Works, now in charge of the building operations and the physical development of the area, had put forward a proposal to erect the new building for the Geological Museum behind the Imperial Institute. Part of the Museum of Practical Geology in Jermyn Street, including its teaching functions, had been moved to the Huxley Building in South Kensington in the 1870s, but the removal of the rest of the collection had been mooted for a long time. A scheme had already been approved by both government and the 1851 Commissioners by which the new building was to be sited south of Imperial Institute Road, and to be used to provide a physical link between the Natural History and Science Museum collections. This somewhat shotgun marriage had been an objective of some of the scientists on the Commission, but had been adopted with less than enthusiasm by the participants, who like other denizens of South Kensington were often reluctant to cooperate. Sir Francis Ogilvie had taken up the cudgels, pointing out that siting the Museum further north would have not only made the 'connecting link' impossible, but impaired an intellectually ordered development of the site containing the Imperial Institute. The Board, anxious 'to promote a common policy and concerted action among the several authorities interested in the development of that part of the estate dedicated to a national exposition of Science and its application in Industry' appointed a subcommittee of Stamfordham and Ogilvie to confer with the Office of Works.[28] The duo managed to keep the Office of Works to the previous plan.

In his last report from the Board of Management, Esher was able to claim that the Museums and Galleries Commission had been influenced by the 1851 Commission's strong representations over the unifying of the science collections. He cited a general comment, pertinently if unkindly, to demonstrate the Museum Commissioners' awareness of 'the need for a common policy and concerted action in the development of the various scientific collections at South Kensington':

> We feel bound to say that we are impressed by the isolation and lack of concerted effort which characterise the present organisation of the National Museums and Galleries . . . Furthermore, while we consider that the evils of overlapping have been exaggerated, we think that the frontiers in the case of certain of the Institutions might be more clearly defined and such definition cannot altogether be brought about by the present casual system of communication.[29]

In general the members of the Museums' Commission had been impressed by the achievements of the 1851 Commissioners. They had praised the Prince Consort's scheme and the way in which the 1851 Commissioners had fulfilled their trust. They had not remarked on the Imperial War Museum then occupying the Western Galleries, but had commended the proposed removal of the Geological Museum to the site south of Imperial Institute Road, in a way which could provide a physical link between the different scientific collections. This had been on the *tapis* since 1911, when Sir Henry Tanner had designed a terracotta building intended to accord with Waterhouse's Natural History Museum. In the event, his successor, Sir Richard Allison, designed a building modelled on his own Science Museum in plan, which was erected with a Portland stone façade attributed to J. H. Markham. Though a connection to the Science Museum was made, that to the Natural History Museum was omitted through a change in plan, and not reinstated because of the British Museum's resistance. The handsome new building was opened by the Duke of York, later George VI, in July 1935.[30]

THE ROYAL ALBERT HALL

Outside 'the main square' was, of course, the Royal Albert Hall, whose future had been causing concern for some time, because of its financial instability. The Commission had virtually washed its hands of the Hall in 1908, when they had surrendered their seats, on which they were paying more seat rate than they obtained in income. However, they still took an interest in the Hall's welfare, and in 1927 a new Act of Parliament was obtained. This had aroused the opposition of the Royal Choral Society, and in the House of Lords it had been referred to a Select Committee, presided over by Lord Esher. Despite this rather incestuous arrangement, the Bill finally passed; it gave the Hall borrowing powers, up to the then considerable sum of £100,000, and permitted it to be used for theatrical and operatic performances, and to be let for periods of up to a year. In addition, the management of the Hall was given powers to exclude seat-holders on some occasions when it was let to outside impresarios. To safeguard the intellectual tone and 'to emphasize the public character of the Hall and the original purposes of its foundation as part of a great educational scheme', the Select Committee recommended that the Council should obtain a Supplementary Charter, providing for five additional members. These were to be nominated by the representatives of five national institutions – the British Museum, the President of the Board of Education (in 2000 represented by the Secretary of State for Culture, Media and Sport), Imperial College and the Royal College of Music, and the 1851 Commission itself.

PAYMENT TOWARDS THE COSTS OF THE SCIENCE MUSEUM

Despite their concern for the proper development of the remainder of their estate, the Commissioners were still anxious to avoid paying for the Science Museum, which they felt would so deplete their capital resources as to damage the scholarship schemes. In 1933, the Treasury reminded

Shaw that the Commission would be expected to honour its offer of a capital contribution towards the projected second block. The Commissioners' contribution to the Science Museum had become a long-drawn-out saga. First made in 1876, but rejected, its renewal in 1910 had coincided with the government's determination to address the deficiencies of scientific education in the country, and it had been accepted. At that time, the estimates for the new museum were between £350,000 and £400,000, of which £150,000 would be spent on the first eastern section, to which the Commission agreed to give £40,000.[31]

The start made in 1913–14 was nullified by the First World War, and considerable disquiet was felt by the scientific community at the continuing delay. An article in *Nature* in 1923 pointed out that despite the importance and variety of its collections, 'in the matter of buildings, this museum has lagged far behind the museums that represent other branches of knowledge and culture'. More space was needed not only for those professionally interested in the machines and inventions but for the 'crowds who visit the galleries . . . when any large section of the public is free of work'.[32]

The first part of the Science Museum was only completed in 1928, when it was opened by George V. It fell to Shaw to remind Stamfordham of the need for a royal opening:

> As you will remember the original South Kensington Museum was established by the Commissioners & it embraced both Science and Art. The new Museum is to be home of the science section of the original Museum just as the Victoria and Albert Museum is the home of its art section.
>
> As the new buildings for the Art Collections of the Nation was opened by King Edward it would seem only right and proper that the new building for the National Science Collections should enjoy a similar mark of distinction at the hands of His present Majesty, and as you will guess the omission of such a ceremony is certain to be keenly felt by men of science.[33]

Despite considerable modification to the original design, the first part of the new building cost £270,000, of which the Commission contributed £35,000 of the promised monies, and was due to provide a further £1275 during 1934 to complete the building. The Museums and Galleries Commission in its Report had given a high priority to the building of the second part, the Central Block, on which it was hoped to make a start in 1934.

Influenced by the success of the Industrial Bursaries Scheme, and alarmed about the Commission's ability to continue funding it if its capital base was eroded, the Board had become increasingly unhappy about the obligation. The details of negotiation have happily survived – giving a graphic insight into Shaw's skill as a negotiator. Late in 1933, Shaw obtained a breakdown of the annual requirements of the Treasury towards the new block. This was estimated to cost £250,000, and the original offer of the Commission still stood, so capital sums totalling £30,000 would be due as the work progressed – £1500 in 1934, £10,000 the following year, then £12,000 in 1936, and £6500 in 1937.[34]

Shaw wrote a memorandum on the problem for the next meeting of the Board of Management, on 20 December, 1933, in which he set out the need for the Commissioners to be relieved from the obligation. Peacock explained the financial dilemma: the Commission's resources could not be reorganized, or supplemented, to meet both demands – the capital required for the Museum, and that needed to generate income for their various scholarships and bursaries. If the capital demanded was paid, equivalent income could be generated only by taking the remainder out of gilts into higher-yielding but less secure investments.

The members of the Board, led by Lord Rutherford[35] endorsed the idea of appealing to the government to renounce the grant, by convincing them that 'the educational interests of the nation would be better served if . . . the Commissioners were released . . . and thus enabled to continue . . . their present policy [their highly successful educational schemes]'. The Chairman was instructed to approach the government in order to bring this about.

Early in 1934, Macmillan approached Lord Irwin about the problem, setting out the Commission's case, which was, in effect, that the proposed contribution would cripple the excellent and fruitful schemes which the Commissioners had started, both the Science Studentships, and the more recent Industrial Bursaries. The former scheme could now claim to have assisted more than forty students to become Fellows of the Royal Society. While the Commission's contribution to the cost of the Science Museum would be relatively small in Treasury terms, he asked the minister to consider 'the very serious injury which the requirement . . . would inflict on an educational enterprise of exceptional merit'.[36]

Shaw was summoned to see J. A. Barlow, the Prime Minister's aide, for an interview on 17 January, 1934, which provoked a rather unsympathetic report to the Prime Minister. Barlow reported that Shaw had explained that the offer had been made by Lord Wolverhampton, when Chairman, 'who regarded scientific research as a waste of money, and whose policy was to get rid of all the funds of the Commissioners and bring them to an end. The late King Edward dissented strongly from this view and got Wolverhampton removed'. Barlow went on to comment that 'Shaw really had no explanation of why the question . . . had not been faced before, except that the scholarship system had grown gradually and steadily, and that the Board of Management had always let the question drift in the hope that something would turn up'. He was also critical of the way in which the Board of Management, which had effectively taken over control from the full body of Commissioners, had not informed the latter, who, of course, included the Prime Minister, as First Lord of the Treasury.

However, he concluded, the matter had ceased to be so urgent, since the second wing of the Museum had been deferred until 1935–6, so it could be sorted out between the Office of Works, the Board of Education and the Treasury.[37]

Macmillan saw Lord Halifax, who was not convinced about the needs of the Commissioners, and asked him to send Shaw to see the permanent officials. Macmillan was dismissive: 'I'm afraid you will have to enter the lion's den, but you will come out unscathed! To my mind the whole case is in our memorandum & this further inquiry is quite superfluous and rather impertinent. However, we must do our best to keep on the right side of the powers that be.'

'My dear Chief', replied Shaw, 'I attend the lacqueys' conference . . . on July 12th to discuss the present and future states of my Master's income. There will be present "someone" from the Office of Works interested in real property.' Shaw was furious that he was not allowed to take the Commissioners' Surveyor, E. R. Canham, and accused the Treasury official, one F. P. Robinson, of relishing 'the idea of a pantry feast'.[38]

The conference took place, with the Treasury taking it upon itself to criticize the Commission, first, for its expenditure on the offices at 1 Lowther Gardens, then to suggest that it would have been more prudent to set aside the capital for the Science Museum. 'In reply to this', reported Shaw, 'I could only express my gratitude that the Commissioners were made of different stuff, and that they deliberately spent the interest on the grant in improving the educational service of the Empire.' A claim that 'by securing the Imperial Institute site for 999 years at . . . £5 a year, the government had taken over a heavy liability' was dismissed by Shaw, equally briskly. The civil servants then put forward a series of suggestions as to how the Commissioners could capitalize on their landed estate, chiefly by selling extensions to the leases and anticipating the capital growth in other ways. To Shaw's glee the upshot was another meeting to discuss this last proposal, this time between J. H. Salmon, OBE, Director of Lands and Accommodation at the Ministry of Works, and Canham.

He was not sanguine about the prospect of being let off the debt, since he thought that

> Government Officials . . . are obviously under orders to torpedo our claims with as much courtesy as possible . . . as an independent Royal Commission we do not possess, as others do, the particular technique which is necessary for dealing with the Treasury. We have stated our case honestly and without exaggeration, and no one else can apparently afford to do this who hopes to secure even a fraction of his demands from the Treasury.[39]

Canham reported on his meeting and the subsequent negotiations which had enabled him and Salmon to agree on the possible value of the sale of outlying properties, and sale of the reversions to the Commission in the main square in cash terms. The domestic properties then owned by the Commissioners, and held on long leases, were Albert Hall Mansions, potentially the most valuable, 11–16 and 17–24 Kensington Gore, houses with stables, whose leases would expire in 1944, and which he anticipated would need rebuilding by 1972. There were several blocks in Queen's Gate (the former Prince Albert Road) – a block at the north end on the eastern side, north of Prince Consort Road, numbers 188–200, with numbers 2–24, 41, 43, 45 Jay's Mews behind, whose leases would fall in at the same time as the Kensington Gore Houses, numbers 177–8 and 181–3, further down, whose leases expired in 1996–9, and finally numbers 186–8, together with their mews, whose leases had about forty years to run. Finally, there were 'outlying properties', that is those 'outside the main square', where the policy had always been to sell them when conditions were favourable to supply the estate with working capital. These were in Queen's Gate Terrace, Queen's Gate Mews, Cromwell Road and

Thurloe Place Mews. The sale of these would be in accordance with the long-standing policy of the estate, which was to retain control of the 'main square' but gradually divest itself of the outer properties when opportunity offered.

In 1933, the Commissioners received a total annual income of £10,550 6s. from these properties, to which they could add £200 from the Royal School of Needlework, £2935 from the Ministry of Works, for the East and West Exhibition Galleries, and £200 for the vaults south of the Royal Albert Hall. Most of the rest of the estate had, of course, been sold or disposed of on lease to government or other public institutions on such favourable terms that there was no benefit to the Commissioners' funds. After more than half a century of inflation, it is difficult to assess the value of the Commissioners' income, but it puts contemporary money values in context to remember that the despised Mr Robinson, Assistant Secretary in the Treasury, received £850 a year, and the Commission paid the senior Science Scholars £450 per annum.[40]

Canham found the proposals of the Treasury valuer 'feasible and not unreasonable', always assuming that the Commissioners wished to raise the capital, and that the lessees were prepared to purchase the reversion, or extend their leases. He estimated that a total of £41,000 could be raised, subject to a deduction of £2000 for costs associated with the transactions, and some £13,267 to purchase gilts to replace the Commissioners' income of £398 per annum from the properties which had been sold. Though it had been demonstrated that it was practicable, Canham did not feel it was desirable, since it would be more advantageous for the Commissioners, as ground landlords, to renew the leases nearer their expiry date, though he privately admitted to Shaw that he was pleased that he had reduced Salmon's original estimate of a capital product of £58,000 to £41,000. He added that 'if it were ever desired to put the proposals into effect, I should expect to get a few thousands more than the £41,000 all told'. However organized, the proposals would have reduced the Commissioners' capital by £28,000, and made any rise in income from the estate unlikely until 1972.

An offer of a further meeting was refused by Shaw, and Robinson agreed in February 1935 to draft a report for the Chancellor, Neville Chamberlain, which he would submit to Shaw for his comments. This report suggested that some £26,000 could be raised without difficulty. Shaw canvassed Sir Edward Peacock, Canham and A. E. Cutforth, the auditor, for their comments on his draft reply. Peacock, like Macmillan, was a little taken aback by the vehemence of Shaw's language, suggesting that to say that Robinson's memorandum was 'clearly an *ex parte* statement' that would 'only serve to keep the Chancellor in blinkers' might give the impression that he 'had written in an exasperated state of mind'.

Shaw was also working on the Commission's *Ninth Report*, which he hoped to get out for the King, while Robinson was concerned that the Chancellor, as an *ex officio* Commissioner, might receive the *Ninth Report* before the promised Treasury memorandum on the Commission's commitment to the Science Museum funding, and be annoyed.[41] By the time the Board of Management met on 11 March, 1935, Shaw had replied to Robinson, but the matter never came to a head-on confrontation between Treasury and Commissioners, thanks to the skilled intervention of the Royal Household.

Stamfordham's role as go-between had been taken on by his successor in the Royal Household, Sir Clive Wigram. The official royal representative on the Commission was its President, Edward, Prince of Wales, and his secretary, Sir Godfrey Thomas, was also a Commissioner, but the personal link with George V was maintained. Occasionally it was called on, as when the King was persuaded to send a letter of congratulation to Dr William Garnett, the sole surviving member of Playfair's original Committee for the Science Scholarships, and on other occasions it proved vital.

The King had been persuaded to take an interest in the matter in September when Chamberlain had been staying at Sandringham, and in March, Wigram took a hand. After the meeting of the Board in 1935, he wrote to Sir Warren Fisher at the Treasury, to express his fellow-Commissioners' concern

> at the possible loss of income which a further contribution . . . must inflict upon the scope of our educational work.
>
> I do not think that people realise the value of the educational work of the Commission in providing Science and Research Scholarships not only for students in this country, but also for students from the Dominions; even India is now clamouring to come within the fold.
>
> Since 1891 we have turned out about 600 scholars . . . No fewer than 40 scholars are now Fellows of the Royal Society . . .
>
> The King always takes the keenest interest . . . and likes to feel

that those handicapped in the race of life are being given a chance of coming to the front.

He concluded by suggesting Fisher should see Lord Macmillan, and the latter was able to report that he 'scarcely expected so rapid and so fortunate a result . . . we are to be entirely released from our obligation to contribute from the funds of the Royal Commission to the second and third instalments to the Science Museum. This is complete success for our application'.

Chamberlain was able to respond to a Parliamentary question by saying that, because the development of the Commissioners' schemes for the provision of scholarships and bursaries 'in this connexion has proved to be of quite exceptional importance and value', he had decided to relieve them of their liability to contribute further to the museum.[42]

The Commission had triumphed, and moreover, what had been seen by civil servants as a somewhat parochial struggle over cash had ended in a public acknowledgement of the educational value of an initiative now half a century old, which had been a carefully thought-out development from the original emphasis on bricks and mortar.

The accommodation with the Treasury over the Science Museum grant and the agreement with Neville Chamberlain was the last service which George V was to render to the Commission which he had served so long and so loyally. His death was followed by Edward VIII's succession to the throne and his resignation from the Commission. He was succeeded as President by his brother, Prince George, Duke of Kent (1902–42), elected in 1937.

FUTURE DEVELOPMENT ON THE ESTATE

It was clear that several institutions on the estate were looking for room to expand, most obviously Imperial College, which since Keogh's day had shown predatory tendencies towards any spare land or property in the vicinity. Some were offered better accommodation away from South Kensington, like the Imperial War Museum, which moved from the Western Galleries to the former Bethlehem Hospital in Lambeth. The Western Galleries, which it had occupied together with part of the Imperial Institute galleries, were leased to the Office of Works. The lease was extended by another twenty-five years,[43] and in due course the Galleries were taken over by the Science Museum.

However, other institutions were finding it difficult to sustain substantial premises on the estate, like the Royal School of Needlework, a craft-based college which found the proximity of the Victoria and Albert Museum useful. Burdened with a mortgage to the Commission for its handsome Arts and Crafts building, the School was forced to let a large part of it to Imperial College. In 1934, the College took over the lease from the Commission, giving a short lease of part of the building to the erstwhile owners.[44]

Another struggling organization was the Imperial Institute, which had been taken over by the government in 1905 as an adjunct to the Board of Trade, and had been shuffled about between the Board and the Colonial Office. Other occupants, including departments of the University of London, took over parts of the building, and the exhibition galleries were used for a variety of purposes.

Despite the comments made by some Commissioners it is clear that even at this date, the income from the estate was just higher than that from investments, some £11,051 as against £10,997 from investments, though the capital value of the estate was higher at £376,328, as against £338,372.

The Commissioners had retained a clear picture of the development they would like to see on their estate, which they put forward to the Museums and Galleries Commission, and to government, though not all the bodies on the estate concurred with their schemes. The simple subdivision of the former South Kensington Museum into Arts to the east and Science to the west of the Exhibition Road had not been fully implemented, and the lofty Huxley Building in Exhibition Road on the north of the Victoria and Albert Museum still contained laboratories and students from Imperial College. On the west, the Commissioners had equally clear ambitions for the 'main square' – to the south of Imperial Institute Road, the 'exhibition of science' containing the three scientific museums, and to the north Imperial College. The College possessed the striking Royal College of Science building on the south, impeding the development of the Science Museum, which the Commissioners, though reluctant to bleed their resources to fund it, wished to see completed.

Sir Henry Tizard (1885–1959), Rector of Imperial College from 1929 to 1942, developed a plan for the college to expand north of Imperial Institute Road, challenging a plan for giving sites to other institutions in the area, including the College of Art and a new museum of ethnology, one of the desiderata of the Royal Commission on Museums and Galleries. This scheme envisaged the College surrendering its holdings elsewhere including the Huxley Building, and the Royal College of Science building. This scheme was given architectural expression by Sir Hubert Worthington in 1936–7, but had to be pigeon-holed in the face of preparations for rearmament under the threat of war. It had, however, set in place a scheme for the most profound changes in the Commissioners' estate for half a century, which was to be implemented after the war. (As this was a continuous process, the details of the Tizard/Worthington scheme will be dealt with in Chapter X.)

THE OUTBREAK OF WAR

The Second World War brought even more profound changes to the Commissioners and their tenants than had its predecessor. Aerial bombardment had been a threat to London in the earlier war, but the development of aerial warfare since, and its demonstration in the Spanish Civil War, made clear the necessity for the partial closure of the museums, and the dispersal of their collections. Any projects for the extension of the Science Museum or for changes on the estate were deferred.

Evelyn Shaw moved the office to Shalford, Surrey, for the duration, closing the office at Lowther Gardens, and Sturch took a job as a civil servant. The Commission's President, the Duke of Kent, was killed on 25 August, 1942, while on active service with the RAF.

The Commissioners met on 6 March, 1945, before even the war in Europe had ended, at the House of Lords, a somewhat diminished band, many members being occupied on matters of national importance, like Winston Churchill, others deterred by the difficulty of travelling. They welcomed their new President, the Princess Royal, whose husband was already a Commissioner. Even more than in the previous war had former Scholars and Industrial Bursars proved the value of the Commission's work, though of course no scholarships or bursaries had been awarded for five years. The Board had been husbanding the Commission's resources against the prospect of being again able to select and assist Scholars. It was some time before the staff were able to return to Lowther Gardens, the Board meeting in a number of makeshift locations, including the Athenaeum Club, until things returned to normal.

The future was still uncertain; it was not clear what sort of scholarship scheme would best serve in the new post-war circumstances. However, arrangements had been made to meet, and reconcile, some of the most pressing needs of major tenants on the estate. A site had been found in Kensington Gore for the Cinderella of the tenants – the Royal College of Art, while Imperial College had been persuaded to cede some ground for the extension of the Royal College of Music.

Evelyn Shaw had held the post of Secretary for thirty-five years, serving the Commission in all some forty-two years, and was ready to retire in 1947, leaving his post to his assistant Digby Sturch, in accordance with an agreement made when the latter returned from the war.[45] Shaw was the longest-serving of any of the Commission's staff and on his retirement the Board unanimously voted to make him a Commissioner. His enthusiasm in his dealings with the Scholars and the Industrial Bursars had done much to make the schemes a success, while his continuing interest and solicitude for the award-holders in later life was remembered by many. He had showed a similar concern for the Rome Scholars and for the work of the British School at Rome, of which he had been Honorary General Secretary since 1912.

His appointment as Assistant Secretary by Ellis so many years before had been an inspired choice. In the words of Macmillan's tribute:

> It is rare to find a man and his vocation so happily wedded. He has never been content to confine himself to the routine performance of his office. To him the varied activities of the Royal Commission have afforded much more than an opportunity for the exercise of his admirable administrative gifts: they have been the absorbing interest of his life, so that he came to be identified with the Royal Commission in a quite exceptional manner. Members of the Board come and go and Mr. Shaw has witnessed many changes in its composition, but he has remained throughout the permanent element in its composition and thus has helped in no small measure to preserve the continuity of its policy.[46]

X

Post-War Reorganization and Reassessment: Rebuilding the Commissioners' Estate 1947–1970

The first opportunity for the Commission to review its plans for the future came in the autumn of 1947, when some eight Commissioners met under their President, the Princess Royal, with their new Secretary Digby Sturch. After quarter of a century they were again having to review the work of the 'royal educational trust', again in the face of a declining income, and with demands on the remaining landed assets of the Commission. The political and educational background had changed yet again, and in place of the more laissez-faire British tradition which the Commission had been set up to supplement, a new more Continental-style command-driven philosophy directed educational policy. The Commission found itself dealing with bodies which it had itself set up, but whose standing and wealth had outgrown that of their sponsor. The future was still uncertain in that it was not clear what sort of scholarship scheme would best serve in the new post-war circumstances. However, Sir Edward Peacock, the financial adviser, had made it clear that whatever the Commissioners wanted to do, there would be less money available; many of the companies in which they were accustomed to invest had been nationalized, inflation was increasing and the value of the pound declining, while the role of landlords had been made increasingly irksome by the rent acts, and restrictions on maintenance and rebuilding.

New Commissioners were recruited, including Evelyn Shaw, who had been made a Knight Commander of the Victorian Order for his life's work, the Liberal lawyer Lord Simonds (1881–1971), and the botanist Sir Edward Mellanby (1884–1955). Shaw was also appointed to the Board and the Science Scholarships Committee, for both of which other new members were recruited. The Chairman of the Science Scholarships Committee was again a former award-holder, Sir Robert Robinson.[1] In future, though the deaths of Commissioners of political standing, such as Earl Lloyd-George, Lord Halifax and Sir Winston Churchill were recorded, active politicians were invited to Commission meetings on a strictly *ex officio* basis, and rarely bothered to attend. Increasingly, recruitment to the Commission was through work on the Science Scholarships Committee, though some non-scientists were recruited. In due course, the Board effectively took over, and only the most formal of business was transacted at Commission meetings, which were presided over less and less by the President.

THE COMMISSION'S AWARDS

The Board's first task was to get the educational awards started again. As in 1914–19, they had been able to accumulate funds during the war, and so were able to provide the British School at Rome with its pre-war grant of £4500 a year for 1946–9, though not all the scholarships in art were awarded in those years. There was also the problem of pre-war Scholars: many of these had married in the course of the war, and for them a year's study in bachelor quarters in Rome was less attractive. A sign of the times was that the British government had seen the necessity of tripling the School's grant of £1000, paid through the British Academy, while the Royal Institute of British Architects had set their Architectural Scholarship at £750. These were increases that the Commission would not find easy to match, and which would make them a less and less significant player.

The scholarship in Naval Architecture failed to attract candidates immediately after the war, and had to be seriously revamped, the award being doubled. Moreover, though the candidates had hitherto been sought only from the four Schools of Naval Architecture, the field was considerably widened to include all universities in the United Kingdom which had schools of naval architecture, engineering science or aerodynamics. These changes were successful, and a promising candidate was found in 1947, who continued for the usual two years, encouraging the Board to declare:

> At present the shipbuilding industry in this country is leading the world. To retain this position will require constant research on ship

design, construction and operation and the Board are glad . . . to encourage able research workers to interest themselves in this important field.[2]

The Industrial Bursaries had ceased at the outbreak of war; again, some of the award-holders had married, and the Board had seen it as proper to continue their awards to enable them to complete their training. However, the post-war pattern of work indicated that proper payment would now be given to trainees, and with some relief the Board was able to discontinue the scheme after the war. However, Commissioners could reflect with pride that some six hundred ill-provided but aspiring applicants had been helped, and enabled to make their contribution to British industry.

The Science Scholarships, however, were not redundant, though again the award-holders of 1937–9 had taken up wartime jobs, and had mostly found good permanent posts. The Science Scholarships Committee looked very carefully at the Senior Studentships and were happy to find many more comparable awards available than had been the case in 1891, or even in 1922, when they had established those particular awards. During the war the government had come to realize the importance of postgraduate training, and there was also concern about post-war scientific manpower, which had led to more awards being made available. Here again increased spending was required from the Board, and they decided to raise the students' stipends from £400 to £500, though not the overall budget, so the number of Senior Studentships was set to fall from five to four.

One of the Board's reasons for avoiding an increase in the cost of the Senior Studentship scheme was to ensure that the Overseas Scholarships, to which they attached the greatest importance, should not be limited by financial constraints. The members looked at the scheme in the year the war ended and decided to give it priority in order

> to attract the best of the young post-graduate research workers in the Dominions and India and to give them an opportunity of extending their scientific experience by two or three years' work overseas . . . the majority elect to study in Great Britain. The Committee welcome this tendency. The need for treating the British Commonwealth in the realms of science as an entity, with the maximum interchange of scientific workers between its constituent coun-

tries, has been amply proved by the war, and the attention of the Royal Society and the Commonwealth Governments has recently been directed to finding means of preserving in peace the links that were forged in times of military stress.[3]

The Committee could congratulate itself 'on the important part . . . in introducing the younger scientists from the Dominions and India to this country' played by the Overseas Scholarships scheme, and proposed its extension by a second scholarship to India, something which Sir James Jeans had been pressing for in 1939.[4] This was necessitated by partition, but may also have been influenced by the fact that one of the first Indian Scholars to hold a Senior Studentship, H. J. Bhabha, had been almost immediately made a Fellow of the Royal Society, in 1941. Accordingly, the first post-war awards were allocated on the basis of one each to Eire and South Africa, two each to Australia, India, and New Zealand (which got an extra Scholar that year), with three to Canada. The stipends were raised in line with the 'greatly increased cost of living', which, with the additional scholarship, put the costs up by £3000 a year.

This additional expenditure was possible immediately after the war, during which the Commission had given no scholarships and had reduced staff salaries, saving some £107,000, which was added to their capital reserves. However, rents and investments had fallen in real terms, since the increase in the latter was largely due to the investment of the wartime surplus.[5] This sanguine approach was soon dented by post-war inflation, increased costs for 1 Lowther Gardens, and for administration generally and for the awards, while there were difficulties in collecting the rents on the estate. Sir Edward Peacock initiated a conservative regime, suggesting that the Commission should start building up a fund for an anniversary record of the award-holders, in 1951.

THE DEVELOPMENT OF THE ESTATE: DEMOLITION AND
RECONSTRUCTION

Like all London landlords, the Commissioners found the post-war problems of their estate difficult to solve. Vigers reported on the problems of war damage, and on buildings taken over by government agencies, like Queen Alexandra's House requisitioned for the ATS.[6] Other properties were being 'squatted in', or were in multiple occupation, while an increasing amount of legislation on landlord and tenant relations was to curb the

London ground landlord's traditional control over such matters as the use to which buildings were put, sub-letting and the rents paid. A number of long leaseholds had been turned into statutory tenancies over which neither the Commission nor its head-lessees had any control. In several cases, the Commission were advised by Vigers, and his successor Holroyd Chambers, either to accept an offer to buy the freehold from a leaseholder, or in desperation, to undertake the redevelopment of a property as the only means of getting rid of an obnoxious protected tenant. Thus, one of the few remaining stables, a livery stables much disliked by the neighbours, and seen as lowering the tone of the neighbourhood, was dislodged on the grounds that the Commission planned to convert the whole building to residential use.[7] Some substantial tenants like Mr Howard, the lessee of the Gore Hotel at number 189 at the north end of Queen's Gate, were able to purchase longer leases to make improvements worthwhile, but generally the outlook was depressing as far as private tenancies went. The result was to encourage the sale of the relatively few remaining privately owned long leaseholds, particularly those outside the 'main square', where institutional tenants occupied almost all the properties.

HOUSING THE INSTITUTIONS: ADAPTING THE PRE-WAR SCHEMES

However, even greater changes were imminent as the Board endeavoured to meet and reconcile some of the most pressing needs of major tenants on the estate. As in so many cases, the post-war rebuilding acted as a midwife to developments which had been discussed and planned in embryo for many years. It had become obvious in the 1930s that there were a large number of competitors for space in South Kensington of which the largest player was Imperial College. The pre-war Rector, Sir Henry Tizard (1885–1959) had developed an elaborate scheme for extension of the College, of which many elements were incorporated in the post-war scheme. It was Shaw who had suggested the Manchester architect Hubert Worthington should be asked to assist Tizard with his ideas.[8] Worthington and Tizard set to work in the early part of 1936 on an ambitious plan to give Imperial College extended facilities and a more collegiate character. There were certain basic premises dating in essence from the 1899 Select Committee on the Department of Science and Art, endorsed by the Museums and Galleries Report. These assumed that the east side of the Exhibition Road was dedicated to art, the west to science, with the Imperial Institute Road providing the frontier between museum uses to the south and educational to the north. This simple plan necessitated the rehousing, or, at worst, the expulsion of non-conforming organizations, of which Imperial College was one of the largest, occupying as it did some 30,000 square feet of teaching space in the Huxley Building, north of the Victoria and Albert Museum, and 130,000 square feet in Aston Webb's Royal College of Science in the 'museums area' south of the Imperial Institute Road. It was accepted that these would have to be surrendered, but it was a lot of space for the College to replace.

In 1937, the College could, however, look forward to the surrender in 1948 by the Royal School of Needlework of its remaining space in what had been its own building, and the removal of the Imperial War Museum to a permanent home had left much of the Western Galleries vacant.[9] The Eastern Galleries housed the rump of the ill-fated Indian Museum, whose exhibits had been largely collected by the servants of the East India Company. When the latter had been wound up in the wake of the Indian Mutiny, it had passed to the Secretary of State for India, whose department seems to have had little appreciation of the importance of the collection. These were partitioned between various institutions, the British Museum claiming some of the most significant of the archaeological objects, the botanical specimens going to Kew and the animal specimens to the Natural History Museum. Those exhibits seen as decorative art or manufactured objects went to the South Kensington Museum, which lodged them in the Eastern Galleries.[10]

HOUSING THE STUDENTS OF THE ROYAL COLLEGE OF ART

The other institution looking for accommodation before the war had been the Royal College of Art, which, as the Government School of Design, had been one of the earliest arrivals on the South Kensington scene, sharing accommodation with the South Kensington Museum. In 1897 it had changed its name from the National Art Training School to the Royal College of Art, which perhaps gave weight to the criticisms of Lewis Day and others that the School was not earning its keep as a trainer of industrial designers. Because of the reorganization of education in 1902, and their take-over by local authorities, it had lost its connection with the provincial colleges of design. In a letter accompanying a critical report on the College in 1910, Day put his criticisms to Sir Robert Morant at the

Board of Education: 'in reality Ornament is very little considered and its practical application to industry is entirely neglected . . . The very fact that Ornament and Design are connected with Trade, and that the Royal Academy ignores them, makes it, I know, difficult to do anything for the subject'.[11]

The somewhat controversial appointment of the Bradford-born William Rothenstein as Principal in 1920 had given the College a new start. As he had put it to the civil servants at the Board of Education, the College should not

> limit itself to the education of designers and industrial craftsmen, while schools elsewhere would provide training for students of fine art. . . The separation between craftsmen and arts is already too wide. Each has lessons of value to learn from the other . . . Nor is it desirable to define and to limit, early in a young aspirant's career, his future activities. From the practice of the arts of design a fine artist may develop naturally; while too many men and women become indifferent painters whose gifts are better fitted for more modest and useful work.[12]

The art students were housed in a variety of accommodation in the area, but had been promised a site in the 'main square' by the Office of Works. The Office of Works was the government department tradition-ally responsible for housing national institutions, and the various leases which the Commission had granted to the South Kensington institutions had, by the 1930s, fallen into its effective control. In April 1937, Leitch of the Office of Works laid out his department's scheme for allocating the space on the Commission's estate. The scheme had been devised to respond to the needs of the art students, and for a site for a new Ethno-graphical Museum of the British Museum material, and a new 'Exhi-bition of Modern Applied Art'. The plan was to place the new Applied Art Museum with the art museums on the east, and the new home for the ethnographical collections with the science museums to the south of the Imperial Institute Road. This ambitious plan, which he admitted 'would involve a considerable exchange and reallocation of properties among the institutions concerned', had been 'generally approved' both by those insti-tutions concerned and by the Standing Commission on Museums and Galleries, and was, of course, dependent on Treasury approval, but, as he conceded, was also dependent on the consent of the Commissioners as ground landlords. In due course, the Board agreed to commend the 'attempt now being made . . . to draw up a long-range and comprehensive scheme for its development on more orderly and efficient lines'. A sub-committee of Sir James Jeans, Thomas Jones and Lord Wigram was appointed to represent the Commissioners over any questions which might arise, and to advise how the Board might help in due course. However, it took the opportunity to point out to the Office that the Royal College of Music was sorely in need of room to expand, and suggested that this should be taken into account. The somewhat lofty approach on the part of the Office of Works aroused irritation in Shaw, who pointed out that most of the land belonged to the Commission, and that a very small rent was paid by the various lessees.[13]

The Office of Works had promised the Royal College of Art a site at the north-west corner of the 'main square', where stood a building belonging to Imperial College. The Royal College of Music also wanted to expand, and felt that the Royal College of Art was taking a desirable adjacent site which would suit it very well. In any case this scheme to house the Royal College of Art on the corner of Prince Consort Road and Queen's Gate conflicted with the Imperial College scheme of expansion promulgated by Sir Henry Tizard.

SIR HENRY TIZARD'S SCHEME FOR IMPERIAL COLLEGE

The scheme worked out by Tizard and Worthington in 1936–7 was very ambitious, with the intention of transforming what had been a series of somewhat disparate teaching bodies into a residential collegiate institution closer to the Oxbridge model. Though the College no longer has the plans for the architectural schemes or the perspectives by J. D. M. Harvey, it is possible to reconstruct the ideas behind the proposed redevelopment from the correspondence. Tizard needed accommodation for 450 students, but because Worthington did not want the halls to be 'too high and flat-like' he suggested six halls, all with individual Junior Common Rooms, with only four hundred students, though Tizard suggested a 'separate small hall for Indian students and such-like, holding not more than 50'. This accommodation seems to have been intended for the north-west corner of the site – in fact, the only space sufficiently large to have given the perspective and the grand entrance which Worthington wanted. A 'hall to dine 500' was also included, but what really inspired him was the Rector's house, which he wanted to set 'at the end of the long vista':[14]

I am scheming a Rectorial Residence on the scale, say, of the Vice-Chancellor's house at Manchester – large drawing room, large dining room, smaller reception room between – good study on first floor, 6 good bedrooms, 2 dressing rooms, 2 bathrooms, waiting room and typist's room, with maids' accommodation in attic over, garage, usual kitchens, etc.[15]

This alarmed Tizard, who pointed out that 'Rectors are unlikely to be wealthy people', and that therefore the residence should not be too large, and preferably sited close to the college kitchens. A Rector would have to entertain, and, if the college kitchens were convenient, then he would not need to have such a large domestic staff. Accommodation for the college staff was also planned, and a 'staff house' with common room, dining room and sitting rooms was discussed, and also the strategic distribution of tutors' 'sets' scattered among student accommodation. Tennis and racquets courts were to be placed in the centre of the various quadrangles.

In due course, Tizard confessed his 'mad, visionary, or statesmanlike' scheme to the Chairman of the Imperial College governing body, the physicist, the 4th Lord Rayleigh (1875–1947), with the request that Worthington should be commissioned to produce a plan, though admitting that 'there would be all sorts of formidable obstacles in the way of carrying it out, not the least one being the financial obstacle of having to find about a million pounds for building and endowment'. The scheme went ahead, with Worthington becoming enthusiastic: 'I am absolutely head and soul in the thing and can think of nothing else'.[16] Both Shaw and various officials from the Office of Works were involved, and after a meeting in February 1937 with Sir James West, architect to the Office of Works and J. H. Salmon, Director of Lands at the Office, Worthington was able to convince the civil servants of the merits of his scheme.

I told him what a shock I had had at the idea of the Royal College of Art spoiling my cross-vista and main entrance and taking a large proportion of our labs, and said that the only thing that would reconcile me to this sacrifice would be that the three houses and part of the road alongside General Makins' house were surrendered to us. [Sir James West] began by saying that this was asking too much . . . and we ought to be able to enter from Imperial Institute Road. I said 'no, as an Architect you must see that this vista is essential' . . . He said that they would ultimately want your building on the new Royal

College of Art site . . . I gather that he jumped at our idea of the Science Library on the ground floor and the basement of the Imperial Institute on the right hand side, with Mathematical School above, provided you could get over London University.[17]

The Office of Works apparently accepted the idea of Imperial College having the whole block, with the exception of the sites of the Royal Colleges of Art and Music, but Tizard found considerable problems in dealing with his own colleagues at London University. A memorandum by the Office of Works, under pressure to meet the competing demands of its South Kensington clients, set out the main lines of development to provide accommodation for the Royal College of Art, Imperial College, the Indian section of the Victoria and Albert Museum and the Imperial Institute Galleries. New clients included the Ethnographical Section of the British Museum and the new blocks of the Science and Natural History Museums; the Victoria and Albert Museum was promised some more room. Existing interests included London University, which occupied the Great Hall, Galleries and Chemical Laboratory in the Imperial Institute Building, the Board of Education Art Examination staff, and an Office of Works Generating Station and depot.

The Office of Works saw the solution as the removal of the London University departments to their new headquarters in Bloomsbury, and the rebuilding of the Fuel Research Laboratory of Imperial College in Prince Consort Road, west of the Royal College of Music, together with the complete removal of the Imperial Institute galleries, and the Eastern and Western Galleries. Part of the problem was the relationship between London University and Imperial College, since London University could not expect any compensation for giving up buildings to a constituent body. The scheme of the Office of Works was to give the Royal College of Art a new building in Prince Consort Road, west of the Royal College of Music, with a possibility of extension westwards on to the Fuel Research Laboratory site. To provide 'an adequately impressive site from the West' for the new Imperial College buildings it was thought that 178 and 179 Queen's Gate would have to be demolished. Imperial College would also be offered the Imperial Institute building. In recompense, Imperial College would be expected to give up the Royal College of Science building on the south of Imperial Institute Road, which would serve as the missing third block of the Science Museum. On the east side of

Exhibition Road the proposal was to give the Victoria and Albert Museum additional accommodation by extending over the sites then occupied by the Royal Colleges of Science and Art to the north of the Aston Webb building. The Office of Works set out a programme, starting with the rehousing of the Royal College of Art and ending with the reconstruction of the Victoria and Albert Museum, 'as finances permit and the needs of the Museum require, in the years after 1947'.

This pre-war scheme was driven to some extent by the aim to redistribute the institutions in the tidy 'art to the east, and science to the west' pattern laid down so long ago, but it is also interesting in that there is little reference to the interests of the 1851 Commissioners. In fact, except for the few private houses left in Queen's Gate, and its ultimate control as ground landlord through covenants over existing leases, there was little that the Commissioners could do to affect the outcome. The complicated game of musical chairs amongst its clients was essentially one for the Office of Works, anxious to attain 'an ordered arrangement of the constituent interests, which has hitherto received comparatively little consideration'.

The Office paid homage to Prince Albert's vision, in describing its own attempt at this 'long range scheme of redevelopment of a highly important site, with, as its main object, the attainment in the maximum degree possible of the purposes for which the site was acquired almost a century ago'. Thus the new scheme harked back to the Prince's project, but was considered a matter for government itself, without reference to the Commission.[18]

Tizard's scheme was seen by outsiders as ambitious, if not greedy, since, even though the College was to be given the lion's share of the 'large central site', it was reluctant to give up the outlying sites to other bodies. In addition, there was a suggestion that if the anticipated private backers who were expected to fund the buildings did not materialize, the Treasury would be expected to step in. In a thinly veiled threat, John Beresford, Secretary to the Standing Commission on Museums and Galleries, pointed out that as the government owned the central site they could just as easily put the Royal College of Art and the proposed Ethnographical Museum on it as surrender the whole for Imperial College expansion.[19]

However, as the need for rearmament gradually absorbed government attention and the Treasury's funds, the scheme was pigeon-holed, and both the Treasury and the Office of Works had other priorities. Sir Henry Tizard left Imperial College in 1942, to go to Oxford as President of Magdalen, and by the time the post-war redevelopment of the site was put in train, the scheme had been considerably enlarged by the government's need to promote technological education.

THE PRIVATE ESTATE

Before the war the 1851 Commission had its own development scheme for the private residential part of the estate, which Vigers had set out in good time for the moment when the leases in Kensington Gore, Jay's Mews and the houses at the top of Queen's Gate fell in. These leases were due to fall in in the early 1940s, and the Commission's surveyors had been planning lucrative redevelopment of the traditional London type, when the houses would have either been rebuilt or taken by tenants on a repairing lease at a rack rent.

As it was, at the end of the war, there was no possibility of repairs or rebuilding, and some of the houses were empty or occupied by squatters. The Surveyor presented a very pessimistic report at the Board's meeting in April 1944, even suggesting that Westminster Council should be asked to 'commandeer the houses for the duration'. Macmillan suggested that, as 'the original purpose . . . in acquiring the estate was to devote it not to private buildings but to public purposes', the Board should explore the possibilities of leasing the land for an institutional purpose.[20]

THE ROYAL COLLEGE OF ART

The Secretary therefore offered to the Office, now the Ministry, of Works the site in Kensington Gore for use of the Royal College of Art on a ninety-nine-year lease at £3000 per annum from June 1945, later altered to 140 years from June 1946. The site would comprise the last major sites in the possession of the Commission, offered in three *tranches* – 11–20 Kensington Gore with the Mews behind, 197–200 Queen's Gate with 25–35 Kensington Gore and Jay's Mews behind from 1973, and finally another block of Jay's Mews, of which the lease would not fall in until 1979. On it, they proposed the Ministry should erect buildings for the Royal College of Art, to the satisfaction of the Commissioners and the Royal Fine Art Commission.[21] Another problem was also overcome by this deal with the Royal College of Art, since in return for the coveted north-west site, Imperial College was persuaded to cede some ground for the extension of the Royal College of Music.

The Commission showed a more commercial attitude to letting land to institutions, since the rent for the Royal College of Art site was intended to be a realistic one which would assist the Commission in its scholarship work. Unfortunately, the benefit of the new financial approach was diluted by the effects of dramatic inflation in the post-war period.

This scheme meant the housing of the Cinderella of the tenants, indeed, the last of the Commission's major tenants, in a suitable way. However, because of post-war priorities, and the College's need to raise money, it was a long time before much progress was made in housing the art students. Immediately after the war, they were scattered round the neighbourhood, in the Western Galleries, and in converted private houses in the Cromwell Road. In due course, the College's architects, H. T. Cadbury-Brown and Sir Hugh Casson, presented schemes for three blocks, duly approved by the Board. Increasingly, however, the Board was prepared to take a lead from the Royal Fine Art Commission on aesthetic matters, as they were prepared to leave the matter of non-conforming uses on the estate to the London County Council, to be dealt with under their planning and zoning laws.[22] The first block, the tall studios and workshops block carried out in brick next to the Albert Hall, was completed in 1962. Treasury guidelines for finance proved to be inhibiting on such an important site, but happily a private donor gave the Gulbenkian Hall. A small unobtrusive octagonal block of common rooms followed, but the College was to find difficulty in developing the third site, at the top of Queen's Gate, in 1973.

IMPERIAL COLLEGE

The problems of dealing with the College of Art were relatively minor compared with those of dealing with the Ministry of Works and Imperial College. By May 1954, Sturch was able to outline the scheme to Peacock, observing that the Ministry had gone far with their plans without consulting the ground landlords:

> They propose to hand over to the Imperial College, as part of the Government's plan to promote technological education, all the land between Imperial Institute and the Prince Consort Road in which they have an interest, the intention being that ultimately the whole

site will be covered by the College, except that part occupied by the
Royal College of Music.

The College was also to be allowed to retain the sites south of Imperial
Institute Road, originally to be surrendered to the museum authorities.

Though much of the ground was already occupied by the College,
Sturch pointed out that it would have to take steps to acquire the rest,
including the houses in Queen's Gate. The Commission would need to
ensure that its existing rent on the land was safeguarded, though he was
cynical about the official suggestion that the Commission should be compensated for the destruction of the buildings on its land, including that of
the Imperial Institute. 'From this genial attitude I infer that it is not the
Ministry that will have to face the Treasury, but the University Grants
Committee, seeing that the initiative . . . [now] lies . . . with the
University of London, fortified by a government policy decision to
expand the Imperial College'. He anticipated a 'row that will follow any
decision to pull down the Imperial Institute building, now becoming a
venerable piece of architecture', though he was prepared to leave 'that
battle' to the Fine Art Commission.[23]

The Commissioners were already concerned over their finances, and
experienced as they were in dealing with the Treasury, were anxious that
the value of the new development should be recognized by a rise in rent.
Chambers suggested that the Commission land then occupied by Imperial
College, even if valued at only a sixth of a penny per foot, which he
regarded as half its market value, represented a subsidy of £20,000 per
annum to Imperial College. The promised extension would represent a
further £6000 a year. The matter dragged on: a formal letter from Sturch
to the Ministry in September 1954 asking for information, remained
unanswered for over a year.[24]

When the Ministry finally vouchsafed a reply in January 1956, the
Commission was asked to agree the immediate demolition of the Eastern
Galleries and that of the Western Galleries in July, before there was any
discussion of the general principles of the scheme or of the rent to be
paid. This was an action which Sturch mistrusted, though he felt that as
the Commission was 'dealing with respectable institutions . . . the risk of
being let down is perhaps not great'. He was still apprehensive about the
Commissioners being 'made partners to the crime of destroying a
London landmark'. Several members of the Board, including Sir Frank

Smith, who had a reputation for taking an independent line, were against allowing the demolition of the Imperial Institute, though generally the Board itself was happy to leave such matters to the Royal Fine Art Commission.

The scheme grew and changed considerably over the process of development, as the College's projected intake of students was raised from 3000 to 4700. The new architects, Norman and Dawbarn, with Sir Hubert Worthington as consultant, built on the pre-war ideas, but the new scheme made massive demands on the 'Island site', seen as extending from the Beit Quadrangle in the north to the Royal College of Science, and from Queen's Gate to Prince's Gardens. A large number of students and staff were to be accommodated as well as laboratories, lecture rooms and the well-established Science Museum and Imperial College Library. Fashionable ideas such as pedestrian walkways separated from vehicular traffic, to 'improve human contact', dictated the planning. The Board considered the scheme formally on 2 February, 1956, meeting the Rector, Dr Linstead, and Mr Cunliffe from the Ministry, and approved the scheme generally, though stipulating that the income from the site should be increased. This was not unreasonable since, as Sturch had pointed out earlier in the year, the commercial rental value of the land in question was in excess of £51,000, but the Commission received only £2941 a year.[25] However, apparently driven by Frank Smith, the Board pointed out that there was 'considerable public controversy' over the demolition of the Imperial Institute, and it was were not prepared to give its consent to its demolition until 'HMG' had considered the various representations. They were ready to give permission for the immediate demolition of the East Galleries, and part of the Western ones.

The proposed demolition of so much of Albertopolis, including the Imperial Institute, was challenged by a number of opponents. For the architectural historian H. S. Goodhart-Rendel, who quoted Tennyson in its defence, the Institute was 'one of the most beautiful buildings of its kind and time, not only in England but in Europe'.[26] Christopher Hussey attacked the project in the staid pages of *Country Life*, pointing out that because the government was technically the landowner no statutory safeguards existed either against demolition or to approve the design of the new buildings:

Not only are the character and scenery of an important section of

London to be completely altered without national opinion being regarded: the destruction of a great building, architecturally commensurate with the Law Courts or Westminster Cathedral, and its replacement by something unspecified, has been decreed by the Cabinet . . .

It may be that the old imperial spirit is now so much a thing of the past that the Imperial Institute has outlived its purpose. Undoubtedly technology counts for more than sentiment as a bond to keep together what remains of the colonial empire; engineers and chemists are vastly more necessary than poets. Even if this . . . confined site . . . is suitable for laboratories and residential hostels, has our generation the moral sanction thus to erase from the historic scenery of London a great architectural monument?[27]

A number of eminent figures, including both scientists and architectural historians, took up the cudgels, including, predictably, John Betjeman and Goodhart-Rendel, and, less characteristically, Hugh Casson, Sir Julian Huxley and Sir Albert Richardson.

The battle for the Imperial Institute was joined in the House of Lords by the architect Lord Mottistone and Lord Crawford, as well as by the Royal Fine Art Commission, where very strong representations were made to the University of London and the other authorities responsible. Though the Imperial Institute was seen as the most important loss, other buildings were threatened, including Wade's Royal School of Needlework of 1903, and Waterhouse's City and Guilds Building of 1884, both in Exhibition Road. In Queen's Gate, Imperial College wanted the site of Alexandra Court, Nos 171–5. At least two houses designed by Norman Shaw were threatened, No. 170, on the corner of Imperial Institute Road, and the Makins house at number 180, together with numbers 178 and 179. In the words of the Royal Fine Art Commission,

the scheme . . . did not seem to pay enough regard to the importance, architecturally and historically, to London of some of the existing buildings of the site, particularly the main block of the Institute, and No. 170 Queen's Gate.

In addition, the Royal Fine Art Commission took the view that the secrecy demanded by the College over the discussions of its plans was 'quite unnecessary and undesirable'. Though applauding the preservation of the tower of the Imperial Institute, it was quite rightly concerned over its treatment, pointing out that it 'was not designed to be a free-standing campanile and its architectural treatment will require very careful consideration. The Commission', the report concluded, 'is not convinced that a more sympathetic approach at the outset might not have found some use for the main block'.[28]

At its meeting in June 1956, the Board was told that a decision to retain the central tower of the Institute had been taken, with some reluctance on the part of the architects and the Treasury. This decision was attributed by Peacock to Frank Smith's intransigence, and Sturch's persistence, but nothing could save the main block of the Imperial Institute, or the Makins house, possibly the finest and least altered of Shaw's Queen's Gate houses.[29]

Indeed, the main lines of development had been agreed, and Imperial College in fact went ahead with its scheme over the next ten years. On the financial side of the proposed redevelopment scheme, a rent of some £5000 rising to £25,000 was being negotiated by Chambers, together with the repayment of the Commissioners' long-standing loan to the Royal School of Needlework. On occasion, the College failed to obtain its landlord's consent for further demolitions and changes, a sign of the way in which the Commission was no longer in total control of the estate.

Perhaps more unfortunately for the future appearance of the Commissioners' estate was the fact that the pre-war scheme of Tizard and Worthington with its grand talk of a rectorial residence at the end of a vista was replaced by a utilitarian approach, which lined the site with fashionable modern movement buildings creating a sort of 'science laager'. As the architects set it out:

> Architecture today is either handmade or machinemade . . . This scheme is predominantly machinemade; an architecture that relies on grouping, on patterns and rhythm, on contrast and repetition. It can in gracious surroundings be a living and beautiful expression of our age. It has been suggested that such architecture may stand best on its own merits, without the intrusion of the other arts . . . but the exterior must gain enormously from free-standing sculpture as well as from lawns, trees and fountains; and the interiors from pictures and other works of art. The scheme as now presented can stand equally with or without the Tower. Should this in the end be

removed, and the substantial saving be applied to sculpture and other forms of grace, a great stimulus would be given to living genius to the lasting advantage of the allied arts.[30]

Only Webb's Royal College of Science survived on the outer perimeter, though it too was demolished in the 1960s. The tower from the Imperial Institute, now renamed the Queen's Tower, was saved as a central feature; the rest of the buildings from Imperial Institute Road, once a street of considerable distinction, gradually disappeared over the next three decades, leaving the once despised Post Office as one of the few buildings of distinction in the area.

The only other survivor was 170 Queen's Gate, which had been acquired by Imperial College, and was retained to fulfil the role of 'rectorial residence' and Senior Common Room. Alexandra Court was reprieved, though for a long time it was seen as a potential site for expansion.

THE ANNIVERSARY OF THE GREAT EXHIBITION

The Commission was approached by a number of people and bodies who wished it to help in celebrating the anniversary of the Great Exhibition, but the Board decided that it could not undertake another exhibition.[31] The Festival of Britain in due course went forward without the Commission's participation, though of course, as the Commissioners had hoped, a good deal of publicity was given to the Great Exhibition and the Crystal Palace.

In the summer of 1951, Shaw reminded the Commissioners to ask for a formal commemoration of the anniversary of the Great Exhibition from George VI. Macmillan's reference to the centenary of the Royal Commission and its hundred years of public work was graciously answered, and the King congratulated the Commissioners on the holding of their 151st meeting in May 1951.[32]

The Commission did however hold a dinner for award-holders in the autumn of 1951, a tradition which had been established before the war. The Scholars' Dinner became an annual function in Peacock's chairmanship, but was gradually discontinued and replaced by an annual cocktail party after a Commission or Board Meeting. This appears to have been partly because it was easier for the then President, the Princess Royal, to attend a cocktail party, and meet more award-holders. The practice of

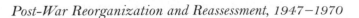

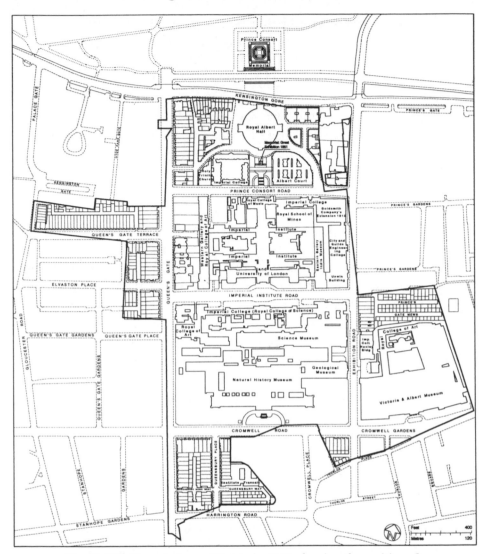

Fig 27. The Commissioners' Estate in 1951, showing the position after
the Second World War.

asking the President to preside over meetings of the Commission gradually fell into disuse, though the Princess Royal occasionally presided.[33]

SIR EDWARD PEACOCK'S CHAIRMANSHIP

Lord Macmillan served the Commission as Chairman for over twenty years, dying in office in 1952, and leaving the Board without an obvious successor. He himself had been recruited by Esher as a potential Chairman of the Board, but his own death seems to have taken his colleagues by surprise.

Sturch turned to the most senior member of the Board, the Canadian financier Sir Edward Peacock (1871–1962), who had joined the Board to manage the Commission's finances in 1934, and was in fact a year or two older than Macmillan. Peacock had had a remarkable career – starting from a modest manse in Ontario, he had worked his way through college at Queen's University, Ontario, going on to teach at the Canadian public school, Upper Canada College, Toronto. From a successful career as a teacher and housemaster, he entered a commercial firm which sent him to London in 1907 to take charge of its new European office. His work was so impressive that he came to the notice of Montagu Norman, the Governor of the Bank of England, who put him on the Court of the Bank of England in 1924. He joined Baring Brothers, and was recruited to the Council of the Duchy of Cornwall, as well as to a number of charities and educational foundations, like the King Edward VII Hospital Fund, and the Rhodes Trust. He kept his connections with Canada, where he was on the boards of the Hudson's Bay Company and the Canadian Pacific Railway.[34]

Peacock was diffident about taking on the chairmanship, possibly because of his age and deafness, and, though he took the chair on Macmillan's death, when he was offered the succession at a Board meeting in November 1952, he declined it. A number of other candidates were mooted, including Humphrey Mynors from the Bank of England, Lord Elton of the Rhodes Trust, (Sir) Oliver Franks and the senior civil servants Sir Edward Bridges and Sir John Maud. Only when Oliver Franks finally turned down the invitation to join the Board in November 1953, did Peacock agree to take on the chairmanship.[35] Possibly, he was influenced by the fact that in 1953 he formally retired, moving from Barings to a London base at the Savoy Hotel.

He was made Chairman at the Board Meeting in December 1953, and for the next nine years, despite increasing deafness, he both managed the Board and kept an eye on the Commission's finances. He was so success-ful that the Commission was able to invest the modest sums obtained from the estate, as well as a respectable surplus on current account, every year. He was also responsible for bringing the Commission's financial arrangements up to date. In May 1953, the Board transferred its invest-ment accounts from the Bank of England to Baring Brothers, and some years later, when the Bank of England closed its Law Courts branch, the Board moved its current account, terminating an arrangement which had lasted since the Great Exhibition.[36] Without infringing the rules con-trolling charities, Peacock gradually moved the Commission's portfolio from its earlier dependence on gilts to commercial preference shares, and even into equities. With Sturch's cooperation and the advice of 'Mr Lloyd' from Barings, his 'scheme to build up our resources as a safeguard against future contingencies' was implemented, as was his insistence on economy in the use of the Commission's resources.[37] Successful attempts were made to get the countries from which the Scholars came to supplement their awards. Starting with Canada and Australia, all the nominating dominions, including India and Pakistan, though not Eire, came to con-tribute.[38] In addition, the major British shipping companies, the Canadian Pacific Railway, Cunard, Union Castle and P & O, were persuaded to con-tinue their pre-war help with travel to overseas Scholars.

Peacock and Sturch were also careful to provide for the succession of new Commissioners, a term which was becoming increasingly identified with membership of the Board of Management, for, as Sturch pointed out, 'if new [Commission] members are needed it hardly seems worthwhile nowadays adding people who are not going to be members of the Board'. In an 'arbitrary classification', Sturch defined the membership of the Board in 1960, as two scientists, Sir Frank Smith and Sir Eric Rideal, two with a 'special interest in the humanities', T. S. R. Boase, President of Magdalen College, Oxford, and Sir Thomas Kendrick, a former Director of the British Museum, one from the City, Mynors, Deputy Governor of the Bank of England, and four with 'general interests', Shaw, Lord Tryon, Sir Keith Murray and the retired civil servant Sir Alan Barlow. As new recruits, he suggested Sir George Mallaby, former Secretary of the National Trust, a High Commissioner to New Zealand, and deputy Chairman of the University Grants Committee, Geoffrey Crowther, man-aging Editor of the *Economist,* and Trenchard Cox, Director of the

Victoria and Albert Museum from 1956 to 1966. To these three were added the scientist Lord Fleck, and Lord Nelson of Stafford.[39]

One reason why the Board had taken such an interest in the rent for the Imperial College site was their increasing unease over the funding of the award schemes.

The British School at Rome, despite an increased contribution from government, which contributed £12,000 out of the total cost of £25,000 in 1961, was badly hit by increased costs and inflation in Italy. Sir Alan Barlow, and later Boase, the Commission's representatives on the School Council, found themselves regularly asking for more money, both for the general running of the School, and for the award-holders. The annual grant rose from £5000 in 1951 to £8000 in 1961. There were also capital costs like the much-needed extension to the library. The Board was still confident of the School's 'valuable service to the humanities and the fine arts', though there was also some concern since the monumental sculpture, classical architecture and engraving, so fashionable when the Art Scholarships were founded before the 1914–18 War, were now regarded as *vieux jeux*, and artists and architects were not as keen to spend time in Rome.[40]

THE SCIENCE SCHOLARSHIPS IN DIFFICULTY

Most disquieting, however, was the position over the funding of the Science Scholarships, awards in which the Board rightly took great pride, particularly in the number of Scholars who had gone on to be Fellows of the Royal Society. In 1951, of a total of 769 Students and Scholars recorded in that year's edition of the *Record of Science Research Scholars*, 91 had become Fellows, about 12 per cent. The Scholarship Committee had agreed to reduce the number of the Senior Studentships to four, in order to finance the Overseas Scholarships, to which the Board attached great importance for their role in bringing young scholars from the different Commonwealth countries together. There was increasing competition for both types of candidates. Companies like Imperial Chemical Industries and Unilever were giving scholarships to attract rising young scientists, while a gradual falling-off in the applications, particularly from Canada, indicated that the mother country was no longer the magnet it had been. In June 1956, Sir Robert Robinson, a former 1851 Scholar who was retiring from the Chairmanship of the Committee, persuaded the Board to raise the value of all the awards. The Scholarship Committee saw that inflation was continually eroding the value of the awards, and considered that the Senior Studentships should rise from a total of £650 to £900, and the Overseas Scholarships from £450, plus an allowance for fees of £100, to £550, together with provision for an additional third year for some Scholars. The Board sanctioned this on the grounds that the Commissioners would not wish to see their awards relegated to second place.[41] A year later, the absence of good Canadian candidates was more marked, but by 1958, the new Chairman of the Scholarships Committee, Sir Eric Rideal, was able to report that the Canadian National Research Council had supplemented the Canadian awards, and this had improved the quality. While Australian Scholars would not be as immediately affected by opportunities in the United States, he thought that the Australian scientific authorities should also be asked to supplement their awards. His Committee considered that the Overseas Scholarships were so important that if necessary the studentships should be reduced in number. A warning against the current trends came from Sir Frank Smith, who stressed the importance of giving 'the best scientific talent in this country a free hand in research. There was a danger that research might be increasingly influenced by industrial requirements, whereas all the greatest scientific advances had sprung from non-industrial investigations'.[42]

The situation varied from year to year: in 1959 the quality of Canadian Scholars still seemed poor, and only eight out of ten Overseas Awards were made, but in 1960 the position was reversed, and six instead of five scholarships were given. In 1961, despite the threatened departure of South Africa from the Commonwealth, eleven awards were given, a full three to Canada, and an extra one to New Zealand. The following year the Committee gave an award to a candidate from Singapore, to replace the Indian one. Further problems were to arise – in a world where the winds of change were beginning to make themselves felt, the Science Scholarships Committee was forced to look at the anomalous situation in which long-standing, but technically departed, members of the Commonwealth, like Eire and South Africa, were given awards while the newly emerging African countries were not catered for.[43]

The last year of Peacock's Chairmanship was exercised from a hospital bed in the Royal Homoeopathic Hospital, whence directions came via his efficient secretary, Miss Dorothy Clarke, and the office at the Savoy. It may have been a measure of the respect in which Sir Edward was held by his fellows, or of the efficient way in which Sturch ran the Commission, but any attempt by the Secretary to get the Board to appoint a new Chairman was resisted, and only on Peacock's death in November 1962 was his successor appointed.

LORD MURRAY'S CHAIRMANSHIP

Sir Keith Murray (1900–93), later Lord Murray of Newhaven, who made his name as an agricultural economist, had had a widely varied career in business and education, from being Rector of Lincoln College, Oxford, and Director of the Bristol Aircraft Company, to advising on the development of arts and technology colleges, as well as being Chairman of the University Grants Commission (1953–63). He had been recruited as a potential Chairman in 1956. As the forthright Sir Frank Smith pointed out, he was one of the few members of the Board under sixty. He had a reputation as an efficient administrator who had worked on a number of public enquiries and government bodies. One of his colleagues on the University Grants Commission recalls how no meeting ever lasted for more than an hour and a half.[44]

Murray's tenure as Chairman was relatively short, under ten years, but he faced a number of very thorny issues. The traditions of the Commission had changed leaving him more freedom to modernize: thus the new President, the Duke of Edinburgh, did not preside over the biennial meetings of the Commission as the Princess Royal had occasionally done, so they became more of a formality; only one *ex officio* member, Geoffrey Ripon, as Minister of Works, took part in a meeting, while the older members began to resign or retire rather than soldier on, though Sir Evelyn Shaw did not retire from the Board of Management till 1970, when he had served on it as Secretary or Commissioner for sixty years.[45]

The financial position of both Commission and its tenants was difficult at this period. Peacock's transfer of the Commission's funds to equities was a sound decision in the long term, but necessarily reduced its income. The struggle to get a fair price out of the District Valuer for properties sold to Imperial College continued. Even some of the established tenants were in difficulties, like the Royal Albert Hall.

KEEPING THE ROYAL ALBERT HALL GOING

The Hall had already done a great deal since the war to put its affairs on a sound footing. The problem was the same one as had led the Commissioners to give up their seats in 1908, that of the cost and the difficulty of funding regular maintenance, and the reluctance of the seat-holders to pay a seat rate adequate to the task. Immediately after the war, with a daunting report on the condition of the fabric and repairs estimated at between £250,000 and £500,000, Sir John Wardlaw-Milne, President of the Hall, appealed unsuccessfully to the government for a loan to assist in the restoration of the fabric. The solution was a further Act of Parliament putting matters on a sounder footing. By the 1951 Act the seat-holders were obliged to contribute a capital charge of £280, payable over forty years, and the Hall's powers to borrow were raised from the 1927 limit of £100,000 to £500,000. Finally, its revenue-earning powers were increased by allowing the management to exclude seat-holders from at least ten public occasions, and eight private functions organized for a specialized audience. This provision increased the revenue-earning powers of the Hall, and made it more commercially viable. Lord Pender, who succeeded as President of the Hall, even managed to persuade the Treasury to provide an interest-free loan of £40,000.[46]

However, some ten years later financial problems had again arisen, and Sir Louis Gluckstein, now President, was forced to contemplate a radical solution. As Evelyn Shaw reported to the Board, 'the financial position of the Hall was now precarious, and there were outstanding loans of some £81,000 secured on the seat rate and capital contributions'. An 'immense amount of repair work' was needed, 'including a new heating system, rebuilding of the organ, reupholstering of the seating . . . their income is not very elastic, and they are . . . feeling the draught from the subsidized establishments such as the Festival Hall, Covent Garden, and so on'.[47]

One of the seat-holders approached the Board to enquire what view the Commissioners, as ground landlords, would take of a proposal to demolish and rebuild the Hall. A recent proposal by the Council to promote a Bill giving them powers to raise the seat rate, and wider powers of exclusion of seat-holders for commercial reasons had failed. The lease reverted to the Board should the management of the Hall fail to carry out its functions, so if the latter were involved in any change of scheme, the Board members were advised that they should insist on a new lease. It was also clear that under the terms of their Charter it would be more suitable to use the Hall or the site for a 'cultural and scientific centre', than allow it to be 'exploited further' as a similar sort of concert hall or place of entertainment. Happily the Commission did not agree to the project to demolish and rebuild the Hall. Had they done so, it is likely that they would have been faced by a storm besides which the 'battle' over the Imperial Institute would have paled into insignificance. In due course, this message was relayed to Sir Louis Gluckstein, and seems to have put an end to the scheme, the problem being solved by a further Act giving the Council of the Hall more commercial powers. Matters were improved by stronger internal management, and a more efficient use of the Hall's resources. In 1971, the Hall's centenary year, Sir Louis organized a successful appeal.[48] This enabled the Hall to soldier on, until some twenty-five years later the National Lottery provided funds to refurbish a building for which the British public have long had a somewhat ambivalent admiration. *The Times* summed it up in 1950:

> We laugh at the Albert Hall, we shrug our shoulders in despair at its acoustics, but we have an affection for it, and we will even grudgingly admit that its Victorian size and accoutrements have a certain swagger and solidity which we envy.[49]

FINANCING THE COMMISSION

A major problem for Murray was finding money to enable the Commission to carry on its work; this issue was to force the Commission to rethink their awards, a process which was to cause individual members of the Board considerable discomfort and indeed some unhappiness, as treasured clients were abandoned, and cherished causes found their funding cut back. Despite his predecessor's shrewd handling of the Commission's finances, and the bargain struck with the Ministry over the land for Imperial College, the resources available for the various awards were increasingly inadequate: there were now more and better financed schemes in the field like the Commonwealth Scholarships, which it was feared would affect the quality of the Overseas Scholarships field.

One concern was the rising cost of the activities being supported by the Commission in a period when trustee securities were not providing much of a return[50] while the Commission's rental income was restricted by the preponderance of academic tenants, and the effect of the rent acts on its remaining residential properties. Despite a bold statement by Frank Smith on the value of the Commission's work at the meeting of the Commission in 1962, and the possibility of outside funding to enable it to carry on, a radical approach was necessary.

Another problem which concerned Murray was whether the Commission was fulfilling its supplementary Charter obligations to encourage the application of art and science in the interests of productive industry, or whether it was spending too much on pure science and pure art.

THE BRITISH SCHOOL AT ROME

In a sense this applied particularly to the funding of the British School, where there were doubts as to whether the support for the Faculty of Fine Arts in Rome was in accordance with the Commission's charter obligation. Financial problems were particularly acute, since the pound sterling was worth less and less. Recent devaluation against the lira had stretched the Commissioners' ability to help. Though the School had completed the extension of the library, financed by a widespread appeal in 1962–4, its buildings were becoming outdated, and needed radical restoration and improvement if it was to continue to attract students of quality. The Commission was heavily involved with the School, since Digby Sturch, the Secretary, was also Honorary General Secretary of the School, whose London office shared premises with the Commission. The School was represented on the Board of Management by Boase, and Shaw, who, having in effect set up the Fine Art Faculties under Lord Esher, had a strong loyalty to the School.

Poised, as it were, between the arts and sciences interests on the Board, Murray turned to Lionel Robbins of the London School of Economics as a respected and independent figure:

> We felt that the time had come to have a look at long term policy; after all, we are merely trustees; we have not really had a general or extensive look at what we are doing since 1911; and we might be open to criticism, when the demands on our funds are growing . . . if we did not review the position.

He wanted Boase and the banker, Sir Humphrey Mynors, to review the position together with Robbins. He thought that they should 'consider such issues as the role of the school today? does it require modification in its general or its particular activities? should there be any change in the system of scholarships, instituted in the circumstances of the last century'. He intended that the School should be told what was going on, and that any change should be gradual.[51]

Sturch was clear that any report 'should be mainly concerned with whether in this day and age the sending of young artists to Rome (or artists of the kind we are dealing with) is a proper use of the Commissioners' funds – and of Treasury funds'. The intention was not to examine the 'competence' of the Executive Committee or the way in which the various faculties conducted business, but comment on such matters could not be entirely ruled out.

John Ward-Perkins (1912–81), who had been Director of the School since 1945, produced his comments on the four Art Faculties supported by the Commissioners, Painting, Engraving, Sculpture and Architecture, urging that they should be shaken up by rotating the senior members as the Faculty of Archaeology had decided to do, and thus getting rid of 'dead wood'.

Shaw responded that Ward-Perkins was the 'best *administrator*' that the School had had since 1911. 'He has managed – as no-one else was able to do – to put the School, its archaeological side, in the fore-front of the foreign academies in Rome, which is a very great achievement. His energy is remarkable and is exercised dispassionately over the whole school' . He was less enthusiastic about Ward-Perkins' scholarship, or his 'understanding of the artist's mind'.[52]

Personalities aside, the Fine Arts faculties were facing considerable problems: the conditions under which the scholarships had been devised had changed radically, and, even in 1912, there had been an element of retrospection. As Shaw told Sturch:

> I knew from our earliest reports that what made the French preeminent in design at the Great Exhibition was their practice of recruiting designers from their most highly trained art students, and . . . what we needed most to carry out the Commissioners' wishes was an opportunity for our ablest students to forget their art school discipline and to devote themselves for 2 or 3 years to unimpeded study and creative work in the atmosphere of a great art centre.[53]

However, Rome in 1964 was no longer the Rome of 1900, in which 'France and the other great nations' maintained 'finishing schools or academies of art'. Then the British painting scholarship had been set up to encourage monumental painting when representational art was all the rage, and Sargent's murals, of 1890–1916, in the Boston Public Library were fresh and new. The inquiry brought out the problem of choosing artists who would benefit from being in Rome, and not just taking candidates who wanted the prestigious prize and the opportunity to spend a year without financial worries. There were complaints about the abstract artists who were 'studio-burrowers', and could not be lured out of them to benefit from the sights and art of Rome. The same problem applied to sculpture, where the School had been set up under the inspiration of men like Thomas Brock, whose over life-size statues had adorned both Buckingham Palace and the British Pavilion in Rome. Again the problem was finding someone, even if his or her work was abstract rather than representational, who 'was genuinely interested in some aspect . . . of the Italian scene – its buildings, its galleries, its people or its countryside'. Engraving, originally funded by Stephen Courtauld, so fashionable when the scholarships were devised, was now much less so, and the so-called engravers who took the engraving prizes appeared to be 'crypto-artists'. The Faculty of Architecture had retained a membership of die-hard classicists – as Ward-Perkins observed, it was hard to see a body which included Arthur Davis (1878–1951), a member of the partnership which had designed the Ritz Hotel, or Sir Albert Richardson (1880–1964), 'as representative of the sort of thing that appeals to the young architect today'. Moreover, there was some difficulty in attracting the newly qualified architects for whom the scholarships were designed; in the heady atmosphere of post-war town-planning and reconstruction, jobs were easy to come by, and Sturch said baldly that the main demand for the scholarships came from Australia. He felt that a shorter tenure aimed at older architects who needed a sabbatical might be preferable.[54]

Boase asked Sturch to provide a list of 'successful scholars' and the posts they held, provoking the brisk reply that 'the after-careers of artists are reflected more in their incomes than their posts'.[55] However, the Commission could point to a number of successful award-holders: prominent sculptors like G. Ledward, Sargeant Jagger, and A. F. Hardiman, and artists like Winifred Knights, Thomas Monnington, PRA, and Edward Halliday. Engraving was far from fashionable, but the long list of architects included the town-planners William Holford, and C. A. Minoprio, and a number who had become Professors of Architecture at Edinburgh and Sheffield.[56]

All these comments were submitted to an authoritative quartet – Boase and Mynors for the Commission, and Robbins and Mortimer Wheeler, the Secretary, for the British Academy. The upshot of this activity was that, in Boase's words, Robbins, whose advice had been so carefully sought, appeared to favour the retention of the status quo:

> The archaeological side of it he is entirely satisfied about. He also thinks that we have been quite right to try and review the position, even though he does not think it calls for any drastic change. In fact I think it is now clear that we shall carry on along similar lines.[57]

However, Sturch had identified that there was a more profound question for the 1851 Commission to answer; he questioned whether the awards were being

> offered in the right sorts of subjects. The emphasis in the Commissioners' Charter is on the applications of science and art. Is it really for them to sponsor awards to students whose interests are only in art for art's sake? The Rome Scholarships were originally offered for *mural* painting and for sculpture which had some architectural setting. Now, owing to the swing to purely subjective work, the competitions can only be maintained by giving the Scholarships for 'pure' painting and sculpture. There would otherwise be no candidates.
>
> I feel that the earlier idea of awards for 'applied art' might be revived and carried further, so that the awards could be offered for such subjects as ceramics, graphic design, industrial design (furniture, silver work, etc).[58]

Shaw agreed that the transfer of funding to applied instead of 'pure' art was a good idea, and would be in line with the Charter; however, no such changes were carried out.

A further investigation into the School was undertaken during Murray's chairmanship, in 1968, this time together with the British Academy, which supported the Faculties of History and Archaeology. As Murray explained to Sir Kenneth Wheare, President of the British Academy:

> Under their Charter the Commissioners are charged to 'increase the means of industrial education and extend the influences of science

and art upon productive industry' . . . The Board of Management has recently been reviewing its activities. There are serious doubts about whether this particular scheme, designed some fifty-seven years ago and centred in the School in Rome, is today the best way of extending the influence of art on industry. It ties up a large part of our limited resources.

. . . Our particular anxiety is to be sure whether it is in the national interest that we should continue to spend a large sum ($£$11,600) on the School and its Scholarships in their present form.[59]

It was agreed that a committee should be set up of members of the Academy, and, on Murray's suggestion, with 'outsiders' like Sir Colin Anderson, the shipping magnate, and the designer Sir Paul Reilly, rather than members of the 1851 Commission. It was a potentially difficult situation, since as Sturch noted, Murray 'would like to curtail, if not abandon, the Commissioners' grant [while] the Academy would like it to continue'. 'Lord Robbins', he observed, 'seems very *pro* Rome scholarships'.[60]

The outcome was the setting-up of a small committee under Robbins, which included Sir Colin Anderson, Sir Anthony Blunt, then head of the Courtauld Institute, Mortimer Wheeler, Milner Gray and Derek Allen, Secretary of the British Academy, the institution which provided the archaeology faculty with its funds. The Committee produced a report in February 1970, which succinctly and clearly reviewed the history of the School and the Royal Commission's contribution. It considered a large number of criticisms, which ranged from those claiming that students did not spend enough time in Rome or with their colleagues at other national academies, to the nature of the funding, and the way in which the School's resources were allocated. It concluded that the School, 'on the present formula, remains a national asset, which this country could ill-afford to lose'. It could not be easily relocated, though Rome was not an ideal centre for industrial design. The Report went on to make a number of suggestions as to the better management of the School, advocating the amalgamation of the three Fine Art disciplines, Painting, Sculpture and Engraving, into a single faculty of Fine Arts, but leaving Architecture independent. The Faculty of Archaeology was on the whole regarded as satisfactory, though the funding of both sides of the School's activities clearly affected the Commission's finances. However, it considered that as long as the Fine Arts side continued, it was 'incumbent on the 1851 Commissioners to give it such support as they can', and in any case, not to withdraw their support before September 1971, and then only if replacement funds were available.

The Commission found the Report on the whole encouraging, and decided to continue the grant at the current level of £11,600 a year, for the next six years with a review in due course.[61]

However, the financial position did not improve, and the demands on the Commission's income did not diminish. The matter of the Science Scholarships was revived a few years later, partly because of the impact of institutions like the University Grants Commission, and the influence of the Department of Education and Science, both of which had funds which dwarfed those of the Commission. The latter had started its grant-giving activities when there were few sources of money available to students; by 1964, grants for students of promise were commonplace, and far larger from government organizations than from the Commission.[62] The competition for scientists of quality was fierce, and Sturch was approached by an American scientist suggesting that if there were a shortage of post-graduate posts in the United Kingdom, young British graduates should be encouraged to take up teaching posts at 'second-flight' American universities. Murray was doubtful: 'I am chary of this proposition. There is a very determined and acknowledged drive by the Americans to recruit our best young scientists and I do not think that a stipulation about returning to this country would be effective in the long run'.

By 1963, Murray was so concerned over this 'drive' that he wrote to Sir Howard Florey, the Australian scientist who had done so much to develop penicillin at Oxford during the war, who was President of the Royal Society. The Scholarship Committee discussed whether some of the Senior Studentships should be specifically targeted at scientists working in America, in the hope of encouraging them to return. This was not carried out, though the decision was taken to raise the stipends in 1964. Otherwise the Committee endorsed the current policy of Senior Studentships in conjunction with postgraduate Overseas Scholarships open to Commonwealth countries, with the addition of Eire and South Africa. They were prepared to give awards for applied science as well as pure science, but not to 'earmark awards' for the former.[63]

By the following year, the retiring Chairman of the Science Scholarship Committee, Sir Eric Rideal, was rather in favour of radical change to the scheme in view of the Commonwealth and other awards available, but thought that such decisions should be taken by the Board rather than the Science Scholarships Committee. The matter was raised at the Board, but the decision was taken to continue the present awards as long as the quality of candidates remained high, though Murray took the opportunity to suggest that the 'Commissioners must soon consider whether the time had come to use their funds in a new way'. Sir Willis Jackson, an electrical engineer at Imperial College and a former Industrial Bursar was recruited to the Committee for his advice in the technological field.[64]

Murray found a powerful ally in his attempt to redirect the efforts of the Commissioners to the 'greater need for supporting research into the application of the arts and sciences rather than for pure research'. The new President, the Duke of Edinburgh, who succeeded the Princess Royal in 1965, was known for his 'great interest in science and technology, and in the exchange of students'. In one of his first messages to the Commissioners, the new President pointed out that 'the 1851 Exhibition was very much a festival of applied science and technology so that it would be quite in keeping to extend the scholarship scheme', suggesting either management training for technologists, or the extension of teaching of technology to schools.[65]

This suggestion bore fruit in 1968 when the Board set up the Senior Industrial Fellowships in conjunction with the Council of Engineering Institutions, agreeing to dedicate some £75,000 to the project over the next seven years. This tempted back to a Commissioners' meeting the most senior of the *ex officio* members, the President of the Institution of Civil Engineers.

The need for a new initiative was underlined by the termination of the long-standing engineering postgraduate award in Naval Architecture for lack of demand. Its funds were absorbed by the Science Scholarships Committee[66] which, even at this difficult time, could congratulate itself on the strong demand for both types of science award.

XI

Technology to the Fore:
Changing the Commissioners' Awards –
A New View of Albertopolis
1970–2000

Digby Sturch retired in the course of 1970, with tributes from the Commissioners, and from the British School, for 'his quiet efficiency . . . and his knowledge of the School and its administration [which] have been of great assistance in their deliberations'.[1] He was appointed to the Board at the next Commission meeting, and was succeeded as Secretary by Anthony James, who had worked with him for over twenty years.

THE BRITISH SCHOOL AT ROME

Changes in the work of the Commission, and in the office, followed, driven to some extent by Murray. As Sturch explained to Boase:

> [Murray] is clearly of the opinion that the School should ultimately be entirely divorced from the Commission, with the exception of the annual grant. On the other hand he seems to picture it as a slow process and is content to carry on as at present with James running the school administration from Lowther Gardens . . . supported not by a junior edition of himself but by some capable person (perhaps a woman) who could do some of the routine work but also understudy him to some extent.[2]

As Sturch recognized, there was to be a break in the tradition of the Secretary being succeeded by the Assistant Secretary. A 'capable woman' was indeed found in Kathleen Stedman, who worked with James until they both retired in 1987. James also brought in a more informal style, in due course addressing Elworthy as 'Sam', whereas Murray had always been addressed by Sturch by his title. The Science Scholarships Committee elected its first woman member, the distinguished chemist Dame Kathleen Lonsdale (1903–71), Professor Emeritus from University College, London.[3]

Murray retired from the Board in July the following year, though remaining on the Commission, and was succeeded as Chairman of the Board of Management by the New Zealander Marshal of the Royal Air Force Sir Charles Elworthy, Constable of Windsor Castle. Elworthy was confronted by many of the same problems, but at least Murray had set in train measures to deal with them, through his insistence that the Commission's 'educational activities deriving from the Charter should be continuously tested in the light of contemporary needs'.[4] The Board was in a position to reduce its commitment to the British School, the Naval Scholarship had come to an end, and the Commission had been relieved of the struggle to compete on equal terms with other bodies giving grants to Commonwealth scholars. Murray was also responsible for establishing the biennial dinner attended by the President for current and past Scholars, and for the informal annual cocktail party when Scholars and their spouses had the opportunity to meet members of the Board of Management and the Science Scholarships Committee.

The new policy towards the British School in Rome was clearly laid down in the Board's Report in 1969, when it had been agreed that the Art Scholarships and the relatively modest grant should be continued annually until 1976. 'During this period the Board will have time to consider alternative means of further education and the application of the creative arts to industry. Their underlying principle is rather to remain flexible in order to meet changing needs than to embark on long-term commitments'.[5]

The awards were continued, though they did not take account of inflation. In 1979, the Board considered a paper produced by Digby Sturch, and decided to continue the two scholarships for architecture and printmaking until 1981. They later reconsidered the matter of the other two scholarships, but gave the School notice that they would not provide support for painting or sculpture beyond 1983, though they would continue with the architecture and the engraving scholarships, which they saw as nearer to applied art.[6]

The Commission's major problem was rampant inflation, which necessitated large increases in the stipends. The story is told in the Commission's accounts: in 1961 the cost of the Senior Studentships was

£6600, by 1971, £14,100, in 1975, £17,600; by 1984 the renamed Science Research Scholarships cost £54,500. The story was the same for the Overseas Scholarships: in 1961 about £15,500, ten years later it was £26,700, and by 1984, shortly before they were discontinued, £176,500. Equally, to attract candidates of quality the stipends had to rise, annually at the end of the period; £900 in 1965 for the Overseas Scholars, twice as much ten years later, and in 1988, their last year, £5080. In the same period the stipends for the Science Research Scholars rose from £1300 in 1965 to between £10,670 and £11,275 in 1988. The problems were compounded by a change in government policy about the funding of universities, and an attempt to get students from abroad, from the Commonwealth or elsewhere, to pay fees. In addition, university departments, conscious of the costs of a well-equipped research environment, were charging students laboratory fees. However, it was not the sheer cost which brought about the changes in the Commission's award policy, so much as a renewed interest in the terms of the Commission's Charter, and disquiet about the state of manufacturing in Britain. It was a return to the same concerns which had led Esher so long ago to create the Industrial Bursars.

This process of rethinking the policy on awards had been begun under Murray, and with considerable encouragement from the President it was pursued with increasing effect over the next fifteen years, in due course revolutionizing the educational work of the Commission.

However, in 1971 the mid-term review of the Senior Industrial Fellowships was so disappointing that the decision was taken to terminate them. It was agreed that no more awards would be given, leaving the money unallocated. A suggestion came from the President for the support of an educational venture, the Standing Conference on Schools Science and Technology (SCSST), set up in 1971 to coordinate the activities of schools committees, devoted to increasing the understanding at school level of the development of applied science and technology. The Board agreed to allocate £5000 a year for 1973–5. Unfortunately, by the third year of the Standing Conference's grant the Commission's finances were so straitened that they had to ask some hard questions as to alternative funding, and to warn the SCSST that the grant might have to be spread over several years or even to cease. Through the intervention of the President, this was averted, and the SCSST was one of the bodies given a start-up grant through the Board's new thrust towards encouraging the teaching of technology and applied science.

Initially, change was gradual, and the Board altered the policy for the existing awards, encouraging the Science Scholarships Committee to focus on applied science and technology. The Committee was already under financial pressure, and in 1976 had to report that it was impossible to continue both the Fellowships and the Overseas Scholarships. At the following meeting the Chairman of the Committee, Sir Harrie Massey, himself a former Senior Student in 1931–3, supported by Sir John Hackett, the Principal of King's College, London, made an impassioned plea for giving preference to the Overseas Scholarships, underlining

> the great goodwill for the United Kingdom which the . . . Scholarships Scheme engenders in the Commonwealth and elsewhere and that, as well as the advantages to British Universities from the presence of overseas post-graduates there was substantial benefit to the UK in the export of scientific and engineering equipment.[7]

Sir Ian Wark, a former Science Research Scholar, and a distinguished industrial chemist from Australia, a member of the Commonwealth Science and Industrial Research Organization, analysed the benefits to Australia from the 1851 awards. By 1961, some 180 Scholars had benefited, 'most drawn to the United Kingdom, where they have been the recipients of unexpected kindness from successive Secretaries'. He paid tribute to the insistence on 'proved capacity for original work', and the shrewd manner in which they were selected. 'Almost without exception scholars have made highly significant contributions to education and science, either back home in Australia or abroad'. He noted that, of the award-winners before 1950, half went into industry, but that since then more had stayed at university, and half of those achieving professorial rank had remained abroad. Though some Australians had made their careers and their names in the United Kingdom, like Sir Robert Robinson (1907), H. S.W. Massie and A. R. Todd, both senior students in 1931, the contribution to Australian science was very considerable. Thomas H. Laby had established the 'strongest university research school in the southern hemisphere' at Melbourne, in due course sending some thirteen of his students to Britain on the Commissioners' awards, and many members of the Australian Academy of Sciences had started their careers as 1851 Scholars. 'At times', he concluded, 'England has been generous beyond measure to the member countries of the Commonwealth – perhaps in no way more handsomely than through this scholarship scheme.'[8]

The Commission avoided the issue of discriminating between the awards, and, in fact, raised the stipends, partly made possible by the increasing returns from the estate. However, the educational policy of the Commission was about to change with the appointment of a new Chairman and the recruitment of more members dedicated to the support of engineering and technology.

SIR RICHARD WAY'S CHAIRMANSHIP, 1978–87

In 1977, Elworthy announced his intention of retiring to New Zealand, and Sir John Hackett was asked to take on the chairmanship, but declined and indeed left the Commission. However, his successor at King's College, Sir Richard Way (1914–98), was offered the job, and accepted. As *The Times* later put it, Way was one of the best administrators of his generation. He had begun with a very distinguished career in the civil service, entering the War Office as a non-graduate and rising to a high post in the War Office, and then to become Permanent Secretary of the Ministry of Civil Aviation. Leaving the civil service in his early fifties, he followed this by a spell in industry, on the board of BOAC, and as Chairman of London Transport 1970–4, adding the chairmanship of the Council of Roedean School and King's College to his portfolio of interests.[9] Unusually, perhaps, for such a high-achiever, 'Sam' Way, as he was universally known, was popular with his colleagues, and this doubtless helped him to push through a number of changes and make his time as Chairman of the Board of Management one of significance.

Way set in train a programme of change, not only in the way in which the Commission's funds were spent, but in the way its resources were managed. In 1981 a small finance Committee was set up to manage investment policy and the estate, to whom Barings Bank and the Surveyor would report.[10] Concern was expressed about administrative costs, and the British School was persuaded to contribute its share of the cost of running the office at 1 Lowther Gardens, though the disposal of the office was also in contemplation with the prospect of the end of the tenants' lease.

More engineers were recruited to the Board, including Hugh Conway, who had been Managing Director of Shorts Belfast, and then of Bristol Siddeley Engines, and who was a prominent advocate of the need for education in industrial design. Another was Sir Arnold Hall, whose distinguished career has included the Chair of Engineering at Imperial College, heading the Royal Aeronautical Research unit at Farnborough, and a range of Board appointments in industry. A third was Sir Denis Rooke, Chairman of British Gas, who had pioneered the use of natural gas in the United Kingdom, and was President of the Fellowship (now the Royal Academy) of Engineering.[11]

Way also revived Sir Edward Playfair's idea, first mooted in the 1960s, that the Board should commission a history of the Commissioners' development of education on the South Kensington estate, proposing that the Professor of History at King's College, London, should be asked to suggest a student, who might be interested in it as a thesis subject. Subsequently, a number of names from the Victoria and Albert Museum were approached, and through a Board member's contact with the newspaper magnate Robert Maxwell, Pergamon Press expressed an interest. A number of avenues were explored and in the event, this book was the outcome.[12]

At the 1979 summer meeting, the question of the awards was raised, and while the Science Scholarships Committee argued that the scholarships offered in technology and applied science did not attract enough strong candidates, Hugh Conway, and Dr Pope from Aston University, took up the cudgels on behalf of technology and engineering. They pointed to the increasing cost of the Overseas Scholarships. They put forward the case that the national interest in engineering and technology had to be stimulated, not only at university and polytechnic level but also earlier, at school; for far too long, they maintained, priority had been given to the pure sciences at the expense of manufacturing industry. The ratio of potential engineers and technologists to scientists was very much out of proportion, and engineering and industry were regarded as poor seconds to scientific careers.

Even the engineers did not agree: Frederick Warner observed that 'the difficulty had been compounded when Colleges of Advanced Technology and polytechnics had moved away from a technological and engineering base towards the sciences, and the schools did little to stimulate the personal creativity which marked out the best future engineers. Engineering was not, indeed, primarily a university or academic activity'. With so little certainty as to the best way forward, the solution was a working party to review educational policy. Meanwhile the Board decided to continue the existing Research Fellowships and Overseas Scholarships on the present scale, and, convinced by Sturch's paper on the British School at Rome, to maintain the two scholarships in architecture and printmaking. It was decided that science and technology would 'also be promoted' through a grant to the Standing Conference on Schools Science and Technology for the next three years.[13]

The two sorts of science awards continued, with efforts to alert vice-chancellors to the fact that they were available for applied science and technology as well as 'pure science'. But the following year the review of educational policy bore fruit in the form of two joint courses suggested by Conway, one between two South Kensington institutions – the Royal College of Art and Imperial College, and the second between the former and Cranfield College of Technology. The Cranfield course was for two Research Fellows with industrial experience to work on problems in engineering design with particular reference to computer-aided design, with the general intention of fostering collaboration in the teaching of engineering design and industrial design. The South Kensington course was an industrial studentship scheme for selected engineering graduates to join a new postgraduate course in industrial design and engineering, jointly promoted by the two Royal Colleges. In the words of the Working Group, both schemes were aimed at 'bridging the long-standing gulf between engineering design based on the applied sciences and industrial design based on the art-school tradition', and also at increasing consciousness of commercial needs by 'promoting the importance of market analysis and the matching of product design to market needs'.[14]

The schemes were launched in September 1980, and celebrated by a dinner at Imperial College on 24 November. Together with the launch of the engineering courses, the Board continued to fund scholarships at the British School at Rome, even agreeing to support painting and sculpture until 1986. Sir Arnold Hall, together with Conway, questioned whether the award was in order, suggesting that 'the present proposal represented an extra allocation for activities in the pursuit of which the Commissioners could conceivably be adjudged as acting *ultra vires*'. They considered that the Commissioners should, in the national interest, be devoting more resources for training engineers and applied scientists.[15]

In marked contrast to the research scholarships, which were nearing their centenary, the engineering awards were not well known, though the Board had assistance in publicizing them from the Fellowship of

Engineering. There was even a suggestion that firms were not always anxious to allow promising young engineers leave of absence for research and training, and indeed that universities were not necessarily the best places for engineers to pursue research. A working party set up with the Fellowship of Engineering had identified *ad hoc* needs rather than long-term initiatives.

However, the well-established Research Fellowships and Overseas Scholarships were advertised to attract more students in applied science and technology, a point made regularly by Sir Denys Wilkinson, the distinguished nuclear physicist, who chaired the Science Scholarships Committee. In addition, it was claimed that scientists who started in 'pure science' often moved on to applied science. In 1985, Wilkinson pointed out that the dilemma was to attract more engineers, without sacrificing 'the distinguished and long-standing awards [which] have been essentially pure-science orientated'. However, as he pointed out, the new direction was succeeding so well that the Scholars whose reports had been circulated were divided almost equally between applied science, pure science and fields with development potential in applied science, which he termed 'strategic science'. Of the successful twelve Overseas Scholars, four could be categorized as pure scientists, four as working in 'strategic science' and four as working in applied science.[16]

Despite these reports, some members of the Board, led by Way, and supported by the President, continued to press for more emphasis on the needs of training in applied science and technology. As the Imperial ideal of bringing British scientists together faded, there was a feeling that the balance between home and overseas was now wrong, and that more should be done for the United Kingdom.[17]

Encouraged by the President's concern about the needs of British industry for research in engineering and applied technology, considerable progress was made by the Board during Way's chairmanship. Nevertheless, there remained a reluctance to change on the part of some veteran members, partly because no inspiring new scheme had emerged from the working party with the Fellowship of Engineering, though a number of useful small schemes had been developed and implemented.

There was also considerable opposition in the Scholarships Committee to the proposed emphasis on engineering and technology, not only as a matter of principle but also because of the competition for scarce funds. However, increases in the property market were benefiting the Commission's funds, while the British School had been put on notice that its awards would be reduced. Moreover, while the Science Scholarships were inflation-proofed, those for the School were continued at the same level. However, a new departure was made easier by changes in office arrangements which brought an increased income in their train.

THE KENSINGTON ESTATE

There was a beneficial side to inflation, since there was a considerable growth in the value of the Commissioners' estate. Immediately after the war, the Board had resigned itself to dispose of all the land known as 'the private estate', that is the part which had not been handed over to academic or education institutions for the national benefit. However, by the 1960s the attitude was changing, with encouragement from the Commissioners' surveyors, Holroyd Chambers, and Stuart Hibberdine, who had succeeded him in 1967. This was partly due to external forces; thus in 1972, a long-planned sale of 186–95 Queen's Gate with the mews behind to Imperial College was turned down by the University Grants Commission, which was unable or unwilling to pay the price agreed between the Commission's Surveyor and the District Valuer. This was a reflection of the way in which houses in South Kensington were rising in value, and it was paralleled by a more long-term approach to investment on the part of the Board.

However, the efforts needed to keep the estate going in a period of inflation were still considerable. There were blocks of flats remaining in Queen's Gate where some of the tenants had protected status, which made it impossible for the Commission to manage the block profitably. Immediately after the war, the Commissioners might have sold them, but by the 1970s they were attempting to regain possession and ensure they were a long-term source of income. This change in approach had been recommended by the surveyor, in a report presented in 1959. Chambers advocated that the Commission should come to terms with the tenants and pay them to leave. The policy of selling freeholds was altered, and a large block at the top of Queen's Gate was retained as long-term rental property to increase the Commission's income.[18] These manoeuvres were ultimately successful despite the considerable depression in the London housing market in the early 1970s.

Thereafter, the Commissioners were more ready to retain their investment in property, on occasion even investing in property elsewhere in

London. Even the Commission's office arrangements came under review; and, when the Physical Society declined to pay a more realistic rent for the top floors of Lowther Gardens than the previous £3175, and decided to move, the Board's Surveyor obtained a commercial rent from a public relations company of £18,750.[19] Even the development of 1–7 Cromwell Gardens, an island block which had been alienated in 1912 to the government, brought a small bonus to the Commission. This site had been sold to the National Theatre Trustees before the Second World War, and they had commissioned a scheme from Lutyens. After the war, the National Theatre was offered a larger site on the South Bank, and the site in the middle of the Brompton Road became redundant. The Board was consulted about the uses and the architectural schemes, and were able to sell a small piece of garden to the ultimate owners the Ismaili Centre. All these capital sums were ploughed back either to obtain possession of protected tenancies or into the Commission's share portfolio.

However, as Richard Way said in the 1978 Report, though these sales had added £1,170,000 to the Commission's funds, there would not be such a bonanza again until the next leases fell in, in forty years' time, and serious thought must be given to the future.[20]

Some of the academic tenants too found conditions difficult: Imperial College was refused permission by government to buy 186–95 Queen's Gate with the Jays Mews houses behind, partly because of a dispute between the University Grants Commission, whose clients they were, and the Department of Education and Science which was responsible for the College of Art. The houses, many of which were occupied by protected tenants, and some of which had been squatted in by students, reverted to the Commission as ground landlords. By 1975, the Commissioners had almost got possession of numbers 192–3 and 186–8, which they hoped to sell to the East Germans as an embassy. In the event, numbers 186–8 were bought by the Bulgarians as embassy tenants, together with the mews houses behind, injecting much-needed capital into the Commission's funds.[21] In the changing conservation climate, and as more importance came to be attached to Victorian buildings, the Royal College of Art was refused permission to demolish 25 Kensington Gore and the houses in Jay's Mews. The College of Art managed to solve its problem by developing the site behind the façade to Queen's Gate, though the Commission insisted on sharing in the commercial profit they made from the site.

Queen Alexandra's House found it impossible to meet the Greater London Council fire regulations in its extensive buildings, and the Chairman, Sir Louis Gluckstein, appealed to the Commissioners for help. Elworthy had to reply that they too 'were in difficulties . . . like so many charities in these inflationary times'. Queen Alexandra's House, which had found an 'anonymous benefactor' to pay its bill when it was £100,000, could not raise £260,000 when the GLC's demands became more stringent, and was forced to sell off a lease of a part of the building to the London Festival Ballet. The purchase and development of the Ballet's part of the premises was funded by grants from the GLC and the Arts Council.[22]

The Royal College of Organists which occupied the handsome building which was the original home of the National Training School for Music, the forerunner of the Royal College of Music, approached the Commissioners for an extension of the lease in 1986. It had hoped to extend on the same terms, but was informed that the College would be expected to pay rather more than the peppercorn rent it had enjoyed for the best part of a century. In fact, the building was too large, and the College was able to depart with a substantial payment for the end of the lease. However, when the building came to be sold, though other tenants on the estate wanted it, it went to the highest bidder, a commercial developer, who has, happily, refurbished the building and has restored the magnificent façade. The Board had to take this approach because of the increasing needs of its award-holders.

REORGANIZATION IN 1988

Anthony James (1922–97) had worked for the Commission since 1947, when he had joined its staff as Assistant Secretary. He was the last of a triumvirate of full-time Secretaries who served the Commission throughout their working lives. The seventy-five years between Shaw's appointment, as the first full-time professional Secretary, and Anthony James's retirement saw the transformation of the Commission into 'a Royal educational trust'. This had been achieved by the development of the Commission's educational schemes through several types of scientific and industrial scholarship, and the initiation of the Fine Art Scholarships at the British School at Rome. James and his assistant Kathleen Stedman were due to retire in 1987, and this coincided with the Board's decision to sell the office at 1 Lowther Gardens, and to seek more modest offices.

The Lowther Gardens office was vacated in the course of 1986, when the Commission's staff was reduced, and transferred to smaller offices within Imperial College. This necessitated the disposal of the furniture, some of which was of a more stately era, and a number of pictures and ephemera.[23] The archives were moved to Imperial College, and an archivist taken on to the staff to index them.

A successor to James was found in the Whitehall Department which had absorbed Sir Richard Way's old ministry. Michael Neale, CB, a civil servant with a background in engineering, and extensive experience of working with industry and the universities, was about to retire from the purchasing department of the Ministry of Defence. He was the man to whom fell the job of effecting the increased emphasis on engineering and industrial design for which Way and others on the Board had long been pressing. Way and Neale had worked together in earlier years and were to transform the organization and educational policy of the Commission. Neale joined the Commission on 1 June, 1987, a month before James retired, serving until the end of 1994.

The Commission's resources were, of course, increasingly circumscribed, particularly by the beneficial leases granted to various institutions on the estate, which severely limited the Commission's rental income. The Finance Committee, under a series of able chairmen, had done its best to ensure the means for the existing awards. This was achieved partly from the astute investment of the Commissioners' liquid funds, still managed by Barings, and partly by investment in commercial property elsewhere in London. Despite the more profitable management of the estate, it was becoming clear that the Board would have to take some difficult decisions as to the proper disposal of its funds, shrinking in relation to the demands upon them, and the best awards to support in the light of its Charter obligations. Moreover, it was clear that any new initiatives would necessitate the abandonment of some or all of the current awards.

RETHINKING THE COMMISSION'S AWARDS

The changes to the Commission's educational policies which had been mooted by different interests took some time to achieve. Their full implementation followed the abandonment of the offices at 1 Lowther Gardens, which provided a welcome infusion of liquid capital. The change in educational policy was carefully argued, and based on the changing national circumstances, where again, as in the 1890s, British industry was seen as under threat from foreign competition, and 'fighting an economic war from a much reduced position'. In the Board's view, 'The need to attract the most able of the country's youth towards careers in industry has never been greater, nor the Commission's charter more pertinent'.[24]

Since the end of the Second World War, the scientific schemes had been the Overseas Research Scholarships, as reorganized in 1922, and the post-doctoral Research Scholarships, which were the lineal descendants of the pre-war Senior Studentships, again dating from 1922. Their critics claimed that the latter had become increasingly dedicated to pure science, rather than to the development of industrial techniques as defined in the Supplementary Charter. In 1960, a scientist from Sussex University, Roy Macleod, had analysed the subjects and universities chosen by award-winners since 1891, using the Commission's own detailed records, and the results had been published in *Nature* in 1968. Macleod's analysis had made much the same point as the schemes' critics. Between 1946 and 1960, over 40 per cent of the awards went to scholars from Oxford and Cambridge, while the favoured subjects were chemistry and physics (approximately 45 and 20–30 per cent respectively), closely followed by the life sciences at about 20 per cent. Engineering and geology, arguably the disciplines most immediately related to industry, each only accounted for 4–5 per cent of the students.[25]

One major change in the Commission's policy was, of course, the 'loosening of the Commission's ties with the British School at Rome', achieved through the separation of the offices. However, despite a number of ultimata, the break took a long time to take place and the School's Architecture and Printmaking Scholarships continued to be supported, to the tune of £12,000 a year, and a representative continued to sit on the Council of the British School. This arrangement was only ended in 1996, when the British government, through its funding of the British Academy, agreed to take over responsibility for supporting the School's work. Thereafter, the Commission terminated the scholarships and gave up its representation on the School Council, though it has since supported occasional appeals.[26]

The changes in the scientific scholarships were put forward by Neale in 'Proposals for Change' at the Board meeting in December 1987. He reminded the Board members that as long ago as 1978 the President had raised the question of whether some of the Commission's activities were consonant with the aims of the Charter, and 'had expressed the view that the Research Fellowships and Overseas Scholarships did not provide sufficiently for applied science and engineering'. He pointed out that the scholarships scheme had been a pioneering scheme in 1891, but today, a century on, there were over 20,000 non-native postgraduates working in British universities, of which about 7534 came from the Commonwealth and British dependencies, 2191 from EEC countries (*sic*) and 10,122 from foreign countries. Against these figures it was beyond argument that the Commission's role had become less important. The growth in institutions from which the Overseas Scholars now came had increased the 'tedious, time-consuming and unproductive work' in the office needed to sort the applications. He suggested that even if the Overseas Scholarships were abandoned, the Commission could still claim to continue the 'promotion of kindly international feelings' as advocated by its founder, through its generosity to Imperial College, which trained a large number of full-time Commonwealth and foreign students, some 1200 out of a total of nearly 5000 full-time students, including 322 from the Commonwealth, 155 from Hong Kong, and 267 from the European Community.

An entirely new scheme for the training of promising engineers was put forward. These were to be identified in their final undergraduate or first postgraduate year, and encouraged to take up the 'advancement of engineering research, design and manufacturing technology' within industry but 'linked to a University Engineering Faculty, and providing for the joint supervision by their line manager in industry and an appropriate member of the University'. Though most of the funding was to come from 1851 scholarships, the industry in question would be expected to foot some of the bill. This dual management was intended to avoid a problem which had already become manifest, of the gulf felt to exist between those working in industry, and what was seen as the more remote approach of the universities. It was also felt that in general terms it would encourage industry and universities to work more closely together. In a manner reminiscent of the destinations of the first 1891 Scholars, it was to be supplemented by visits to 'appropriate centres of expertise overseas'. In addition, it was proposed that three Senior Fellowships should be set up to provide teaching in universities from practical engineers, with recent experience in industry. The ten scholarships at £12,000 a year, for three years, would absorb about half of the Commissioners' income of £600,000, with £120,000 going to fund the

Senior Fellows. Of the remainder of £150,000, £60,000 would be allocated to support projects in 'pure science,' and to projects in art, with the balance going to a 'discretionary fund' to be at the disposal of the 'Chairman in conjunction with the Secretary' for small grants to minor causes. All the new awards were to be managed by a new Engineering Awards Committee especially created for the purpose. Both sets of Science Scholarships would therefore cease after the current year, being replaced by the engineering schemes in 1989 or 1990.

It was conceded that these changes might seem 'draconian', but, it was pointed out, it had become clear over the previous twenty years of 'tinkering' that no significant changes had been achieved, and that the Commission's resources in manpower and money were not up to supporting two schemes. Though concern was expressed that the arts were being neglected,[27] and the members of the Science Committee on the Board expressed considerable misgivings, the proposals were accepted by the Board, though it was agreed that the Committee should discuss them further.

With the submission of the paper outlining these proposals, Way felt that the time had come for him to retire as Chairman of the Board, a post which he had held for nearly ten years. Following discussions with his close associates on the Board, and with the President, a distinguished figure from British industry, the former chairman of the British Gas Council, Sir Denis Rooke, was appointed to succeed him. The new chairman was Chancellor of Loughborough University, and therefore had important contacts with universities and technical colleges. He had been party to the recent negotiations over the changes to the awards, and was well equipped to deal with the various reactions to them as they developed in the ensuing months.

The scheme was indeed radical, implying as it did 'the abolition of the present scholarships and fellowships schemes', and to the unconcealed dismay of the Committee members meant the '*ipso facto* abolition' of the Science Scholarships Committee.[28]

A number of individual members of the Science Scholarships Committee, including some who were also members of the Fellowship of Engineering, expressed their concern. A Cambridge biochemist, with three 1851 Scholars working in his department, argued that he was

not persuaded of the need to put all our eggs into the engineering basket. Whilst . . . not dissenting from the actions already taken, I think it is wrong to equate 'applied science' with 'engineering'. The present explosion in biotechnology rests as much, if not more, on advances in basic science as it does in the application of those basic discoveries to useful ends by technologists . . . I do hope that the Committee can persuade the Board and Commission not to throw out the scientific baby with the bath water![29]

A geneticist from another university expressed his 'unequivocal opposition':

It has become fashionable to emphasise the applications of science, and basic science is now threatened . . . The Universities . . . are under continual pressure to obtain money from industry, and they are in danger of becoming merely cheap Research and Development outfits subsidized by government.[30]

Even members recruited from the world of engineering were against the abolition of the scientific awards, one offered to resign, another working at GEC pointed out that, as a physicist turned engineer, he would not have been eligible for the new awards, and that his company employed many types of scientists, not only engineers.[31] Former Overseas Scholars too, could ask, as Rutherford had in 1935, where, without the Overseas Scholarships scheme, would their careers have lain?

The members of the Science Scholarships Committee volunteered to assist in working out a new approach to the 1851 awards in conjunction with the new Engineering Committee. However, the members also expressed their concern to the Board in a measured paper recording the long and prestigious history of the 1851 awards, the cost-efficient way they had been carried out through a 'considerable labour of love', and their contribution in serving 'a real social need through cultural diplomacy within the Commonwealth'. They did not feel that the proposed changes would remedy 'an admittedly unsatisfactory position as regards engineering', and were concerned that there would be a loss of good science candidates with a potential contribution to industry.

We particularly regret that the Commonwealth ties should be broken. The needs of the Old Commonwealth and the New admittedly differ greatly but valuable links to both have been carefully forged over the years and we are dismayed that their value is not recognized

. . . the reputation at present enjoyed by the Royal Commission rests firmly on many decades of dedicated work. If lost, it will not be readily rebuilt . . . Our concern is that the Royal Commission's prestige in the universities will be frittered away to little purpose.[32]

The Board gave careful consideration to these arguments, but the Commission's funds were not adequate both to support the old awards, and to introduce the new scheme with its emphasis on industry for which its advocates had been pressing for so long. However, the financial position had been so improved by the successful sale of the Lowther Gardens office that this windfall, and possibly the protests, encouraged the Board to think again at its meeting in July 1988.[33] The Science Scholarships Committee was to remain in being to manage the Research Fellowships, partially reprieved, and reorganized to comprise four general awards, and two specifically for engineers every year. The industrial awards were to be managed in parallel by a new Industry and Engineering Advisory Committee, under Oscar Roith, former Chief Engineer of British Petroleum, and Chief Scientist and Engineer of the Department of Industry.

The Overseas Scholarships were awarded for the last time in 1988, thus breaking 'a link of tremendous historical importance' and 'signalling another explicit movement of the UK away from its ancient associations'.[34] In defence of the decision to abolish them, it was pointed out that scholars from various parts of the former British Empire did, in effect, often obtain postdoctoral Research Scholarships under the Commission's scheme, and therefore the overseas universities were still participants by proxy through their alumni.

There were a number of resignations from the Committee, including that of Wilkinson, succeeded as Chairman by Professor Rex Richards, a distinguished Oxford chemist and Chancellor of Exeter University.[35]

The decision to reprieve the Research Fellowships had a happy outcome in that the Commissioners could celebrate both old and new awards at a centenary dinner in 1991. Taking all the scientific schemes together, in a hundred years the Commission had made awards to nearly 1400 scholars from British universities at home and overseas; by 1991 of these some 130 had become Fellows of the Royal Society, with three former Presidents, ten had won a Nobel Prize, and five the Order of Merit. The Chairman, Sir Denis Rooke, marked the occasion with a speech commemorating the achievements of earlier award-holders, but reminding his audience of 'our objectives in seeking to get the best brains into industry and, at the same time, working to raise the standards of industrial design'.[36]

Less publicized than the scientific and industrial scholarships, but significant in its reflection of the breadth of the Commission's interests, was the establishment of a bursary in 1991. This stemmed directly from the fire at Windsor Castle, following on which the Commissioners, conscious of their debt to and longstanding relationship with consecutive members of the Royal Family, had submitted an expression of profound loyalty, as they had done on appropriate occasions throughout the Commission's history. They resolved to follow this up with a tangible expression of loyalty likely to be both useful and welcome to the Sovereign.

It so happened that on the morning of the fire, staff and students from the Textile Conservation Centre were working at the Castle, and were instrumental in saving tapestries from the reach of the fire, and thus preserving historic works of art of great value. The Commission thought it appropriate to institute a bursary at the Centre to commemorate this. The bursary enables the holder to study for the Diploma awarded jointly with the Courtauld Institute of the University of London, and is awarded on a regular basis.[37]

Michael Neale retired as Secretary in 1994, and was succeeded by Patrick Middleton, CB, a retired rear admiral from the engineering branch of the Royal Navy with a distinguished career as submariner.

THE WORK OF THE COMMISSION AT THE MILLENNIUM

The development of the three committees, Finance, Science Scholarships and Engineering, has meant that the Board has become more like the old Commission had been, in that decisions are largely taken elsewhere, to be ratified by the Board. A further refinement has been a planned reduction in numbers to about nine, to make the Board more manageable, as it was in the days when it was the driving force behind the Commission, and reported to the other Commissioners, once or even twice a year. This was achieved at Sir Richard Way's suggestion, when he persuaded the Board to vote for a limitation of membership by age to 75, and by years of service to 15.

Meetings of the Commission are still held, when the *ex officio* Commissioners, the First Lord of the Treasury, the Chancellor of the

Exchequer, the Minister for Education, the President of the Civil Engineers, and so forth, are invited, but they rarely attend. In addition, the President no longer chairs the meetings of the Commission, as had been the practice earlier, though this does not preclude his appearing at receptions for award-holders, and taking a great practical interest in the doings of the Board of Management, to which a presidential nominee continues to be appointed.

The Commission continues to fund young scientists or engineers of exceptional promise by giving them two further years in which to conduct research. These awards are open to candidates from Britain or the British Commonwealth, or from former members of the British Commonwealth who are of postgraduate or doctoral standing. These Research Fellowships therefore carry on the tradition of the old Overseas Scholarships.

The new industrial awards are open only to British nationals, resident and working in Britain. They are of two types, replacing a scheme linking university engineering departments with the industrial design departments of Colleges of Art, modelled on an established relationship between Imperial College and the Royal College of Art. The Industrial Fellowship scheme makes grants to up to six engineering graduates to pursue research in conjunction with some industrial firm, while also maintaining connection with the engineering department of a suitable university or polytechnic. The scholar is funded by the Commission for three years, as to half his or her salary, and all the University fees, but with a contribution being made by the industry in question to underline its involvement. On the successful conclusion of an Industrial Fellowship the Commission makes an *ex gratia* payment to the University *pour encourager les autres.* A similar number of Industrial Design Studentships is given for British postgraduates who wish to pursue a career in industrial design. The candidate has to have obtained a place in a postgraduate course, and is then funded as far as fees and a small stipend are concerned for one year. Satisfactory scholars can expect to be funded for a second year.

The obligation to the arts has not been forgotten, and is now served through a number of awards, including a new 'Built Environment' award, set up in 1996, and given annually for two years to a British subject, or a partnership, working in an environmental discipline like architecture, town planning or civil engineering for work which will lead to a doctorate, or similar distinction. Each year the Commissioners select a suitable theme, such as 'Urban Issues' or 'Human Habitation'.

At Way's suggestion, his successor as Chairman was provided with a discretionary fund which can be used for all types of minor award which complies with the supplementary charter.[38] The reduced contribution to the arts side has, therefore, been compensated by a series of *ad hoc* awards to institutions involved in art and industry, who appeal to the Secretary and Chairman for individual projects. These projects are referred to the relevant institutions for assessment and are awarded by the Board after taking advice. Beneficiaries have included the National Portrait Gallery, the Victoria and Albert Museum and the Textile Conservation Centre, where awards are made on a regular basis.

Thus both scientific and engineering scholarships and industrial awards continue, with the competition for the former still very healthy. In the same tradition as in the nineteenth century, the Commission has based its recent efforts to increase educational provision in the scientific, manufacturing and engineering fields on the development of novel educational initiatives, which will later be taken up by government or organizations with deeper pockets. As in the days of Evelyn Shaw, it sees the need to ensure, if practicable, that its innovative ideas, when successful, are taken up as widely as possible. The Commission is still playing its part in British scientific and engineering education, but in a global marketplace this is not as straightforward a matter as when Playfair persuaded the Commissioners to found the Science Scholarships. Indeed, as a columnist in *The Times* pointed out in 2000, flagship British companies, both in the City and in manufacturing and engineering, are increasing owned and managed from abroad.

> Britain's schools and universities now put far more emphasis on creativity and independent thinking than they do on obedience, rigour and attention to detail . . . [thus] the British approach to education . . . can put British managers at a disadvantage in competition [with Americans, Germans or Japanese].
>
> Secondly, public policy in Britain is far less attuned than it is in other countries to building and strengthening great national institutions.

From this the author concluded that many of the best minds would end up working for foreign bosses, as so many Britons increasingly found themselves doing.[39] Thus the 'unity of all mankind' so welcomed by Prince Albert has increased, with side-effects unforeseen in the mid-nineteenth century. Globalization has given the world new challenges, presenting some difficulties to smaller nationally based industries. This may be an isolated opinion, but it might be argued that it is time for the Board to look again at the training of future 'captains of industry', as they did under Lord Esher. The Commission may need to resuscitate its industrial bursaries to encourage management skills in graduates who might otherwise end up working for foreign owners.

ALBERTOPOLIS IN 2000

Since its first triumphant Report of 1852, the Commission has reported regularly to Parliament, and one of the regular features was a description of the development of the estate. This might well be known today as a 'Science and Culture Park': at the time bystanders labelled it, equally tongue in cheek, 'Albertopolis'. Though today the immediate business of the Commissioners is that of 'a royal educational trust' and rests on the scientific and industrial awards for which they are known to the academic and educational communities, to the general public the institutions on the South Kensington estate are the main monument to both Prince Albert and to the Commission he founded. The area claims to have the largest concentration of museums on a single site anywhere in Europe, with five million visitors a year, 6000 employees, and some 8000 students.

Prince Albert saw the importance of linking museums and galleries with teaching institutions, and this has remained the central theme of the estate. For most people the trio of museums dominates the estate – the Victoria and Albert and Science Museums deriving from the South Kensington Museum, and the Natural History Museum (formerly part of the British Museum), which owes its origin to Sir Hans Sloane's collections so unwelcome in Bloomsbury. The Royal College of Art can look to the Victoria and Albert, while the Imperial College of Science and Technology, long connected to the Science Museum with which it shares a Library, has gathered up a number of long-standing, older but more modest foundations like the Royal College of Science, the School of Mines, and the City and Guilds Institute. Most recently it has added to its portfolio a number of medical schools including those of St Mary's Hospital, Paddington, and the Westminster Hospital.

The National Gallery and the Royal Academy were never tempted

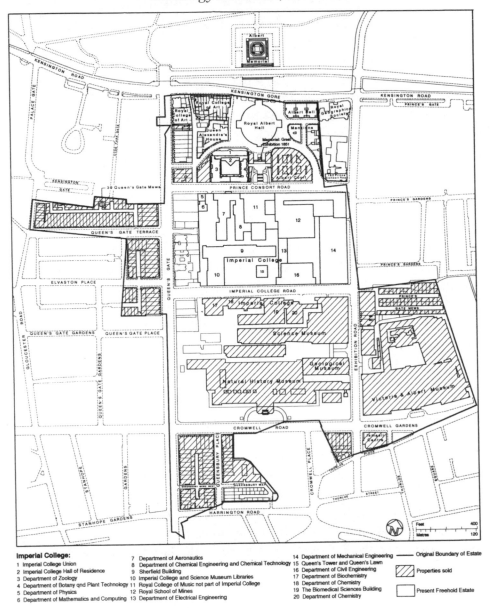

Imperial College:

1 Imperial College Union
2 Imperial College Hall of Residence
3 Department of Zoology
4 Department of Botany qnd Plant Technology
5 Department of Physics
6 Department of Mathematics and Computing

7 Department of Aeronautics
8 Department of Chemical Engineering and Chemical Technology
9 Sherfield Building
10 Imperial College and Science Museum Libraries
11 Royal College of Music not part of Imperial College
12 Royal School of Mines
13 Department of Electrical Engineering

14 Department of Mechanical Engineering
15 Queen's Tower and Queen's Lawn
16 Department of Civil Engineering
17 Department of Biochemistry
18 Department of Chemistry
19 The Biomedical Sciences Building
20 Department of Chemistry

——— Original Boundary of Estate

▨ Properties sold

☐ Present Freehold Estate

Fig 28. The Commissioners' Estate in 1997.

away from Central London to the remote western suburb, but it is arguable that this left more space for Albertopolis to develop the industrial bias laid down in its charter. A number of other organizations have started out on the estate, whose ample galleries and exhibition space served as a springboard for many enterprises. Thus, though the Tate Gallery was barred from the estate by the lobbying of the scientific community, the National Portrait Gallery and the Imperial War Museum began in South Kensington, as did the Royal College of Organists, and the National Training School for Cookery. The major institutions which remain in the area have 'colonies' elsewhere, not only the Museum of Childhood at Bethnal Green, but the many outstations of the Science Museum, probably the national institution the Commissioners worked hardest to promote. Though the links have been almost entirely snapped, the British School at Rome would not be the thriving and well-known establishment it is today without the vision of a Chairman of the 1851 Board, and the devoted work of one of its Secretaries.

All the institutions are now self-governing with their own boards of trustees, perhaps less dominated by government in the shape of the Ministry of Works, but still dependent on Treasury whims and *fiats*. Cooperation exists in South Kensington, less pronounced as in the days when Henry Cole's South Kensington Museum dominated the area, providing architects and designers for its neighbours, as for the Horticultural Gardens and the Albert Hall.

There is considerable interchange of membership: thus the Commission appoints members to the boards of several institutions – Imperial College, the Royal College of Art, the Royal Albert Hall and Queen Alexandra's House, amongst others. Equally, there is a long tradition of recruiting Board members from locally based institutions, often after they have retired from active involvement in the latter to avoid any suspicion of conflict of interest.

In 1967, the heads of the various bodies wrote a letter to *The Times* to complain about the damage that uncontrolled public access with its attendant traffic could do to 'one of the most important and educational and cultural areas of London'. The signatories were led by Robin Darwin of the Royal College of Art, and included the Directors of the Institute of Geological Sciences, Royal College of Music, Science Museum, Royal Geographical Society, Royal College of Organists, British Museum (Natural History), Victoria and Albert Museum, the President of the

Corporation of the Royal Albert Hall and the Acting Rector of Imperial College. A subtext was the area's lack of 'any sense of cultural or physical unity'.[40] This, of course, had been given for a short time by the magnificent but short-lived Horticultural Gardens, which provided a central recreational space for Albertopolis, linking museums and galleries with the entrance to the Albert Hall.

The traffic, the coaches and the ice-cream vans have been curbed to some extent, as elsewhere in London, but the sense of physical unity is still lacking, possibly because of the number of organizations in the area. There was a millennium scheme, much discussed in 1994–6, to the design of Sir Norman Foster, *Albertopolis: The Vision*, which was designed to coordinate the plans of all of the denizens of Albertopolis in their sometimes disparate extensions and developments. The eight major institutions were all involved – the Royal Albert Hall, the Victoria and Albert Museum, the Science Museum, the Natural History Museum, the Imperial College of Science and Technology, the Royal College of Art, and the Royal College of Music. The backbone of this was to be a Millennium Mall, running under Exhibition Road, as the original tunnel

Fig 29. 'Spiral', cartoon by Louis Hellman, about a proposed addition to the Victoria and Albert Museum.

still does, but extended northwards to the Royal Albert Hall, as originally intended. It also included an ambitious programme for linking the
Albert Memorial with the Prince's creation to the south, by lowering
Kensington Gore, and placing it in a tunnel.[41] In fact, the scheme never
took off, partly perhaps because of the objections of local residents to the
idea of living in a 'culture complex', but also because of the difficulty of
coordinating and funding such a massive scheme, even with support from
the National Lottery. However, almost all the institutions have their own
millennium schemes, ranging from the Royal Albert Hall's major face-lift
and restoration to the Norman Foster extensions to Imperial College,
and the exciting and controversial Liebeskind building for the Exhibition
Road frontage of the Victoria and Albert Museum.[42] Thanks to National
Lottery grants and private patronage, all are looking forward to developing new galleries and extensions. In consequence, the face of the area
is still changing rapidly.

The Albert Memorial has been splendidly restored and regilded, being
unveiled by the Queen in 1998. The less well-known Memorial to the
Great Exhibition of 1851, also with a statue of its founder, originally the
centrepiece to the Horticultural Gardens and now situated south of the
Albert Hall, has also been restored and reinstated in the sesquicentenary
year of the Great Exhibition, 2001.

The Commission can look with pleasure on the institutions of South
Kensington, which are well established nationally and internationally. It
could perhaps be argued, though, that the links between those institutions and the Commission are more tenuous than they used to be, and
that the Commission is now more remote from their day-to-day considerations than it might have been in the days of Edgar Bowring or Evelyn
Shaw.

The Commission, which celebrated its 150th anniversary recently, will
doubtless find a new set of challenges in the twenty-first century.
Throughout its existence, the men who have run it have shown an ability to identify the needs of British industry, and to take steps to meet
them. First of all it was the need to exhibit British goods, and to provide
a showplace for industry. Then when that revealed the deficiencies in
native manufacturing, steps were taken to provide museums and colleges
for those going into industry. Scientific scholarships followed, and the
imaginative Industrial Bursaries to enable poorer graduates to make a
career in manufacturing.

However, there are always new challenges. Ironically, today one of the concerns is the one which was tacitly assumed to be possible in the nineteenth century – the mutual understanding between scientists and arts graduates. By the end of the nineteenth century this had become difficult, and by the 1950s, the Secretary's report described 'the need for a bridge between the scientific and the humane elements in our society' as one of the most important problems. This has led to a certain polarization in the Commission's work, where a greater emphasis on the support of scientific education, as opposed to training in art, has developed. This may be because the former is seen as needing more assistance, but may also reflect the make-up of the Board of Management, which has tended to recruit from the scientific and engineering constituencies.

Prince Albert's dream of an international centre celebrating the arts and sciences has been achieved, through the determination and dedication of those who served the Commission over the intervening century and a half, either as members or officers. They have created the world-class museums of art and science, which he wanted to see founded in the wake of the successful international exhibition, and colleges in both cultures now train students from all over the world. 'Albertopolis' celebrates its founder's ideals and ambitions for his adopted country, but also exemplifies the truly international quality of the man himself and the institutions he created.

Appendix I
Commissioners for the Exhibition
of 1851

‡ Names of Commissioners who signed the *First Report*, 24 April, 1852
† Commissioners appointed in 1850 who did not sign either through death or because they were appointed *ex officio*
* Later appointments

Notes:
Cubitt: *ex officio* as President of the Institution of Civil Engineers. When his term ended he was made Commissioner in his own right.
Derby: appointed as Edward Geoffrey Lord Stanley.
Overstone: appointed as Samuel James Loyd.
Sir Archibald Galloway: appointed *ex officio*: Chairman of East India Company, deceased by 14 August, 1850.
Lyell: *ex officio* as Chairman of the Geological Society of London for the time being. Elected Commissioner in his own right when replaced by Hopkins.
Rendel: appointed in succession to Cubitt as President of the Institution of Civil Engineers.
Shepherd: replaced Galloway as Chairman of the East India Company.
Stephenson: appointed later at time of incorporation, 15.8.1850, originally a member of the Executive Committee.

25.01.1853   Benjamin Disraeli (1804–81) (p)
30.06.1855   Sir Roderick Murchison (1792–1871) (sc)
14.02.1857   Lord Portman (Viscount Portman) (1799–1888) (p)
01.05.1858   Sir George Cornewall Lewis (1806–63) (p)
03.05.1861   Marquis of Chandos (Duke of Buckingham) (1823–89)
             Thomas Fairbairn (Sir Thomas Fairbairn) (1823–91)
             Henry Thring (Lord Thring) (1818–1907) (cs)
30.06.1863   Robert Lowe (Viscount Sherbrooke) (1811–92) (p)
             Sir Stafford Northcote (Earl of Iddesleigh) (1818–87) (p)
             Sir Morton Peto (1809–89) (£)
30.07.1866   Henry Austin Bruce (Lord Aberdare) (1815–95)
             Sir Francis Grant, PRA (1803–78) (a)
08.07.1869   Edgar Bowring (1826–1916) (formerly Secretary, later Treasurer)
             Gen. the Hon. Charles Grey (1804–70) (rn)
             Sir Francis Sandford (Lord Sandford) (1824–93) (cs)
             Dr Lyon Playfair (Lord Playfair) (1818–98) (SSC) (sc)
18.02.1870   HRH Prince Christian (1831–1917) (CBM, 1881–1904) (rn)
             Edward Henry Stanley, 15th Earl of Derby (1826–93) (rn)
12.05.1870   Major Gen. Sir Thomas Biddulph (1809–78) (rn)
             Col. Ponsonby (Sir Henry Ponsonby) (1825–95) (rn)
18.07.1870   HSH the Duke of Teck (1837–1900)
             Earl de Grey and Ripon (Marquis of Ripon) (1827–1909) (p)
             Sir William Tite (1798–1873) (a)
             Alexander Beresford Hope (1820–87) (a, p)
16.02.1872   HRH the Duke of Edinburgh (1844–1900) (Chairman 1872) (rn)
             HRH Prince Arthur (Duke of Connaught) (1850–1942) (rn)
13.08.1872   Sir William Anderson (1835–98)
             Henry Cole (Sir Henry Cole) (1808–82) (resigned)
21.10.1872   HRH Duke of Cambridge (1819–1904) (rn)
             Marquess of Lansdowne (1845–1927) (p)
22.02.1873   Earl of Carnarvon (1831–90) (CBM 1873–4)
             R. C. Childers (1838–76) (India Office)
             Sir Anthony de Rothschild (1810–76) (£)
             Sir Richard Wallace (1818–90) (collector)
             Sir Henry Bartle Frere (1815–84) (p, rn)
08.12.1873   Gen. Sir William Knollys (1797–1883) (rn)
             Major Gen. Sir Dighton Probyn (1833–1924) (rn)
25.03.1874   5th Earl Spencer (1835–1910) (CBM 1874–81) (p)
09.05.1874   Earl of Rosebery (1847–1929) (p)
24.05.1876   Marquess of Salisbury (1830–1903) (p)
20.07.1877   Admiral Sir Alexander Milne (1806–96)
             Col. Ellis (Sir Arthur Ellis) (1837–1907) (resigned when appointed
             Secretary, 1889–1907) (rn)
29.07.1878   Duke of Sutherland (1828–92) (rn)
26.07.1879   Earl of Dudley (1817–85)
             Sir Frederick Leighton (Lord Leighton) (1830–96) (a)
12.07.1881   Lord Selborne (Earl of Selborne) (1812–95) (p)
             Sir Sydney Waterlow (1822–1906) (£, p)

Frederick Bramwell (Sir Frederick Bramwell) (1818–1903) (sc)

25.07.1883 Anthony Mundella (1825–97) (educationalist, p)

12.03.1887 Lord Herschell (1837–99) (Lord Chancellor)

16.05.1889 Henry Fowler (1830–1911) (Sir Henry Fowler, then Lord Wolverhampton) (CBM 1904–10) (p)

27.07.1891 Duke of Fife (1849–1912) (rn)

Baron Ferdinand de Rothschild (1839–98) (rn)

Sir William Thomson, Lord Kelvin (1824–1907) (sc)

Sir Henry Roscoe (1833–1915) (SSC) (sc)

Prof. T. H. Huxley (1825–95) (sc)

1894 Marquis of Lorne (Duke of Argyll) (1845–1914) (rn)

Prof. Sir Norman Lockyer (1836–1920) (SSC 1891–1920) (sc)

15.06.1896 Lord Welby (1832–1915)

Lord Rayleigh (1842–1919) (SSC) (sc, Nobel Prize for Physics, 1904)

Lord Courtney of Penwith (1832–1918) (SSC) (p)

Sir Fleetwood Edwards, RE (1842–1910) (rn)

Sir John Millais (1829–96) (a)

Sir Charles Ryan (1831–1920) (cs, private secretary to Gladstone and Disraeli)

Sir Edward Hamilton (1847–1908) (cs)

26.07.1897 Sir Henry Campbell-Bannerman (1836–1908) *ex officio*

Dr Garnett (1850–1932) (SSC)

25.07.1898 Lord James of Hereford (1828–1911) (p)

H. H. Asquith (1852–1928) *ex officio*

31.07.1899 6th Earl Spencer (1857–1922)

10.02.1903 Viscount Esher (1852–1930) (CBM 1910–30) (rn)

Sir Francis Mowatt (1837–1919) (cs)

Sir Arthur Bigge (1849–1931) (Secretary, 1907–10) (rn)

10.07.1908 Duke of Norfolk (1847–1917)

Sir Archibald Geikie (1835–1924) (SSC) (sc)

Sir George Herbert Murray (1849–1936) (cs)

Sir Robert Morant (1863–1920) (cs)

Mr (Sir Francis) Ogilvie (1858–1930) (cs)

13.03.1911 Sir Arthur Rücker, FRS (1848–1915) (SSC) (sc)

Sir Richard Glazebrook (sc) (1854–1935) (SSC, Chairman)

24.06.1912 Lord Revelstoke (1863–1929) (£)

Rt. Hon. Winston Churchill (1874–1965) *ex officio*

Rt. Hon. Bonar Law (1858–1923) *ex officio*

Sir Aston Webb (1849–1930)

16.03.1914 Viscount Harcourt (1863–1922). *ex officio*

J. S. Sargent, RA (1856–1930) (a)

23.02.1921 Earl of Birkenhead (1872–1930) (p)

Earl Lloyd-George (1863–1945) (p)

Viscount Ullswater (1855–1947)

Marquis Curzon of Kedleston (1859–1925) (p)

Viscount Haldane (1856–1928) (p, London University)

Viscount Buckmaster, GCVO (1861–1934) (p, Imperial College)

Rt Hon. H.A.L.Fisher (1865–1940) (rn)

Lt Gen. Sir Alfred Keogh (1837–1936) (sc, Imperial College)
Sir Frederick Kenyon, GBE (1863–1952)
Lord Rutherford, OM, FRS (1871–1937) (sc)
Sir William M'Cormick (1859–1930)
Sir John Farmer, FRS (1865–1944) (sc)
Thomas Jones, CH (1870–1955) (cs)

14.05.1924 Rt Hon. J. Ramsay McDonald (1866–1937) (p)
Rt Hon. Stanley Baldwin (1867–1947) (p)
Montague James, OM (1862–1936)
Sir William Bragg, OM, KBE, FRS (1862–1942) (sc)
Sir Frank Heath (1863–1946)

15.12.1926 Earl of Harewood (1882–1947) (rn)
Marquis of Londonderry (1878–1949)
Marquis of Hartington, 10th Duke of Devonshire (1895–1950)
27th Earl of Crawford & Balcarres (1871–1940)
Viscount Chelmsford (1868–1933) (Viceroy)
Viscount Snowden (1864–1937) (p)
Rt Hon. William Graham (1887–1932)
Lord Macmillan (1873–1952) (CBM 1930–52)
Rt Hon. Walter Elliott (1882–1956)

09.07.1930 Viscount Sankey (1866–1948)
Sir Godfrey Thomas, Bt, KCVO (1889–1968) (rn)
Sir George Marjoribanks, KCVO (1856–1931) (£ Coutts)
Sir D. Y. Cameron (1865–1945) (a)
Sir Henry Lyons, FRS (1864–1944) (Director, Science Museum)
Sir James Jeans (1877–1946) (SSC) (sc)
Sir Frank Smith KCB, FRS (1879–1970) (sc)

18.10.1934 Sir Edward Peacock, GCVO (1871–1962) (CBM 1952–62) (£)
Col. the Rt Hon. Clive Wigram (1873–1960) (rn)
Viscount Halifax, KG (1881–1959)
Sir Edward Harding, KCMG (1880–1954)
Sir Frederick Gowland Hopkins, PRS, OM (1861–1947) (sc)
Sir James Colquhoun Irvine, CBE, FRS (1877–1952) (sc)
Sir William Llewellyn, GCVO, PRA (1863–1941) (a)
Sir Josiah Stamp, GCB (1880–1941) (cs)

08.07.1937 Sir Henry Dale, OM, GBE, FRS (1875–1968) (sc)
Sir Warren Fisher, GCB (1879–1948) (cs)
Lord Greene, MC, FSA (1883–1952) (Pilgrim Trust)
Marquess of Lothian, KT, CH (1882–1940)
Lord Eustace Percy, DCL (1887–1958 (p)

06.03.1945 Sir Ulick Alexander, GCVO (1889–1973)
Sir Lawrence Bragg, MC, FRS (1890–1971) (sc)
28th Earl Crawford & Balcarres (1900–75) (a)
Rt Hon. Sir Percy Loraine, Bt, GCMG (1880–1961)
Sir Robert Robinson, OM, FRS (1886–1975) (SSC) (sc)
Sir Henry Tizard, GCB, FRS (1885–1959) (Imperial College,)

24.10.1947 Sir Edward Mellanby, GBE, FRS (1884–1955) (sc)
Sir Evelyn Shaw, KCVO (1881–1974) (Secretary, 1910–47)

Lord Simonds (1881–1971)
06.05.1949 Lord Elton (1892–1973)
Gen. Lord Ismay, GCB, CH (1887–1968)
Mark R. Norman, (1910–95) (£)
1951 Sir Alan Barlow, Bt (1881–1968) (cs)
Sir George Dyson, KCVO (1883–1964) (Royal College of Music)
1953 Sir Thomas Kendrick (1895–1979) (British Museum)
H. C. B. Mynors, (1903–89) (£)
Brig. Lord Tryon, KCVO, DSO (1906–76) (rn)
1956 T. S.R. Boase, MC (1898–1974)
Sir Keith Murray, later Lord Murray of Newhaven (1900–93)
(CBM 1962–1971)
Sir Eric Rideal, MBE, FRS (1890–1974) (SSC) (sc)
1960 Sir Trenchard Cox, CBE (1905–96) (a)
Sir Geoffrey Crowther (1907–72)
The Lord Fleck, KBE, FRS (1889–1968) (sc)
Sir George Mallaby, KCMG (1902–78)
Lord Nelson of Stafford (1887–1962)
1962 Sir John Cockcroft, OM, KCB, FRS, etc. (1897–1967) (sc)
Dr P. B. Medawar, CBE, FRS (BM) (1915–87)
1964 A. H. Carnwath, (1919–1996) (£)
Professor R. S. Nyholm, FRS (1917–71) (SSC) (New Zealand)
1968 Gen. Sir John Hackett, KCB, CBE, DSO, MC (1910–77) (King's College)
Sir John Pope-Hennessy, CBE (1913–94) (a)
Dr E. G. Woodroofe (1912–) (Unilever)
Professor Lord Jackson of Burnley, FRS (1904–1970) (SSC)
(former Industrial Fellow 1929–30) (e)
1970 Marshal of the Royal Air Force Sir Charles Elworthy, GCB, CBE, DSO,
MVO, DFC, AFC (1911–93) (CBM 1972–8) (rn)
1972 Prof. Sir Harrie Massey, FRS (1908–83) (SSC) (sc, Australia)
Lord Rupert Nevill, JP, DL (1923–82) (rn)
A. G. Sheppard Fidler, CBE, FRIBA (1909–90) (a)
W. D. Sturch, CVO (1909–95) (Secretary, 1947–70)
1974 Prof. B. B. Boycott, FRS (1924–2000) (King's College)
1976 Sir Arnold Hall, FRS, FEng (1915–2000) (e)
Sir Frederick Warner, FRS, FEng (1910–) (e)
1978 Sir Richard Way, KCB, CBE (1914–98) (CBM 1978–87) (King's College)
1978 Hugh Conway (1914–89) (Design Council) (e)
Dr J. A. Pope (Sir Joseph Pope) (1914–89) (e, Aston University)
1980 Sir John Hale (1923–99) (a)
1982 Michael Welman (1921–) (£)
1983 Hermione Hobhouse, MBE, FSA (1934–)
Sir Rex Richards, FRS (1922–) (SSC)
Sir Denis Rooke, CBE, FRS, FEng (1924–) (CBM 1987–20) (e)
Sir Denys Wilkinson (1922–) (Chairman, SSC, 1983–90)
1984 Sebastian Z. de Ferranti, (1927–) (rn)
D. H. Maitland, CVO (1922–) (£)
1985 Sir Diarmid Downs, CBE, FRS, FEng (1922–) (sc)

	Professor John Phillips (1933–87)
1986	Sir Peter Gadsden, GBE, FEng (1929–)
	Dame Margaret Weston, DBE (1926–) (e, sc)
1987	R. Clutton, FRICS (1929–) (£)
	K. M. H. Mortimer (1946–) (£
1988	O. Roith, CB, FEng (1929–) (e, sc)
1989	Sir Randolph Quirk, CBE, FBA (1920–) (Life Peer, 1994)
	I. R.Yates, CBE, FEng (1929–) (e)
1990	Sir Robert Honeycombe, FRS, FEng (1921–) (SSC) (e, sc)
	Sir William Whitfield, CBE, FRIBA (1920–) (a)
1995	Sir John Meurig Thomas, ScD, FRS (1932–) (SSC) (sc)
1996	W. L. Banks, (1938–) (£)
1997	Sir Alan D. W. Rudge, CBE, FRS, FEng (1937–) (e)
1998	Lord Linley (rn) (1961–)
	Dr C. L. Vaughan (1941–) (£)
2000	Alan Baxter, FIStructE, MICE, MCONSE (1938–) (e)
	J. Dyson, CBE (1947–)
	I. Macgregor (1937–)
2001	Prof. A. H. Windle, FRS (1942–)
	Prof. D. J. Wallace, CBE, FRS, FREng (1945–)

£	man of money, banker
a	artist or architect, aesthete
CBM	Chairman of the Board of Management (after 1872)
cs	civil servant, treasury official
e	engineer
p	MP or minister, politician
rn	royal nominee
sc	scientist

After 1970, all the Commissioners are automatically members of the Board of Management.

After 1989, all Commissioners sit on the Board of Management, and the numbers are drastically reduced by an age limit of 70 or 75, and a limited term.

Appendix II
Chairmen of Committees of the Royal Commission for the Exhibition of 1851

THE SCIENCE SCHOLARSHIPS COMMITTEE

1891–6	Lord Playfair
1896–1915	Sir Henry Roscoe, FRS
1915–35	Sir Richard Glazebrook, KCB, FRS
1935–45	Sir James Jeans, OM, FRS
1945–56	Sir Robert Robinson, OM, FRS
1956–64	Sir Eric Rideal, MBE, FRS
1964–8	Sir Ronald Nyholm, FRS
1968–70	Lord Jackson of Burnley, FRS
1970–1	Sir Ronald Nyholm, FRS
1972–83	Sir Harrie Massey, FRS
1983–9	Sir Denys Wilkinson, FRS
1990–7	Sir Rex Richards, FRS, FBA
1997–	Sir John Meurig Thomas, ScD, FR

THE FINANCE COMMITTEE*

1850–72	Earl Granville
1982–5	Sir Andrew Carnwath, KCVO
1986–97	D. H. Maitland, Esq., CVO
1997–	W. L. Banks, Esq.

THE INDUSTRY AND ENGINEERING ADVISORY COMMITTEE

1989–1999	Oscar Roith, Esq., CB, FEng
1999–2001	Sir Alan Rudge
2001–	Prof. D. J. Wallace

THE ARCHITECTURAL AND ENVIRONMENTAL COMMITTEE

1996–2000	Sir William Whitfield, CBE, FRIBA
2000–	Alan Baxter, Esq.

*ceased in 1872, when it was superseded by the Board of Management; re-established in 1982.

Appendix III

Secretaries to the Royal Commission for the Exhibition of 1851

1850–2	Sir Stafford Northcote, Bt, CB *Joint Secretaries*
	John Scott Russell, FRS
1850–2	Edgar Bowring Esq., CB *Acting Secretary*
1852–69	Edgar Bowring, Esq., CB *Secretary*
1869–83	Major Gen. H. Y. D. Scott
1883–9	Sir Lyon Playfair, KCB, FRS *Honorary Secretary*
1889–1907	Major Gen. Sir Arthur Ellis, GCVO
1907–10	Lt Col. Sir Arthur Bigge, GCVO
	(later Lord Stamfordham)
1910–47	Sir Evelyn Shaw, KCVO
1947–70	W. D. Sturch, Esq., CVO .
1970–87	C. A. H. James, Esq.
1987–94	M. C. Neale, Esq., CB
1995–	Rear Admiral J. P. W. Middleton, CB

Notes

INTRODUCTION

1. Henry Cole, quoted C. H. Gibbs-Smith, *The Great Exhibition of 1851*, HMSO, 1981, p. 7a.
2. RA VIC/F25/7, M. L. A. T. Quetelet to Prince Albert, 8.9.1849.

CHAPTER 1. THE FOUNDING OF THE ROYAL COMMISSION

1. For the history of the Society see Sir Henry Trueman Wood, *A History of the Royal Society of Arts*, 1913; Derek Hudson and Kenneth W. Luckhurst, *The Royal Society of Arts 1745–1954*, 1954.
2. A. Rupert Hall, *The Royal Society of Arts: Two Centuries of Progress in Science and Technology*, Trueman Wood Lecture for 1974. *RSA Journal* CXXII, September 1974
3. Hall, *The Royal Society of Arts*, p. 648.
4. Wood, *History*, p. 324.
5. Theodore Martin, *The Life of His Royal Highness the Prince Consort*, 5 vols, 1875–80, vol. i, p. 334, n. i.
6. Wood, *History*, pp. 360–1.
7. Kenneth W. Luckhurst, pamphlet, *The Great Exhibition of 1851*, Three Cantor lectures, March 1951, pp. 1–6; Resolution passed at Council of RSA, May 1845.
8. Henry Cole's own major work is *Fifty Years of Public Work*, 2 vols, 1884, completed by his children after his death. Elizabeth Bonython is working with Anthony Burton on a full-length biography; meanwhile there is her catalogue of an exhibition at the Victoria and Albert Museum in 1982, *King Cole, A Picture Portrait of Sir Henry Cole, KCB, 1808–1882*.
9. Wood, *History*, p. 358.
10. *Field*, 4.6.1887, p. 709; *The Times*, 7.6.1887, p. 11e; Letter, 16.5.1848, RSA Archives, D12/180; Wood, *History*, p. 404, n. 1.
11. Luckhurst, pamphlet, *The Great Exhibition of 1851*.
12. J. M. Robinson, *The Wyatts, An Architectural Dynasty*, 1979, p. 201, generally pp. 200–18.
13. RSA, Scott Russell Collection, Francis Fuller's Diary.
14. Cole, *Fifty Years*, i, p. 123.
15. *Field*, 4.6.1887, p. 709.
16. Cole, *Fifty Years*, i, p. 126; Hermione Hobhouse, *Thomas Cubitt: Master Builder*, 1971, p. 444; RSA.
17. Uncorrected proof of minutes of meeting of 30.6.1849. RC 1851 archive. MS copy reproduced Cole, *Fifty Years*, i, p. 126.
18. RC Minutes of meeting, 14.7.1849.
19. Bonython, *King Cole*, p. 3; Wood, *History*, p. 413. Drew also had an office at 28 Parliament Street, from the Munday contract, and I assume that he is the George Drew of the Westminster Committee.
20. *ILN*, vol. 20, 6.3.1852, p. 201. An article on Francis Fuller and Crystal Palace gives Munday's risk at £100,000; Luckhurst, *Great Exhibition*, pp. 202–4 .
21. Wood, *History*, p. 413; Yvonne

ffrench, *The Great Exhibition: 1851*, Harvill Press, pp. 28–9; RSA, *Earliest Proceedings I*, pp. 609–11; Henry Cole, Diary, 25.8.1849: 'Mr Drew signed agreement; and wd. pay £500 deposit.'

22. Bonython, *King Cole*, p. 3; HCD, entry for 31.7.1849, 1.8.1849.

23. RA VIC/F24/1, Prince Albert to Labouchere, 9.7.1849.

24. RA VIC/F24/1A; RA VIC/F24/2. Cole to Col. Phipps, 16.7.1849; RA VIC/F24/3, Phipps to Cole, 17.7.1849.

25. RA VIC/F24/6.

26. Jagow, *Letters of the Prince Consort*, 1938, p. 153. Prince Albert to Stockmar, 10.9.1849.

27. Martin, *Life*, ii, p. 226; Martin, ii, p. 227, Prince Albert to Phipps, 14.9.1849

28. Cole, *Fifty Years*, i, pp. 141–2; RC WA/I/64 and 65.

29. RC WA/I/88,89,90: RA VIC/F24/15. Grey to Prince Albert

30. RC WA/I/91; *The Times*, 21.12.1849; RC WA/II/2, John Potter to Lord John Russell, 27.12.1849; RC WA/II/3, John Potter to Lord John Russell, 28.12.1849; WA/II/9: 'Is the Exhibition to be a job?', article in *Patent Journal*, 29.12.1849.

31. See Appendix I for a complete list.

32. Galloway had died by 14 August, 1850, when he was replaced as Chairman of the East India Company by John Shepherd. Stephenson was appointed later at the time of the incorporation of the Commission, 15 August, 1850.

33. Cole, *Fifty Years*, i, p. 148; RC WA/IX/38; E. Bowring to Phipps, 4.12.1851.

34. RC 1850/24, Munday to Scott Russell; *First Report*, 1852, p. xvii.

35. Rendel acting for the Commission told Granville that Mundays were not the only party, apparently indicat-ing Fuller. ffrench, *Exhibition*, pp. 58–9.

36. ffrench, *Exhibition*, pp. 43, 170–1.

37. 1 Com., 11.1.1850; 2 Com., 18.1.1850.

38. See Reid's obituary in Cole, *Fifty Years*, i, pp. 157–61, n. 1.

39. 8 Com., 28.2.1850, App. E, p. 6.

40. See *First Report*, App. IX; H.-R. Hitchcock, *Early Victorian Architecture in Britain*, 1954, i, pp. 533–4, for Turner's and Horeau's designs. Peter Berlyn and Charles Fowler Jr, *The Crystal Palace: Its Architectural History and Constructive Marvels*, London, 1851, has a detailed description of the complicated building history. A researcher working in the 1970s investigated the archives of the Royal Commission for the 1851 Exhibition, the Royal Society of Arts, and the Institution of Civil Engineers and the Victoria and Albert Museum without result. Anthony Bird, *Paxton's Palace*, 1976, p. 19.

41. *ILN*, vol. 16, 22.6.1850, p. 446; *Builder*, 15.6.1850, p. 277.

42. *First Report*, p. xxv.

43. Cole, *Fifty Years*, i, p. 164; Hitchcock, *Early Victorian Architecture*, p. 534; information from John Kenworthy-Browne, who is working on Joseph Paxton, henceforth JKB; British Architectural Library, Wolfe Archive, WOJ/1/2/1 (xcvii); information from Guy Booth, who is working on Charles Barry, henceforth GB.

44. 17 Com., 16.5.1850.

45. *ILN*, vol. 16, p. 445, 22.6.1850, 'Proposed Building for the Industrial Exhibition'; Cole, *Fifty Years*, i, p. 163; *Punch*, Cartoon, July 1850, p. 22.

46. DNB; Martin, *Life*, i, pp. 59–60.

47. *Westminster and Foreign Quarterly Review*, April–June 1850, pp. 94–5.

48. *The Times*, 27.6.1850, quoted Bird, *Paxton's Palace*, p. 25; Martin, *Life*, ii, pp. 285–6.

49. PRO, Work 6/126/27: 15.6.1850.

Seymour and A. Milne advising
Treasury; 22.6.1850. Minutes of
meeting at Treasury, . Conditions on
which ground will be let; Work
6/126 (2)/3, 15.8.1850; Draft
Warrant authorising Commissioners
to 'enter upon a piece of ground in
Hyde Park, 15.8.1850; (37–40)
Warrant correspondence from Crown
to 1851 Commission; 6/126 (2)/1–2
Warrants

50. Cole, *Fifty Years*, i, p. 163.

51. Hitchcock, *Early Victorian Architecture*,
i, p. 535; George F. Chadwick, *The
Works of Sir Joseph Paxton*, 1961, *passim*.

52. Chadwick, *Paxton*, pp. 105–110;
Paxton to Sarah Paxton, n.d. but
24.6.1850 (JKB). I am indebted to
John Kenworthy-Browne, who is
working on a biography of Paxton,
for access to unpublished information,
and help over the exact sequence of
events.

53. Cole, *Fifty Years*, i, pp. 165–6; *ILN*,
vol. 17, p. 13, 6.7.1850.

54. *Hansard*, vol. 112, pp. 866–90;
Hansard, vol. 112, pp. 901–35; RA
VIC/F24/43, Lord J. Russell to
Prince Albert, 4.7.1850.

55. Chadwick, *Paxton*, pp. 111–12.

56. RC 1850 Corr. 1/6, 13.2.1850.

57. Martin, *Life*, ii. pp. 247–8;

58. Cartoon by Leech, *Punch*, vol. xviii, p.
229. According to his biographer,
Theodore Martin, the Prince enjoyed
a joke at his own expense, and preserved this cartoon among the
records of the Exhibition. Martin,
Life, ii, p. 298, n. 5.

59. Cole, *Fifty Years*, i, pp. 168–71.

60. RA VIC/F25.109, Sir Alexander
Spearman to Bowring; RA
VIC/F25/110. The Bond itself gives
the names.

61. 27 Com., 26.7.1850; ffrench,
Exhibition, p. 101; see Davis, *Great
Exhibition*, p. 84, n. 98; GB. Wolfe

Archive, BAL WOJ/1/2/1 (xcvii).

62. 27 Com., 26.7.1850.

63. 25 Com., 16.7.1850. Resolution
adopted Tuesday, 16 July, 1850: 'this
Commission is not in a position to
commit itself to a legal acceptance of
any tender'.

64. *First Report*, p. xii; pp. xvii–xviii. *Art
Journal Illustrated Catalogue: The
Industry of All Nations*, George Virtue,
London, n.d., pp. xvi–xviii.

65. *ILN*, vol. 19, 7.7.1851, p. 22, Fox,
after-dinner speech at Derby.

66. Mrs C. H. Smith (*née* Fanny Riviére),
Wanderings of my Memory over my Life,
privately printed 1890, quoted
Journal of the London Society, 1989,
no. 417; *Art Journal Illustrated
Catalogue*, p. xvii.

67. Chadwick, *Paxton*, p. 118; *First
Report*, pp. xxvi–xxix.

68. *Proceedings of the Institute of Civil
Engineers*, x, 1850–1, p. 189.

69. *ILN*, vol. 19, p. 22, 5.7.1851; *ILN*,
vol. 17, 19.10.1850, pp. 322–3.

70. *Proceedings of the Institute of Civil
Engineers*, x, pp. 132–3 (quote); pp.
127–192, lecture by M. D. Wyatt, and
contributions: 14, 21, 28.1.1851; *Proc.
ICE*. x, p. 165; Charles Downes, *The
Building erected in Hyde Park for the
Great Exhibition*, 1851, Weale,
London, p. 3.

71. 30 Com., 14.11.1850, pp. 4–5; 32
Com., 6.1.1851, App. A, pp. 2–3.

72. *The Civil Engineer and Architect's
Journal*, 1857, p. 273. Obit. Charles
Heard Wild, Civil Engineer.

73. DNB; Simon Jervis, *Penguin
Dictionary of Design and Designers*,
1984; Michael Darby, *The Islamic
Perspective*, 1983.

74. 31 Com., 5.12.1850, pp. 1–2; Downes,
Building, part 2, pp. 2–3,
Introduction.

75. The *ILN* carried stories and illustrations throughout the autumn of 1850,
and early 1851. There were a number

of specialist books on the building itself such as Downes, *Building*, and Peter Berlyn and Charles Fowler Jr, *The Crystal Palace 1851*; *First Report*, pp. xxvi–xxix, xxxv; Chadwick, *Paxton*, p. 118; *ILN*, vol. 17, 14.12.1850, p. 453.

76. Chadwick, *Paxton*, p. 118.
77. See plan and engraving *ILN*, vol.18, p. 203. Berlyn and Fowler, *Crystal Palace*; *First Report*; Downes, *Building*; Chadwick, *Paxton*, pp. 104–24.
78. RA VIC/F24/66, Prince Albert to Duke of Wellington; RA VIC/F24/74,75, Wellington to Prince Albert, January 1851.
79. J. S. Curl, *The Life & Work of Henry Roberts*, 1983, pp. 97–8; Hobhouse, *Prince Albert*, 1983, pp. 57–8.
80. *ILN*, vol. 18, 1.2.1851, p. 71.
81. *First Report*, pp. xxix–xxx.

CHAPTER II. THE GREAT EXHIBITION OF 1851

1. *First Report*, p. xxxii
2. RA VIC/F24/10, Normanby to Phipps, 20.9.1849.
3. See *First Report*, p. 56, for effect on would-be exhibitors of machinery of lack of protection.
4. 9 Com., 6.3.1850, App. B, Hepworth Dixon's Report.
5. *ILN, Supp.* vol. 18, 28.6.1851, pp. 623–4.
6. *First Report*, p. xxiii, App. I., pp. 4–6; see also pp. 51–6.
7. 15 Com., 2.5.1850, mins.
8. RC Corr. 1850/2, Bundle of papers relating to East India Company.
9. RA VIC/F24/10, Normanby to Phipps, 20.9.1849; RA VIC/F24/13, Address from French manufacturers presented by M. Sallandrouze de la Mornaix, member of the Jury for the Expositions of 1839, 1844, 1849, 1.11.1849.
10. 18 Com., 21.6.1850, John Capper,

Secretary Asiatic Soc. from Colombo, 15.4.1850; RC Corr./1850, British Consul in Stockholm.
11. 22 Com., 6.7.1850, p. 55. Notice from Austrian Committee.
12. *First Report*, p. 58; 22 Com., 6.7.1850, p. 5, Translation of notice in Official Vienna Gazette, 12.6.1850. Forwarded by the Foreign Office.
13. RC Corr/1850/115, Copy letter from Lord Cowley to various authorities.
14. *First Report*, App. XLI, Jury Awards.
15. RC 1850 Corr./I/113; Box I/77.
16. RC Corr./1850/I/98. Copy letter Abbott Lawrence to Sec. American Institute, New York, 22.2.1850.
17. *First Report*, App. 1, pp. 1–3, List of Committees; Report of Medals and Medals Inscription Committees.
18. 38 Com., 15.4.1851, Dupin to Prince Albert, 8.4.1851.
19. 42 Com., 12.5.1851; Edward Miller, *That Noble Cabinet*, 1973, pp. 133–5.
20. 46 Com., 26.7.1851, Jury Awards; 45 Com., 5.7.1851.
21. 42 Com., 12.5.1851; *First Report*, p. 156; 52 Com., 1.3.1852.
22. 47 Com., 19.8.1851, App. B, p. 4.
23. 24 Com., 15.7.1850, App. A, pp. 2–3.
24. *First Report*, p. xlix; 11 Com., 23.3.1850, App. E, Memorandum on Catalogue, Wentworth Dilke, 20.3.1850.
25. *First Report*, App. XXVII, pp. 132–8.
26. 51 Com., 14.1.1852.
27. *First Report*, App. XXVII and XXVIIa, pp. 132–46.
28. Patricia Spencer-Silver, *Pugin's Builder, The Life and Work of George Myers*, 1993, pp. 40–2; Cole: *Fifty Years*, i, p. 174; *First Report*, pp. 76–7, App. XIV, Reception of Foreign and Colonial Goods Liable to Customs Duty, Numbers of Foreign Packages.
29. RA VIC/F24/58–62, 4.1.1850. The Prince's reply was sent via Lord John Russell, who softened it a little; RA VIC/F24/78–9, March 1850.

30. RA VIC/F24/69–70, Bunsen to Prince Albert, 23.1.1851; *First Report*, App. XXIV, pp. 120–2.

31. RA VIC/F24/85, W.[illiam] Temple to Palmerston, 3.4.1851; RA VIC/F24/83, Bloomfield (St Petersburg) to Palmerston, 2.4.1851; RA VIC/F24/87, Cowley to Palmerston, from Vienna, 5 April, 1851.

32. RA VIC/F24/86, Cowley to Palmerston, April 1851; RA VIC/F24/88, Lord Westmoreland to Palmerston, 10.4.1851.

33. RA VIC/F24/91, Normanby to Palmerston, April 1851, enclosing report from French Préfet de Police to Normanby, RA VI/F24/92.

34. RA VIC/F24/95, Normanby to Palmerston, April 1851.

35. RA VIC/F24/89, King of Prussia to Prince Albert, 8 April, 1851.

36. RA VIC/F24/96, Playfair to Col. Grey, 17.4.1851. RA VIC/F24/98, Cole to Phipps.

37. RA VIC/F24/99, Thomas Bazley to Prince Albert, 17.4.1851.

38. RA VIC/F24/106, Lord J. Russell to Prince Albert, 19.4.1850; RA VIC/F24/107, Prince Albert to Lord J. Russell, 22.4.1850.

39. RA VIC/F24/122, Prince Albert to Palmerston, 26.4.1851; RA VIC/F24/120, Palmerston to Russell, 24 April, 1851; RA VIC/F24/122, Prince Albert to Lord John Russell, 26.4.1851.

40. RA VIC/QV. HM Journal, 1 May, 1851, quoted Gibbs- Smith, *The Great Exhibition of 1851: A Commemorative Album*, HMSO, 1950, p.16.

41. *First Report*, p. 85; *First Report*, App. XV, p. 80.

42. Cole, *Fifty Years*, i, p. 179, fn 1.; Martin, *Life*, ii, pp. 367–8.

43. RA VIC/QV, HM Journal, 1.5.1851, quoted Cole, *Fifty Years*, i, p. 178.

44. RA VIC/F24/115, Russell to Prince Albert, April 1851.

45. RA VIC/F24/142, King of Belgians to HM , 5 May, 1851; RA VIC/F24/130, Lord J. Russell to HM , 1 May, 1851; RA VIC/F24/139, Lady Lyttelton to HM , 3 May, 1851; RA VIC/F24/133. Mr E. Kater, letter sent to HM

46. *C. G. Greville's Journal of the Reign of Queen Victoria*, 1885, iii, p. 405.

47. RA VIC/F24/127a, cutting, *The Times*, 30.4.1851.

48. M. Schlesinger, *Saunterings in London*, 1853, p. 107.

49. Cole, *Fifty Years*, i, pp. 194–5.

50. *First Report*, App. XVI, p. 85.

51. *Art Journal Illustrated Catalogue 1851*, London, *c*.1851, p. xxv; Cole, *Fifty Years*, i, pp. 182–5.

52. *The Times*, 25.6.1851.

53. ffrench, *Great Exhibition*, p. 248; Walter Bagehot to his mother, 8 [1].5.1851. Norman St John-Stevas, *The Collected Works of Walter Bagehot*, vol. xii, *The Letters*. The date must be incorrect, as the Exhibition was opened on 1 May.

54. Delia Millar, *The Victorian Watercolours and Drawings in the Collection of H. M. the Queen*, 1995. The watercolours are in the Royal Collection, Joseph Nash, nos. 4007–55, and Louis Haghe, nos. 2332–7. The first four seem to have been produced by Nash as a speculation, and subsequently sold to the royal couple, the rest were commissioned by Prince Albert. They were published as chromolithographs by Dickinson, as *Views of the Great Exhibition*.

55. L. T. C. Rolt, *Isambard Kingdom Brunel*, Pelican Books, 1970, p. 299; *Jury Reports*.

56. *Art Journal Illustrated Catalogue*, pp. 245, 280.

57. *Art Journal Illustrated Catalogue*, Ralph Nicholson Wornum, 'The Exhibition

as a Lesson in Taste', R. N. Wornum. pp. I–VII*** (*sic*).

58. RA VIC/F24/149, Lord Ashley to Prince Albert, 17.5.1851, enclosing RA VIC/F24/151, letter from George Browne, 16.5.1851.

59. RA VIC/F24/111, Palmerston to Normanby, April 1851.

60. *Builder*, 10.5.1851, vol. ix, no. 431, pp. 291–2.

61. *First Report*, p. 88.

62. Quoted Sir D. Brewster, 'Prince Albert's Industrial College', *North British Quarterly*, August 1852, pp. 519–88.

63. *First Report*, p. 113. Report from Committee, pp. 111–26.

64. *First Report*, App. XVIII, pp. 92–100.

65. *First Report*, App. XVIII, p. 97.

66. *Builder*, 18.10.1851, p. 652; *The Times* 13.6.1851.

67. *First Report*, Report of the Working Classes Committee, p. 116; 52 Com., 1.3.1852.

68. PRO/Work/6/126/Map (Xerox); Memorandum Mayne to Seymour, 4.4.1851. PRO/WORK/6/126/42–4.

69. *First Report*, p. 118.

70. *First Report*, pp. 179, 164; *First Report*, pp. 196–203.

71. RA VIC/F24/156, Granville to Grey, 23.7.1851; RA VIC/F24/157, Phipps to Granville; RA VIC/F24/164–6, Granville to Phipps.

72. *Builder*, 18.10.1851.

73. *First Report*, p. 104; *First Report*, App. XIX, pp. 103–4.

74. 48 Com., 13.10.1851.

75. RA VIC/F25/22, Prince Albert to Lord John Russell, 14.10.1851; RA VIC/F25/35, Granville to Grey, 15.10.1851. Dilke received his baronetcy, almost as a form of 'dissolution honour', after Prince Albert's sudden death in December 1861.

76. RA VIC/F25/35, Granville to Prince Albert, 15.10.1851.

77. RA VIC/F25/24–9, Prince Albert to

Reid, Playfair, Cole, Dilke, Northcote and Scott Russell, 15.10.1851; RA VIC/F25/37–8, Prince Albert to W. Cubitt 15.10.1851; Granville, 16.10.1851; RA VIC/F25/30–4, Grey to Fuller, Bowring, Wyatt, Lloyd and Drew, 15.10.1851.

78. RA VIC/F25/45, Messrs Munday to Prince Albert, 16.10.1851; RA VIC/F25/63, Scott Russell to Grey, 22.10.1851; RA VIC/F25/52, Col. Phipps to HRH, Prince Albert, 17.10.1851.

79. RA VIC/F25/26, Prince Albert to Henry Cole, 15.10.1851.

80. *Builder*, vol. ix, no. 454, 18.10.1851, p. 651.

81. 'The Industrial Exhibition of 1851', by 'Helix' in *Westminster Review*, vol. liii, April–July 1850, pp. 85–100.

82. *Hansard*, vol. cxviii, col. 1725.

83. *Hansard*, vol. cxviii, col. 1733.

84. 51 Com., 14.1.1852.

85. PRO/WORK/6/126/68.

86. PRO/WORK/6/126/71.

87. PRO/WORK/6/126/83.

88. *ILN*, vol. 20, pp. 337–8. 1.5.1852, .

89. *ILN.*, vol. 20, p. 350, 1.5.1852.

90. RA VIC/F25/88, Lord Derby to Prince Albert, April 1852.

91. RA VIC/F25/97, Grey to Prince Albert, 13.5.1852.

92. PRO/WORK/6/126/113, Fox and Henderson to Molesworth, 4.2.1853.

93. PRO/WORK/6/126/128/129 Alfred Austin to Edgar Bowring; PRO/WORK/6/126/132, Bowring to Austin, 21.3.1859.

CHAPTER III. 1852–1857: THE GRAND DESIGN

1. *ILN*, 11.10.1851, vol. 19, p. 441.

2. *ILN*, 11.10.1851, vol. 19, pp. 457–8.

3. *First Report*, App. XLI.

4. *The Times*, 6.6.1851.

5. Playfair, *Lectures on the Results of the Great Exhibition of 1851, delivered*

before the Society of Arts, etc., London, 1852.

6. *Hansard*, 29.7.1851, vol. cxviii, p. 1727; Lord Granville, Speech at Mansion House, June 1851.

7. 'The industrial Exhibition of 1851', by 'Helix', *Westminster Review*, vol. LIII, 1850, pp. 93–5; Warrington Committee; RC. Correspondence, Clonmel Mechanics ?53/54 meeting.

8. PRO/WORK/6/126/137.

9. RA VIC/F25/1 (Transcript), dated 'Osborne 10/8 1851'.

10. Cole, *Fifty Years*, i, p. 315.

11. PP 1851 (642) XXII (545), Correct name of Inquiry. For the background to the problem see M. Port, *Imperial London, Civil Government Building in London, 1851–1915*, 1996, pp. 84–6.

12. RA VIC/F25/77, Prince Albert to Lord J. Russell, 13.1.1852; RA VIC/F25/108, Lord J. Russell to Prince Albert, 10.7.1852.

13. RA VIC/F25/2. There is a column of questions by Cole, answered on the left by Prince Albert. Copy among Windsor Archives. See also Cole, *Fifty Years*, i, pp. 314–17.

14. RA VIC/F25/3, the Prince's Memo. Dr Playfair's additions and amendments; RA VIC/F25/5, Playfair to Phipps, 26.9.1851.

15. RA VIC/F25/6, Phipps to Playfair, 27.9.1851; RA VIC/F25/74, Grey to Playfair, 18.11.1851.

16. 47 Com., 19.8.1851.

17. *First Report, passim*; 51 Com., 14.1.1852.

18. Algernon Bowring presented Edgar Bowring's presentation set of Exhibition medals to the Board of Management, together with a bookcase and its contents which had belonged to him, in 1955.

19. Evidence to the Sel. Com. on Nat. gallery., p. 605, no. 8541/2; *ILN*, vol.18, 28.6.1851; *The Times*, 11.8.1911; *WWW*, 1897–1916; 54

Com., 24.4.1852.

20. *ILN*, vol. 19, 11.10.1851, p. 441.

21. 50. Com., 6.11.1851, App. B.

22. RC WA. IX. c.25–31.

23. RA VIC/F25/130, Disraeli to HM, 6.12.1852.

24. *DNB; Proceedings of the Institute of Civil Engineers*, vol. 87, pp. 451–5 *obit.*

25. The subsequent development of the Commissioners' estate is the subject of volume xxxviii of *The Survey of London*, Athlone Press for the Greater London Council, 1975.

26. *Survey*, xxxviii, pp. 7–8.

27. Cubitt's dealings in the South Kensington estate are given in Hobhouse, *Cubitt*, pp. 445–55.

28. RA VIC/F25/83, Memorandum by Col. Grey, 27.1.1852; *Survey*, xxxviii, p. 54.

29. Hobhouse, *Cubitt*, p. 451.

30. RA VIC/F25/105, 14.6.1852.

31. RA VIC/F25/101, Disraeli to Prince Albert, 10 June, 1852.

32. RC WA: X.29, Bowring to Grey, 9 June, 1852.

33. Hobhouse, *Cubitt*, pp. 451–2.

34. *Survey*, xxxviii, p. 54, n.58.

35. RC WA:x.27, T. Cubitt to Grey, 24.12.1852.

36. *Survey*, xxxviii, p. 8.

37. *Survey*, xxxviii, p. 56.

38. RA VIC/F25/86, Prince Albert to Derby, 4.4.1852.

39. RA VIC/F25/137, Prince Albert to Granville, 15.1.1853.

40. RA VIC/F25/138, Granville to Prince Albert, 17.1.1853.

41. RA VIC/F25/139, Prince Albert to Aberdeen. 18.1.1853.

42. RA VIC/F25/132–4, Prince Albert & Woodcroft; RA VIC/F25/144–5 *passim*; RA VIC/F25/159, Granville to Prince Albert, 9.4.1853.

43. RA VIC/F25/114 Grey to Brewster, 29.7.1852; RA VIC/F25/118, Prince Albert to Derby, 3.8.1852.

44. RA VIC/F25/112. *North British*

Quarterly, August 1852, pp. 519–88, Sir D. Brewster, 'Prince Albert's Industrial College of Arts and Manufactures'.

45. RA VIC/F25/119, Grey to Prince Albert, 3.8.1852.
46. 58 Com., 23.2.1853; App. B, Treasury minute dated 15.2.1853.
47. Port, *Imperial London*, p. 86.
48. Sel. Com. on Nat. Gall. nos. 10177, 10178.
49. RA VIC/F25/168, Memorandum, 20.8.1853.
50. RA VIC/F25/175 Barry to Prince Albert, 15.10.1853.
51. Port, *Imperial London*, pp. 88–9.
52. 71 Com., 19.2.1859. Financial arrangements with Treasury.

CHAPTER IV. 1857–1869: THE CREATION OF A QUARTIER LATIN

1. *Vanity Fair*, 19.8.1871.
2. Sel. Com. on Nat. Gall. p. 612 1.
3. RA VIC/F25/132, conversation with Professor Woodcroft, 29.12.1852.
4. 61 Com., 21.2.1854, App. D, pp. 9–10.
5. E. A. Bowring, 'South Kensington', articles in *The Nineteenth Century*, June (i) (pp. 563–82) and August (ii) (pp. 62–81), 1877. I. p. 575.
6. Murray, A., *The Book of the Horticultural Society*, 1863, pp. 47–8.
7. RA VIC/F27/15, 'Rough estimate of probable result of forming a Horticultural Garden at Kensington', undated note by Prince Albert.
8. 72 Com., 2.7.1859, App. D, p. 10.
9. RA VIC/F27/17, Plan of labyrinth; RA VIC/F27/18, Grey to Nesfield, 9.12.1859.
10. A survivor of this project is Foley's 'Youth at a Stream', now in the Albert Hall.
11. *Athenaeum*, 8.6.1861, p. 766, quoted *Survey*, 38, p. 129.
12. Martin, *Life*, ii, p. 537.
13. *Survey*, xxxviii, pp 134–5.

14. Murray *Hort. Soc.* p. 61.
15. Anon., 'The Exhibition of 1861. Why it should be. What it should be . . .', reprinted from *The Globe*, 1859, pp. 4–5.
16. 71 Com., 19.2.1859, p. 16. Thomas Farquhar to C. Wentworth Dilke, 11.12.1858.
17. RA VIC/F27/9, Grey to Prince Albert, 8.1.1859.
18. Cole, *Fifty Years*, i, p. 230.
19. RA VIC/F27/9, Cole to Grey, 21.5.1860.
20. 73 Com., 28.6.1860, App. C, pp. 15–17. Bowring to Le Neve Foster, 28.6.1860.
21. RA VIC/F27/36, Granville to Prince Albert, 19.6.1860.
22. RA VIC/F27/73, Bowring to Grey, 17.9.1860.
23. RA VIC/F27/82, Memo, enc. in letter of 13.12.1860.
24. Granville to Canning, 24.1.1861, quoted Lord E. Fitzmaurice, *The Life of Lord Granville*, 2 vols, 1905, i, p. 390.
25. See Wood, *History*, pp. 420–2.
26. Granville to Canning, 24.2.1861, Fitzmaurice, *Life*, i, p. 391.
27. *Survey*, 38, p. 145; Cole: *Fifty Years*, i, pp. 240–1; *Art Journal Catalogue*, pp. x–xii.
28. *Survey*, 38, p. 139.
29. RA VIC/F27/130, Granville to Phipps, 22.3.1862.
30. *Survey*, xxxviii, p. 140.
31. *The Times*, 31.1.1862, p. 10a; 25.2.1862, p. 5; 7.2.1862, p. 12d. Sandford 5.2.1862.
32. Bowring, 'South Kensington', August, ii. p. 79.
33. Granville to Canning, 14.12.1861, Fitzmaurice, *Life*, i, p. 404.
34. Phipps to Dilke, 24.12.1861, Horticultural Soc. Mins. 27.12.1861, p. 440.
35. RA VIC/F27/130, Granville to Phipps, 22.3.1862.

36. *The Times*, 1.5.1862, p. 10.
37. *The Times*, 1.5.1862, p. 10c.
38. *Report of 1862 Commission*, 1863, p. xliii.
39. *The Times*, 2.5.1862., p. 10b.
40. *Record of 1862 Exhibition*, 1862, William Mackenzie, Glasgow.
41. *ILN*, vol. 41, p. 168, 9 August 1862. (Platt's Mule).
42. *Art Union Journal Catalogue*, p. x; *Report of 1862 Commission*, pp. 93–111; 1862 Report, p. 62; 1862 Report, p. lxii.
43. *Art Union Journal Catalogue*, p. x.
44. *ILN*, vol. 41, 8.11.1862, p. 502.
45. *ILN*, vol. 41, 5.7.1862, p. 17; *Survey*, xxxviiii, p. 146, quoting *Report*, 1863, p. 87.
46. *Art Union Journal Catalogue*, p. xii.
47. Bowring to Sandford, 2.3.1863., App. A, 78th meeting, RC.
48. Mins. of 76 Com., 7.2.1862, RC 1851.
49. *Fifth Report*, 1867, p. 14; 84th meeting, mins.
50. 78 Com., 21.5.1863, p. 4; 78 Com., 21.5.1863, p. 4, pp. 7–8.
51. Bowring, 'South Kensington', ii, August, p. 70; W. Gregory, *Autobiography*, ed. Lady Gregory, 1894, p. 208.
52. Gregory, *Autobiography*, p. 223.
53. Gregory's speech, quoted Bowring, 'South Kensington', ii, p. 66; Palmerston to HM, 3.7.1863, *Letters of Queen Victoria, 1862–1878*, ed. G. E. Buckle, 2 vols, 1926, i, p. 98; Gregory, *Autobiography*, p. 208.
54. Bowring, 'South Kensington', ii, p. 69.
55. Port, *Imperial City*, pp. 98–101.
56. 79 Com., 30.6.1863, pp. 9–12, App. G; Bowring, 'South Kensington', ii, p. 71.
57. RA VIC/F28/51. Derby to HM; RA F28/52–4; 81 Com., 16.4.1864.
58. Bowring 'South Kensington', ii, p. 72; for Cole's account, see *Fifty Years*, i, pp. 358–65.
59. RA VIC/F28/56, Cole to Grey, May 1864; RA VIC/F28/55, Grey to

Derby, 18.5.1864; RA VIC/F28/61, Grey to HM, 4.12.1864; RA VIC/F28/68, Memorandum drawn up by Grey, amended by Bowring, March 1865; RA VIC/F28/72, Grey to HM, 24.3.1865.
60. Cole, *Fifty Years*, i, p. 361.
61. RA VIC/F28/74, Derby to HM, 6.4.1865; RA VIC/F28/76, Grey to HM, 9.4.1865.
62. 82 Com., 29.5.1865, Special Report of Finance Committee, 29.5.1865, App. A.
63. WA XXI/9, Bowring to Grey, 27.6.1865.
64. *Survey*, xxxviii, pp. 66–7, and *passim*; WA/XX/19, Scott biog.
65. WA/XXI/36, Scott to Grey, 6.12.1865; WA/XXI/40, Fisher to Grey, 12.12.1865.
66. WA/XXI/41, Fisher to Grey, 12.12.1865.
67. WA/XXI/48 Fisher to Grey, 17.1.1866; WA/XXI/49, Derby to Prince of Wales; WA/XXI/50, Derby to Grey.
68. WA/XXI/54, Grey to Derby, 15.2.1866.
69. WA/XXI/97, G. G. Scott to Grey, 24.7.1866.
70. *Survey*, xxxviii, p. 184; *Survey*, xxxviii, Chapter 11, pp. 192–3.
71. WA/XX1/2, Albert Hall Prospectus, June 1865.
72. WA/XXI/42, H. Scott to Grey, 28.12.1865.
73. WA/XXI/53, Cutting from *Pall Mall Gazette*, Feb. 1866.
74. WA/XXI/65, Grey to Cole, 13.4.1866.
75. RA VIC/F28/102, List of Subscribers, April 1866.
76. 83 Com., 30.7.1866, App. F, pp. 21–3; 84 Com., 15.8.1867.
77. RA VIC/F28/75, HM to Derby, 6.4.1865.
78. WA/XXI/88, Bowring to Grey, 14.6.1866; WA/XXI/80, Derby to

members of Royal Academy, 14.5.1866; WA/XXI/86, Grant to Grey, 20.5.1866; WA/XXI/95, Grey to Grant, 17.7.1866.

79. 86 Com., 17.3.1869, App. C, pp. 6–7, Bowring to Granville, 12.12.1868; WA/XIX/136, Bowring to Grey, 14.1.1864; WA/XIX/155, Bowring to Grey, 29.2.1864.

80. 87 Com., 8.7.1869, Bowring to Derby.

CHAPTER V. 1869–1878: THE LATE
LAMENTED PRINCE

1. 88 Com., 10.2.1870.
2. Bowring, 'South Kensington', August 1877, p. 71.
3. Henry Cole's Diary (HCD). 8.7.1869; *DNB*.
4. Robert Lowe, quoted Bowring, 'South Kensington', ii, p. 70.
5. Mark Girouard, *Alfred Waterhouse and the Natural History Museum*, 1981, pp. 7–8; *4th Report*, pp. 22–4.
6. RC 68,3/6/1911, quoted *Survey*, xxxviii, p. 72, n. 314.
7. William T. Stearn, *The Natural History Museum at South Kensington*, 1981, pp. 43–8.
8. Bowring, 'South Kensington', i, p. 572.
9. Grey referred to him as 'in his dotage', HCD, 13.5.1869.
10. *Survey*, xxxviii, pp. 196–7; 85 Com., 18.7.1868, App. C, letter from Scott, Sec. to Provisional Committee to Bowring, 16.7.1868; 87 Com., 8.7.1869, App. D., 'Remarks on the revised plans for International Exhibitions'.
11. HCD 1869, *passim*; Cole, *Fifty Years*, i, pp. 264–7.
12. RA VIC/F28/108, Grey to HM, 20.1.1869; HCD 15.7.1869, Meeting Grey and Teck with Cole; RA VIC/F28/109, Grey to HM, 28.6.1869.
13. 87 Com., 8.7.1869, pp. 6–8,

Memorandum by Sir Alexander Spearman, App. C; 91 Com., 18.7.1870.; 87 Com., 8.7.1869, App. D., 'Remarks on the revised plans for International Exhibitions'. *Survey*, xxxviii, pp. 196–8; 88 Com., 10.2.1870.

14. 92 Com., 3.4.1871., pp. 3–4, App.
15. 93 Com., 30.5.1871, App. E.
16. RC Thring, Memorandum, November 1871.
17. 97 Com., 17.7.1872.
18. 98 Com., 13.8.1872.
19. 99 Com., 21.10.1872.
20. HCD, 17.6.1873; HCD, 8.1.1874.
21. Report 19 Com., Man., 27.2.1873.
22. *Sixth Report*, p. 9.
23. 104 Com., 25.3.1874, p. 4.
24. HCD, 27.4.1874; HCD, 30.4.1874.
25. *Sixth Report*, p. 10, App. E. The offer was renewed in 1879, and duly accepted by Cole (10th Rep. of Special Committee, Mins. 115th Meeting, 20.7.1879, p. 13., Accounts, Mins. 117th Meeting, p. 7).
26. RA VIC/Add. MSS A/36/180, H. Ponsonby to M. Ponsonby, 10.6.1870; Bowring, 'South Kensington', i, p. 572; HCD, March–April 1874, *passim*.
27. He did suggest repaying the royal loan in 1874, but was discouraged by Granville, who seems to have seen the suggestion as some sort of 'lèse majesté' (HCD, 1874).
28. RA VIC/F38/60, Phipps to HM, 1.11.1862; RA VIC/F28/123, Ponsonby to HM, 4.12.1874.
29. RA VIC/F28/129, cutting, *The Times*, 17.6.1874; Lord Sandon, reply in Commons; RA VIC/F28/131, Richmond to HM, 18.6.1874.
30. RA VIC/Add. MSS A.36/667, H. Ponsonby to M. Ponsonby, 10.10.1873; RA VIC/A47/84, Disraeli, 18.12.1874.
31. RA VIC/F28/137, enc. within RA VIC/F28/136, Cole to Ponsonby, 17.1.1876; RA VIC/F28/140–144.

32. RA VIC/F28/145, D. of Edinburgh to Ponsonby, 18.2.1876; RA VIC/F28/142, Spencer to Ponsonby, 6.2.1876.

33. RA VIC/F28/148, Memorandum, 'Suggestions from Sir Henry Cole', n.d. *c.* April 1876.

34. RC 99, Hunt to Scott, 9.7.1872. The purchase of a ground rent was similar to the purchase of an annuity, enabling the purchaser to enjoy the modest rent due to the ground landlord, for the remainder of the original leasehold term, usually 99 years.

35. *Sixth Report*, p. 35.

36. Andrew Saint, *Richard Norman Shaw*, 1976, pp. 194–7; *Survey*, xxxviii, pp. 342–5.

37. Andrew Saint, *Richard Norman Shaw*, pp. 232–5, 243–52, *passim*; *Survey*, xxxviii, pp. 331–40.

38. Bowring, 'South Kensington', i, p. 579; H. R. Fletcher, *The Story of the Royal Horticultural Society, 1804–1968*, Oxford University Press, 1969, p. 207, quoting *Gardeners' Chronicle and Agricultural Gazette*, 1873, p. 216.

39. *Gardeners' Chronicle*, 15 February, 1873, p. 219.

40. *Survey*, xxxviii, p. 357; *Gardeners' Chronicle*, 15.2, 22.2, 29.3, 4.4.1873.

41. Fletcher, *Royal Horticultural Society*, p. 209.

42. RA VIC/F28/135, Ponsonby to HM, 5.11.1875; RA VIC/F28/153; Biddulph to HM, 3.8.1876.

43. *Sixth Report*, p. 43; *Survey*, xxxviii, p. 131; Fletcher, *Royal Horticultural Society*, p. 210.

44. Fletcher, *Royal Horticultural Society*, p. 233; *Sixth Report*, p. 44.

45. The figure of two-sevenths was chosen because the Commissioners' seats were two-sevenths of the total number available for the public (*Sixth Report*, p. 23).

46. *Sixth Report*, pp. 21–7, App. I, K, L, M, N.

47. *Seventh Report*, pp. 15–16.

48. Michael Robbins, 'Up and Down the Exhibition Road', *London Transport Newsletter*, 36, Mar. 1994, p. 5.

49. Ronald Clark, *Albert Hall*, 1958, p. 94.

50. RA VIC/F28/161, H. Ponsonby to HM Queen Victoria, 1.6.1886; RA VIC/F28/162–3, H. Ponsonby to HM, 1886.

51. Clark, *Albert Hall*, pp. 98–115; *Seventh Report*, p. 4, App. C, 478.

52. RA VIC/F28/176, H. Ponsonby, to HM, 24.11.1889.

53. Giles Britwell, lecture on 'Henry Cole and the National Training School for Music' at the Royal Society of Arts, 17.4.2000; 83 Com., 30.7.1866, App. F, pp. 21–3.

54. *Sixth Report*, pp. 27–31, App. O, p. 103; H. C. Colles, *The Royal College of Music, 1883–1933*, 1933, p. 4.

55. *Seventh Report*, App. G, p. 68.

56. Colles, *Royal College of Music*, p. 5; *Survey*, xxxviii, pp. 217–19.

57. *Survey*, xxxviii, p. 288.

58. *Survey*, xxxviii, p. 346; *Seventh Report*, pp. 25–6; *Queen Alexandra's House, 1884–1984, passim*.

59. *Sixth Report*, p. 12.

CHAPTER VI. 1878–1896: FOR SCIENCE, THERE IS NO ADEQUATE PROVISION

1. *Sixth Report*, p. 47.

2. Playfair to Taunton, 15.5.1867, *Fifth Report*, App. O, p. 119.

3. Professor John Tyndall to H. J. Roby, 3.6.1867, *Fifth Report*, App. O, p. 123.

4. Select Committee Report, PP. 1867–8 (13) LIV. 67.

5. R. Bud and G. K. Roberts, *Science Versus Practice, Chemistry in Victorian Britain*, 1984, p. 86.

6. Bud and Robert, *Science*, pp. 133–4.

7. Bud and Roberts, *Science*, p. 147, n. 105, citing Dev. Commission, vol. i, pp. vii–viii.

8. Bud and Roberts, *Science*, p. 125; S.

Forgan, 'The Architecture of Science and the Idea of a University', *Studies in the History of the Philosophy of Science*, vol. 20, no. 4., 1989, pp. 405–34.

9. Sophie Forgan and Graeme Gooday, 'Constructing South Kensington: the buildings and politics of T. H. Huxley's working environments', *British Journal for the History of Science*, 1996, pp. 442–8.

10. Lecture by Professor Ruth Barton, 'Huxley and the X Club, mutual support and conspiracy', *T. H. Huxley and Victorian Culture*, International Conference held at Imperial College, 1–20 April, 1995.

11. Forgan and Gooday, 'Constructing South Kensington', p. 447; H. G. Wells, *Experiment in Autobiography*, 2 vols, London, 1934, i, p. 201, quoted Forgan and Gooday, *op. cit.*, p. 452.

12. F. Greenaway, *A Short History of the Science Museum*, 1951, p. 7; *Sixth Report*, 1878, p. 34.

13. John Hewish, *The Indefatigable Mr. Woodcroft, The Legacy of Invention*, n.d. [1979] to accompany an exhibition at the British Library.

14. RA F25/132, Note of conversation, 29.12.1852; Hewish, *Woodcroft*, pp. 20–1.

15. *Third Report*, 1856, pp. 35–7; Trueman Wood, *History of Royal Society of Arts*, 1913, p. 381, n. 2.

16. *Sixth Report*, pp. 110–13.

17. Greenaway, *Science Museum*, p. 8.

18. *Survey of London*, vol. xxxviii, p. 69; 115 Com., 29.7.1879, Enc. III, Letter from Treasury to 1851 Commission, 5.3.1879.

19. 113 Com, pp. 4–6, 17–18.

20. *Sixth Report*, App. S, pp. 117–26.

21. PP XXXX, *Report of Royal Commission on City of London Livery Companies*, 1884 (C–4073), pp. 28, 36; p. 67, n. 1; *op. cit. Dissent Report*, pp. 66–7.

22. *Survey*, xxxviii, p. 238, n. 50; Livery Companies' Committee, Report 1878.

23. RC 71/Box 1/fos. 155–6. Scott to Lord Spencer, 31.10.1878; fos. 149–50, January 1879, Add. Note; fos. 151–2, Scott to Bramwell, 16.5.1879; fos. 144–6, 'Suggestions for Statements . . .', 23.5.1879; 113 Com., 20.7.1877, p. 10, Report of Special Committee.

24. *Survey*, xxxviii, p. 239; RC 71/Box 1/fos. 144–6. 'Suggestions . . .', RC Archives.

25. RC 71/1/133–4, Executive Committee of City of London Institute to Prince of Wales.

26. RC 71/1/125, Huxley to Scott, Feb. 1880; RC 71/1/123–4. Spencer to Scott, 24.2.1880.

27. RC 71/1/96, A. Waterhouse, Specification and description of the proposed building, 15.2.1881; Huxley, quoted Forgan and Gooday, 'Constructing South Kensington', p. 459.

28. *Survey*, xxxviii, pp. 239–40.

29. *Survey*, xxxviii, pp. 241–2; Forgan, 'College architecture and scientific education', *History of Universities*, vol. xiii, pp. 153–92.

30. RC 99, Letter on the Kensington Estate. Cole to Granville, 18.12.1874; Granville to Cole.

31. RC 99, Memorandum on the Proposals of the Royal Commissioners for dealing with their Trust.

32. 115 Com., 20.7.1879, p. 12.

33. A. Somers-Cocks, *The Victoria and Albert Museum: The Making of the Collections*, Phaidon, 1980, p. 127.

34. Spencer was twice viceroy of Ireland: 1868–74, 1881–5, Carnarvon once from 1885 to 1886. Ripon was governor-general of India from 1880 to 1884.

35. 117 Com., 12.7.1881, p. 5; 118 Com., 15.7.1882, pp. 3, 10.

36. 115 Com., 20.7.1879, pp. 3–4, Report of Special Committee, pp. 12–13, 15.

37. 118 Com., 15.7.1882, pp. 6–7; *Seventh Report*, 1889, pp. 9–10.

38. Official Catalogue to *Colonial and Indian Exhibition 1886*; Philip Magnus, *King Edward the Seventh*, 1964, p. 199.

39. 119 Com., 25.7.1883, pp. 16–17; 118 Com, 15.7.1882, Capital Account of Commissioners.

40. 121 Com., 12.3.1887, Board Report, 10.3.1887, p. 14.

41. 122 Com., 19.7.1888, Board Report, p. 12, Enc. IV; *Seventh Report*, pp. 2, 33–4.

42. *Seventh Report*, p. 36.

43. *Survey*, i, pp. xxxi–xxxii, xxxvi.

44. 122 Com., 19.7.1888, p. 10; Fletcher, *Royal Horticultural Society*, p. 236.

45. *Survey*, xxxviii, p. 42; Board Report, 28.7.1885, 10.3.1887.

46. RC 74/244–7. Lord Playfair's memorandum for the consideration of HRH the President, Dec. 1886.

47. 121 Com., 12.3.1887; p. 12; 120 Com., 15.12.1883; Forgan, *History of Universities*, vol. XIII, 1994, College Architecture and Scientific Education, pp. 176–82.

48. RC, letter 13.9.1886, Prince of Wales to the Lord Mayor; 121 Com., 12.3.1887, Enclosure 1, pp. 19–26, *Report of the Committee . . . appointed to frame a Scheme for the Imperial Institute.*

49. RC 74/244–7, Memorandum by Playfair; 121 Com., 12.3.1887, Board Report, 10.3.1887, p. 18.

50. 121 Com., 12.3.1887, Board Report, 10.3.1887, pp. 15–16; *Seventh Report*, p. 73.

51. A. Stuart Gray, *Edwardian Architecture*, Duckworth, 1985, p. 144; *British Architect*, 1.7.1887, p. 4, quoted *Survey* xxxviii, p. 220.

52. Goodhart-Rendel, *English Architecture since the Regency*, 1953, p. 172; *Survey*, xxxviii, plates 70 c, d; *Imperial College, A Pictorial History*, 1988, illus. of staircase.

53. H.-R. Hitchcock, *Architecture in the Nineteenth and Twentieth Centuries*, 1958, pp. 218–19.

54. C. Langdon Davies, *The Facts of the Imperial Institute*, 1898; RC 74/248, pp. 16–17, 19.

55. *Survey*, xxxviii, pp. 220–4.

56. Philip Magnus, *King Edward the Seventh*, Murray, 1964, pp. 199–200 (Magnus was the son of the first director).

57. 128 Com., 15.6.1896, Accounts, p. 47; RC 74/240–2, Statement of Income of Royal Commission; RC 74/236–7, Memorandum by Lord Playfair, 28.3.1898, RC 74/222–8, Abel to Ellis, 1.12.1898.

58. 125 Com., 27.7.1891, pp. 7–10.

59. RC 20/2/fo. 141, Grove to Playfair, 17.3.1887.

60. RC 20 139–41, Draft Memorial of the Council of the RCM, Feb. 1888.

61. RC 20/2, Grove to Playfair, 6.2.1888.

62. RC 20, Grove to Prince Christian, 28.5.1888.

63. RC 20/2/127–8, Ellis to Playfair, 3.7.1888.

64. RC 20/2, Copy of Agreement as to site; RC 20/124, Playfair to Grove offering site in Exhibition Road, 23.7.1888; Playfair to HRH, Prince of Wales, 13.8.1888.

65. 122 Com., 19.7.1888, p. 10; Fletcher, *Royal Horticultural Society*, p. 236; RC 20, Feb and March 1889; RC 74, Playfair memo; RC 74, Plan.

66. Priscilla Metcalf in *Victorian London*, Cassell, 1972, pp. 74–5, says one was re-erected on Clapham Common, but I understand that the South Kensington bandstands were bought by the London County Council. Information from Hazel Conway.

67. RC 84, Catalogue.

68. 124 Com., 23.7.1889, Report of Board of Management, 20.7.1889; RC 46/6,

Memorandum on S. Kensington estate. 1889.

69. *The Times*, 15.3.1895, p. 3c; RC 100, printed précis *c.* March 1895, and *passim* 1892–5; *The Times* Law Report, 29.5.1895, p. 3e-f.

70. *Survey*, xxxviii, p. 348, n.133, citing RC 100, 23.5.11.11.1895.

71. RC 72/632, Roscoe to Ellis, 13.12.1897.

72. RC 101/528, Drawing, Hunt to Ellis, 19.4.1898; RC 101/523, Fowler to Sayles, 19.5.1899; RC 101/520, Fowler to Ellis, 6.6.1899; RC 101/503.

73. RC 72/514–15, Hunt to Ellis, 21.7.1899.

74. RC 101/506, Hunt to Ellis, 22.11.1899; RC 101/488–501.

75. RC 101/477.

76. RC 101/479.

77. RC 101, *passim*, see correspondence Fladgate, Shaw Vigers 1908–1923.

78. RC 72/82–5, See estimate dated 3.7.1908.

79. RC 72/22, Shaw to Sturch, 5.10.1959.

80. RC 72/57, R. Auriol Barker to E. Shaw, 21.6.1928; RC 72/56, Shaw to Barker, 22.6.1928.

81. RC 72/36. Shaw to Macmillan, 8.6.1948; RC 72/37, Shaw to Macmillan, 8.6.1948.

82. RC 72/20, *The Times*, 21.10.1959, cutting; RC 72. Chambers to Sturch, 21.10.1959.

83. Millar, *Victorian Watercolours*, 1995, no. 1698, p. 297; RA VIC/Z469/23; Sir F. Ponsonby, *Recollections of Three Reigns*, 1951, pp. 124–5.

84. Board Report, 1889, p. 8; *WWW*, 1897–1916.

85. 123 Com., 15.5.1889, Board Report 14.5.89.

86. 126 Com., 26.7.1892, pp. 9–10.

87. The full list of annual scholarships was: Edinburgh, Glasgow, Mason College of Science, Birmingham, Bristol University College, Durham College of Science, Newcastle, Yorkshire College, Leeds, Liverpool University College, Owens College, Manchester, Nottingham University College, Firth College Sheffield. Shared awards: St Andrews and Aberdeen; Aberystwyth, Bangor, Cardiff (1); Belfast, Cork, Galway, Dublin Royal College of Science (2); McGill, Montreal, and University of Toronto; Universities of Sydney, Melbourne, Adelaide and New Zealand (2).

88. 125 Com., 27.7.1891, pp. 4–7; Enclosure 1, pp. 22–5. The University of Sydney was unable to find a suitable student, and preferred not to send one, rather than to nominate one 'who might fail to fulfil the objects of the Scholarship'.

89. 128 Com., 15.6.1896, p. 16, Science Scholarships Committee.

90. 128 Com., 15.6.1896, List of Science Research Scholars whose scholarships expired in 1894, p. 20; *Record of the Science Research Scholarships of the Royal Commission for the Exhibition of 1851, 1891–1960*, 1961, p. 11. All the award-holders are listed in a series of records issued by the Royal Commission.

91. 128 Com., 15.6.1896. p. 18. £9,996 19s was invested. London and North-Western Railway Stock.

92. 129 Com., 26.7.1897, Board Report, pp. 13, 42.

93. 128 Com., 15.6.1896, p. 50, App. B., Memorandum by Lord Playfair to Prince Christian, KG, 9.6.1896.

CHAPTER VII. 1896–1910: CHANGE AT SOUTH KENSINGTON

1. RC Ch. Corr., Ellis to Esher, 15.9.1902.

2. At the 137th meeting in 1908, Lloyd-George as Chancellor of the Exchequer and Winston Churchill as

President of the Board of Trade were both reported as *ex officio* members by Sir Arthur Bigge; see also 130 Com., 25.7.1898; 137 Com., 10.7.1908, p. 3; *Tenth Report*, p. 23.

3. RC Ch. Corr., Ellis to Esher, 15.9.1902.

4. *POD* 1886, 1900; 136 BM, 5.2.1901; 152 BM, 17.1.05.

5. Shown in *POD* 1890s as Assistant Secretary; BM *passim*, 1904–6.

6. 125 BM, 1.7.1898.

7. Information supplied by the firm of Fladgate Fielder, through kind assistance of Mr A. M. Baker.

8. 152 BM, 17.1.05.

9. 126 Com., 26.1.1892, p. 23; 137 Com., 10.7.08. p. 15.

10. 125, 126, 127 BM, 1, 15, 25.7.1898; 129 BM, 15.4.1899; 136 BM, 5.2.1901; 132 Com., 10.2.1903, p. 10.

11. *Epitome*, p. 18; 138 BM, 21.6.1901; 140 BM, 31.1.1902; 132 Com., 10.2.1903, pp. 7–8.

12. Forgan, 'College Architecture', pp. 176–82.

13. 126 BM, 15.7.1898; 144 BM, 8.6.03.

14. 121 BM, 7.12.1897; 140 BM, 31.1.1902; 132 Com., 10.2.1903, fos. 7–8; 143 BM, 21.1.03.

15. 140 BM, 31.1.1902; 132 Com., 10.2.1903, p. 6; *Seventh Report*, 1889, pp. 14–17; 125 Com., 27.7.1891, pp. 34–5; 130 Com., 25.7.1898, p. 9.

16. RC Ch. Corr., Fowler to Edward VII, 15.3.1904; *Ninth Report*, pp. 23–4; RAH, Second Supplementary Charter 1928; 137 Com., 10.7.1908, pp. 6–8.

17. Ellis makes the position about the Chairmanship of the Board clear: 'This Board nominally presided over by Prince Xtian [*sic*] is really managed by Sir H. Fowler'. RC File Chairman's Correspondence, Ellis to Esher, 15.9.1902.

18. James Lees-Milne, *The Enigmatic Edwardian*, 1986; F. Ponsonby, *Recollections of Three Reigns*, 1951, p. 92.

19. C. Iriarte, letter to *The Times*, quoted A. Somers-Cocks, *The Victoria and Albert Museum, The Making of the Collections*, Windward, 1980, pp. 11–12.

20. *The Deutsches Museum, Guide through the Collections*, Munich, 1988, p. 126.

21. John Physick, *The Victoria and Albert Museum, The History of its Building*, Phaidon, 1982, p. 183, and *passim*.

22. *The Crawford Papers*, ed. John Vincent, 1984, p. 55.

23. Quoted David Follett, *The Rise of the Science Museum under Henry Lyons*, Science Museum, 1978, p. 6.

24. *Report of the Science and Art Department for 1899 and 1900*, App. A, p. 1, List of Organizations . . . responsible for Science and Art instruction. 28 County Councils are listed.

25. *First Report of the Select Committee on Museums of the Science and Art Department, 26 April, 1898*, Cmd. 175, 1898, p. ii–iv; Port, *Imperial London*, p. 101.

26. *Report of Select Committee on Museums*, pp. xliv. III. The Buildings at South Kensington, p. xlv. IV. Staff.

27. *The Crawford Papers*, p. 56.

28. *Survey*, xxxviii, *The Museums Area*, 1975, pp. 120–1; Follett, *Rise of the Science Museum*, p. 7.

29. Quoted Physick, *The Victoria and Albert Museum*, p. 224.

30. Memorandum signed Devonshire, Rosebery, Balfour, August 1902, RC 71/2, fos. 70–81.

31. Report of LCC Technical Education Committee, quoted *Eighth Report*, 1911, p. 21.

32. Memorandum signed Devonshire, *et al.*

33. Memorandum on sites at South Kensington, RC 71/2/fo. 2.

34. 145 BM, 14.7.03.

35. *Eighth Report*, 1911, pp. 22–3, Departmental Report.

36. RC 71/36–9, Memorandum: 'A Brief

History of the Charlottenburg Scheme'.

37. 153 BM, 17.1.1905.

38. 158 BM, 22.11.06.

39. RC 71/1/66, Morant to Ellis, 11.2.1907.

40. RC 71/53–4, Ellis and Morant, letters 14.2.1907; RC 71/2/46–7, Fowler to Ellis, 19.2.1907.

41. *Eighth Report*, App. J and K; Follett, *Science Museum*, p. 7.

42. *Survey*, vol. xxxviii, pp. 242–4.

43. *Survey*, vol. xxxviii, p. 245; 166 BM, 24.3.1908; 164 BM, 4.2.08.

44. *Survey*, vol. xxxviii, pp. 244–6.

45. *Epitome*, p. 20.

46. *Eighth Report*, 1911, App. D. List of Science Scholars appointed from 1891–1910. There is a complete record of the careers of these Scholars published incrementally by the 1851 Commissioners. Details of the scholar, his or her home institution, career, posts held, and distinctions are given. The numbers in square brackets are the numbers given to the Scholars in sequence.

47. RC 68/188–91, Norman Lockyer, 'Memorandum on the Proposed Science Museum; RC 68/151, Lockyer to Shaw.

48. 137 Com., 10.7.1908, p. 8.; RC Ch. Corr., Fowler to Bigge, 17.2.1908; RC Ch. Corr. Roscoe to Fowler, 7.3.1908; RC 68/149–51.

49. *Eighth Report*, 1911, App. L, pp. 138–44, 'Memorial addressed to the President of the Board of Education . . .'.

50. RC Ch. Corr., Fowler to Shaw, 12.4.1910; RC. Esher–Bigge Corr., Bigge to Esher, n.d.; Bigge to Esher, 23.3.1910.

51. RC. Esher–Bigge Corr., Memo. Bigge to Esher, n.d. but written before Edward VII's death in May 1910.

52. 169 BM, 22.4.1910; RC 68/136, Bigge to Runciman, 18.6.1910.

53. RC. Esher–Bigge correspondence, Esher to Bigge, 3.6.1910.

54. RC. Esher–Bigge correspondence, Bigge to Esher, 2.6.1910.

55. RC Ch. Corr., Bigge to Wolverhampton, 1.7.1910.

56. RC Ch. Corr., Bigge to Esher, 10.7.1910; 170 BM 18.7.10.

CHAPTER VIII. 1910–1921: NEW INITIATIVES IN EDUCATION

1. Thomas Jones, *A Diary with Letters 1931–1950*, 1954, p. xix.

2. RC Ch. Corr. Bigge–Esher, 2.6.1910.

3. 138 Com., 13.3.11.

4. *Eighth Report*, presented to Rt Hon. Winston Churchill, 13.3.1911.

5. 170 BM, 18.7.10.

6. 138 Com., 13.3.1911 pp. 10–11; App. B., Report of Science Scholarships Committee.

7. Report of Committee on Education, 1867, quoted David Follett, *The Rise of the Science Museum under Henry Lyons*, Science Museum, 1978, p. 2; Fourth Report of the Royal Commission on Scientific Instruction and the Advancement of Science, 1874, p. 23; Report of the Interdepartmental Committee on the National Science Collections, 25.6.1886.

8. *Survey*, xxxviii, pp. 251–2; *Hansard*, cccxi, 1396–7.

9. Follett, *Science Museum*, pp. 41–2.

10. *Bell Report*, quoted Follett, *Science Museum*, pp. 21–2.

11. RC 68/1/7/fos. 226–9, Esher to Lloyd George, Chancellor of the Exchequer, 7.7.1912; RC. 1 Chairman's Policy Notes, fo. 225; RC 68/1/fo. 192. Copy of letter from Chancellor of the Exchequer to Lord Esher, 4.2.1913; Corr. between Esher and Chancellor, 1912–13.

12. Port, *Imperial London*, p. 196; *Deutsches Museum*, p. 126; *Survey*,

xxxviii, Chapter xix.

13. RC Ch. Corr.1/277, Shaw to Esher, 31.3.1911; RC Ch. Corr., Esher, Typewritten draft, anon., Box 1/fos. 254–6; 139 Com., 24.6.12. pp. 15–17; 140 Com., 16.3.1914, pp. 26–7.

14. *Ninth Report*, 1935, pp. 13–14; 139 Com., 24.6.1912, Enc. II, pp. 25–6; 180 BM, 7.5.1915; *Tenth Report*, 1951, pp. 11–12.

15. RC 44/III, fo. 24.

16. RC 44/1, fo. 272, Shaw to Esher, 12.4.1911; Hugh Petter, *Lutyens in Italy*, British School at Rome, 1992, p. 21; RC 44/III/fo. 21, Report by Evelyn Shaw, 25.4.1911.

17. T. P. Wiseman, *A Short History of the British School at Rome*, British School at Rome, n.d. *c.*1990, pp. 7–9.

18. British School at Rome (BSR), Rodd to Esher, 14.6.1914.

19. Material provided by the *Survey of London*, inc. Note by David C. Humphreys, 1987; Advert for 'Humphreys Complete Hospital, *c.* 1900'; Prospectus for Humphreys & Co. Ltd, 1891.

20. BSR 44/IV/1/3, *The Times*, 19.11.1910, with speech of Sir R. Rodd; Christopher Hussey, *The Life of Sir Edwin Lutyens*, 1950, p. 217; Hussey, *Lutyens*, p. 225.

21. Lutyens to Lady Emily, April 1911, BAL, Lutyens papers, Ser.1.95.

22. RC 44/IV/90, Counsel's opinion, 2.5.1911; BSR (Rome) 116. Telegram Esher to Rodd, British Embassy, Rome, 3.5.1911; RC 44/IV/30, Agreement between British gov. and Syndic of Rome, 25.7.1911.

23. RC 44/IV/51–3. Memo; Hussey, *Lutyens*, p. 226; see BSR (Rome) archives for Freeman; Hussey, *Lutyens* p. 272.

24. RC 44/IV/59–61.

25. 175 BM, 19.12.1911; RC 44/IV/51–3, memo.

26. Letter, Lutyens to Lady Emily

Lutyens, quoted Hussey, *Lutyens*, p. 227.

27. RC 44 6th meeting of Subcommittee, 10.5.1912.

28. 139 Com., 24.6.1912, p. 2; *ibid*, p. 9.; 139 Com., pp. 8–9, BM Report.

29. RC 44/I Dec. Painting fos. 21–3, Sculpture fos. 210–11, Architecture fos. 209–10; RC 44/I 'Scheme of Competitions for Scholarship in Architecture, November 1912.

30. RC NPL/Box 1/fos. 202–3, 'The Work of the National Physical Laboratory', Memorandum by Director, July 1912; RC NPL/Box 1/fos. 204–5, National Physical Laboratory appeal, November 1912.

31. 139 Com., 24.6.1912, p. 10, BM Report.

32. Lutyens to Lady Emily Lutyens, quoted T. P. Wiseman, *The British School at Rome*, p. 13.

33. BSR – Finance Notes, Nov. 1912, p. 3; RC 44/I/fo. 206–7; RIBA Drawings collection, LUT/AOS (Drawings of BSR on loan); Petter, *Lutyens*, pp. 46–9.

34. BSR 94/1, Squire to Shaw, 27.6.1915; Petter, *Lutyens*, p. 43; Shaw to Squire, quoted Petter, *Lutyens*, pp. 44–5.

35. Lutyens to Lady Emily, June 1915, quoted Petter, *Lutyens*, p. 41.

36. RC 44/Envelope, 'Furnishings', fos. 38–43; RC 44/VI/88, quotation from Müntzer.

37. 180 BM, 7.5.15.

38. 180 BM. 7.5.15.

39. POD 1886 and 1900; 183 BM, 13.4.1920, the Board discussed the matter of a government contribution towards their accommodation.

40. BSR Rome, File 117, Esher to Shaw, 8.3.1920; Esher to Shaw, 21.3.1920.

41. RC 62, Shaw to Vigers, 31.3.1920; Vigers to Shaw, 12.4.1920; Shaw to Esher, fos. 118–20.

42. RC 62, Shaw to Esher, 12/13.5.1920, fos. 67–9; Rackley to Shaw, 5.5.1920,

fos. 81–3; Esher to Shaw, fo. 54; Shaw to LCC, 8.6.1920, fo. 26.

43. RC Ch. Corr.I, Esher to Shaw, 23.9.1920; 141 Com., 23.2.1921, p. 11.

44. RC Ch. Corr. Esher to Shaw, 23.9.1920.

45. RC 68, Science Museum.

CHAPTER IX. 1921–1947: SERVING THE BRITISH EMPIRE

1. James Lees-Milne, *The Enigmatic Edwardian*, 1986, p. 332; Esher to Hankey, 18.2.1919, quoted Lees-Milne, *op. cit.*, p. 322.

2. 199 BM. 2.3.1932.

3. 207 BM. 14.4.1937.

4. 145 Com., 18.10.1934, App. A, Report of the Board of Management, pp. 4–7. Record of Industrial Bursars, 1929: *ibid.*, p. 5.

5. 141 Com., 23.2.1921, p. 37. Report of Consultative Committee on Scholarships for Higher Education, 1916, quoted Report of Sci. Schol. Cttee. 18.11.1920.

6. RC 80, Science Scholarships, Overseas Scholarships, Glazebrook to Conference, 22.6.1921, fo. 99.

7. 142 Com., 14.5.1924, App. B, p. 45. Report of Sci. Schol. Cttee; RC Ch. Corr. Box 1/fo. 101. Minutes of a Conference with DSIR, 22.6.1921.

8. RC Ch. Corr. Box 1/fos. 108–9, Esher to Shaw, draft letter; fos. 105–6, Shaw to Esher, 9.6.1921; 185 BM 18.5.1921; Chair. Box 1/fo. 95, Shaw to Esher, 17.11.1921, report of meeting with McCormick at Athenaeum.

9. The universities entitled to recommend candidates were in Canada: McGill, Montreal, Toronto, Kingston, Dalhousie, Manitoba, Saskatchewan, Alberta, Vancouver; Australia: Sydney, Melbourne, Adelaide, Queensland, Perth, Tasmania; South Africa: Cape Town, University of South Africa, Stellenbosch, Johannesburg; University of New Zealand.

10. RC Statement of Revised Conditions for . . . Science Research Scholarships allotted to overseas Universities, Evelyn Shaw, 22.11.1921.

11. BSR Archive, Rome, Esher to Shaw, 29.11.1922.

12. RC 44, Report 1937; Report of annual meeting of Faculty of Archaeology, 8.2.1938; Macmillan to Rennell, 24.1.1939; Petter, *Lutyens, passim.*

13. Wiseman, *The British School at Rome*; obituary J. B. Ward-Perkins, 1912–81, by J. J. Wilkes, *Proceedings, British Academy*, vol. lxix, 1983, pp. 631–55.

14. RA PS/GV/PS 40859, Esher to Stamfordham, 10.4.1924; Stamfordham to Esher, 11.4.1924; Esher to Stamfordham, 12.4.1924; Stamfordham to Esher, 14.4.1924; Esher to Stamfordham, 23.4.1924.

15. RC Ch. Corr., Shaw to Esher, 16.4.1924.

16. RC Ch. Corr. Box 1/fos. 2–3, Shaw to Lady Esher, 19.2.1930.

17. 198 BM, Macmillan tribute; Glazebrook tribute, 22.7.1931.

18. 147 Com., Report of the Science Scholarships Committee, 8.7.1937.

19. *Nature*, 28.6.1930, reprint, p. 23.

20. Macmillan Memoirs, unpublished chapter on the 1851 Commission, RC Archives; 198 BM, 22.7.1931; 199 BM, 2.3.1932.

21. 202 BM, 19.7.1933; *Record of the Science Research Scholars of the Royal Commission for the Exhibition of 1851 (1891–1960)*, 1961.

22. 212 BM/fo. 127, 24.4.1944.

23. Royal Commission on Museums and Galleries, *Interim Report*, 1928, pp. 26–8.

24. Royal Commission on Museums and Galleries, *Report*, Reply p. 280.

25. Standing Commission on Museums and Galleries, *8th Report*, 1965–9, p. 31.

26. Royal Commission on Museums and Galleries, *Interim Report*, 1928, p. 304. Evidence of Dr M. J. Friedlander, 21.11.1927.
27. 195 BM, Schedule of Estate, 19.2.1930.
28. 190 BM/fos. 407–8, 7.5.1924.
29. 144 Com., 2.1929, BM Report, February 1929, p. 14, quoting *Report of the Royal Commission on Museums and Galleries*, 1928.
30. *Survey*, xxxviii, pp. 257–9.
31. RC 68/2/33–40, Draft memo '1851 Commissioners and the New Science Museum, 1934', by F. P. Robinson for Chancellor of the Exchequer.
32. *Nature*, 30.6.1923.
33. RA PS/GV/PS 42464, Shaw to Stamfordham, 26.9.1927.
34. RC 68/2/fo. 10, Barrett to Shaw, 8.12.1933.
35. RC Ch. Corr. (Peacock)/fo. 380, Peacock to Sturch, 3.2.1955, Peacock recalled two decades later Rutherford's outburst: when the potential damage to the Science Scholarships scheme was being debated by the Commissioners, Rutherford burst out 'Without the Science Scholarships, there would have been no Rutherford'.
36. 203 BM, 20.12.1933; RA PS/GV/PS 42464, Macmillan to Irwin, 8.1.1934.
37. RA PS/GV/PS 42464, Copy Report to PM, 19.1.1934.
38. RC 68/2, Science Museum Debt, Macmillan to Shaw, MSS 24.6.1934; Shaw to Macmillan, 27.6.1934.
39. RC 68/2, Memo. on Conference held at the Treasury on 12.7.1934; Shaw to Macmillan, 14.7.1934.
40. RC 68/2, Draft report by Canham, December 1934, pp. 87–93.
41. RC 68/2/fo. 77, Env. Canham to Shaw, 17.12.34; fo. 48, Peacock to Shaw, 14.2.1935; Note on telephone conversation, 25.2.1935.
42. RA PS/GV/PS 42464, Wigram to Fisher, 13.3.1935; Macmillan to Wigram, 27.3.1935; Hansard: H. of Commons, 9.4.1935.
43. 147 Com., 8.7.1937, p. 7.
44. *Survey*, xxxviii, p. 232; 147 Com., 8.7.1937, p. 35.
45. 216 BM, 5.12.1946. Sturch turned down the offer of a better-paid job as a permanent civil servant in return for the reversion of the secretaryship on Shaw's imminent retirement.
46. 216 BM, Macmillan tribute to Evelyn Shaw, 5.12.1947.

CHAPTER X. 1947–1970: POST-WAR REORGANIZATION AND REASSESSMENT

1. 149 Com., 24.10.1947.
2. Board of Management report, 1949, p. 4.
3. 149 Com., 24.10.1947. pp. 8–9. List of Senior Students of 1937, 1938, 1939, who have relinquished their awards; App. B, p. 5., Rep. Science Scholarships Com.; App. B, p. 4., Rep. Science Scholarships Com.
4. 209 BM/fo. 106, 19.4.1939.
5. 149 Com., 24.10.1947, Rep. Science Scholarships Com. App. B, p. 4; Report of Board of Management, p. 11.
6. 216 BM, 5.12.1946.
7. 234 BM, 14.11.1956; RC Ch. Corr. (Peacock)/fo. 367, Sale of 46 Queen's Gate Terrace.
8. Imperial College Archives (henceforth ICA), Tizard to Rayleigh, 19.3.1936.
9. The Royal College of Art occupied these galleries for a brief period after the 1939-45 war.
10. Ray Desmond, *The India Museum, 1801–1879*, 1982.
11. Lewis Day to Sir Robert Morant, quoted Christopher Frayling, *The Royal College of Art*, 1987, p. 79.
12. Quoted Frayling, *The Royal College of Art*, p. 90.

13. 207 BM/fos. 91–2, 14.4.1937; 208 BM/fos. 101–2, 2.3.1938; 207 BM, Leitch's evidence, 14.4.1937.

14. ICA, Worthington to Tizard, 6.2.1936; Tizard to Worthington, 10.2.1936; Worthington to Tizard, 12.2.1936.

15. ICA, Worthington to Tizard, 6.2.1936.

16. ICA, Tizard to Lord Rayleigh, 19.3.1936; Worthington to Tizard, 10.12.1936.

17. ICA, Worthington to Tizard, 19.2.1937.

18. ICA, 'South Kensington Estate Development' marked 'Personal and Confidential', 25.2.1937; Memorandum 25.2.1937, p. 9.

19. ICA, Beresford to Tizard, 1.4.1937.

20. 212 BM, 24.4.1944.

21. 213 BM, 6.3.1945, Secretary's report; 149 Com., 24.10.1947, p. 10. Report of Board of Management.

22. RC Ch. Corr. (Peacock), Sturch to Peacock, 20.11.1953.

23. RC Ch. Corr. (Peacock)/fo. 416, Sturch to Peacock, 31.5.1954.

24. 231 BM mins./fos. 355–6, Chambers Report, 6.7.1955; Ch. Corr. (Peacock)/fo. 403, Sturch to Ministry of Works, 3.9.1954; fo. 343, Sturch to Peacock, 27.1.1956.

25. RC Ch. Corr. (Peacock)/fo. 343, Sturch to Peacock, 27.1.1956; fo. 341, Sturch to Peacock, 14.2.1956.

26. *RIBA Journal*, January 1956, quoted Hussey in *Country Life*, 23.2.1956, p. 329.

27. *Country Life*, 23.2.1956, pp. 329–30.

28. Royal Fine Art Commission (henceforth RFAC) files on Imperial Institute; RFAC File, 22.1 Imperial College, Mottistone to Sir Edward Bridges, 28.2.1958; RFAC archives, quoted H. Hobhouse, *Lost London*, 1971, p. 133; Report of RFAC, 1955 and 1956, p. 9.

29. 233 BM, 27.6.1956; RC Ch. Corr.

(Peacock)/fos 315–18, Peacock to Sturch; see photos from NMR archive, reproduced in Hobhouse, *Lost London*.

30. Report of Norman and Dawbarn, Jan. 1958, p. 3, RFAC, File 22.1.

31. 215 BM, 25.7.1946.

32. 151 Com., 29.5.1851, p. 3.

33. RC Ch. Corr. (Peacock)/fo. 280.

34. Tribute from L. W. Brockington, *Toronto Globe & Mail*, Obit. *The Times*, 19.11.1962; Lord Monckton of Brenchley at Memorial Service, St Margaret's Westminster, 5.12.1962.

35. RC Ch. Corr. (Peacock), Sturch to Peacock, 19.11.1953.

36. 228 BM 18.5.1953; RC Ch. Corr.

37. RC Ch. Corr. (Peacock)/fo. 31, 1960–2, Sturch to Peacock, 11.9.1961.

38. RC Ch. Corr. (Peacock), Board Meeting, 4.12.1961.

39. RC Ch. Corr. (Peacock), Sturch to Peacock, 24.4.1960.

40. RC Ch. Corr. (Peacock)/fos. 19–24, Draft Report to Commission, 1962; *Tenth Report*, 1951, p. 13.

41. 231 BM, 6.7.1955. Board mins., fos. 261–2; 233 BM, 27.6.1956. Board mins., fos. 276–7

42. 238 BM mins., 27.5.1958, fo. 308.

43. RC Ch. Corr. (Peacock), fo. 19, Draft Report 1962, p. 1, Report of Science Scholarships Committee.

44. *Who's Who*; information from Lord Briggs, 12.9.1999.

45. 157 Com., 12.1962; 161 Com., 7.12.1970.

46. Clark, *RAH*, p. 239 – 41.

47. BM 3.2.1965, fos. 410–11; RC Ch. Corr./fo. 391, Murray to Sturch, 7.4.1965.

48. 161 Com., Report of Board of Management, item 5.

49. Quoted Clark, *Albert Hall*, 1958, p. 239.

50. 151 Com., Peacock, 20.5.1951, p. 2.

51. RC 44/256, Draft letter Murray to Robbins.

52. RC 44/224, Sturch to Mynors, 14.4.1964; RC 44/211, Shaw to Sturch, April 1964.
53. RC 44/155, Shaw to Sturch, 17.11.1968.
54. RC 44/225–33. Ward-Perkins, Memorandum on the Rome Scholarships, n.d. but *c.* April 1964 and covering letter, 2.4.1964; RC 44/214–18, Sturch Memo, 20.4.1964.
55. RC 44/203 Boase to Sturch; RC 44/202, Sturch to Boase, 27.5.1964.
56. RC 44/197.
57. RC 44/191, Boase, 10.7.1964.
58. RC 44/217, Sturch, Memo, 20.4.1964.
59. RC 44/168–9, Murray to Wheare, 8.11.1968.
60. RC 44, Note of a Meeting at the British Academy, 13.1.1968.
61. RC 44, Report of Robbins Com. 1970; Report of British School at Rome, 1970.
62. RC Ch. Corr. (Murray)/fo. 545, Sturch to Murray, 13.2.1963.
63. RC Ch. Corr. (Murray)/fo. 527, Murray to Sturch, 9.4.1963; fo. 513, Murray to Florey, 5.6.1963; fo. 503, Sturch to Murray, 25.6.1963.
64. RC Ch. Corr. (Murray)/fo 452, Draft Mins. of Board meeting, 17.6.1964; fos. 468–9, Sturch, Notes for Sir Keith Murray, n.d. *c.* 3.4.1964.
65. Murray to Bonham Carter, 19.7.1965; HRH Duke of Edinburgh to Murray, 16.11.1966; 159 Com., 13.12.1966, p. 1.
66. 160 Com., Establishment of the 1851 Industrial Fellowships, no. 4, p. 1, 11.12.1968; RC Ch. Corr., Murray to Chairman of CEI, 27.1.1967; 161 Com., 7.12.1970; BM, October 1970.

CHAPTER XI. 1970–2000:
TECHNOLOGY TO THE FORE

1. Report of BSR, 1970, p. 23.
2. RC Ch. Corr. (Murray), Sturch to Boase, 13.11.1969.
3. 161 Com., 7.12.1970.
4. BM Report 1972, p. 1.
5. BM Report 1970, p. 4.
6. 279 BM, 2.7.1979; 281 BM, 1.7.1980; 283 BM, 2.7.1981; Wiseman, *The British School at Rome*, pp. 19–25.
7. 273 BM, 7.12.1976; 274 BM, 29.6.1977.
8. 274 BM, 29.6.1977; Ian. W. Wark, '1851 Science Research Scholarship Awards to Australians', article in the *Records of the Australian Academy of Science*, vol. 3, no. 3/4, Nov. 1977, pp. 47–52.
9. *Who's Who*, 1998; *The Times*, 7.10.1998, p. 23.
10. 283 BM, 2.7.1981.
11. *Who's Who, The Times*, obits. Conway, Hall. Information from Michael Neale.
12. 277 BM, 28.6.1978; 278 BM, 12.12.1978; 279 BM, 2.7.1979, Meeting with Maxwell; 283 BM, 2.7.1981.
13. 279 BM, 2.7.1979.
14. 281 BM, 1.7.1980, Report of Working Group.
15. 283 BM, 2.7.1981.
16. 290 BM, 27.11.1984.
17. 285 BM, 30.6.1982.
18. RC 99, 1974 Report.
19. 280 BM, 4.2.1980, Purchase of 169 Clapham Road, Coach and Horses yard.
20. BM Report 1978.
21. Ch. Corr. (Elworthy), RC James to Elworthy, 19.5.1975; James to Elworthy, 17.2.1976; 271 BM, 10.12.1975. Hibberdine suggested that any profit should be shared with the Commission on a 50/50 basis. In the event the Commissioners received 40 per cent.
22. Ch. Corr. (Elworthy), RC Gluckstein to Elworthy, 1.5.1975; RC Elworthy to James, 8.5.1975; 271 BM, 10.12.1975.

23. BM Report 1985; the ephemera were sold at Christie's South Kensington the following year.
24. BM Report, August 1989, p. 2.
25. *Nature*, 15.6.1968, vol. 218, no. 5146, pp. 1011–26.
26. BM Report 1989; Info. from BSR fundraiser, 17.2.2000.
27. The concern was expressed by the writer, then a Commissioner and a member of the Board of Management. 296 BM, 2.12.1987, printed minute was amended by request as a subsequent correction.
28. 296 BM, 'Proposals for Change' paper in Science Scholarships File, 2.12.1987; RC SSC Box, Ch. Corr./fos. 70–3, Notes on 'Proposals for Change,' drawn up by Bishop, and adopted by Science Scholarships Committee, 1987–9.
29. RC SSC. Chair Corr./fo. 65, Sir Hans Kornberg to Neale, 8.2.1988.
30. RC SSC, Ch. Corr./fo. 66, Bryan C. Clarke, Prof. Genetics, Notts. to Wilkinson 9.2.1988.
31. RC SSC, Ch. Corr./fo. 35, Bishop; SCC Ch. Corr./fos. 63–4, Hilsum.
32. RC SSC, Ch. Corr./fos.38–9, Paper headed 'The 1851 Proposals', n.d. unsigned.
33. I am indebted to Michael Neale for his recollections of this period of the Commission's history.
34. RC SSC/fo. 52–3, 'Observations of the S and F Committee, Note by the Chairman', n.d.; Information from Michael Neale.
35. RC SSC/fos. 25, 19, Richard Southwood, Head of Zoology, Oxford; RC SSC. c./fo. 80. Wilkinson to Neale, 'looking forward to a long period of happy collaboration', 3.7.1987.
36. BM Report 1991, p. 7. Rooke, Speech at dinner, 19.2.1991; *Record of the Science Research Scholars*, 1961, 1891–1921 Science Research Scholars: 471; Overseas Scholars 1922–61: 295; Senior Students 1922–61: 152; 1961–89, Overseas Scholars, say: 124; 1961–91, Senior Students, say: 120. Information from archivist.
37. Information from Michael Neale.
38. *Outline of Activities*, 1991, 1997.
39. Anatole Kaletsky, *The Times*, 27.1.2000.
40. *The Times*, 1.7.1967, Letters page.
41. *Evening Standard*, 21.2.1994, pp. 27–8, 45, 'A brave New World for SW7', article by Mark Honigsbaum; see also *Daily Telegraph*, 2.3.1994, 'No way to celebrate the Millennium', article by Richard Dorment.
42. *Journal of Design History*, vol. 10, nos 1, 3, 1997. Charlotte Benton, 'Daniel Liebeskind's extension for the V & A and its context'; Hellmann cartoon at exhibition at the Soane Museum.

Bibliography

This only includes works cited more than once in the text.

Albert, Prince Consort, *Principal Speeches and Addresses, etc.*, John Murray, London, 1862.

Allwood, John, *The Great Exhibitions*, Studio Vista, 1977.

Art Journal Illustrated Catalogue, London, c.1851

Berlyn, Peter, and Charles Fowler Jr, *The Crystal Palace: Its Architectural History and Constructive Marvels*, James Gilbert, London, 1851.

Bonython, Elizabeth, *King Cole, A Picture Portrait of Sir Henry Cole, KCB, 1808–1882*. Catalogue of an Exhibition at the Victoria and Albert Museum in 1982.

Bonython, Elizabeth, and Anthony Burton, *The Great Exhibitor: The Life of Henry Cole*, Victoria and Albert Museum, forthcoming.

Bowring, E. A., 'South Kensington', articles in *The Nineteenth Century*, (i) June (pp. 563–82) and (ii) August (pp. 62–81), 1877.

Bud, R. F., and G. K. Roberts, *Science versus Practice, Chemistry in Victorian Britain*, Manchester University Press, 1984.

Chadwick, George F., *The Works of Sir Joseph Paxton*, The Architectural Press, London, 1961.

Clark, Ronald, *The Royal Albert Hall*, Hamish Hamilton, London, 1958.

Cole, Henry, *Fifty Years of Public Work*, 2 vols, completed by his children after his death, George Bell & Sons, London, 1884.

Colles, H. C., *The Royal College of Music, 1883–1933*, Macmillan, London, 1933.

The Crawford Papers, The Journals of David Lindsay, 27th Earl of Crawford and Balcarres, Manchester University Press, 1984.

Davis, John R., *The Great Exhibition*, Sutton Publishing, 1999.

Downes, Charles, *The Building Erected in Hyde Park for the Great Exhibition*, Weale, London, 1851.

ffrench, Yvonne, *The Great Exhibition: 1851*, The Harvill Press, London, 1950.

Fitzmaurice, Lord Edmond, *The Life of Lord Granville, 1815–1891*, 2 vols, Longmans & Co., 1905.

Fletcher, H. R., *The Royal Horticultural Society, 1804–1968*, Oxford University Press, 1969.

Follett, David, *The Rise of the Science Museum under Henry Lyons*, Science Museum, 1978.

Forgan, Sophie, 'College Architecture and Scientific Education', *History of Universities*, Oxford University Press, 1984, vol. xiii, pp. 153–92.

Forgan, Sophie, and Graeme Gooday, 'Constructing South Kensington: The Buildings and Politics of T. H. Huxley's Working Environments', *British Journal for the History of Science*, 1996, pp. 135–68.

Frayling, Christopher, *The Royal College of Art, One Hundred and Fifty Years of Art and Design*, Barrie & Jenkins, London, 1987.

Gibbs-Smith, C. H., *The Great Exhibition of 1851*, HMSO, 1981.

Girouard, Mark, *Alfred Waterhouse and the Natural History Museum*, Yale University Press, London, 1981.

Gray, A. Stuart, *Edwardian Architecture*, Duckworth, London, 1985.

Greenhalgh, Paul, *Ephemeral Vistas, The Expositions Universelles, Great Exhibitions and World's Fairs, 1851–1939*, Manchester University Press, 1988.

Hall, A. Rupert, 'The Royal Society of Arts: Two Centuries of Progress in Science and Technology', Trueman Wood Lecture for 1974, *Royal Society of Arts Journal*, vol. CXXII, September 1974, pp. 641–58.

Hewish, John, *The Indefatigable Mr. Woodcroft, The Legacy of Invention*, n.d. [1979], to accompany an exhibition at the British Library

Hitchcock, H.-R., *Early Victorian Architecture in Britain*, 2 vols, Yale University Press, New Haven, 1954.

Hobhouse, Christopher, *1851 and the Crystal Palace*, John Murray, London, 1950.

Hobhouse, Hermione, *Thomas Cubitt: Master Builder*, Macmillan, London, 1971.

Hobhouse, Hermione, *Prince Albert, His Life and Work*, Hamish Hamilton, London, 1983.

Hudson, David, and Kenneth W. Luckhurst, *The Royal Society of Arts 1745–1954*, John Murray, London, 1954.

Hussey, Christopher, *The Life of Sir Edwin Lutyens*, Country Life, 1950.

Jagow, Kurt, *Letters of the Prince Consort, 1831–1861*, John Murray, London, 1938.

Lees-Milne, James *The Enigmatic Edwardian*, Sidgwick & Jackson, London, 1986.

Luckhurst, Kenneth W., *The Great Exhibition of 1851*, Three Cantor lectures, pamphlet, March 1951.

Macleod, R. M., and E. Kay Andrews, 'Scientific careers of the 1851 Exhibition Scholars', *Nature*, vol. 218:5146, 15 June, 1968, pp. 1011–26.

Magnus, Philip, *King Edward the Seventh*, John Murray, London, 1964.

Maré, Eric de, *London 1851: The Year of the Great Exhibition*, Folio Society, London, 1972.

Martin, Theodore, *The Life of the Prince Consort*, 5 vols, Smith, Elder & Co., 1875–80.

Millar, Delia, *The Victorian Watercolours and Drawings in the Collection of HM the Queen*, 2 vols, Philip Wilson, London, 1995.

Morris, Barbara, *Inspiration for Design, The Influence of the Victoria and Albert Museum*, Victoria and Albert Museum, 1986.

Murray, A., *The Book of the Horticultural Society*, Bradbury & Evans, London, 1863.

Petter, H., *Lutyens in Italy*, British School at Rome, London, 1992.

Physick, John, *The Victoria and Albert Museum, The History of its Building*, Phaidon Christie's, Oxford, 1982.

Ponsonby, Sir Frederick, *Recollections of Three Reigns*, Eyre & Spottiswoode, London, 1951.

Port, M., *Imperial London, Civil Government Building in London, 1851–1915*, Yale University Press, New Haven, 1996.

Rhodes James, Robert, *Albert, Prince Consort*, Hamish Hamilton, London, 1983.

Rolt, L. T. C., Isambard Kingdom Brunel, Penguin Books, London, 1970.

Saint, Andrew, *Richard Norman Shaw*, Yale University Press, New Haven and London, 1976.

Sheppard, F. H. W. (ed.), *Survey of London*, volume XXXVIII, *The Museums Area of South Kensington*, Athlone Press for the Greater London Council, London, 1975.

Spencer-Silver, Patricia, *Pugin's Builder: The Life and Work of George Myers*, University of Hull, 1993.

Stearn, W. T., *The Natural History Museum at South Kensington*, Heinemann, London, 1981.

Wark, Ian W., '1851 Science Research Scholarship Awards to Australians', *Records of the Australian Academy of Science*, vol. 3:3/4, Nov. 1977, pp. 47–52.

Wiseman, T. P., *History of the British School at Rome*, British School at Rome, London, n.d. [*c.*1990].

Wood, Sir Henry Trueman, *A History of the Royal Society of Arts*, John Murray, London, 1913.

Publications of the Royal Commission for the Exhibition of 1851 (HMSO)

First Report, 1852. *Second Report*, 1852. *Third Report*, 1856. *Fourth Report*, 1861. *Fifth Report*, 1867. *Sixth Report*, 1878. *Seventh Report*, 1889. *Eighth Report*, 1911. *Ninth Report*, 1935. *Tenth Report*, 1951. *Eleventh Report*, 1961. *Epitome*, 1908.

An Outline of its Activities Past and Present, 1924, revised 1932, 1951, 1962, 1974, 1980, 1983, 1991, 1997.

Record of the Science Research Scholars of the Royal Commission for the Exhibition of 1851, 1916, 1922, 1930, 1951, 1961, 2001.

Archives

A number of original sources have been used, and the references are given in the Notes. There collections have been particularly valuable:

The Royal Archives, Windsor Castle
The Royal Commission for the Exhibition of 1851
   Minutes of meetings of the Royal Commission
   Minutes of meetings of the Board of Management
   The Windsor Archives
The Royal Society of Arts

Meetings of the Commission itself were held almost weekly at the beginning, in 1850–2, but less frequently later, and today are purely formal.

Index